TRUTH AND MEANING

TRUTH AND MEANING

ESSAYS IN SEMANTICS

EDITED BY

GARETH EVANS

AND

JOHN McDOWELL

FELLOWS OF UNIVERSITY COLLEGE
OXFORD

CLARENDON PRESS · OXFORD
1976

Oxford University Press, Ely House, London W. I

GLASGOW NEW YORK TORONTO MELBOURNE WELLINGTON
CAPE TOWN IBADAN NAIROBI DAR ES SALAAM LUSAKA ADDIS ABABA
DELHI BOMBAY CALCUTTA MADRAS KARACHI LAHORE DACCA
KUALA LUMPUR SINGAPORE HONG KONG TOKYO

ISBN 0 19 824517 3

TEXT SET IN 10/12 PT. MONOTYPE TIMES NEW ROMAN, PRINTED BY LETTERPRESS, AND BOUND IN GREAT BRITAIN AT THE PITMAN PRESS, BATH

Contents

ACKNOWLEDGEMENT

P. F. Strawson's contribution is reprinted, by permission of the publisher's from *Freedom and Resentment and Other Essays* (Methuen, London, 1974). The other essays have not been previously printed.

Introduction

THIS introduction makes no pretensions to expressing some joint doctrine common to all contributors to this volume. Indeed, it will be evident that they are not in agreement about the general nature which acceptable theories of meaning might have. We have allowed ourselves, rather, to produce a tendentious sketch, from our own perspective, of some of the general issues about meaning which strike us as important. This non-conciliatory purpose will involve us in some disagreements, both explicitly and by implication, with some of our fellow contributors, from all of whom we have learned a great deal. Our hope is that the one-sided picture we shall outline, for which we make no claims of novelty,[1] will help to place at least some of the papers which follow in a clearer focus.

Many of the papers in this volume take their departure from a proposal about the nature of theories of meaning made by Donald Davidson.[2]

One way of appreciating the attractiveness of Davidson's conception of a theory of meaning is to consider the inadequacies of an alternative conception, found in the work of some linguists.[3] The alternative conception originates with the thought—surely correct—that a theory of meaning for a natural language must at least give the

[1] In particular, D. K. Lewis presented in a paragraph ('General Semantics', in Davidson and Harman (eds.), *Semantics of Natural Languages*, D. Reidel, Dordrecht, 1972, pp. 169–70) the points against 'translational semantics' which we believe bear spelling out again. And naturally no one has been clearer in the presentation of the virtues of Davidson's programme than Davidson himself.

[2] See especially 'Truth and Meaning', *Synthese*, xvii (1967), 304.

[3] See, for example, J. J. Katz and J. A. Fodor, 'The Structure of a Semantic Theory', *Language*, xxxix (1963), 170; J. J. Katz and P. M. Postal, *An Integrated Theory of Linguistic Descriptions* (M.I.T. Press, Cambridge, Mass., 1964). Our criticisms apply also to those linguists who choose artificial languages studied by logicians as the basis for their representation of meanings. Such an approach has some virtue if the artificial language chosen is one for which we can construct a recursive semantics, but casual enrichment by devices which preclude that (e.g. a sentential operator '*X* believes that . . .') makes it clear that it was not their possession of that property which attracted linguists to such languages. See, e.g., J. D. McCawley, 'Meaning and the Description of Languages', *Kotoba no Uchū* ii (1967), 10, 38, 51 (reprinted in J. F. Rosenberg and C. Travis (eds.), *Readings in the Philosophy of Language* (Prentice-Hall, Englewood Cliffs, N. J., 1971)); and 'Where do noun phrases come from?', in R. A. Jacobs and P. S. Rosenbaum (eds.), *Readings in English Transformational Grammar* (Blaisdell, Waltham, Mass., 1970), p. 166.

meanings of each of its sentences. However, since any theory must be stated in some language, the meanings of sentences of the object language must be given by means of expressions of the theory's language. This prompts remarks like the following:

It has often been stated that, essentially, meanings cannot be described in language. Sometimes they can be demonstrated by ostensive definition, but any description in terms of a language, natural or artificial, is bound to have its own meaning in turn, a description of which will again have its own meaning, etc. If this is true, we can only set up sets of synonymous expressions.[4]

On this view, then, the most that can be expected of a semantic theory is the setting up of translation rules.

If no restriction were placed upon the language into which object-language sentences are translated, semantic theory would be too easy. Since it is undeniable that 'Snow is white' gives the meaning of, is a semantic representation of, 'Snow is white', we could meet the requirements, as so far stated, by allowing the translation relation to be the identity function. (This excessive ease might have persuaded us that there was something wrong with our conception of a semantic theory.)

It is normally required that the theory's language *L* be, not just not identical with the object language, but also such that the map of sentences of the object language on to it conform to the following conditions:

(1) If *S* is meaningful and unambiguous, there is exactly one sentence of *L* on to which *S* is mapped.

(2) If *S* is *n*-ways ambiguous, there are *n* distinct sentences of *L* on to which *S* is mapped.

(3) If *S* lacks a meaning, there is no sentence of *L* on to which *S* is mapped.

(4) If *S* entails *S′*, there is an effectively decidable relation which holds between the sentences of *L* on to which *S* and *S′* are respectively mapped.

Conditions (1), (2), and (3) require that *L* be a logically perfect language, with sentences free from structural or lexical ambiguity. Condition (4) is usually taken to require that we do some apparently interesting work of *conceptual breakdown*. For it is held that the theory should account for the entailment, say, from 'John is a bachelor'

[4] Pieter A. M. Seuren, *Operators and Nucleus* (Cambridge University Press, Cambridge, 1969), p. 219. See also pp. 84–8.

to 'John is unmarried'; accordingly the semantic representation of 'John is a bachelor' cannot be as simple as 'John is a bachelor', but must be at least as complex as 'John is an unmarried man'.

This whole conception is objectionable: not so much because it builds into the very statement of the aims of a semantic theory a highly controversial distinction between analytic and synthetic statements,[5] nor because the conceptual breakdown, if pursued seriously, would be without evident limit; but because what we are doing if we engage in this enterprise (difficult and interesting though it may be) serves only to enable us to conceal from ourselves our utter incapacity to do what we ought to be doing. What we ought to be doing is stating what the sentences of the language mean, stating something such that, if someone knew it, he would be able to speak and understand the language.

It would be unfair to claim that the theorists of meaning whom we have been considering were unaware of the need to provide a theoretical articulation of a speaker-hearer's competence. Indeed conditions (1)—(4) were imposed precisely to ensure that someone who knew the theory would have some of that competence: he would be able to tell when a sentence was ambiguous, or without a meaning, or when one sentence entailed another. But there is no escaping the fact that one could have a competence thus based upon the mapping relation, and yet not know what a single sentence of the language meant. A speaker-hearer would know that only if he knew what sentences of the theory's language meant; but this is knowledge of precisely the kind that was to be accounted for in the first place.

We call this view, according to which the job of a theory of meaning is to provide rules relating sentences to their semantic representations, 'translational semantics'. It has been widely felt that such theories would leave what is really important out of account. But no doubt one form or another of the argument which we quoted from Seuren persuaded people to accept the limitations of those theories; for this argument suggests that trying to transcend them would involve trying, impossibly, to get outside the circle of language, to state the meanings of sentences using no language.

There is a fallacy in the argument. Of course, we cannot express meanings other than with words. But it does not follow that if we give the meaning of a sentence, *S*, by means of a sentence *S*′, we must

[5] See W. V. Quine, 'Two Dogmas of Empiricism', in *From a Logical Point of View* (Harvard University Press, Cambridge, Mass., 2nd edn., 1971), p. 20.

be stating or reporting upon a relation between *S* and *S*′. We may give the meaning of *S* by not mentioning *S*′, but using it, in the standard use which it has in talk about the world.

The sentence

(5) 'Snow is white' is true if and only if snow is white

does not report a relation which the sentence 'Snow is white' has to itself, but states at any rate *one* semantic property of the sentence by using it, in an exemplification of the very use which we might put it to in expressing our belief that snow is white. Similarly with a false sentence:

(6) 'Snow is black' is true if and only if snow is black

states a semantic property of 'Snow is black' by using that sentence in an exemplification of the very use which we might put it to—augmented with a negation sign—to express our belief that snow is not black.

A theory which uses expressions to state meanings would be immune to the objection which devastates translational semantics, namely that someone could know it without understanding the language of which it is a theory. To say, for example, that Pierre knows that something satisfies '*chauve*' if and only if it is bald is not to credit Pierre with knowledge of some relation between '*chauve*' and the English word 'bald'—knowledge which he could have without knowing what either meant. It is to credit him with knowing a relation between '*chauve*' and bald men: knowledge which would, together with similar knowledge, help to explain competent employment of French in talking about the world. We can state the relation that way because the use to which we put 'bald' in stating it is the use to which we put 'bald' in our talk about the world, notably in saying, of various people, that they are bald.

It is difficult to emphasize sufficiently the importance of the shift in theoretical perspective which takes place when we see, even as generally as this, the way to state a theory of meaning. We are entirely freed from the idea that there is something ineffable in the native speaker's mastery, or something which we can capture only by getting outside the circle of words and pointing at things. And we are entirely freed from the idea that our semantics must be trivial unless we effect conceptual breakdown and construct a special *characteristica universalis* in which to state the meanings of words.

For we can see how the meanings of expressions in, say, English can be given, if we like, even by themselves without the result being trivial. There is nothing trivial stated by

(7) Something satisfies 'bald' if and only if it is bald.

That proposition states an eminently learnable and forgettable relation between an English word and a set of men.

A semantic description of a language in this style, dealing with vague predicates by using those very predicates, would be systematic without being vulnerable to Wright's accusations, in his contribution to this volume, of incoherence. Wright's paper is in fact a valuable attack on the underpinnings of the view that semantics must effect conceptual breakdown.

It would be quite wrong to claim this theoretical perspective as the exclusive property of those who hold Davidson's views about the nature of a theory of meaning. The improved perspective results simply from seeing that meaning-giving expressions can be expressions in use, and there are other ways than Davidson's of incorporating that insight. It is, however, a cardinal merit of Davidson's proposal that it does incorporate that insight.

Transformational grammar was originated by men who had a lively appreciation of the native speaker's ability to understand new sentences, and therefore of the requirement that a theory of meaning show how to derive a statement of the meaning of each one of an infinite number of sentences from a finite number of principles governing their parts and modes of combination. But when the aim is the construction of a translational semantics this is not a tremendously difficult task. Certainly it is not as difficult as it ought to be.

To illustrate this point, consider the problem posed by predicates of the form 'ξ is a picture of an *F*' where, of course, '*F*' may be replaced by a predicate of arbitrary complexity. Suppose that we had stated a series of rules which enabled us to map each of the infinite number of possibly complex English predicates which do not contain 'picture of' on to their semantic representations. The additional semantic problem posed by 'picture of'-predicates is, on the translational view, not difficult; we may extend the mapping to them by a rule to this effect:

If *W* is the canonical translation of *F*, then 'is a picture of a'$\frown W$ is the canonical translation of 'is a picture of a'$\frown F$.

(Or more likely, since that seems a little thin:

> If *W* is the canonical translation of *F*, then 'is a representation upon a surface, the result of the action of painting or drawing, of a'⌒*W* is the canonical translation of 'is a picture of an a'⌒*F*.)

However, with the change of perspective, this problem becomes enormously difficult. And with Davidson's version of the improved perspective, we acquire a sharp conception not only of the difficulty but also of what a solution might be like. Let us suppose ourselves to have a theory which entails, for each of the possibly complex English predicates, *F*, which do not contain the expression 'picture of', a theorem of the form:

> (8) x satisfies *F* if and only if Wx;

where what replaces '*W*' is an expression of the metalanguage in use. The problem is to construct additional clauses which, together with the original clauses, will entail, by principles faithful to the senses of the expressions used in them, theorems on the pattern of

> (9) x satisfies 'is a picture of a lion' if and only if x is a picture of a lion;

one such theorem for each of our original predicates. The additional clauses are to be what, in our theory, gives the meaning of the 'picture of' construction. In the standard way, they are to do that by means of expressions in use: possibly, but not necessarily, the expression 'is a picture of' itself. The fact that expressions are used, in the clauses which give the meanings of object-language expressions, and the consequent requirement that the manipulations permitted in the derivations of the required theorems be faithful to their sense pose a grave obstacle to any solution. In fact, the construction of such additional clauses remains an unsolved semantical problem.

This formal difficulty is no more than a reflection of the obligation imposed upon a semantic theorist by the complexity of sentences. He must state the semantic properties of semantically simple expressions, not by relating them to mentioned metalinguistic expressions, but by using metalinguistic expressions. And he must do so in such a way that the semantic properties of complex expressions, above all those of sentences, can be derived from the clauses which state the semantic properties of the simple expressions which combine to

form them.[6] He will have satisfactorily answered the question, posed by the occurrence of the words $e_1 \ldots e_n$ in a complex expression Σ ($e_1 \ldots e_n$), 'What are these familiar words doing here?',[7] only if he can state a general clause for the construction Σ (   ) which will combine with the clauses he already has for $e_1 \ldots e_n$ in derivations of statements of the meanings of arbitrary exemplifications of that construction.

We have touched, in the last few paragraphs, upon two related virtues possessed by Davidson's conception of a theory of meaning. First, it provides us with a way of giving the slogan 'The meaning of an expression is a function of the meaning of its parts' a precise and non-metaphorical sense. And, second, by providing us with an idea of how to solve them, it provides us with a sharp conception of the problems posed for semantic theories by what Chomsky calls 'creative' language use.

Another advantage which has been claimed for the conception must now be deemed illusory. This was the hope of reconstructing the concept of meaning from the concept of truth alone. The hope was, in Davidson's words, that of 'extracting a rich concept (here something reasonably close to translation) from thin little bits of evidence (here the truth values of sentences) by imposing formal structure on enough bits'.[8]

The idea was that one could conclude that a sentence *p* would constitute an adequate translation, into the metalanguage, of a sentence designated by a structural description *s*, and thus that the sentence ('T-sentence')

(10) $s^\frown$'is true if and only if'$^\frown p$

[6] This makes it desirable not, in general, to succumb to the temptation to complete sentences of the form 'The meaning of *e* is . . .'. Series of such clauses do not easily combine to give the meanings of sentences. Often, at least, the way to meet the requirement that one use, not mention, metalinguistic expressions in giving the meanings of subsentential expressions is to use the expression itself whose meaning one is giving, or one to the same effect. Thus not: 'The meaning of "and" is . . .', but rather: For any two sentences S and S', $S^\frown$'and'$^\frown S'$ is true if and only if S is true and S' is true.

[7] Davidson, 'On Saying That', in D. Davidson and J. Hintikka (eds.), *Words and Objections* (Reidel, Dordrecht, 1969), pp. 158–74, at p. 160.

[8] Davidson, 'In Defense of Convention T', in H. Leblanc (ed.), *Truth, Syntax, and Modality* (North-Holland, Amsterdam, 1973), p. 84.

was a meaning-giving T-sentence, provided merely that two conditions held:

(a) the T-sentence was true;

(b) the T-sentence was a theorem of a finitely axiomatized theory which entailed a true T-sentence for every sentence of an infinite language (upon the basis of discerning structure in those sentences).

It was hoped that the obvious counter-examples to the adequacy of condition (a) alone, such as the true, but not meaning-giving,

(11) 'Snow is white' is true if and only if grass is green,

would be ruled out by condition (b). For it was difficult to see how a theory which had (11) as a consequence could be capable of an infinite pairing of object-language truths with metalanguage truths and object-language falsehoods with metalanguage falsehoods. (11) could result only from a semantical connection of 'white' with green things and of 'snow' with grass which, although striking lucky here, would be bound to lead us wrong (extensionally wrong) somewhere else.

The fact that each axiom of a truth theory has its impact upon an infinite number of T-sentences does indeed have the consequence that it is difficult for counterfeit theories to pass the tests provided by (a) and (b). But, as two contributors[9] point out, it is not impossible. Axioms for individual expressions may be chosen which, even though they disperse their inaccuracy, if construed as giving the meanings of those expressions, over as many T-sentences as there are sentences in which the expressions occur, nevertheless preserve the truth of all the T-sentences. Such inaccuracy is undetectable by the tests provided by (a) and (b).

It is thus obvious that more stringent conditions must be imposed upon a theory of truth, if it is to serve as a theory of meaning, than that its T-sentences be true.[10] These conditions must have the effect of ensuring that the sentences used on the right-hand sides of the theory's T-sentences do indeed give the meaning of those mentioned on the left. Obviously the most interesting case is that of a theory for one language in another: in that case the conditions must ensure that

[9] Foster and Loar

[10] Cf. Davidson, 'In Defense of Convention T', p. 84: 'I suggest that it is enough to require that the T-sentences be true.' But see also Davidson's 'Reply to Foster' (in this volume), p. 35.

the sentences used on the right translate those mentioned on the left.

In our view it is over-hasty to conclude, from recognition of the need for such additional conditions, that we have now come full circle, after a useless detour through theories of truth, face to face once more with 'the Problem of Meaning'. The virtues we have sketched remain untouched. And although we have to abandon the aspiration to reconstruct the concept of meaning out of the concept of truth alone, that does not seem to us to compel abandonment of the idea that it is theories of truth which we should think of as being subjected to the required further conditions. Thus we ourselves would wish to retain the hope of a theory which, by meeting these conditions, is guaranteed to give the meanings of expressions, even though the theory itself remains extensional in syntax and only minimally extends the ontology of its object language.[11]

We have so far left the nature of the required further conditions quite unspecified. It is clear what they must do, namely ensure (in the case of a theory for one language in another) that the theory yields a translation relation from the first language into the second. We have not said how they are to do that. It seems evident, however, that formulation of the conditions in such a way as to ensure what they must ensure would involve employing psychological concepts; and some may see this as raising hopes for the reduction of the concept of meaning to psychological concepts.

Principles which link pairs of concepts may simply display conceptual constraints upon the joint application of concepts which are of equal status, not a possibility of reducing one to the other. Reduction requires that there be some ground for claiming an asymmetry. Now it seems unlikely that an epistemological asymmetry holds in the case we are considering: that is, that the psychological material which might figure in the conditions we are looking for might be empirically more accessible than the deliverances of the semantic theory on which the conditions are to bear. As Davidson points out,[12] when we are confronted with hitherto uninterpreted linguistic behaviour, we cannot tell what utterances mean without at least guessing at what speakers believe; but equally, it is quite implausible that we

[11] Foster and Loar both draw different conclusions from the arguments we have borrowed from them.

[12] See, e.g., 'Truth and Meaning', 313.

can even guess at more than the crudest specifications of what they believe without at least guessing at what their utterances mean. The same would go for propositional attitudes in general. And it seems reasonable to suppose that the conditions we are looking for will do their work by connecting determinations of the meanings of sentences with propositional attitudes whose content is given with at least the same degree of specificity. In that case, we cannot envisage the conditions as enabling us to fix the truth values of semantic statements by way of first fixing the truth values of the requisite propositional-attitude statements.

But it might be held that there is an asymmetry of a different kind. Suppose it is granted that there is no access to the specific propositional attitudes which, we are imagining, constrain particular determinations of meaning, independent of those determinations of meaning themselves. Nevertheless, it might be said, the concepts of the propositional attitudes as such are independent of the concepts of semantics: for there is no requirement, if we are to ascribe propositional attitudes to an organism, that it possess a language. And it might be argued that such asymmetry, conceptual but not epistemological, is enough to justify the view that the further conditions we are looking for might be reductive. Something like this must be the view of H. P. Grice and his followers, who offer principles connecting semantic and psychological concepts—the connection being made with the aid of the notion of practice or convention—in a reductionist spirit.

We should like, however, to explore the possibility of incorporating some version of Grice's insights into the conception of a theory of meaning which we have sketched, without reliance on reductionism.[13]

As we saw, Davidson views the construction of a theory of meaning, for hitherto uninterpreted linguistic behaviour, as requiring the simultaneous fixing of meanings and beliefs. Neither can be determined first and then be used to get leverage on the other. The predicament could seem impossible, but Davidson suggests a way of, so to speak, working our way in. Without knowing what a sentence *S* means, and without knowing what a person *X* believes about the

[13] We urge the reader to consult for himself a series of writings to which, in pursuing this aim, we shall inevitably be doing less than justice: Grice's articles, 'Meaning', *Philosophical Review*, lxvi (1957), 377; 'Utterer's Meaning, Sentence-Meaning, and Word-Meaning', *Foundations of Language*, iv (1968), 1; 'Utterer's Meaning and Intentions', *Philosophical Review*, lxxviii (1969), 147; Stephen R. Schiffer, *Meaning* (Clarendon Press, Oxford, 1972); P. F. Strawson, 'Intention and Convention in Speech Acts' and 'Meaning and Truth', both in *Logico-Linguistic Papers* (Methuen, London, 1971); and Loar's essay in this volume.

world, we can nevertheless, in imaginable circumstances, find it plausible that *X* holds *S* to be true. The idea is that we amass as many good guesses as we can about the conditions under which people hold sentences to be true, and then[14] construct a theory which, in the way we considered above, permits the derivation of truth conditions for sentences on the basis of some articulation perceptible within them, in such a way that the conditions under which, according to the theory, sentences *are* true acceptably relate to the conditions under which, according to our initial guesses (which may, of course, need to be revised), people *hold* them true. Adoption of a theory as a theory of meaning, together with the initial guesses as to which sentences people hold true, will (as far as these sentences go) fix our view of their beliefs about the world; and the theory relates acceptably to the data on the basis of which it is constructed only if the beliefs which the theory and the data thus jointly require us to ascribe can be accounted for on general psychological principles.[15] Ideally, we should be able to say, about each belief thus ascribed, that, in the circumstances, we can see how they might have come to believe *that*.[16]

If the thesis that truth, in a theory of truth, is sufficient for it to constitute a theory of meaning is to be maintained, a procedure like that outlined above has to be viewed as no more than a way of telling whether a theory of truth is true. That emphasizes the untenability of the thesis. For, given a theory of truth warranted as true by the above procedure, we could use the devices discussed by Foster and Loar in order to construct a theory of truth whose truth follows, by the plainest extensional logic, from the truth of the first theory and certain facts, known to us but not, on any plausible view, believed by our subjects. Nevertheless, since those surplus facts will show up in the truth conditions assigned to sentences, and hence in the beliefs ascribed to the subjects in consequence of adoption of the new theory, the new theory will *not* be certified to be true by the above procedure.

[14] This is an idealization: in practice theory construction and data collection would proceed together.

[15] Davidson tends to limit this requirement to the ascription of error, thus making a principle of charity seem to be built into the conditions for adequate translation. But true beliefs need to be accountable for too. (See R. Grandy, 'Reference, Meaning, and Belief', *Journal of Philosophy*, lxx (1973), 439.) Charity is merely good advice in the opening stages.

[16] Other attitudes to sentences (e.g. wishing them true, wondering whether they are true) might be reasonably identifiable before translation, and thus yield similar psychological constraints on determinations of meaning. But we shall ignore this for simplicity's sake.

We have already urged abandonment of the thesis that truth, in a theory of truth, is sufficient for it to constitute a theory of meaning. We can thus regard the condition of adequacy embedded in the above outline as a Davidsonian formulation of the further condition required, as already noted, by abandonment of the thesis.[17]

The condition uses, in order to put restrictions upon acceptable determinations of meaning, limitations imposed by general psychological principles upon intelligible ascriptions of belief: limitations like that which precludes our supposing that illiterate African tribesmen might have beliefs about, say, William the Conqueror.[18] Reduction, of the sort which is warranted as such by relations of epistemological priority, is not in question, since we started from a predicament arising from precisely those considerations which make such reduction seem implausible. And we can recognize the correctness of conditions of adequacy on those lines without *needing* to ground our acceptance of them on reductionism of the second variety distinguished above.

In Davidson's view, as we saw, construction of a theory of meaning for a foreign language would begin with plausible guesses to the effect that certain people hold certain sentences true. The behaviour which is construed as manifesting those attitudes is regarded as the joint result of the people's beliefs about the world and their beliefs about what the sentences mean: the problem being, so to speak, to solve a set of simultaneous equations, fixing the beliefs and the meanings together.

Independently of reductionism, a Gricean might protest that the picture, as so far sketched, is too simple: it suffers by ignoring the fact that most linguistic behaviour is conversation.[19] Conversational behaviour is not happily regarded as supporting generalizations which report relations between speakers, on their own, and sentences of their language. The primary data of linguistic behaviour—assent

[17] The following is still true, and seems to be in the spirit of that thesis: there is no hope of constructing a theory of truth for a foreign language, reliably held to be both true and *not* suited to serve as a theory of meaning for it, except by inference from a theory certified to be both true and suited to serve as a theory of meaning by Davidson's procedure, or some improvement on it.

[18] Cf. Gareth Evans, 'The Causal Theory of Names', *Proceedings of the Aristotelian Society*, Supplementary Volume xlvii (1973), 187.

[19] The protest has nothing to do with our limitation to utterances construed as expressing beliefs (see p. xix, n. 16). It applies within the class of such utterances; a similar protest could be made against a spelling-out, on parallel lines to those above, of the constraints made available by considering attitudes to sentences other than holding them true.

to, and dissent from, utterances of sentences by others, and utterances of sentences in the direction of others—support generalizations, not of the form '*X* holds *S* true', but of the form '*X* holds true the utterance of *S* by *Y* at *t*'.[20] Such attitudes to utterances, and hence the behaviour which is construed as manifesting them, are not best viewed, according to the Gricean protest, as resulting from just the two factors: *X*'s belief as to what *S* means and *X*'s belief about the facts of the appropriate matter. Rather, we can fix that belief of *X*'s which, as semantic theorists, we want to fix—his belief as to what *S* means—only by simultaneously ascribing to *X*, in addition to a belief about the facts of the appropriate matter, a whole network of beliefs about some appropriate *Y*. If *X* is responding to an utterance of *Y*'s these might include, notably, *X*'s belief about what *Y* intends in regard to himself ('Is *Y* speaking ironically, or seriously, or . . . ?'), *X*'s belief about what *Y* believes *S* means, and also perhaps, *X*'s belief about what *Y* believes *X* believes *S* means . . . If *X* is directing an utterance at *Y*, the relevant beliefs are *X*'s beliefs about *Y*'s possession, about *X*, of the network of beliefs which we have just gestured at.

The idea would be that a detailed account of the complex network of beliefs and intentions involved in conversation, in the characteristic Gricean style (but purged of the reductionist refusal even to entertain the possibility that semantic matter might figure in the specification of the content of the beliefs and intentions), might yield a richer set of simultaneous equations for us to regard ourselves as solving when we construct a theory of meaning: and hence a richer set of constraints, imposed, not necessarily in a reductive spirit, by bringing general psychological principles to bear upon determinations of meaning in order to make the constructed theory fit the data on the basis of which it is constructed. Apart from this greater richness, the constraints would operate in much the same way as that already considered in connection with the Davidsonian procedure.

How far we went along this path would depend on how much credence we gave to its starting point. How complex a view should we take of the psychological factors which issue in those utterances, and reactions to utterances, which we conjecturally regard as manifestations of holding the sentence uttered to be true—psychological

[20] *Y* may *be X:* see below. (In that case we shall still need, according to the protest, to consider a different *Y*.)

factors which, because of our crediting that effect to them, become, in our view, variables to be solved for in constructing our theory of meaning?

Do people really, in the most straightforward and ordinary communicative exchanges, stop to think whether, say, others have the same beliefs as they do about what sentences mean? It began to seem that we were obliged to view conversation as dependent on beliefs whose content was of apparently endlessly ramified complexity (*X*'s belief about *Y*'s beliefs about *X*'s beliefs . . .). Our own suspicion is that we should be more reluctant to lose sight of the habitual, unthinking character of most ordinary human use of language; we should not be content to describe, instead, the perfectly reflective awareness which might characterize communication between ideally rational superhumans, whose movements were neither impeded nor facilitated by the friction provided by sheer habit.

Consider an analogy. It might be suggested that an ordinary person's acceptance of a coin (something with no intrinsic value) in payment for goods or services should be seen as a consequence of a peculiarly complex network of propositional attitudes, the special character of its complexity being due to its including beliefs about the presence of just such a complex network of propositional attitudes in others. His acceptance is a monetary transaction only because it is determined by his belief that other members of his community will accept that and similar coins in payment for goods and services, not because they value them intrinsically, but because they believe this: other members of their community will accept them and similar coins in payment for goods and services, not because . . ., and so on. But it is surely utterly implausible to attribute any such beliefs to ordinary people, and therefore utterly implausible to attribute them to extraordinary people, engaging in monetary dealings with ordinary people, either.[21] The point is not that acceptance of the coin depends on possession of that endlessly complex belief, but rather this: if our ordinary person disbelieved that others would accept coins, or believed that others disbelieved that others would, or believed that others believed that others disbelieved that others would, or . . ., then either he would not accept the coin at all, or at least such acceptance would be debarred from being rightly viewed as a move within the institution of money. It is not that there is a complex

[21] People extraordinary enough to contemplate them would realize that others have no such beliefs.

belief he must *have*, but rather that there is a series of beliefs each of which he must *lack*. (If the series is seen in this way, the endless ramifications present no problem.)

If we take seriously the unreflectiveness which characterizes ordinary monetary transactions, we shall be inclined to rest content with seeing ordinary acceptance of a coin as the outcome of the belief that it is *worth* so much. That would be an abandonment of any hope of a reductive account of the concept of non-intrinsic value in terms of convention and propositional attitudes; for in a reductive account the contents of the propositional attitudes would have to be specified without use of the concept to be reduced.

Similarly with the ordinary, unreflective use of language. The complex network of beliefs gestured at above need not be positively ascribed to *X*. Rather, a detailed and satisfactory account of the network would yield a specification of a different series of beliefs, generated from the network by means of negation ('*Y* does not share my belief about what *S* means', etc.), such that we must take *X* to *lack* each of them if we are to view his behaviour, in the same way as before, as issuing from his semantic and factual beliefs. This seems unlikely to yield much in the way of richer constraints to be imposed, in the light of general psychological principles, on acceptable theories of meaning. If we take seriously the unreflectiveness of ordinary linguistic behaviour, we shall be inclined to return to seeing *X*'s behaviour, in normal cases at least, as the resultant of just the two factors: *X*'s belief about what *S* means on *Y*'s lips at *t*, and *X*'s belief about the facts of the appropriate matter. The simultaneous equations look much the same;[22] and, as before, the use of semantic terminology in giving the content of one of the beliefs ascribed looks like the abandonment of reductive ambitions.

We can imagine someone protesting that we are taking the unreflective nature of actual everyday linguistic behaviour too seriously. He might admit that those complex networks of propositional attitudes fit, not ordinary behaviour, but a frictionless superhuman substitute. Nevertheless, he might claim that it is of the essence of the conventions exemplified by our ordinary proceedings, unthinking as they are, that those proceedings would be duplicated by the imagined superhuman beings. We behave, unthinkingly, just as if we were behaving utterly reflectively, and proper understanding of

[22] We have brought in what would anyway have been necessary: relativity of semantic properties to speakers and times.

the character of our unthinking actions depends essentially upon appreciating this fact. (If the contents of the propositional attitudes in the network can be kept free of semantic matter, a sort of reductionism might be defended on such grounds.)

Such a view seems to us to be profoundly attractive. We ourselves are nevertheless disinclined to accept it; but we find the question extremely difficult, and we are conscious of the insufficiency of the remarks which follow. The attractiveness of the view, we think, lies in the peculiar phenomenological duplicity of language which leads Wittgenstein to say: 'Every sign *by itself* seems dead. *What* gives it life?'[23] A sort of answer to this question might seem to be afforded by the remark that our use of the sign duplicates the highly reflective behaviour of the imagined superhuman beings. But to the question 'How can it be that the phenomenology of language should be as it is?' we suspect that such an answer would be exactly wrong. For it seems that, whatever life could be conferred on signs by the imagined frictionless use, it would not be the life which our signs have for us. The phenomenological fact which generates the original perplexity is that we see or hear their life *in* the signs: and this excludes reading their life into them as the conclusion of a piece of ratiocination.

Seeing cheerfulness in a face is not inferring that its owner is cheerful from the way his face looks.[24] (Of course it is only because his face looks that way that we can see the cheerfulness in it.) To see a familiar scene in a photograph, we need to forget that we are dealing with a creased piece of paper with patterns of black and white on it: we cannot get life into the photograph by treating such, or any, properties as premisses in an argument. (Of course, again, it is only because it has appropriate properties that we can see the life in it.) Just so, we suspect, with language: that is, it is essential to language as we know it that our understanding of meanings should normally be *perception* of meanings, and hence precisely *not* a matter of inference.[25]

We said above that complex specifications of propositions about one another which people in communicative situations must *not* believe seemed unlikely, in view of their negative formulation, to yield much in the way of richer constraints on the construction of

[23] L. Wittgenstein, *Philosophical Investigations* (Blackwell, Oxford, 1963), §432.

[24] Cf. Wittgenstein, op. cit., § 568: 'Meaning is a physiognomy'.

[25] We speak and respond as we do because of the way we and others have spoken and responded in the past. This captures, not, in general, our *reasons* for doing as we do (to be spelled out employing such concepts as that of *precedent*), but rather the causes of our having the habits we have.

acceptable theories of meaning. But that is not where the real utility of such subtle descriptions is to be looked for. The real point bears not upon our conception of the method of constructing a theory of meaning but upon our conception of what we are doing in doing so. When we interpret a man's language we are making him intelligible to us, not as a mere blurter-out of what he believes, but as a communicator to others and as an interpreter, himself, of their communications to him.

I

Meaning and Truth Theory

J. A. FOSTER

I. WHAT IS A THEORY OF MEANING?

A speaker of English hears the sounds 'the sun is hot' and knows that they mean that the sun is hot. This episode of semantic insight is part of the general competence of an English speaker to interpret the expressions of his language on the basis of their physical makeup. Given the epistemic character of this competence, we may be led to seek for an explicit statement of the knowledge which sustains it. What facts about English does one who has mastered it thereby know? Since his competence spans an infinite number of expressions, the knowledge cannot be stated by listing his separate interpretations of each. Rather, we have to ascribe to him some general theory from which these intepretations flow, some finitely stated corpus of knowledge from which the meaning of each expression can be extracted. Such a theory must exploit the (not accidental) fact that the infinitely many English expressions are constructed from a finite stock of elements, and that their meanings are systematically determined by the semantic material which these elements contribute. The theory yields the full range of interpretations by specifying the semantic significance of the elements and isolating the general principles by which different concatenations produce different meanings. Thus what began as the demand for an account of linguistic competence turns out to be the demand for a theory of meaning for English—a theory which gives the meaning of each English expression on the basis of its structure. This is hardly surprising. For meaning is precisely what fills the slot that the epistemic character of competence creates. However elaborate its philosophical ramifications, however lofty its ontological representation, meaning resides in just those facts about a language which its mastery implicitly recognizes.

But having seen the generality of the theory required, we may wonder whether we should ascribe it to the speaker at all. The knowledge we would have to attribute to him is not, typically, what he would

attribute to himself. His mastery of English equips him to interpret its expressions, but not to state the general principles to which these interpretations conform. Is it not unnatural, even incoherent, to ascribe states of knowledge to which the subject himself has no conscious access? This question could only be decided by putting the concept of knowledge through the mills of analysis. But despite the interest in what might result, we can capture all that matters to the philosophy of meaning by putting the original project the other way round. Rather than ask for a statement of the knowledge implicit in linguistic competence, let us ask for the statement of a theory whose knowledge would suffice for such competence. Instead of demanding a statement of those metalinguistic facts which the mastery of a language implicitly recognizes, let us demand a statement of those facts explicit recognition of which gives mastery. What we are then demanding is still a theory of meaning, but without the questionable assumption that one who has mastered the language has, at some deep level, absorbed the information which it supplies. The theory reveals the semantic machinery which competence works, but leaves undetermined the psychological form in which competence exists.

Why then bring competence in at all? If what we are looking for is a way of constructing a theory of meaning for a language, why not simply characterize such a theory as one which specifies the meanings of all significant expressions? Why insist that the specification suffice for a mastery of the language? In any case, does this extra requirement really add anything? For what more could one need for mastery than a complete specification of the meanings? Taking the last question first, it is easy to show that what more one needs and what the requirement adds is, in a word, scrutability. Let us call a theory which suffices for mastery an *interpretative* theory. Suppose we have a language L for which we seek a theory of meaning. What interpretativeness ensures is that the references to the expressions of L and the assignments of meaning to them are scrutable in the right way, that we are able to tell what expressions the theory refers to on the basis of their physical makeup, and which meanings it assigns to them in terms of how in our language these meanings are expressed. We can envisage theories, superficially theories of meaning, where such scrutability is lacking. In the first place, we can envisage some way of defining an ordering O_1 of all L-sentences such that there is no procedure for deciding, for each integer n, the physical makeup of its nth element. Given this ordering, we can envisage a

theory θ_1 which, for each *L*-sentence *S*, entails what is got from the schema 'The *n*th element of O_1 means that *p*' by substituting for '*n*' the numeral for the place which *S* occupies in O_1 and for '*p*' the English translation of *S*. It is undeniable that, in some sense, θ_1 assigns the correct meaning to every *L*-sentence and therefore, implicitly, to every *L*-expression. But because we cannot correlate the physical makeup of a sentence with its mode of designation in the theory, we cannot use the consequences of θ_1 as a means for interpreting the *L*-sentences we physically identify.

In a genuinely interpretative theory, the expressions of the object language are designated by what are called *structural descriptions*, descriptions which are built from names of the simplest symbols of the language together with a predicate or function-term signifying concatenation. Designation by structural description has the right kind of scrutability: we can discern the physical makeup of an expression in its mode of designation. But a theory with a scrutable system of reference to the object language may fail to be interpretative on account of the inscrutability of its assignments of meaning. Thus, ignoring, for the sake of the example, the questionable status of propositions, we can envisage defining an ordering O_2 of all the propositions expressed by *L*-sentences, such that there is no procedure for finding, for each *n*, a sentence of English which expresses its *n*th element. We can further envisage a theory θ_2 which, for each *L*-sentence *S*, entails what is got from the schema '*x* expresses the *n*th element of O_2' by substituting for '*x*' the structural description of *S* and for '*n*' the numeral for the place which the proposition expressed by *S* occupies in O_2. In some sense θ_2 assigns the correct meaning to every *L*-sentence and therefore, implicitly, to every *L*-expression. Moreover, we can tell which sentences are being referred to on the basis of their physical makeup. But because we cannot correlate the designations of the propositions assigned with English sentences which express them, we cannot use the consequences of θ_2 to gain an understanding of the sentences of *L*. The theory gives the meanings of *L*-sentences, but not in a form in which we can discern them.

The requirement of interpretativeness, therefore, is by no means vacuous. But wherein lies its importance? Not presumably in its practical advantages in the sphere of language tuition, for these are hardly of philosophical concern. Our aim is not to provide a handbook for language students, not even for those exceptional students who could digest a language in the compressed form in which the theory

would characterize it. No, the point of investigating the conditions for an adequate theory of meaning is to gain philosophical insight into the *nature* of language and meaning, to bring the semantic character of language into the right philosophical perspective. This perspective is not provided by a theory of meaning itself, which only purports to give the meanings of the expressions in some particular language. The idea is rather that if we put the right constraints on what giving-the-meanings involves, then characterizing the general method by which such theories can be constructed and verified reveals what meaning-in-language really amounts to. By showing what for certain purposes counts as a theory of meaning, we show what meaning is. There is an analogy here with the philosophy of science. A scientific theory does not explain the concept of natural law, but there is no better way of explaining it than by uncovering the canons of scientific method to which such theories must conform. Likewise a theory of meaning does not explain meaning, but there is no better way of explaining it than by uncovering the conditions which such theories must meet and the form in which these conditions can be implemented. It is in this framework that the requirement of interpretativeness must be understood. The point is not that a noninterpretative theory is no help to a would-be learner of the language, but that the character of interpretative theories gives philosophical insight at the level where the problem of meaning originates. The problem originates not in some platonic realm that philosophers have created, but in the mundane comprehensibility of our linguistic tokens. Meanings are first and foremost those properties of sounds and marks that comprehension discerns, those properties in virtue of which there is something there to be understood. Our philosophical account will not go far enough unless it reveals how physical tokens have comprehensible meaning, how expressions of language can be interpreted on the basis of their physical makeup. The link with competence cannot be discarded, for it is only in the character of interpretative theories that we can hope to bring meaning into the right perspective. In short, our philosophical aims demand that a theory of meaning be a theory of mastery.

When I say, of an interpretative theory, that it suffices for mastery, I should, to be precise, say that *what it states* suffices for mastery. This correction reflects an important distinction. Suppose we have a theory θ_3 which tells us, and scrutably, how to translate each sentence of L into a sentence of English, a theory formulated in English which,

for each *L*-sentence *S*, entails what is got from the schema '*x* translates *y*' by substituting the structural description of *S* for '*y*' and the structural description of the English translation of *S* for '*x*'. Now in one sense θ_3 suffices for a mastery of *L*. For because θ_3 is formulated in English, anyone who understands it can understand those English sentences which it cites as translations. And if he understands these translations, then by knowing them to be translations he can construe the corresponding sentences in *L*. (There is the pedantic objection that understanding θ_3 may not guarantee an understanding of the translations, since the fragment of English used in formulating θ_3 may not include all the words the translations contain. This can be met by including in θ_3 some long vacuous clause that uses all the relevant words, though without contributing anything to the business of translation.) But what suffices for the mastery of *L* is not what θ_3 states, but the combination of what it states and the language in which it states it. Our understanding of English has, as it were, to play a double role, the role of allowing us to grasp the theory, and the role of allowing us to construe those sentences which the theory cites as translations. By reformulating θ_3 in another language we can make these roles come apart, and where they come apart the link with mastery breaks. Thus suppose we translate θ_3 into French. The French version will state all the facts which θ_3 states: it will say which structural types in English translate which structural types in *L*. But because this version is not formulated in the same language as the translations it refers to, one who grasps it may be unable to interpret any sentence of *L*. What ensures mastery of *L* is not knowing the facts which θ_3 states, but knowing these facts in the medium of English.

It is quite clear that, for our purposes, θ_3 does not count as a theory of meaning: it can be used for mastering *L*, but it does not *specify* those meanings which mastery discerns. As such it is not genuinely interpretative. Yet it comes close to meeting the earlier demands of scrutability. It takes us from sentences of the object language structurally identified to sentences of our own language which express their meanings. There is no objecting that the *L*-sentences referred to cannot be picked out on the basis of their physical makeup, nor that the meanings assigned cannot be discerned in terms of how we would express them in English. The defect is the simpler, more fundamental one that the meanings never get assigned. The theory pairs *L*-sentences with English sentences when it should be pairing

L-sentences with the meanings which English sentences express. But if so, there seems to be an equally simple remedy: retain the format of moving from *L*-sentences to their English translations, but refashion it as a move from the *mention* of the former to the *use* of the latter, from *L*-sentences structurally designated to English translations used to specify their meanings. The obvious way of doing this would be to fuse the scrutable aspects of θ_1 and θ_2, taking, as our model for a theory of meaning, a true theory which, for each *L*-sentence *S*, entails what is got from the schema '*x* means that *p*' by substituting the structural description of *S* for '*x*' and the English translation of *S* for '*p*'. Such a theory seems to be just what we want: it yields a correct and unique interpretation of each *L*-sentence on the basis of its physical makeup. Feed in a structural description and the theory tells you how what it designates is to be construed.

This model, however, is less helpful than it seems. In the first place, there is the problem of getting a theory to deliver the goods, of finding a finite set of axioms which yield the full range of interpretative consequences. The chief obstacle here is the intensional form in which the consequences are expressed: the extension of a predicative expression of the form 'means that *p*' is not determined by the truth value or even the extensional structure of the sentence we substitute for '*p*'. Even granted the sophistication of modern semantic techniques, it is hard to envisage an acceptable theory which handles this intensionality in the general terms the model requires: it is hard to see how, without doing violence to our syntax or our logic, we can condense the infinite set of consequences into a finite set of axioms. But even if, *per impossibile*, the intensionality proved tractable, our philosophical aims would be better served without it. The point of showing how to construct theories of interpretation is to gain insight into the nature of meaning; this insight will be diminished if, to gain it, we have to take intensional idiom for granted, for to understand such locutions as 'means that', 'says that', and 'it is necessary that' requires an implicit grasp of the very concept of meaning which we hope to explicate. If possible, the syntax of the theory should be kept extensional simply because the problem of intensional idiom is part of the problem of meaning itself. We want the theory to tell us, in some scrutable way, what the expressions of the object language mean, but we also want the method of telling us to shed the maximum light on what meaning is.

This aim, of course, puts restrictions not only on the syntax of the

theory, but also on its primitive vocabulary. In short, we do best to avoid using *any* linguistic material which, by involving the concept of meaning, casts shadows over the region where we want light. But there is a qualification. In the case of the *vocabulary* these restrictions apply only to that material which is essential to the method of the theory, not to that which is contingent on the particular features of the language with which it deals. If, as suggested, the general format is to be the systematic linking of *L*-sentences mentioned with English sentences used—if the theory is to do its interpretative work by entailing, for each *L*-sentence, a theorem in which the sentence is structurally designated and its English translation used—we must distinguish between the accidental, *L*-oriented vocabulary from which we draw the translations and the essential, methodological vocabulary which we use, in combination with the former, to generate the theorems. The essential, methodological vocabulary is independent of the particular interpretations which the theory offers: it holds constant through other theories of the same type dealing with other languages of the same grammatical structure. The accidental vocabulary is what adapts the general method to a particular object language: it provides descriptive resources to match the resources of the language to which that method of interpretation is applied. Such restrictions on vocabulary as we think appropriate (the avoidance, for example, of such terms as 'meaning' and 'necessity') fall only on the methodological sector. For it is from the method of the theory that we hope to gain our insight into the nature of meaning. To impose restrictions on the vocabulary of the translations is to get entangled in a different problem, namely how the concepts employed in the object language can be analysed into ones that are philosophically more basic. This is an interesting problem, but not the one that here concerns us.

II. DAVIDSON'S INITIAL THESIS

To summarize the discussion so far, we are seeking a method of constructing theories of meaning for particular languages which will yield the greatest philosophical insight into the nature of meaning and language in general. To yield this insight the theories must be genuinely interpretative: the facts they state must suffice for the mastery of the languages they characterize. In addition, their syntax should be extensional, their logic sound and their essential vocabulary free

from the concept of meaning and other concepts of an intensional kind. For a theory to be interpretative, its designations of expressions in the object language and its characterization of their meaning must be relevantly scrutable, and, given the primacy of sentences as vehicles of meaning, this suggests, as a general format, the presence of a finite set of axioms which, for each sentence of the language, entail a theorem in which that sentence is structurally designated and its English translation used. So our task could be construed as that of devising formulations of such suitably interpretative theorems that we can get a finite theory, meeting our other constraints, to generate. As far as I know, there is, in the literature, only one concrete proposal as to how this can be done. It is the proposal put forward by Donald Davidson in his celebrated paper 'Truth and Meaning'.[1] In that paper Davidson argues that what we are looking for as a theory of meaning we find in a theory of truth conforming, in effect, to Tarski's Convention T, a theory which, for each sentence *S* of the object language, entails what is got from the schema '*x* is true if and only if *p*' by substituting the structural description of *S* for '*x*' and our English translation of *S* for '*p*'.[2] I say '*in effect* conforming to Convention T' for two reasons. In the first place, as formulated by Tarski, the convention states the conditions for an explicit definition of truth for a language, without the use, in the methodological sector, of primitive semantic terms; and granted we are meeting the formal requirements of a definition, the entailing of the relevant biconditionals, in which on the right-hand side all references to *L*-expressions disappear, is the criterion of when an adequate definition has been achieved. In the hands of Davidson the convention tests the adequacy not of a definition, but of a theory of truth, of a set of axioms which entail the biconditionals by employing truth and certain related semantic properties as formally primitive. Secondly, as formulated by Tarski the convention applies only to object languages which are context-free, languages in which what each sentence can be used to state does not vary with the circumstances of utterance. In the hands of Davidson this restriction is lifted: truth becomes a three-place relation between a sentence, a person (potentially uttering it) and a time (when he potentially utters it), and the biconditionals are reformulated as universally quantified sentences of the form

[1] *Synthese*, xvii (1967), 304.

[2] A. Tarski, 'The Concept of Truth in Formalized Languages' in *Logic, Semantics, Metamathematics* (Clarendon Press, Oxford, 1956), p. 152.

'$(P)(t)(S$ is true for P at t if and only if . . .)' where what fills the blank translates not S itself, but S relative to P at t. This second disparity between Tarski and Davidson is one which, for simplicity of discussion, I shall ignore. I shall assume the object language to be context-free so that the references to speakers and times are unnecessary. On the first point, however, I shall follow Davidson quite strictly, for the difference is of crucial importance—an importance which is not sufficiently emphasized in his paper. If the characterization of the truth predicate for L serves to explicate its sense, to say exactly what is meant by 'is true in L', it cannot also serve to interpret the expressions of L. The characterization can only serve as a theory of meaning if the truth predicate, thus employed, is already understood; for although the characterization tells us how in L truth applies, it is only by knowing that it is *truth* which thus applies that we can hope to gain an understanding of L. Thus the difference in the form of the characterization between Tarski and Davidson reflects a difference in their aims. Tarski is seeking to explain the concept of truth for a particular language, and to this end nothing could be better than the explicit definition of a previously uninterpreted predicate. Davidson is seeking to construct an interpretative theory of meaning, and this requires using the concept of truth as formally primitive. Of course, in saying that truth must be formally primitive, I mean primitive relative to the T-style truth theory. There is nothing to prevent this theory forming part of a larger theory in which the truth predicate is defined. What we cannot have is its definition by those very clauses which, by generating the Tarski biconditionals, form the theory of interpretation.

Given the task we have set ourselves, the merits of Davidson's proposal are obvious. A theory of truth meeting the modified version of Convention T, a *T-theory* as I shall call it, exemplifies the general format we envisaged: for each sentence of the object language, it entails a theorem in which that sentence is structurally designated and its English translation used. But the method of linking the designated and the used has changed for the better: the intensional concept of meaning has given place to the extensional concept of truth, and the intensional idiom of oratio obliqua to the extensional idiom of material equivalence. Moreover, the prospects for constructing T-theories are favourable. Tarski's own method, suitably reconstrued, suffices for elementary quantificational languages, while Davidson and others have shown, and continue to show, how to adapt this

method to languages of a richer grammatical structure.[3] So far, so good. But the crucial question is whether a T-theory is fully interpretative. And here, even before a detailed investigation, one has the suspicion that in relinquishing the intensional idiom we have relaxed our grip on meaning. Can we really hope that a characterization of truth for a language will also constitute a full characterization of meaning?

The suspicion of inadequacy may be due in part to a misunderstanding of how a T-theory is supposed to do its interpretative work. In shifting from the intensional to the extensional idiom, we diminish the interpretative force of each individual theorem. An extensional theorem of the form '*S* is true if and only if *p*' says less than an intensional theorem of the form '*S* means that *p*'. But it is not intended that a T-theory should interpret each sentence of the language by that unique theorem which states its truth conditions. It is not intended that our understanding of each sentence be based wholly on the truth-conditional for it which the theory entails. Rather, the theory purports to interpret each sentence by locating its position on the lines of truth determination for the language as a whole, by stating its truth conditions in the framework of the general principles by which the truth conditions of *any* sentence are determined by its structure. The meaning of each sentence *S* is given not by that unique theorem which refers to it, but by that infinite set of theorems which refer to all sentences that contain any *S*-component. In effect, the interpretation of *S* is the interpretation of the whole language in the perspective of that sentence. This gives an interesting slant to the dictum that the meaning of a sentence depends on the meanings of its elements, a slant in which the lines of dependence run in both directions. The meaning of a sentence does depend on the meanings of its elements, but, on a T-theoretical view, the meaning of each element consists in what it contributes to the truth conditions of the sentences which contain it. On such a view, the meaning of each expression, whether simple or complex, consists in the particular form in which its structure channels the contributions to truth conditions.

Once we have grasped how the work of interpreting each sentence is diffused throughout the whole theory, the weakness of the individual theorems is less alarming. But here there is room for a second mis-

[3] E.g. Davidson, 'The Logical Form of Action Sentences', in *The Logic of Decision and Action*, ed. N. Rescher (Pittsburgh University Press, 1967), 81, 'Causal Relations', *Journal of Philosophy*, lxiv (1967), 691, and 'On Saying That', *Synthese*, xix (1968), 130

understanding, this time one which puts Davidson's thesis in a more favourable light than it deserves. Just as we might wrongly demand that the individual theorems accomplish more than they are supposed to, so we might mistakenly suppose that they accomplish more than they do. I have said that these theorems, T-sentences as Davidson calls them, state the truth conditions of the sentences they refer to. But this is so only in a special sense. As ordinarily understood, the truth conditions of a sentence are those conditions necessary and sufficient for its truth: two sentences are said to have the same truth conditions just in case they would, with their meaning held constant, have the same truth value in all possible circumstances—just in case there could not be circumstances of a kind which accords with what is stated by the one which were not also circumstances of a kind which accords with what is stated by the other. Similarly, as ordinarily understood, to state the truth conditions of a sentence is to say what (indirect question) is necessary and sufficient for its truth, to demarcate, within the total range of possible circumstances, that subset with which the sentence accords. But this is not the sense in which a *T-sentence* states truth conditions. A T-sentence does not say that such and such a structural type *would be* true (meaning held constant) in all and only those circumstances in which it *was* the case that . . ., but merely that, things being as they are, this structural type *is* true if and only if . . . It suffices for the truth of a T-sentence that what fills the blank has the same truth value as what it structurally designates, and the only sense in which a T-sentence states truth conditions is a sense whereby two sentences have the same truth *conditions* if and only if they have the same truth *value*. This point may be obscured by the fact that to qualify as a T-sentence it is not enough that what is designated on the left have the same truth value as what is used on the right: it is necessary, in addition, that the latter be a *translation* of the former. Replacing either sentence by one that is materially equivalent preserves the truth value of the biconditional, but such replacements do not guarantee that what emerges is qualified to go in a T-theory. This may foster the illusion that T-sentences are stronger than they are: it may persuade us that the constraints on their formulation are reflected in the force of what they state, that a T-sentence states truth conditions in the ordinary, strong sense, because the English translation expresses just that range of circumstances with which the designated sentence accords. I would hesitate to ascribe this illusion to Professor Davidson. But on the other hand,

once it has been dispelled, it becomes all too apparent, as I shall now show, that his thesis (as he *then* stated it) is mistaken.

To keep things simple, let us examine the form of a T-theory for an elementary quantificational language of the kind for which Tarski's own method, minus its definitional aspect, suffices. Let *L* be a language which consists, or can be represented as consisting, of a two-place predicate *P*, the truth-functional connective stroke with its normal meaning, the universal quantifier '$\bigwedge$' with its normal meaning, a denumerable stock of individual variables ordered as $v_1, v_2, v_3, \ldots$, the brackets '(' and ')', and all sentences, open and closed, formed from these elementary symbols by the standard formation rules of the predicate calculus. Assuming these formation rules have already been stated, the first step in constructing a T-theory for *L* is to introduce, either by explicit set-theoretical definition or as a primitive characterized by appropriate axioms, the concept of an infinite sequence of objects drawn from the universe of things over which the variables of *L* range. These sequences we shall call *assignments*, for, by its role in the theory, each sequence in effect assigns a unique value to each *L*-variable, the value of v_n for the sequence Σ being simply the *n*th element in Σ. (For the range of sequences to constitute the full range of assignments it is, of course, necessary that the same object *can* occur many times in the same sequence.) The next step is to find an English translation of the *L*-predicate *P*, and this, we will suppose, is provided by the predicate 'part of'. This brings us to the meat of the theory, which consists in the recursive characterization of the relation of satisfaction between assignments and sentences. We begin by saying that an assignment Σ satisfies an atomic *L*-sentence—a formula consisting of *P* followed by a pair of variables—if and only if the object which Σ assigns to the first of these variables is a part of the object which Σ assigns to the second. By similarly exploiting our translations of stroke and '$\bigwedge$' we can then characterize satisfaction for sentences of higher complexity. Thus Σ satisfies a sentence of the form $A^\frown$stroke$^\frown B$ if and only if Σ fails to satisfy either *A* or *B*; and Σ satisfies a sentence of the form '$\bigwedge$'$^\frown v_n{}^\frown A$ if and only if *A* is satisfied by every assignment which differs from Σ, if at all, in at most its *n*th place. With satisfaction fully characterized, the final step is to say that an *L*-sentence is true if and only if it is satisfied by all assignments. Suitably formalized, and enriched with the appropriate axioms of structural description and sequence theory, these clauses collectively constitute a T-theory for

L: for each closed *L*-sentence *S*, they entail what is got from the schema '*x* is true if and only if *p*' by substituting the structural description of *S* for '*x*' and the translation of *S* for '*p*'.

This theory—we will call it θ—gives an adequate characterization of truth in *L*. But it does not, however obliquely, give an adequate characterization of meaning. For, for every *L*-sentence, there are infinitely many and importantly different interpretations with which θ is consistent. Knowing the facts which θ states does not suffice for so much as an approximate understanding of a single sentence. This is most clearly seen by considering what θ says of the simple elements of which *L*-sentences are composed. For *P*, the crucial clause (we will call it the *P-clause*) is that which states that, for any integers *i* and *j*, an assignment satisfies $P^\frown v_i{}^\frown v_j$ if and only if its *i*th element is a part of its *j*th element. The other clauses are not crucial, since they are obviously consistent with any interpretation of *P* which is consistent with its grammatical parsing as a two-place predicate. But just what does the *P*-clause tell us? Only, in the context of the other clauses, that *P* applies to all and only those ordered pairs of objects that are related as part to whole. But this, while not compatible with *every* interpretation of *P*, *is* compatible with every interpretation which accords with its extension. If P' is any predicate with the same extension as *P*, we can substitute in the *P*-clause the designation of P' for the designation of *P* without altering its truth. Hence if there is or could be a predicate P' with the same extension as *P*, but with a different sense, nothing in the *P*-clause or in any other clauses of θ precludes our falsely interpreting *P* to mean whatever it is that P' means. All that remains is to show that there could be such a predicate. This is easy. Take any contingently true sentence of English, (say) 'the earth moves', and envisage P' as what would be correctly translated by the English expression 'the earth moves and . . . is a part of . . .'. Since it is true that the earth moves, *P* and P' are coextensive: there is no pair of objects to which one applies and the other does not. But they differ in meaning; P' is, to put it technically, a proper determinate of *P*: it implies all that *P* implies and in addition the contingent proposition that the earth moves. There are obviously infinitely many examples of this type, as many as there are distinct truths of English. And there are also examples, again infinitely many, of other types. One type, closely related, would be to take any contingently false English sentence, (say) 'the earth is still', and envisage P' as what would be correctly translated by 'either

the earth is still or . . . is a part of . . .'. Again P and P' would be coextensive, but this time P' would be a proper determinable of P, implied by anything that implies P, and in addition by the contingent proposition that the earth is still. Types of example and instances of each type could be multiplied indefinitely. But it is the principle they illustrate which matters, namely that θ, while it fixes the extension of P, comes nowhere near fixing its sense. For for each such P', θ says nothing to exclude a false interpretation of P along the lines of the correct interpretation envisaged for P'.

There is an exactly parallel argument to show that θ fails to interpret the connective and quantifier. We can envisage a connective stroke$^+$ translatable in English as 'the earth moves and either it is not the case that . . . or it is not the case that . . .', and we can envisage a quantifier '$\wedge^+$' translatable as 'for every object . . ., the earth moves and . . .'. These new operators have the same *truth-relevant* force as their counterparts in L, and θ says nothing to exclude a false interpretation of stroke along the lines of stroke$^+$, or a false interpretation of '$\wedge$' along the lines of '$\wedge^+$'. θ is obviously in a bad way. To ram the point home, consider any analytically true sentence of L, (say) '$\wedge$'$\frown v_1 \frown P \frown v_1 \frown v_1$. This sentence states the trivial truth that everything is a part of itself. But θ says so little about '$\wedge$' and P that there is absolutely no contingent truth which we could not, compatibly with θ, construe this sentence to be stating. And if this is so, then whatever its merits as a theory of truth, θ is a very bad theory of meaning indeed.

The failure of θ to capture the meanings of the elements of L reflects the attenuated sense in which, quite generally, a T-theory for a language states the truth conditions of its sentences. Whatever these sentences mean, each T-sentence is true simply because the English sentence used on the right has the same truth value as the sentence designated on the left. Given a language X and its T-theory Y, a false interpretation of X is compatible with Y if revising the meanings of the X-sentences to accord with this interpretation preserves, in all cases, their grammar and truth values; and grammar and truth values are systematically preserved if the revision preserves all that the elements contribute to the truth values of the sentences which contain them. Because on such a revision Y would remain true (though no longer a T-theory), an interpretation which ascribes the revised meanings is both false of X as it actually is, and compatible with all that Y states. It is just this which the case of L and θ exemplifies.

And from this case we can now draw the general conclusion which demolishes Davidson's thesis, namely that T-theorizing fails to be genuinely interpretative for all languages where the full significance of the elements, gauged by their contributions to what is stated by the sentences which contain them, exceeds their truth-relevant significance, gauged by what they contribute to the truth or falsity of these sentences. These languages will include, at the very least, all languages of an extensional kind, of which the elementary quantificational languages, exemplified by *L*, are the paradigm case.

There are four ways in which this conclusion, or the importance I attach to it, might be attacked. First, there is the argument, possibly ascribable to Hintikka, that I am reading more meaning into an extensional language than the austerity of its syntax allows, that in such a language the full significance of the elements does *not* exceed their truth-relevant significance, and that the extra meaning I thought I discerned has been, so to speak, misappropriated from the richer resources possessed by an extensional fragment of a larger *non*-extensional language.[4] Secondly, it might be argued that, while the case of extensional languages is as I have represented it, no natural, autonomous language could be purely extensional, since to speak a language requires having propositional attitudes, and to have such attitudes requires the ability to ascribe them to oneself and others by means of nonextensional idiom. So granted that Davidson's concern is with theories of meaning for natural languages, my arguments do not touch him. Thirdly, and more weakly, it might be argued that, while there *could be* an extensional natural language, all known natural languages *are*, as a matter of fact, nonextensional, so that my conclusions are of little consequence. Fourthly, and finally, it could be argued that if the method of T-theorizing suffices for certain kinds of nonextensional language, we can readily adapt it to an extensional language by merely constructing the theory for some hypothetical nonextensional language of which that language would be a fragment. These four objections, while different and in certain cases inconsistent with each other, are variations on a common theme, namely that the defects I have ascribed to Davidson's thesis stem not from this thesis, but from my failure to grasp the peculiarity of those languages by which I have tested it. In their different ways they claim

[4] Thus see J. Hintikka, 'Semantics for Propositional Attitudes', in *Philosophical Logic*, ed. J. W. Davis *et al.* (Reidel, Dordrecht, 1969), p. 21.

that I have misrepresented either the character or the importance of those extensional languages I have chosen as my battleground.

It would be nice to examine these objections in detail and expose all their misconceptions and mistakes. But I can afford to be brief, for I think that neither Davidson, nor anyone familiar with his work, would wish to press them. To begin with, someone who, along the lines of the last two objections, regards intensional idiom as something to draw out the true strength of T-theorizing is simply ignorant of the kind of problems such idiom creates, problems which might make one despair of providing a T-theory at all. Nonextensionality in the object language is not an invigorating tonic which ensures that the lines of truth determination encompass richer fields of meaning, but a disease which threatens to prevent the truth theory ever developing. Davidson's own solution, and I can see no other, is, before applying the T-theory, to reconstrue the seemingly nonextensional idiom in extensional terms, an example of this being the paratactic analysis of oratio obliqua, as presented in his paper 'On Saying That'.[5] This paratactic analysis also disposes of the second objection; for even if we thought the analysis unsatisfactory for (say) English as it is, there obviously could be a language in which the ascription of propositional attitudes worked in the paratactic way. Finally. once we have accepted that an extensional language can, by such devices, do all the descriptive work of a natural language, the first objection loses even that modicum of plausibility which it had. The objection, if coherent at all, must amount to the claim that, given a community with an extensional language, there could be no grounds, in the observable features of linguistic usage, for deciding between the different interpretations compatible with its T-theory. But to claim such a degree of indeterminacy is absurd; for if extensionality does not as such restrict descriptive resources, it does not as such restrict the kind of empirical evidence relevant to interpretation.

III. DAVIDSON'S REVISED THESIS

Professor Davidson will, I think, accept the essentials of my argument so far. There may be dispute over detail, but I think he will concede that the thesis he put forward in 'Truth and Meaning', and endorsed, with only minor adjustments, in certain subsequent papers,[6] is wrong for the reasons I have given. But recently his position has undergone

[5] *Synthese*, xix (1968), 130.

[6] See especially his 'Semantics for Natural Languages', in *Linguaggi nella Società e nella Tecnica* (Edizioni di Comunità, Milan, 1970), p. 177.

an important change, a change which appears to protect him from the particular criticisms I have made. So I want next to state this new position, if I have understood it correctly, and assess its merits.[7]

The right starting point is to note again something which has already come up, namely the disparity between the weakness of what T-sentences state and the constraints on their construction. Any sentence of the form '*x* is true if and only if *p*' is true just in case the sentence designated by what we substitute for '*x*' has the same truth value as the sentence we substitute for '*p*'. But for this biconditional to qualify as a T-sentence, as a theorem of a theory meeting Convention T, it is necessary in addition that the sentence substituted for '*p*' be a translation of the sentence designated by what we substitute for '*x*'. But if so, it seems that a T-theory can, in some sense, serve as a theory of meaning. For although a T-theory is not itself a theory of meaning—since the facts it states do not suffice for mastery—if one knows a T-theory and knows that it *is* a T-theory, one knows enough to interpret the language. Let us develop this for the case of L and θ. θ fails as a theory of meaning because, while it captures what the elements of L contribute to the truth or falsity of the sentences which contain them, it fails to capture all that they contribute to what these sentences state. But suppose we add the knowledge that θ is a T-theory. Then for each L-sentence S, we know that θ's theorem for S is a T-sentence, in which the sentence on the right translates S. But this sentence on the right is one which we understand, indeed *have* to understand to understand θ; and if we both understand this sentence and know that it translates S, then we know what S states. In effect, equipped with a grasp of θ and the knowledge of its T-theoreticity, we can systematically reread each T-sentence as of the form '*x* states that *p*'. With these rereadings in mind, we only have to work back from the T-sentences to their axioms to net all that the elements contribute to what L-sentences state. And to have netted this is to know how to interpret any L-sentence on the basis of its structure.

This thesis, that within the framework of the knowledge that we are T-theorizing a T-theory serves as a theory of interpretation, is the first layer of Davidson's new account. Behind it is a second and older layer, which now takes on a new importance. This older layer con-

[7] My representation of Davidson's new position is based on certain unpublished papers he delivered in Oxford in Trinity Term 1974.

sists, in effect, of an empirical account of the notion of translation.[8] So far, in formulating the conditions for being a T-theory, we have, like Tarski, taken this notion for granted: we have assumed that we understand what it is for a sentence on the right of a truth-conditional to translate what is designated on the left. If we were ever to use the character of T-theories to give leverage on the concept of meaning, there obviously had to come a time when this assumption was abandoned. And abandon it is just what Davidson does. In its place he holds that to be a T-theory is to be a theory which meets certain formal and empirical constraints. The formal constraints ensure the form of a fully developed theory of truth: they require the entailment of the characteristic truth-conditionals with structural designators on the left and no structural designators on the right. The empirical constraints ensure, or are intended to ensure, that the theory is accurate and, within the limits of indeterminacy, exemplifies, in its truth-conditional theorems, an accurate manual of translation: here, the main requirement is the maximizing of agreement between the truth-claims of the native speakers and the truth-claims of the theory —the better the theory, the more it represents the speakers as correct in what they hold true. This, the Principle of Charity as it is sometimes (mis)called, is the main empirical constraint, but once it has allowed the theory to take off, it is to be tempered by other considerations, such as the likelihood, in given circumstances, of native error, and the degree to which the beliefs ascribable to speakers on the basis of the theory are supported by independent behavioural evidence.

Davidson's new thesis is, then, that a theory of truth meeting certain formal and empirical constraints serves as a theory of meaning for one who knows that it meets these constraints. It may be possible to question whether Davidson's constraints are strong enough, whether they ensure the closest fit that indeterminacy allows between sentences of the object language and sentences of English. But such questions are, from my point of view, a matter of detail. The crucial point is that, given the right constraints, the new thesis appears to escape my earlier objections. My only achievement, it seems, is to have shown, perhaps more decisively than Davidson himself, *why* this new thesis should be adopted. However, matters are not so simple. Look again at the case of θ and L. The claim is that,

[8] The origins of the account date back to 'Truth and Meaning'.

given the knowledge that it is a T-theory (as defined by the relevant constraints), θ serves as a theory of meaning for *L*. This claim does not, of course, mean that, given the relevant knowledge, θ *becomes* a theory of meaning for *L*, that θ comes to state facts which suffice for a mastery of *L*. For obviously, however useful this extra knowledge, it cannot make any difference to what θ states. The claim is, rather, that knowing the facts which θ states and knowing that θ is a T-theory between them suffice for a mastery of *L*. But is this so? Suppose that θ' is an exact reformulation in French of all that θ states, and suppose that Pierre, a Frenchman with no understanding of English, accepts θ' on the authority of a compatriot François, who is an expert linguist. François, however, omits to mention that θ' is a T-theory. So Pierre, while he knows the facts which θ' states and, since they are the same, the facts which θ states, cannot yet use this knowledge to interpret *L*. Now suppose that next François, overrating his friend's linguistic capacities, writes out θ, specifies its rules of inference, informs Pierre that these English sentences, in the framework of these rules, constitute a T-theory for *L*, and supplies a formal criterion by which Pierre can recognize its T-sentences. Thus informed, Pierre knows that θ is a T-theory for *L* and can, by deriving the T-sentences, work out the English translation of any selected *L*-sentence. So Pierre has both items of knowledge whose conjunction, it was claimed, suffices for mastery. He knows the facts stated by θ and he knows that θ is a T-theory. But, not knowing English, and not knowing that θ and θ' state the same facts, he cannot convert this knowledge into an understanding of *L*. Indeed, in his circumstances, the information that θ is a T-theory is wholly gratuitous.

This point, of course, harks back to the objections to a translation theory discussed much earlier. If formulated in English, a theory of translation from *L* to English can pose as a theory of meaning; for anyone who, in virtue of understanding English, understands the theory can interpret the sentences of *L* on the basis of their translation. But such a theory is not genuinely interpretative, since the understanding of *L* is not derived wholly from what the theory states. Davidson's new thesis is defective in the same way. What in effect he is offering, as a theory of meaning, is the combination of a T-theory and, by adding a clause which claims its T-theoreticity, a translation theory dressed up in empirically respectable terms. Given that we understand θ, claiming its T-theoreticity provides a translation manual from *L* to a language we understand, and we only have to inspect the

manner in which the T-sentences, exhibiting the translations, are derived, to gain a full understanding of any expression of *L*. But the conjunction of θ and a clause which states that it is a T-theory is not, as the case of Pierre demonstrates, an adequate theory of meaning. What it *states* does not suffice for a mastery of *L*. Indeed, it is no more interpretative than θ on its own, since the additional clause states nothing which bears on the interpretation of *L* unless supplemented by an interpretation of English.

Thus if I have correctly represented it, Davidson's new thesis is no better than the original. Indeed, if anything it is worse, since it increases the complexity of the supposed theories of meaning without any gain in their interpretative power. There is, however, a closely related thesis which is seemingly more effective and perhaps what Davidson is trying to convey. The trouble with the present version is that the claim of T-theoreticity and the content of the T-theory do not interlock: our knowledge that θ is a T-theory has no direct contact with our knowledge of the facts which θ states. But the idea behind this thesis may be sound. For in effect what we need to know, for the mastery of *L*, are both the facts which θ states and that these facts, as known by us, are T-theoretical; we need to know both the θ-facts and that, in knowing these facts, we are T-theorizing. How then are we to put this, granted that the predicate 'T-theory' applies not to facts or knowledge, but to sets of sentences? The answer must surely be this: the facts which suffice for a mastery of *L* are those stated by the single sentence (θ^*): 'Some T-theory for *L* states that . . . .' where we fill the blank with the conjunction of all the clauses of θ. θ^* employs the predicate 'T-theory' in its established sense, but in it the claim of T-theoreticity encompasses the content of the truth theory—it tells us what we need to know, for an understanding of *L*, about the facts which θ states. Generalizing, we obtain the following revised thesis: for any language *X*, the theory of meaning for *X* is what is got from the schema 'Some T-theory for *y* states that *p*' by substituting a designator of *X* for '*y*' and a T-theory for *X* for '*p*'.

This revision takes care of the problem of interpretativeness. For consider again the trivial *L*-sentence '$\bigwedge$'$^\frown v_1{}^\frown P^\frown v_1{}^\frown v_1$, whose structural description, just used, we will abbreviate to '*D*'. In θ this sentence has as its T-sentence: '*D* is true if and only if $(x)(x$ is a part of $x)$'. Since this T-sentence is a logical consequence of θ, we can deduce from θ^* (not, of course, by means of standard extensional

logic) that (1) some T-theory for *L* has as a logical consequence a sentence which states that *D* is true if and only if $(x)(x$ is a part of $x)$. And since any sentence which states this must be a T-sentence of any T-theory which logically entails it, we can deduce from (1) (again not by means of standard extensional logic) that (2) some T-theory for *L* has a T-sentence whose left half contains a designation of *D* and whose right half states that $(x)(x$ is a part of $x)$. But knowing the significance of the T-constraints, we can deduce from (2) that (3) a sentence which states that $(x)(x$ is a part of $x)$ is a translation of *D*. From which we can immediately deduce that (4) *D* states that $(x)(x$ is a part of $x)$. Since this same procedure is available for every *L*-sentence, by knowing the facts which θ^* states we can, with our wits about us, work out what any selected sentence states. And this general capacity, encompassing the totality of *L*-sentences, implies the capacity to interpret each sentence on the basis of its structure, since it implies the capacity to discern, not only what this sentence states, but what each of its elements contributes to what it states.

Interpretativeness, however, is θ^*'s only merit. In all other respects it falls short of our requirements. For it brings back the kind of intensionality which conflicts with our philosophical aims: it takes for granted the concept of stating and the nonextensional syntax which goes with it. There is not much to be gained in letting the claim of T-theoreticity and the content of the T-theory make contact, if the only means of connecting them are by the intensional idiom of 'stating that'. Why, after all, take the trouble to give an empirical account of translation, if such idiom can be assumed to be unproblematic? This idiom, moreover, is all the worse because the only genuinely semantic clauses, laying semantic conditions on structural types, fall on its opaque side. We have lost the explicit identification of *L*-expressions and the explicit description of their semantic significance. All that θ^* says of *L* is that some T-theory for it states that such and such, and we are left, as it were, to work out the semantics by discerning the concealed implications.

At this point Davidson may be tempted to press his paratactic analysis of oratio obliqua, reformulating θ^* as:

—. Some T-theory for *L* states that

where θ fills the left hand blank and the demonstrative 'that' refers back to that particular θ-utterance. For this not only extensionalizes

the syntax, but leaves *stating* as a relation which, like translation before it, may yield to analysis. But thus construed, θ^* ceases, as I shall now show, to be interpretative. To avoid terminological confusion, I shall use the word 'states' in its normal, non-Davidsonian sense and use the expression 'stands in the stating relation to' for that special relation, expressed in the reformulation, which holds between a theory and an utterance. Let us call that particular θ-utterance '*U*'. Now obviously someone may be able to identify *U*, (say) as the utterance made by so and so at such and such a time, without knowing what it is that *U* states. And consequently, someone who does not know what it is that *U* states may know, on good authority, that some T-theory for *L* stands in the stating relation to it. But if he does not know what it is that *U* states, knowing that some T-theory for *L* stands in the stating relation to it does not help him to interpret *L*. Moreover, someone who does not know what it is that *U* states may nonetheless know all the facts which *U* does state. So someone may know all that is stated by both components of the reformulated θ^* without being able to interpret *L*: he may know both the facts stated by θ and that some T-theory for *L* stands in the stating relation to *U*, without having any more interpretative knowledge of *L* than what is provided by θ alone. In effect, by formulating θ^* paratactically we sever that direct link between the claim of T-theoreticity and the content of θ which the intensional idiom secured.

It may be objected that it is *I* who have severed the link by failing to discern the subtle way in which the two components of the paratactic whole interact. If Smith says to a French audience: 'The earth moves. Galileo said that', his interpreter (*interpreter* in the ordinary, not my special sense), who, we may think, is trying to stand in the same-saying relation to him, says: 'La terre tourne. Galilée a dit cela', in which the demonstrative 'cela' refers not to Smith's utterance of the English sentence 'The earth moves' but to his own utterance of the French sentence 'La terre tourne'. So it may be argued that to know the facts stated by the paratactic θ^*, to stand in the same-knowing relation to its utterer, is to know, not that some T-theory stands in the stating relation to *U*, but that some T-theory stands in the stating relation to one's own last utterance—where one's own last utterance is of a sentence stating the same facts as θ. Well, this may be so. But if it is so, it can only be because the paratactic version of oratio obliqua is not what it purports to be. For the Davidsonian analysis of 'Galileo said that', as uttered by Smith, is 'some utterance

of Galileo and my last utterance make Galileo and me same-sayers', and a strict French rendering of what Smith thereby *states* must preserve the reference to Smith's previous utterance. To insist, contrariwise, that rendering the *whole* of what Smith states requires changing the reference in the suggested way, is, in effect, to construe the paratactic version of oratio obliqua as a notational variant of the intensional version, to construe the apparent demonstrative as an intensional operator on the previous sentence. There is no denying, of course, that a good interpreter, in the ordinary sense, would change the reference from Smith's utterance to his own. But that is because a good interpreter would convey the information which Smith wants conveyed, not restate the facts or propositions which Smith states. Our concern, it must be emphasized, is with the stating of facts, not the conveying of information; otherwise we could have settled for a translation theory long ago.

That, I think, is the *coup de grâce* for Davidson's new approach. I, at any rate, cannot see any way of harnessing the claim of T-theoreticity that both secures interpretativeness and avoids intensionality. And if there is no way, and if a T-theory on its own is inadequate, Davidson's grand design is in ruins. The only remaining question is what we should put in its place.

IV. TARSKI WORLD-RELATIVIZED

Although Davidson's design is in ruins, there are two central ideas in it which we can salvage, ideas which we might label his *holistic conception of meaning* and his *holistic conception of translation*. In the first place, I think Davidson is right to maintain the dependency of meaning on truth conditions, provided truth conditions are construed in their ordinary, strong sense. In any language, the meaning of each element consists in what this element contributes to the truth conditions of the sentences which contain it, and the meaning of each expression consists in the particular form in which its structure channels such contributions.[9] And granted this conception of meaning, what we are looking for as a theory of interpretation is a finite set of axioms which, for each sentence of the language, yield a theorem stating its truth conditions. Secondly, I think Davidson is right to

[9] This needs qualification: there are aspects of meaning (e.g. the difference in tone between the sentential connectives 'and' and 'but', and the difference in force between indicative, interrogative and imperative moods) which the truth-conditional account does not (and is not intended to) capture. The account is offered as a characterization of the central core of meaning, roughly what is usually called *sense*.

construe the requirement of translation, relating to the theorems, in terms of holistic constraints, of a formal and empirical kind, on the provision of an acceptable theory. An accurate translation manual is not something which we start with, prior to the construction of the theory, but something which we discover by finding that a certain theory of the required form has the right kind of empirical support. If we accept these fundamental ideas on meaning and translation, then what remains might be represented as a purely technical problem, the problem of formulating truth-conditional theorems that are both extensional and of the required strength—of finding some extensional filling between the structural designator and the English sentence that makes the relation of translation relevant to the correctness of what is stated.

But if these are the terms of our project, we face not a technical *problem*, but a technical *impossibility*. If we retain the structural designator and English translation found in a T-sentence, and look merely for a more effective way of linking them, the requirement of extensionality and the requirement of strength are simply incompatible. The theorem will only have the required strength if the correctness of what it states depends on the fact that the English translation has the same truth conditions as the sentence structurally designated. But the theorem will only be extensional if its truth cannot be affected by any replacement of this translation by a sentence with the same truth value. Obviously we cannot have it both ways: we cannot have *both* extensionality of syntax *and* the demands of translation reflected in the force of what is stated. From which it follows that either there are no truth-conditional theorems of the kind we want, or, if there are, we cannot formulate them quite as we have supposed, by the linking of structural designator and English translation. Given our present approach, this is a somewhat depressing conclusion. Indeed, it might make one suspect that my conception of a theory of meaning is incoherent.

However, with a little ingenuity, I think we can see our way towards an acceptable solution. I am going to begin at a point which does not look too promising. To state the truth conditions of a sentence is to specify what circumstances are required by and suffice for its truth—to demarcate within the total range of possible circumstances that subset with which the sentence accords. Thus if we could accept an ontology of possible worlds, entities which embody the hypothetical circumstances with which sentences accord or fail to accord, and if

we introduce a two-place truth predicate 'true-of' to hold between a sentence and a world with which it accords, then one way of formulating truth-conditionals of the required strength would be by means of the schema '(*w*) (*x* is true-of *w* if and only if, if *w* obtained, it would be the case that *p*)', where for '*x*' we put the structural description of the relevant sentence and for '*p*' we put an English sentence with the same truth conditions. Such a formulation is, of course, predictably nonextensional: the truth-conditional would cease to be true if the sentence in the place of '*p*' were replaced by another materially equivalent sentence with different truth conditions. But what makes these truth-conditionals important is that, provided there is not further nonextensionality within the sentence in the place of '*p*', they can, as I will shortly demonstrate, be reformulated extensionally with no loss of strength.

Reformulating these conditionals would, of course, be an easy task if we could recognize as objects of reference the imaginary constituents of other worlds. For suppose the sentence *S* of the object language is translated as 'all humans are mortal', so that, in its original form, the truth-conditional *C* for *S* is '(*w*)(*S* is true-of *w* if and only if, if *w* obtained, it would be the case that all humans are mortal)' or, more idiomatically, '(*w*)(*S* is true-of *w* if and only if, if *w* obtained, all humans would be mortal)'. If we could count among the values of our variables objects which *would* exist (but do not) if some other world obtained, we could reformulate *C* as '(*w*)(*S* is true-of *w* if and only if (*x*) (if *x* is human-in *w*, then *x* is mortal-in *w*))', where 'human-in' and 'mortal-in' are relations which hold between objects (not necessarily existent) and worlds whose actualization would humanize or mortalize them. This procedure obviously generalizes to other truth-conditionals, once we have got the translations into canonical form. To each of the predicates used in the translation we simply add an extra place, to be filled by a reference to a world. We then cross out from the truth-conditional the middle chunk 'if *w* obtained, it would be the case that', replace the old predicates by the new, and relocate the variable '*w*' in its new positions. The result is an extensional truth-conditional with the same force as the original.

In my view, I know not shared by everyone, the cost to our ontology of such a procedure is too high a price to pay. Indeed, to talk of a *high price* is too lenient, for no amount of pride-swallowing or special pleading can get our variables to range over objects that do not exist.

There is an absolute distinction between recognizing a queer sort of entity, like Platonic Forms, and imaginary versions of tangible things like humans—the distinction (to be provocative) between eccentricity and madness. The method of reformulation I advocate is quite different. In it we preserve, in a sense, our links with imaginary entities, but through the medium of real things that stand proxy for them.

To begin with an example, consider again the open sentence employed in the rejected reformulation of *C*:

(1) $(x)(\text{if } x \text{ is human-in } w, \text{ then } x \text{ is mortal-in } w)$.

Retaining the bogus ontology of imaginary objects, we can re-express (1) set-theoretically as:

(2) $$(y)(s)(t)((y = \langle s,t \rangle \ \& \ s = \hat{v}(v \text{ is human-in } w) \ \& \ t = \hat{v}(v \text{ is mortal-in } w)) \supset (x)(x \in s \supset x \in t))$$

i.e. (y)(if y is an ordered pair whose first element is the class of all humans in w and whose second element is the class of all mortals in w, then all members of the first element are members of the second element).

Now let us say that two sets or sequences are structurally equivalent just in case each can be transformed into the other by consistent replacement of its atomic constituents. In other words structurally equivalent sets or sequences are those which possess the same set-theoretical structure and, within that structure, atoms that exhibit the same relations of identity and difference. Given this concept, (2) can be re-expressed in an even more complicated way as:

(3) $$(y)(y')(s)(s')(t)(t')((\text{Structurally Equivalent }(y, y') \ \& \ y = \langle s, t \rangle \ \& \ y' = \langle s', t' \rangle \ \& \ s = \hat{v}(v \text{ is human-in } w) \ \& \ t = \hat{v}(v \text{ is mortal-in } w)) \supset (x)(x \in s' \supset x \in t'))$$

i.e. $(y)(y')$(if y and y' are structurally equivalent and y is an ordered pair whose first element is the class of all humans in w and whose second element is the class of all mortals in w, then all members of the first element of y' are members of the second element of y').

(3) is logically equivalent to (2) since if y and y' are structurally equivalent, all members of the first element of y are members of the second element of y just in case all members of the first element of y' are members of the second element of y'. It is at this point that we can make our ontological saving. For although we cannot admit,

among the values of our variables, the ordered pair whose first element is the class of humans in w and whose second element is the class of mortals in w—unless perchance all the members of these classes are constituents of the real world—we nonetheless can and must admit pairs to which it is structurally equivalent. And as shown in (3), by describing the set-theoretical properties of a structurally equivalent pair, we can say all that has to be said about the imaginary humans and mortals in w. Thus let us introduce a two-place predicate 'R' explained thus: 'R' holds between x and y just in case y is a world and x is a sequence structurally equivalent to what would, if y obtained, be the ordered pair of the class of humans and the class of mortals. We can then re-express (3) as:

$$(4) \quad (y)(s)(t)((Ryw \ \& \ y = \langle s, t\rangle) \supset (x)(x \in s \supset x \in t))$$

i.e. (y)(if y is R-related to w, then all members of the first element of y are members of the second element of y).

And (4) states, within a universe of actual objects, exactly what we were trying to state, in the bogus ontology, by (1). Hence we can reformulate the truth-conditional C as:

$$(w)(S \text{ is true-of } w \equiv (y)(s)(t)((Ryw \ \& \ y = \langle s, t\rangle) \supset (x)(x \in s \supset x \in t)))$$

i.e. (w)(S is true-of w if and only if (y)(if y is R-related to w, then all members of the first element of y are members of the second element of y)).

And this sentence is both extensional in syntax and involves no commitment to imaginary objects.

Given an object language L_o and a canonical English translation of each L_o-sentence, this method can be generalized for all relevant truth-conditionals. Thus suppose the lexical vocabulary of these translations consists of the predicates 'F_1' . . . 'F_k', where 'F_1' is a one-place predicate defining the universe of L_o for all possible circumstances. In place of these ordinary English predicates we introduce a single two-place predicate 'F^*', explained as holding between x and y if and only if y is a world and x is a k-element sequence structurally equivalent to what would, if y obtained, be the k-element sequence of the class of F_1-type objects, the class of F_2-type n-tuples of F_1-type objects, the class of F_3-type n-tuples of F_1-type objects, . . . and the class of F_k-type n-tuples of F_1-type objects—in each case n being the place-number of the relevant predicate. Now suppose

S_1 is an L_o-sentence, S_2 its canonical English translation, and 'α' any variable not occurring in S_2. Let S_3 be the open sentence we obtain from S_2 by the following procedure: for each integer i and each integer n, if 'F_i'$\frown v_1 \frown \ldots \frown v_n$ is an atomic sentence contained in S_2, we replace it by the set-theoretical sentence '$\langle$'$\frown v_1 \frown \ldots \frown v_n \frown$'$\rangle$'$\frown$'$\in$ the ith element of α' (e.g. 'F_3xy' gets replaced by '$\langle x,y \rangle \in$ 3rd element of α'). The reformulated truth-conditional for S_1 is then what we get from the schema '(w)(x is true-of w if and only if (α)(if $F^*\alpha w$, then p))' by substituting the structural description of S_1 for 'x' and S_3 for 'p'.

This extensionalizes our syntax and eliminates the spurious constituents of other worlds. But what of the worlds themselves, the worlds we explicitly quantify over? Are not these just larger versions of the imaginary objects we are trying to avoid? Or if not this, the imaginary situations in which these objects are depicted? Well, not as I construe them. How I construe them is a long story, but to cut it short, let me appeal to the work of Quine, a philosopher not given to ontological extravagance. From the admittedly restricted viewpoint of Democritean materialism, Quine shows, in his essay 'Propositional Objects', how possible worlds can be construed as complex set-theoretical arrangments of real numbers.[10] Given the viewpoint, each world, prior to its construal, is conceived as a distinct distribution of homogeneous matter in space-time. Representing space-time by a 4-axis system, Quine construes a world as the set of those quadruples of real numbers which identify its materially occupied points.[11] Thus demythologized, worlds are rendered ontologically and conceptually respectable: ontologically, since we can locate them in the familiar set-theoretic universe; conceptually, since the predicate 'world' can be defined without recourse to intensional concepts. Only a Goodmanian nominalist would still have qualms. Are my worlds, then, the ones Quine has constructed? Not necessarily. The Quinean worlds are what emerge when the initial possibilities are sifted through the grid of a narrowly materialistic world-view. There are other world-views—Dualism, Phenomenalism and richer forms of Physicalism—which sift the possibilities in other ways. What is valuable in Quine is not the end-product, but the method,

[10] W. V. Quine, *Ontological Relativity and Other Essays* (Columbia University Press, New York, 1969), p. 139.

[11] To be precise, he construes a world as a set of sets of quadruples of real numbers, a set such that any two sets it contains represent the same spatiotemporal distribution on a relativistic conception of position and distance.

the method of using set theory to encode the range of possibilities which our philosophical convictions allow. My own convictions happen to be phenomenalistic, which is why the story of how *I* construe worlds would be such a long one.

But even granted a Democritean metaphysic, Quine's worlds do not quite provide all that we want, for the possible states of affairs they represent are purely qualitative. Suppose our object language contains a sentence S' whose English translation is 'Socrates is mortal', so that, unreformulated, the truth-conditional for S' is C': '$(w)(S'$ is true-of w if and only if, w obtained, Socrates would be mortal)'. We can easily enough reparse 'Socrates' as a one-place predicate 'Socratizes' and obtain the canonical reformulation of C' by the prescribed method. The trouble is that, even if we construe Socrates in purely material terms, neither C' nor its reformulation makes sense for the kind of worlds Quine has constructed. Each world has its own space-time frame of reference by which we can identify and reidentify the material particulars within it. But there is no common frame of reference, relating space-time points in one world with space-time points in another, by which we can trace an actual particular, such as Socrates, from the real world into the ones we envisage. The problem is not merely that in some nonactual world the extension of 'Socratizes' may be undecidable, for many predicates may be extensionally undecidable in virtue of their vagueness relative to the ultimate qualitative possibilities. The problem is that a crucial factor which bears on the decision has been omitted from the construction: for we do not know where and when to look for Socrates in the fictional setting unless we can locate and date its material events in our own spatiotemporal framework.

To remedy things, we must set up an axis system for space and time fixed by particular, identifiable events in the real world, and we must conceive of a possible world not just as a qualitative arrangement of material particles, but as such an arrangement sited in a determinate way within this system, as, in effect, a possible history and geography of *our* world. Worlds remain sets of quadruples of real numbers, but the same numbers represent the same positions in different worlds, positions which we can identify in our own space-time framework. With such a construction, we can now trace a particular from the real world into its fictional setting by the same procedure we use to trace it through its actual career. Certain questions of transworld identity may remain undecidable, for there may be alternative

'manuals of identity' consistent with the same data. But what matters is that the data now contain all the factors on which these questions turn. With possible worlds superimposed, as it were, on the real world, we can significantly ask of each whether, if it obtained, Socrates would be mortal.

Let us assume that, whatever our metaphysic, we have constructed an adequate range of worlds, worlds which represent not only the ultimate qualitative possibilities, but these possibilities mapped out on the dimensions which create particularity in the real world. Knowing the kind of truth-conditionals which a theory of meaning must entail, how are we to formulate the theory itself? Well, in the case of an elementary quantificational language like *L*, the solution lies in a simple adaptation of the Tarski characterization of truth: Tarski, as it were, world-relativized. The vocabulary of *L*, it will be recalled, consists of the two-place predicate *P* (meaning 'part of'), the universal quantifier '$\wedge$', the sentential connective stroke, a denumerable stock of variables v_1, v_2, . . ., and brackets; and the sentences of *L* are generated from these elements by the standard formation rules of the predicate calculus. Let us suppose that the universe of *L* is defined by the English predicate 'material', which we will assume applies to any material particle or aggregate of particles. To construct a theory of meaning for *L*, we begin by introducing the primitive two-place predicate 'matpart to', which we explain as holding between *x* and *y* just in case *y* is a world and *x* an ordered pair structurally equivalent to what would, if *y* obtained, be the ordered pair whose first element was the class of all things material, and whose second element was the class of all ordered pairs of material things part-whole related. Given a world *W*, a pair which is matpart to *W* may be called an *extensional projection* of L for *W*, for it encodes, in an ontology of real objects, the hypothetical universe of *L* for *W* and the hypothetical extension of *P* within that universe. We next say that Σ is an α-assignment if and only if α is matpart to some world and Σ is a denumerable sequence of objects drawn from the first element of α. The theory then proceeds, predictably, to give a recursive characterization of satisfaction between *L*-sentences, assignments and extensional projections. Thus if Σ is an α-assignment, $\langle\Sigma, \alpha\rangle$ satisfies an atomic sentence $P^\frown v_i{}^\frown v_j$ if and only if the ordered pair of the *i*th element and the *j*th element of Σ is a member of the second element of α. Moving to complex sentences, $\langle\Sigma, \alpha\rangle$ satisfies $A^\frown$stroke$^\frown B$ if and only if it fails to satisfy either *A* or *B*; and $\langle\Sigma,$

$\alpha\rangle$ satisfies '$\wedge$'$\frown v_i \frown A$ if and only if (Σ')(if Σ' is an α-assignment which differs from Σ, if at all, in at most its *i*th place, then $\langle\Sigma', \alpha\rangle$ satisfies *A*). The final step is the characterization of the truth relation between sentences and worlds: for any *L*-sentence *S* and world *w*, S is true-of *w* if and only if $(\alpha)(\Sigma)$(if α is matpart to *w* and Σ is an α-assignment, then $\langle\Sigma, \alpha\rangle$ satisfies S). Backed by suitable axioms of set theory and structural description, this theory entails all the truth-conditionals of the required strength and prescribed form.

It might be thought that the theory should be taken one stage further, by defining the matpart-relation in terms of the predicates by which the worlds are constructed. The problems of providing such a definition will obviously depend on the kind of worlds we have, the kind of possibilities they embody. If our worlds are Quine's Democritean ones, the definition is straightforward: α is matpart to *w* just in case α is structurally equivalent to an ordered pair $\langle x, y\rangle$ in which *x* is the set of all unions of particle-representing sets of quadruples in *w*, and *y* is the set of all ordered pairs $\langle v, z\rangle$ such that *v* and *z* are members of *x* and *v* is a subset of *z*. And particle-representation can itself be expressed in purely numerical and set-theoretical terms. But to provide a comparable definition of 'matpart to' for a range of phenomenalistic worlds would be far from straightforward. Indeed, there are grounds for thinking it impossible, the same grounds, in fact, for thinking that any materialistic predicate would be, from a phenomenalistic viewpoint, irreducibly vague. However, the demand for the reduction of the matpart-relation is misplaced. The role which this relation plays in the theory of meaning is equivalent to the role which 'material' and 'part of' play in a T-theory—the role, in effect, of translating *L* into English. The only difference is that in the new theory translation, like truth, is world-relative: 'matpart to' is used to express, in our modified English, what each *L*-sentence states relative to a given world. It belongs, to hark back to an earlier distinction, to our accidental, *L*-oriented vocabulary;[12] to insist on its reduction to the predicates of world-construction is to insist on converting a theory of meaning into a theory of analysis—on converting what suffices for an interpretation of *L* into what suffices for its reinterpretation in the perspective of one's overall metaphysic.

In conclusion, I state my thesis thus:[13] a theory of meaning for an object language L_o consists in the construction of an appropriate

[12] See the final paragraph of section I.
[13] With the qualification already indicated in note 9.

range of worlds, exhausting the possible total states of affairs which our philosophical viewpoint allows, together with a finite set of axioms which are true and entail, for each L_0-sentence *S*, the relevant canonical reformulation of that truth-conditional got from the schema '(*w*)(*x* is true-of *w* if and only if, if *w* obtained, it would be the case that *p*)' by substituting the structural description of *S* for '*x*' and the canonical English translation of *S* for '*p*'. The provision of such a theory for a natural language would be a monumental task, beset with problems. Some of these problems, such as how to make natural idiom amenable to truth theory and how to give an empirical account of translation, are shared by the weaker, T-theoretical programme proposed by Davidson. The progress which has been made in these fields carries over into my programme, as do the residual impediments. Other problems, such as establishing an overall metaphysic and constructing a range of worlds to accord with it, are distinctively mine, and what I have said about them has been conspicuously sketchy. Still, if my arguments are sound, the little that has been achieved is not without value: in knowing the adequacy conditions for a theory of meaning and possessing a rough plan of how they can be met, we already have a deeper grasp of what meaning is.

II

Reply to Foster*

DONALD DAVIDSON

THERE is much with which I agree, and more I admire, in Mr Foster's paper. I share his bias in favour of extensional first-order languages; I am glad to keep him company in the search for an explicitly semantical theory that recursively accounts for the meanings of sentences in terms of their structures; and I am happy he concurs in holding that a theory may be judged adequate on the basis of holistic constraints. I especially applaud Foster for what he passes over: just as *Lear* gains power through the absence of Cordelia, I think treatments of language prosper when they avoid uncritical evocation of the concepts of convention, linguistic rule, linguistic practice, or language games.

Still on the positive side, I think Foster is right in asking whether a proposed theory explicitly states something knowledge of which would suffice for interpreting utterances of speakers of the language to which it applies. (I avoid the word 'mastery', and the special competence of a speaker, if any, for reasons that will not, I believe, affect our discussion.) I was slow to appreciate the importance of this way of formulating a general aim of theories of meaning, though elements of the idea appear in an early paper of mine, 'Theories of Meaning and Learnable Languages' (1965),[1] as well as in 'Truth and Meaning'.[2] I am grateful to a number of Oxford friends for prompting me to try to clarify my views on this subject—and here I should especially mention Michael Dummett, Gareth Evans, John McDowell and John Foster.

In a paper first read in Biel, Switzerland, in May 1973, I criticized my own earlier attempts to say exactly what the relation is between a theory of truth and a theory of meaning, and I tried to do better.

* Read in reply to the first three parts of J. A. Foster, 'Meaning and Truth Theory' (in this volume), at the Oxford Philosophical Society on 13 June 1974.

[1] Y. Bar-Hillel (ed.), *Logic, Methodology and Philosophy of Science, Proceedings of the* 1964 *International Congress* (North-Holland, Amsterdam, 1965), p. 383.

[2] *Synthese*, xvii (1967), 304.

I read this paper again in Windsor (November, 1973), and it became the basis for much discussion in a seminar Michael Dummett and I gave in Oxford in Trinity Term, 1974. The criticisms I there levelled against my earlier formulation are (I believe) essentially those elaborated by Foster in the second part of his present paper, and my attempt at something better is among the views he attacks in the third part of his paper.

I am in general agreement with Foster that I have yet to give a completely satisfactory formulation of what it is, on my approach, that it suffices to know in order to be able to interpret a speaker's utterances. On the other hand, I hope I am not as far off target as he thinks, and I am not persuaded by his arguments that my 'grand design is in ruins'. Indeed it still seems to me right, as far as it goes, to hold that someone is in a position to interpret the utterances of speakers of a language *L* if he has a certain body of knowledge entailed by a theory of truth for *L*—a theory that meets specified empirical and formal constraints—and he knows that this knowledge is entailed by such a theory.

Tarski says, nearly enough for our purposes, that a theory of truth for a language *L* is satisfactory provided it entails (by a finite set of non-logical axioms and normal logic), for each sentence *s* of *L*, a theorem of the form:

s is true-in-*L* if and only if *p*

where '*s*' is replaced by a standardized description of *s* and '*p*' is replaced by a translation of *s* into the language of the theory. If we knew such a theory, and that it was such a theory, then we could produce a translation of each sentence of *L*, and would know that it was a translation. We would know more, for we would know in detail how the truth values of sentences of *L* were owed to their structures, and why some sentences entailed others, and how words performed their functions by dint of relations to objects in the world.

Since Tarski was interested in defining truth, and was working with artificial languages where stipulation can replace illumination, he could take the concept of translation for granted. But in *radical* interpretation, this is just what cannot be assumed. So I have proposed instead some empirical constraints on accepting a theory of truth that can be stated without appeal to such concepts as those of meaning, translation, or synonomy, though not without a certain

understanding of the notion of truth. By a course of reasoning, I have tried to show that if the constraints are met by a theory, then the T-sentences that flow from that theory will in fact have translations of *s* replacing '*p*'.

To accept this change in perspective is not to give up Convention T but to read it in a new way. Like Tarski, I want a theory that satisfies Convention T, but where he assumes the notion of translation in order to throw light on that of truth, I want to illuminate the concept of translation by assuming a partial understanding of the concept of truth.

That empirical restrictions must be added to the formal restrictions if acceptable theories of truth are to include only those that would serve for interpretation was clear to me even when I wrote 'Truth and Meaning'. My mistake was not, as Foster seems to suggest, to suppose that *any* theory that correctly gave truth conditions would serve for interpretation; my mistake was to overlook the fact that someone might know a sufficiently unique theory without knowing that it was sufficiently unique. The distinction was easy for me to neglect because I imagined the theory to be known by someone who had constructed it from the evidence, and such a person could not fail to realize that his theory satisfied the constraints.

Foster notes the difference between two questions that might be raised about my proposal. One is, whether the constraints I have placed on an acceptable theory are adequate to ensure that it satisfies Convention T—i.e. to ensure that in its T-sentences, the right branch of the biconditional really does translate the sentence whose truth value it is giving. The other question is whether I have succeeded in saying what a competent interpreter knows (or what it would suffice for him to know). Foster is concerned here only with the second question; he is willing to grant, for the space of the argument, that the constraints are adequate to their purpose.

It is in this light that we must understand Foster's discussion of theories of truth that correctly give the extension of the truth predicate—theories all of whose T-sentences are true—but which do not satisfy Convention T. Thus Foster is going along with me (for the moment) in supposing that my criteria will not allow a theory that contains as a T-sentence the following:

> '*a* is part of *b*' is true if and only if *a* is a part of *b* and the Earth moves.

Foster's point is rather that although my interpreter has a theory that satisfies Convention T, nothing in the theory itself tells him this.

The same point comes up when Foster says,

> as ordinarily understood, to state the truth conditions of a sentence is to say what . . . is necessary and sufficient for its truth, to demarcate, within the total range of possible circumstances, that subset with which the sentence accords. But this is not the sense in which a *T-sentence* states truth conditions. A T-sentence does not say that such and such a structural type *would be* true . . . in all and only circumstances in which it *was* the case that . . ., but merely that, things being as they are, this structural type *is* true if and only if . . .

A theory that passes the empirical tests is one that in fact can be projected to unobserved and counterfactual cases, and this is apparent to anyone who knows what the evidence is and how it is used to support the theory. The trouble is, the theory does not state that it has the character it does.

We get a precise parallel if we ask what someone must know to be a physicist. A quick answer might be: the laws of physics. But Foster would say, and I agree, that this is not enough. The physicist must also know (and here I speak for myself) that those laws *are* laws—i.e. that they are confirmed by their instances, and support counterfactual and subjunctive claims. To get the picture, you are to imagine that a budding scientist is told that the mass of a body has no influence on how long it will take for it to fall a given distance in a vacuum. Then he is asked, 'Suppose Galileo had dropped a feather and a cannon ball from the top of the Empire State Building, and that the earth had no atmosphere. Which would have reached the ground sooner, the feather or the cannon ball?' The wise child replies, 'I have no idea. You told me only what *does* happen, things being as they are; you did not say what would happen if things were otherwise.'

Foster offers, as a thesis he thinks I may have 'tried to convey' but failed to get right, the following: 'what we need to know, for the mastery of *L*, are both the facts which [a T-theory] states, and that those facts as known by us, are T-theoretical.' He then puts it in a nutshell: what someone needs to know is that some T-theory for *L* states that . . . (and here the dots are to be replaced with a T-theory). I am happy to accept this version, since it is equivalent to my own. (So far as I know, I never held the view he attributes to me which leaves unconnected

the knowledge of what a theory of truth states and the knowledge that the theory is T-theoretical.)

Now let us consider the view which Foster thinks I should, and I know I do, hold. It cannot be said that on this view, knowledge of a language reduces to knowing how to translate it into another. The interpreter does, indeed, know that his knowledge consists in what is stated by a T-theory, a T-theory that is translational (satisfies Convention T). But there is no reason to suppose the interpreter can express his knowledge in any specific linguistic form, much less in any particular language.

Perhaps we should insist that a theory is a sentence or a set of sentences of some language. But to know a theory it is neither necessary nor sufficient to know that these sentences are true. Not sufficient since this could be known by someone who had no idea what the sentences meant, and not necessary since it is enough to know the truths the sentences of the theory express, and this does not require knowledge of the language of the theory.

Someone who can interpret English knows, for example, that an utterance of the sentence 'Snow is white' is true if and only if snow is white; he knows in addition that this fact is entailed by a translational theory—that it is not an accidental fact about that English sentence, but a fact that *interprets* the sentence. Once the point of putting things this way is clear, I see no harm in rephrasing what the interpreter knows in this case in a more familiar vein: he knows that 'Snow is white' in English *means that* snow is white.

It is clear, then, that my view does not make the ability to interpret a language depend on being able to translate that language into a familiar tongue. Perhaps it is worth reinforcing this point by tidying up a matter so far passed over. In natural languages indexical elements, like demonstratives and tense, mean that the truth conditions for many sentences must be made relative to the circumstances of their utterance. When this is done, the right side of the biconditional of a T-sentence never translates the sentence for which it is giving the truth conditions. In general, an adequate theory of truth uses no indexical devices, and so can contain no translations of a very large number and variety of sentences. With respect to these sentences, there is not even the illusion that interpretation depends on the ability to translate. (The 'means that' idiom does no better here.)

Foster thinks my grand plan is in ruins because in trying to harness the claim of T-theoreticity to secure interpretation I must use an

intensional notion like the 'states' in 'The interpreter knows that some T-theory states that . . . '. But here he foists on me a goal I never had. My way of trying to give an account of language and meaning makes essential use of such concepts as those of belief and intention, and I do not believe it is possible to reduce these notions to anything more scientific or behaviouristic. What I have tried to do is give an account of meaning (interpretation) that makes no essential use of unexplained *linguistic* concepts. (Even this is a little stronger than what I think is possible.) It will ruin no plan of mine if in saying what an interpreter knows it is necessary to use a so-called intensional notion—one that consorts with belief and intention and the like.

Of course my project does require that all sentences of natural languages can be handled by a T-theory, and so if the intensional idioms resist such treatment, my plan has foundered. It seems to be the case, though the matter is not entirely simple or clear, that a theory of truth that satisfies anything like Convention T cannot allow an intensional semantics, and this has prompted me to try to show how an extensional semantics can handle what is special about belief sentences, indirect discourse, and other such sentences. Foster thinks my analysis will not do, but it is not easy to see how this is relevant to our debate. If his point is that *no* T-theory can give a satisfactory semantics for sentences that attribute attitudes, then all the discussion of how exactly to describe the competence of a speaker is simply irrelevant. But if some analysis is possible, mine or another, then what works for indirect discourse and sentences about belief and intention will presumably work also for the 'states' relation that worries Foster.

Foster is certainly right that the expression 'a T-theory states that' is what would usually be called a non-truth-functional sentential operator, since following it with materially equivalent sentences may produce results with divergent truth values. This leaves us with two problems (between which Foster does not perhaps sufficiently distinguish). The first is whether the paratactic analysis of indirect discourse can properly be applied in the present case; the other is whether my account of radical interpretation is threatened if the relevant notion of stating (whatever its semantics) conceals an unanalysed linguistic concept. The former problem is, I have just suggested, only marginally germane to our discussion; the latter is obviously central. I would, however, like to say something on both topics, since unless it is shown incompetent I do propose a paratactic semantics for 'states that'.

The paratactic semantic approach to indirect discourse tells us to view an utterance of 'Galileo said that the Earth moves' as consisting of the utterance of two sentences, 'Galileo said that' and 'The Earth moves'. The 'that' refers to the second utterance, and the first utterance is true if and only if an utterance of Galileo's was the same in content as ('translates') the utterance to which the 'that' refers. (Foster wrongly says my analysis of 'Galileo said that' is 'Some utterance of Galileo and my last utterance make Galileo and me same-sayers'. This is not an analysis, but a rephrasal designed to give a reader a feeling for the semantics, an expository and heuristic device.)

Foster tries to prove my semantic analysis wrong by showing that it fails a translation test. This test requires that the translation of an utterance (as analysed) must state the same fact or proposition (I am using Foster's words) as the original utterance. Then he points out a translation of 'Galileo said that' into French that preserved the reference of 'that' (on my analysis) would fail to convey to a French audience anything about the content of Galileo's remark. He takes this to show that on my analysis an ordinary utterance of a sentence like 'Galileo said that the Earth moves' fails to state what Galileo said; and so a parallel analysis of the 'states that' which my theory of interpretation needs will suffer from the same failure.

But what is this relation between utterances, of stating the same fact or proposition, that Foster has in mind? All he tells us is that reference must be preserved. This is surely not enough, however, since if any two utterances state the same fact when reference is preserved, it is very difficult to block a familiar proof that all true utterances state the same fact. The use of the word 'proposition' suggests that meaning must be preserved as well as reference. But if both reference and meaning must be preserved, it is easy to see that very few pairs of utterances can state the same fact provided the utterances contain indexical expressions. Leaving aside bilinguals, no French utterance can state any fact I do by using 'I', and I cannot twice state the same fact by saying 'I'm warm' twice. To judge my analysis wrong by these standards is simply to judge it wrong because it supposes that indirect discourse involves an indexical element. Failing further argument, the conclusion throws doubt on the standards, not the analysis.

Like Foster, I assume of course that a translator will render English indirect discourse into French in the usual way. In my view, he will

do this by referring to a new utterance which he will have to supply. (The same thing goes on if I utter 'Galileo said that the Earth moves' twice.) To admit this is not 'to construe the paratactic version of oratio obliqua as a notational variant of the intensional version', as Foster urges. Notation has nothing to do with it; both the possible world semanticist and I accept the same notation. We differ on the semantic analysis. The point is that the translator is stating the same fact, not in Foster's sense, but in some more usual sense which often allows, or even requires, that translation change the reference when that reference is, to use Reichenbach's phrase, token reflexive.

Turning back to the prospects for a paratactic analysis of that troublesome 'states', we ought first to note that a slightly more appropriate word would be 'entails'. What we want is the semantics for utterances of sentences like 'Theory T entails that "Snow is white" is true in English if and only if snow is white'. And the claim must be that an utterance of this sentence is to be treated, for the purposes of semantic theory, as the utterance of two sentences, the first ending in a demonstrative which refers to the second utterance. Entailment (of this sort) is thus made out to be a relation between a theory and an utterance of the speaker who claims entailment. What is this relation? A reasonable suggestion is that it is the relative product of the relation of logical consequence between sentences and the relation of synonymy between sentences and utterances (perhaps of another language). If a theory T entails that 'Snow is white' is true in English if and only if snow is white, then T has as logical consequence a sentence synonomous with my utterance of ' "Snow is white" is true in English if and only if snow is white'.

Does not the second component bring in an appeal to a specifically linguistic notion—that of synonomy? Certainly: it is just the concept of translation we have been trying to elicit by placing conditions on a theory of truth. This does not make the account circular, for those conditions were stated, we have been assuming, in a non-question-begging way, without appeal to linguistic notions of the kind we want to explain. So the concept of synonomy or translation that lies concealed in the notion of entailment can be used without circularity when we come to set out what an interpreter knows. Indeed, in attributing to an interpreter the concept of a translational theory we have already made this assumption.

On a point of some importance, I think Foster is right. Even if everything I have said in defence of my formulation of what suffices

for interpretation is right, it remains the case that nothing strictly constitutes a theory of meaning. A theory of truth, no matter how well selected, is not a theory of meaning, while the statement that a translational theory entails certain facts is not, because of the irreducible indexical elements in the sentences that express it, a theory in the formal sense. This does not, however, make it impossible to say what it is that an interpreter knows, and thus to give a satisfactory answer to one of the central problems of the philosophy of language.

III

Truth Conditions, Bivalence, and Verificationism*

JOHN McDOWELL

1. If there can be such a thing as a theory of meaning for any language, meaning cannot be anything but what any such theory is a theory of. Hence a clear and convincing description of the shape which a theory of meaning for any language would take, not itself uncritically employing the notion of meaning, ought to remove all perplexity about the nature of meaning in general.

Frege held that the senses of sentences can be specified by giving truth conditions, and that the sense of a sentence-constituent is its contribution to the senses of sentences in which it occurs.[1] ('Sense' may be paraphrased as 'cognitive meaning'.[2]) Those two ideas of Frege's are captured by the following conception of a theory of sense for a language: it assigns a suitable property to each simple sentence-constituent discerned in the language by an appropriate syntax, and states rules which determine suitable properties for complex expressions formed in each of the ways permitted by that syntax, given the relevant properties of their components; the property thus determined for a complete sentence is that of being true if and only if some specified condition holds. A theory of sense for a language, then, shows how to derive, for any indicative sentence, a theorem of the form '*s* is true if and only if *p*', where '*s*' is replaced by a suitable designation of the sentence and '*p*' by a sentence. Briefly, a theory of sense, on this conception, is a theory of truth.

* This paper's debts to others' published work will be obvious. Michael Dummett's forbearing comments, when confronted by an earlier version, helped me to understand his position better. (I may still have it wrong.) I have been helped also by Gareth Evans, Samuel Guttenplan, Christopher Peacocke, and Mark Platts.

[1] Gottlob Frege, *The Basic Laws of Arithmetic: Exposition of the System*, translated and edited by Montgomery Furth (University of California Press, Berkeley and Los Angeles, 1967), pp. 89–90.

[2] See Michael Dummett, *Frege: Philosophy of Language* (Duckworth, London, 1973), e.g. pp. 92–3.

Tarski's work shows how theories of truth, conforming to the above schematic description of a Fregean theory of sense, may be constructed for certain sorts of formalized languages;[3] and Donald Davidson has urged optimism about the possibility of doing the same sort of thing, one way or another, for natural languages.[4]

A promise to illuminate the notion of sense by way of the thesis that a theory of sense, for any language, is a theory of truth for that language involves an apparent obligation to say what, in general, a theory of truth for a language—any language—is. Discharging the obligation would be elucidating a general notion of truth, not relativized to some particular language or other. It would be suspect to rely on an assumed prior understanding of 'true', as used in specifying the form which the theorems would take; and the promise of general illumination seems to block retreating to the position that what is at issue is a different predicate for each language, on the pattern 'true-in-*L*', in which 'true' is semantically inert.[5] An attractive strategy, now, would be to stipulate an appropriate general condition on the relation between replacements for '*s*' and replacements for '*p*', in theorems whose form is, initially, to be represented thus: '*s* is *f* if and only if *p*'. The hope would be that a general condition which ensures that '*f*' may acceptably be replaced by 'true' would constitute the apparently required answer to the question what, in general, a theory of truth is.

Frege, in whose terminology the sense of a sentence is a thought, says that when the sense of a sentence is specified by giving truth conditions, the thought is determined as the thought that those conditions are fulfilled.[6] That implies the following general condition on the theorems: '*p*' must be replaced by a sentence which expresses the same thought as, that is, has the same sense as, the sentence designated by what replaces '*s*'. Such a condition would ensure that '*f*' might acceptably be replaced by 'true', but only by employing the notion of sameness of sentence-sense; which must presumably be disallowed, in the context of a promise to illuminate the notion of sense.

Another formulation of the desired general condition might

[3] Alfred Tarski, 'The Concept of Truth in Formalized Languages', in *Logic, Semantics, Metamathematics* (Clarendon Press, Oxford, 1956), p. 152.

[4] Notably in 'Truth and Meaning', *Synthese* xvii (1967), 304.

[5] Cf. P. F. Strawson, 'Meaning and Truth', in *Logico-Linguistic Papers* (Methuen, London, 1971), p. 170 ff., at p. 180. See also Christopher Peacocke, 'Truth Definitions and Actual Languages', in this volume.

[6] Loc. cit.

require conformity to Tarski's Convention T, thus: what replaces '*p*' must be the very sentence designated by what replaces '*s*', if the theory is stated in the language with which it deals; if not, a translation of it into the language in which the theory is stated.[7] But unless something can be said about when one sentence translates another, other than that they have the same sense, that is no improvement on the Fregean condition.

A better line is, at least apparently, a change of tack: spelling out the function of a theory of sense in a systematic description of what is involved in understanding a language. For that purpose, the form of the desired theorems can, initially, be represented still more schematically, thus: '*s* . . *p*'; where, as before, '*s*' is to be replaced by suitable designations of object-language sentences, and '*p*' by sentences in the language in which the theory is stated.

A theory of sense must interact with a theory of force for the language in question.[8] A theory of force would do two things: first, license the identification of linguistic actions, given enough information about them, as performances of propositional acts of specified types (assertion, question, and so on); and, second, show how to recover, from a sufficiently full description of an utterance, which may be an utterance of an elliptical or non-indicative sentence, a suitable designation of a suitable indicative sentence. The idea is that a theory of sense and a theory of force, in combination, should enable one to move, from a sufficiently full description of a speaker's utterance, uninterpreted, to a description of his performance as a propositional act of a specified kind with a specified content, that is, a description on the pattern of 'He is asserting that *p*', 'He is asking whether *p*', and so on; where what replaces '*p*' is (waiving some syntactic complications) the sentence used on the right-hand side of the theorem which the theory of sense entails for that indicative sentence which is warranted by the theory of force as being suitably related to the utterance (possibly the sentence uttered).

Acceptability, in a bipartite theory of the sort constituted by combining a theory of sense with a theory of force, would require that the descriptions of propositional acts which it yields should fit coherently into a wider context, in which the speakers' behaviour in general, including both their linguistic behaviour, under those descriptions, and their non-linguistic behaviour, under suitable

[7] Tarski, op. cit., pp. 187–8.
[8] Cf. Dummett, op. cit., p. 416.

descriptions, can be made sufficiently intelligible in the light of propositional attitudes (centrally, beliefs and desires) whose ascription to them is sufficiently intelligible in the light of their behaviour, again, and of the facts which impinge on them. Actions are made intelligible by finding descriptions under which one can see how they might have seemed reasonable: on the conception sketched here, that applies, as it ought, to linguistic actions just as much as others. Understanding linguistic behaviour, and hence understanding languages, involves no more than a special case of what understanding behaviour, in general, involves.

Understanding a language consists in the ability to know, when speakers produce utterances in it, what propositional acts, with what contents, they are performing: that is, the ability to know what would, with suitable input, be the output of a bipartite theory of the sort described above. Capacity to interact with a theory of force, in the appropriate way, would certify a theory as part of a systematic description of such understanding, and hence as part of a theory of meaning.[9] By way of Frege's doctrine that sense determines the content of propositional acts, it would certify such a theory as, precisely, a theory of sense. [10]

Certification of a theory as a theory of sense requires it to be capable of functioning in the ascription of propositional acts. That might suggest that the position outlined here promises elucidation of the notion of sense in terms of the notions of the propositional acts, assumed to be conceptually prior. But that would be a misrepresentation. Acceptable ascriptions of propositional acts must simultaneously meet two requirements: not only the requirement, from outside the envisaged bipartite theory, that the acts ascribed be intelligible, but also a requirement from within, evidently compulsory given even the dimmest insight into how language works, that it be possible to represent the content of propositional acts performed by uttering a sentence as dependent on the repeatable contribution of its components. The second requirement suggests that the notion of the

[9] See Dummett, op. cit., pp. 92–3.

[10] Frege, 'On Sense and Reference', in Peter Geach and Max Black, *Translations from the Philosophical Writings of Gottlob Frege* (Basil Blackwell, Oxford, 1952), pp. 56 ff., at p. 59. If the theory worked by determining conditions for the application of a predicate to sentences, it would conform to the Fregean condition and Convention T; the requirement of interaction might be said to elucidate those formulations. Indexical elements in natural languages introduce complications about the claim of conformity: but the topic of this paper can be pursued at a level of abstraction at which that may be ignored.

content of a propositional act cannot be viewed as accessible in advance of, at least, an adumbration of the idea that the determination of such contents by the words used should be describable by a theory which works systematically across a language, generating a specification of the content of propositional acts potentially performed in the utterance of any sentence, by way of its structure and properties assigned to its components.[11] That idea simply is the idea of a theory of sense. What is proposed here, then, is not elucidation of the notion of sense in terms of other notions, still less any hope of reducing it to those others, but simply a description of its relation to those others: the hope being that a notion which is at first sight problematic may be rendered less so by an explicit account of its location, so to speak, in a conceptual space in which we normally find our way about without thinking.

An ordinary indicative sentence can be used to say something about the world. Quotation and similar devices yield expressions suitable for the construction of remarks about sentences, insulated, in general, from that normal concern with extra-linguistic reality. But appending a truth predicate to a designation of a sentence produces a sentence apt, once more, for saying something about the world: the very thing, in fact, which could have been said by using the original sentence.[12] That guarantees the following: if a necessary and sufficient condition for the application of some predicate to any indicative sentence of a language is given by a sentence which can be used to specify the content of propositional acts potentially performed by uttering the former sentence, then the predicate applies to exactly the true sentences of the language. Thus if the lacuna, in '*s* . . . *p*', is filled, as before, by (schematically) 'is *f* if and only if', the requirement of interaction with a theory of force ensures that an acceptable theory of sense will remain acceptable if '*f*' is replaced by 'true'.[13] So it might seem that the change of tack was only apparent: the requirement of interaction, on that assumption about the filling of the lacuna, serves the purpose for which the Fregean condition and Convention T were found wanting.

The concept of truth as such, however, need not figure in the certification of a theory as a theory of sense. A theory of force need not be

[11] Unstructured sentences, if such are possible, could be viewed as a special case, each being its own sole component.

[12] See W. V. Quine, *Philosophy of Logic* (Prentice-Hall, Englewood Cliffs, 1970), pp. 10–13.

[13] Cf. Davidson, op. cit., pp. 310–11.

sensitive even to the syntactic form of what fills the lacuna, let alone to its substance. Of course the lacuna must be filled somehow, if the theory of sense is to permit, as it must, the derivation of an acceptable theorem of the form '*s* . . . *p*' for every indicative sentence on the basis of its composition out of parts. We know, from Tarski, that 'is *f* if and only if' will meet the bill, at least for languages with certain logical structures. And we know, from the considerations given above, that '*f*' may then be written 'true'. But that fact is not one which needs to be appreciated *en route* to acquiring, from the description of the requirement of interaction, a general conception of the nature of a theory of sense. So although the apparent obligation to elucidate a general notion of truth has indeed been discharged, the result is to show that there was, in fact, no need to undertake exactly that obligation in the first place. The thesis should be, not that sense is what a theory of truth is a theory of, but rather that truth is what a theory of sense is a theory of.[14]

It remains the case that, on that assumption about the lacuna, a theory of sense would conform to the original specification of a Fregean theory. And even if the lacuna were filled in some quite different way, the above considerations ensure that the theorems would continue to be acceptable if that unknown other filling were replaced by 'is true if and only if'. So either way a theory of sense would, as Frege thought, specify truth conditions for sentences: either directly or by justifiable conversion.

2. Michael Dummett has suggested that there is an opposition between a truth-conditions conception of sense, on the one hand, and, on the other, verificationism: which, for present purposes, is the doctrine that ordinary mastery of a language, and hence of the application of the concepts of truth and falsehood to its sentences, is a state acquired solely by the acquisition of, and therefore consisting

[14] Given a theory meeting the requirement of interaction, we could construct a theory matching it except, say, that some arbitrary true sentence was conjoined with what previously replaced '*p*' in each theorem. If the first was a correct theory of truth, the second would be, too. Such possibilities (see J. A. Foster, 'Meaning and Truth Theory', and Brian Loar, 'Two Theories of Meaning', in this volume) constitute a prima facie objection to Davidson's suggestion that a theory of truth for a language L_1 in a language L_2 will characterize an acceptable translation scheme from L_1 to L_2 (constitute an acceptable theory of sense for L_1 in L_2) if its theorems of the form '*s* is true if and only if *p*' are true: see 'In Defense of Convention T', in H. Leblanc, ed., *Truth, Syntax, and Modality* (North-Holland, Amsterdam, 1973), pp. 76 ff., at p. 84. The present position is immune to such objections.

solely in, dispositions to suit one's linguistic behaviour to evidence for the truth and falsehood of sentences.[15]

In one version, the envisaged verificationist objection to a truth-conditions conception of sense turns on the thesis that such a conception presupposes the principle of bivalence (the principle that every significant indicative sentence is either true or false). If the truth value of sentences in a language cannot always be settled, then purported knowledge, nevertheless, that every sentence is either true or false might be held to go beyond anything which can possibly be comprised, on the verificationist view, in competence with the concepts of truth and falsehood. It would follow that, in the presence of undecidable sentences, a verificationist is debarred from a truth-conditions conception of sense.

Adherence to the principle of bivalence, even in the presence of undecidable sentences, is, according to Dummett, characteristic of realism, a doctrine whose defining thesis I shall take to be that the truth condition of a sentence may obtain, or not, independently of our capacity to tell that it obtains, or that it does not.[16] An appropriate alternative conception of sense for a verificationist who rejected a truth-conditions conception would, Dummett suggests, replace the notion of truth, as the fundamental notion of a theory of sense, with the notion of verification or warranted assertibility. A notion of truth would still be employed; but truth would be thought of only as a product of verification, not as something which may obtain independently of verification. That would be an abandonment of the defining thesis of realism. The alternative conception of sense would require a novel, anti-realist conception of the world: if truth is not independent of our discovering it, we must picture the world either as our own creation or, at least, as springing up in response to our investigations.[17] So verificationist objections to a truth-conditions conception of sense would have far-reaching metaphysical implications.

[15] Op. cit., *passim* (see the Brief Subject Index, under 'Verificationism versus realism, as theories of meaning'). For the opposition, see also 'Truth', *Proceedings of the Aristotelian Society*, lix (1958–9), 141, reprinted in P. F. Strawson, ed., *Philosophical Logic* (O.U.P., Oxford, 1967), pp. 49 ff., to which page references are given henceforth. This paper was substantially completed before I had seen Dummett's contribution to this volume.

[16] Dummett seems not to distinguish the defining thesis from adherence to bivalence: see, e.g., *Frege*, p. 466, and his British Academy lecture, 'The Justification of Deduction' (O.U.P., London, 1973), p. 30. I shall be arguing that they are distinct (§6).

[17] Cf. 'Truth', p. 68.

The verificationist attitude towards bivalence which I want to consider is a refusal to assert the principle, combined with a refusal to deny it. It might be thought that undecidable sentences, on which the refusal to assert the principle depends, would afford counter-instances and hence grounds for denying it. But a claim to know, in the absence of evidence, that a sentence is neither true nor false should be no less suspect than a claim to know, in the absence of evidence, that a sentence is either true or false. If an adherent of such a position decides, on the basis of arguments like that sketched above, that he may not think of truth as being independent of verification, he must not take himself to be thereby entitled to infer untruth from absence of verifying evidence. His proper course would be to withhold all pronouncements about the truth or falsehood of sentences whose truth value is not determined by evidence.[18]

My main aim is to show that it is not because verificationism justifies such an attitude towards bivalence—if it does, a question which I shall not discuss—that it requires, if it does, an alternative conception of sense. I want to suggest that the real interest of verificationism, in its bearing on general issues about meaning, is to be sought elsewhere than at any rate one of the places where Dummett, on occasion, finds it, namely in the metatheory of intuitionistic logic.

3. At first sight, Dummett appears to argue on the following lines for the thesis that a truth-conditions conception of sense presupposes the principle of bivalence.[19] First, a theory which specifies truth conditions for sentences can be taken to determine their senses only, if at all, in the context of a theory which gives an account of their actual use in the performance of speech acts of the various types which occur, including, centrally, assertion.[20] Second, in contrast with, say, betting, 'the linguistic act of assertion makes, as it were, no intrinsic provision

[18] If there is such a thing as an identifiable, decidably undecidable sentence, there is perhaps room for a different position, in which (on the ground that evidence that there *can* be no evidence that a sentence is true counts as evidence that it is not true, and similarly for falsehood) the principle of bivalence is denied. By what is conceded, in §5, to the argument of §3, that position would be debarred from a truth-conditions conception of sense. But I shall not discuss it in this paper.

[19] To find this argument in Dummett would be to misconstrue his intentions, as he points out in his contribution to this volume. (His argument was not meant to be for a stronger conclusion than that conceded in §5 below.) In earlier versions of this paper I did thus misconstrue Dummett's intentions: I have retained discussion of the argument as a convenient way of bringing out the lack of necessary connection between realism and acceptance of the principle of bivalence.

[20] 'Truth', pp. 50–2, 56–7; *Frege*, pp. 295–7, 413–17. I have formulated the premiss in a way reminiscent of §1, though Dummett's account of the need for a theory of force does not exactly match that given there. (Cf. §5.)

for the introduction of a gap between two kinds of consequence which the making of an assertion might be supposed to have'.[21] The truth value of an assertion is determined, by its content and the facts, in such a way that there are only the two possibilities, truth and falsehood. Hence the principle of bivalence must hold for sentences suited to be used in making assertions.[22] Combining that with the first premiss, it would follow that the principle of bivalence is a prerequisite for a truth-conditions conception of sense.

The above sketch ignores a concession of Dummett's that, even in the context of a truth-conditions conception of sense, the dictates of smoothness and generality, in an account of how sentences affect the truth values of complex sentences in which they occur, may yield reasons for calling sentences of certain kinds 'neither true nor false'. Dummett reconciles the concession with the requirement derived from the nature of assertion thus: when one is concerned with the truth value of a sentence of one of those kinds, used on its own with a view to making an assertion, one must regard the conceded status as a way of being true or a way of being false.[23] The concession is remote from my concerns in this paper: for what is yielded by the verificationist considerations sketched in §2 is, at most, a disinclination to assert the principle of bivalence, not an inclination, like that which is partly indulged by Dummett's concession, to cite counter-instances.

4. A theory of truth, serving as a theory of sense for a language, must show how to derive, for each indicative sentence of the language, a theorem of the form '*s* is true if and only if *p*', where what replaces '*p*' in each case is (to summarize the requirement of interaction with a theory of force) a sentence giving the content of propositional acts which speakers of the language can intelligibly be regarded as performing, or potentially performing, with utterances of the sentence designated by what replaces '*s*'. In theories of truth of the sort which Tarski showed how to construct, derivation of such a theorem would start with a biconditional obtained by applying, to a suitable designation of a sentence, an outright definition of truth in terms of a

[21] *Frege*, p. 417.

[22] Passages which at first sight seem to argue on these lines for this second premiss are 'Truth', pp. 57–63; *Frege*, pp. 344–8, 417–24.

[23] Discussion of the concession pervades the passages cited in n. 22.

subsidiary semantic concept, that of satisfaction; and would then eliminate semantic vocabulary from the right-hand side of that biconditional, by applying clauses from a recursive characterization of satisfaction and, possibly, clauses from recursive characterizations of other subsidiary semantic concepts, for instance that of denotation. So a theory of truth must incorporate a proof theory adequate for any transformations which are needed in that systematic elimination of semantic vocabulary. Tarski's specimen truth definition, for the language of the calculus of classes, incorporates a classical proof theory.[24] But that does not seem essential to the application of Tarski's methods. On the contrary, it seems obvious that a fundamentally Tarskian theory, for a suitable language, could be given in the context of a proof theory which was, say, intuitionistic.[25]

Tarski's specimen truth definition, unsurprisingly in view of its proof theory, yields a proof that, whatever object-language sentence one takes, either it or its negation is true.[26] A corollary, given the principle that a sentence is false if its negation is true, would be the principle of bivalence for sentences of the object language. But a Tarskian theory with an intuitionistic proof theory would not yield those conclusions. On the face of it, then, such a theory might seem apt to serve as a truth-conditions theory of sense, interacting in the standard way with a theory of force in which assertion is central, for a language for which, because of the verificationist scruples sketched in §2, we are disinclined to insist on the principle of bivalence.

5. If the argument of §3 were sound, that suggestion would be incoherent. For the suggestion involves appeal to interaction with a theory of force mentioning assertion, in order to justify the idea that a theory of the sort envisaged is a truth-conditions theory of sense; but that mention of assertion ought, according to the argument, to import the principle of bivalence, which a theory of the sort envisaged is designed, precisely, not to require.

Intuitionists do not accept the principle of bivalence. Hence, if intuitionists may consistently regard themselves as making assertions, it cannot be true that employment of the concept of assertion requires acceptance of that principle. And it is difficult to see how adoption of

[24] Tarski, op. cit., p. 175, n. 2.

[25] See Gareth Evans, 'Semantic Structure and Logical Form', in this volume, at p. 204.

[26] Op. cit., p. 197.

intuitionistic logic could preclude one from regarding oneself as making assertions.[27]

What about the argument of §3? Some form of its first premiss seems unquestionable, but the second is open to objection.

In the first place, it should be pointed out that those passages in Dummett which look, at first sight, like a justification of the second premiss are suspiciously redolent of the view that a truth-conditions conception of sense must, by way of something like the first premiss, imply a conceptual priority of the notion of the content of an assertion over the notion of sense. We seem to be invited to extract a requirement which applies to assertions in any language whatever, from a purported grasp of the notion of the content of an assertion which is independent of exigencies deriving from the need to construct systematic theories of sense for particular languages. The idea that something like that can be done is especially clear in Dummett's handling of the concession mentioned in §3. He allows, for instance, that the dictates of a systematic theory of sense may require atomic sentences containing bearerless names to be viewed as neither true nor false, but insists, nevertheless, that an utterance of such a sentence with honest assertoric intent must, in deference to the requirement derived from the nature of assertion, be regarded as the assertion of a falsehood. That insistence could be warranted only by a conception of the content of an assertion which is independent of (since the content is not necessarily determined by) the sense of the sentence uttered, as specified by a systematic theory of sense.

From the standpoint of §1, the invitation to aim at comprehending that prior notion of the content of an assertion may be simply declined. Assertion is not a casually observable phenomenon, correctly describable, wherever it occurs, independently of the construction of a systematic theory for the language in which it is occurring. Assertions are made only in languages, and what (if anything) is asserted by uttering a sentence cannot diverge from what would be said about the sentence by a systematic theory for the language which contains it.[28]

[27] If intuitionists were precluded from assertion, there would be an incoherence in the suggestion ('Truth', pp. 66–7) that a theory of sense suitable for intuitionists would centre on the notion of assertibility-conditions.

[28] Thus if a systematic theory does not allow atomic sentences containing bearerless names to be either true or false, and accordingly does not equip them with fulfillable truth conditions, the right position will be that nothing can be asserted by the use of such sentences. The intention of making an assertion does not guarantee its own success. (Of course if nothing is asserted by the use of such sentences, *they* pose no threat to a link between assertion and bivalence.)

Alleged general truths about assertion, announced in advance of systematic theories for particular languages, cannot survive if not preserved, for some language, by a systematic theory adequate on all other counts. And that, it might be said, is the situation with any alleged requirement that the principle of bivalence should be accepted; such a requirement is not preserved by an intuitionistic theory of truth.

However, although the protest against the implication about conceptual priority is justified, that line of attack is inconclusive. No doubt our grasp of the concept of assertion, as we apply it to ourselves, should be thought of as simultaneous with, not prior to, our acquiring mastery of our first language, that is, our coming to be correctly describable by a bipartite theory of the sort sketched in §1; so that that grasp could not equip us with general truths about assertion, and its content, which would be independent of what an adequate theory of sense for our language would say about the appropriate sentences. Still, not just any type of speech act performed by others can be intelligibly viewed by us as assertion, the very speech act we sometimes ascribe to ourselves under that name. That suggests that we can reasonably require our grasp of the concept, as we apply it to ourselves, to yield general controls on intelligible application of the same concept to others: such controls being in some sense, after all, prior to the construction of systematic theories for the languages which others speak, even if not prior to what such a systematic theory would say about our own language. And now it may be suggested that bivalence does hold in our own language, and that that fact is essential to our grasp of the concept of assertion, as we apply it to ourselves; so that bivalence is, after all, a prerequisite for the extension of that concept to others. Certainly there is something plausible about the claim that assertion, as such, leaves no room for contemplating possibilities other than that one is saying something either true or (at worst, so to speak) false.

In the context of intuitionistic logic, however, there is a way of conceding that claim without accepting that assertion requires the principle of bivalence. For although the law of excluded middle is not a theorem of intuitionistic logic, its double negation is. Thus, although it would not be provable, in an intuitionistic theory of truth, that, whatever object-language sentence one takes, either it or its negation is true, nevertheless any purported counter-instance to that generalization would be provably inconsistent. Given that a sentence is false if

and only if its negation is true, purported counter-instances to the principle of bivalence would be similarly inconsistent, even though the principle itself is not assertible. Hence an intuitionist who regards himself as making an assertion need not contemplate possibilities other than truth and falsehood for the sentence which he uses, and indeed, granted the equivalence between falsehood and truth of the negation, must not, on pain of contemplating the possibility of something which would be, by his own lights, inconsistent. In the context of classical logic, of course, such refusal to contemplate counter-instances amounts to acceptance of the principle of bivalence; but it would be peculiar to use that fact in arguing the insufficiency, for justifying the claim that the speech act in question is indeed assertion, of a refusal which does not amount to acceptance of the principle. If, as seems plausible, such refusal is sufficient, then there need be no incoherence, after all, in the suggestion that a Tarskian theory with an intuitionistic proof theory might serve, for a suitable language, as a truth-conditions theory of sense, certified as such by interacting, in the standard way, with a theory of force mentioning assertion. [29]

The verificationist doubts about bivalence described in §2 yield, at most, disinclination to assert the principle, not an inclination to cite counter-instances. That point is respected in the suggestion defended above.

6. Severing the connection, alleged by the argument of §3, between a truth-conditions conception of sense and insistence on the principle of bivalence leaves the realist conception of truth conditions untouched.

Suppose that the understanding of sentences in some language is represented by a bipartite theory which incorporates, as its theory of sense, an intuitionistic theory of truth, and hence combines a truth-conditions conception of sense with avoidance of the principle of bivalence. Strictly, the articulation of the bipartite theory—its division into the two sub-theories, and the deductive machinery of the sub-theories—need not articulate anything literally known by a competent speaker. The articulation answers, not to requirements of the speaker, but to requirements of the theorist who aims at a compendious description of the speaker's capacity to know, given suitable observations, an indefinite number of particular truths. Strictly, then, a

[29] On one interpretation, the thesis that assertion requires bivalence is conceded here. What is not conceded is that assertion requires the *principle* of bivalence.

speaker's understanding of a sentence is represented as consisting, not in actual knowledge of anything, but in the capacity to know, on suitable occasions of utterance of the sentence, something which a theoretical description of his capacity would generate by combining, with the deliverances, for those utterances, of the theory of force, that theorem of the theory of sense which specifies what it is for the sentence to be true. But it seems a harmless abbreviation to say, loosely, that a speaker's understanding of a sentence is represented as knowledge of what it is for it to be true. That goes, in particular, for sentences whose truth value is not decidable by appropriate evidence. Absence of decisive evidence does not block understanding; and understanding is thought of, here too, as knowledge of a truth condition. Thus speakers are credited (in a similar harmlessly abbreviated idiom) with a conception of truth conditions as possibly obtaining, or not, quite independently of the availability of appropriate evidence.

That position is essentially realist, even though, by virtue of intuitionistic logic in the envisaged theory of sense, it concedes the verificationist doubts (§2) about the principle of bivalence. In the context of intuitionistic logic, to say, on the one hand, that the truth condition of a sentence may obtain even if we cannot tell that it does, and may not obtain even if we cannot tell that it does not, is not to say, on the other, that the truth condition of any sentence either does obtain or does not, even if we cannot tell either that it does or that it does not. For the position outlined combines, coherently if intuitionistic logic is coherent, refusing to say the latter with continuing to say the former.

7. Intuitionistic theories of truth would not necessarily be apt for imparting, *ab initio*, an understanding of their object languages. A theory which used sentences to state their own truth conditions would be intelligible only if the sentences were already understood. A theory in a different metalanguage could in principle impart understanding of its object language; but it would do nothing for someone who professed not to understand speakers of its metalanguage: an adherent of classical logic, for instance, who professed general incomprehension of intuitionists' talk.

The point is not special to intuitionistic theories: an analogous point holds for classical theories of truth. And in itself the point is no objection to the adequacy of such theories as theories of sense. Any

theory is intelligible only to someone who understands the language in which it is stated. A theory of sense can reasonably be required to play a part in a systematic description of what is involved in understanding the language of which it is a theory (§1); that is quite different from its being called upon to serve as a possible means to the acquisition of a command of its object language.

The possibility of general incomprehension of intuitionists, on the part of an adherent of classical logic, might seem to imply the existence of special intuitionistic logical constants, differing in sense from the classical constants. On that view, the intuitionist could not be correctly regarded as refusing to accept some of the laws of classical logic. Certainly he refuses to assert some sentences which, in the mouth of an adherent of classical logic, would express, say, instances of the law of excluded middle; but in his mouth, since his logical constants differ in sense, they would not express instances of just that law.[30]

But the thesis of a divergence in sense between intuitionistic and classical logical constants is not entailed by the possibility of incomprehension. Understanding a linguistic action, like understanding any action, is a matter (executive failures aside) of finding a description under which it can be seen how it might have struck the agent as a reasonable thing to do. Theories of sense would be parts of larger theories whose aim would be the systematic generation of such descriptions for linguistic behaviour (§1). Now in the case of intuitionists and adherents of classical logic, there is not only massive correspondence in linguistic behaviour, but also a possibility of explaining the residual divergence in terms of what seem to be arguments, on the intuitionists' part, against accepting the residue: notably the verificationist argument that, in the presence of undecidable sentences, we cannot know that every sentence is either true or false (§2). If we can understand the arguments as really being what they seem to be, that is, arguments against asserting the surplus classical laws, then it must be acceptable to translate the logical constants used in intuitionistic logic by their counterparts in classical logic: for it must, in that case, be acceptable to translate the intuitionists as refusing to assert precisely those classical laws. The translation would involve ascribing, to intuitionists, linguistic behaviour which, from a classical standpoint, is bizarre: for example, refusing to assert some instance of the law of excluded middle. But if we can see why they might suppose it reasonable to refuse to assert that, we can agree that it is indeed that which

[30] So Quine, op. cit., pp. 80–91.

they refuse to assert. General incomprehension of intuitionists, on the part of an adherent of classical logic, might be explained, compatibly with the thesis that there is no divergence in the senses of the logical constants, in terms of a failure on his part to appreciate intuitionists' reasons for proceeding as they do.[31]

If intuitionism need not import novel senses for the logical constants, it could hardly require, on those grounds, at least, a novel general conception of sense. That it does not is a conclusion already argued above (§§ 4–5) by a different route.

8. The metatheory of intuitionism standardly contains systematic specifications of the conditions under which we have proofs of complex formulae, in terms of the conditions under which we have proofs of simpler formulae. If intuitionistic logic is to be applied to non-mathematical subject matter, the notion of proof, in such specifications, would need to be replaced with a notion, sufficiently general to suit all areas of discourse, of a sentence's having been verified. So a generalized version of something which intuitionists do in fact feel called on to provide would conform to Dummett's description of the nature of a theory of sense appropriate for a verificationist who objects to a truth-conditions conception of sense. Of course that is no surprise: Dummett indeed holds that those systematic specifications of proof-conditions constitute explanations of the senses of special intuitionistic logical constants, and hence embody a conception of sense different from a truth-conditions conception.[32]

Those systematic specifications are intuitionistic substitutes for classical model theory. Suppose, for simplicity, that we have to deal with a language containing only unstructured sentences and truth-functional connectives. Specification of a particular classical interpretation would assign, to each simple sentence, a truth value (on the interpretation), truth or falsehood; common to the specification of all interpretations would be general clauses explaining how the truth values (on an interpretation) of complex sentences depend on the truth values (on the interpretation) of simpler sentences. Sentences true on all interpretations which share those general clauses would be the logical truths. Soundness in a proof theory requires it to be able to prove nothing but logical truths, and completeness requires it to be

[31] See Adam Morton, 'Denying the Doctrine and Changing the Subject', *Journal of Philosophy*, lxx (1973), 503.

[32] See, e.g., *Frege*, pp. 507, 611; 'The Justification of Deduction', pp. 7–8, 19.

able to prove all of them. Those properties of a proof theory are of more than merely technical interest,[33] from a classical standpoint, since the common general clauses, if correct, capture that systematic dependence of the truth values of complex sentences on the truth values of simpler sentences which constitutes the contribution of the connectives to the senses of sentences in which they occur, that is, the senses of the connectives. Sentences true on all interpretations must owe their actual truth to what is invariant between the interpretations. Thus the model theory renders precise the conception of logical truths as owing their truth solely to the senses of the logical constants. Soundness in a proof theory is a matter of its not being unfaithful to the senses of its logical constants: completeness is a matter of its capturing all that those senses require.

Each such interpretation would determine, for every sentence constructible out of the vocabulary of the language, one or the other of the two truth values (on the interpretation), truth and falsehood. With orthodox general clauses, that would secure that the logical truths included all instances of those laws of classical sentential logic at which the intuitionist jibs.

The intuitionist's inability to accept such a model theory need not reflect inability to accept its general clauses. Suppose the general clauses set out the information contained in the standard (two-valued) truth tables. Although such general clauses determine the truth values of complex sentences on the basis of assignments to simpler sentences of only the two truth values, true and false, they do not themselves say that every sentence has one or the other of those two truth values. The intuitionist does not deny the principle of bivalence, but simply refuses to assert it; and that refusal does not involve willingness to contemplate counter-instances (§5). Hence the intuitionist need not deny that general clauses corresponding to the standard truth tables entirely capture the systematic dependence of truth values on truth values which, as before, constitutes the senses of the connectives. Whichever of the two truth values the constituent sentences have, the clauses determine the truth values of sentences composed out of them; and there is no further status which he is required to envisage the constituent sentences as possibly having, for which the clauses would leave the truth values of complex sentences undetermined, thus being vulnerable to accusations of incompleteness. Sentences determined as true on all the classical interpretations

[33] See 'The Justification of Deduction', pp. 5–9.

owe that status, not just to the general clauses, but to the general clauses in conjunction with a built-in assumption of the principle of bivalence. The general clauses do not themselves assert the principle; on their own, they need not be unacceptable to the intuitionist. So far, then, the intuitionist's inability to accept classical model theory need not imply that his connectives differ in sense from the classical connectives, let alone that he requires a different general conception of sense.

It might now seem that definition of soundness and completeness for intuitionistic proof theory, in the context of preservation of the thesis that the intuitionist's connectives do not differ in sense from the classical connectives, would require a model theory matching the classical model theory at all points except that the built-in assumption of the principle of bivalence is dropped. But that thought leads nowhere. The general clauses determine truth values on the basis of truth values; so something, in the envisaged intuitionistic model theory, would have to correspond to the assignment, in a classical interpretation, of a truth value to each simple sentence. General clauses which say, at least, what the standard truth tables say could be prevented from ensuring the truth, on all such interpretations, of the undesired theorems only if, in some interpretations, some simple sentences were assigned a status other than those of being true (on the interpretation) or false (on the interpretation). That would require, after all, additions to the general clauses, to deal with cases where constituents of sentences have that further status: hence an admission, contrary to the position we are trying to reflect, that the general clauses do not entirely capture the senses of the connectives.[34] Preservation of the general clauses leaves no room for an intuitionistically acceptable conception of logical truth according to which, as before, it is owed solely to the senses of the logical constants.

The verificationism described in §2 implies not that the principle of bivalence is false but, at most, that it is not known to be true. If such a verificationist accepts, as he has, so far, no reason not to, that the general clauses capture the senses of the connectives, then he can say, in the light of the classical model theory, that if the principle of bivalence is true (as it may be), then the classical theorems are true;

[34] If there are only two (or indeed any finite number of) conditions other than truth, the envisaged model theory will in any case not yield the right set of logical truths.

indeed, if the principle of bivalence is true (as it may be), then the senses of the connectives guarantee the truth of the classical theorems. The trouble is that since he does not know that the antecedent is true, he cannot detach and assert the consequents of those conditionals. In his view, the classical logical truths are picked out, in the classical model theory, by a property amounting to no more than this: being such that, for all we know, the senses of the connectives guarantee their truth. Since that property does not ensure even the truth of sentences which have it, there is no particular point in a procedure which generates all and only the sentences which have it: which is what a sound and complete classical proof theory would be.

The position described in the last paragraph requires a conception of the truths of logic, not as true solely in virtue of the senses of the logical constants—without assuming the principle of bivalence, there is no telling which sentences have that status—but as knowable solely in virtue of the senses of the logical constants. Such a conception could be made precise, in a way analogous to the way in which, on the assumption that the principle of bivalence holds, the other conception is made precise in classical model theory, by a systematic specification of the conditions under which we may claim to know the truth of complex sentences, in terms of the conditions under which we may claim to know the truth of simpler sentences. Keeping to the simplifying assumption that the only logical constants are the sentential connectives, such a specification may be thought of as constructed by considering how claims to know the truth of complex sentences could be justified by knowledge of the truth of simpler sentences, in the light of, first, that systematic dependence of truth values on truth values which, we continue to assume, constitutes the senses of the connectives; and, second, the verificationist insistence that we cannot claim to know that every sentence is either true or false. Any such systematic specification would certify sentences of some forms as knowable to be true whatever the epistemic status of their components, and, on the new conception, those would be the truths of logic. Soundness and completeness in a proof theory are definable, as before, in terms of the notion thus rendered precise. Those properties have a more than merely technical interest, analogous to, but not the same as, the interest possessed, on the assumption of the principle of bivalence, by the classically defined notions. In particular, unsoundness no longer necessarily indicates unfaithfulness to the senses of the logical constants. Classical proof theory is unsound not because it

misrepresents the senses of the logical constants but because it purports to prove sentences which cannot be known to be true.

The metatheoretical utility of those systematic specifications of proof-conditions mentioned at the beginning of this section lies in the need, if interesting notions of soundness and completeness in an intuitionistic proof theory are to be defined and investigated, for an interesting non-proof-theoretical specification of the intuitionistic truths of logic. That utility has been accounted for, here, without abandoning, and indeed on the basis of preserving, the thesis that intuitionism imports no novel senses for the logical constants, and therefore requires, on such grounds, at least, no novel general conception of sense.

A common generalization states that theses of soundness and completeness connect a syntactically (proof-theoretically) defined notion of logical truth (or logical consequence) with a semantically defined notion.[35] That might make the position adopted here seem impossible: for, surely, radical differences in the nature of definitions of semantic notions of logical truth would reflect radical differences in the underlying conception of meaning. But according to the position adopted here, the generalization is simply wrong. In the classical case, certainly, it is reasonable to regard the non-proof-theoretically defined notion of logical truth as a semantic notion: logical truth is viewed as owed solely to the senses of the logical constants. But the whole point of the argument above is that no purely semantic notion of logical truth is available to a verificationist who adopts the attitude towards the principle of bivalence described in §2; an impurely semantic notion (so to speak) nevertheless serves analogous purposes. If the non-proof-theoretically defined notion which figures in the definitions of intuitionistic soundness and completeness need not be a semantic notion, its novel character cannot be used to argue that intuitionism requires a novel conception of meaning.[36]

9. If I am right, then, the verificationist attitude towards bivalence which I have considered requires a novel logic and a novel conception

[35] 'The Justification of Deduction', p. 1.

[36] The considerations of this section undermine an objection which might be raised against the suggestion of § 7, on these lines: the fact that the classical inter-definabilities of the connectives are not matched in intuitionistic logic shows that the connectives must diverge in sense. From the intuitionistic viewpoint described here, those classical inter-definabilities reflect not just the relations between the senses of the connectives but those relations together with the assumption that the principle of bivalence holds.

of how the senses of the logical constants enter into the marking out of the truths of logic. But it does not require a novel conception of sense, either directly (§§4–5) or by way of the required novel logic (§§7–8). There is no route, on these lines, from verificationism, through non-acceptance of the principle of bivalence, to the abandonment of our common-sense picture of reality.

10. A quite different verificationist argument for a novel conception of sense demands consideration at this point. The different argument would be a head-on attack, leaving bivalence aside, against the realist notion of truth conditions, which, as we saw (§6), can survive non-acceptance of the principle of bivalence. The argument would be that the realist notion of truth conditions involves viewing ordinary command of the concepts of truth and falsehood as something which it cannot possibly be: something which cannot possibly have been acquired in the way in which ordinary command of those concepts must have been acquired, namely by acquiring habits of sensitivity to evidence (cf. §2).

It is certainly the case that a theory of sense taking the form of a Tarskian theory of truth would not include an account of the evidence appropriate to the sentences with which it deals. It does not follow, however, that a bipartite theory containing such a theory of sense as a part (cf. §1) would represent understanding as something independent of sensitivity to evidence. We should miss the point of the verificationist objection if we took it to be a complaint on those lines. Such a complaint (call it 'the weak verificationist objection') would be too easy to meet.

If a bipartite theory is to be acceptable, its output—ascriptions of propositional acts with specified contents—must be intelligible in the light of intelligible ascriptions of propositional attitudes (§1). Now ascriptions of belief to a person are intelligible only if the beliefs ascribed can mostly be viewed as states partly formed by, or at least potentially sensitive to, evidence for their truth. Ascription of a whole set of beliefs to someone who has never been exposed to anything which one can count as evidence (even bad evidence) for their truth would be simply baffling. If a bipartite theory is to treat a speaker's (potential) utterances of sentences as assertion that $p_1, \ldots,$ assertion that p_n, such assertions being, standardly at least, made intelligible as manifestations of the belief that $p_1, \ldots,$ the belief that p_n, then it

must be possible, in general, to regard the (potential) actions which are viewed as manifestations of those beliefs, like the beliefs themselves, as partly prompted by, or at least potentially sensitive to, evidence for those beliefs. The content of the belief appropriate to a given sentence would be given by the replacement for '*p*', in the relevant theorem entailed by the theory of sense. Hence assessment of a theory of sense for acceptability would essentially involve speakers' sensitivity to evidence, and the weak verificationist's point seems to have been met.

It would be a mistake to suppose that each theorem of the form '*s* . . . *p*' requires a theory-independent justification, involving observation of what actually prompts speakers' utterances of the sentence designated by what replaces '*s*'. A representation of mastery of a language must be articulated primarily in terms of sentence-constituents and modes of combination, and only secondarily in terms of sentences. Thus the warranting of a theory of sense as meeting the weak verificationist's point could reasonably require, at most, that its representation of understanding be appropriately related to evidence in respect of each simple sentence-constituent and each mode of combination. That would be secured, ideally, by direct consideration of the evidential prompting of some sentences containing each. The systematic nature of the theory would involve its consequently representing the understanding of other sentences (in the abbreviated idiom explained in §6) as consisting—as with all sentences—in knowledge of truth conditions, even though there might be no possibility, with those other sentences, of such direct consideration of evidential prompting. Even in the absence of such direct consideration, the theorist could claim, wholly on the basis of the acceptability, elsewhere, of his theory, that speakers' (potential) uses of those other sentences were potentially sensitive to appropriate evidence.

Opposition to the above, it seems, would have to involve the idea that mastery of one sentence is a state independent of mastery of the next, as if sentences were always learned as disconnected units. But that idea, which leaves no room for the fact that a competent speaker can understand new sentences, is totally unacceptable.

The weak verificationist objection, then, seems to be untenable. But from the standpoint of a strong verificationism that is beside the point. The strong verificationist objection insists, not that mastery of a language should be represented as not independent of sensitivity to evidence, but that it should be represented as consisting solely in sensitivity to evidence. Perhaps we have seen how a truth-conditions

conception of sense can meet the former insistence, but that is not to see how it can meet the latter.

11. In acquiring mastery of his language, the native speaker had nothing more to go on than encouragement and discouragement of his vocalizings in observable circumstances, together with the observable vocalizings of others in observable circumstances. He cannot have acquired anything more, thereby, than a set of dispositions to suit his vocalizings to observable circumstances. The radical translator, who sets out without benefit of tradition to give a systematic description of competence in some foreign language, has nothing more to go on than the infant learner. That summarizes a well-known doctrine of W. V. Quine.[37]

It captures, also, almost exactly, the position of the strong verificationist. The only difference is that the verificationist reference to evidence is replaced by a reference to observable circumstances, which presumably need not be restricted to (what is construed as) evidence for the truth and falsehood of sentences. Dropping the restriction will make no difference to the argument.

Suppose we believe that members of some community understand some of their own and one another's utterances as assertions: that is, we regard them as knowing, on suitable occasions of utterance of some sentence, something which we can specify by descriptions of actions on the pattern of 'So and so is asserting that *p*'. A systematic description of their capacity to know such things would represent them as knowing (in the abbreviated idiom explained in §6), concerning that sentence, that it is true if and only if . . . (here should follow the sentence which replaces '*p*' in that schematic description). Now suppose we regard the truth value of assertions made by uttering the sentence as undetermined by what is observable: suppose, say, we regard it as expressing a theoretical statement belonging to an empirical theory which we construe realistically. In that case we credit our subjects (in the other abbreviated idiom explained in §6) with a conception of truth as being independent of what is observable. According to the strong verificationist, that is to credit them with something which they cannot have acquired, and so cannot possess.[38]

[37] See *Word and Object* (M.I.T. Press, Cambridge, Mass., 1960), Chapter Two (pp. 26 ff.); and especially a remark in *Ontological Relativity and Other Essays* (Columbia University Press, New York and London, 1969), p. 26.

[38] See, e.g., Dummett, *Frege*, p. 467. In Dummett's contribution to the present volume, the point is overlaid with other concerns which I believe are both inessential to it and mistaken; but obviously I cannot argue that here.

A scheme of translation would be a scheme for systematically generating, from suitable designations of uninterpreted sentences, appropriate replacements for '*p*' in (among other things) the schematic description 'So and so is asserting that *p*'.

It is thus possible to regard Quine's celebrated thesis of the indeterminacy of translation[39] as a version, not quite happily formulated, of the strong verificationist objection to realism in a theory of meaning: or, rather, of an objection which mirrors that objection, but differs in that the starting point replaces the reference to evidence, as noted above, by a reference to observable circumstances. The unhappiness of Quine's thesis, construed as making the verificationist point, lies in the fact that it is an indeterminacy thesis: its burden seems thus to be that the choice of a scheme of translation is underdetermined by the data on the basis of which it is undertaken, and that suggests that, in order to defend it, one is obliged to produce, or at least to show the possibility of, alternative schemes of translation in concrete cases. In the context of the strong verificationist objection to realism, availability of alternative schemes would be, at most, an inessential extra, and it would be a misrepresentation to describe the situation in terms of underdetermination by data. It does not matter, for the profound point which the verificationist is making and which, according to this suggestion, Quine was attempting to make, if there is only one way of making a scheme of translation fit people's dispositions to vocalize in observable circumstances. The point is that, even so, adoption of the scheme would involve going beyond the data: not because there are alternative schemes which would fit equally well, but because no scheme genuinely fits at all—adoption of any scheme involves crediting its subjects with conceptions which they cannot have acquired.[40]

Obviously if the objection applies at all, it applies equally to our crediting ourselves, in similar circumstances, with similar conceptions.[41]

[39] *Word and Object*, loc. cit.; and especially 'On the Reasons for Indeterminacy of Translation', *Journal of Philosophy*, lxvii (1970), 178: note the argument called 'pressing from above' (183), which locates the indeterminacy precisely in sentences whose truth value is not determined by observation.

[40] Critics of Quine, notably Noam Chomsky, have objected that indeterminacy of translation would be no more than the standard underdetermination of empirical theories by data: see Chomsky, 'Quine's Empirical Assumptions', in Donald Davidson and Jaakko Hintikka, eds., *Words and Objections: Essays on the Work of W. V. Quine* (Dordrecht, Reidel, 1969), p. 53. On the present construal of the point Quine was aiming at, such objections simply lapse.

[41] As Quine says, 'radical translation begins at home': *Ontological Relativity*, p. 46.

From the standpoint of a strong verificationist, then, the only hygienic concept of meaning would be something like Quine's concept of stimulus meaning,[42] which is tailored precisely to avoid going beyond what is accessible in dispositions to linguistic behaviour in observable circumstances. Any other conception of meaning, such as that which we ascribe to ourselves and others when we describe ourselves and others as making, and knowing that we are making, assertions whose content goes beyond what is observable, must be simply mythical: a conception which we pretend that we and they possess, when that cannot be the case.

An adherent of such a position is under an obligation to show how we might make linguistic behaviour, in general, intelligible to ourselves, satisfactorily answering the question 'What are we all doing when we talk?', without employing the conceptual materials which he stigmatizes as merely mythical. It seems evident that, in any detailed attempt at discharging the obligation, the principle of bivalence would go by the board: but the line of argument would be, not through doubts about bivalence to rejection of realism (cf. §9) but through rejection of realism to doubts about bivalence.

Anyone who is sceptical (as I am) about the prospects for a coherent and satisfactory anti-realism is under an equally stringent obligation to defuse the strong verificationist argument, or its generalized version. Even if we had a proof of the impossibility of anti-realism, the obligation would not lapse. What is required is to show how, in face of the strong verificationist argument, a realistic account of the understanding of language is so much as possible. That seems to me to be a profoundly important task, but I am not at present sure how to begin on it.[43]

[42] *Word and Object*, pp. 31 ff.

[43] Quine has come close to posing the problem. But he thinks he can have things both ways: preserving a realism of first intention in genuine scientific theorizing, while relegating realism of second intention (the mythical conceptual scheme) to everyday unscientific talk, where the standards can be relaxed (see *Word and Object*, pp. 216 ff.: 'The Double Standard'). The trouble is that the mythical scheme is needed, not just for the mundane purposes Quine recognizes, but for a coherent account of what we are doing when we engage in (realist) science. (See further Dummett, *Frege*, pp. 377–8.) Dummett has drawn attention to the problem, but he is less sceptical than I am about anti-realism.

IV

What is a Theory of Meaning? (II)*

MICHAEL DUMMETT

I

Does the meaning of a sentence consist in its truth condition? Does the meaning of a word consist in the contribution it makes to determining the truth condition of any sentence in which it occurs?

It is unnecessary to labour the observation that an affirmative answer to these questions represents by far the most popular approach, among those philosophers who would not jettison the concept of meaning altogether, to an account of that concept, and that it has been explicitly contended for by Frege, by the Wittgenstein of the *Tractatus*, and by Davidson. I am far from being certain that an affirmative answer is wrong. I am quite certain, however, that such an answer faces formidable difficulties, and that we have no right to assume it correct until we have shown how it is possible to overcome them. It is, to my mind, very far from obvious why we should need, or how we can use, the notion of truth (or, rather, the twin notions of truth and falsity) in this connection, that is to say, as the basic concept, or pair of concepts, in the theory of meaning: a case needs to be made out that it is either necessary or possible to do so before we have any title to presume that meaning and truth are connected in anything like the way Frege supposed them to be.

Because more philosophers have favoured an affirmative answer to the above question than a negative one, and because Frege, in particular, was so great a genius, we have more grasp on what a theory of meaning given in terms of truth conditions looks like than on the general form of a theory of meaning of any rival kind; indeed, the

* This paper is intended as a sequel to 'What is a Theory of Meaning?', in *Mind and Language*, ed. Samuel Guttenplan (Clarendon Press, Oxford, 1975). It can, however, be read independently

In a discussion of this sort, it is hard to retain lucidity while making due allowance, in one's formulations, for the phenomenon of indexicality, and I have preferred to aim at lucidity; thus my use of 'sentence' and 'statement' is very inexact. I do not think that this has vitiated the thought or obscured its expression, if the reader will grant me a little licence.

retort that equally formidable difficulties face the construction of any rival theory is entirely just. However, the difficulties are of different kinds. Thanks to the work of Frege, Tarski and many others, the difficulties that face the construction of a theory of meaning in terms of truth conditions are not difficulties of *detail*: they are difficulties of *principle*, that face us at the very outset of the enterprise. We know well enough how to build the machine: but we have no grounds for confidence that we can set it in operation. There are some problems of detail, of course, concerning the adaptation to natural language of the techniques devised by Frege and Tarski for formalized languages; but we may reasonably feel optimistic about finding solutions to problems of this kind. By contrast, theories of meaning of alternative types, in which the central concept is not taken to be that of truth, do not face an objection of principle before their construction is even undertaken; but, just because no serious attempt has ever been made to work out such a theory, even as applied to a formalized version of natural language (i.e. a quantificational language for everyday use), we encounter difficulties of detail as soon as we start to think how such a construction might proceed. I do not in the least rule out the possibility that a thorough investigation would reveal these difficulties to be, after all, difficulties of principle, blocking the construction of any such theory of meaning; the discovery that such difficulties existed for any such theory of meaning would enable us to give grounds for regarding it as necessary to employ the concept of truth as our basic notion in explaining meaning, and it is because I think that there may be such grounds to be discovered that I conceded at the outset that I am not certain that meaning is not to be explained in terms of truth conditions. A proof that it is *necessary* to use the concept of truth for this purpose would not, in itself, show how it is *possible* for it to play this role; it would not of itself overcome the initial objections to a theory of meaning in terms of truth conditions, but it would guarantee that there was a way of overcoming them to be found. But, at present, we do not have any proof that it is necessary to take the concept of truth as the basic notion for the theory of meaning, and hence we ought to treat the objections to the possibility of doing so with more respect; and, if we are to discover any such proof, we shall most probably do so by investigating the construction of rival theories of meaning.

Before we can look at this topic any more closely, we have to be clearer about what it means to say that the meaning of a sentence

consists in its truth condition: for it is, I believe, a common experience that this idea, though luminous at first glance, is maddeningly difficult to state coherently. A step in the right direction is taken by conforming to what is, I believe, the correct observation that philosophical questions about meaning are best interpreted as questions about understanding: a dictum about what the meaning of an expression consists in must be construed as a thesis about what it is to *know* its meaning. So construed, the thesis becomes: to know the meaning of a sentence is to know the condition for it to be true. This is a step to elucidation, but only a small step: the really elusive notion is that of truth conditions itself. What *is* it to know the truth condition of a sentence?

We can make no progress with this question without taking account of the fact that we want that knowledge of the truth condition of a sentence which is to constitute an understanding of that sentence to be derived from an understanding of the words which compose the sentence and the way they are put together. It is obvious that we do not want to say that, whenever it is the case that a certain sentence is true if and only if certain circumstances obtain, anyone who knows that fact is to be credited with an understanding of the sentence; the condition is much too weak. What we are after is an account of the sort of understanding which a speaker of the language has. It may be that, for someone to be said to know the meaning of a sentence, including one from a language which he does not know, it is too strong a requirement that he should know the meanings of all the individual words in the sentence; or it may be that there is no definite answer to this question. That does not matter—the question is unimportant. What we need to have is an account of what it is to know a language; and a speaker of a language derives his understanding of any sentence of that language from his knowledge of the meanings of the words.

Our problem is, therefore: what is it that a speaker knows when he knows a language, and what, in particular, does he thereby know about any given sentence of the language? Of course, what he has when he knows the language is practical knowledge, knowledge how to speak the language: but this is no objection to its representation as propositional knowledge; mastery of a procedure, of a conventional practice, can always be so represented, and, whenever the practice is complex, such a representation often provides the only convenient mode of analysis of it. Thus what we seek is a theoretical representation of a practical ability. Such a theoretical representation of the mastery of

an entire language is what is called by Davidson, and will be called here, 'a theory of meaning' for the language; Davidson was, perhaps, the first to propose explicitly that the philosophical problems concerning meaning ought to be investigated by enquiring after the form which such a theory of meaning for a language should take.

A theory of meaning will, then, represent the practical ability possessed by a speaker as consisting in his grasp of a set of propositions; since the speaker derives his understanding of a sentence from the meanings of its component words, these propositions will most naturally form a deductively connected system. The knowledge of these propositions that is attributed to a speaker can only be an implicit knowledge. In general, it cannot be demanded of someone who has any given practical ability that he have more than an implicit knowledge of those propositions by means of which we give a theoretical representation of that ability. But, in the particular case when the ability is the ability to speak a language, it would be self-defeating to require that the speaker's knowledge of the propositions constituting the theory of meaning for the language should be manifested in an ability to formulate them verbally, since the fundamental aim of the theoretical representation is to explain what it is that someone who does not yet know any language has to acquire in order to come to know the given language. It would, moreover, be palpably incorrect to hold that, once someone had mastered a language, he could give, in that language or any other, an explicit formulation of a theory of meaning for the language.

A theory of meaning of this kind is not intended as a psychological hypothesis. Its function is solely to present an analysis of the complex skill which constitutes mastery of a language, to display, in terms of what he may be said to know, just what it is that someone who possesses that mastery is able to do; it is not concerned to describe any inner psychological mechanisms which may account for his having those abilities. If a Martian could learn to speak a human language, or a robot be devised to behave in just the ways that are essential to a language-speaker, an implicit knowledge of the correct theory of meaning for the language could be attributed to the Martian or the robot with as much right as to a human speaker, even though their internal mechanisms were entirely different. At the same time, since what is being ascribed to a speaker is *implicit* knowledge, the theory of meaning must specify not merely what it is that the speaker must know, but in what his having that knowledge consists, i.e. what

counts as a manifestation of that knowledge. Without this, not only are we left in the dark about the content of ascribing such knowledge to a speaker, but the theory of meaning is left unconnected with the practical ability of which it was supposed to be a theoretical representation. It is not enough that a knowledge of the theory of meaning as a whole be said to issue in a general ability to speak the language: for the whole point of constructing the theory was to give an analysis of this complex ability into its interrelated components. Rather, certain individual propositions of the theory must be correlated with specific practical abilities, the possession of which constitutes a knowledge of those propositions. The demand that every proposition of the theory be correlated with some practical ability would, indeed, be far too strong. For example, a knowledge of a language involves a knowledge of its syntax, and this requires a classification of words and phrases into syntactic categories, so that we may attribute to one who has the capacity to speak grammatically a tacit knowledge that a given word is, e.g., a noun. There is obviously no single ability which manifests this piece of knowledge, taken in isolation: the capacity to recognize certain sentences containing that word as well-formed, and others as ill-formed, depends upon knowing the syntactic categories of other words and the complex rules of sentence-formation which may be expressed in terms of those categories. Here, an implicit grasp of certain general principles, naturally represented by axioms of the theory, has issued in a capacity to recognize, for each sentence in a large, perhaps infinite, range, whether or not it is well-formed, a capacity naturally represented as the tacit derivation of certain theorems of the theory. To each of these theorems corresponds a specific practical ability, i.e. the ability to recognize of a particular sentence whether it is well-formed or not; but this is not true of the axioms. A knowledge of certain axioms, taken together, issues in a general capacity, in this case to recognize of any sentence whether or not it is well-formed; and the ascription to the speaker of an implicit knowledge of those axioms is based on the confidence that he has a general capacity which embraces all the specific abilities which correspond to theorems derivable from that set of axioms. An axiom earns its place in the theory, however, only to the extent that it is required for the derivation of theorems the ascription of an implicit knowledge of which to a speaker is explained in terms of specific linguistic abilities which manifest that knowledge.

What holds good at the syntactic level also holds good for the

semantic part of the theory. A theory of meaning will contain axioms governing individual words, and other axioms governing the formation of sentences: together these will yield theorems relating to particular sentences. If a theory correlates a specific practical capacity with the knowledge of each axiom governing an individual word, that is, if it represents the possession of that capacity as constituting a knowledge of the meaning of that word, I shall call it *atomistic*; if it correlates such a capacity only with the theorems which relate to whole sentences, I shall call it *molecular*. I know of no demonstration that an atomistic theory of meaning is in principle impossible; but since, with unimportant exceptions, the unit of discourse (the shortest expression whose utterance effects a significant linguistic act) is the sentence, there can be no general requirement, of a theory of meaning, that it be atomistic. What a speaker knows, in knowing the language, is how to use the language to say things, i.e. to effect linguistic acts of various kinds. We may therefore require that the implicit knowledge which he has of the theorems of the theory of meaning which relate to whole sentences be explained in terms of his ability to employ those sentences in particular ways, that is, that the theory be molecular. But his employment of words consists only in his employment of various sentences containing those words, and hence there need not be any direct correlation of that knowledge which is taken as constituting his understanding of any one word with any specific linguistic ability. The ascription to him of a grasp of the axioms governing the words is a means of representing his derivation of the meaning of each sentence from the meanings of its component words, but his knowledge of the axioms need not be manifested in anything but the employment of the sentences.

We should not have the least idea how such a theory of meaning might be constructed if we were not familiar with the distinction, introduced by Frege, between sense and force. Without such a distinction, a speaker's understanding of any given sentence would have to be taken to consist in nothing less than his awareness of every feature of the use of that sentence, that is, of the entire significance of any possible utterance of the sentence. Wittgenstein's celebrated slogan 'Meaning is use' can be interpreted in many ways, most of which probably tally with some aspect of his understanding of it. One very radical way of interpreting it is as repudiating altogether any distinction between sense and force; but the fact is that we have no conception of how to set about describing the employment of any one

particular sentence without the help of any general machinery which would involve making a distinction of that kind, and hence we should have to despair of constructing any systematic account of language whatever. A distinction between sense and force is implicit in any thesis such as the one which we are considering, that to know the meaning of a sentence is to know its truth condition. Someone who knows, of a given sentence, what condition must obtain for it to be true does not yet know all that he needs to know in order to grasp the significance of an utterance of that sentence. If we suppose that he does, we are surreptitiously attributing to him an understanding of the way in which the truth condition of a sentence determines the conventional significance of an utterance of it: but, since the theory of meaning is intended to display explicitly all that a speaker must implicitly know in order to be able to speak the language, the presumed connection between the truth condition of a sentence and the character of the linguistic act effected by uttering it must be made explicit in the theory. This is made apparent by the phenomenon of mood (which need not actually be signalized by the inflection of the verb): in most languages, there are many sentences whose utterance would not normally be described as saying anything that could be true or false, although they bear a systematic syntactic relation to sentences the utterance of which would be so described. The theory of meaning may be formulated so as not to attribute truth or falsity to such sentences but to associate with them conditions of a parallel kind, e.g. obedience-conditions in the case of imperatives; in that case, it must make explicit what may be done by uttering a sentence which has a truth condition, and what other things may be done by uttering a sentence which has a condition of some other kind. Alternatively, the theory may be formulated so as to associate truth conditions with all sentences: but, in that case, the theory must include an explicit explanation of the significance of the various moods, that is, it must explain the different relations which the truth condition of a sentence has to the act of uttering it, according to the mood of the sentence. Even if we considered a language without mood, it would hold good that the conventional significance of a given utterance was not uniform —one and the same sentence could be used to do different things; and the theory would still have to give an account of the different ways in which the truth condition of a sentence might, according to context, be related to the significance attached to an utterance of it.

The simplest way to put the point is this. If we suppose that, by

knowing the condition for a sentence to be true, a speaker thereby knows the whole use of the sentence, this can only be because of his grasp of the concept of truth. That part of the theory of meaning which stipulates the truth conditions of the sentences of the language merely specifies the extension of the concept: it therefore does not display those features of it which allow the whole use of a sentence to be derived from its truth condition. If, in place of the term 'true', taken as already understood, the theory had employed some primitive technical term which had no existence outside the theory, it would be impossible to maintain that, by knowing only the principles governing the application of this predicate, a speaker thereby knew the use of each sentence: rather, there would have to be a supplementary part of the theory which stated, by the use of this term, the connection between its application to any sentence and the use of that sentence. This supplementary part of the theory of meaning would embody those principles relating to the concept of truth which someone would have to grasp if he were to be able to derive the use of a sentence from a specification of the condition for it to be true.

A theory of meaning which takes the concept of truth as its central notion will, therefore, consist of two parts. The core of the theory will be a theory of truth, that is, an inductive specification of the truth conditions of sentences of the language. This core would be better called 'the theory of reference', since, while among its theorems are those stating the conditions under which a given sentence, or utterance of it by a given speaker at a given time, is true, the axioms, which govern individual words, assign references of appropriate kinds to those words. Surrounding the theory of reference will be a shell, forming the theory of sense: this will lay down in what a speaker's knowledge of any part of the theory of reference is to be taken to consist, by correlating specific practical abilities of the speaker to certain propositions of the theory. The theory of reference and the theory of sense together form one part of the theory of meaning: the other, supplementary, part is the theory of force. The theory of force will give an account of the various types of conventional significance which the utterance of a sentence may have, that is, the various kinds of linguistic act which may be effected by such an utterance, such as making an assertion, giving a command, making a request, etc. Such an account will take the truth condition of the sentence as given: for each type of linguistic act, it will present a uniform account of the act of that type which may be effected by the utterance of an arbitrary sentence whose truth condition is presupposed as known.

It is only against such a background that it makes any sense to say that to know the meaning of a sentence is to know the condition for its truth; what is intended is not that to know the condition for the application of the predicate 'true' to the sentence is, in itself, *all* that a speaker has to know in order to be able to use that sentence or understand the utterance of it by another, but that it is all that has to be known that is *specific* to that sentence; all else that has to be known is of a general character—a set of general principles by means of which we can determine uniformly, from the truth condition of any arbitrary sentence, every feature of its use. And the same holds good for any other thesis according to which there is some one property of a word or sentence an awareness of which constitutes a grasp of its meaning, for instance that the meaning of a sentence is the method of its verification. In this latter case, what is being proposed as constituting the meaning of a sentence is, unlike the truth condition of the sentence, a feature of its use; but it is only one particular feature. If the sole activity in which our use of language consisted were the verification of sentences, then the thesis would be a platitude; but plainly it is not. Learning to use language involves learning to do many other things: to act on, or respond verbally to, the assertions of others; to make assertions on grounds which fall short of being conclusive; to offer grounds for our assertions; to draw inferences; to ask and answer questions; to give, obey or flout commands; and so on. The thesis that the meaning of a sentence is the method of its verification is not a denial that there are all these different aspects of the use of language, but a claim that there is some uniform means of deriving all the other features of the use of any sentence from this one feature, so that knowledge of that one feature of a sentence is the only specific piece of knowledge about it that we need to know its meaning. Such a claim involves, precisely, an acknowledgement of a distinction between sense and force: a conception of the correct theory of meaning as falling into two parts, a central part giving the theory of sense and reference (here conceived of as an inductive specification, for each sentence, of the method of its verification), and a supplementary part giving a uniform means of deriving, from that feature of any sentence determined by the central part, every aspect of its use.

As I have said, we have no idea how to construct a systematic theory of meaning which does not embody a sense/force distinction. The question before us is whether the concept of truth is the right choice for the central notion of a theory of meaning, that in terms of which its core theory is stated, or whether we need to employ some

other notion in this role. One large question concerning this choice is whether a viable supplementary theory (theory of force) can be constructed in terms of the notion chosen as central; whether there really is a uniform means of describing our whole linguistic practice in terms of it. So far, we have very little conception of what such a supplementary theory, formulated without appeal to a prior understanding of notions, such as assertion, relating to linguistic behaviour, would look like: attention has been concentrated more on the form of the core theory. It is because the core theory represents a grasp of the sense of an expression, not as the mastery of its entire use, but as the apprehension of one particular property of it, that we have no general argument to show the impossibility of an atomistic theory of meaning, any more than we have one to show the necessity of a theory of that type. To know the sense of a sentence is to know one particular thing about it—the condition for its truth, or the method of verifying it, or the like, according to what is taken as the central notion for the given theory of meaning; or, more accurately, it is to have derived that knowledge from the way the sentence is put together out of its component words. I have argued that an acceptable theory of meaning must be at least molecular; its theory of sense must state how a speaker's knowledge of the meaning of any sentence is manifested. But because the supplementary part of the theory is available to explain how he derives, from his grasp of its sense, a complete understanding of its use, it is quite unnecessary that what is stipulated as constituting his knowledge of its meaning should cover every aspect of his ability to use that sentence as it is used in the language: it may, rather, be some quite restricted ingredient of that ability (for instance, an ability to carry out a verification of the sentence). By the same token, therefore, there is no reason why the theory of sense should not identify a speaker's grasp of the sense of each individual word with some specific ability of his relating to that word, say his grasp of the senses of some very specialized range of sentences containing that word.

II

The question, 'Does the meaning of a sentence consist in the condition which must obtain for it to be true?', thus amounts to this: Is the choice of the notion of truth as the central notion for a theory of

meaning which admits a distinction between sense and force the right one?

One of the reasons for the great popularity of the conception that the meaning of a sentence is given by its truth condition is its intuitive obviousness. If we take the notion of truth for granted, if we credit ourselves with a grasp of that notion, but do not stop to ask how it should be analysed, it appears evident that no other notion but that of truth can be adequate to explain our understanding of a sentence, and, equally, that nothing more is needed. This impression is in large part due to the equivalence principle, i.e. the principle that any sentence *A* is equivalent in content to the sentence ⌜It is true that *A*⌝. This seems to show that truth *must* be the right notion to use to explain meaning: we could not say, for example, that to know the meaning of a sentence *A* is to know what has to hold good for *A* to be known to be true, for ⌜It is known that *A*⌝ is much stronger than *A* itself; nor could we say that it is to know when there are adequate grounds for asserting *A*, since these could exist even though *A* was false.

The equivalence principle provides a basis for an acceptable explanation of the role of the word 'true' *within* the language. If someone already understands a language *L*, and *L* is then extended, to a language L^+, by the introduction of the predicate 'true', regarded as applicable to sentences of *L* and as subject to the equivalence principle, such a stipulation makes it quite intelligible that the speaker will be equipped to understand sentences of L^+. (The stipulation would actually have to be made more complex, to take account of indexicality, but these complications need not detain us.) We can even see why the extension would be useful; if the word 'true' is treated as an ordinary predicate, not confined to contexts of the form 'It is true that . . .', but allowed also in such contexts as 'He said something to me which was not true', then it will not always be eliminable, but its extension will be determinate. Of course, such an account will not serve to explain the word 'true' when it is used to give the semantics of a language, in particular when it is used as the central notion of a theory of meaning for the language, since it depended upon supposing that the speaker had a prior understanding of those sentences of the language which did not contain the word 'true'. It will also not do for an account of the word 'true' as it actually functions in natural language, since such a language aspires to be what Tarski called 'semantically closed', i.e. to contain its own semantics. This is not merely a matter of the extension's being impredicative, i.e. of our

allowing the predicate 'true' to be applied also to sentences of the extended language; we also use the word 'true', and many other words, to enunciate propositions belonging to a theory of meaning for the language, that is, we attempt to use the language as its own metalanguage, and, in so doing, admit as principles governing the use of the word 'true' ones which are not covered by the stipulation of the equivalence principle. For the most part, however, we continue to require that the equivalence principle be maintained.

As long as we take the notion of truth for granted, then it seems obvious that it is in terms of it that meaning must be explained. The moment that we cease to take it for granted, however, and start to enquire into the correct analysis of the notion, to ask where we get it from, this obviousness evaporates. To ask such questions is to ask where, in the process of acquiring a mastery of language, an implicit grasp of the notion of truth comes in. If the notion of truth is to serve as the basic notion of a theory of meaning for the language, then we cannot think of it as introduced by a stipulation of the equivalence principle, for that, as we have seen, is in effect to suppose that we may acquire a mastery of the greater part of our language in advance of having any apprehension of the concept of truth: if we want to maintain that what we learn, as we learn the language, is, primarily, what it is for each of the sentences that we understand to be true, then we must be able, for any given sentence, to give an account of what it is to know this which does not depend upon a presumed prior understanding of the sentence; otherwise our theory of meaning is circular and explains nothing.

If the notion of truth is to serve as one belonging to our theory of meaning, which serves to display in what our knowledge of the language consists, the equivalence principle cannot fulfil an explanatory role; but, as already remarked, it may still play a very important part in our grasp of the concept of truth, in that we continue to require that the concept be so understood that the equivalence principle remains correct. Now any acceptable theory of meaning must give recognition to the interconnectedness of language. Since words cannot be used on their own, but only in sentences, there cannot be such a thing as a grasp of the sense of any one word which does not involve at least a partial grasp of the senses of some other words. Equally, an understanding of some one sentence will usually depend on an understanding not merely of the words which compose that sentence, and of other sentences that can be constructed from

them, but of a certain sector of the language, often a very extensive one. The difference between a molecular and a holistic view of language is not that, on a molecular view, each sentence could, in principle, be understood in isolation, but that, on a holistic view, it is impossible fully to understand any sentence without knowing the entire language, whereas, on a molecular view, there is, for each sentence, a determinate fragment of the language a knowledge of which will suffice for a complete understanding of that sentence. Such a conception allows for the arrangement of sentences and expressions of the language in a partial ordering, according as the understanding of one expression is or is not dependent upon the prior understanding of another. (That it be, or approximate to being, a partial ordering, with minimal elements, seems to be required if we are to allow for the progressive acquisition of a language. On a holistic view, on the other hand, the relation of dependence is not asymmetric, and in fact obtains between any one expression and any other: there can be nothing between not knowing the language at all and knowing it completely.)

In particular, it is evident that, in practice, once we have reached a certain stage in learning our language, much of the rest of the language is introduced to us by means of purely verbal explanations; and it is reasonable, as well as traditional, to suppose that such explanations frequently display connections between expressions of the language a grasp of which is actually essential to an understanding of the words so introduced. That is to say, in effect, that the possibility of explaining certain expressions by purely verbal means is an essential characteristic of the meaning they possess; if so, this must be reflected in any correct theory of meaning for the language. Now if we want to offer a purely verbal explanation of a certain form of sentence, we cannot do better—indeed, we cannot do other—than state the conditions under which a sentence of that form is *true*: for, in virtue of the equivalence principle, to do that will be precisely to state the content of a sentence of that form, and there is no other property a statement of the condition for the possession of which by such a sentence would serve that purpose. Here, again, therefore, is another reason, once more traceable to the equivalence principle, why the idea that to give the meaning of a sentence is to give its truth condition should be so compelling; moreover, it indicates a respect in which any correct theory of meaning must conform to that idea.

A theory of meaning which takes truth as its central notion has to supply an explanation of what it is to ascribe to someone a knowledge

of the condition which must obtain for a sentence to be true. If the sentence is of a form which a speaker can come to understand by means of a verbal explanation, then there is no problem: his knowledge of the truth condition of the sentence is explicit knowledge, knowledge which is manifested by his ability to state that condition. An explanation of this form obviously presupposes that the speaker already knows a fairly extensive fragment of the language, by means of which he can state the condition for the truth of the given sentence, and in terms of which he came to understand it. It follows that, however large the range of sentences of the language his understanding of which can be explained in this way, this form of explanation will not suffice generally. Since, in virtue of the equivalence principle, to state the condition for the truth of a sentence is simply to give the content of that sentence in other words, an explicit knowledge of the truth condition of a sentence can constitute a speaker's grasp of its meaning only for sentences introduced by means of purely verbal explanations in the course of his progressive acquisition of the language: it would, notoriously, be circular to maintain that a speaker's understanding of his language consisted, in general, of his ability to express every sentence in other words, i.e. by means of a distinct equivalent sentence of the same language. His understanding of the most primitive part of the language, its lower levels, cannot be explained in this way: if that understanding consists in a knowledge of the truth conditions of sentences, such knowledge must be implicit knowledge, and hence the theory of meaning must supply us with an account of how that knowledge is manifested.

The difficulty of giving a suitable explanation of that in which a speaker's knowledge of the truth condition of a sentence consists does not lie in deciding what to count as displaying his recognition that that condition is satisfied. It is true that there is no single universal and unmistakable sign of acknowledgement of the truth of a given sentence, nor any absolutely standard means of eliciting such a signal: but it is reasonable enough to suppose that, in relation to the speakers of any one language, we can devise a criterion for a speaker's recognition of the fulfilment of the condition which establishes any given sentence as true. If we allow this, then we have no difficulty in stating what constitutes a speaker's knowledge of the condition for the truth of a sentence, provided that the condition in question is one which he can be credited with recognizing whenever it obtains: that knowledge will consist in his capacity, perhaps in response to suitable

prompting, to evince recognition of the truth of the sentence when and only when the relevant condition is fulfilled. Plainly, however, an explanation of this form covers at best a very restricted range of cases; there are very few sentences the condition for whose truth cannot obtain without its being recognized as obtaining. Such a form of explanation may be generalized to cover any sentences which are, in practice or even in principle, decidable, that is, for which a speaker has some effective procedure which will, in a finite time, put him into a position in which he can recognize whether or not the condition for the truth of the sentence is satisfied. For any such sentence, we may say that the speaker's knowledge of the condition for it to be true consists in his mastery of the procedure for deciding it, that is, his ability, under suitable prompting, to carry out the procedure and display, at the end of it, his recognition that the condition does, or does not, obtain. (Of course, this characterization contains a number of general terms which would not occur in an actual theory of meaning, which would mention only the specific decision procedures involved and the particular means by which the speaker displayed his recognition that the condition for the truth of a sentence was satisfied: the general characterization is intended only to show that there is no difficulty in principle in doing that.)

The difficulty arises because natural language is full of sentences which are not effectively decidable, ones for which there exists no effective procedure for determining whether or not their truth conditions are fulfilled. The existence of such sentences cannot be due solely to the occurrence of expressions introduced by purely verbal explanations: a language all of whose sentences were decidable would continue to have this property when enriched by expressions so introduced. Many features of natural language contribute to the formation of sentences not in principle decidable: the use of quantification over an infinite or unsurveyable domain (e.g. over all future times); the use of the subjunctive conditional, or of expressions explainable only by means of it; the possibility of referring to regions of space-time in principle inaccessible to us. Of course, for any given undecidable sentence, the possibility may well be open that we may find ourselves in a position to recognize that the condition for its truth is satisfied, or that it is not. But, for such a sentence, we cannot equate a capacity to recognize the satisfaction or non-satisfaction of the condition for the sentence to be true with a knowledge of what that condition is. We cannot make such an equation because, by hypothesis,

either the condition is one which may obtain in some cases in which we are incapable of recognizing the fact, or it is one which may fail to obtain in some cases in which we are incapable of recognizing that fact, or both: hence a knowledge of what it is for that condition to hold or not to hold, while it may demand an ability to recognize one or other state of affairs whenever we are in a position to do so, cannot be exhaustively explained in terms of that ability. In fact, whenever the condition for the truth of a sentence is one that we have no way of bringing ourselves to recognize as obtaining whenever it obtains, it seems plain that there is no content to an ascription of an *implicit* knowledge of what that condition is, since there is no practical ability by means of which such knowledge may be manifested. An ascription of the knowledge of such a condition can only be construed as *explicit* knowledge, consisting in a capacity to *state* the condition in some non-circular manner; and that, as we have seen, is of no use to us here.

The problem which here confronts the attempt to construct a theory of meaning which uses the notion of truth as its central notion does not relate to the supplementary part of the theory, to which I have given the title 'the theory of force'. That part of the theory is concerned with displaying the connection between the truth condition of a sentence and the actual practice of using it in discourse; unless it proves possible to devise such a theory of force in a convincing way, the whole enterprise of constructing a theory of meaning of this type collapses. But it would be rash at the present time to base any predictions on the feasibility of this task; we know as yet hardly anything about how to go about it. The problem which I am here discussing relates to the theory of sense, which I depicted as a shell about the core theory. The core theory states the way in which the references of the component words of each sentence determine its truth condition; or, better, how the application to each sentence of the predicate 'true' depends upon the references of its component words. The shell—the theory of sense—relates this theory of truth (or of reference) to the speaker's mastery of his language; it correlates his knowledge of the propositions of the theory of truth with practical linguistic abilities which he displays. Now when someone learns a language, what he learns is a practice; he learns to respond, verbally and non-verbally, to utterances and to make utterances of his own. Acknowledging sentences as true or as false is among the things which he learns to do; more precisely, he learns to say and do various things as expressions of such acknowledgement. But knowing the condition

which has to obtain for a sentence to be true is not anything which he *does*, nor something of which anything that he does is the direct manifestation. We have seen that, in some cases, we can explain acceptably enough, in terms of what he says and does, what it amounts to to ascribe such knowledge to him. But in other, crucial, cases, no such explanation appears to be available: and so we fail to attain a genuinely explanatory account of what the practice that he acquires consists in.

Where does the concept of truth come from? Its most primitive connection is plainly with the linguistic act of assertion, as is seen from the fact that we naturally call assertions 'true' or 'false', but not questions, commands, requests, bets, etc. If we apply a Fregean sense/force analysis to our sentences, we see the sentence as falling into two parts, that which conveys the sense of the sentence (the thought), and that which indicates the force which is being attached to it, assertoric, interrogative, imperatival, etc. It is the thought alone which is, from this standpoint, properly said to be true or false, whether we are asserting it to be true, asking whether it is true, commanding that it be made true, or whatever. On such a view, therefore, someone who asks a (sentential) question or gives a command can be said to be saying something true or false with as much right as one who makes an assertion; and it is as much of a solecism to call the *assertion* 'true' or 'false' as it is so to call a question or command. However attractive this way of speaking may be, it is a revision of our natural mode of expression; and this is not due solely to the fact that we lack an assertoric mood corresponding to the interrogative and imperatival ones, but use the same form of words in a co-ordinate clause, or, in English, in a subordinate one, as we do when the sentence is used on its own assertorically. To say something true is to say something correct, to say something false is to say something incorrect. Any workable account of assertion must recognize that an assertion is judged by objective standards of correctness, and that, in making an assertion, a speaker lays claim, rightly or wrongly, to have satisfied those standards. It is from these primitive conceptions of the correctness or incorrectness of an assertion that the notions of truth and falsity take their origin.

An utterance may be criticized in different ways. Certain kinds of criticism—as that a remark was impolite, a breach of confidence or in bad taste—are directed, not at what is said, but at the saying of it. This intuitively clear distinction is difficult to draw without invoking

problematic concepts. We might say, for instance, that what is criticized is the external utterance rather than the interior act, e.g. of judgment; but the fact that certain linguistic acts, such as assertion, can be internalized is itself a puzzling one which we should expect a theory of meaning to throw light on, not to take for granted. Perhaps the least question-begging way to draw the distinction between the two types of criticism is as follows. Any linguistic act can be cancelled, at least if the cancellation is sufficiently prompt: a speaker may withdraw an assertion, a command, a request or a question. A criticism which is directed solely at what is said—as that an assertion is untrue, a command unjust or a question unfair—no longer stands if the utterance is cancelled. A criticism which is levelled at the act of saying, on the other hand, may be weakened, but is not wholly met, by its cancellation: if someone, by his utterance, broke a confidence or wounded his hearer's feelings, his withdrawal of the utterance mitigates, but does not wipe out, the offence. The distinction thus drawn does not fully coincide with that we should obtain by reference to the speaker's interior state: if we object to a question as being unfair, the objection is wholly met if the question is withdrawn, so that, on this principle, the objection is to what is said rather than to the saying of it; but we are not objecting to the speaker's desire to know the answer, but only denying his right to ask. I think, however, that the distinction as I have drawn it is closer to what we want in this context than one drawn by reference to interior states.

The notion of an assertion's being incorrect or correct relates only to the existence or non-existence of valid criticisms directed against what is said, rather than against the saying of it: I think it is important to filter out the possibility of criticisms of the latter kind; an undifferentiated concept of the acceptability of an utterance—of an utterance's not being open to criticism of *any* kind—would be of little use for our purposes. The notion of truth takes its rise from the more primitive notion of the correctness of an assertion; but it does not coincide with it. It is integral to the notion of truth that we can draw a distinction between the truth of what someone says and the grounds which he has for thinking it true; the idea that an assertion is judged by standards of correctness or incorrectness does not yet supply a basis for this distinction. An assertion which is made on inadequate grounds is open to criticism, criticism which is directed against what is said rather than against the saying of it, and hence is incorrect: the question is why we want to introduce a distinction between different

ways in which an assertion may be incorrect, and on what basis we draw this distinction. Once we are supplied with a conception of the condition for the truth of the sentence used to make the assertion, then we know how to draw this distinction; but the question is where we got that conception from. We cannot suppose it given with the most primitive employment of assertoric sentences: for this, we require only a general distinction between the cases when a sentence may correctly be uttered assertorically and when it may not. This may be clearly seen when we consider sentences, such as the indicative conditionals of natural language, to which we are not ordinarily accustomed to apply the predicates 'true' and 'false'. Philosophers dispute over the proper criteria for applying these predicates to such sentences: and they do so precisely because they are in disagreement about how much is to be reckoned to the condition for the truth of such a sentence, and how much to the grounds which a speaker may have for considering it true. Such disputes reflect no ambiguity in the everyday use of indicative conditionals. All parties to the dispute are agreed on the circumstances in which an assertion made by means of an indicative conditional is warranted, that is, when a speaker is entitled to make such an assertion; and this is all that we need to know in order to interpret an assertion of this type when it occurs in everyday discourse. In consequence of such knowledge, we know when to make such an assertion, how to support it when challenged, what makes it reasonable to accept it or reject it, how to act on it or to draw conclusions from it if we do accept it. What the philosophers argue about is the further question what makes an indicative conditional sentence *true*. Some hold that it is true just in case the corresponding material conditional is true; others that, when the antecedent is true, the conditional is true or false according as the consequent is true or false, but that, when the antecedent is false, the conditional is true or false according as the corresponding counterfactual conditional is true or false, further argument relating to the truth conditions of counterfactuals; others, again, would accept the first part of this, but hold that, when the antecedent is false, the indicative conditional is neither true nor false; and yet others demand that, irrespective of the truth or falsity of the antecedent, the truth of the conditional demands the existence of some connection between antecedent and consequent. These disputes leave the ordinary understanding of the indicative conditional untouched: a grasp of the use of such conditionals in everyday discourse does not appear to turn on our having any conception of the truth conditions of conditional

sentences as opposed to the condition for the correctness of a conditional assertion. But, if this holds good in this case, why does it not hold good in every case? Why cannot we make do in all cases with the more primitive notion of the correctness of an assertion, without invoking the notion of the truth of a sentence, with its concomitant distinction between saying something false and saying something on inadequate grounds?

At least part of the answer lies in the formation of compound sentences. This comes out very clearly with the future tense. If our use of the future tense were confined to atomic sentences, there would be no saying how the line should be drawn between the condition for the truth of such a sentence and the grounds upon which it might reasonably be asserted; we should need no such distinction in order to understand future-tense assertoric utterances. Indeed, it would not only be that we should have no basis for denying that conditions prevailing at the time of utterance, including the speaker's intentions, were part of the truth condition of the sentence; we should not be compelled to allow that what subsequently happened, when it belied the tendencies prevailing at the time of utterance, had any direct bearing on the truth of the sentence, since we should not have to regard a subsequent utterance of the negation of the sentence, or of its present-tense form, as a contradiction of the original assertion. What forces us to distinguish between the truth of the sentence and the speaker's warrant for its assertion is the behaviour of the sentence as a clause in a compound sentence, and, more particularly, when it figures as the antecedent in a conditional, as well as the use of compound tenses, in particular the past future ('was going to . . . '). In explaining the use of indicative conditionals, we do not need the notion of the truth value of the conditional, as opposed to the circumstances which warrant its assertion; but we do need that of the truth of its antecedent.

The behaviour of future-tense sentences as constituents in compound sentences forces on us a distinction between their truth conditions and the conditions which warrant their assertion, and therefore allows a differentiation between the genuine future tense, which yields a sentence true or false according to what subsequently happens, and the future tense used to express present tendencies, which yields one which is true or false according to the conditions prevalent at the time of utterance. The recognition of the truth conditions of sentences involving the genuine future tense is also

prompted by the use of future-tense sentences to effect certain linguistic acts other than assertion, e.g. commands, requests and bets. The existence of these linguistic acts depends upon there being certain conventional consequences which follow on their being made, consequences determined solely from the content of the sentence used in making them; the understanding of the force attached to the sentence in these cases therefore itself provides a basis for separating the speaker's grounds for his utterance from the content of the utterance itself. Thus, although the notion of truth originates in connection with the making of assertions, we are assisted in disentangling it from the more general notion of the correctness of an assertion by our understanding of certain types of utterance which carry a non-assertoric force. This does not mean that the notion of truth can be satisfactorily explained solely in terms of commands, bets, etc. The behaviour of a form of sentence when it carries one kind of force may be quite different from its behaviour when it carries another: the interpretation of conditional commands and bets is a useless analogy for the explanation of conditional assertions; disjunctive questions behave quite differently from disjunctive statements. Unless we had a reason for appealing to a notion of truth conditions for future-tense assertoric sentences which coincides with that required for commands relating to the future, we should not import the notion from one context to the other.

There is thus built into the concept of truth from the outset a contrast between the semantic and pragmatic aspects of an assertion; truth is an objective property of what the speaker says, determined independently of his knowledge or his grounds for or motives in saying it. Naturally, some such distinction arises as soon as enough language has been learned for a speaker to be capable of making mistaken assertions, where the mistake does not lie in an erroneous grasp of the language: but the contrast is greatly heightened by our need to discriminate between failure to say what is true and failure to say what is warranted.

To explain why we need the concept of truth, for semantic purposes, is not in itself to explain how the concept is to be applied. It is apparent from the foregoing that, in acquiring our mastery of language, we make a tacit appeal to the notion of the truth of a sentence in learning to form compound sentences and to construe assertions made by means of them, and that this process is assisted by our simultaneous learning of the use of certain sentences carrying non-assertoric force.

The notion of truth thus tacitly acquired must be capable, in turn, of yielding the more primitive notion of the correctness of an assertion: this means that whatever further conditions, beyond the truth of the sentence, are in fact required for an assertion to be justified must be able to be explained as conditions for the speaker to have reasonable grounds for supposing the sentence to satisfy the condition for its truth; if that were not so, we should not be able to take the content of the sentence as being determined by its truth condition. That is not to deny that there is an element of convention governing the claim which we take to be made by an assertion. It is, for example, a conventional matter that a mathematical assertion is construed as a claim that a proof of the statement is known (not necessarily to the speaker); our understanding of mathematical statements themselves would be quite unaffected if it were normal practice to make an unqualified assertion of such a statement on the basis only of plausible reasoning (in Polya's sense). But it is a requirement on the notion of truth—i.e. on what we take the truth condition of any sentence to be—that whatever else is conveyed by an assertion effected by means of that sentence, beyond the satisfaction of its truth condition, e.g. in the mathematical case the existence of a proof, can be represented as a ground for taking it to be true (or, as with Grice's principles of conversational implicature, a reason for uttering that sentence rather than a simpler and stronger one): all that remains for convention to determine, for assertions of different kinds, is how strong the ground is required to be if the assertion is to be justified.

None of this, however, does anything to resolve the difficulty about a theory of meaning based on the notion of truth which arises from the fact that the truth of many sentences of our language appears to transcend our powers of recognition. The case of future-tense sentences is instructive, because the truth conditions we are forced to associate with such sentences in order to account for their behaviour as constituents of compound sentences are such as to make it impossible for a speaker to have conclusively established the truth of such a sentence at the time of utterance, and this compels us to make the sharpest possible distinction between the condition for the truth of a sentence and that which entitles a speaker to make an assertion. But, so long as we consider a future-tense sentence whose present-tense form remains decidable, we are still concerned with truth conditions a knowledge of which can be directly manifested by the speaker, since, at a time subsequent to the utterance, he can display his recognition

of whether or not the condition for its truth is satisfied. We are still no further towards explaining the content of an ascription to a speaker of a knowledge of the condition for the truth of a sentence, when that condition is not one which he is, in any circumstances, capable of directly recognizing.

III

In order to get clearer about what is involved in the ascription of truth to a statement, we need a fresh start, and this is provided by considering the principle: If a statement is true, there must be something in virtue of which it is true. This principle underlies the philosophical attempts to explain truth as a correspondence between a statement and some component of reality, and I shall accordingly refer to it as the principle *C*. The principle *C* is certainly in part constitutive of our notion of truth, but is not one which can be directly applied. It is, rather, regulative in character: that is to say, it is not so much that we first determine what there is in the world, and then decide, on the basis of that, what is required to make each given statement true, as that, having first settled on the appropriate notion of truth for various types of statement, we conclude from that to the constitution of reality.

Because it is a regulative principle, the principle *C* may at first strike one as empty. We feel its force only when we consider something which appears a violation of it. The most obvious such violation is provided by a counterfactual conditional alleged to be true even though there is nothing which, if we knew of it, we should accept as a ground for its truth: for instance, those counterfactuals asserted by one school of theologians to be the objects of God's *scientia media*, relating to the behaviour, had they been created, of beings endowed with free will whom, on the basis of such knowledge, God decided not to create. Most people naturally feel a strong objection to such a conception, precisely on the ground that, in such a case, there would be nothing to *make* the counterfactual true. This objection is based upon the thesis that a counterfactual cannot be, as I shall say, *barely true*, that is, that a counterfactual cannot be true unless there is some statement, not involving the subjunctive conditional, whose truth renders the counterfactual true; in other words, there must, for any true counterfactual, be a non-trivial answer to the question, 'What makes it true?'.

Here the principle *C* yields substantial information, but only

because combined with a more specific thesis, the thesis that a counterfactual cannot be barely true. In general, we can learn something by applying the principle *C* to a specific type of statement only when we have already decided something about the sort of thing in virtue of which a statement of that type can be true; and, in particular, this requires a basis on which to determine which types of statement can be barely true and which cannot. However, even in the case of counterfactuals, we have not yet obtained a very sharp conclusion until we know which statements are to be classified as involving the subjunctive conditional.

Our present considerations link up with our previous discussion just because, as then observed, the subjunctive conditional is one of the sentence-forming operations which allow us to construct sentences which are not effectively decidable. Why should anyone think that a counterfactual may be barely true? His only possible ground can be that he supposes it to be a matter of logical necessity that either that counterfactual or its opposite should be true (the opposite of a conditional being that conditional which has the same antecedent and the contradictory consequent), but does not think that there is necessarily any ground for the truth of either of the sort on which we usually base assertions of such counterfactuals. Now no one could rationally take it as a quite general logical necessity that, of any pair of counterfactual conditionals, one or other should be true: but we are strongly disposed to make this assumption of certain such pairs. The reason is that we readily equate the truth of certain statements, not overtly involving the subjunctive conditional, with the truth of certain subjunctive conditionals, and their falsity with the truth of the opposite subjunctive conditionals. If, then, we assume the law of bivalence for the statements of the first kind, we are forced into granting that, for any subjunctive conditional corresponding to such a statement, either it or its opposite must be true.

A clear case of a type of statement thus correlated with conditionals is provided by statements ascribing abilities to people. A statement like '*X* is good at learning languages' is, of course, normally tested by observing how quickly the subject acquires fluency in a foreign language. If, now, we consider the statement applied to someone who has never had any contact with a language other than his mother-tongue, we are confronted by three possible attitudes to the question, 'Must this statement be either true or false?' (i) It is not necessarily either; there just does not have to be any determinate answer to the

question whether or not this individual would learn a foreign language quickly if he were to attempt to learn one. (ii) Linguistic ability must be correlated with, or consist in, some feature of brain structure, not at present known to us; the brain of this individual must either exhibit this feature or not; hence the statement must be determinately either true or false, whether or not we ever find out which. (iii) Linguistic ability need not be correlated with any physiological feature, but, nevertheless, any one person either has it or lacks it; hence the statement must be either true or false.

That the truth of '*X* is good at learning languages' stands or falls with the truth of 'If *X* were to attempt to learn a language, he would quickly succeed', and its falsity with the truth of the opposite conditional, is not at issue between the upholders of these three positions: it must be granted by anyone who understands the phrase 'good at learning languages'. Hence the question whether it is a matter of necessity that one or the other of the two opposite subjunctive conditionals is true coincides with the question whether the law of bivalence holds for the overtly categorical statement '*X* is good at learning languages'. The upholder of position (iii), recognizing that there is no necessity by which, when the antecedent of the conditional remains unfulfilled, we could, if we knew enough, recognize the truth either of that conditional or its opposite, frankly allows, in effect, that one or other of these conditionals may be barely true. The upholder of position (ii) feels impelled to maintain the law of bivalence for the overtly categorical statement, but, since he finds the idea of a counterfactual conditional's being barely true repugnant, makes it a matter of necessity that the truth or falsity of the statement which ascribes the ability to the given individual should depend upon the truth or falsity of a statement of another type, namely about physiology. The upholder of position (i) shares with the proponent of (iii) the conviction that there need be nothing which would enable us to determine the categorical statement as true or as false, however much we knew; but, since he also shares with the proponent of (ii) a distaste for allowing as a possibility the bare truth of a counterfactual, he escapes the dilemma by rejecting the law of bivalence.

Of course, someone who takes up position (iii) is not compelled to admit that a counterfactual conditional may be barely true. He may, if he likes, deny this, and claim that what makes the statement 'If *X* were to attempt to learn a language, he would quickly succeed' true (if it is true) is the truth of the statement '*X* is good at learning

languages'. If this claim is to qualify as a denial that the counterfactual can be barely true, then he must hold that a statement like '*X* is good at learning languages' does not involve the subjunctive conditional. This may seem a futile contention, reducing the thesis that counterfactual conditionals of this kind cannot be barely true to utter triviality: for it is hardly to be disputed that we actually learn to apply such a predicate as 'good at learning languages' to one who performs in a certain way under certain conditions, or to one who we have reason to think would perform in that way if those conditions were to be fulfilled, so that this seems to be a prime case of an expression which is introduced by means of the (subjunctive) conditional. He must, therefore, concede that the sentence, '*X* is good at learning languages', does indeed *involve* the subjunctive conditional, 'If *X* were to attempt to learn a language, he would quickly succeed', in the sense that we come to understand the former by means of the latter, and that any ground for the truth of either is a ground for the truth of the other. But he may also retort that it does not follow that the overtly categorical sentence *reduces to* the subjunctive conditional, and that the criterion for a counterfactual conditional's being barely true ought to be that there is no statement the truth of which renders the counterfactual true and which does not actually itself *reduce to* a subjunctive conditional. His ground for denying that '*X* is good at learning languages' reduces to the corresponding subjunctive conditional, i.e. that the meaning of the one is to be strictly equated with that of the other, is precisely that '*X* is good at learning languages' can according to him, be barely true, while a subjunctive conditional cannot. We cannot in general assume, of any random pair of opposite subjunctive conditionals, that one or other must be true: but of certain such pairs we do make precisely this assumption, and we do so because we regard them as reflecting some permanent feature of reality which we cannot directly observe. In allowing the transition from the conditional form of sentence to the categorical form, such as '*X* is good at learning languages', we are, on his view, giving expression to just this conviction. That is why the categorical form of sentence does not simply reduce to the conditional form: it embodies the assumption that a man's facility in learning a language reflects a permanent but not directly observable condition. That form of sentence can be correctly understood only when it is seen as embodying such an assumption, an assumption which does not underlie the use of the merely conditional form of sentence.

This version of position (iii) must not be dismissed as a mere attempt, by juggling with words, to render the thesis that a subjunctive conditional cannot be barely true nugatory, while conforming to it. On the contrary, it distinguishes between cases in which the application of that thesis forces us to allow that neither of two opposite counterfactuals may be true, and cases in which, if we maintain the law of bivalence for certain overtly categorical statements, we need make no such concession. What it does not do is to delineate any principle upon which the two kinds of case may be distinguished, save by appeal to our customary linguistic practice; it therefore supplies no justification of that practice. That we are obliged to draw some such distinction cannot be denied; for the range of expressions within our language which may be said to be introduced by appeal to a conditional of some sort is vast. It includes every term for a property the possession of which is determined by a test, or for a quantity the degree of which is determined by measurement. We interpret some such tests and measurement-procedures as revealing states of affairs which existed antecedently to and independently of the execution of the test or measurement; and we proceed to make the assumption that a sentence ascribing the property to something, or assigning to something a specific degree of the quantity, is determinately true or false independently of whether the test or measurement was or could be carried out.

In making such an assumption, we are adopting a realistic attitude towards the property or quantity in question; and it should now be apparent how it is that, as was claimed at the beginning of this section, the notion of truth which we take as governing our statements determines, via the principle *C*, how we regard reality as constituted. We may, in fact, characterize realism concerning a given class of statements as the assumption that each statement of that class is determinately either true or false[1]. Thus positions (ii) and (iii) amount

[1] This embraces the principle of bivalence for statements of that class; but it amounts to a little more than that, since the word 'determinately' is not included merely for rhetorical effect. The formulation also embraces that semantic principle which is related to the distributive law as the principle of bivalence is related to the law of excluded middle; let us call it the principle of dissection. From the principle of bivalence, we know that, in relation to a single statement *A*, there are just two possibilities: that *A* is true, and that *A* is false. But we need to invoke also the principle of dissection if we are to conclude that, in relation to two statements *A* and *B*, there are just four possibilities: that *A* and *B* are both true, that *A* is true and *B* false, that *A* is false and *B* true, and that *A* and *B* are both false. I owe this point to Hilary Putnam, although he would not, I think, agree that the assumption either of the principle of bivalence or of the principle of dissection was required for a realistic interpretation. For the purposes of the present discussion, however, we may inaccurately identify realism concerning a class of statements with the assumption, for them, of the principle of bivalence.

to different versions of a realistic view of statements about human abilities, whereas position (i) is a rejection of realism concerning those statements. Position (ii) is, however, a reductionist one: assuming that any statement ascribing a specific ability to a particular individual must be determinately true or false, its proponent concludes that there must be some physiological fact which renders it true or false. Reductionism does not, of course, have to take the strong form of asserting the translatability of statements of one class into statements of another; it is fundamentally concerned with the sort of thing which makes a statement of a given class true, when it is true. The thesis that statements of a class M are reducible, in this sense, to statements of another class R takes the general form of saying that, for any statement A in M, there is some family $\bar{A}$ of sets of statements of R such that, for A to be true, it is necessary and sufficient that all the statements in some set belonging to $\bar{A}$ be true; a translation is guaranteed only if $\bar{A}$ itself, and all the sets it contains, are finite. In such a case we may say that any statement of M, if true, must be true in virtue of the truth of certain, possibly infinitely many, statements in R.

Armed with this notion of reducibility, we may now say generally that a statement is barely true if it is true but there is no class of statements, not containing it or trivial variants of it, to which any class containing it can be reduced. While position (ii) represents a reductionist form of realism concerning human abilities, position (iii) embodies a naive realism concerning them: naive realism about statements of some class D consists in a combination of realism concerning that class with the thesis that statements of that class are capable of being barely true, i.e. that there is no class of statements to which they can be reduced. This amounts to holding that we cannot expect a non-trivial answer to the question, 'In virtue of what is a statement of the class D true when it is true?' Our view of the constitution of reality—our metaphysical position—depends in part on which are the classes of statements of which we take a realistic view, i.e. for which we assume the principle of bivalence, and in part on which are those which we admit as capable of being barely true.

We are now in a better position to understand what is involved in the ascription to a speaker of the knowledge of the truth condition of a sentence. If a sentence S is such that statements made by uttering it are not capable of being barely true, then there will be some class R of statements such that an utterance of S can be true only if the statements in some suitable subset of R are all true; and a grasp of the truth

condition of *S* will consist in an implicit grasp of the way in which its truth depends upon the truth of statements in *R*. It may be that this dependence may actually be displayed within the theory of truth itself, so that, if we conceive of this theory as expressed in a metalanguage which is an extension of the object language, the T-sentence for *S* will be non-trivial, i.e. will not have *S* itself on its right-hand side. It may be, alternatively, that the obstacle (if there is one) to giving an actual translation of *S* within the object language will also prevent the construction of such a non-trivial T-sentence; in that case, the theory of sense, which explains in what a speaker's grasp of the propositions of the theory of truth consists, will have to make explicit the relation between *S* and the class *R*. In either case, the notion of a grasp of the truth condition of *S* is not problematic.

Matters stand differently when *S* is understood as a sentence used to make a statement capable of being barely true. In this case, the corresponding T-sentence cannot but be of the trivial form. The explanation of what it is for a speaker to know the truth condition of *S* must, therefore, in this instance, fall wholly to the theory of sense. Our model for such knowledge, in the case of a sentence capable of being barely true, is the capacity to use the sentence to give a report of observation. Thus if someone is able to tell, by looking, that one tree is taller than another, then he knows what it is for a tree to be taller than another tree, and hence knows the condition that must be satisfied for the sentence, 'This tree is taller than that one', to be true.

The notion of a report of observation is a very loose one. Without attempting to go into all the problems which arise if one wishes to make it sharper, we are here concerned to pick out those cases in which an ability to use a given sentence in order to give a report of observation may reasonably be taken as a knowledge of what has to be the case for that sentence to be true; bearing in mind that this criterion is intended to apply only when the sentence is one for which we have no non-trivial way of *saying* what has to be the case for it to be true. The following conditions appear to be required. First, the making of the observation-report must not rest upon any extraneous inference (must not represent 'a conclusion of the witness'), as, e.g., in 'I see that the Smiths forgot to cancel their newspapers'. Secondly, in every case in which the sentence is true, it must be in principle possible that it should be observed to be true. And, thirdly, the possibility of observing it to be true cannot involve any operation

which effects a transformation of the constitution or situation of any object referred to in the sentence. It is the last of these three conditions which is the delicate one; I am unsure whether there is any precise intuitive principle, let alone whether I have stated it accurately. The point can, however, be illustrated from our example of human abilities. Everyday discourse will certainly permit the use of a sentence like 'I observed that he was good at languages'. But, if we take a naively realistic view of sentences ascribing abilities to people, we can hardly accept a capacity to observe manifestations of such abilities as sufficient to guarantee a knowledge of what it is, in general, that makes such a sentence true. If each individual determinately either possesses or lacks any one given ability, regardless of whether an occasion ever arises for his possession or lack of it to be manifested, then the possession of such an ability cannot *consist* in its manifestations. It cannot even consist in whatever renders true the appropriate subjunctive conditional, when this is considered as understood antecedently to the use of the vocabulary of permanent abilities, for otherwise an individual might neither possess nor lack the ability. Rather, in a particular case it may be the mere possession of the ability which renders the corresponding subjunctive conditional true, in the absence of anything else which would show that conditional to be true, or, therefore, that the ability was present. Hence, given a naively realistic view of human abilities, we ought not to count observing that someone learns a language quickly as an observation of the ability itself, but only as an observation of a manifestation of it, from which his possession of it is inferred; the ability itself must be regarded as something not directly observable by us. Now it may be said that the second of our two principles is enough to yield this result, since, of a man now dead, who had lived his whole life in a totally monolingual environment, it would be in principle impossible to observe whether or not he had linguistic ability; and a similar difficulty would attend making such observations before the building of the Tower of Babel. However, this would be to appeal to rather special features of our particular example. What seems of more significance is the fact that, if one tests out a person's linguistic ability by creating an incentive and an opportunity for him to learn a foreign language, and then observing the outcome, one has materially altered the situation; and it is for this reason that we should be reluctant to say that an understanding of how to carry out such a test amounted to a knowledge of what it is for someone to have linguistic

ability even though it is never called into play; reluctant, that is, to say this in the context of a naively realistic view of human abilities. It was in order to sanction such reluctance that the third requirement was included above, unsatisfactory as its formulation undoubtedly is. We should contrast this case with that of observation of, say, shape. Although, as is well known, some philosophers have gone down this path, it would seem quite unreasonable to deny that someone who was capable of telling, by looking or feeling, whether or not a stick is straight knew what it was for a stick to be straight, on the ground that he would not thereby show that he knew what it was for a stick which no one had seen or touched to be straight; and the best way that occurs to me to explain the intuitive difference between the two kinds of case is to say that looking at or feeling the stick effects no alteration in it. It is not, indeed, that the modification effected by the test is in respect of the property being tested: by testing somebody's linguistic ability, we are supposed to establish the degree of ability he would have had even if it had not been tested; it is not only the case in which the test affects the relevant property that is being excluded. It may be said, with some justice, that it is again a matter for metaphysical decision which observation procedures are reckoned as effecting some modification in the object; but that is another matter.

We may, on the other hand, legitimately extend the notion of a report of observation to include assertions based upon the execution of the sort of operation of which counting is the prototype, something which does not operate upon the object observed, but serves to impose an order on the observations. Statements of number might be ranked among sentences whose truth conditions can be informatively stated; but perhaps statements of equality of number might be regarded as ones the knowledge of whose truth conditions consists in a capacity for reporting the result, not of passive observation, but of observation accompanied by an intellectual operation. Sentences which record the outcome of measurement or observations effected by instruments form an intermediate case, or rather a spectrum of intermediate cases, which approach, at the further end, those registering the result of a test of just that kind which we have tried to rule out. I do not know how to draw a sharp line, nor whether any can be drawn. It is not, indeed, part of my case that it is imperative to draw one, for I do not believe that, in the end, the conception of meaning as truth conditions can be defended. All that I feel sure of is that we have just two basic models for what it is to know the condition for the truth of a

sentence. One is explicit knowledge—the ability to state the condition; this, as we have seen, is unproblematic, and, moreover, is the model that we actually need in a large range of cases; but, as we have also seen, it is not a model that can be used if we want the notion of a grasp of truth conditions to serve as our general form of explanation of a knowledge of meaning. The other is the capacity to observe whether or not the sentence is true. This notion may legitimately be stretched a certain way. It is not important to determine exactly how far it may be stretched: the important fact is that it cannot be stretched as far as we need.

It was argued earlier that the notion of a grasp of truth conditions is problematic only when it is applied to a sentence not in principle decidable. This is actually more generous than the immediately foregoing discussion, since it would credit a speaker with a grasp of the truth conditions of a sentence whenever there is some test which can in principle always be applied. The point is of relatively minor importance, however. It was also maintained earlier that there are three principal sentence-forming operations which are responsible for our capacity to frame undecidable sentences: the subjunctive conditional; the past tense (or, more generally, reference to inaccessible regions of space-time); and quantification over unsurveyable or infinite totalities. Now the claim that we tend to appeal to the mastery of observational sentences as a model for the knowledge of the truth conditions of a sentence is borne out by our surreptitious, or sometimes explicit, appeal to such a model when sentences involving these operations are in question. Since the sentences in question are not in principle decidable, the observations which we imagine as being made are not ones of which we are capable: they are observations which might be made by some being with a different spatio-temporal perspective, or whose observational and intellectual powers transcend our own, such powers being modelled on those which we possess, but extended by analogy. Thus, for example, a naive realist about mental abilities is disposed to appeal to a picture of the mind as an immaterial substance, whose constitution we can know about only indirectly, by inference, but which could be directly inspected by a being on whom spiritual substance made an impact like that made on us by material reality. Again, we are inclined to think of statements in the past tense as being rendered true or false by a reality no longer directly accessible to us, or, perhaps, only fragmentarily so, in memory, but which nevertheless is in some sense still there; for if there were, as it were,

nothing whatever left of the past, then there would be nothing to make a true statement about the past true, nothing in virtue of which it would be true. On such a picture, we are for the most part forced to rely on inference in order to ground our statements about the past, that is, on indirect evidence; but our knowledge of what it is that actually makes such statements true or false involves our understanding of what it would be to apprehend their truth directly, i.e. by that which actually rendered them true. To be able to do this would be to be capable of observing the past as we observe the present, that is, to be able to survey the whole of reality, or, at least, any temporal cross-section of it at choice, from a position outside the time-sequence. The most celebrated example of this way of thinking relates to quantification over an infinite domain. We gain our understanding of quantification over finite, surveyable domains by learning the procedure of conducting a complete survey, establishing the truth value of every instance of the quantified statement. The assumption that the understanding so gained may be extended without further explanation to quantification over infinite domains rests on the idea that it is only a practical difficulty which impedes our determining the truth values of sentences involving such quantification in a similar way; and, when challenged, is defended by appeal to a hypothetical being who could survey infinite domains in the same manner as we survey finite ones. Thus Russell spoke of our incapacity to do this as 'a mere medical impossibility'.

In this way, we try to convince ourselves that our understanding of what it is for undecidable sentences to be true consists in our grasp of what it would be to be able to use such sentences to give direct reports of observation. We cannot do this; but we know just what powers a superhuman observer would have to have in order to be able to do it—a hypothetical being for whom the sentences in question would *not* be undecidable. And we tacitly suppose that it is in our conception of the powers which such a superhuman observer would have to have, and how he would determine the truth values of the sentences, that our understanding of their truth conditions consists. This line of thought is related to a second regulative principle governing the notion of truth: If a statement is true, it must be in principle possible to know that it is true. This principle is closely connected with the first one: for, if it were in principle impossible to know the truth of some true statement, how could there by anything which *made* that statement true? I shall call this second principle the principle *K*: its application depends heavily upon the way in which 'in principle possible' is

construed. One who adopts a realistic view of any problematic class of statements will have to interpret 'in principle possible' in a fairly generous way. He will not hold that, whenever a statement is true, it must be possible, even in principle, for *us* to know that it is true, that is, for beings with our particular restricted observational and intellectual faculties and spatiotemporal viewpoint; it may be possible only for beings with greater powers or a different perspective or scale. But even the most thoroughgoing realist must grant that we could hardly be said to grasp what it is for a statement to be true if we had no conception whatever of how it might be known to be true; there would, in such a case, be no substance to our conception of its truth condition. Moreover, he would further grant that it would be useless to specify in a purely trivial manner the additional powers which a hypothetical being would have to have if he were to be capable of observing directly the truth or falsity of statements of some given class. We could not, for example, explain that a being who had a direct insight into counterfactual reality would be able to determine by direct observation the truth or falsity of any counterfactual conditional, because the expression 'a direct insight into counterfactual reality' provides no picture of what these powers consist in. Even the realist will concede that the picture of the required superhuman powers must always bear a recognizable relation to the powers which we in fact possess; they must be analogous to, or an extension of, our actual powers. It is precisely for this reason that the thesis that counterfactuals cannot be barely true is so compelling, since we cannot form any conception of what a faculty for direct recognition of counterfactual reality would be like.

The foregoing account is offered as a diagnosis, not as a defence. It gives, I believe, an accurate psychological account of how we come to suppose so readily that, for the sentences belonging to the less primitive strata of our language, we possess such a thing as a knowledge of what has to be the case for them to be true: but it provides no justification of this supposition. There is, so far as I can see, no possible alternative account of that in which our grasp of the truth conditions of such sentences consists: but this one works only by imputing to us an apprehension of the way in which those sentences might be used by beings very unlike ourselves, and, in so doing, fails to answer the question how we come to be able to assign to our sentences a meaning which is dependent upon a use to which we are unable to put them. This difficulty faces any explanation of the meanings of certain

expressions which consists solely of saying that we understand those expressions by analogy with or extrapolation from other expressions whose meanings we have come to grasp in some more direct way. There is no way of distinguishing such an account from the thesis that we treat certain of our sentences as if their use resembled that of other sentences in certain respects in which it in fact does not; that is, that we systematically misunderstand our own language.

IV

What is the way out of this impasse? To find this, we must first ask what led us into it. The plain answer is that our difficulties all arise because of our propensity to assume a realistic interpretation of all sentences of our language, that is, to suppose that the notion of truth applicable to statements made by means of them is such that every statement of this kind is determinately either true or false, independently of our knowledge or means of knowing. For decidable statements, the assumption of the principle of bivalence does little or no harm, since, by hypothesis, we can at will determine the truth value of those statements. It is when the principle of bivalence is applied to undecidable statements that we find ourselves in the position of being unable to equate an ability to recognize when a statement has been established as true or as false with a knowledge of its truth condition, since it may be true in cases when we lack the means to recognize it as true or false when we lack the means to recognize it as false. When we are in this position, we can explain the attribution to a speaker of a knowledge of the truth condition of the statement only when this can be represented as explicit knowledge, i.e. when that truth condition can be informatively stated, and an understanding of the statement may be represented as consisting in an ability to state it. When this is not the case, we are at a loss to explain in what a speaker's implicit knowledge of the truth condition of the statement can consist, since it apparently cannot be exhaustively explained in terms of the actual use which he has learned to make of the sentence.

If the realism which we adopt in regard to some class *M* of statements is of a reductionist type, then we have a means of enquiring whether or not the principle of bivalence holds good for statements in *M*. There will be a class *R* of statements to which the reduction is made, and the question will be comparatively easy to settle if we take a realist view of the class *R* itself. In that case, for any statement *A* in *M*,

there either will or will not be some set, belonging to the family $\bar{A}$ of sets of statements of *R*, all the members of which are true, and hence *A* itself will either be or not be true. Whether or not this is sufficient to guarantee the principle of bivalence for the class *M* will depend upon how we interpret the notion of falsity in respect of that class. If we interpret 'false' as meaning simply 'not true', then the principle of bivalence will hold trivially; but we are more often disposed to interpret 'false' so that '*A* is false' is to be equated with 'The negation of *A* is true', where the negation of a statement of the kind in question is to be identified by straightforward syntactic criteria. If the class *M* is closed under negation, the enquiry whether any statement *A* of *M* must be either true or false reduces to the question whether, if there is no set belonging to $\bar{A}$ all of whose members are true, there will always be some set belonging to $\overline{\text{Not-}A}$ all of whose members are true; even if the answer is negative, the situation will be unproblematic. There will then be statements of *M* which are neither true nor false, and, provided that we wish to represent the operation of negation as the result of applying a genuine sentential operator, we shall require a many-valued semantics for statements of the class *M*; but there will be no particular obstacle to the construction of such a semantics.

The case which gives rise to our difficulties is that of a class *M* of statements which are not in principle decidable and our view of which is that of naive realism: we assume the principle of bivalence for the members of *M*, but do not think that there is any non-trivial way of specifying what it is that makes a statement of *M* true when it is true. In any such case, we are bereft of any means of justifying our assumption of the principle of bivalence, save by appeal to the conception, discarded in the foregoing discussion, of a being with powers superior to ours for whom the statements of *M* would be decidable. It may, indeed, be the case that accepted linguistic practice is to treat as valid, in application to such statements, forms of inference which hold in classical two-valued logic; and it is this fact which impels us to suppose that we do in fact possess a notion of truth, applicable to those statements, according to which each statement is determinately either true or false. But a mere training in the acceptance of certain forms of inference cannot, by itself, endow us with a grasp of such a notion of truth, if we did not have it already, or, at least, if it is impossible to explain what it is to have such a notion of truth without reference to our acceptance of those forms of inference. Classical two-valued logic depends, for its justification, upon our having notions

of truth and falsity which license the assumption that each statement has, determinately, just one of those truth values; it cannot, of itself, generate those notions. It is true enough that classical logic can be justified in terms of a different semantics, specifically, any in which the truth values, whether finite or infinite in number, form a boolean algebra. This is of no particular help, however, since the use of any semantics based upon some range of truth values always presupposes that each statement has some one determinate truth value in that range; and this assumption presents just the same difficulties as the assumption of bivalence (which is simply a special case of it).

In such a case, there is no possibility of constructing a workable theory of meaning which will apply to the sentences in this class unless we first abandon the assumption of bivalence. Without doing so, we are committed to attributing to ourselves, as speakers, a grasp of a notion of truth which, in application to these sentences, is transcendental, that is, which goes beyond any knowledge which we might manifest by our actual employment of the language, since the condition for the truth of such sentences is one which we are not, in general, capable of recognizing as obtaining when it obtains. If we abandon the assumption of bivalence, we must construct a semantics for these sentences which is not formulated in terms of truth values; and it is probable, though not certain, that the outcome will be that we can no longer acknowledge a classical logic as governing them. In so far as our ordinary unreflective practice is to accept all classical forms of inference as valid for such sentences, this will mean that our theory of meaning is no longer purely descriptive of our actual practice in the use of our language, but, on the contrary, has compelled us to propose a revision in that practice, namely the rejection of certain classically valid forms of argument. However, this development provides no ground of objection against that theory of meaning, for the possibility was present from the outset. Obviously, of any two viable theories of meaning, that which justifies our actual linguistic practice is always to be preferred to that which demands a revision of it; but we have no ground to assume in advance that our language is in every respect perfectly in order. Frege supposed that various features of natural language—the presence of vague expressions and of predicates undefined for certain arguments, and the possibility of forming singular terms lacking a reference—made it impossible to construct a coherent semantics for it as it stood; Tarski likewise asserted that the semantically closed character of natural language

rendered it inconsistent. Such views may or may not be correct, but they cannot be ruled out a priori as absurd. The possibility that a language may stand in need of adjustment, that, in particular, the principles of inference conventionally recognized may require reassessment, is implicit in the idea that a language ought to be capable of systematization by a theory of meaning which determines the use given to each sentence from the internal structure of that sentence, that is, by an atomistic or molecular theory of meaning; for there can be no guarantee that a complex of linguistic practices which has grown up by piecemeal historical evolution in response to needs felt in practical communication will conform to any systematic theory.

This is, indeed, especially obvious when the theory of meaning is taken to have, as its core, a specification of the truth conditions of sentences. If such a theory is to be adequate for a language containing counterfactual conditionals, to take them once more as our example, the truth conditions assigned to those counterfactuals must allow us to determine the content of an assertion of any such counterfactual. What is given in linguistic practice is the content of a counterfactual assertion: the sort of grounds which a speaker may have for such an assertion, and the understanding which a hearer thereby has of what prompts the speaker to make such an assertion. Whatever is selected as providing the condition for a counterfactual conditional to be true must accord with this practice: the theory of force—the supplementary part of the theory of meaning which determines, from the truth condition of a sentence, the content of an utterance of that sentence when endowed with assertoric (or other specific types of) force—must enable us to derive from the truth condition of the counterfactual, as specified by the theory of truth, the content of an assertion made by uttering it. Now suppose that the speakers of the language accept as a valid principle of inference the alternation of opposite counterfactuals, mentioned earlier as a principle which we should reject: whatever follows both from some counterfactual conditional and from the opposite conditional is to be accepted as true. It is very likely that the truth conditions determined for counterfactual conditionals will not justify this principle, i.e. will not yield the result that, of any pair of opposite counterfactuals, one or other must be true; likely, that is, if the content of counterfactual assertions in this language coincides with that of such assertions in our language. Now it is possible that there may be some way of rectifying this so as to provide a justification

for the acceptance by the speakers of this language of the principle of the alternation of opposite counterfactuals. That is, it is possible that there is some way of broadening the truth conditions of counterfactuals, of allowing them to be true in cases in which, under the original specification, they were not true, so as after all to guarantee that one out of each pair of opposite counterfactuals must be true, without conferring on counterfactual assertions a content weaker than that which, in the actual practice of using the language, they in fact bear. But it is more likely that there is not: that we are driven to the conclusion that the speakers of this language are the victims of an error in permitting reasoning which depends upon the assumption that one of each pair of opposite counterfactuals must be true, and that they ought, in consistency, to reject such forms of argument. The idea, which Wittgenstein had, that acceptance of any principle of inference contributes to determining the meanings of the words involved, and that therefore, since the speakers of a language may confer on their words whatever meanings they choose, forms of inference generally accepted are unassailable by philosophical criticism, has its home only within a holistic view of language. If a language ought to be capable of systematization by means of an atomistic or molecular theory of meaning, we are not free to choose any logic that we like, but only one for which it is possible to provide a semantics which also accords with the other uses to which our sentences are put; in accepting or rejecting any particular form of inference, we are responsible to the meanings of the logical constants, thought of as given in some uniform manner (e.g. by two- or many-valued truth tables).

We are thus in the position of having to abandon, for certain classes of statements, the principle of bivalence, or any analogous principle of multivalence. We cannot, therefore, employ as our general representation of a grasp of the meaning of a sentence a knowledge of the condition under which it possesses, independently of our knowledge, a particular one out of two, or any larger number of, truth values. Instead, we shall have to construct a semantics which does not take, as its basic notion, that of an objectively determined truth value at all.

One well-known prototype for such a semantics already exists: the intuitionistic account of the meanings of mathematical statements. This is most easily thought about, in the first instance, in application only to statements of elementary arithmetic. In this case, there is no problem about the meanings of atomic statements, namely, in this

context, numerical equations, since these are decidable: a grasp of their meaning may be taken as consisting in a knowledge of the computation procedure which decides their truth or falsity. The whole difference between the classical or platonistic and the intuitionistic interpretation of arithmetical statements therefore turns upon the way in which we are given the meanings of the logical constants—the sentential operators and the quantifiers.

At this point some remarks are needed about the way that I have handled the phrase 'true in virtue of'. As explained above, a true statement is barely true only if there is no set of true statements, none of them trivial variants of the original statement, the truth of all of which determines the original statement as true. Whenever a sentence is capable of being barely true, the T-sentence relating to it in the theory of truth will, when the metalanguage is an extension of the object language, be of the trivial Tarski form, i.e. the sentence occurring on the right-hand side of the biconditional will be the same as that named on the left-hand side. When it is not capable of being barely true, the T-sentence may or may not be trivial, according to the resources of the metalanguage. Now on the explanation given, no conjunctive, disjunctive, universal or existential statement can be barely true. A conjunctive statement, when true, will be true in virtue of the truth of both its conjuncts. A disjunctive statement, when true, will be true in virtue of one of its disjuncts; we must allow that a given statement may be true in virtue of each of two or more distinct things. A true universal statement will be true in virtue of the truth of all its instances, and a true existential statement in virtue of the truth of any one of its true instances. This way of speaking accords with what has prompted philosophers to say such things as that there are no disjunctive facts; but the principal reason for adopting it is that it falls out as a by-product of the most convenient way of characterizing the notion of reducing one class of statements to another. It is plainly not a convenient way of speaking, however, when our interest is concentrated on the meanings of the logical constants themselves; it involves that the class of classical truth-functional combinations of sentences reduces to the class of atomic sentences and their negations, and, likewise, that the class of *EA* sentences (Σ_2^0 sentences) reduces to the class of quantifier-free sentences, and thus simply sweeps the problem of accounting for the meanings of the logical constants out of sight.

It is sometimes claimed that, while a theory of truth of the type envisaged in a Davidsonian theory of meaning does not itself give the

meanings of the non-logical primitives of the language, it does give the meanings of the logical constants. In order to understand the meanings of the non-logical primitives, we have to look outside the theory of truth itself (presumably because the axioms governing those primitives are of a trivial form, such as '"London" denotes London'), to the evidence, taken from the linguistic behaviour of the speakers, on which the theory of truth is based; or, as I should prefer to say, to the theory of sense, which explains what it is for a speaker to know the propositions expressed by the axioms. But, in order to understand the meanings of the logical constants, we need look to nothing but the axioms governing them within the theory of truth.

Presumably this claim is based on the notion that if, e.g., the sentential operators of the language are classical, the theory of truth will embody the truth-table explanations of those operators. It is, however, entirely misguided. The question whether an axiom of the theory of truth itself displays that in which an understanding of the expression which it governs consists, or whether we have to look for that to the theory of sense, is the question whether or not that axiom is trivial. A trivial axiom is one which, when rendered in a metalanguage which is an extension of the object language, will yield, in combination with suitable axioms for the other expressions, a trivial T-sentence for each sentence of the object language containing the expressions which it governs. Now, notoriously, the axioms governing the classical logical constants are trivial in this sense: they take such forms as 'For every sentence S and T, $\ulcorner S$ or $T\urcorner$ is true if and only if S is true or T is true' and 'For every finite sequence of objects $\vec{b}$ having the same length as the sequence $\vec{y}$ of variables, $\vec{b}$ satisfies $\ulcorner$For some x, $A(x, \vec{y})\urcorner$ if and only if, for some object a, $\langle a\rangle * \vec{b}$ satisfies $A(x, \vec{y})$'.

Now it is indeed true that the use as the core theory of a theory of truth, that is, of a theory which issues in T-sentences for the sentences of the object language, does not compel us to assign classical meanings to the logical constants. If we wish to impose upon the logical constants of the object language some non-classical meanings, and are prepared to presume that the logical constants of the metalanguage are interpreted in a similar non-classical manner, then we can often endow the logical constants of the object language with these non-classical meanings by adopting trivial axioms of just the same kind as in the classical case. This will be so whenever the relevant notion of truth distributes over the logical constants, as, for example, in the

intuitionistic case. At first sight, truth will not distribute over the logical constants within the many-valued logics; for instance, in a three-valued logic, when *B* is false but *A* is neither true nor false, the statement 'If *A* is true, then *B* is true' will be true although the statement ⌜If *A*, then *B*⌝ is not. However, this is so only because we are assuming, as can hardly be disputed, that the statement '*A* is true' is false when *A* is neither true nor false: for the purpose of constructing a theory of truth in which we may derive trivial T-sentences, we shall not want to use the predicate '. . . is true', construed as meaning '. . . has the value *true*', but a different predicate, say '. . . is True', which satisfies the requirement that, for any atomic sentence *A*, '*A* is True' has the same truth value as *A*. If we can devise axioms for the primitive terms and predicates, and for the condition for an atomic sentence to be True, which satisfy this requirement, then the property of being True will distribute over the sentential operators, and hence the requirement will be satisfied for complex sentences also.

There will be difficulties in various cases: for instance, in a many-valued logic which has more than one designated truth value; or when a logical constant, such as the modal operators, induces a context in which the variables of quantification must be taken as having a domain distinct from that which they have in other contexts. But there is certainly a large range of non-classical logics for which it would be possible to construct a theory of truth which yielded trivial T-sentences.

Whenever this can be done, however, the situation is exactly the reverse of what is claimed for a Davidsonian theory of truth. A trivial axiom for any expression, whether a logical constant or an expression of any other kind, does not, in itself, display in what an understanding of the expression consists, but throws the whole task of explaining this upon the theory of sense, which specifies what is to be taken as constituting a grasp of the proposition expressed by that axiom. An axiom of the form '$\vec{b}$ satisfies ⌜*S* or *T*⌝ if and only if $\vec{b}$ satisfies *S* or $\vec{b}$ satisfies *T*' (e.g. '$\vec{b}$ satisfies ⌜If it had been the case that *S*, then it would have been the case that *T*⌝ if and only if, if it had been the case that $\vec{b}$ satisfied *S*, then it would have been the case that $\vec{b}$ satisfied *T*') is no more explanatory of the meaning of the logical constant which it governs than is ' "London" denotes London' explanatory of the

meaning of the word 'London'; in either case, if there is to be any explanation at all, it will have to be found in the account of what a knowledge of the axiom consists in.

What is significant about a logical constant is not whether it is possible to construct a theory of truth so as to adopt a trivial axiom governing it, but, on the contrary, whether it is possible to devise a *non*-trivial axiom for it. If only a trivial form of axiom is possible, then the next significant question is whether the theory of sense can provide a non-circular account of what it is for a speaker to grasp its meaning, i.e. to have implicit knowledge of the trivial axiom governing the constant. Now, while it is possible to adopt trivial axioms for the intuitionistic constants, the standard explanations of these constants yield axioms of a different kind, not stated in terms of truth but in terms of proof. The meaning of a logical operator is given by specifying what is to count as a proof of a mathematical statement in which it is the principal operator, where it is taken as already known what counts as a proof of any of the constituent sentences (any of the instances, where the operator is a quantifier). In so far as the logical operator being explained is itself used in the explanation, the circularity is harmless, since it is a fundamental assumption that we can effectively recognize, of any mathematical construction, whether or not it is a proof of a given statement; thus, when it is explained that a construction is a proof of ⌜*A* or *B*⌝ if and only if it is either a proof of *A* or a proof of *B*, the 'or' on the right-hand side stands between two decidable statements, and is therefore unproblematic; we are explaining the general use of 'or' in terms of this special use. To put the matter differently, such an explanation of disjunction can be taken as a representation of implicit knowledge possessed by the speaker, knowledge which is fully manifested by his practice in the use of mathematical statements: he displays his understanding of the operator 'or' by acknowledging a construction as a proof of a disjunctive statement when and only when it is a proof of one or other disjunct. By contrast, the explanation in terms of truth conditions is irremediably circular if the statements to which the disjunction operator is applied are not decidable, that is, if the condition for the truth of such a statement is not effectively recognizable; for then we have no way of explaining what it amounts to to ascribe to someone a knowledge that ⌜*A* or *B*⌝ is true if and only if either *A* is true or *B* is true. This is just how matters stand with the quantifiers, when they are understood classically and the domain of quantification is infinite.

The truth conditions of quantified statements are stated by the use of quantification over the same domain; and, because we have no effective means of recognizing in every case whether or not they are satisfied, we cannot find in a description of our linguistic practice a means of escaping that circularity.

The intuitionistic explanations of the logical constants provide a prototype for a theory of meaning in which truth and falsity are not the central notions. The fundamental idea is that a grasp of the meaning of a mathematical statement consists, not in a knowledge of what has to be the case, independently of our means of knowing whether it is so, for the statement to be true, but in an ability to recognize, for any mathematical construction, whether or not it constitutes a proof of the statement; an assertion of such a statement is to be construed, not as a claim that it is true, but as a claim that a proof of it exists or can be constructed. The understanding of any mathematical expression consists in a knowledge of the way in which it contributes to determining what is to count as a proof of any statement in which it occurs. In this way, a grasp of the meaning of a mathematical sentence or expression is guaranteed to be something which is fully displayed in a mastery of the use of mathematical language, for it is directly connected with that practice. It is not in the least required, on such a theory of meaning, that every intelligible statement be effectively decidable. We understand a given statement when we know how to recognize a proof of it when one is presented to us. We understand the negation of that statement when we know how to recognize a proof of *it*; and a proof of the negation of a statement will be anything which demonstrates the impossibility of finding a proof of that statement. In special cases, we shall possess an effective means of discovering, for a given statement, either a proof of it or a proof that it can never be proved; then the statement will be decidable, and we shall be entitled to assert in advance the relevant instance of the law of excluded middle. In general, however, the intelligibility of a statement in no way guarantees that we have any such decision procedure, and hence the law of excluded middle is not in general valid: our understanding of a statement consists in a capacity, not necessarily to find a proof, but only to recognize one when found.

Such a theory of meaning generalizes readily to the non-mathematical case. Proof is the sole means which exists in mathematics for establishing a statement as true: the required general notion is, therefore, that of verification. On this account, an understanding of a

statement consists in a capacity to recognize whatever is counted as verifying it, i.e. as conclusively establishing it as true. It is not necessary that we should have any means of deciding the truth or falsity of the statement, only that we be capable of recognizing when its truth has been established. The advantage of this conception is that the condition for a statement's being verified, unlike the condition for its truth under the assumption of bivalence, is one which we must be credited with the capacity for effectively recognizing when it obtains; hence there is no difficulty in stating what an implicit knowledge of such a condition consists in—once again, it is directly displayed by our linguistic practice.

This characterization of a type of theory of meaning alternative to that which takes truth as its central notion requires one caveat and two reservations. The caveat is this: that, if a theory of meaning of this type is to be made plausible at all, it must take account of the interlocking or articulated character of language, as emphasised by Quine's 'Two Dogmas of Empiricism'. The great contribution of that essay was that it offered an essentially verificationist account of language without committing the logical positivist error of supposing that the verification of every sentence could be represented as the mere occurrence of a sequence of sense-experiences. Such a representation is approximately correct only for a restricted class of sentences, those which, in Quine's image, lie on the periphery; for other sentences, the actual process which we have learned to treat as leading to their being conclusively established will, in general, involve some inferential procedure; in the limiting case, e.g. for mathematical theorems, it will involve *only* this. For any non-peripheral sentence, our grasp of its meaning will take the form, not of a capacity to recognize which bare sense-experiences verify or falsify it, but of an apprehension of its inferential connections with other sentences linked to it in the articulated structure formed by the sentences of the language. A generalization of the intuitionistic theory of meaning for the language of mathematics must follow Quine in treating the verification of a sentence as consisting in the actual process whereby in practice we might come to accept it as having been conclusively established as true, a process which will usually involve the tacit or explicit use, in inference, of other sentences; proof, which is verification by inference alone, thus becomes merely a limiting case, not a distinct species.

The first of the two reservations is this. In the mathematical case, it is unnecessary to take the understanding of a statement as consisting

both in the ability to recognize a proof of it and the ability to recognize a refutation of it, since there is a uniform way to explain negation, i.e. to explain how to recognize a disproof of a statement. More exactly, we might regard the meanings of negations of numerical equations as being given directly in terms of the computation procedures by which those equations are verified or falsified: a proof of the negation of any arbitrary statement then consists of an effective method for transforming any proof of that statement into a proof of some false numerical equation. Such an explanation relies on the underlying presumption that, given a proof of a false numerical equation, we can construct a proof of any statement whatsoever. It is not obvious that, when we extend these conceptions to empirical statements, there exists any class of decidable atomic statements for which a similar presumption holds good; and it is therefore not obvious that we have, for the general case, any similar uniform way of explaining negation for arbitrary statements. It would therefore remain well within the spirit of a theory of meaning of this type that we should regard the meaning of each statement as being given by the simultaneous provision of a means for recognizing a verification of it and a means for recognizing a falsification of it, where the only general requirement is that these should be specified in such a way as to make it impossible for any statement to be both verified and falsified.

The second reservation is more far-reaching. In a theory of meaning in which truth plays the central role, the content of any assertion is fully determined by the condition that the sentence uttered be true. In this sense, we know the meaning of any sentence when we simply know what has to be the case for it to be true: provided with this knowledge, we know the content of any utterance of that sentence with assertoric force, and, equally, with imperatival, interrogative, optative force, etc. There is, however, no a priori reason why we should thereby know enough to know the meaning of any complex sentence into which the given sentence enters as a constituent; that is to say, there is no a priori reason why the truth condition of a complex sentence should depend only on the truth conditions of its constituent sentences. If we are able to represent the sentential operators of the language truth-functionally at all, we may be able to do so only by distinguishing different ways in which a sentence may be false, that is to say, different undesignated 'truth values' that it may have, or, perhaps, different ways in which it may be true, that is, different designated 'truth values'. These distinctions are irrelevant to the understanding of an utterance

of the sentence on its own, with whatever variety of linguistic force the utterance is made: they are needed for a grasp of the way in which a sentence may contribute to determining the truth condition of a complex sentence of which it is a constituent (i.e. the condition for such a sentence to have a designated 'truth value').

Now, in a theory of meaning in which the central notions are those of verification and falsification, rather than those of truth and falsity, the same thing applies. In intuitionistic logic, a sentence serving as a constituent of a complex sentence contributes to determining what is to count as a proof of that complex sentence solely through the definition of what counts as a proof of *it*, that is to say, solely through its meaning considered as a sentence capable of being used on its own. In this respect, intuitionistic logic resembles two-valued logic as opposed to a many-valued logic, since in two-valued logic a sentence contributes to determining the truth condition of a complex sentence of which it is a constituent solely through its own truth condition, whereas in many valued logic this is not so (if, as is intuitively natural, we identify the condition for a sentence to be true with the condition for it to have a designated value). But, just as the general conception of a theory of meaning in terms of truth conditions carries with it no presumption that the truth condition of a complex sentence can be determined solely from the truth conditions of its constituents, i.e. that the semantics of the theory will not require the use of more than two 'truth values', so, likewise, the general conception of a theory of meaning in terms of the conditions for the verification and falsification of a sentence carries no presumption that the meanings of the sentential operators will be able to be explained in the comparatively simple way that they are in intuitionistic logic. It may well be that, when we generalize the conception of such a theory of meaning to our language as a whole, we shall be unable to explain the meanings of the logical constants uniformly in terms of whatever constitutes a verification of each of the constituent sentences. The resulting logic will not be classical logic, and it therefore will not hang together with a realistic interpretation of all the sentences of our language: we shall have abandoned the assumption that every statement which has a definite sense is determinately either true or false, independently of our knowledge. But it will not necessarily very closely resemble intuitionistic logic either. The principal difference between the language of mathematics and our language as a whole lies in the fact that, within the former, the property of decidability is stable. A statement to the

effect that some particular large number is prime can in principle be decided, and it is therefore legitimate to assert the disjunction of that statement and its negation, or any other statement which can be shown to follow both from the statement and from its negation, since at any time we wished we could, at least in theory, determine the statement as true or as false. But the decidability of an empirical statement is not in the same way an enduring feature: if we regard the statement 'There is now either an odd or an even number of ducks on the pond' as assertible on the ground that we could, if we chose, determine one or other disjunct as true, we cannot offer the *same* ground for the assertibility of 'There was either an odd or an even number of geese which cackled on the Capitol' and if, nevertheless, we want to regard the latter statement as assertible, then either the assertion has to be explained as making a claim weaker than that the statement asserted is even in principle verifiable, or the specification of what counts as verifying a complex statement cannot be given uniformly in terms of what counts as verifying the constituents. For instance, we may wish to lay down that a disjunctive statement is conclusively established by a demonstration that an effective procedure would, if it were or had been applied at a suitable time, yield or have yielded a verification of one or other disjunct. This would be contrary to the intuitionistic meaning of disjunction, since it would involve that a disjunctive statement might be verified by something which not merely did not verify either disjunct, but did not guarantee that either disjunct could be verified at all. If this interpretation of 'or' were admitted, many instances ⌜*A* or not *A*⌝ of the law of excluded middle would be assertible when *A* could not be decided. (The effect of this, in achieving a greater rapprochement with classical reasoning than any permitted by a strictly intuitionistic interpretation of the logical constants, would probably be mitigated by the fact that, in such a case, a certain number of conditionals ⌜If *A*, then *B*⌝, whose antecedents were subject to the law of excluded middle, and which would be plausible on a realistic interpretation, would not be assertible on the appropriate verificationist interpretation of 'if'.) All will, however, remain within the spirit of a verificationist theory of meaning, so long as the meaning of each sentence is given by specifying what is to be taken as conclusively establishing a statement made by means of it, and what as conclusively falsifying such a statement, and so long as this is done systematically in terms only of conditions which a speaker is capable of recognizing.

V

I have argued that a theory of meaning in terms of truth conditions cannot give an intelligible account of a speaker's mastery of his language; and I have sketched one possible alternative, a generalization of the intuitionistic theory of meaning for the language of mathematics, which takes verification and falsification as its central notions in place of those of truth and falsity. This does not mean that the notion of truth will play no role, or only a trivial one, in such a theory of meaning. On the contrary, it will continue to play an important role, because it is only in terms of it that we can give an account of deductive inference; to recognize an inference as valid is to recognize it as truth-preserving. If, in the context of such a theory of meaning, the truth of a statement were to be identified with that statement's having been explicitly recognized as having been verified, deductive inference which proceeded from premisses which had been conclusively established could never lead to new information. More accurately stated, it could lead to new information only when it represented the most direct route to the establishment of the conclusion of the inference; for, as we have noted, any adequate theory of meaning must recognize that the sense of many statements is such that inference must play a part in any process which leads to their verification. Within any theory of meaning, the way in which the sense of a sentence is determined in accordance with its structure will display what we may regard as the most *direct* means of establishing it as true. This applies to a theory of meaning in terms of truth conditions as much as to one in terms of verification: the difference is that, in the former case, the most direct means of establishing the sentence will sometimes be one that is not available to us. For example, the classical representation of a universally quantified sentence as having a truth value which is the product of the truth values of the instances displays as the most direct means of determining its truth value a process of determining the truth values of all the instances in turn, a process which we cannot carry out when there are infinitely many of them. Any adequate theory of meaning must, however, account for the fact, not merely that we base many of our assertions upon evidence that falls short of being conclusive, but also that there exist ways of conclusively establishing the truth of statements which do not proceed by the direct route which is determined by the way in which their senses are given; one case of this is when we arrive at the

truth of a statement as the conclusion of a deductive argument. In order to account for the possibility of establishing a statement conclusively but indirectly, it is essential to appeal to some notion of the *truth* of a statement, which, evidently, cannot be equated merely with the statement's having been directly verified. This holds good as much for the intuitionistic account of mathematics as for the generalization of this account to empirical statements; it would be plainly contrary to the facts of the matter to maintain that mathematical reasoning, even within constructive mathematics, always proceeds along the most direct possible path: that would involve, for example, that we never in practice concluded to the truth of a statement by universal instantiation or by modus ponens. The most that can be plausibly maintained is that any valid proof provides us with an effective means whereby we could construct a proof of the conclusion of the most direct possible kind. Hence, even in intuitionistic mathematics, a notion of the truth of a statement is required which does not coincide merely with our actually possessing a proof of the kind which is specified by the explanation of the sense of the statement in accordance with its composition out of primitive symbols. It is far from being a trivial matter how the notion of truth, within a theory of meaning in terms of verification, should be explained. What differentiates such a theory from one in which truth is the central notion is, first, that meaning is not directly given in terms of the condition for a sentence to be true, but for it to be verified; and, secondly, that the notion of truth, when it is introduced, must be explained, in some manner, in terms of our capacity to recognize statements as true, and not in terms of a condition which transcends human capacities.

A theory of meaning in terms of verification is bound to yield a notion of truth for which bivalence fails to hold for many sentences which we are unreflectively disposed to interpret in a realistic manner. It will therefore compel us to accept certain departures from classical logic, and hence a certain revision of our habitual linguistic practice. Obviously, the theory would lose plausibility if this revision was too extensive; although, as I have argued, we cannot rule out a priori the possibility that the adoption of a correct theory of meaning may lead to some revision, the principal purpose of a theory of meaning is to explain existing practice rather than to criticize it. Whether a plausible theory of meaning in terms of verification can be constructed, I do not know; there are many problems which there is no space in this general discussion to investigate. But such a theory of meaning is not

the only conceivable alternative to one in terms of truth conditions; I shall devote a little space to describing a quite different possibility.

What is the content of an assertion? According to a theory of meaning in terms of truth conditions, the content is, simply, that the statement asserted is true. It may be that we are able to recognize it as true only in certain cases, and to recognize it as false only in certain cases; there may be states of affairs under which it is true, although we shall never know that it is true, and other states of affairs under which it is false, although we shall never know that it is false: but what the speaker is *saying* is that it is true. We have considered the difficulties—insuperable difficulties, if I am right—of explaining what it is for the speaker, or the hearer, to know what it is for the sentence to be true, in the general case; and there will be an equal difficulty in explaining what it is for the hearer, or the speaker, to act on the truth of the assertion. There is a general difficulty in explaining this notion, on any theory of meaning, namely that how one's actions are affected by a statement that one accepts depends upon what one wants. But, on a theory of meaning in terms of truth conditions, there is an additional difficulty: even given the desires of the hearer, what is it for him to conform his actions to the obtaining of a condition which he cannot, in general, recognize as obtaining? The supplementary part of a theory of meaning, its theory of force, must, in giving an account of the linguistic activity of assertion, be able to explain what it is to act on an assertion, as part of an explanation of what it is to accept an assertion: and, within a theory of meaning in terms of truth conditions, this explanation will be very difficult to construct.

According to a theory of meaning in terms of verification, the content of an assertion is that the statement asserted has been, or is capable of being, verified. It was conceded above that such a theory may have to allow that what is taken to constitute the falsification of a statement may have to be separately stipulated for each form of sentence. But, if so, this can only be for the purpose of laying down the sense of the negation of each sentence, no uniform explanation of negation being available: it cannot be for the purpose of fixing the sense of a sentence, considered as being used on its own. For, if we supposed otherwise, we should have to say that the content of an assertion was that the sentence asserted was capable of being verified, and, further, that it was incapable of being falsified. It may be said that this complication is quite unnecessary, since the stipulations are always required to be such that no statement can be both verified and falsified;

hence the correctness of an assertion will always guarantee the weaker claim that the sentence cannot be falsified, which will be expressed by the double negation of the sentence. This retort is fully justified if the determination of what counts as falsifying the sentence need not be considered as affecting the sense of that sentence when used on its own; but, when it is so considered, it must play some role in fixing the content of an assertion made by means of the sentence. It would then follow that a speaker might be neither right nor wrong in making an assertion: not wrong, because it could be shown that the sentence could not be falsified; but not right either, because no way was known of verifying the sentence. This consequence would be fatal to the account, since an assertion is not an act which admits of an intermediate outcome; if an assertion is not correct, it is incorrect. A bet may have conditions; if they are unfulfilled, the bettor neither wins or loses. But there is nothing corresponding for an assertion; it is a reductio ad absurdum of any theory of meaning if it entails that there is.

It may be said that, even if the condition for a sentence's being falsified does not enter into the determination of the sense of that sentence as used on its own, a verificationist theory of meaning must leave open the possibility of an assertion's being neither right nor wrong: for the speaker's claim to be able to verify the statement may be unjustified, even though there is nothing to rule out the possibility of its coming to be verified at some future time. This situation, however, is one which cannot be ruled out by appeal to our understanding of the linguistic practice of assertion, though how it is described depends upon our background theory of meaning. If we hold a theory of meaning in terms of truth conditions, then we shall describe such a situation as one in which the speaker was not entitled to make the assertion, but in which it has not yet been shown whether the speaker was right or wrong. Admittedly, some explanation is required of our having a place for such a distinction: on the face of it, if assertion is simply a linguistic act governed by objective conditions of correctness, and these are not fulfilled, then the assertion was simply wrong, without more ado. This point was discussed earlier: it is due to our understanding of sentences as constituents of more complex sentences, and of their use with, e.g., imperatival force, that we are led to distinguish between the truth of an assertion and the speaker's entitlement to make it. Under a theory of meaning in terms of verification, we cannot say that every assertion is either right or wrong, but we can draw a similar distinction between a speaker's having the means to

verify his assertion and his saying something a means of verifying which later became available. Such a distinction is indeed forced on us in exactly the same way as under a theory of meaning in terms of truth conditions: given that notion of the verification of a sentence which is required for explaining its role in complex sentences, we cannot, in general, consider an assertion as a claim already to have a means of verifying the statement asserted, but only as a claim that such a means will be arrived at; for example, when the statement is in the future tense. Thus to say in *this* sense that an assertion may be neither right nor wrong is in full harmony with the nature of assertion as a type of linguistic act.

The sense which we have been discussing, in which it can legitimately be said that an assertion may be neither right nor wrong is, as we have seen, that which relates to the distinction between a speaker's entitlement to make the assertion and the truth of what he says, i.e. between *his* being justified in saying it and there being a justification not known to him at the time. We may say that the *speaker* is right if he is, at the time of speaking, able to verify what he says, but that his *assertion* is correct if there is some means of verifying it, a knowledge of which by the speaker at the time of utterance would have made him right. The sense in which it is false to the nature of assertion to say that an assertion may be neither right nor wrong is that in which, in this terminology, the assertion itself is neither correct nor incorrect. That is, there cannot be a piece of knowledge the possession of which by any speaker would show both that he would not be right to make a certain assertion and that he would not be wrong to make it. If someone makes a conditional bet, someone else, by knowing that the condition is unfulfilled, may know that he will neither win nor lose his bet: there is no piece of knowledge which is related in this way to an assertion.

Now, certainly, a verificationist theory of meaning rules out the possibility that an assertion may be both correct and incorrect, just because no statement can be both verified and falsified. But, even if the specification of what falsifies a sentence does not go to determine the sense of the sentence as used on its own, such a theory of meaning does come dangerously close to allowing that an assertion may be neither correct nor incorrect. If our logic at all resembles intuitionistic logic, there is indeed no possibility of discovering, for any statement, that it can neither be verified nor falsified, since whatever would serve to show that it could not be verified would ipso facto verify its negation.

But, for any statement which is not stable in Brouwer's sense (which is not equivalent to its double negation), there is a possibility of our discovering that it can never be falsified without our yet having a verification of it. In such a case, we may say that we know that an assertion of the statement would not be incorrect, without knowing that it was correct. Admittedly, the possibility of verifying the statement would always remain open, so that this could never become a case of knowing the assertion to be neither correct nor incorrect; but it points to an obscurity in the representation, within such a theory, of the force of an assertion. What more is someone saying, when he makes an assertion, than that his statement is not incorrect? What more does he say, when he affirms a statement, than when he simply denies its negation? In so far as we are considering his assertion as a claim to have verified a statement, these questions are not hard to answer, since, in general, more is needed in order to verify a statement than is needed to verify its double negation; and so, in the mathematical case, when assertion always amounts to a claim that the statement asserted has actually been proved, no problem arises. But we have seen that, in the general case, we have to consider as primary, in determining the content of an assertion, not the speaker's personal entitlement to make the assertion, but the condition for its objective correctness; and, in connection with that, it is impossible to distinguish between the supposedly stronger content and the supposedly weaker one. If a speaker claims to have verified a statement, and we find that he has verified merely its double negation, his claim fails: but our present question is not this, but what we are doing if we accept his assertion as objectively correct, regardless of his personal entitlement to make it. To acknowledge it as not incorrect is, obviously, to rule out the possibility of its ever being falsified; what more is involved in accepting it as correct must, therefore, be to expect it at some time to be verified, or at least to hold the possibility open. Holding the possibility open adds nothing whatever to recognizing that it can never be falsified; if we have recognized this, then the possibility of its at some time being verified just *is* open; since we can never close it, we do not have to *hold* it open. But even expecting that it will at some time be verified amounts to nothing substantive, when there is no bound on the time within which this will happen; in knowing that the statement can never be falsified, we already know that that expectation can never be disappointed; and, given that the expectation will never be disappointed, the supposition that it will at some time be realized is

consistent with *any* sequence of events over any finite interval, however long, and therefore adds nothing.

It is a well-known fact that some philosophers have wished to consider assertion as a linguistic act which may have an intermediate outcome, in a sense analogous to that in which a conditional bet has an intermediate outcome when the condition is not fulfilled. That is, they have wanted to hold that certain sentences will, under certain determinate conditions, be neither true nor false; and they have wanted to make a direct connection between the notions of truth and falsity here employed and the correctness and incorrectness of assertions, so that someone making an assertion by the utterance of a sentence which proves to be neither true nor false will have made an assertion which is neither correct nor incorrect. (Sometimes this is expressed by saying that he has made no assertion at all; but this form of expression cannot disguise the fact that he has made a significant utterance, that he has performed a linguistic act.) I have elsewhere argued against this that we can attach no sense to the notion of an assertion's being neither correct nor incorrect, except in so far as it is vague or ambiguous, and that the proper interpretation of a sentence's being neither true nor false is that it has an undesignated truth value distinct from that which we label 'falsity', or else a designated truth value distinct from that which we label 'truth'; and, accordingly, that the state of being neither true nor false is of significance only in connection with the behaviour of the sentence as a constituent in complex sentences, for which we wish to employ a many-valued semantics, and not with the use of the sentence on its own to make an assertion, for which we need to know only the distinction between its having a designated and an undesignated truth value.

Now what is the proper way to argue for this? One approach might be to say the following. If the content of an assertion is specific, then it must be determinate, for any recognizable state of affairs, whether or not that state of affairs shows the assertion to have been correct. If some recognizable state of affairs does not suffice to show the assertion to have been correct, there are two alternative cases. One is that this state of affairs serves to rule out the possibility of a situation's coming about in which the assertion can be recognized as having been correct: in this case, the state of affairs must be taken as showing the assertion to have been incorrect. The other is that the given state of affairs, while not showing the assertion to have been correct, does not rule out the possibility of its later being shown to have been so: in this case, the

correctness of the assertion has simply not yet been determined. What is not possible is that any recognizable state of affairs could serve to show both that the assertion was not correct and that it was not incorrect, since the content of the assertion is wholly determined by which recognizable states of affairs count as establishing it as correct: hence any state of affairs which can be recognized as ruling out the correctness of the assertion must be reckoned as showing it to be incorrect. Hence, if a sentence is held to be neither true nor false in certain recognizable circumstances, this cannot be explained by saying that an assertion made by uttering the sentence would, in those circumstances, be neither correct nor incorrect.

This argument is not intended, as some have taken it, as a demonstration that every assertion must be either correct or incorrect. It allows the possibility that an assertion may never be recognized either as being one or as being the other; and a realistic metaphysics—or better, a realistic theory of meaning—needs to be invoked if we wish to claim that, nevertheless, it must actually *be* one or the other. It is therefore certainly not an argument to the conclusion that only those sentences can be used to make assertions for which the principle of bivalence holds good, or a derivation of the principle of bivalence from the nature of assertion. It is merely an argument that there can be no circumstances in which an assertion can be recognized to be neither correct nor incorrect. It would be consistent with this to hold that there were some assertions which were neither correct nor incorrect, although we are incapable of recognizing the fact for any particular assertion. However, I should repudiate such a view as an indefensible hybrid. If we are able to understand a description of a state of affairs which we are incapable of recognizing as obtaining, and to entertain the supposition that it *does* obtain, then there is no reason not to conceive of meaning as given in terms of truth conditions which we cannot in general recognize, and for which the principle of bivalence holds good. In this case, the content of an assertion will be able to be given in terms of conceivable, though not necessarily recognizable, states of affairs, i.e. by which among such states of affairs render it correct, and the above argument goes through without the restriction of the states of affairs considered to recognizable ones. It would follow that, not only can an assertion not be recognized as being neither correct nor incorrect, but it could not in fact *be* neither correct nor incorrect. Indeed, since, on this realistic conception, the non-occurrence of any state of affairs which rendered the assertion correct would again be a state of affairs (which is not so if we restrict ourselves to recognizable

states of affairs), every assertion would be either correct or incorrect. If, on the other hand, we are not able to form the conception of a state of affairs which we cannot recognize as obtaining, then we cannot attach any content to the notion of an assertion's *being* correct or incorrect other than our being able to recognize it as one or the other, in which case the fact that an assertion cannot be recognized to be neither correct nor incorrect is sufficient to show that it cannot be neither. Only on a realistic assumption, therefore, which the argument does not invoke, does the argument lead to the principle of bivalence. By itself, it establishes only the weaker conclusion that a statement cannot be neither true nor false, where the notions of truth and falsity are those directly connected with the correctness and incorrectness of assertions, i.e. a sentence is true if an assertion made by means of it is correct, and false if such an assertion is incorrect.[2] It requires a classical logic to allow us to pass from saying that no statement is neither true nor false to saying that each statement is either true or false; and the argument does not presuppose the validity of classical logic.

The argument, as presented above, leads directly to a verificationist theory of meaning; at least, it does so if the restriction to recognizable states of affairs is justified. But *is* that the proper way to present it? Suppose that we are considering some assertoric sentence which we understand perfectly well in practice—that is, we have no uncertainty about the content of an assertion made by means of it—but the application to which of the notions of truth and falsity is intuitively obscure. How do we decide whether or not any given state of affairs shows an assertion made by means of the sentence to be correct? For instance, the sentence is an indicative conditional, and the state of affairs is one in which the antecedent is recognizably false. To make a fair test, we must of course take a sentence to which the application of the predicate 'true' is obscure, since otherwise we shall simply (perhaps quite rightly) identify the correctness of the assertion with the truth of the sentence, whereas we are here concerned with whether an understanding of the content of the assertion alone determines what is to be taken as showing it to have been correct. The answer is, I think, that we have no clear direct guide to what should be regarded

[2] By this, I do not mean notions of truth and falsity so crude that we cannot distinguish a man's saying something false from his saying what he had no right to say on the evidence available, but only those notions of truth and falsity which correspond, in a many-valued logic, to the possession of a designated and of an undesignated value.

as showing the assertion to have been correct; and the reason is that it is not the *correctness* of an assertion which should be taken as the fundamental notion needed in explaining assertion as a linguistic act. An assertion is not, normally, like an answer in a quiz programme; the speaker gets no prize for being right. It is, primarily, a guide to action on the part of the hearers (an interior judgment being a guide to action on the part of the thinker); a guide which operates by inducing in them certain expectations. And the content of an expectation is determined by what will surprise us; that is, by what it is that is *not* in accord with the expectation rather than by what corroborates it. The expectation formed by someone who accepts an assertion is not, in the first place, characterized by his supposing that one of those recognizable states of affairs which render the assertion correct will come to obtain; for in the general case there is no bound upon the length of time which may elapse before the assertion is shown to have been correct, and then such a supposition will have, by itself, no substance. It is, rather, to be characterized by his *not* allowing for the occurrence of any state of affairs which would show the assertion to have been incorrect; a negative expectation of this kind has substance, for it can be disappointed. The fundamental notion for an account of the linguistic act of assertion is, thus, that of the *incorrectness* of an assertion: the notion of its correctness is derivative from that of its incorrectness, in that an assertion is to be judged correct whenever something happens which precludes the occurrence of a state of affairs showing it to be incorrect. (In just the same way, as I have argued elsewhere, the fundamental notion in an account of the linguistic act of giving a command is that of *disobedience*, the notion of obedience being derivative from it.)

This comes out very clearly when we ask, of some sentence the assertoric content of which we understand in practice, but to which the application of 'true' and 'false' is obscure, which states of affairs we should take as showing an assertion made by uttering it to have been incorrect. By making an assertion, a speaker *rules out* certain possibilities; if the assertion is unambiguous, it must be clear which states of affairs he is ruling out and which he is not. From our practical understanding of the assertoric sentence, we can answer at once whether, by such an assertion, a speaker is to be taken as ruling out this or that state of affairs. In answering such a question, we do not need to seek guidance from the intuitive application of the predicate 'false' to the sentence, and our answer may even run counter to this;

nor do we have to think whether we should *consider* the assertion to be incorrect in this or that case (as we have to think whether we should *consider* a conditional assertion to be shown to have been correct when the antecedent proves false). We know at once, for example, that the maker of a conditional assertion is *not* ruling out the possibility that the antecedent is false, and that therefore its falsity does not render the assertion incorrect, and, indeed, precludes the occurrence of the case which he *is* ruling out; and we know this independently of any decision as to whether the conditional sentence which he uses is to be called 'true' in this case. Likewise, we know at once that a speaker who makes an assertion by means of an atomic sentence containing a proper name or definite description *is* meaning to rule out the possibility that the name or description lacks a reference; and, again, we know this quite independently of any decision as to whether, when a reference is lacking, the sentence should or should not be called 'false'.

Thus, in the order of explanation, the notion of the incorrectness of an assertion is prior to that of its correctness. Why has this fact been so persistently overlooked? Partly because of the tendency to concentrate on the decidable case: an expectation as to the outcome of a test may indifferently be described as an expectation that the result will be favourable or as an expectation that it will not be unfavourable. Even, perhaps, in part because of a tendency to think particularly of future-tense assertions which predict the occurrence of an observable state of affairs within or at a specified time; for then the positive expectation has a bound, and hence has substance—if it is not satisfied within the given time, it will be disappointed. But principally, I think, because of the tacit assumption of a realistic theory of meaning in terms of non-effective truth conditions. If the conditions in terms of which the content of an assertion is given are ones which we can recognize, then it makes a very substantial difference whether we take the notion of correctness or that of incorrectness as primary: it gives quite a different effect to say that an assertion is shown to be correct if something occurs which excludes the possibility of its being shown incorrect, from that yielded by saying that it is shown to be incorrect if something occurs which precludes the possibility of its being shown correct. But, if the conditions in terms of which the content is given are ones which we can grasp without, in general, being able to recognize, then it makes no effective difference, since the condition for the incorrectness of the assertion will obtain whenever

that for its correctness does *not* obtain, and vice versa. That is not to say that, in the context of a realistic theory of meaning, the point is devoid of significance: even in this context, it remains true that, in the order of explanation, the notion of the incorrectness of an assertion is primary.

These considerations prompt the construction of a different theory of meaning, one which agrees with the verificationist theory in making use only of effective rather than transcendental notions, but which replaces verification by falsification as the central notion of the theory: we know the meaning of a sentence when we know how to recognize that it has been falsified. Such a theory of meaning will yield a logic which is neither classical nor intuitionistic[3]. In one respect, it stands on the other side of a theory of meaning in terms of truth conditions from a verificationist theory. A verificationist theory comes as close as any plausible theory of meaning can do to explaining the meaning of a sentence in terms of the grounds on which it may be asserted; it must of course distinguish a speaker's actual grounds, which may not be conclusive, or may be indirect, from the kind of direct, conclusive grounds in terms of which the meaning is given, particularly for sentences, like those in the future tense, for which the speaker cannot have grounds of the latter kind at the time of utterance. But a falsificationist theory does not relate the meaning of a sentence directly to the grounds of an assertion made by means of it at all. Instead, it links the content of an assertion with the commitment that a speaker undertakes in making that assertion; an assertion is a kind of gamble that the speaker will not be proved wrong. Such a theory therefore has obvious affinities, not only with Popper's account of science, but also with the language-game type of semantics developed by Hintikka and others.

[3] Let us write f_A for the set of recognizable states of affairs in which A is falsified, and $\bar{f}$ for the set of recognizable states of affairs which preclude the occurrence of any state of affairs in f. Plainly, $f \cap \bar{f} = \emptyset$, $f \subseteq \bar{\bar{f}}$ and, if $f \subseteq g$, then $\bar{g} \subseteq \bar{f}$; hence $\bar{f} = \bar{\bar{\bar{f}}}$. We may also assume that $\overline{f \cup g} = \bar{f} \cap \bar{g}$ and that $\bar{f} \cup \bar{g} \subseteq \overline{f \cap g}$. It seems reasonable to take $f_{\neg A} = \overline{f_A}$, $f_{A \vee B} = f_A \cap f_B$, $f_{A \& B} = f_A \cup f_B$ and $f_{A \rightarrow B} = f_B \cap \overline{f_A}$, and to define $A_1, \ldots, A_n \vdash B$ as holding when $f_B \subseteq f_{A_1} \cup \ldots \cup f_{A_n}$, so that $\vdash B$ holds just in case $f_B = \emptyset$; on this definition, however, $\vdash A \rightarrow B$ may hold when $A \vdash B$ does not. On this basis, we have $\neg\neg A \vdash A$ and $\vdash A \rightarrow \neg\neg A$, but not $A \vdash \neg\neg A$. We also have $\vdash A \vee \neg A$, $\vdash \neg (A \& \neg A)$, $\neg (A \& B) \dashv\vdash \neg A \vee \neg B$ and $\neg (A \vee B) \vdash \neg A \& \neg B$, but not $\neg A \& \neg B \vdash \neg (A \vee B)$. However, I do not feel at all sure that this approach is correct.

VI

Any theory of meaning was earlier seen as falling into three parts: first, the core theory, or theory of reference; secondly, its shell, the theory of sense; and thirdly, the supplementary part of the theory of meaning, the theory of force. The theory of force establishes the connection between the meanings of sentences, as assigned by the theories of reference and of sense, and the actual practice of speaking the language. The theory of reference determines recursively the application to each sentence of that notion which is taken as central in the given theory of meaning: if truth is the central notion, it issues in a specification for each sentence of the condition under which it is true; if verification is the central notion, it specifies, for each sentence, the condition under which it is verified; and similarly when falsification is the central notion. It does this, for each of the infinitely many sentences of the language, by assigning to each minimal significant sentence-constituent (each word) a reference, which takes whatever form is required in order that the references of the components of any sentence shall jointly determine the application to that sentence of the central notion. Thus, when the central notion is that of truth, the referent of a one-place predicate is a set of objects (or function from objects to truth values); when it is that of verification, it is an effective means of recognizing, for any given object, a conclusive demonstration that the predicate applies to that object; or that it does *not* apply, when the central notion is that of falsification.

The theory of sense specifies what is involved in attributing to a speaker a knowledge of the theory of reference. When the theory of reference takes the form of a theory of truth, this is necessary whenever an axiom of T-sentence assumes a trivial form, and therefore fails to display in what the speaker's implicit knowledge of it consists. When, however, the central notion is an effective one—one the conditions for the application of which a speaker can recognize as obtaining whenever they obtain, like the notions of verification and of falsification—then there appears to be no need for a theory of sense to round out the theory of reference; we could say that, in a theory of meaning of such a type, the theories of reference and of sense merge. In a verificationist or falsificationist theory of meaning, the theory of reference specifies the application to each sentence of the central notion of the theory in such a way that a speaker will directly manifest his knowledge of the condition for its application by his actual use of the language.

The distinction between sense and reference derives, of course, from Frege, who gave two quite different arguments for making it. One was that it is unintelligible to attribute to a speaker a bare knowledge of the reference of an expression; e.g. to say that the speaker knows, of a certain object, that it is the bearer of a given proper name, and to add that this is a *complete* characterization of that item of the speaker's knowledge. On Frege's view, such a piece of knowledge must always take the form of knowing that the object, considered as identified in a particular way, is the referent of the name; and that mode of identification of the object which enters into the characterization of what it is that the speaker knows constitutes the sense of the proper name. Exactly parallel considerations apply to expressions of other semantic categories.

This argument goes halfway in the same direction as the argument used in the present paper, to the effect that a theory of sense is needed to characterize that in which a speaker's knowledge of the meanings of expressions of the language, as determined by the theory of reference, consists. Frege's argument is that the theory of reference does not fully display what it is that a speaker knows when he understands an expression—what proposition is the object of his knowledge. I have here endorsed that argument, but have, in addition, gone one step beyond it, by maintaining that, since the speaker's knowledge is for the most part implicit knowledge, the theory of sense has not only to specify *what* the speaker knows, but also how his knowledge is manifested; this ingredient in the argument here used for the necessity of a theory of sense is not to be found in Frege.

Frege's other argument for the sense/reference distinction also concerns knowledge, but, this time, the knowledge that is acquired when a sentence comes to be accepted as true by one who already knows its meaning, rather than the knowledge of its meaning; it relates, therefore, to the use of language to convey information. Frege is not, of course, interested in the information that may be communicated to an individual by means of an assertion, for that will vary according to the information already possessed by that individual: he is interested in the informational content of the sentence in itself, which we might explain as the information which would be acquired, on coming to learn the truth of the sentence, by someone who previously knew nothing save the meaning of that sentence. Now it is obvious that the informational content of a sentence depends upon its meaning: a man can acquire no further information from learning the

truth of a sentence of whose meaning he is unaware, and what information he does acquire will vary according to the particular meaning he attaches to it. Frege's argument is that a plausible account of the informational content of a sentence is impossible if the hearer's understanding of the sentence is represented as consisting, for each of the constituent words, in a bare knowledge of its reference (as this was characterized above). The celebrated example used by Frege is that of an identity-statement, the truth value of which would already be known by anyone to whom it was—per impossibile—correct to ascribe a bare knowledge of the references of the terms on either side of the identity-sign (assuming, of course, that he also understood the identity-sign); such a statement would therefore have no informational content whatever, if a knowledge of meaning consisted in a bare knowledge of reference. Actually, a parallel argument works for *any* atomic statement.

The notion of sense is thus connected, from the outset, with that of knowledge. Now a very extensive body of theory is required to carry us from a knowledge of the meanings of sentences of the language, as specified jointly, in terms of the central notion of the given theory of meaning, by the theories of reference and of sense, to an understanding of the actual practice of speaking the language. We seldom think explicitly about the theory which effects this transition; as language-users, we have had an implicit grasp of it from early years, and, because it is so fundamental, philosophers find it elusive and do not contrive to say much about it. But we can recognize how extensive it would be if made explicit if we try to imagine how a Martian might be instructed in the use of human language. Martians are highly intelligent, and communicate with one another, but by a means so different from any human language that it is a practical impossibility to set up any translation from a human language into the Martian medium of communication. The only means, therefore, by which a Martian can come to learn a human language is by studying a fully explicit theory of meaning for that language (compare a speaker's mastery of the grammar of his mother-tongue and his learning that of a foreign language by means of a grammar-book). The Martian first masters the theories of reference and of sense for some one of our languages; but, since his ultimate objective is to visit Earth as an alien spy, disguised as a human being, he needs to acquire a practical ability to speak the language, not just a theoretical understanding of it; he needs to know, not only what he may say, and when, without

betraying his alien origin, but also, within these constraints, how he can use the language as an instrument to further his own ends of gaining knowledge and of influencing the actions of the human beings around him. Obviously, having mastered the theories of reference and of sense, he has a great deal more to learn; he has to be provided with an explicit description of our linguistic practice, in terms of our utterances of sentences whose meanings (conceived of as given in terms, e.g., of their truth conditions) are taken as already known, and of our responses to such utterances on the part of others.

All of this additional information, which is required if one is to pass from a knowledge of meanings as given in terms of the central notion to a complete practical mastery of the use of the language, I have promiscuously gathered into the supplementary part of the theory of meaning; and it may be a valid criticism that I have thereby lumped together under the single title of the 'theory of force' multifarious propositions concerning the language of very disparate kinds. Following a proposal of Donald Davidson's, we may distinguish two stages in the passage from the theory of reference to the actual employment of the language. The first takes us to the actual judgments which we make concerning the truth and falsity of sentences. At least, that is how Davidson expresses it. He is, however, more concerned with the stages in the process of constructing a theory of reference for a language which we do not originally know, but the use of which we observe; we begin with the raw data provided by our observations of the actual utterances of the speakers, and an intermediate stage in the construction of a theory of truth for the language will consist in our assigning to particular speakers particular judgments as to the truth values of sentences at various times. I have been concerned, on the other hand, not with the upward process of constructing a theory of reference from the records of initially uninterpreted utterances, but with the downward process of deriving, from the theory of reference, the practice of using the language, this process of derivation itself to be incorporated into a theory which forms part of the total theory of meaning for the language; if the claim that a given theory of reference is the correct one, i.e. can serve as the core of a viable theory of meaning for the language, is to be substantiated, such a downward process of derivation must be possible. We do not expect, nor should we want, to achieve a deterministic theory of meaning for a language, even one which is deterministic only in principle: we should not expect to be able to give a theory from which, together with all other relevant

conditions (the physical environment of a speaker, the utterances of other speakers, etc.), we could predict the exact utterances of any one speaker, any more than, by a study of the rules and strategy of a game, we expect to be able to predict actual play. Hence what is to be derived, in accordance with the supplementary part of the theory of meaning, is not a detailed account of the utterances which will actually be made in given circumstances, but only general principles governing the utterance of sentences of the language, those principles a tacit grasp of which enables someone to take part in converse in that language. From our point of view, therefore, the intermediate stage in the downward process of derivation will yield, not actual individual judgments of the truth or falsity of sentences, but the general principles which govern our making such judgments.

The second stage in the downward process of derivation carries us from the judgments that we make, under given conditions, concerning the truth and falsity of sentences, to our actual utterances, assertoric, interrogative, imperatival, etc.; here, again, we can expect to obtain no more than a formulation of the general principles in accordance with which the language-games of assertion, question, command, request, etc., are played. It is this second stage which may be said to constitute the theory of force properly so called.

What, then, of the first stage, which determines, from the meaning of a sentence, the principles governing the conditions under which we judge it to be true or false? To what part of the theory of meaning do those principles belong? It can hardly be denied that there *are* such principles: what but the meaning of a sentence can determine what we count as a ground for accepting it as true? Admittedly, when the grounds fall short of being conclusive—and also when we cannot recognize with certainty that we have conclusive grounds (as with a very complex mathematical proof or computation)—there is an element of choice as to whether or not we accept the sentence as true; the term 'judgment', in its technical use, is well chosen. But the meaning alone determines whether or not something *is* a ground for accepting the sentence, independently of whether we decide to treat that ground as sufficiently strong. That might be because the specification of what counted as a ground for the truth of the sentence was an integral part of fixing its meaning; but none of the three types of theory of meaning at which we have looked has allowed this to be so. According to a theory of meaning in terms of truth conditions, we know the meaning of a sentence when we know what it is for it to be true; to know

that is not, in itself, expressly to know what counts as evidence for its truth. A verificationist theory represents an understanding of a sentence as consisting in a knowledge of what counts as conclusive evidence for its truth. Even on such a theory, that understanding does not immediately involve a capacity to recognize evidence which is less than conclusive. Indeed, as we have seen, it does not even take the meaning of the sentence as relating directly to everything that could serve as conclusive evidence for its truth, but only, as it were, to a canonical method of establishing the truth of the sentence—what we called its 'direct' verification; I argued that, even in the context of a verificationist theory, an adequate account of deductive inference must acknowledge the possibility of establishing the truth of a sentence conclusively but indirectly, that is, by a route distinct from that immediately provided for by the way in which the meaning of the sentence is given. Hence, within any theory of meaning of the types we have considered, the principles which govern what counts as evidence for the truth of a sentence must be systematically derivable from its meaning, since they are not immediately given with it, but are determined by it. By means of what part of the theory of meaning is this derivation effected?

In the previous discussion, I assigned it vaguely to that part of the theory of force which treats of the linguistic act of assertion. Now there is here a distinction to be made. It is certainly part of the conventions governing the assertoric use of language what kind of claim we take a speaker who makes an unqualified assertion to be advancing, i.e., what kind of ground or warrant is required for the assertion not to be misleading. This is something *not* uniformly determined by the meaning of the sentence used to make the assertion, and may vary from one area of discourse to another, and also from one context to another. We already noted, for example, that our convention requires the unqualified assertion of a mathematical statement to be backed by the existence of an actual proof, and that this convention, quite different from that governing assertions of other kinds, could be changed without altering in any way the meanings of mathematical sentences. The enunciation of these conventions does indeed belong to the theory of assertoric force. This is, however, an entirely separate matter from that with which we are here concerned. What we are concerned with is what determines that something is evidence of a certain strength for the truth of a given sentence, not with whether the existence of evidence of a particular strength is sufficient reason for

accepting the sentence as true (that is a matter of personal strategy), nor yet with whether it warrants an assertion of the sentence (that is a matter of independent commonly agreed linguistic convention).

Now since, as we have seen, sense is a cognitive notion, it may seem that this epistemological component of the theory of meaning should belong to the theory of sense rather than to the theory of force. Even if the theory of reference merely states what has to be the case for a sentence to be true, should not the theory of sense state, not merely how we know the truth condition of the sentence, but also how we can know, or on what basis we may judge, the sentence to be true? Does this not follow if Frege was right in thinking that the notion of sense can be employed not only to make the theory of meaning at the same time a theory of understanding, i.e. to give a representation of our grasp of the meanings of our expressions, but also to give an account of the use of language for the communication of information, since information is a cognitive notion, and the amount of information conveyed must depend upon what steps the original informant needed to take to obtain it?

Frege would certainly have answered 'No' to these questions. For him, the sense of a sentence gives its cognitive value (informational content) only inasmuch as it determines *what* someone who understands the sentence knows when he knows it to be true, not *how* he might come to know it of his own knowledge, still less what might lead him to think it true without knowing it. In knowing the sense of the sentence, he knows that it expresses a certain thought, i.e. he knows that the sentence is true if and only if a certain condition obtains; so, in coming to accept the sentence as true, the thought which he takes it as expressing represents the information he has acquired, the information, namely, that the condition for the truth of the sentence is satisfied; *how* that information was obtained in the first place is an altogether different matter, which belongs to epistemology and not to the theory of meaning at all.

At first sight, this doctrine appears clear and sharp; but a little investigation disturbs this impression. If the sense of a sentence is not related to our methods of determining its truth, why does Frege refuse to allow that two analytically equivalent sentences have the same sense? The doctrine that in modal contexts a sentence stands for its sense would not be violated by such a concession, since, of two such sentences, it would not be possible for one to be true and the other false; and the concession is tempting, since Frege had a well-developed

theory of analyticity, whereas, if two analytically equivalent sentences may differ in sense, no obvious criterion for identity of sense is forthcoming. Of course, if the concession were granted, it could not be maintained that the senses of sentences (thoughts) were the objects of belief and knowledge, i.e. that the referent of a sentence is its sense when it forms a clause governed by a verb for a 'propositional attitude': but this doctrine itself requires that sense be connected with the mode of knowledge or ground of belief.

Our question is: Can we say that sense determines only the *object* of knowledge or belief—*what* is known or believed, rather than *how* it is known or *why* it is believed? The difficulty is that the two things, at first sight so distinct, are bound together too tightly to be prised apart. Why cannot two sentences, *A* and *B*, have the same sense? It may be that the only argument against their doing so is that $\ulcorner X$ believes (knows) that $A\urcorner$ may be true, while $\ulcorner X$ believes (knows) that $B\urcorner$ is not. What makes *this* possible is that a ground of belief in the truth of *A* is not a ground of belief in that of *B*; and the conclusion is that, since in these oblique contexts *A* and *B* stand for their respective senses, those senses must be distinct, otherwise the truth values of the compound sentences would coincide. It follows that a difference in the possible grounds for one and the other belief, or in the mode of this and that item of knowledge, entails a difference in the objects of belief or of knowledge; and this corroborates our original contention that, in apprehending a possible object of belief or knowledge, i.e. in grasping the sense of a sentence, we must thereby know what grounds that belief may have or how that knowledge may be arrived at. Frege's conception of a thought as a possible object of knowledge or belief did not have to be surrounded by doctrines which forced this conclusion on us; but it was.

Two analytically equivalent sentences cannot, in general, have the same informational content, nor, therefore, the same sense, because one could know the one to be true without knowing the other to be true; someone knowing the one to be true would consequently acquire information by coming to learn the truth of the other, and hence the information conveyed by each must be different. It follows that the means by which a sentence can be recognized as true bears on the sense of that sentence. It might be argued that all that is shown is that, if the information conveyed by one sentence can be acquired without acquiring that conveyed by another, the two pieces of information must differ, since different things are true of them,

without its following that to specify what they are involves specifying how they can be acquired. But, against that, the fact stands that, for Frege, the notion of analyticity and the more general notion of aprioricity are defined in terms of the way in which a sentence can be known to be true; and surely the sense of a sentence is sufficient to determine whether it is analytic or synthetic, a priori or a posteriori. And yet there is little indication in Frege's account of how the way in which the sense of a sentence is given connects with the grounds on which we may base a judgment as to its truth.

I think that the defect in Frege's account of sense which is responsible for this hiatus lies in Frege's failure to insist that the theory of sense must explain in what a speaker's grasp of sense is manifested; and this failure is due to the exigencies of constructing a theory of sense within the framework of a realistic theory of meaning in terms of truth conditions. Sense is supposed by Frege to be something objective; that is, it can be definitely ascertained whether two speakers are using an expression in the same sense, and one speaker can effectively convey to another the sense which he attaches to any expression. This is possible only if the sense of a word is uniquely determined by the observable features of its linguistic employment (i.e. only if sense is use); it follows that a grasp of its sense is fully manifested by the manner in which the speaker employs it. If it were necessary to represent a speaker's grasp of the sense of a word as his knowledge of some proposition an awareness of which transcended all mere practical knowledge, that is, could not be exhaustively accounted for in terms of the ability to use in a particular way sentences containing the word, then sense would not be intrinsically fully communicable: we could never be sure that, by teaching someone to adopt a certain linguistic practice, we had really induced him to attach the right sense to the word. Frege's thesis that sense is objective is thus implicitly an anticipation (in respect of that aspect of meaning which constitutes sense) of Wittgenstein's doctrine that meaning is use (or of one of the family of doctrines so expressed): yet Frege never drew the consequences of this for the form which the sense of a word may take. Thus, in the case of proper names, the crudest picture of a speaker's grasp of the sense of a name would be as consisting in an ability to determine effectively, for any given object, whether or not it is the bearer of the name. On any credible theory of meaning, this account must be generalized. On either a verificationist or falsificationist theory, we should have to say that a grasp of the sense of a name consisted in a

capacity to recognize whatever is to be taken as conclusively establishing, of a given object, that it is the bearer of the name. On a realistic theory, however, even this is too restricted an account: we must say, rather, that a grasp of the sense of a name consists in a knowledge of what has to be true of any given object for it to be the bearer of the name; and, since the condition to be satisfied by the object may be one our apprehension of which will transcend our capacity to recognize, in special cases, whether or not it obtains, an understanding of the name, as so conceived, will not, in general, be something that can be fully manifested by the use of the name. Similarly, Frege's insistence that a predicate ought to be everywhere defined is expressed by him as the demand that it be determinate, for every object, whether the predicate applies to it or not; but he explicitly allows that *we* may not be able to determine this. Our recognition that it is, nevertheless, determinate must therefore depend upon our attaching to the predicate such a sense that we can tell that there is a definite condition for its application without knowing how to tell whether that condition is satisfied or not; once more, it follows that our grasp of the sense of the predicate cannot be fully manifested by the use which we make of it. One might maintain that certain features of that use, for example our willingness to assert certain instances of the law of excluded middle involving it, manifest our conviction *that* the predicate stands for some condition which is determinately either satisfied or not satisfied by each object; but our use of it can never fully display *which* the condition that we associate with the predicate is. The first of Frege's two arguments for the sense/reference distinction is to the effect that one cannot attribute to a speaker the knowledge, about the referent of an expression, that it is the referent, without going further and attributing to him the knowledge of a specific proposition; but he failed to face the problem how an explanation of a speaker's understanding of an expression in terms of his knowledge of a proposition can avoid circularity if knowledge of that proposition cannot in turn be explained save by an ability to enunciate it. It is precisely because of this failure that he failed to give a convincing account of the connection between sense and knowledge.

To replace a realistic theory of meaning by a verificationist one is to take a first step towards meeting the requirement that we incorporate into our theory of sense an account of the basis on which we judge the truth values of our sentences, since it does explain meanings in terms of actual human capacities for the recognition of truth. I have,

however, already pointed out that this step does not, in itself, take us all the way towards meeting this requirement, and I have no clear idea how it may be met. It is a natural reaction to regard the requirement as excessive, as asking the theory of meaning to take over the functions of a theory of knowledge. If we were convinced that we understood in principle how the sense of a sentence determined what we took as being evidence for its truth, and that the problems in this area, however intricate, were ones of detail, then it might be satisfactory to relegate them to a different philosophical discipline: but the difficulty is that we have no right to be satisfied of this. A conception of meaning—that is, a choice of a central notion for the theory of meaning—is adequate only if there exists a general method of deriving, from the meaning of a sentence as so given, every feature of its use, that is, everything that must be known by a speaker if he is to be able to use that sentence correctly; unquestionably, among the things that he must know is what counts as a ground for the truth of the sentence. Most of us serenely assume that a theory of meaning in terms of truth conditions is capable of fulfilling this role, without stopping to scrutinize the difficulties of devising a workable theory of this type. On our present exceedingly imperfect comprehension of these matters, reflection should make us admit that a verificationist theory of meaning is a better bet than a thoroughgoing realistic one, and, probably, a falsificationist theory a better bet still. But until we have, for some one choice of a central notion for the theory of meaning, a convincing outline of the manner in which every feature of the use of a sentence can be given in terms of its meaning as specified by a recursive stipulation of the application to it of that central notion, we remain unprovided with a firm foundation for a claim to know what meaning essentially is. And, so long as we remain in this shaky philosophical condition, any problem the possibility of solving which, given a choice of a central notion for the theory of meaning, will help to decide the correctness of that choice, must be regarded as the business of the philosophy of language.

V

Two Theories of Meaning

BRIAN LOAR

The leading question in the general theory of meaning is what the form of a theory of meaning for a particular language should be. What is the empirical status of the semantical description of a language? How does it fit into our other empirical theories? What kind of apparatus is sufficient to do the job? There is no general agreement about these matters.

The account which I am going to give locates semantical notions within the general framework of propositional attitudes, and, hence, makes essential use of intensional entities. But there is, these days, a not uncommon idea that empirical semantics can be done within a wholly extensional framework, without intensional entities. This is due, in large part, to Davidson, who has claimed[1] that the apparatus of (what we might call) extensional truth-condition semantics is sufficient for theories of meaning for natural languages. His suggestion may seem to have the merits of a compromise: the attack led by Quine against intensions might be granted success, without requiring the wholesale abandonment of intuitions that there exist some kind of semantical facts. But it is my view that this compromise makes no sense. Semantics without intensions is *Hamlet* without the Prince of Denmark.

The overall constraints are obscure. Part of what is at issue is whether certain intuitive philosophical and pre-philosophical notions of meaning can be explicated, or suitably replaced, in such a way that something of these notions is both preserved and shown to have empirical application. So my arguments against Davidson, and for my own account, will perforce rely on intuitions about these notions of meaning; indeed, how could a theory which cut all ties with such intuitions properly be called a theory of *meaning*?

I shall begin with some arguments against Davidson's theory, and then sketch a quite different account. The upshot will be that semantics

[1] Donald Davidson, 'Truth and Meaning', *Synthese*, xvii (1967), 304–23.

is part of propositional-attitude psychology, and stands or falls with it. If propositional attitudes cannot be accommodated in a scientific conception of reality then neither can semantics; but, if they can, there is no need to cast about for anaemic approximations to our red-blooded intuitive semantical notions.

I

According to Davidson, an adequate theory of meaning for a particular language will satisfy these conditions: first, it will, in some appropriate sense, 'give the meaning' of each sentence of the language; secondly, it will show how the meaning of a sentence is a function of its parts and structure; and, thirdly, it will do these things in a testable way; it will be suitably empirical. There is no arguing with these constraints; they are partially definitive of the enterprise. That there is a further desideratum which Davidson does not, and cannot, recognize—namely, that the semantical theory of a particular language should be couched in such terms as to make it possible to relate the theory to a broader psychological framework—will emerge.

The theory for *L* which satisfies these constraints, according to Davidson, would be a Tarski-type truth theory for *L*, or rather a certain modification of a truth theory which accommodates indexical sentences. A truth theory for *L* is a finite set of conditions which, for each sentence *S* of *L*, implies an equivalence of the form ⌜*S* is true iff . . .⌝; examples are ' "Snow is white" is true iff snow is white', and ' "La neige est blanche" is true iff snow is white'. If a truth theory for *L* implies only true equivalences of that form, and does so in such a way as to exhibit how the truth conditions of each sentence are a function of its parts and structure, then that is all we can reasonably require of a theory of meaning for *L*—its implied equivalences will count as 'giving the meaning' of each sentence of *L*. Notice that it is not made an explicit requirement for a truth theory's counting as a theory of meaning that the sentence on the right-hand side of each such equivalence be a translation of the sentence mentioned on the left. But the implication seems to be that if a truth theory for a natural language meets the other conditions, the right-hand side will be at least an approximation to a translation of the sentence mentioned on the left.

The initial appeal of Davidson's suggestion lies in the platitude that to give the meaning of an indicative sentence is to give its truth conditions. The plausibility of the platitude, however, may rest on an

interpretation on which it is of no service here. For to know the meaning of a sentence may indeed be to know under what conditions it would be true in any *possible* state of affairs; it does not follow that knowing *S*'s meaning is the same as knowing the material conditional '*S* is true iff *p*'. Not that that is a point which anyone is likely to miss for long.

Perhaps the most striking and significant feature of extensional truth-condition semantics is its eschewing sentential meanings as entities. Davidson's avowed reason for rejecting intensional entities is curious: 'my objection to meanings is . . . that they have no demonstrated use.'[2] There are several issues here: first he claims that meanings, as entities, are not specifiable independently of descriptions like 'The meaning of "Theaetetus flies"'. If that were so then meanings would indeed have no use, since one could never informatively say *what* the meaning of 'Theaetetus flies' is. Secondly, he thinks that one cannot specify relations among such entities in such a way as to be able informatively to say how the meaning of a sentence depends on the meanings of its parts. And, of course, if expressions of the form 'The meaning of ". . . "' were the best we could do in specifying meanings, such generative relations among meanings could not be informatively specified.

But the point is that meanings can be specified independently of such expressions—if, for example, you allow yourself enough possible world and set-theoretic apparatus. And functions may be specified which map the meanings of parts on to the meanings of wholes. In the time that has elapsed since Davidson's paper that has become old hat.[3]

The real question about meanings is this: are they required for expressing generalizations which are essential to the very nature of a semantic theory? If the answer to that is yes, then the choice is simple: are we to allow that some semantic theories or other might be true, or do we, out of physicalist asceticism, reject the possibility of any such theory?

Let us get on to Davidson's positive account. Suppose one were to add to an otherwise acceptable truth theory for English the equivalence ' "Snow is white" is true iff grass is green'. Would the resulting theory be a theory of meaning for English, and would that equivalence therefore 'give the meaning' of 'Snow is white' on Davidson's account?

[2] Op. cit., p. 307.

[3] Cf. David Lewis, 'General Semantics', in D. Davidson and G. Harman, eds., *Semantics of Natural Language* (D. Reidel, Dordrecht, 1972), 169–218.

The answer is no: Davidson's claim is that such an equivalence 'gives the meaning' of the mentioned sentence only if it follows from a truth theory by virtue of the more general contributions which its parts and structure make to the sentences in which they occur. And it is difficult to see how there could be a truth theory for English which satisfied that structural requirement (as I shall call it) and yet still implied the equivalence. So the theory is not threatened by such simple wholesale refutation.

On this point, Davidson says something rather puzzling. If a theory which satisfied the requirement *were* to imply '"Snow is white" is true iff grass is green', he would, he claims, remain true-blue to his identification of meaning and extensional truth conditions, for 'then there would not . . . be anything essential to the idea of meaning that remained to be captured'.[4] This loyalty to theory is excessive. Knowing the truth of that equivalence could not remotely be construed as *understanding* the sentence 'Snow is white', and if a theory of meaning for L is not (partially) the theory of what any speaker of L understands by its sentences, then it is hard to see what else it might be. To urge the *replacement* of theories of meaning with truth theories, regardless of the connection with understanding, would be to change the subject. And to what avail?

The structural requirement does not eliminate all difficulties of the kind which arise from (as I would want to interpret it) trying to get intensional refinements from extensional apparatus. For an equivalent difficulty arises at the level of satisfaction conditions for lexical items. Probably, 'x is a camel' has a finite extension. Hence, armed with the complete catalogue of camels '$c_1 \ldots c_n$', we could provide extensionally adequate enumerative satisfaction conditions for 'x is a camel': it is satisfied by y iff $y = c_1$ or . . . or $y = c_n$. This will have a systematically perverse effect on the truth conditions of every sentence which contains 'camel'. For each such sentence S, $\ulcorner S$ is true iff . . .$\urcorner$ would not intuitively 'give the meaning' of S; for knowing the equivalence would not be to understand S. Blithely accepting the result would again raise the charge of changing the subject; as we shall see, there are essential connections between the meaning of a sentence and certain propositional attitudes.

Of course if we were constructing a truth theory for English, we would not use the enumeration, given our laziness and our ignorance.

[4] Davidson, op. cit., p. 312.

But that is beside the point; the structural requirement (for a truth theory to be a theory of meaning) does not eliminate enumerative satisfaction conditions. Apart from simply accepting the result—a move whose disadvantage I have mentioned—one might now try to impose a further requirement on the appropriate class of truth theories.

One possibility is to try directly to eliminate from the acceptable truth theories those troublesome admixtures of extralinguistic fact. Let us invent the *cautious semanticizer*: he attends only to his knowledge of his language in constructing a truth theory. So perhaps a truth theory for *L* is a theory of meaning for *L* only if it would be constructed by the cautious semanticizer. (An implicit assumption of something like this possibility may, for some, add to the plausibility of Davidson's theory.) But, of course, the distinction between knowledge of language and knowledge of extralinguistic fact presupposes the very thing we are in search of: what it is for a sentence of *L* to mean such and such. And Davidson, of course, must reject the distinction, a fact which raises the further question: how can a theory which fails to make such a distinction be a 'theory of meaning' except by changing the subject?

Another possible device for eliminating enumerative satisfaction conditions is to require that for a truth theory to be a theory of meaning it should meet certain standards of *simplicity*; and the condition '"*x* is a camel" is satisfied by *y* iff *y* is a camel' is far simpler than the enumerative one. There are various possible difficulties here: the requirement may be too strong, and simplicity is a vague notion, but let us waive them.

The acount which is emerging, then, is this: ⌜*S* is true iff *p*⌝ gives the meaning of *S* in *L* just in case it is implied by a truth theory for *L* which meets the *structural* and *simplicity* requirements; any such truth theory can be counted a theory of meaning for *L*. What could be more straightforward than that?

Unfortunately, these restrictions do not alchemize a truth theory into a theory of meaning; to think they might is to fall prey to a simple confusion. To see this let us experiment with Smith, who as yet knows nothing about *L*. Suppose that ⌜*S* is true iff *p*⌝ follows from a truth theory for *L* which meets the requirements, and let us even assume that this means that, by our intuitive notion of 'translation', the sentence in the '*p*'-position is an acceptable translation of the sentence of *L* which is mentioned in the '*S*'-position. Now let Smith be informed only that

(*T*) *S* is true iff *p*.

Does he thereby know what *S* means, or something approximating thereto? Of course not, for although *T*, *ex hypothesi*, does follow from a suitable truth theory, that information is not contained within *T*. All Smith now knows is that either *S* is true and *p* or both *S* is not true and not-*p*. Virtually nothing about what *S* means follows from that. The upshot is that, even when an equivalence of form *T* follows from a suitable truth theory, it does not in itself 'give the meaning' of *S*. That is too obvious.

What more does Smith have to know to know what *S* means in *L*? The preceding discussion of requirements on a theory of meaning makes *that* clear. Smith has to know at least that

> (*TT*) some expression *X* denotes *S*, and ⌜*X* is true iff *p*⌝ is implied by a truth theory for *L* which meets the structural and simplicity requirements and which is true.

We might further require that Smith should know by virtue of which aspects of its composition the equivalence follows from the truth theory.[5]

Now, *TT* is meta*meta*linguistic with respect to *L*; it asserts a relation between the sentence *S* of the object language and the sentence of the metalanguage which is in the '*p*'-position. It would follow, then, that (1) to say what *S* means in *L* is to assert a *relation* between *S* and a certain sentence in the language of some truth theory for *L*—that is, the sentence in the '*p*'-position in *TT*; and (2) *a theory of meaning for L*—i.e., a theory which implies, for each sentence *S* of *L*, something which says what *S* means—is *not* simply a *truth theory* for *L*, but rather is metalinguistic with respect to such a truth theory; it consists of the single assertion that a certain correct truth theory for *L* meets the structural and simplicity requirements. This is certainly quite a different account from what Davidson's seemed to be.

It is not too surprising that this should be the result. ⌜*S* is true iff *p*⌝ is far too permissive to capture even approximately what *S* means. One advantage of entified meanings is that they demarcate what a sentence means from everything else which is true of it. In rejecting meanings, one creates the need for some other entity to do that job: in Davidson's account, it is smuggled in surreptitiously as the sentence mentioned in the '*p*'-position of *TT*, despite first appearances of a de-entified theory of meaning.

[5] Davidson often implies that knowing this is part of knowing the meaning. This is not my view; see below, p. 145.

An account in which *TT* is the basic form of meaning ascription is radically at variance with the original Tarskian position that semantics treats of certain relations between the linguistic and the extralinguistic; this seemed to be fundamental to Davidson's suggestion. Let us remind ourselves why that is such an important requirement for a semantic theory.

First, if sentences stand in translational relations to other sentences —for example, the relation which 'Snow is white' has to 'La neige est blanche'—that would seem to be so by virtue of properties which they have independently of the relation. The meaning of a sentence in a particular population is some function of its psychological and social role; its relations to other sentences in other populations are beside the point. Whatever the relevant connections with the population of speakers are, *they* are what constitute the semantics of a sentence.

Secondly, what is it that the monolingual speaker knows when he knows what a certain sentence of his language means? Whatever it is, it is not in general that it stands in a translational relation to some other sentence.

A second problem I find in Davidson's theory concerns the basic, as it were, pre-analytic notion of sentential meaningfulness which the theory is intended to elucidate. A straightforward way of getting at the problem is to consider *simple signals*—that is, utterance-types which are conventionally meaningful in a group of communicators but which do not have semantical structure. They show that meaningfulness is independent of membership in a language; most importantly, they have their meaningfulness in common with sentences: a certain type of hand wave could conventionally mean just what 'Here is what we have been looking for' means.

The upshot of this is as follows. If you try to extend the notion of truth conditions to simple signals, as if a simple signal belonged to a one-sentence language, you get the 'grass is green' problem with a vengeance. No consideration of structure or simplicity could rule out arbitrary true equivalences ⌜*S* is true iff *p*⌝ as giving the meaning of simple signal *S*. Consequently, if simple signals have meaning, there must be some non-truth-conditional manner of ascribing their meanings to them. But, since simple signals can mean the same as some sentences, that non-truth-conditional style of ascribing meanings must apply to sentences as well, and so there has to be more to a theory of meaning for *L* than a truth theory for *L*.

This argument raises the question as to what the connection between a sentence's meaning and its semantic structure is. Confusion is possible here. That the meaning of a sentence is a function of its parts and structure does not entail that meaningfulness in general implies semantic structure. A way of viewing the matter is this: there are certain communicational and expressive roles (which will be outlined later) to be played by utterance-types: for any given role, either it may be *directly* assigned to a certain utterance-type (a simple signal), or it may be assigned indirectly, by a system of rules, to an utterance-type which is, therefore, semantically complex.

Confusion on this point may possibly be engendered by a certain ambiguity in the notion of what it is to know a sentence's meaning. A person may authoritatively be informed as to what a certain sentence of an otherwise unknown language means, without knowing any facts of its structure—in that sense he knows its meaning, and that is how I shall use the notion. Of course, one might want to say that such a person does not *fully* know its meaning; but I would rather say what he does not know are further facts about its semantical structure; facts as to *how* its language assigns it its meaning.

The third difficulty with Davidson's theory is its inability to cope with certain essential connections between the semantical properties of sentences and the propositional attitudes of language users. This has two distinct aspects.

First, the already discussed incapacity of a truth theory to discriminate certain extensionally equivalent meanings is relevant in a new connection. Here is a fact:

(A) If a sincere, linguistically informed, attentive, sane English speaker who wished to speak literally were to utter the sounds 'A zebra is a cordate', then (generally) it would be the case that he believed that a zebra is a cordate.

This is not trivial, as may be seen by imagining (A) translated into Italian, preserving the reference to the English sentence.

Now substitute for the one quoted occurrence of 'A zebra is a cordate' in (A) a quoted occurrence of 'A zebra is a renate'. The resulting generalization will not be, as it were, true to the same extent. It is slightly more likely that there will be counterexamples to it than that there will be counterexamples to (A). The point is that these two extensionally isomorphic sentences have different connections with propositional attitudes, and the difference in the

connection reflects the intuitive difference in their semantical properties. One might even say that it is because extensionally equivalent propositional attitudes are not thereby identical propositional attitudes that extensional semantical notions are not adequate for expressing all semantical properties of sentences.

This becomes especially important when we consider the connections with propositional attitudes which are constitutive of a sentence's being meaningful in a certain group—connections, as we shall see, with communicative intentions to produce beliefs and actions in a hearer. Utterances of extensionally isomorphic sentences may affect the beliefs of the hearer in quite distinct ways.

The second aspect of this problem is more general and more basic. Intensional *entities* are needed to express generalizations which are essential to such questions as what makes a particular language the language of a given population. As we shall see, it is necessary to quantify over, as it were, the semantical content of sentences in order to generalize their relation to the content of the propositional attitudes of language users. As Davidson would be the first to insist, the '*p*' position in an equivalence of the form ⌜*S* is true iff *p*⌝ does not admit a genuine quantificational variable. The point of extensional truth-condition semantics is to avoid postulating meanings as entities; the effect of the austerity is to prevent semantics from being tied correctly to the psychology of language use.

II

As you may anticipate, in the positive account of sentence meaning I am going to offer, the semantical properties of sentences are a certain function of the propositional attitudes of language users. It is a matter of some importance, therefore, whether 'propositional' attitudes are not best explicated as being certain relations to sentences or other linguistic entities. If so, there would be implicitly a vicious circle in an explication of sentence meaning in terms of the propositional attitudes of language users.

There are only two such explications of propositional attitudes, as relations to linguistic entities, that I know of which can be taken seriously—namely, Carnap's, and one which can be extrapolated from a theory of Davidson's, his analysis of indirect discourse.

On Carnap's account,[6] ⌜Jones believes that *S*⌝ asserts a relation

[6] Rudolf Carnap, *Meaning and Necessity* (The University of Chicago Press, Chicago, 2nd ed., 1956), 53–5.

between Jones and the sentence *S*. But, as Church and others have pointed out, there must also be some implicit reference to *S*'s *meaning*. How is that to be expressed except by making propositional attitudes a relation between Jones, *S*, and a certain intensional entity: (*R*(Jones, *S*, *p*))?[7] But then the reference to the sentence becomes otiose, since the form of words used is irrelevant to what is being asserted to be believed, once one has got the proposition. Frege's theory is much better: ⌜that *S*⌝ denotes the entity which is in fact *S*'s meaning, without referring to *S* itself *as* having a certain meaning.

Davidson's theory of indirect discourse,[8] extrapolated to propositional attitudes, is much more subtle, and escapes, at least overtly, the objection to Carnap. According to Davidson, an utterance of 'Galileo said that the Earth moves' asserts a relation between Galileo and a certain historical event—namely, the utterance, by the speaker of the whole, of 'the Earth moves' as having a certain sense and reference. So its logical form is '*S*(Galileo, that)'. The relation thereby asserted is not, of course, the direct discourse relation; it is this: *x* asserted something which makes him and the utterer of *y* same-sayers. 'Same-saying' is taken as unanalysed.

The generalization, not made in that paper by Davidson, to other propositional attitudes is obvious. The relation asserted by 'Galileo believed that the Earth moves', between Galileo and the current utterance of 'the Earth moves', is: what-*x*-believes-is-the-same-as-what-is-said-by-the-utterer-of-*y*, where that, again, is taken as unanalysed.

Davidson's theory, thus extended, has great attractiveness. First, it eliminates, at one stroke, those difficulties about the logical form of propositional-attitude sentences which arise from the variable number of referential positions in the that-clause. Secondly, the analysis, at least ostensibly, precludes the need for supposing that intensional entities are referred to in propositional-attitude assertions. For, one might say, the utterer of the whole no more refers to the *meaning* of his utterance of 'the Earth moves' than he would have, had he just asserted 'the Earth moves'. In both cases he is producing a meaningful utterance; in neither case is he referring to a meaning.

[7] It might seem that the implicit reference is to *S* as belonging to a certain *language* rather than as having a certain *meaning*. That that won't do can be seen by considering cases in which *S* has more than one meaning in its language, but where 'Jones believes that *S*' is asserted, in its context, unambiguously.

[8] Davidson, 'On Saying That', D. Davidson and J. Hintikka (eds.), *Words and Objections* (D. Reidel, Dordrecht, 1969), 158–74.

Now the main difficulty I find with Davidson's theory—or, rather, this extension of it—is that if my assertion of 'Galileo believed that the Earth moves' is true, it is impossible to see how this could be so unless something rather substantial was true of Galileo quite independently of the existence of my utterance. The theory makes beliefs irreducibly relations to the utterances of those who describe them. Aren't there actual beliefs which no one has ever uttered something equivalent to? If so, beliefs are not in themselves relations to the utterances of their describers. How then can the fundamental mode of *ascribing* beliefs be *as* related to utterances? Is there something ineffable about their more intrinsic properties? Of course not. When I ascribe a belief to someone, I am not asserting something which logically implies that I have spoken and which therefore could not have been so had I kept quiet.

Here is a possible reply. The description of an object's *length* (it might be said) essentially relates the measured object to some other object—a standard. But it does not follow that had no such standard existed, the measured items would not have had precise length. A metre-long object on Mars (the reply continues) could have been that length had the standard metre bar never existed.

Now, the point is that what the last consideration *really* shows is that 'x is one metre long' is *not* to be analysed as 'x is as long as the standard metre bar'. Rather what it means is 'x has that length—i.e. the length which, as it happens, is the length of the standard metre bar'.[9] The former analysis implies that had the bar not existed nothing could have been one metre long. On the latter analysis, measurement asserts a relation to a certain abstract entity.

The Davidson-style analysis of belief sentences cannot be conservatively repaired by a similar move. If 'Galileo believed that the Earth moves' is supposed to pick out some particular *independent* fact about Galileo via helpful reference to my utterance, then the analysis should be 'Galileo believed *that*—i.e. that which happens to be expressed by this utterance of mine'. Now that asserts a relation between Galileo and what is presumably an intensional entity.

The consequence is that, for both Carnap's analysis and the extension of Davidson's analysis to propositional attitudes, suitable repairs introduce intensional entities, and the reference to linguistic entities becomes superfluous. Hence, a potential impediment to taking

[9] This is essentially Saul Kripke's point; see 'Naming and Necessity', *Semantics of Natural Language*, 274.

propositional-attitude notions as presupposed by semantical notions is removed. What I want to show is that the theory of meaning is part of the theory of mind, and not the other way around.

III

There is a tradition in the philosophy of language which would locate all facts about the communicative intentions and beliefs of language users, and regularities concerning them, in *pragmatics* and not *semantics*. Since the semantics of a language includes facts about the meanings or senses of its terms and sentences (or, if you are an extensionalist, about their extensions), it would follow that those semantical notions are not to be construed as being about the communicative intentions and beliefs of language users. So, the nature of the semantics-pragmatics distinction is no mere terminological matter, but involves the question of the fundamental nature of semantic concepts.

One enormously influential view as to what semantics includes has been that of Tarski, for whom semantical notions are definable entirely via abstract correlations between terms and their denotata and via abstract Tarski-type truth definitions, which employ only syntactical and logical notions together with a vocabulary adequate for paraphrasing the object language.

There is an intensionalist counterpart to this formalist Tarskian conception of semantics—one on which semantic concepts are definable entirely in terms of abstract correlations between expressions and certain intensional entities.

Suppose, for example, that we were to define a *language* as a function from sentences to sentence-sized intensions (which we might identify with functions from possible worlds to truth values). Would we, in specifying any such function, thereby be defining a *semantical* notion? Is all there is to a certain sentence's meaning such and such that some such abstractly defined function maps it on to a certain intension?

Verbal quibbling is a risk here, but some terminologies are more sensible than others. What a sentence means is, of course, always relative to a language; and a language may be identified with a certain abstractly defined function (although not, in general, one which is quite as simple as the one just mentioned). But it does not follow that all there is to semantical notions is captured by the notion of such

abstract correlations, with all facts about the psychology of their use being consigned to pragmatics.

To see this, all that is needed is to see that such functions can be embodied in, or abstractions from, facts of a kind which we would not at all be tempted to call linguistic or semantical. As an example, suppose that on a certain planet in a certain possible world cloud formations occurred in striking correlations with subnubilar phenomena as follows. The set of physically possible cloud formations is definable by formation rules over their spatial arrangement, by extrapolation from actually occurring cloud formations.[10] Most importantly, the correlation between the occurrence of cloud formations and facts on the ground may be lawlikely generalized by employing a function L from cloud formation types to sets of possible worlds, thus: if $L(N)$ = the intension I, then N occurs only if I is realized. So if I is the intension *snow is white*, and $L(N) = I$, then it is derivable from natural law, on that planet, that cloud formation N occurs only if snow is white.

Is L in that context a *language*? Not until the dawning of nubisemantics.

Notions like 'language' and 'means' should always be thought of as intrinsically relativized to a population of language users. The real semantical notions are not 'L is a language', or 'S means M in L', but 'L is the language of population P' and 'S means M in the language of P'. Clearly, *those* notions cannot be reduced formalistically to logical and syntactical notions. Facts about the *use* of language in a population have to be introduced—and so psychological notions are needed in the analysis of semantical concepts.[11]

The implausibility of formalist analyses of semantical concepts is more striking if one considers non-indicative semantical features, and certain nonmodal features like the second-person pronoun. That a sentence is imperative, or that 'you' is a second-person pronoun, are *semantical* matters. How is one adequately to define such notions

[10] Perhaps the formation rules contain a transformational component, and cloud formations have deep structures. Such a fantasy might dispel misconceptions about those over-romanticized entities, deep structures.

[11] A certain abstractly defined function may be called a language, *tout court*, in the way in which a certain abstract correlation of numbers with persons' names may be called a telephone listing. They are abstractions from communicational or electronic facts about a population. The substantial import of those terms is a matter of what makes such an abstract entity a language of, or a telephone listing for, a given population.

except by reference to the standard use of those forms with certain communicative intentions?

There *is* a distinction between semantics and pragmatics, and where the line gets drawn is a hard question. Pragmatics is to be defined negatively, relative to the definition of semantics; the pragmatics of the language of a population is all the facts of a certain kind about language use in that population which are not semantical facts. Some of these facts are general facts about the psychology of communication; others are about the particular communicative practices of that population. The key question, of course, is what belongs to semantics, and to that we should now turn.

IV

What facts about a sentence constitute its meaning—that is, its meaning in abstraction from any particular utterance, and in so far as it belongs to the language of a particular population? If *L* is the language of *P*, then there are in *P* conventional associations of utterance-types and types of communicative intention; *L* is a kind of generalization of those associations. The language associates with the sentence a range of possible communicative intentions—those which a speaker may have in uttering the sentence conventionally.

Before giving the account, I shall give the basic notions out of which it is constructed; you can see that they are essentially *psychological* notions and *logical* notions.

(1) There are various notions specifically involving types of communicative intentions:

(1a) *Speaker's* or *utterer's meaning*, introduced by Grice as the fundamental notion in the theory of meaning.[12] So, this account of mine is an essay in what is often referred to as 'Grice's programme'. Both Grice[13] and Schiffer[14] have provided elaborate accounts of this basic notion; its core is the identification of a speaker's meaning something with his intending, in a certain way, to activate in his hearer a certain belief or action. The theoretical utility of speaker's meaning lies in its providing a concept of communication which does not presuppose anything conventional or linguistic. Hence, linguistic meaning can be explained in terms of conventions over such intentions.

[12] H. P. Grice, 'Meaning', *Philosophical Review*, lxvi (1957), 377–88.
[13] Grice, 'Utterer's Meaning and Intentions', *Philosophical Review*, lxxviii (1969) 147–77.
[14] S. R. Schiffer, *Meaning* (Clarendon Press, Oxford, 1972), Chs. I–III.

The subsequent notions of referring and of illocutionary force are similarly non-conventional in their definition.

(1b) Possibly a distinct notion of *reference*, to be defined in terms of a speaker's intention that his hearer should recognize, in certain ways, which particulars are the subjects of his communication.

(1c) Notions of various *illocutionary act-types*, like requesting, asking, telling, objecting. Schiffer has provided an excellent general theory of their definition, in terms of specifications of concepts already present in the definition of speaker's meaning.[15]

(2) There is *convention*, to be defined as a regularity in action which is mutually known to obtain, and which is conformed to because it is expected to be conformed to. This is a simplification; for detailed accounts, see Lewis, *Convention*,[16] and Schiffer, *Meaning*, Ch. V.

(3) There are the notions of various types of abstract entity: *property*, *relation*, and *proposition*, taken primitively; or *possible worlds* and *sets*, from which various intensional notions can be defined.

(4) Possibly an epistemic notion of *presupposition*, which might be needed in the assignment of a certain level of semantical properties.

A sharp distinction is to be made between what a speaker's communicative intentions are on a given utterance—what *he* means—and what the overall semantical properties of a sentence are in so far as it belongs to the language of a population—what *it* means. Facts of the latter kind are a function of regularities involving facts of the former kind. A certain inconvenience arises from using 'means' in two such distinct senses, but, I think, the advantage of continuity with previous philosophical usage overrides that inconvenience.

In the preceding section, I mentioned as a kind of language a function from sentences to intensions.[17] One might use such a function in the description of the communicative practices of a group of speakers who utter only indicative, non-indexical, unambiguous sentences: a speaker utters a sentence *S* of that language with its conventional force only if he does so with the intentions which constitute his meaning thereby that *p*, where *p* is the intension which that language—that function—assigns to *S*. So the intension, or sentential meaning, which such a language assigns to a sentence in its

[15] Ibid., Ch. IV.

[16] D. K. Lewis, *Convention* (Harvard University Press, Cambridge, Mass., 1969).

[17] The terminology may be confusing. *Intensions* are certain abstract entities; '*intention*' is being used, not in the Brentano sense, but as derived from the ordinary usage of 'intends'.

way *determines* (given the kind of convention to be defined shortly) what communicative intentions its utterer may have if the utterance is conventional or literal.

Similarly, a language which has indexical, non-indicative and ambiguous sentences—any natural language—will be identified with a function which assigns to each sentence a set (because of ambiguity) of certain entities—sentential meanings—which are rather more complex than just sentence-sized intensions, and which determine what range of communicative intentions a literal or conventional utterer of the sentence may have.

The definition of what makes a language, however complex, the language of a particular population will take this form:

> L is the language of P iff
>
> there exists in P the convention that, if $L(S) = \{M_1 \ldots M_n\}$, then one utters S, in certain serious circumstances to be explicated, only if one's intentions in uttering S are within the range determined by one of $M_1 \ldots M_n$.

Before specifying the relevant 'serious' circumstances involved in such a convention, and thereby completing the definition in that respect, let us first see what kinds of entities are to count as sentential meanings.

Consider a language with just indexical indicative sentences. A first shot at saying what its sentential meanings are like is this: the meaning of such a sentence is something which determines what proposition a conventional speaker means *given* the referential parameters of that particular utterance. I say 'referential parameters' here so as to avoid raising questions about whether indexicals—pronouns, demonstratives and definite descriptions—should be regarded as introducing uniqueness conditions or the actual referents themselves into the communicative content of an utterance of an indexical sentence. So it might seem that the meaning of an indexical sentence should be viewed as a function from the referential parameters of an utterance to the proposition meant on that utterance. Now that that is not all that is involved in the meaning of such a sentence may be seen by comparing 'She took some cheese' and 'He took some cheese'. The functions which map arbitrary referential parameters of utterances of these sentences on to the propositions which may be conventionally meant thereby are one and the same. Those sentences differ, rather,

in what their pronouns connote; and that is a matter of how the referent is conventionally determined, and not of how, given the referent, the proposition which is thereby meant is determined.

So we might represent the meaning of an indexical indicative sentence in two stages: first, there is the *content* function, which maps an utterance's referential parameters on to the proposition which is thereby meant; and, secondly, there is the ordered *n*-tuple of what might be called the sentence's *referential qualifiers*—roughly, what is connoted by the sentence's referring expressions. Referential qualifiers are sometimes themselves complex; if you represent, at their different levels of embedding, the various properties and relations connoted by the referring expressions in 'the cat which chased the mouse which ate the cheese' you get a complex entity. But this is not the place for the details.

So, then, the communicative intentions of an utterer of such a sentence lie within the range determined by one of its meanings—the utterance *fits* that meaning—provided that (a) the proposition which he means is the one determined by the relevant content function together with the referential parameters determined by his referential intentions, and (b) his referential intentions—that is, roughly, his intentions that his hearer recognize which particular items or uniqueness conditions figure in the content of what he means—are in accordance with the referential qualifiers.[18]

Non-indicative sentences may be accommodated by adding a third stage to the specification of a sentence's meaning. Some sentences are simply conventional devices for meaning *that* such and such, and others for meaning *that* the hearer *is to do* such and such. They are the simple indicatives and imperatives, and the more specific illocutionary forces of their particular utterances are determined by intentions which are to be recognized from generally non-conventional, or at least non-linguistic, features of the context of utterance. But some sentences are conventional devices for performing quite specific ranges of illocutionary acts—that is, for making known those intentions which constitute an utterance an illocutionary act of a

[18] This does not imply that x counts as a referent of a conventional utterance of S only if the relevant referential qualifier of S is *true* of x. (See Keith S. Donnellan, 'Reference and Definite Descriptions', *Philosophical Review*, lxxv [1966], 281–304.) Referential intentions accord with a referential qualifier F provided that, roughly, the speaker intends the hearer to recognize x as his referent by virtue of his and his hearer's mutual belief that x is the F which is such and such.

particular kind.[19] Here we have interrogatives, sentences which begin 'I hereby . . .' where the verb is illocutionary, and so on.

The third element in the meaning of a sentence, then, is the type of illocutionary act conventionally performed on its utterance or just, simply, the relation *x means that p*, or *x means that H is to do A*. The other two elements remain as before, the content function being now the general determinant, with the referential parameters, of the content of the illocutionary act or of what is meant.

So a sentence's meaning may be represented, in an abstract way, as an ordered triple consisting of (a) something which determines whether the sentence is simple indicative, simple imperative or has a conventionally more specific illocutionary force: this element can just be the appropriate act-type; (b) the content function; and (c) the ordered *n*-tuple of the sentence's referential qualifiers, which may themselves be complex embeddings of referential qualifiers.

A particular utterance of a sentence *fits* one of its meanings provided that the speaker's referential intentions are appropriate to the referential qualifier, the illocutionary force is in the right range, and the content of the illocutionary act is the value of the content function for the referential parameters of that utterance.

The question now arises as to what the overall convention is which makes L the language of P. The most straightforward candidate—one which would certainly establish a sufficiently strong correlation between sentence-types and kinds of intentions—is:

> C: the convention that, if $L(S) = \{M_1 \ldots M_n\}$, then any member of P utters S only if his utterance *fits* one of $M_1 \ldots M_n$.

But that convention is too strong. There are many circumstances in which sentences are uttered without being accompanied by intentions of a kind conventionally associated with them, and no confusion, obscurity or frustration of the purposes of language attends such utterances. Examples are: creative metaphors, hyperbole, telling jokes, acting, testing microphones and typewriters, and, in general, utterances such that the speaker knows that his hearer will not take his utterance literally.

One can imagine such non-literal utterances of sentences of L being very widespread, without their existence interfering in the least with

[19] For the general theory of illocutionary acts, and their definition in terms of kinds of intention, see Schiffer, op. cit., Ch. IV.

L's being the language of *P*. But a convention like *C* would not then obtain, since the appropriate underlying regularity would not exist; hence *C* is not the right convention.

What, then, is the right correlation between utterances of sentences and the communicative intentions of their utterers? It would seem to be something like: when a speaker utters *S* in 'serious' circumstances, his communicative intentions fit one of the meanings in *L*(*S*). But that, on the face of it, introduces a circularity, for what are 'serious' circumstances except those in which the speaker is going to be taken literally—that is, in accordance with what his sentence *means* in *P*?

Compare these cases:

(a) Seeing a lachrymose acquaintance approaching, Jones says to Smith, 'It's about to rain'. Smith correctly takes Jones to mean, not that it is about to rain, but that they are in for some weeping.

(b) The sky is solidly blue; Jones says 'It's about to rain'. Smith does not infer that Jones means that it is about to rain, but he is at a loss as to why Jones uttered those words.

(c) The sky is cloudy, and Jones kicks a pebble. Smith does not infer that he means thereby that it's about to rain.

The first two cases differ in a certain striking respect from the third. In them there is no lack of a generally appropriate association between the words uttered and the intentions which would be involved in meaning that it's about to rain—there is an association founded in past communicative practice. Rather, the hearer is in a position to judge that it is improbable that the speaker means that it is about to rain, in the first case, because there is some other much better explanation of his uttering those words, and, in the second case, because, given the circumstances, the speaker would not want to be taken to mean that it's about to rain by *any* utterance of his. This would normally be mutually known by speaker and hearer.

In the third case, however, the improbability that Jones means, by kicking the pebble, that it is about to rain rests on the lack of an appropriate association between that action and that meaning. We might say, then, that in case (c) there is an *associative improbability* that *x* means such and such by his 'utterance', whereas in cases (a) and (b) there is a *non-associative improbability* that *x* means such and such by his utterance.

If there is in circumstances *C* *no* non-associative improbability (excuse the negatives, please; they are not cancellable) that *x*'s communicative intentions in uttering *S* are within the range of *M*, then, I

shall say, x's utterance of S is free, in C, for M-ing. Obviously, one's utterance may be free for M-ing, and yet there may still be an *associative* improbability that one is thereby M-ing. So the convention employed in the following is quite substantial, and sets up, non-trivially, that correlation which exists between sentences of L and their literal meanings even when there exist widespread non-literal utterances of sentences of L.

> L is the language of P iff
>
> there is in P the convention that if $L(S) = \{M_1 \ldots M_n\}$, then any member of P utters S in circumstances in which his utterance is free for M_i-ing only if his intentions in uttering S are within the range determined by M_i.

The definition of sentence-meaning follows simply: S means M_i in P iff, for some L, $L(S) = \{M_1 \ldots M_n\}$ and L is the language of P.

The regularity which underlies the convention, then, is such that if x utters 'It's about to rain' when there exists, for his hearer, no non-associative improbability that he means thereby that it's about to rain, he has thereby meant that it's about to rain. This gives us an idea, at a rather simple level, of one central factor in the inferences which speakers of a language make to each other's communicative intentions.

It is interesting to see how the account accommodates sentences with more than one meaning. If S means M and also M', then on a normal literal utterance of S the speaker's intentions conform to one of them—say M—and he can expect his hearer to infer from the relevant contextual factors that that explanation of his utterance *overrides* the alternative of his having uttered it with intentions conforming to M'. Hence, there is a non-associative improbability that he is M'-ing, his utterance is not then *free* for M'-ing, and therefore the fact that he is *not* M'-ing is not at variance with the regularity.

V

A convention in P is a regularity in action among members of P which they mutually know to obtain. Does that imply that, if L is the language of P, its members *know* the 'rules'—i.e. the syntax and semantics—of L? Is their knowledge of L *under* its description *as* having such and such formation rules and mappings from sentences to meanings?

There may be a Chomsky sense of knowledge—having an internal representation—in which a speaker knows the rules of his language, but that is a psychological hypothesis and, however reasonable it is, we do not want to build it into an *explication* of what it is for L to be the language of P. Better that it should be offered, at a later stage, as an *explanation* of how it is possible for a complex entity like English to be the language of the population of English speakers.

David Lewis has suggested[20] that the mutual knowledge of the relevant regularity involves knowledge of all the sentences of L *in sensu diviso* and not *in sensu composito*. Applied to my account, that is the difference between:

K_D For each sentence S of L, if $L(S) = M$, then all members of P know (potentially or implicitly) that, if anyone were to utter S in circumstances in which it is free for M-ing, the utterer thereby would M.

K_C All members of P know that for each sentence S of L if $L(S) = M$, then if anyone etc.

Adopting interpretation K_D would certainly avoid having to attribute to speakers knowledge of the rules of their language, but it has its own difficulties. Do we really want to say that K_D holds for very complex sentences of English? Our interpretative abilities with regard to sentences of our own language are quite limited; after so many embeddings we fail to discern sense.

It is not wholly far-fetched to claim that the incomprehensibly complex English 'sentences' are not really part of *our* language at all —after all, we cannot understand them! If English were thus reduced to a finite fragment of what it would be if our brains were larger, there would be no problem for K_D. But that is a wildly controversial solution—and an avoidable one. The solution I prefer proceeds in two stages—the second of which generates notions which there are independent reasons for wanting.

The sentences of English we understand are enormous though finite in number. We certainly have potential knowledge of a much greater number of sentences than we have ever heard and, indeed, than have ever been uttered. Let us call the sentences which a person understands —or could understand after some thought—the sentences of his *effective* language. So now we can make the convention, and hence the

[20] Lewis, op. cit., pp. 64–8, 182–3.

relevant mutual knowledge, relative to the *effective* language of the members of the population,[21] as follows.

> L is the language of P *only if*
>
> there is a large (enough) restriction L' of L such that there is in P the convention that if $L'(S) = \{M_1 \ldots M_n\}$, then any member of P utters S in circumstances in which his utterance is free for M_i-ing only if his intentions in uttering S are within the range determined by M_i.

The knowledge of the regularity which underlies the convention has the form of K_D—knowledge of the generalization *in sensu diviso*.

The preceding condition, though necessary, is obviously not sufficient; so we come to the second stage of the solution. As it is stated, no language which arises from adding arbitrary non-English sentences-cum-meanings to English is excluded by the condition. Call some such language English-plus. What, then, is the difference between those sentences of English-plus, on the one hand, and those sentences of real English, on the other, which are left when you subtract *effective* English?

The difference is that the incomprehensibly complex sentences of English have parts and structural features which are realized in effective English as making certain contributions to the meanings of its sentences. English is a projection from effective English. But what selects the projectible pairings of sentential features and meaning contributions? Might there not be more than one simple way of extending effective English?

It is, I think, part of our pre-philosophical conception of language that speakers learn their language and, much more importantly, maintain their linguistic competence, by virtue of some kind of learned associations or other between sentential features (words and types of construction) and meaning-constituents. This is not to retreat from my earlier denial that knowledge of the *rules* or grammar is to be brought into the explication of what it is for L to be the language of P. Something weaker is required: let us say that L is *grounded* in P, with regard to its restriction L', just in case those correlations of sentential features and meaning contributions which

[21] This, of course, will vary from group to group. One should think of the set of 'English speakers' dividing up into many sub-populations each with their own language. 'English' may be identified with the intersection or union (depending on what we want such an entity for) of these various 'languages'.

figure in the correct psychological explanation[22] of the continuing mastery of L' (i.e. effective L) by members of P will generate, when extended, the full language L, including its incomprehensibly complex sentences.

This allows us to eliminate English-plus, and to keep real English in its infinite complexity as the language of English speakers, thus:

> L is the language of P iff
>
> there is a large (enough) restriction L' of L such that there is in P the convention that if $L'(S) = \{M_1 \ldots M_n\}$ then any member of P utters S in circumstances in which his utterance is free for M_i-ing only if his intentions in uttering S are within the range determined by M_i, and L is grounded in P with regard to L'.

David Lewis, supporting Quine's position on the inscrutability of reference, has denied that the language of a given population can be assigned a unique grammar, except relative to some more or less *arbitrarily* chosen method of evaluating grammars.[23] Now a grammar is just the system of correlations of sentential features and constituents of meaning which figure in the definition of groundedness.

It is, indeed, always possible that one and the same language may be abstractly carved up in several equally simple ways—into different lexicons and compensatingly different interpretations of sentential structures. But once we have decided on a scheme of attributing propositional attitudes to a population[24]—and *that* is presupposed, in Lewis's theory and in mine, in assigning a *language* to a population—then there is a non-arbitrary way of selecting one grammar. *The* grammar of the language of a population is just the one which grounds that language in that population.

From this we get an account of word meaning: a word's meaning in P is what gets assigned to it by the lexicon of the grammar of P together with whatever general type of contribution words of that kind make to the meaning of the sentences in which they occur. Hence there is no need to postulate distinct *conventions* which make words meaningful; the conventionality of word meaning is derivative from the overall convention which makes L the language of P.

[22] A system of internal representation, or of Chomsky-type knowledge of rules, would be *one* possible such explanation.

[23] Lewis, op. cit., pp. 197 ff.

[24] If there is an indeterminacy in the ascription of semantical notions, then it is derivative from an indeterminacy, with respect to behaviour and all physical fact and theory, of propositional-attitude attribution.

What is the empirical status of a semantic theory? The place of the theory of meaning among the rest of our empirical theories can be represented in two stages.

First, there is the attribution of communicative intentions to a speaker on a particular occasion. The question of its empirical basis is, of course, an instance of the broader question concerning the empirical basis of propositional-attitude attribution in general.

Secondly, as the definition shows, the ascription of *L* to a given population is a kind of generalization of facts about what speakers mean on particular occasions, taken together with the assumption of potential mutual knowledge of the generalization *in sensu diviso*, and the influence of this knowledge on conformity. So problems about the empirical status of semantics are likely to be instances of more general problems about the status of theories of the mental life of individuals and groups.

VI

Truth Definitions and Actual Languages*

CHRISTOPHER PEACOCKE

I

ACCORDING to Davidson, his Tarski-style theory of truth for a natural language is an *empirical* theory, and 'like any theory, it may be tested by comparing some of its consequences with the facts'.[1] Of particular importance among the consequences of the truth theory for a particular language are the so-called T-sentences it yields as theorems, and Davidson holds that 'the verification of instances of the T-sentences, or rather their surrogates in a theory relativized to speakers and times, remains respectably empirical'.[2] A T-sentence of a truth theory for a language with indexicals is a theorem of the form

$$\forall p \, \forall t \, (\text{true}\,(s, p, t) \equiv A\,(p, t))$$

where *s* is a 'structural-descriptive name' of a sentence of the language, and $A(p, t)$ is some formula possibly containing '*p*' and '*t*' free which does not contain 'true' or 'satisfies'; '*p*' and '*t*' range over persons and times, respectively. The T-sentences, then, contain the predicate 'true'; so it is not unreasonable to claim that to be able to verify the T-sentences, we must be possessed of *some* access to the notion of truth independently of a recursion for a number of particular languages. Put without the epistemological slant, the question is what it is for one truth theory rather than another to be applicable to the actual language of a population. Wallace writes that 'we are interested in

* My thanks to David Bostock, John McDowell, Colin McGinn and especially Gareth Evans for criticisms of drafts of this paper.

[1] D. Davidson, 'Truth and Meaning', *Synthese*, xvii (1967), 311.

[2] D. Davidson, 'In Defense of Convention T' in *Truth, Syntax and Modality*, ed. H. Leblanc (North-Holland, Amsterdam, 1973), p. 85.

"true-in-L" for various particular L';[3] but we can hardly avoid raising the question of the sense of 'true in the language of population P' for *variable* P. To request an answer to this question is not to criticize Davidson's programme: it is only to suggest that a lacuna be filled.

It might be suggested that this request is already met in the requirement that any truth definition conform to Convention T. This suggestion only postpones the problem. Convention T as originally formulated by Tarski[4] employs the notion of *translation* from one language (the object language) to another (the metalanguage). 'Translation' here must mean *adequate* translation: a recursive definition that pairs French sentences with English sentences that, intuitively, give their falsity conditions is no definition of *truth* for French. The dependence of the relevant notion of translation on the concept of truth is shown explicitly in Davidson's talk of his 'assimilation of a translation manual to a theory of truth'.[5] Thus this form of Convention T simply leads us back to the general notion of truth about which we were asking. Davidson has, indeed, proposed that when the theory of truth goes empirical, we alter Convention T so that *any* sentence of the form

$$\forall p\, \forall t\, (\text{true}\, (s, p, t) \equiv A(p, t))$$

counts as a T-sentence, and the modified Convention requires of an adequate theory only that all its derivable T-sentences be true.[6] Once again, the facts that the T-sentences contain 'true' and that the modified Convention concerns *their* truth bars this as an elucidation of the general notion of truth; our request just was for the conditions under which such sentences are true.

Davidson has also suggested, in lectures, that a truth theory T for the language of a population P will be adequate if, subject to certain constraints irrelevant here, it maximizes the number of sentences held true by members of P that are indeed true according to the truth conditions specified by T, in the light of our own beliefs about the world. Once again this does not fill the lacuna since 'true'

[3] J. Wallace, 'On the Frame of Reference', in *Semantics of Natural Language*, eds. D. Davidson and G. Harman (Reidel, Dordrecht, 1972), p. 225. P. F. Strawson has pressed a similar demand in a different way in his Inaugural Lecture 'Meaning and Truth' (Clarendon Press, Oxford, 1970), p. 14.

[4] A. Tarski, *Logic, Semantics, Metamathematics* (Clarendon Press, Oxford, 1956), pp. 187–8.

[5] D. Davidson, 'On Saying That', in *Words and Objections*, eds. D. Davidson and J. Hintikka (Reidel, Dordrecht, 1969), p. 173.

[6] 'In Defense', p. 84.

in 'hold true' is not semantically inert, and it must be the general notion of truth that is meant at this occurrence of 'true' if the suggestion is to be a criterion of acceptability of truth theories for arbitrary languages. All of the objections already raised can also be reproduced in reply to the suggestion that the Ramsey schema itself, 'It is true that *p* iff *p*', supplies all we can reasonably ask for about the general notion of truth; the problems arise again when we ask how the schema is to be applied, directly or indirectly, to 'Pierre spoke truly in saying "Il pleut" '.

This issue over the general notion of truth is intimately tied to the question of what makes an interpreted language the actual language of a population. For if we have an account of that relation (the 'actual language relation'), together with a principle for demarcating those sentences of an interpreted language that may strictly and literally be used to *say* something about the world, we shall implicitly have fixed the application of the predicate 'true in the language of population *P*': it applies to a sentence σ, very roughly, iff σ is in the class of demarcated sentences mentioned and the condition associated with σ in the interpreted language which is the actual language of *P* obtains. Conversely, we are a long way towards knowing which interpreted language a population uses when we know the truth conditions of those sentences of its language that can be used for sayings. We can also relate the issue to the commonly agreed point that some combinations of truth theory and propositional-attitude ascriptions result in not making the speaker make sense;[7] if we can make explicit the connections that must not be severed, we shall have a necessary condition of adequacy of a truth theory. If we can fill this out to a sufficient condition, we could reasonably claim to have met the demand for elucidation of 'true in the language of population *P*' for variable *P*.

There is some reason to think that the general notion of truth, for an arbitrary natural language, is not only intimately tied to the actual language relation, but that this relation, or something very similar, is needed if that notion is to be explained without circularity. The reason for saying this can be stated in terms of an illuminating analogy given by Michael Dummett. Dummett observes that a full specification of the game of chess must say what winning at chess consists in; for there are games that differ from chess *only* in what

[7] D. Davidson, 'Mental Events', in *Experience and Theory*, eds. L. Foster and J. Swanson (Duckworth, London, 1970), p. 97.

counts as winning in them. Further, to understand fully this specification of chess, one must be possessed of some general notion of winning, beyond what winning in bridge, winning in whist, etc., each consist in: 'the rules of a game do not themselves explain, but take for granted, the significance of the classification which they impose upon final positions into winning ones and losing ones'.[8] But Dummett goes further, and makes two more claims. 'The class of true sentences [of an actual language]', he says, 'is the class the utterance of a member of which a speaker of the language is aiming at when he employs what is recognizably the assertoric use'.[9] When we pass in turn to Dummett's remarks on *assertion* we find him trapped in a circle, for he characterizes it in terms, in effect, of truth: 'An assertion in the strict sense may then, in the framework, be characterized as a quasi-assertion the criterion for whose justification coincides with that for the *truth* of the thought which constitutes its sense'.[10] We do not have to construe Dummett's remarks as the whole truth about truth and assertion for the circle to be closed; it is enough that the notions of truth and assertion are each an essential component in the full account, whatever it is, of the other. We have to avoid or neutralize this circle; but we must also remember that it is a condition of adequacy on any account here that it yield the *connection* between truth and assertion (better: saying) expressed in the familiar formula: a man's utterance is true iff things are as he says they are in issuing that utterance. How then are we to proceed?

Let us consider the parallel connection in the case of games. It seems to be approximately this: a man wins a game iff he fulfils the aims he has *qua* player of that game. The parallel is tight: it is tempting to analyse this general notion of winning in terms of the idea of the aims a man has *qua* player of a game. One way out of the problem is to give an analysis of the 'actual game relation', that relation that is constitutive of a group's playing one game rather than another, where the vocabulary of this analysis does not employ expressions like 'winning', 'aims one has *qua* player of the game' and so forth. It is then open to us to use the actual game relation in the analysis of *both* 'wins' and 'aims', in such a way as to fulfil our condition of adequacy.

[8] M. A. E. Dummett, *Frege: Philosophy of Language* (Duckworth, London, 1973), p. 413.

[9] Ibid., p. 320.

[10] Ibid., p. 359; my emphasis.

My claim is that we should take the same course in the linguistic case, and meet the condition of adequacy in a similar way. Thus, in analysing the actual language relation we must employ no semantical vocabulary: that analysis is then available for use in the explanations of the concepts of truth, saying, and adequacy of translation schemes between used languages.[11] The already mentioned condition of adequacy on an account of truth is important in another respect too: it seems, when fulfilled, to capture the *evaluative* aspect of the concept of truth (as something *worth* aiming at). For it follows from it that if we know what a man said on a particular occasion, and know that he spoke truly, then we know that the world is a certain way; it is not clear that there is any interest that the true/false distinction has for us that remains uncovered by this consequence.

It might be said that it is an error even to attempt to break the circle linking truth and assertion: it is just a refusal to take semantic predicates seriously. It must be true of any finite class of expressions that they cannot *all* be defined in terms of each other without circularity. Since this patently does not show that they do not have empirical conditions of application, why should not the class of semantical predicates be a class for which there is no such consequence? The objection, then, is that we are presupposing a certain form of reductionism there is no obvious reason to accept: that of the *semantic* to the *psychological*. Spelled out in more detail, the objector's position will be that there is no open sentence containing only psychological predicates and logical and set-theoretic constants that can define any given semantic predicate. (This statement makes the claim analogous to the irreducibility of the mental to the physical that some defend; and an important special case arises when psychological facts are 'brute relative to' semantic facts, in Miss Anscombe's sense.)[12] It is no argument against this objection that once all the psychological facts about a community are fixed, so are the semantic ones: for this kind of supervenience does not entail the existence of any kind of recursive translation scheme from psychological to semantic predicates. There may be an infinite number of kinds of situation psychologically specified in which a given semantic predicate applies, and nothing specifiable in the psychological vocabulary that they all have in

[11] Despite the criticism by which it has been introduced, the programme stated in this paragraph and indeed the problems it is intended to resolve are close to those mentioned by Dummett (op. cit.) in the paragraph spanning pp. 416–7.

[12] G. E. M. Anscombe, 'On Brute Facts', *Analysis*, xvii (1957-8), 69.

common. Moreover the objector can say that the recognized connection between truth and saying itself suffices to give further content to the general notion of truth.

If this objection is sound, adequate definitions should be unattainable; we should find that whenever we try to define a piece of semantical vocabulary, not only is the definition not quite right, but also that it is plainly the injection of semantic concepts that is needed to put matters right. This part of the objection one can meet only by attempting to supply adequate definitions. But the objection as stated is also importantly misleading in its suggestion that it is *only* a kind of reductionism that can motivate the search for an account of the actual language relation that does not use semantical vocabulary. That is false. For suppose we agreed that we could not ascribe very finely discriminated beliefs and desires to a creature with a language prior to, in some sense, translating his language. Then an account of the actual language relation, though it uses finely discriminated propositional attitudes, would still be needed both to fill the lacuna mentioned earlier and as a specification of the constraints that exist on the joint, simultaneous ascriptions of propositional attitudes and sayings; to fulfil *these* roles it is not required that finely discriminated propositional attitudes be ascribable to a creature in advance of translating his utterances. In this respect at least there is no analogy with the cases cited by Miss Anscombe: for there is no plausibility in the suggestion that (say) we cannot apply predicables like 'ξ had potatoes carted to ζ's house' to people in advance of settling who owes whom what.

To reduce needless complexity in what follows, I shall ignore in this paper such phenomena as indexicality, ambiguity and multiplicity of mood of a given sentence; ignoring the second of these is less of a restriction than it may seem, for we can take into account the possibility of multilingual speakers, and the principles relevant to 'disambiguation' of their utterances arguably carry over to disambiguation within a given language.

II

There is one way of analysing the actual language relation that forges, by way of the notion of convention, a direct link between Davidson-style truth theories and the concept of speaker's meaning (*s*-meaning) that Grice and Schiffer attempt to dissect. Let us temporarily oversimplify even more drastically and ignore bilingual speakers and

moods other than the indicative. Let us too, again temporarily, say that an *interpreted language* is a finitely axiomatized theory in English which contains as theorems *inter alia* sentences of the form

$$T(s) \equiv p$$

where s is a structural-descriptive name of a sentence, and p some sentence of English. 'T' is an uninterpreted predicate, not itself a predicate of English; the theory will also contain in general a relation 'sats' between sequences of objects and expressions. The *sentences* of an interpreted language L are just those referred to by some closed term s such that there is a theorem of L of the form $T(s) \equiv p$. The proposal is then simply this, where 'L' ranges over interpreted languages and 'P' over sets of creatures;

> L is an actual language of P iff it is a convention in P that $\forall\alpha$ (if α is a sentence of L, one utters α only if $\exists p$ ($\vdash_L T(\alpha) \equiv p$, and one s-means by uttering α that p)).[13]

Both the quantifiers in this criterion are substitutional; otherwise quantification into the quoted context governed by '$\vdash_L$' is nonsense. There is a host of problems here I will not touch upon; for instance, how to write the criterion without attributing knowledge of L as a *theory* to the members of P. The general intent is clear: if this view is correct, and a particular interpreted language L is the actual language of P, then L becomes, when 'T' is replaced in it throughout by 'true', or rather 'true in the language of P' (and correspondingly for 'sats'), the very theory that Davidson takes as an *empirical* one about the truth conditions of sentences of P's language.

Appropriate analyses of the relevant notion of convention that occurs in this criterion contain, quite rightly, a clause that ensures that a regularity R is a convention in a population P only if there is some distinct regularity R' that could have obtained in P and (to telescope a long story) would have served the same purpose tolerably well.[14] Does this condition really have to be met in every case in which an interpreted language is the actual language of a population? On at least one way of construing it, it would seem not. Suppose a

[13] In this criterion, '$\vdash_L T(\alpha) \equiv p$' plays the same role that 'σ C-determines p' plays for S. R. Schiffer in his book *Meaning* (Clarendon Press, Oxford, 1972) at p. 164. If we transform the clauses of Schiffer's definition of 'σ meets C' into the axioms of a theory, and replace 'C' by 'T', we get an interpreted language in the sense defined; the proposal then secures the effect of Schiffer's criterion at p. 164 without the irrelevant importation of talk of 'some minimum degree of rationality'.

[14] See, e.g., D. K. Lewis, *Convention* (Harvard University Press, Cambridge, Mass., 1969), p. 78, clause (5).

community has evolved in which one particular interpreted language is transmitted genetically, so that the newly-born member of the community does not need to undergo any training or learning process before understanding the utterances of his fellow creatures, or producing such himself. Are there alternative, equally expressive, languages that *these* creatures could adopt? One may be inclined to say there must be, since they could simply come to a communal decision to adopt another language; but this consideration can at most show that for creatures of sufficient intellectual sophistication to possess the concept of language use and possible alternatives, there must always be an alternative. For lesser creatures, there may be for *them* in the genetic case no equally rich alternative they could now use. (The impossibility envisaged here is relative to a time; it is not denied that if the conditions obtaining during the earlier history of the species had been different, a distinct and possibly equally rich language would have been spoken.) To suppose the creatures thus lesser is not to suppose that utterances of sentences of their language are not under their intentional control, or not to be explained in terms of their beliefs and desires. David Lewis writes: 'Chomsky and his school have argued that there is less conventionality than one might have thought. But so long as even two languages are humanly possible, it must be by convention that a population chooses to use one or the other.'[15] This is puzzling: for how in the limiting case in which *no* other (equally rich) language is possible for a community can that fact prevent one possible language from being their *actual* language? (If we allow the fact that these creatures could perhaps switch to a different language but one of less expressive power, then the sense in which it is a matter of convention that they speak the language they do is correspondingly attenuated.) It seems that it could be a matter of convention that L_1 is the language of a population P_1, and not a matter of convention that L_2 is the actual language of P_2; *ipso facto*, the actual language relation is not to be analysed immediately in terms of convention.

It may fairly be replied that at best this objection shows that at most we should define a predicate 'is a *C*-regularity' by omitting the clause in Lewis's definition that requires the existence of a possible alternative regularity, and simply replace 'convention' in the preceding criterion by '*C*-regularity'. The concept of a *C*-regularity

[15] Lewis, op. cit., p. 16.

remains an important one, for in capturing mutual expectations in the community,[16] it explains what sustains a given regularity or practice. The only objections I have to the suggestion thus modified are objections that apply equally to the early accounts suggested below, and the devices used to meet the objections there can be transferred to do the same work for the *s*-meaning theory. My reason for not pursuing the *s*-meaning suggestion is rather that another, not incompatible, analysis of the actual language relation can be given that is simpler in that it embeds much less complex propositional attitudes than *s*-meaning within such common knowledge conditions as will be present in any account. There need be no incompatibility with the *s*-meaning account because it is plausible from the analysis below that if *L* is an actual language of *P* on the simpler account, and members of *P* are capable of acts of *s*-meaning, then there will indeed be *C*-regularities in *P* relating to *s*-meaning.

III

The notion of *understanding* provides both a starting point for and a constraint upon any alternative analysis of '*L* is an actual language of population *P*'. For, with certain qualifications, we can take it that *L* is an actual language of *P* only if members of *P* understand utterances of sentences of *L* (as utterances of *L*). So, suppose that creature *x* utters the unambiguous sentence σ of *L* as a sentence of *L*, and suppose too that in uttering σ, *x* says something (in the indirect sense). What is it for a man to understand *x*'s utterance?

One answer immediately comes to mind: a man understands *x*'s utterance iff he knows what was said in it (or, put in a more tendentious but ambiguity-free way: iff he knows of what was said that *it* was said in the utterance). But this condition is not sufficient.

Prior to making a speech from the balcony of the Kremlin, Brezhnev tells you, who are unversed in Russian, in English that in the first sentence of his speech he will say that production doubled in 1973. We can fill out the story in such a way that you *know* what he said in uttering the first Russian sentence of his speech. But you do not understand his utterance.

What feature does this example lack which standard cases of

[16] Lewis, op. cit., p. 78, clauses (1) and (2).

understanding possess? Someone might say that the feature is this: the utterance is not in any language of which you have mastery. This may be true but is unhelpful: for one has mastery of a language only if one understands utterances in it (roughly speaking). The feature seems rather to be approximately this: your knowledge of what Brezhnev said in uttering his first sentence is not based on anything which supplies a basis for knowledge of what, if anything, is said in an utterance of an arbitrary sentence of Russian built up using atomic expressions and iterative devices that occur in Brezhnev's first sentence. To supply an account of the conditions such a basis must meet for knowledge of what is said to count as understanding provides a constraint on analyses of the actual language relation.

It may be objected that understanding cannot properly provide a constraint upon the analysis since one can think of cases in which a certain language is the actual language of a group, yet members of the group do not understand sentences of the language. Suppose we placed a number of monolingual speakers of different nationalities together on an island, and equipped each with a device (a machine, or a phrase book) that translated between their language and a certain language L which we had constructed. It could be common knowledge between these people that this was their situation; and they could exchange information, commands and requests by uttering sentences of the constructed language that they do not understand. But we have a good ground for considering such cases as of secondary importance in that they seem to arise only when members of the group each already understand utterances of sentences of *some* language or other.

We cannot use what little we have so far on the notion of understanding in the definition of the actual language relation, for what we have uses the concept of saying, and our aim is to use no semantical concepts in the definition. As a preliminary, let us now say that an interpreted language is an ordered pair, the first component of which is an interpreted language in the sense of the previous section of this paper, and whose second component is a function from sentences of its first component to propositional attitudes (if one likes, one can get by for our purposes with propositional-attitude words). If L is an interpreted language in our present sense, let T_L be its first component. Then the idea very roughly indeed is that, if $\langle T_L, f\rangle$ is an actual language of P and $\vdash_{T_L} (T(\sigma) \equiv p)$ and $f(\sigma) = \psi$, then members of P will take each other's utterances of σ as prima facie

evidence that the utterer ψ-s that p: later in this section some attempt will be made to remove the many crudities here. That is, as a first shot we have:

> $\langle T_L, f\rangle$ is an actual language of P only if $\forall\psi\ \forall x \in P\ \forall y \in P\ \forall\sigma\ \forall p$ (x notices that y utters σ, and $\vdash_{T_L}(T(\sigma) \equiv p)$ and $f(\sigma) = \psi\ .\supset.$ x takes y's utterance of σ as prima facie evidence that y ψ-s that p).

Some remarks:

(i) The values of 'ψ' may be any propositional attitude (word)—believing, wanting, fearing, even *s*-meaning—so long as they presuppose no semantical concepts; roughly, the permissible values are specified by English verbs such that on completion by 'that *s*', for any sentence *s*, they yield a predicable whose application conditions depend solely upon the psychological state of the subject of predication and not on facts about his society.

(ii) '$\forall p$' and '$\forall\sigma$' are substitutional quantifiers.

(iii) 'Prima facie evidence' is used in such a way that the fact that the grass is wet is prima facie ('p.f.') evidence that it has rained recently. Prima facie evidence may be overruled, for example by the observation that there are some operating sprinklers nearby. But to say that certain p.f. evidence that q is overruled is not (as I propose to use the term) to say that it is not after all p.f. evidence that q, but rather that it is not, all things considered, evidence that q. Properly,

> ——is prima facie evidence that . . .

is a relation between properties or type-situations; syntactically, at a first level of analysis, it is a sentence-forming operator on pairs of open sentences. I am also using 'prima facie evidence' in such a way that if something's being F is p.f. evidence that it is G, and object x is F, then this evidence that x is G can be overruled only on the basis of facts about the particular object x.

(iv) There are some circumstances and some substituends for p such that in those circumstances you will not take any action of mine, utterance or anything else, as even p.f. evidence that I believe that p ('We are on Venus', '$2 + 3 = 4$'); perhaps there are even some statements such that there are *no* circumstances in which you would take any action of mine as p.f. evidence that I believed them. Yet we

want a theory that makes the actual language of Englishmen have as its first component something containing the theorem

$$T(\underline{1 + 1 = 3}) \equiv 1 + 1 = 3.$$

Plainly what gives such sentences as '1 + 1 = 3', 'Snow is white and it's not the case that snow is white' the truth conditions they have in English is a matter of the 'contribution' of their parts to other sentences in which they occur; we shall return to the question of capturing this in the actual language relation. For the present, we can say that appended to all occurrences of

> x takes y's utterance of σ as p.f. evidence that y ψ-s that p

is to be understood the qualification:

> in any circumstances in which it is not, for x, so improbable that y ψ-s that p that x would not take any action of y's as p.f. evidence that y ψ-s that p.

This necessary condition for the actual language relation is of course far from sufficient. Above all, it could be satisfied without any member of P having any reason at all to think that if *he* uttered σ (where $\vdash_{T_L}(T(\sigma) \equiv p)$ and $f(\sigma) = \psi$, say), other members of P would take this as p.f. evidence that he ψ-s that p. Perhaps everybody has a psychological hypothesis about the causal origins of the noises emitted by his fellow creatures, but no one believes that others have such hypotheses about himself.

Should we then instead use a stronger necessary condition that rules out such cases? We might add this to our given condition:

> $\forall\psi\,\forall\sigma\,\forall p\,\forall x \in P\,(\vdash_{T_L}(T(\sigma) \equiv p), \&\, f(\sigma) = \psi\,.\supset.\, x$ knows that $\forall y \in P\,(y$ notices that he (x) utters $\sigma\,.\supset.\, y$ takes x's utterance of σ as p.f. evidence that x ψ-s that $p))$.

Familiar problems arise at this point. Would L be the actual language of P if it were not the case that everyone in P believed that everyone in P had the beliefs specified in this second necessary condition? Intuition has no firm grasp at this point; while some such

common knowledge conditions are necessary for the existence of a convention, it is unclear that we need them for L to be an actual language.

Imagine certain cases where just the two necessary conditions we have already are fulfilled. Certainly, members of P would reasonably utter sentences of L and expect them to be taken in just the way they *would* be taken if L were the actual language of P; and by the first condition, they would be so taken. Moreover, if we took the conjunction of these two conditions as sufficient, we would already have the desirable consequence that from the fact that L is the actual language of populations $P_1, \ldots, P_n$ that comprise P, it does not follow that L is the actual language of P.

It would not, however, be at all detrimental to the conclusions I later draw to alter this second necessary condition to

> $\forall p\, \forall \sigma\, (\vdash_{T_L}(T(\sigma) \equiv p)\ \&\ f(\sigma) = \psi\ .\supset .$ it's common knowledge in P that $\forall x \in P\, \forall y \in P$ (x notices that y utters $\sigma\ .\supset .\ x$ takes y's utterance of σ as p.f. evidence that y ψ-s that p))

where 'common knowledge' is taken in the sense of David Lewis. Given our earlier scruples about unsophisticated creatures, it might be appropriate to use a notion of common knowledge that finitely generates this paradigm:

> It is common knowledge between x and y that p iff all these conditions hold:
>
> (a) x knows that p
> (b) y knows that x knows that p
> (c) x does not *disbelieve* that (b)
> (d) y does not disbelieve that (c)
> (e) x does not disbelieve that (d) . . .
>
> (a′) y knows that p
> (b′) x knows that y knows that p
> (c′) y does not disbelieve that (b′) . . .

This definition does not imply that if x and y commonly know that p, then they are capable of highly complex propositional attitudes.

There are still a number of major reasons why these conditions, with or without common knowledge, are not sufficient. The first concerns altered versions of languages. Let English* be just like

English, except that the *T*-condition for some simple conjunctive sentence is altered; for instance

$\vdash_{T_{\text{English*}}}$ *T*(Susan is blonde and Jane is short) ≡ Susan is blonde.

(Such a theory can still be finitely axiomatized: it is a matter of conditionalizing the satisfaction axioms in such a way that (a) they do not serve up the English *T*-condition for the sentence 'Susan is blonde and Jane is short' (b) the contribution that sentence makes to the *T*-conditions of more complex sentences in which it occurs remains as it is in ordinary English. We then add a special axiom for 'Susan is blonde and Jane is short'. In this way we can always adjust the *T*-conditions of finitely many sentences without dropping finiteness of axiomatization.) Suppose that in fact English is the actual language of a population *P*. Then if we took our present conditions as sufficient, it would follow that English* is also an actual language of *P*. For it could be common knowledge in *P* that if any member believes that *p* & *q*, that member believes that *p*. A parallel problem can be made to arise for alternation with such attitudes as disbelief: if a man disbelieves that *p* v *q*, he disbelieves that *p*.

English and English* are however asymmetrically related. Given that English meets (with respect to *P*) the condition on the actual language relation we have already laid down, we can, by appealing to purely psychological facts about members of *P* that do not relate to their attitudes to sentences of English or English*, explain why English* also meets the specified conditions w.r.t. *P*; here the purely psychological fact is just that it is common knowledge in *P* that if a member of *P* believes that *p* and *q*, he believes that *p*. But it is not true that there are facts not relating to sentences of the two languages in terms of which we can account for English meeting the specified conditions, given that English* meets them. When languages *L′* and *L* are related as English and English* are in this way (w.r.t. a community *P*) let us say that *L′ ranks above L* w.r.t. *P*. Now if *L′* ranks above *L* w.r.t. *P*, we need to say that *L′* (or something that ranks above *it*) is an actual language of *P* anyway; why say that *P* has the other distinct language *L*, when the facts that make *L′* rank above *L* w.r.t. *P* still hold even if we said that? Thus we can add as another necessary condition for *L* to be an actual language of *P* that

$\sim \exists L'$ (*L′* ranks above *L* with respect to *P*).

In effect, this comes down to adopting the maxim: 'Count as *linguistic* knowledge only what you *have* to'. Of course in some cases there will be genuine idioms, and it is in just such cases that interpreted languages which adjust the *T*-conditions of single sentences will not have others ranking above them. There is no hope of explaining the sense of 'Let's hit the road!' in terms of the senses of its parts in English combined with psychological facts about Englishmen that do not relate to sentences of English.

These conditions are still not sufficient. Consider a community *P* in which it is common knowledge that everyone watches television from 9 to 9.30 every evening, and that everyone believes everything they hear stated on it between those times. A scientific discovery is announced on television one evening at 9.15 to the effect that members of *P* blush when and only when they want the conversation they are presently engaged in to end because they find it embarrassing. Now consider the language L_0 whose only utterance-type is a blush, whose second component is a function that maps this type to the propositional attitude *wanting* and whose first component consists of the theory whose sole axiom is

T(the type blush, u, t) $\equiv$ the conversation in which u is engaged at t, if any, ends.

When sentences with indexicals are considered, the first component of an interpreted language will have to specify *T*-conditions for sentences relative to (at least) an utterer u and a time t, and contain theorems of the form $T(\sigma, u, t) \equiv A(u, t)$: and the actual language relation will have to be cashed out in some such terms as: if x and y are in P, $\vdash_{T_L} (T(\sigma, u, t) \equiv A(u, t))$ and $f(\sigma) = \psi$, then x takes an utterance by y of σ at time t as p.f. evidence that y ψ-s that $A(y, t)$ (better: that $A(y\text{-self}, t)$). The example of the preceding paragraph is then a counter-example to the sufficiency of our previous conditions when thus relativized to utterers and times; the conditions can be checked out. (Note that there are no facts *not relating to* sentences of L_0, viz. the type blush, in terms of which one could explain why L_0 meets the conditions already given.) But L_0 is not a language of such a group.

One might tack on the further necessary condition that

$\forall\sigma$ (if σ is a sentence of L, it's common knowledge in P that uttering σ is under the intentional control of members of P).

But this will not cope with yet another kind of case that can be constructed.

Consider an interpreted language L_1 whose first component is a theory which in one way or another contains as theorems all sentences of the form

$T(\sigma, u, t) \equiv u$'s utterance of σ at t, if any, is heard by someone or other

where σ is replaced by a structural-descriptive name of an English sentence; the second component of L_1 maps every English sentence to *belief*. Plainly there can be (indeed there almost certainly are) populations that, intuitively, speak English, and which would be construed as having L_1 as an actual language too if we took the present conditions, including that of the previous paragraph, as sufficient. There are or could be groups in which, because of minimal physiological and psychological knowledge of one another, member x takes member y's utterance of σ as p.f. evidence that y believes that his utterance is heard by someone; it can be common knowledge that this is so.

It seems to be wrong to say that the reason L_1 is not an actual language of the group in these circumstances is that T_{L_1} fails to satisfy the condition

there is no formula $R(\sigma, u, t)$ not containing 'T' or'sats' such that for any sentence σ of $\langle T_{L_1}, f\rangle$, $\vdash_{T_{L_1}} (T(\sigma, u, t) \equiv R(\sigma, u, t))$;

for some interpreted languages that could be actual languages of groups also fail to satisfy this condition. In particular, all one-sentence languages do not meet it: consider the interpreted language L_2, where T_{L_2} has the sole axiom

$T(\sigma, u, t) \equiv$ there are man-eating tigers in the vicinity of u at t

for some σ, and L_2's second component maps σ to *belief*. We can if we like deny that such simple communication systems are languages, but we cannot deny that the relation between them and a group using them is similar to (if not the same as) that between more full-blooded languages and *their* users; and it is that relation we are chasing.

Nor does it help to invoke the condition that L is an actual language of P only if no language 'ranks above' it w.r.t. P. We can imagine a simple language which uses all of the finitely many types of sound which it is common knowledge in P that members of P can both reproduce and hear; then it will not be true that there are facts

not relating to the sentences of the language in question in terms of which we can explain why L_1 meets the other necessary conditions for being an actual language of P. We might get round this if we could individuate sentences by reference to their truth (fulfilment...) conditions, but this is not open to us since we are eschewing all use of semantical concepts in the analysis.

We should rule out L_1 rather for the reasons that members have for taking each other's utterances as p.f. evidence that the utterers believe that their utterances are heard by someone. In the case of a genuine language, anyone will take another's utterance of 'It's raining' as p.f. evidence that the utterer believes that it's raining in part for the reason that it is common knowledge that everyone expects that anyone will take another's utterance of 'It's raining' as p.f. evidence that the utterer believes that it's raining. (Generally this common knowledge will result from common knowledge about utterances of 'It's raining' in the community in the past, but it need not; it could come from express agreement or stipulation for the future.) In the case of L_1, hearers do not have this type of reason; not do they in the 'blushing' example. I should note that to have at the heart of the actual language relation the concept of one creature's taking a second's utterances of certain expressions as p.f. evidence of certain propositional attitudes in the utterer, in part for the reason that it is common knowledge that every creature expects any creature so to take such utterances, is not thereby to oust *intention* from the field. For the way this reason operates is in an inference on the audience's part to the likely intentions of the utterer. So we may be tempted to expand our necessary condition for L to be an actual language of P to

> $\forall\sigma\,\forall p(\vdash_{T_L}(T(\sigma) \equiv p)\ \&\, f(\sigma) = \psi\ .\supset .$ it's common knowledge in P that $\forall x \in P\ \forall y \in P$ (x notices that y utters $\sigma\ .\supset .\ x$ takes y's utterance of σ as p.f. evidence that y ψ-s that p, and x's reason for doing so is in part that it's common knowledge in P that every member of P expects that $\forall x \in P\ \forall y \in P$ (x notices that y utters $\sigma\ .\supset .\ x$ takes y's utterance of σ as p.f. evidence that y ψ-s that p))).

But before we rush to add this, we must take account of a related point. In any case in which an interpreted language L has infinitely many sentences, it follows from the conditions already imposed on

the actual language relation that L is an actual language of P only if the members of P bear certain complex propositional attitudes to the infinitely many sentences of L. It is highly plausible that human beings can be thus related to infinitely many sentences only if these relations can be represented as resulting from finitely many propositional attitudes in relation to finitely many kinds of element or expression. The fact that finiteness of axiomatization has been required of the first component of any interpreted language does not suffice to do this as long as the actual language relation ties the propositional attitudes of members of the community to the infinitely many sentences of the language *one by one*. The same problem arises for analyses in terms of convention and *s*-meaning; in the criterion mentioned in the previous section:

> it's a convention in P that $\forall\alpha$ (if α is a sentence of L, one utters α only if $\exists p(\vdash_{T_L} T(\alpha) \equiv p$ and one *s*-means by uttering α that p)),

one convention relates the members of P to infinitely many sentences. If we move '$\forall\alpha$' so that it precedes 'it's a convention', each convention concerns only a single sentence; but then there are infinitely many conventions.

A closer tie between the actual language relation and the (finitely many) 'recursive' axioms of the first component of an interpreted language is required. One way we can obtain the closer tie can be illustrated by considering a particular language L_3. L_3 has atomic sentences s_1, s_2 and s_3, with *T*-conditions p_1, p_2 and p_3, and has just two iterative devices, $\underline{\&}$ and $\underline{\sim}$. Now suppose the following five statements are true of a community P.

(1)–(3) It's common knowledge in P that any member x will take any member y's utterance of s_i as p.f. evidence that y believes that p_i, and x will do so in part because it's common knowledge in P that any member of P expects that any member x will take any member y's utterance of s_i as p.f. evidence that y believes that p_i;

(for $i = 1, 2, 3$).

(4) It's common knowledge in P that any member x will take any member y's utterance of any (complete) sentence of the form

(*A* & *B*) as p.f. evidence that *y* believes that *q* & *r*, for any *q* such that it's common knowledge in *P* that any member *x* will take any member *y*'s utterance of the (complete) sentence *A* as p.f. evidence that *y* believes that *q*, and for any *r* such that it's common knowledge in *P* that any member *x* will take any member *y*'s utterance of the (complete) sentence *B* as p.f. evidence that *y* believes that *r*; and it's common knowledge that *x* will do so in part for the reason that it's common knowledge in *P* that every member of *P* expects that any member will take . . .

[as in what precedes the above semicolon].

(5) It's common knowledge in *P* that any member *x* will take any member *y*'s utterance of any (complete) sentence of the form ($\sim A$) as p.f. evidence that *y* believes it is not the case that *q*, for any *q* such that it is common knowledge in *P* that any member *x* will take any member *y*'s utterance of the (complete) sentence *A* as p.f. evidence that *y* believes that *q*; and it's common knowledge that *x* will do all this in part for the reason that it's common knowledge in *P* that every member of *P* expects that any member will take . . .

[as in what precedes the last semicolon].

For every sentence *s* of L_3 we can deduce from (1)–(5) that if $\vdash_{T_{L_3}} T(s) \equiv p$, then it's common knowledge in *P* that any member *x* will take any member *y*'s utterance of *s* as p.f. evidence that *y* believes that *p*. (The further point about *x*'s reasons for doing so we intentionally keep only in the atomic and 'recursive' facts (1)–(5).) To prove this formally one would proceed by induction on the length of *s*, but a single example should suffice to bring home the general plan. Consider the sentence (s_1 & ($\sim s_2$)). Using (2) and (5) together with the principle that if it is common knowledge in *P* that $\forall x(Fx \supset Gx)$ and it is common knowledge in *P* that *Ft*, then it is common knowledge in *P* that *Gt*, we can conclude that:

> it is common knowledge in *P* that any member *x* will take any member y's utterance of the complete sentence ($\sim s_2$) as p.f. evidence that *y* believes that it is not the case that p_2.

Then once again using this deduced fact, (2), (4) and the principle about common knowledge, we reach

> it is common knowledge in P that any member x will take any member y's utterance of the complete sentence $\underline{(s_1 \,\&\, (\sim s_2))}$ as p.f. evidence that y believes that: p_1 and it is not the case that p_2.

(The qualifications about complete sentences are present since we want L_3 to be an actual language of some populations even though members don't take each other's utterances of $\underline{(s_1 \,\&\, s_2)}$ as p.f. evidence of a belief that p_1 and p_2 when uttered within the larger sentence $\underline{((s_1 \,\&\, s_2) \vee s_3)}$. In a fuller treatment, one can avoid these complications by speaking in clauses (4) and (5) about utterances of sentences of the form $\underline{(A \,\&\, B)\,.}$ and $\underline{(\sim A)\,.}$; ' . ' then functions as a completion-indicator, in the way the full stop does in written English.)

Thus from the finite conjunction of (1)—(5) follow the infinitely many conditions specified in our earlier necessary conditions for L_3 to be an actual language of a population. This treatment can be immediately generalized to accommodate arbitrary interpreted languages whose only iterative devices are sentential connectives. In particular, for the subcase in which f_1 maps every sentence of T_L to belief, we have:

> $L = \langle T_L, f_1 \rangle$ is an actual language of P only if:

(1) for any atomic sentence σ of L, if $\vdash_{T_L} T(\sigma) \equiv p$, it's common knowledge in P that: any member x of P will take any member y's utterance of σ (that x notices etc.) as p.f. evidence that y believes that p, in part for the reason that it's common knowledge in P that every member expects that any member x will take any member y's utterance of σ as p.f. evidence that y believes that p;

and

(2) for any n-place connective c,

> if $\vdash_{T_L} \forall A_1 \ldots \forall A_n \,(T(\underline{c(A_1, \ldots, A_n)}) \equiv \mathscr{C}\,(T(\underline{A_1}) \ldots, T(\underline{A_n})))$ then it's common knowledge in P that: any member x of P will take any member y's utterance of a sentence of L of the form $c(\alpha_1, \ldots, \alpha_n)$ as p.f. evidence that y believes that $\mathscr{C}\,(p_1, \ldots, p_n)$, for any $p_1, \ldots, p_n$ such that for each α_i it's common knowledge

in *P* that any member *x* will take any member *y*'s utterance of α_i as p.f. evidence that *y* believes that p_i $(1 \leqslant i \leqslant n)$; and that any member *x* will so take any member *y*'s utterance of a sentence of *L* of the form $c(\alpha_1, \ldots, \alpha_n)$ in part for the reason that it's common knowledge in *P* that every member expects that any member *x* of *P* will take any member *y*'s utterance of a sentence of *L* of the form $c(\alpha_1, \ldots, \alpha_n)$ . . . etc.

It seems a reasonable conjecture that these conditions, subject only to minor adjustments, provide a sufficient condition for the actual language relation when the clause that no *L'* ranks above *L* w.r.t. *P* is added; sufficient, that is, for languages of this restricted form. In a formulation applicable to languages exhibiting more logical structure, the bulk of the changes that are needed are formal rather than philosophically substantive. Three points worth mentioning are that

(i) we must represent the second component of interpreted languages as operating recursively too, since in general the domain of such functions is infinite;

(ii) and this must be done in a way that does not conflict with the insight that mood-indication devices should be regarded as attaching to the whole sentence, even in the case of complex sentences;

(iii) for languages containing quantifiers, the actual language relation must be tied to the recursive satisfaction axioms. One should add too that recursive conventions about *s*-meaning can be designed, along lines exactly parallel to the account just given; the ideas given in the last few paragraphs can in fact be fitted into almost any theory of what propositional attitudes lie at the heart of the actual language relation.

We are now in a position to make a point about the concept of understanding. Earlier we noted that knowledge of what is said in a particular utterance is not sufficient for understanding that utterance; only certain ways of reaching such knowledge give understanding. We can circumscribe the ways that yield understanding by appealing to the recursive statement of the common knowledge conditions. Suppose we have some account of the concept of saying that (for which see the next section) and some account also of the notion of a sentence being uttered *as* a sentence of *L*. Then the following seems to be a sufficient condition for *x* to understand *y*'s utterance of σ:

if L is the interpreted language such that y uttered σ *as* a sentence of L, then x knows what y said in his utterance of σ in part on the basis of an inference from

(a) his perception of certain physical features of y's utterance, where these features suffice to determine the T-condition in L of the uttered sentence, and from

(b) his knowledge (in general 'recursive') relating to those features, which knowledge is part of the knowledge required on our definitions of the members of any group for L to be their actual language.

This condition says, roughly, that x understands y's utterance if he knows what was said in it by way of inferences analogous to those we ourselves drew above from statements (1)–(5). The creatures possessing translation machines fail to meet this condition, as does also the hearer in the Brezhnev example. It is attractive to see this necessary condition for understanding as an acceptable elucidation of Ziff's talk of the 'analytical data processing' involved in understanding.[17] (See also note (a) added in proof, p. 188 below.)

IV

If we are to give some account of truth in terms of the actual language relation, we need to note that there are two distinct but related notions of truth to be elucidated:

(i) that expressed in English by 'what he said on that occasion was true', 'he spoke truly';

(ii) that in which we can assert ' "I am bored" is true in the language of Englishmen as uttered by person p at time t iff p is bored at t'. It is not hard to explain notion (ii) in terms of the actual language relation: where '$\exists p$' is a substitutional sentential quantifier, we may say that

σ is true in the language of population P iff $\exists p \exists T_L \exists f$ ($\langle T_L, f\rangle$ is the actual language of P & $f(\sigma)$ = belief & $\vdash_{T_L}(T(\sigma) \equiv p)$, & p).

But there is no immediate account of notion (i) in terms of (ii). Even under the supposition that any many-membered community of creatures speaks at most one language, an individual person may be bilingual, utter a sentence σ common to two of the languages he

[17] Paul Ziff, 'Understanding', in his *Understanding Understanding* (Cornell University Press, London, 1972), pp. 17–20.

speaks, where σ has different truth conditions in each, and yet *say* only one thing. The point is parallel to one regarding disambiguation of ambiguous predicates and singular terms on an occasion within a single language.

We can approach notion (i) via the analysis of saying that. Let me use the abbreviation-schema:

> σ is suitable for p in $P =_{df.} \exists T \exists f (\langle T, f \rangle$ is an actual language of P & $\vdash_T T(\sigma) \equiv p$, & $f(\sigma) =$ belief).

Then the remark of the preceding paragraph shows that it is not sufficient for u's saying that p in uttering σ (in utterance-event e) that

> $\exists P$ ($u \in P$ & σ is suitable for p in P).

Reflection shows too that it is not sufficient that this stronger condition hold:

> $\exists P$($u \in P$ & σ is suitable for p in P & u's reason for uttering σ in utterance-event e is in part that σ is (believed by his audience to be) suitable for p in P).

For there are many ways in which u might have such reasons for uttering σ and yet not say that p. Perhaps a bet is in force with his interlocutor that he (u) can answer a question he has been asked in a sentence that is also suitable for p in some community of which they are both members; or perhaps it is a question of a ('bilingual') pun. Something more is needed.

Not all cases of *saying* that p are cases of *asserting* that p. If in response to a remark that one's tape recorder is malfunctioning, another replies 'Nixon will be pleased to help you with any difficulties you have with the "Erase" button' as a joke, he does strictly and literally say that Nixon will be pleased to . . . etc. But he does not *assert* that Nixon will be pleased . . .&c. Falsity is a defect in an assertion, but is not necessarily so in a saying. (Of course in this example it may be misleading to say *only* that the speaker said that Nixon will be pleased . . . etc. But the misleadingness can be explained on pragmatic grounds: generally, sayings *are* assertings.) The following example may be found more convincing. Suppose x propounds to y an economic hypothesis that clearly entails that U.K. exports rose last year; and suppose it is common knowledge between x and y that inflation proceeded apace last year. y may try to refute x's

theory by saying 'Since exports rose last year, there was no inflation then'. *y* does not *assert* that since exports rose last year, there was no inflation then; but he does say that, and a report of his utterance in indirect speech would legitimately say that he said it. There is perhaps an element of stipulation in the appropriation of the English words 'say' and 'assert' to mark the distinction we want; but it is a motivated stipulation, for the class of so-called sayings are just those utterances that are *truth-evaluable*. In general in such cases, only one 'proposition' is propounded even if the expression-type a token of which is uttered is common to two of the languages the utterer speaks.

It may be said that sayings that are not assertings are possible only in a social context in which there is, at least potentially, a practice of full-blooded assertion; and this is indeed plausible. But, if true, it does not show that saying cannot be defined without use of the notion of assertion. It simply supplies a condition of adequacy on any pairs of definitions of saying and asserting, viz. that this relation can be shown to hold between them on the basis of the given definitions.

The prospects look very dim for any claim that part of what we need to add to the above necessary conditions for *u* to say to *a* that *p* is that *u* intend *a* to have the (activated) belief that *p*. It can hardly be denied that when one says to a man one knows to be counter-suggestible on certain topics 'Your wife spent the evening at the school concert' one strictly and literally *says that* his wife spent the evening at the school concert; yet one does not intend him to believe it, and *a fortiori* one does not *s*-mean it.[18] Nor will switching from the intention that *a* believe that *p* to the intention that *a* believe that *u* intends him to believe that *p* help: any case in which, for one reason or another, one intends *a* to believe one is lying will be a counter-example. The system in these counter-examples combined with the heterogeneity of cases of saying in our wide intended sense suggests that we will not make progress by having the intention to get *a* to believe that *p* at the heart of an account of saying. (We should remember that by having the necessary condition that the sentence *u* utters be suitable for *p* in some community containing *u*, we have

[18] Yet the claim that one says that *p* only if one *s*-means thereby that *p* is to be found in Grice, Schiffer and Strawson. In 'Utterer's Meaning, Sentence-meaning and Word-meaning' (*Foundations of Language* iv (1968)) Grice objects to 'by uttering *x*, *U* meant that *p and when uttered by *U*, *x* meant "*p" ' only as a *sufficient* condition of 'in uttering *x*, *U* said that *p'. Schiffer (op. cit.) makes the claim explicitly at p. 114 and Strawson in a more guarded way for 'stating or asserting' in 'Meaning and Truth', pp. 14–15.

already captured much if not all of what proponents of definitions of the kind just rejected intended they should cover.)

As a rough first approximation for an analysans of

u said to *a* in uttering σ that *p*

(which itself only approximates to the notion one finally wants since there are audienceless sayings) one might offer

> $\exists P(u \in P$ & σ is suitable for *p* in *P* & $\exists F$(*u* intends it to be common knowledge between *u* and *a* that the statement that *p* has *F*, which intention *u* intends to realize
> (a) via his uttering σ
> (b) on the basis of his (*u*'s) belief that it's common knowledge between *u* and *a* that σ is suitable for *p* in *P*
> (c) via *a*'s recognition that *u* has this intention)).

In the 'refutation' example, for instance, the relevant value of *F* might be the property of following from *a*'s economic theory. In a case where a detective is tracing out loud a possible sequence of events that leads to the murder, and says (but does not assert) that the murderer enters the house and waits a few hours for his victim to enter, the value might be: being a hypothesis consistent with all known facts and the immediately preceding conjectures. In the more familiar cases of sayings that are assertings the value *might* be: is believed by *u*; or indeed: is *s*-meant by *u* in this utterance of σ. But a definition of the notion of asserting would certainly have to wait upon the definition of the general notion of truth, to which in fact in our construction the definition of saying forms an input.

It would be rash to hold that this account of saying is watertight; but it does not seem rash to claim that something along similar lines using the concept of suitability (and thereby the actual language relation) can be made to work, an account fit for the service we require of it.

We can now turn directly to truth of kind (i). For simplicity, we shall again restrict our attention to sayings with audiences, in which furthermore only one thing is said in the utterance of the uttered sentence. We can define notion (i) in the familiar and notorious formula

> *u* spoke truly in uttering σ iff for some *a* and for some *p*, *u* said that *p* to *a* in that utterance of σ, and *p*.

Such a definition trivially meets the condition of adequacy that it has as a consequence that a man speaks truly iff things are as he

says they are in so speaking; and both truth and saying have been explained in terms of the actual language relation. But it is time for a belated consideration of whether the widespread use of substitutional quantification in the preceding paragraphs (especially blatant in the last definition) belies the claim to have avoided the use of semantical vocabulary; for the sentences containing such quantifiers, when expanded, explicitly use a *truth* predicate. '$\exists p(\ldots p \ldots)$' is true iff there is a sentence which when inserted into the context '. . . . . .' yields a *true* sentence.

One might reply that the substitutional quantifiers are to be taken as primitive, and that paradoxes obtainable from substitutional quantification and quotation together are to be met by hierarchies of languages corresponding to hierarchies of quoted contexts; or one might question the legitimacy of some of the singular terms used to derive the paradoxes. But the challenge can also be met head-on. For the concept of truth used in the definitions when substitutional quantification is not primitive is *not* the *general* notion of truth (the one analogous to the general concept of winning), but only truth in English, or truth in this language. But this last concept we can impart to a person by an outright recursion, or we could train him in its use; we would certainly not need to presuppose possession on his part of any concept of truth (the property according to which he would have acquired the ability to sort English sentences might just be labelled 'property *P*'). Our definitions would allow him to work outwards from this basis to the application of predicates like 'ξ_1 is an actual language of ξ_2'. True, what makes a particular recursive definition of '*P*' or training programme an appropriate recursion or programme is the fact that the sentences written in this essay are addressed to members of a community of which a certain language is an actual language. But that that is so can be seen from the pattern of the definitions written out in French and then applied to our English-speaking community. Understanding of those definitions then requires what is, in its application conditions, truth in French. No one starting point is required, but it is required that one start somewhere. It remains, on these definitions, an empirical fact that (the interpreted language corresponding to) any proper part of English is an actual language of Englishmen. Lewis in his analysis in *Convention* avoids the need for any discussion of the present point but the price is quantification over possible worlds, or at least conditions or propositions.

Those who quantify over possible worlds avoid another complication too. On inductive grounds, there is every reason to believe that the language of twenty-first century Englishmen, or indeed of present-day Eskimos, contains predicates that cannot be translated by any open sentence of present-day English. So there are, or will be, and certainly could be, communities using a language, although no interpreted language in our parochial sense is an actual language of theirs. (The Davidsonian conception faces the same problem.) The best I can offer in reply is that what is important about my tentative definitions is the *pattern* they instantiate: one can extract from them a technique for defining the actual language relation in an arbitrary richer (more expressive) language that one understands. We need this reply to meet another point, too. With some plausibility, a man might insist on no impredicativity in the specification of truth conditions for substitutionally quantified sentences. To this end, we might index all substitutional quantifiers with numerals, and say that '$\underset{n}{\exists} pA$' is true iff there is some sentence with quantifiers having index at most (n–1) which when substituted in A for 'p' yields a true sentence. (This could be made more precise.) Since then the substitutional quantifiers in the definition of the actual language relation must have index higher than the index of any quantifiers in the interpreted languages in its domain, it follows that the language in which the actual language relation is defined is not an actual language of any community *on that definition*. It will, however, be so on a definition cast in a richer language. The analysis of the actual language relation must not be taken as the definition of that relation in any single language, but rather as given by the technique for defining a 'restriction' of that relation in an arbitrary language.

Additional Notes

(a) The conditions on p. 183 are only sufficient, not necessary, for understanding an utterance. I have tried to state the conditions for understanding in the absence of 'recursive' knowledge in paper X of *Proceedings of the Aristotelian Society*, lxxv (1974), on p. 152.

(b) Because of the provability in truth theories of such formulae as the final one displayed on p. 322, throughout the paper occurrences of '$\vdash_{T_L} T(\sigma) \equiv p$' must be understood with the qualification that '$T(\sigma) \equiv p$' has a certain canonical kind of proof in T_L. In standard cases this will be the *shortest* proof of a theorem of the form $T(\sigma) \equiv p$, where p is free of 'T', 'sats', and sequence apparatus.

VII

On Understanding the Structure of One's Language

P. F. STRAWSON

ACTION-ASCRIBING sentences are susceptible of adverbial modification of such a kind that a proposition expressed by a sentence so modified entails any proposition obtained from it merely by shearing away some or all of the modifiers. Different theories are current which purport to explain our grasp of the structure of these entailments. In general there is a contrast between a theory, like Professor Davidson's,[1] which explains these relationships by reference to well-understood logical structures represented as underlying the surface forms of action-ascribing sentences, and any theory which finds an explanation closer to the surface of ordinary language by recognizing a more complicated basic syntax than a Davidsonian theorist is prepared to allow for. A theory of the second sort might deserve the name of an 'Adverbial Theory'. Indeed I shall pretend that we have to do with some particular theory of this sort, which I shall call *the* Adverbial Account, to be set over against the Davidsonian Account.

This contrast between theories obviously points to a question of considerable depth and generality—a question which relates not simply to Davidson's analysis of action-sentences but to any theory whatever which seeks to explain our general understanding of types of sentence and our general grasp of types of logical relation by reference to a true or underlying logical structure which differs more or less radically from the superficial grammatical form of the sentences in question. If this claim to explain is made, we must surely take it seriously and ask what it involves; and not just assume that the answer to this is obvious or that we know it perfectly well. For it is not at all obvious and really, when we look into it, seems to

[1] 'The Logical Form of Action Sentences', in *The Logic of Decision and Action*, ed. N. Rescher (Univ. of Pittsburgh Press, 1967), 81.

involve a great mystery—or, alternatively, the making of highly unplausible or quite unverifiable claims.

So what exactly is involved in such a claim? (I shall call it the 'explanation-claim'.) Let us try to get at the answer to this by contrasting the type of claim in question with something much more modest. A philosopher first points to the well-understood semantics of a language with the grammatical structure of the predicate calculus. He then points out that by quantifying over actions etc. we can frame Davidsonian action-sentences, and also that our understanding of the logical relations of these sentences is explained by our grasp of the semantics of any language which exhibits the grammatical structure they manifestly possess. Finally he points out that we can see very well that our ordinary action-sentences are equivalent to Davidsonian action-sentences: i.e. that given any pair of ordinary action-sentences, S_1 and S_2, such that S_1 entails S_2 (and this relation is an instance of the kind we are concerned with) then we can frame a pair of Davidsonian sentences, DS_1 and DS_2, such that DS_1 is equivalent to S_1 and DS_2 is equivalent to S_2 and DS_1 entails DS_2; and our grasp of *this* entailment relation (i.e. the entailment of DS_2 by DS_1) is explained by our grasp of the semantics of any language possessing the grammatical structure of the predicate calculus.

Now these are interesting things to point out, and they are not things that are in dispute. But simply to point them out evidently falls a long way short of making the claim that our ordinary grasp of the class of logical relations such as the entailment of S_2 by S_1 is *explained* by these facts. The claim is expressed by saying (1) that sentences of the form of DS_1 and DS_2 exhibit the true or underlying structure of sentences of the form of S_1 and S_2 and (2) that it is because this is so that we understand the logical relations of sentences of the form of S_1 and S_2. We still do not know quite what this means. Contrast it, whatever it means, with yet another modest claim: if our ordinary action-sentences had the manifest form of sentences of the *DS* type, then our grasp of their logical relations (or those of the kind we are currently interested in) could be easily understood and explained as just one instance (or class of instances) of our general grasp of the semantics of any language with the grammatical structure of the predicate calculus. This wistful hypothetical, however, makes no pretence of explaining our understanding of the logical relations between action-sentences as we find them.

Could the explanation-claim come to this: it is *because* we grasp or understand our ordinary action-sentences *as* equivalent to *DS* sentences (with *their* well-understood semantics) that we have the general understanding we do have of the logical relations of our ordinary action-sentences? Now it may be that this interpretation of the explanation-claim can itself be understood in more than one way. Indeed I rather think this is the case; and on one way of understanding the explanation-claim, it is exposed to a type of reaction or challenge it is not exposed to on another way of understanding it. By looking first at reactions of this type, we may come to be better placed later on to see how the claim might be understood in a different way which is not exposed to this type of reaction.

So let us look first at a very impatient reaction. What is the evidence, one might ask, for the view in question? Surely such evidence as there is is all against it. For ordinary speakers of the language understand their action-sentences and grasp their logical relations very well without ever having dreamed of *DS* sentences; and when they are introduced to these unfamiliar objects, some time may have to be spent and explanations gone through before they can be got to understand *DS* sentences and hence to see the equivalences in question. So understanding our ordinary action-sentences as equivalent to *DS* sentences is not even a condition, let alone an explanatory condition or underlying ground, of our understanding of the logical relations of our ordinary sentences. It may be said that this is far too crude an interpretation of the claim: that the claim refers to underlying general capacities: that it is only because we have the *capacity* to see our ordinary action-sentences as equivalent to *DS* sentences (when the latter are introduced and explained to us) that we have the general understanding we do have of the logical relations of our ordinary action-sentences. But to this the impatient reply is again obvious. Of course this capacity and this understanding may be expected to go together; for if the two forms of sentence are indeed equivalent and we understand them both, we may be expected to appreciate their equivalence: our not doing so would count against our truly understanding one or the other. But no reason whatever has been given to invoke one capacity (the generally unrealized because generally untested capacity to appreciate the equivalences) to explain our possession of the other (the generally realized capacity to grasp the logical relations of ordinary action-sentences). One might just as plausibly, indeed far more plausibly,

invoke our ordinary understanding of the logical grammar of ordinary action-sentences to explain our capacity to appreciate the possibility of Davidsonian equivalents.

Let us put these impatient reactions on one side for the moment and consider what appears to be a subtler difficulty. Suppose it were the case that our understanding of the relevant logical relations among ordinary action-sentences (call them *SS* sentences—the first '*S*' for 'surface') is somehow dependent on the fact that, in some as yet unclarified sense, we do indeed understand them as equivalent to corresponding *DS* sentences, understanding of the corresponding logical relations among which is explained by the semantics of the predicate calculus. Then we have another problem of explanation on our hands: viz., the problem of explaining our general grasp of the logical relations of mutual entailment between *SS* sentences and the corresponding *DS* sentences. Evidently the semantics of the predicate calculus cannot be invoked to solve *this* problem. Equally evidently it will not be satisfactory to appeal to an intuitive grasp of these equivalences. For if that were satisfactory, there would have been no problem in the first place and we could simply have appealed to an intuitive grasp of the logical relations among *SS* sentences.

How might the reply to this objection go? I imagine that it might go like this. There is a limited set of what might be called transformation or translation rules in accordance with which any *SS* sentence can be represented as derived from the corresponding *DS* sentence, and any *DS* sentence as recoverable from the corresponding *SS* sentence. The fact that the ordinary speaker of the language understands his *SS* sentences as equivalent to the corresponding *DS* sentence is to be explained by crediting him with a 'tacit' or 'implicit' mastery of these rules. His mastery of these rules must be supposed to be a part of his acquisition of the language. Credit him both with a mastery of these rules and with a grasp of the semantics of the predicate calculus, and the task of explaining what was to be explained is completed.

I said the objection to which this is a possible reply was to be a subtler, a less impatient, objection. But you will see that it really leads simply to a more thorough and careful statement of the impatient reaction. We have a theory which sets out to explain our ordinary grasp of a set of relations which we might represent like this:

$$\text{I} \qquad \begin{array}{c} SS_1 \\ \downarrow \\ SS_2 \end{array}$$

The theory proceeds by crediting us with mastery of sets of rules and relations which we might represent like this

$$\text{II} \qquad \begin{array}{c} SS_1 \rightleftarrows DS_1 \\ \qquad\downarrow \\ SS_2 \rightleftarrows DS_2 \end{array}$$

where the horizontal arrows represent our translation or transformation rules and the vertical arrow represents relations which result from the well-understood semantics of the predicate calculus; the theory then claims that our mastery of system I is explained by our mastery of system II.

The simple objection is that the *DS* sentences of system II are for the most part relatively unfamiliar objects and that, on the evidence of verbal behaviour, many ordinary language-speakers show a perfectly competent mastery of system I but would require a certain amount of instruction to get the hang of system II; so it cannot be the case that mastery of system II is a condition of, let alone the explanation of, mastery of system I. If it is said that this is to misinterpret the notion of 'mastery' of a system, and that what is meant is a kind of implicit mastery the existence of which is quite consistent with the facts just mentioned, the retort must be that the claim has now become quite mysterious and unverifiable. If it is now said that the claim is not at all unverifiable, that part of what is meant is simply that one could not show competence in system I unless one were *capable* of mastering system II (i.e. learning to make the translations and inferences of system II), then this claim (or part of the claim) must be conceded as at least plausible; but the further claim that *actual* mastery of system I is *explained* by *potential* mastery of system II remains both unsupported and mysterious.

Here, then, is a profound and surely important difference between any explanation in general semantico-syntactical theory which, like our supposed adverbial account, applies pretty directly to the surface structure of our sentences, and any explanation which, like the Davidsonian account of action-sentences, appeals to an underlying structure differing more or less radically from the superficial grammatical form of the sentences in question. An explanation of the latter kind, it seems, has to face a certain kind of challenge, as to what exactly it is claiming and how these claims are verified; an explanation of the former kind, whatever other challenges it has to face, does not have to face just this kind of challenge. This is not

to say that such a challenge, when it has to be met, can never be met successfully. Nor is it to deny that our theoretical understanding of our grasp of the semantic-syntactic structure of sentences of a certain class may be assisted by the production of paraphrases, or more or less equivalent sentences, of a different grammatical structure, even when no claim that the latter make manifest the true or underlying structure of the former can be sustained.[2] Nevertheless the contrast I have drawn does carry weighty implications for those concerned with the systematic semantics of natural languages; concerned (I quote Davidson) to 'elicit in a perspicuous and general form the understanding of logical grammar we all have that constitutes (part of) our grasp of our native tongue'. It really diminishes the attractions of any programme, like the general Davidsonian programme, which is committed in advance to explaining our grasp of all truly structural semantic relations in terms of a very restricted set of underlying structures, viz., those of the predicate calculus. By the same token it encourages the use in our explanations of a wider range of (more specific) categories than those merely of individual name, individual variable and predicate; and of the ideas of kinds of combination over and above that of simple predication plus sentence-composition and quantification.

If this is truly the way to proceed, then it is futile to lament the fact. Of course it may be natural to do so, in so far as the logical grammar of the predicate calculus stands before us, clearly articulated, a model of clarity and intelligibility.[3] If we cast ourselves adrift from it, what guidelines have we except a vague sense of what categories and combinations are fundamental in our thinking and our discourse? But things are not quite as bad as this. We have checks on our vague sense of the appropriate in the degree of success we achieve in elaborating a plausible theory; and checks on plausibility which linguists and psychologists can combine to supply.

[2] Nor, of course, does the point in any way touch or impinge upon the activities of theorists of language who do not claim to contribute in any way to the explanation of our understanding of the structures of our languages. For instance, if you are simply concerned to draw up a set of classifications and rules which will generate the structures recognized in a given language, you may proceed in any way which you find most convenient and economical. Or if, like Quine, your interest is in producing structures which appeal by virtue of their clarity and economy, your concern with ordinary structures may go no further than the concern to produce, where you feel the need of them, intelligible alternatives which satisfy your ideals of clarity.

[3] Granted, that is, that we understand the 'basic combination' of predication—but do we?

But is it not after all possible that this doctrine of challenge—the challenge to the theory of underlying structure which the Davidsonian account seems to fail to meet—rests on a misunderstanding? If there is any possibility that this is so, then it is important to investigate that possibility. And I think it might be held that it *is* so.

Consider again one of our ways of formulating the claim to explain. It ran: it is *because* we understand our ordinary action-sentences as equivalent to *DS* sentences (with their well-understood semantics) that we have the general understanding we do have of the logical relations of our ordinary action-sentences. Now this formulation, it might be held, is ambiguous. It *can* be interpreted, as just now it was, as claiming that our understanding of our ordinary action-sentences depends on, and is explained by, our having knowledge or mastery, in some sense, of translation-rules relating *SS* to *DS* sentences etc.; and, so understood, it is at best unplausible, at worst totally mysterious. But it can be read quite differently. It might be read as implying rather that the difference between the formal arrangement of parts in an *SS* sentence and the formal arrangement of parts in a *DS* sentence is, in a sense, a quite superficial difference; somewhat as the difference between indicating which is the subject and which is the object of a transitive verb by word order, as in English, or by case-inflection, as in Latin, is a superficial difference. What is fundamental in the latter case is that, in any language containing two-place non-symmetrical predicates, there must be some provision for indicating the order of the two elements in an ordered pair. It does not matter what the provision is: we understand the related forms just so long as we understand them as doing just this. (Only philosophers, or logicians, would express the condition of our understanding the forms in this way; nevertheless this technical description is a perfectly correct general description of the condition of our understanding such forms.)

If this comparison holds good, it will be seen that there is a sense in which we cannot understand our *SS* sentences at all without understanding them as equivalent to *DS* sentences. Not that we need have dreamt of *DS* sentences: the sense is closer to that in which a man might be said not to understand 'Brutus is wiser than Caesar' unless he understood it as equivalent to 'Caesare Brutus sapientior'. And the point will be that to understand the logical grammar of *SS* sentences is to see their actual formal arrangements as indicating

certain combinations of semantic or meaning-elements, precisely those combinations of precisely those elements which are indicated, by means of differential formal arrangements, in the corresponding *DS* sentences. Our ordinary language-speaker satisfies this condition *directly*: we don't have to credit him with mastery of translation-rules etc. (with mastery of system II) any more than we have to credit the man who understands 'Brutus is wiser than Caesar' with the ability to write out the equivalent in the style of logical notation, or in Latin.

SS sentences, then, and corresponding or equivalent *DS* sentences are alike in indicating, by different formal arrangements in each case, precisely the same combinations of precisely the same elements. Moreover they do so—and this is how the challenge is avoided—equally directly in each case, though not equally perspicuously. The difference between an *SS* sentence and its *DS* equivalent—and this is also the reason for bringing *DS* sentences into the picture at all—is that the elements in question and their modes of combination are simply *more clearly represented* by the formal arrangements employed in a *DS* sentence. For practical purposes the differences do not matter. Each way of indicating what elements are combined in what way may be as good as the other, and indeed what is in one sense the less clear way may be the better, e.g. the more economical of breath. But for theoretical purposes the *DS* form is preferable for the reason just given. By looking at the *DS* sentences we can see straight off how the semantics, the logical grammar, of our action-sentences is already taken care of in the predicate calculus. This is not obvious from looking at the ordinary forms, though in fact it *is* taken care of in just the same way.

(Now there is no danger of misunderstanding, we can reintroduce system II, translation-rules and all. We do not have to think of this as something that the ordinary speaker has mastered in any ordinary sense; or in any extraordinary sense either. It is just a devious way, useful for theoretical purposes, of representing the fact that he directly understands his *SS* sentences as indicating just those combinations of just those elements which they do, in their theoretically unperspicuous way, indicate.)

I think this defence or reinterpretation successfully meets the challenge it has so far been confronted with in the sense that the theory as now presented is not exposed to that challenge. But it is exposed to another. By hypothesis, we have available an alternative

account (the Adverbial) of the elements and modes of combination involved, according to which these elements and combinations are not at all unperspicuously represented by the formal arrangements of *SS* sentences as they stand. And why, indeed, should they be? True, the Adverbial Account has something to explain: viz., the possibility of the equivalent, structurally different, *DS* forms. This problem can be solved with the help of a theory of nominalization and attendant predication: a theory which squares with our unreflective sense that the forms which figure in *DS* sentences are grammatically derivative forms. The Davidsonian account, on the other hand, on its present interpretation, has what looks like a much less tractable problem to face: the problem of explaining the striking lack of perspicuousness of our ordinary forms of action-sentences. One who holds the Davidsonian position dogmatically can perhaps afford to view this problem fairly lightly: it exists, but it need not worry us overmuch. But for one who holds the position non-dogmatically, who is prepared to envisage the possibility of a theory of structural semantics which is not confined *a priori* within these narrow limits, there must seem to be a serious worry here.

But by now another and uneasy impression may begin to gain ground. It may begin to seem as if the whole issue is unreal. For it may begin to seem that we could finally settle it only if there were something to appeal to, extraneous to the forms of language itself, to decide what the basic categories of semantic element and modes of their combination were. It seems almost as if we wanted to ask: *forms of language*—natural or artificial—*apart*, is the underlying semantic element expressed by 'kiss' (or 'kill' or 'kick') really apt for entry into predicative combinations as a two-place predicate (of agents and objects) or as a three-place predicate (of actions, agents and objects) or as a one-place predicate (of actions) usually in conjunction with a three-place predicate (of actions, agents and objects)? And this may seem absurd.

But the situation is not really so bad; for two reasons.

(1) The general question regarding semantic categories and modes of combination is this: given a natural language as we have it—and our understanding of it—what is the simplest *realistic* theory of (a) semantic categories and modes of combination, and (b) formal arrangements for expressing the latter, which will cover the facts? It is not really a matter of 'forms of language apart'. Forms of language as we find them must, of course, be considered when we assess our

theories for plausibility, simplicity, realism. It is precisely here that the Davidsonian account encounters difficulties, encounters one or another of the challenges above-mentioned.

(2) The second reason is that it *is* possible to bring extra-syntactic considerations, considerations from outside the philosophy of language, from general philosophy, to bear on the question. Davidson's own arguments relating to the philosophy of action, though easily rebutted, are a case in point. And arguments can be produced on the other side. Thus, it could be argued that what underlies the linguistic grammatical fact that actions and events generally (when they are happenings to things) normally appear as individuals as the result of nominalization is the point that actions and events suffer in general from identity-dependence on substances; and that what underlie this in turn are more general facts about our existence in, orientation in and knowledge of, an objective world.

VIII

Semantic Structure and Logical Form*

GARETH EVANS

THE validity of some inferences is to be explained by reference to the meanings of the particular expressions occurring in them, while that of other inferences is due, rather, to the way in which the sentences are constructed out of their parts. The inference from 'John knows that snow is white' to 'Snow is white' is given as an example of the first type of inference; for it is said to be explained by providing an analysis of the semantical primitive 'knows'. The inferences from 'John ran breathlessly' to 'John ran' and from 'John is a large man' to 'John is a man' may, tentatively, be taken to be examples of the second type.

The distinction I have gestured towards is not without its intuitive appeal, and for many years philosophers have been trying to provide a basis for it in harmony with what they took to be its importance. The debate centred upon, and eventually ran aground upon, the problem of identifying a set of expressions as the logical constants. For if we are determined to say that the inference from ⌜*P* and *Q*⌝ to *P* is valid in virtue of structure, then the distinction between it and the detachment inference with 'knows' must reside in some difference between 'knows' and 'and'.

Donald Davidson has given the notion of structurally valid inference new life and importance by locating it within a highly suggestive theory of semantic theories. In his writings there appears to be support both for the conviction that there is an important difference between the two types of inference, and also for the view that, when an inference has been shown to be structurally valid, a

* An earlier version of this paper was read at a weekend conference on 'Language and Meaning' at Cumberland Lodge, in November 1973. I would like to thank the following for their help and encouragement: D. Davidson, D. Isaacson, J. H. McDowell and P. F. Strawson. Special thanks are due to B. Taylor for help with both technical and theoretical problems.

deeper explanation of its validity will have been provided. He writes concerning one inference:

> By saying exactly what the role of [a certain recurrent element] is and what the roles of the other significant features of the sentence are, we will have a deep explanation of why one sentence entails the other; an explanation that draws upon a systematic account of how the meaning of each sentence is a function of its structure[1].

My interest in the notion of structurally valid inference was awakened by these writings of Davidson, and like him I am ambitious to make precise that distinction which underlies the intuitions with which we began in such a way as would support the claim that, by showing an inference to be structurally valid, we thereby provide a deep explanation of its validity.

In the first part of this paper I shall examine the account of structurally valid inference which Davidson's writings suggest and try to indicate why I think that we have not there reached a finally satisfactory account of the matter. In the second part of the paper I shall sketch another approach to the idea with which I began. Finally from the vantage point provided by the sketch I shall look briefly at some recent and not so recent proposals concerning semantic structure.

I

We can distinguish two kinds of definition or explication in semantics which I shall label 'immanent' and 'transcendent'.

One provides an immanent definition of some semantical term *W* if one does not define it absolutely but rather defines the notion ⌜*e* is *W* according to theory T⌝. One provides a transcendent definition when the definition contains no such relativity to a theory; when one says, rather, what a theory *ought* to treat as *W*.

Our pre-systematic theorizing about semantics has provided us with a set of terms not all of which may suitably be provided with transcendent definitions. Although some theories will be right to treat an expression *e* as *W* (for such a term), and some wrong, this will be because some theories are right or wrong overall. In so far as empirical considerations bear upon the correctness of the claim that an expression is *W*, they bear globally upon the theory according to which it is *W*, and cannot be brought into any more direct relation

[1] D. Davidson, 'Action and Reaction', *Inquiry* xiii (1970), 144.

with that feature of the internal constitution of the theory in virtue of which it may be said to be treating *e* as *W*.

An example of such a semantical term might be 'is a designator'. If there is a theory of meaning, satisfying the global constraints upon such theories, which treats some expression *e* as a designator, and another such theory which does not, there is, perhaps, no sense to the question 'Is *e* really a designator?' because, perhaps, no evidence can additionally be brought to bear upon it.

However, this is not always the case. Consider the notion '*e* is (semantically) composite'. If the theories with which we are concerned are recursive definitions of truth, an immanent definition of this notion is readily obtainable:

> *e* is semantically composite according to T iff
> (i) *e* is a semantical unit according to T and
> (ii) there is no base or recursive axiom assigning *e* a semantical property in T.

But we should not rest content with such an immanent definition, since there is a consideration which bears directly upon the correctness of a theory's decision as to whether to treat an expression as semantically composite. It is this. Are the speakers of the language for which T is a semantical theory capable of understanding new expressions constructed in the way *e* is constructed, upon the basis of their understanding of the (syntactic) parts of those expressions? This consideration provides materials for the construction of a transcendent definition of the notion '*e* is semantically composite'.

Clearly, a question which we must constantly keep in mind is whether the notion of structurally valid inference admits of a transcendent definition; whether there are considerations which bear directly upon the correctness of decisions concerning the structural validity of inferences.

I shall not attempt to answer this question now. My present concern is with the way in which Davidson has made the notion of structural validity precise. It seems evident that he has provided an immanent definition, which I shall now try to make explicit.

I shall assume familiarity with Davidson's conception of a theory of meaning as a theory of truth. It seems clear from his work that a semantic theory for any natural language would in his view have the following two tiers:

(1) a theory of truth, conforming to Tarski's Convention T, for

a suitably chosen, regimented, but still interpreted, language, which will probably be, in large part, a fragment of the natural language, but could be a constructed language;

(2) a set of translation rules mapping any sentence of the natural language not provided with truth conditions at level (1) on to a sentence for which truth is defined directly.

Showing an inference to be structurally valid has a slightly different significance when the sentences concerned are in the fragment for which truth is directly defined and when they are not. I shall consider these in turn, starting with the fundamental case of sentences for which truth is directly defined.

Davidson writes: 'there is no giving the truth conditions of all sentences without showing that some sentences are logical consequences of others'.[2] This is explained as follows: 'A truth definition does not distinguish between analytic sentences and others except for sentences which owe their truth to the presence alone of the constants which give the theory its grip on structure.'[3] In a later paper he expands this idea: 'but it will be evident from a theory of truth that certain sentences are true solely on the basis of the properties assigned to the logical constants. The logical constants may be identified as those iterative features of the language which require a recursive clause (not in the basis) in the definition of truth or satisfaction.' He continues, in an explicit acknowledgement of the immanence of the definition: 'Logical form, on this account, will of course be relative to the choice of a metalanguage (with its logic) and a theory of truth'.[4]

Let us say that the conditional ⌜If S_1 is true, . . ., and S_{n-1} is true, then S_n is true⌝ is the *validating conditional* of the inference $S_1 \ldots S_{n-1} \vdash S_n$. I think Davidson's idea is that an inference is structurally valid according to a theory T if and only if its validating conditional is a *semantic* consequence of the theory's recursive clauses.

Thus to take a perhaps excessively simple case, a theory of truth which has the clause

for any sentences S and S', $S^\frown$'and'$^\frown S'$ is true if and only if S is true and S' is true

[2] D. Davidson, 'Semantics for Natural Languages' in *Linguaggi nella Società e nella Tecnica* (Edizioni di comunità, Milan, 1970), pp. 184–5.

[3] D. Davidson, 'Truth and Meaning', *Synthese* xvii (1967), 318.

[4] D. Davidson, 'In Defense of Convention T', in H. Leblanc (ed.), *Truth Syntax and Modality* (North-Holland, Amsterdam, 1973), p. 81. This way of identifying the logical constants is also to be found in M.A.E. Dummett, *Frege* (Duckworth, London, 1973), p. 22.

treats 'and' as a logical constant and attributes to it the semantic property of forming truths when and only when conjoining truths. It is a (semantic) consequence of this characterization, independent of the characterization of elements given in the base clauses, that if $\ulcorner P$ and $Q\urcorner$ is true, then P is true. The theory thus treats the inference $\ulcorner P$ and $Q\urcorner \vdash P$ as a structural inference.

However, it appears possible to treat a great many expressions which are not typically regarded as logical constants in recursive clauses of the truth definition. (I ignore the fact that, on this view, the standard semantic treatment of identity shows it not to be a logical constant.) In particular, such a treatment appears possible for an attributive adjective, such as 'large'. The full details are given in the appendix, but the leading idea would be to have a clause in the definition of satisfaction along the lines of:

> for all (possibly complex) monadic predicates ϕ, a satisfies 'large'$\frown\phi$ if and only if a is a large satisfier of ϕ.

Such treatment takes seriously the grammatical status of 'large' as a predicate modifier. We will of course need some deductive machinery allowing for substitution within the scope of the metalinguistic modifier 'large', if the semantical material introduced into the right-hand side is to be eliminated and a homophonic biconditional thus to be derived. But an obviously valid rule permitting merely the substitution of predicates which are provably equivalent in the metalanguage will suffice.

Then, such a theory will have shown the inference from '*X* is a large man' to '*X* is a man' to be formally valid. And if the theory were to treat 'small' in a parallel fashion, with *its* recursive clause, the same will hold for the inference from '*X* is a large man' to '*X* is not a small man', since it would be a semantic consequence of the two axioms taken together with the axiom for 'not' that if an object satisfies 'large man' it also satisfies 'not a small man'.

I am not claiming that this is an admirable semantical proposal. The point of the example is to cast doubt upon the idea that we have here captured the basis of the distinction with which we started, even in its application to those cases (e.g. the truth-functional connectives and the quantifiers) for which the background theory is more orthodox. For we were surely encouraged to entertain hopes that a theory which showed an inference to be structurally valid would provide us with a kind of explanation of its validity which would *contrast* with

those in which final appeal is made to the inferential properties of particular expressions. And the conviction that the recursive clause for 'large' provides us with no insight into why the detachment inference is valid is surely reinforced by the observation that an entirely parallel recursive treatment will suffice for such apparently heterogeneous modifiers as 'good' and 'breathlessly', and for 'fake', which does not even sustain the inference.

If you feel like saying that you have as yet no idea of what kind of semantic role 'large' is supposed to be playing in the recursive clause of the metalanguage, what kind of function from what kinds of elements to what kinds of elements it introduces, I must ask you to be patient in the knowledge that the drift of the paper is on your side. But you should also realize that you seem to be appealing to semantic notions richer than any Davidson appeals to in characterizing the notion of structurally valid inference.

I have interpreted Davidson's talk of a theory's *entailing* a validating conditional in terms of semantic consequence. But this is to render uninterpretable his own observation that what inferences count as structural will be relative to the *logic* of the metalanguage. I adopted this interpretation because to introduce mention of the deductive apparatus of the metalanguage simply invites the question: 'How much is relevant to determinations of structural validity?' In general, the inference pattern in the metalanguage which is necessary for proving the validating conditional with respect to a certain object-language pattern of inference is that very same pattern of inference. If the logic of the metalanguage contains the detachment inference for the metalinguistic modifier 'large' we can validate the detachment inference in the object language, if not, not.

Perhaps there is a limit upon metalinguistic logic which would save the notion of structurally valid inference, interpreted in terms of what consequences are provable from the axioms, from free-wheeling entirely. Count as logic for deducing the relevant validating conditionals just the logic the theory requires for deriving its T-sentence theorems.

Certainly this is far from arbitrary, but the results are meagre, since very little logic is necessary. It is known that an adequate theory of truth for a first-order language susceptible of a classical interpretation can be constructed in a metalanguage whose logic is intuitionistic, and so, on this account, not all classically valid inference patterns will be structural. Proof of the T-sentences requires,

on the whole, substitution inferences; it is certain that, provided the biconditional is undefined, neither the detachment inference with 'and', nor that with 'large', will be required for such proofs.

Let us now turn to the other way in which an inference may, on Davidson's view, be shown to be formally valid; when the sentences concerned do not have their truth conditions defined directly by the theory of truth, but are mapped on to sentences which do. If $F(S)$ is the sentence in the fragment on to which S is mapped by the translation rules, then $S_1 \ldots S_{n-1}$ formally entail S_n iff $F(S_1) \ldots F(S_{n-1})$ formally entail $F(S_n)$.

Since this manoeuvre rests upon the idea of formally valid inference we have discussed it clearly inherits any difficulties we were able to point to in that idea. But there are additional questions and a slightly new perspective.

I do not think Davidson would want to claim that the methodology underlying this section of the semantic theory has been entirely worked out. What considerations should guide us in our choice of the background language which is to provide the kernel? Save for eschewing any commitment to first-order languages, little has been said about this. Does the chosen fragment even have to be a fragment of any natural language; and if not, what defence can be provided for, or significance attached to, the requirement that the semantics for a natural language be statable as a homophonic truth theory? Is the relation between S and $F(S)$ to be incorporated into the idea of a semantic theory as having something to do with how speakers understand a natural language, and if so, how?

However our immediate task is to consider the impact the construction of this additional tier of our theory has upon the notion of formally valid inference. It appears at first that it must reinforce the impression of arbitrariness which we brought away from our consideration of the leading idea.

For consider again the sentence 'John is a large man'. If we decide that our fragment is to be first-order, and thus without predicate modifiers, it appears that we have the choice of mapping our sentence either on to the sentence

Large-for (John, $\{y\colon \text{Man}(y)\}$)

or on to the sentence

Large-for* (John, $\{y\colon \text{Man}(y)\}$) & John $\in \{y\colon \text{Man}(y)\}$.[5]

[5] This latter is a suggestion found in S. C. Wheeler, 'Attributives and their Modifiers', *Nous* vi (1972), 310.

If we adopt the first we determine that the detachment inference is to be accounted for by the analysis of the primitive relation 'Large-for', while if we adopt the second, using the primitive relation 'Large-for*', different in being satisfiable by objects and sets of which those objects are not members, the inference will be formally valid in virtue of the presence of the logical constant '&'. We may well wonder what is to stop someone adding ⌜. . . & *p*⌝ on to whatever translation his colleague provided for ⌜*X* knows that *p*⌝, claiming to show thereby that the detachment inference with 'know' is formally valid.

However, I think a deeper and more sympathetic reading of Davidson's ideas would reveal that at least *this* charge of arbitrariness is unfair. Davidson writes: ' . . . we must uncover enough structure to make it possible to state, for an arbitrary sentence, how its meaning depends upon its structure . . .'[6] and the suggested continuation is ' . . . and no more'. In 'On Saying That' he writes: 'For the purposes of the present paper, however, we can cleave to the most austere interpretation of logical consequence and logical form, those that are forced upon us when we give a theory of truth'.[7] We can discern the following plan. In order to provide for the sentence 'John is a white protestant American' a suitable sentence of, say, a first-order fragment with only a finite number of semantical primitives, we *have to* uncover a conjunctive structure. But the addition ⌜. . . & *p*⌝ adds nothing to the enterprise of providing a suitable translation for ⌜*X* knows that *p*⌝, nor, incidentally, does the addition of the conjunct '. . . & John $\in \{y\colon \text{Man}(y)\}$'. The only way in which we can incorporate ⌜John stopped ϕ-ing at *t*⌝ into a fragment with a finite number of semantical primitives (given that it is to contain no expression syntactically parallel to 'stopped') is to map it on to a sentence which contains ϕ occurring in its basic predicative role. Perhaps the only way to do that is to uncover the structure ⌜John ϕ-ed up to *t* and after *t* John did not ϕ⌝. If and only if this is the situation, we shall have shown that the inference from ⌜John stopped ϕ-ing at *t*⌝ to ⌜John ϕ-ed before *t*⌝ is a formally valid one.

This certainly provides us with a far from arbitrary account of what counts as revealing form and what as philosophical analysis. But there are still some grounds for reservation as to whether we

6 D. Davidson, 'The Logical Form of Action Sentences', in N. Rescher (ed.), *The Logic of Decision and Action* (University of Pittsburgh Press, Pittsburgh, 1967), p. 82.

7 D. Davidson, 'On Saying That', in D. Davidson and J. Hintikka (eds.), *Words and Objections* (D. Reidel, Dordrecht, 1969), pp. 160–1.

have provided a finally satisfactory foundation for that distinction with whose allure we began.

First: it is not wholly nugatory to point to the fact that upon this conception the inference from 'John is a large man' to 'John is a man' will almost certainly not count as formally valid.

The second ground I have already mentioned. It is clear that what inferences come out as formally valid will vary radically, depending upon which language is used as the canonical fragment, and this imports an arbitrariness we might feel misplaced in a wholly explanatory account of the matter. Briefly, we miss transcendence.

Finally, and more seriously: it appears that the constraint upon how much structure to uncover will not, without considerable supplementation, achieve the intended results.

Consider the two radically different kinds of attributive adjectives exemplified by 'large' and 'good'. 'Large'-type attributives sustain all the inferences 'good'-type attributives sustain, although the former in addition sustain coextensive predicate substitution. Consequently, it is difficult to see why the general type of translation provided for 'good' will not also serve for 'large'. Suppose, merely for illustration, that we discerned a reference to the attribute 'being a man' in the sentence 'X is a good man', thus

$$\text{Good-in}\ (X, \lambda y\ [\text{Man}(y)]).$$

This would certainly also be a type of structure that would work for 'large'. From the point of view of merely being able to generate the T-sentences, the incorporation of reference to a set in the translation provided for the latter attributive was as gratuitous as the incorporation of the additional conjunct.

This difficulty is quite general. Provided we have a scheme for the suitable translation of what are inferentially the weakest members of a certain grammatical category, we seem to be enjoined to run that scheme quite generally, treating the inferences which the inferentially stronger members sustain as being consequences of their analysis. It is obvious that the maxim 'Translate so as to maximize formally valid inferences' simply sends us back to wreck upon the shore of the superfluous conjuncts.

It would be foolish to hold that no more refined criterion could be forthcoming, but I find it difficult to believe that it can be drafted without drawing upon the slightly richer conception of semantics which I shall develop in the next section. Before proceeding to that,

I should like to draw the comments I have been making together by putting forward a more general observation.

Although Davidson's main conception of formally valid inference drew its inspiration from wholly novel considerations, it rests squarely within that tradition which distinguishes formally valid inferences as those which depend upon the presence of certain favoured words, the logical constants. The novelty lay in two points. First: in the idea that those words would receive a special treatment in any semantic theory through being recursive elements. Second, and, of course, connected, was the stress placed upon a profoundly important *necessary* condition for the inference from $\Sigma(e)$ to $\Sigma'(e)$ to be formally valid. This was the condition that e should be shown to occur as a semantical unit in both $\Sigma(e)$ and $\Sigma'(e)$. Davidson was at pains to point out that, although a syntactic transformation can easily be made to be sensitive to the occurrences of e in $\Sigma(e)$ and $\Sigma'(e)$, nevertheless unless e can be shown to occur there semantically, by some theory of truth, there will be no hope of showing that the transformation is valid, i.e. generally truth-preserving. For example, there is no difficulty whatever in writing a syntactic rule of inference which captures the inference pattern exemplified by

> *X* is a tall man
> *Y* is taller than *X*
> *Y* is a man
>
> ---
>
> Therefore *Y* is a tall man

But in the absence of a semantic theory which discerns 'tall' in 'taller than' (presumably by the construction of a recursive clause for the element '. . . er than'), we will have no hope of proving that each of the infinite number of inferences licensed by the syntactic rule is valid.

But, important though this second idea is, it does only provide us with a necessary condition. For even when a theory of truth has shown e to occur in $\Sigma(e)$, there is the additional question: 'Is the mode of containment $\Sigma(\ \ )$ by itself of a kind that warrants certain inferences, or are they rather due to certain special features of the particular constituents exemplifying that mode of containment?'

In addressing ourselves to that question, we have been following Davidson, and taking the way a theory of truth validates the inference from $\ulcorner P$ and $Q\urcorner$ to P as the model of the way in which a semantic

theory shows an inference to be structurally valid. But following that model with 'large' provided us with the very reverse of that explanation of which our original intuition seemed to encourage the expectation. The possibility that suggests itself is that this model is wrong. Perhaps there is a notion of structurally valid inference, for which we have been groping, which does not comprehend inferences which rely upon the logical constants, and which thus cannot be married with the traditional notion of logical validity without disappearing. If there is such a different conception, whatever its merits and whether or not anyone else has been groping for it, we can only benefit by having it distinguished from its more traditional rival. It is this that I attempt in the next section.

II

Let us return to the intuition about structurally valid inferences with which we began. Surely the natural way of defending the claim that the inference from ⌜John knows that *p*⌝ to *p* is not structurally valid would not mention the logical constants at all, but would rather run as follows: the inference cannot be a matter of structure, since the sentence ⌜John believes that *p*⌝ has precisely the same semantic structure as, is composed in exactly the same way out of the same types of semantic elements as, the sentence ⌜John knows that *p*⌝, and yet it does not sustain the inference.

We have here the idea of a contrast between inferences whose validity depends merely upon the *kind* of semantic elements out of which a sentence is constructed, and its manner of construction, on the one hand, and inferences whose validity depends upon the special variation a particular semantic element is playing upon the theme all expressions of its kind must play, on the other. Can we make anything of this idea?

The central task, if we are to make anything of it, will be to provide a way of telling when two expressions are of the same semantic category, and our hopes of doing this might appear rather dim. For we seem to be confronted with the following dilemma. If we are allowed to consider all the valid inferences involving some expression in determining the kind of semantic contribution it makes, there is nothing to stop us inventing a category of *factive attitudinatives*, unified in being like 'know' and sustaining the detachment inference. If we are not allowed to take all inferences into account, we will have

to decide upon a partition amongst inferences as a preliminary to an enterprise whose object was the construction of just such a partition.

What makes a parallel problem in the taxonomy of natural kinds tractable is the conception of kinds as being differentiated by underlying structures from which the characteristics we use in classification may be regarded as flowing. To solve our problem for semantic kinds we need to find room for a parallel conception of something from which an expression's inferential properties may be regarded as flowing.

Just such a conception is provided by what I shall call an *interpretational semantics*. A semantic theory of that type specifies, for each kind of semantic expression, an entity—a set, a truth value, a function from sets to truth values, or whatever—which may appropriately be assigned to members of that kind upon an arbitrary interpretation of the language. We can regard the specification of the kind of assignment as a specification of the underlying real essence which a word has in common with many other words, and of which the validity of certain inferences involving it is a consequence. These will be the structurally valid inferences; inferences which are truth-preserving no matter how we permute assignments within the limits laid down as appropriate for members of that category.

Thus, to take a central but simple case, we justify the intuition that there is a unitary semantic category of *n*-place predicates, and provide a general characterization of their role, by stating that upon any admissible interpretation of the language each *n*-place predicate must be assigned a set of *n*-tuples of the domain, and by providing an adequate definition of truth upon an arbitrary interpretation using assignments of that type.

A slightly less obvious case is the following. We can justify the belief that there is a semantic category to which 'large', 'tall', 'expensive' and 'heavy' all belong (the extensional attributive adjectives), by showing that there is an assignment which may suitably be made to each (a function from sets to subsets of those sets, possibly satisfying certain additional conditions), and which provides the basis for an adequate definition of truth upon an interpretation. It is again clear that certain inferential features will flow from this underlying real essence. We see why the detachment inference is valid, why substitution of coextensive predicates within the scope of such adjectives is valid, and why commuting the adjectives will not in general be valid.

The metaphor of underlying essence suggests that we are attempting to *explain* why the expression has certain inferential properties, but is there any more justification in speaking of explanation here than there was when validation of the inference followed merely from the presence of the parallel inference in the metalanguage? Are we not merely restating, in set-theoretical terms, the various inferences we are concerned to explain?

I think this charge can be resisted. A certain, syntactically identified, pattern of inferential behaviour is a feature which can and does flow from many different underlying constitutions. For example, both standard adverbs—like 'breathlessly'—and intensional attributives—like 'good' in 'good (as a) king'—sustain a parallel detachment inference; yet it is clear that the 'restatement' we are supposed to have provided is inappropriate for both kinds of expressions. Neither can be seen as involving functions from sets to subsets of those sets. Davidson can be seen as providing a quite different explanation for the detachment inference in the case of adverbs (making assignments of sets of events to adverbs, and sets of $n + 1$-tuples, of events and n-tuples of objects, to verbs). No one yet knows how to provide an adequate explanation of the detachment inference for 'good'.

The requirement that one provide an account of an expression's contribution by specifying an appropriate kind of assignment is not an easy one to meet, and certainly puts a quite different complexion upon the taxonomic problem. Some groupings of expressions upon the basis of shared inferential behaviour will be simply impossible, for no coherent kind of assignment to the members of the heterogeneous class which results will be available. While we are merely concerned with grouping expressions together in a way which imposes the best organization upon their inferential behaviour, we are bound to feel the force of a certain arbitrariness since it appears certain that an equally good scheme which organizes the data in another way can always be put together. Locating the taxonomic problem in the context of an interpretational semantics puts an end to this free-wheeling. What we expect, then, is the provision of the most determinate and yet economical statement of the kind of semantic contribution made by any expression of a given type, thereby making structurally valid as many inferences as possible. One hopes that this will not involve one restriction upon the assignment for every inference validated; we aim at the sort of illumination that can come from an economical axiomatization of the behaviour of

groups of expressions. Then we can say: '*This* is the kind of expression *e* is, and that is why these inferences are valid.'

But this may simply be to raise another, deeper problem. I have spoken of making structurally valid as many inferences as possible. Does this not raise the old difficulty? For will we not be obliged to subdivide the class of attitudinatives, and discover a category of factive attitudinatives, the assignment to which differs from the assignment to their non-factive brothers solely in requiring the contained sentence to be true?

Now that we are working within the context of an interpretational semantics, I think we can quiet this worry. We should regard our construction of, and assignments to, categories in the following spirit: if two expressions behave in the same way but are in different categories, this is a lost generalization. If we regard the enterprise in this light, we will construct a new category out of an older and more comprehensive category only when we can make an assignment to members of the new category which provides a *different* explanation for the behaviour which members of the new category had in common with the old, the provision of which explanation would show that the apparent unity in the behaviour of members of the old category was deceptive, concealing deep differences of functioning. Only in this case will the discovery of a new category not lose us a significant generalization. By imposing this requirement we make the notion of structural validity transcendent.

Thus, to recognize a category of factive attitudinatives would require the provision of a different explanation, for its members, of the inferential properties they share with words like 'believe'; an explanation which would unify these properties with the detachment inference. It is by no means out of the question that just such an explanation ought to be provided. Zeno Vendler has provided arguments which cast doubt upon the apparent similarity of 'knows' and 'believes',[8] while the causal theory of knowledge provides us with a rationale for treating the contained sentence as designating a state of affairs with which the knower is stated to have come into epistemological contact. If we did so treat the contained sentence, this would be to treat 'know' like 'enjoy' in one of its uses, as introducing a function from states of affairs and persons to truth values. This is to provide an explanation of the detachment inference. And

[8] 'On What One Knows', in Z. Vendler, *Res Cogitans* (Cornell University Press, Ithaca, 1972), p. 89.

provided the identity conditions of states of affairs are sufficiently fine-grained, the explanation unifies that inference with the expression's other inferential properties, for example, its opacity.

If we are to preserve the promise in the notion of semantic structure, we have to steer between two courses. We must resist saying, with Montague, that no detachment inference with a predicate modifier is structurally valid, on the ground that the expression 'fake' must be regarded as belonging in that category.[9] But equally we must not allow the freedom to subdivide and form new categories to lead to that proliferation of categories which threatens our interest in the notion. We can steer this middle course only if we require that an appropriate assignment be provided for each category, and illuminatingly different assignments be provided for different categories.

The construction of an interpretational semantics for a natural language will doubtless follow a rather different course from that taken in the construction of such theories for artificial languages, not merely in the heterogeneity of entities assigned. In the first place, there is no reason for the different interpretations to have different domains. Secondly, instead of a single unsorted domain, it will be convenient to have a domain divided into fundamental sorts of objects: places, times, material objects, animate objects, events . . . (This would enable us to describe the admissible assignment to an action verb, e.g., as 'a set of pairs of animate objects and times'.) Fundamental arguments can be expected on the question of how many, and which, sorts of objects we need, and on which we ought to take as primitive and which we can define. Is the sort of object, *Events*, fundamental or can it be defined? Do we need *Facts*, or *States of affairs*, and if so can they be defined?

Argument can also be expected upon how we are to extend the programme to intensional areas of a natural language—how we are to represent meaning-sensitive functions. Perhaps by associating with each semantical primitive an intension and recursively defining intensions for complex expressions. But perhaps not.

All these are interesting, indeed fundamental, questions, but from the lofty viewpoint I have adopted in this paper, matters of detail. What is important is that we should have a general picture of the enterprise, and that it should be recognizable as a representation of

[9] R. Montague, 'English as a Formal Language', in *Linguaggi nella Societá e nella Tecnica*, pp. 212–4.

at least part of what philosophers have been aiming at in their exploration of the semantic structure of sentences of natural languages. They are seen to have been asking questions like: 'What kind of element is this? Does it introduce a class?' (cf. Davidson's remark 'Intentional actions are not a class of actions'[10]), 'Can vague predicates introduce classes?', 'If what this expression introduces is a function, what are its inputs and outputs?'

It seemed that questions of this kind were not necessarily answered by the construction of a truth theory (except in a mildly perverse way, when the background language is taken to be first-order). More interestingly, the answers have little to do with the logical constants.

How do standard inferences involving the logical constants fare? In any interpretational semantics for English the propositional connectives, 'not', 'and', 'or', and so on, would surely fall into a common semantic category, to which, on the classical conception, there would be assigned functions from truth values to truth values. In the definition of satisfaction upon an arbitrary interpretation, *I*, we would have a clause for any sentence involving any *n*-ary connective θ (possibly joining open sentences), and for any infinite sequence *s*:

$$\text{Sats}_I\,(s, \theta\,(S_1 \ldots S_n)) \leftrightarrow \text{Assig}_I\,(\theta)\,[\langle \text{Val}_I\,(s, S_1) \ldots \text{Val}_I\,(s, S_n)\rangle] = \text{T}$$

where

$$\text{Val}_I\,(s, S_1) = \text{T} \leftrightarrow \text{Sats}_I\,(s, S_1).$$

Consequently, with the exception of inferences involving substitution of sentences with the same truth value, none of the standard inferences involving the sentential connectives is structurally valid. Briefly, the sentences ⌜*P* and *Q*⌝ and ⌜*P* or *Q*⌝ have the same semantic structure; the former's entailing *P* is due to the special variation the word 'and' plays upon a theme it has in common with 'or'.[11]

In view of this, it is not surprising that we found the manoeuvrings necessary for validating the inference from ⌜*P* and *Q*⌝ to *P* an unilluminating model, and it is clear why, when we followed it with

10 'The Logical Form of Action Sentences', p. 94.

11 'One might surely have expected that if any pair of non-synonymous expressions exhibit non-difference of type or category, "or" and "and" would be one such pair and "all" and "some" another.' P. F. Strawson, 'Categories', in O. P. Wood and George Pitcher (eds.) *Ryle* (Macmillan, London, 1970), p. 184.

'large', the distinction we were trying to capture between structurally valid inferences and those requiring proper axioms petered out into nothing. To put the point succinctly, there *is* no deep explanation of why ⌜*P* and *Q*⌝ entails *P*.[12]

Quantifiers are more complicated but they too can be seen as falling into a single semantic category. There is work by Lindstrom and Mostowski on generalized quantifiers in which the characterization of the category is attempted.[13]

It is now time to deal with something I have left unclear up to this point. I spoke of the structural inferences as being those whose validity was due to the types of semantic element involved *and* the significance of their construction. What is meant by the semantic significance of a grammatical construction?

An interpretational semantics must not only provide appropriate assignments to expressions; it must also provide an adequate definition of truth upon an arbitrary interpretation making use of those assignments.[14] Each clause in that definition can be regarded as making explicit the significance of one kind of grammatical construction, and certain inferential consequences will follow from the significance thus characterized.

To understand this idea consider the following simple example. Suppose we have a language like English in that attributive adjectives can be stacked, yet unlike English in that from 'John is a strong tall man' it follows both that John is a strong man and also that John is a tall man, and the former sentence is entailed by these taken together. One way of capturing these facts is by making (to such attributive adjectives) the assignments we have earlier suggested (functions from sets to subsets), and writing the following clause in the definition of satisfaction upon an interpretation:

> Where *M*, *M′*... range over object-language attributive modifiers, ϕ over object-language monadic (possibly complex) predicates, and 'Var$_i$' designates the *i*th object-language variable, for any infinite sequence of elements *s*,

[12] It is worth observing that intuitionistic sentential connectives cannot be regarded as representing truth functions in any finite many-valued logic. See K. Gödel, 'Zum intuitionistischen Aussagenkalkül', *Ergebnisse eines mathematischen Kolloquiums*, iv, 1933, pp. 34–38.

[13] Per Lindstrom, 'First Order Predicate Logic with Generalized Quantifiers', *Theoria* xxxii (1966), A. Mostowski, 'On a Generalization of Quantifiers', *Fundamenta Mathematicae* lxiv (1957).

[14] What constitutes adequacy will be considered later, see pp. 217–18.

$$\text{Sats}_I\,(s,\, M\,(M'(\phi))^\frown\text{Var}_n) \leftrightarrow \text{Sats}_I\,(s,\, M\,(\phi)^\frown\text{Var}_n) \text{ and } \text{Sats}_I\,(s,\, M'(\phi)^\frown\text{Var}_n).$$

A consequence of this clause will be that upon the designated interpretation,[15] 'John is a large strong man' is true iff John is a large man and John is a strong man.

If what has gone before is correct, it would be a mistake to try to render explicit the semantical potential lodged in the construction of stacking modifiers by saying that our original sentence has the same semantic structure as some sentence containing the connective 'and'. For such a sentence achieves what is admittedly the same net effect by means of different semantic elements and different constructions.

Just as one can never dispense with rules of inference by enriching one's axioms (though a limited trade-off is possible) so, no matter how interlocking the assignments to interacting expressions are made, one can never obviate the need for *some* semantic potential to be lodged in the grammatical constructions—even if it is merely that concatenation signifies functional application.[16]

The need for the distinction between inferences whose validity is due to the semantic significance of grammatical constructions and those which depend upon the logical words would certainly evaporate if we could see our way to accepting Quine's suggestion[17] that the logical constants should be regarded as 'absorbed into the constructions' they signalize. But, as Quine recognizes, we lack a clear reason for distinguishing them in this way.

It is not part of the thesis of this paper that no satisfactorily transcendent account of the logical constants can be produced, nor, consequently, that there is no well defined notion of logical form, logical consequence, and logical validity. It is merely that there is another, deeper notion, of semantic structure and of structural validity, from which those notions should be distinguished.

Does it follow from what has gone before that we are only interested in relative truth—truth upon an interpretation (truth$_I$)—and not simple truth? Certainly not: no theory of meaning which fails to

[15] For an explanation of the notion of the designated interpretation see below, p. 217.

[16] As it does in the system put forward in D. K. Lewis, 'General Semantics', in D. Davidson and G. Harman (eds.), *Semantics of Natural Languages* (D. Reidel, Dordrecht, 1972), p. 169.

[17] W. V. Quine, *Philosophy of Logic* (Prentice-Hall, Englewood Cliffs, 1970), pp. 28–30.

state the actual truth conditions of sentences of a language is worthy of the name. But since an interpretational semantics will comprise a definition of 'true$_I$' there is a very natural way of modulating to truth by specifying, for each semantical primitive of the language, what assignment it is to receive on the designated interpretation, I^*, and thus enabling us to derive for each sentence of the language its truth$_{I^*}$ (= truth) conditions.[18] In other words, we require not merely that we are told what *kind* of function 'large' is, but *which* function of that kind it is. Thus we will expect the specification of I^* to include such clauses as

$$\text{Assig}_{I^*}(\text{'large'}) = \{\langle\alpha, \beta\rangle : a \in \beta \leftrightarrow \text{large } \hat{y}[y \in \alpha]a\};$$

i.e. on the designated interpretation 'large' is to be assigned that function from sets to sets such that an object is a member of the output set iff it is a large member of the input set.

When the whole weight of the notion of structurally valid inference was being placed upon them, we found clauses like these—clauses in which a term is used to state its own semantic contribution—threateningly trivial. But now that the structurally valid inferences are fixed without their help, they can play their part, for it is an essential one.

Such a modulation to absolute truth is not merely desirable, it is necessary. For it is only by testing consequences of this kind generated by an interpretational semantic theory that we can impose any criterion of adequacy upon such theories. The truth$_I$-conditions of a sentence will necessarily be stated in rich semantical and set-theoretical notation, and in that condition they are immune from empirical control. We must bring an interpretational semantics down to earth by insisting that it should meet just the constraints that Convention T imposes; that it generate for each sentence of the language under consideration a true sentence of the form

$$\ulcorner S \text{ is true}_{I^*} \text{ iff } p \urcorner$$

where p is a translation of the sentence S names.[19] This means *at*

[18] See Montague, op. cit., p. 211.

[19] Given what I have said about clauses in the definition of truth$_I$ stating, with the use of logical constants, the significance of grammatical constructions not containing such expressions, I cannot require homophonic truth$_I$*-biconditionals. How important a difference this is between myself and Davidson depends upon the view one takes of the significance of requiring a homophonic truth theory merely for the regimented fragment, and allowing sentences of the natural language to be mapped on to sentences of the fragment which are very different.

least that *p* should be no richer in conceptual content or ontology, and thus should contain no semantic terms not obviously present in the original.

To summarize, then, an *interpretational semantics for a language L* is a theory consisting of three main parts:

(i) a definition of an *admissible interpretation of L*, which proceeds, in part, by stating, for each grammatical category of semantical primitives of *L*, what constitutes an appropriate assignment to a member of that category;

(ii) a definition of *truth upon an arbitrary interpretation of L*;

(iii) a definition of the *intended or designated interpretation of L*, which identifies, for each semantical primitive of *L*, which of all the appropriate assignments it is to receive on the designated interpretation.

It is important to observe that we can now allow the deductive apparatus of the metalanguage in which we state the interpretational semantics to comprise any *complete* proof theory for expressions of that language, without the danger of trivializing the notion of structurally valid inferences.

Now let us say that a phrase-structure grammar, *G*, is adequate for an interpretational semantics of *L* iff it generates a structural description of every sentence of *L* such that:

(a) There is an effective procedure for determining, upon the basis of this description of any sentence *S*, which clauses of the definition of truth_I are to be used in deriving the truth_I conditions of *S*, and in what order. (This is needed to deal with scope.)

(b) Where a *penultimate non-terminal node* is a node directly dominating only a terminal node (i.e. a lexical item of *L*): at each *penultimate non-terminal node* of each tree generated by *G* is a symbol for a category an appropriate assignment to the members of which is given by the definition of an admissible interpretation of *L*.

Then we may say: two sentences have the same semantical structure relative to an interpretational semantics iff the grammar adequate to that semantics assigns them structural descriptions which agree up to all non-terminal nodes.

The effect of this definition is that two sentences have the same semantical structure iff they are composed out of elements of the same semantic categories in the same way—where 'composed in the same way' means that they will trace exactly parallel courses through the definition of truth_I in the generation of their truth_I conditions.

And finally let us say that an inference from $S_1 \ldots S_{n-1}$ to S_n is structurally valid iff S_n is true upon every admissible interpretation on which $S_1 \ldots S_n$ are true; or more strictly, for every interpretation, every sequence which satisfies $S_1 \ldots S_{n-1}$ upon that interpretation also satisfies S_n upon that interpretation.

III

A logically perfect language would have one-to-one correspondence between its semantic and syntactic categories. I see no reason to suppose that natural languages are logically perfect, at any level.[20] There can be a breakdown of the one-to-one correspondence in either direction. We may find it necessary to subdivide a syntactically unitary category, so that, for example, even if 'It is certain that . . .' and 'It is not the case that . . .' were everywhere substitutable *salva congruitate*, they could be members of different semantic categories. And equally we may find it convenient to make assignments of the same kind to expressions of different syntactic categories. Thus we might find it convenient to assign to an adverb and also an adjective a set of events (indeed, if they stand in some morphological relationship, we may even require that they be assigned the same set of events). We do not have to gerrymander the grammar to get the two expressions into the same syntactic position; we have room for the idea of one and the same semantic element's being realized by expressions of different syntactic categories, no one of which is basic in a transformational sense.

In addition, logical constants will appear only when they appear to appear. We leave the clauses in the theory of truth$_l$ to capture the semantic significance of the constructions.

These features taken together mean that the structures we regard as exhibiting semantic structure can be relatively close to object-language syntactic structures; close, that is, relative to some recent proposals concerning semantic structure. A good example is provided by Davidson's proposal that the semantic structure of 'John ran breathlessly' is that of 'There is an event *e* such that John ran *e* and *e* was breathless'.

Now there is no doubt that proposals of this kind have tended to mystify people. I quote James Cargile as a representative example:

[20] Here, it seems to me, I depart from D. K. Lewis (op. cit.).

First: we might think that this sentence ['Shem kicked Shaun'] consisted of two names and a two-place relation . . . But this is wrong! Wrong? Yes, wrong! Second: the sentence really is of a three-place relational form, with two names and an existential quantifier. An existential quantifier? Where is it?[21]

It is not difficult to make sense of proposals such as Davidson's from the standpoint of the theory we have been developing, if we regard the sentence which is claimed to exhibit the semantic structure of a natural-language sentence as doing two related things. First, it indicates to what semantic category an expression is to be regarded as belonging, by representing it by an expression in the new sentence which belongs to a grammatical category of a canonical syntax, the admissible assignments to which are taken to be well understood. Secondly, it makes explicit with logical constants the semantic significance of the grammatical constructions employed in the original sentence.

Thus, instead of saying that 'breathlessly' should be assigned a set of events, we say that it is *really* a predicate, and instead of saying that to 'runs' should be assigned a set of pairs of agents and events, we say that *really* it is a two-place predicate.

This is a perfectly natural way to proceed; indeed, there has been a long tradition of representing intuitions about semantic functioning as intuitions about syntactic position (in some, admittedly rather mysterious, level of syntax). For example, philosophers have said that 'John feels a pain' has the form 'John feels painfully' (the 'adverbial analysis'), that 'carelessly' is a sentential adverb, that 'before' is not a sentential connective, that 'exists' is not a predicate, that definite descriptions are not terms, and so on.[22] It was natural to present semantic proposals in this way since it represented, before the development of formal semantic theories, one way of registering one's intuition that two expressions did or did not belong to the same semantic category.

Thus I think we can understand proposals like Davidson's as involving much more than claims to mere logical equivalence or regimentation without being mystified by them. The theorist is representing in a favoured, logically perfect, notation the types of semantic element which figure in the original sentence, and represent-

[21] J. Cargile, 'Davidson's Notion of Logical Form', *Inquiry* xiii (1970), pp. 137–8.

[22] See, for example, G. Ryle's notion of 'adverbial verbs' (including 'hurry' and 'think') in 'Thinking and Reflecting', *Collected Papers*, vol. ii (Hutchinson, London, 1971), p. 467.

ing as explicitly as possible the significance of the construction which it exemplifies.

However, there is no need to make semantic proposals in this way; and if one is going to go for it one must be sure that one has a canonical syntax rich enough to accommodate all the types of semantic element one wishes to discover, and that one has an interpretational semantics for the language specified by the canonical syntax. It would seem preferable to short-circuit the canonical language, constructing an interpretational semantics for the natural language directly, where this is possible.

I said earlier that translation into a first-order language did force one to confront the right questions, but led one to answer them in a mildly perverse way. I want to end by explaining why I think that this is so.

We have put into the centre of the picture Frege's idea that some expressions can be regarded as introducing functions. This means that we are obliged to ask, concerning the function introduced by some expression like 'fake' or 'carelessly', 'What are its inputs and outputs?' Now if we translate such expressions into first-order languages, we will probably represent them as relational expressions whose terms designate objects of the type determined to be suitable as inputs. Thus instead of introducing a function from sets, 'large' becomes the relational expression 'large-for' holding between individuals and sets. In a way we register the extensionality of the function, but it is a different way.

Why is it perverse? The perversity lies in the fact that we attribute to the speakers of the language the ontological commitments which properly belong to the *theorist*. We are in fact no more justified in holding that the speakers' ontology encompasses sets, on the basis of the existence of expressions of theirs which introduce functions on sets, than we are in supposing that they require an ontology of truth values in order to have expressions for the truth functions. Delicacy on this issue will pay off when we come to consider intensional areas of language.

APPENDIX. Fragment of a homophonic truth theory for a regimented language containing extensional attributive adjectives as predicate modifiers.

The syntax is as for standard first-order theories save, in addition: where A is any one-place open sentence, $\hat{x}_i[A]$ is a one-place predicate abstract. A complex predicate of degree one is any one-place predicate abstract possibly preceded by one or more modifiers $M, M' \ldots$ If ϕ is a complex predicate of degree one, ϕx_j is a wff.

We let $a, b, \ldots$ be metalinguistic variables over objects, and $s, s', \ldots$ metalinguistic variables over infinite sequences, and we write '$s \underset{i}{\approx} s'$' for '$s$ differs from s' in at most the ith place'. We presuppose the standard two-place function * from infinite sequences and object-language variables to objects such that $s^*(x_i)$ = the ith member of s.

The recursive definition of the two-place relation of satisfaction ('Sats') holding between sequences and object-language expressions is enriched by the following clauses:

$$\text{Sats}\ (s, \phi x_i) \leftrightarrow \text{SAT}\ (s^*(x_i), s, \phi).$$
$$\text{SAT}\ (a, s, \text{`large'}^\frown\phi) \leftrightarrow \text{large}\ \hat{b}[\text{SAT}\ (b, s, \phi)]\ a.$$
$$\text{SAT}\ (a, s, \hat{x}_j[A]) \leftrightarrow (s')[(s' \underset{j}{\approx} s\ \&\ s'^*(x_j) = a) \leftrightarrow \text{Sats}\ (s', A)].$$

Note

We are obliged to define satisfaction for modified wffs by way of the three-place relation SAT for the following reason. If we attempted the most direct manoeuvre

$$\text{Sats}\ (s, \text{`large'}^\frown\phi x_j) \leftrightarrow \text{large}\ \hat{b}[\text{Sats}\ (b, \phi)]\ s^*(x_j)$$

then the predicate abstract $\hat{b}[\text{Sats}\ (b, \phi)]$ would have to be true of individuals, not sequences. But in general ϕ cannot be assumed to be replaced by an expression which an individual can be regarded as satisfying directly. For we need to keep relativity to the sequence s to deal with any free variables which the predicate abstract replacing ϕ may contain.

IX

Language-Mastery and the Sorites Paradox*

CRISPIN WRIGHT

I

Throughout Frege's writings are scattered expressions of the conception that the vagueness of ordinary language, and especially the occurrence of predicates for which it is not always determinate whether or not they may truly be applied to an object, is a defect. His reason for such a view seems to have been that orthodox logical principles fail when applied to sentences containing expressions whose range of application has been defined only partially.[1] Thus Frege seems not to have considered, or not to have thought worth considering, the possibility that vague terms might require a *special* logic. Vagueness is rather something which can and should be expurgated from language, if it is to be suitable for 'scientific purposes'. The same conception is to be found in Russell's Introduction to the *Tractatus*. Ordinary language is always more or less vague, but a logically perfect language would not be vague at all; so the degree of vagueness of a natural language is a direct measure of its distance from being everything which it 'logically' ought to be.

Of course, we have since learned a greater respect for language as we find it; we no longer regard the vagueness of ordinary language as a defect. But a higher-order analogue of the Frege-Russell view continues to figure in our thinking about language: even if many predicates in natural language are vague, there can still be a precise semantics for such expressions and indeed for the whole language, i.e. a theoretical model of the information assimilated in learning it as

* This discussion is a synopsis of, or, better, a series of excerpts from my 'On the Coherence of Vague Predicates', forthcoming in *Synthese*.

[1] Excluded Middle is the obvious example. But, as Frege points out, contraposition also fails: *Grundgesetze der Arithmetik, begriffsschriftlich abgeleitet*, Band ii (Hermann Pohle, Jena, 1903, and Olms, Hildesheim, 1962), p. 65.

a first language or, equivalently, of the conceptual apparatus possession of which constitutes mastery of the language. There need be no imprecision, it seems, in such a model; at any rate, none occasioned purely by the vagueness of the expressions of mastery of whose senses it is to provide an account.

We tend to picture our use of language as something essentially *regular*. We tend to think of language-learning as ingestion of a set of rules for the combination and application of expressions. Thus the task of a philosophical theory of meaning, in one natural sense of that phrase, would be to give a systematic account of the contribution made by the constituents of a semantically complex expression to its overall sense; and the theory would be concerned especially with the epistemology of the transition from understanding of subsentential components of a new sentence to recognition of the sense of the whole. Such a philosophical theory will normally only be concerned with *types* of contribution made by constituent expressions; in just this connection arise the familiar questions concerning the nature of the distinction between proper names and other singular terms, between singular terms generally and predicative expressions, whether the notion of reference may illuminatingly be extended to predicative expressions, etc. So the completion of such a theory would only be a preliminary to what we think of as a full semantic description of a natural language; for it is not just the type of contribution but the *specific* contribution which a constituent expression makes to complex expressions containing it which we think of as determined by rule.

It is worth emphasizing that no obstacle to such a conception is posed by the fact that we cannot in general state such rules in such a way as to explain the sense of an expression to someone previously unfamiliar with it. Consider a schematic rule for a one-place predicate, F:

> F may truly be applied to an individual, a, if and only if a satisfies the condition of being ϕ.

How should we specify ϕ if F is 'red'? Clearly the only completion of the rule which is actually constitutive of our understanding of 'red', rather than a mere extensional parallel, is to take ϕ as the condition of being red. In general we cannot expect instances of such a schematic rule to be of explanatory use if they are stated in a given language for a predicate of the same language; in consequence, it will not generally

be possible to appeal to such rules to settle questions about the applicability of an expression. Nevertheless we may still legitimately regard such a rule as an exact expression of (part of) what is understood by someone who understands e.g. 'red', for it states conditions recognition of which is sufficient to justify him in describing an object as 'red'; the statement of the rule is uninformative only in the sense that such a capacity of recognition cannot be imparted just by stating it.

So our picture is that correct use of language is essentially nothing other than use of it which conforms with a set of instructions, a set of semantic rules, which we have learned. Of course we handle language in general in a quite automatic way. But a chess player's recognition of the moves allowed for a piece in a certain position can be similarly automatic; it remains true that an account of his knowledge is to be given by reference to the rules of chess.

If language-mastery is thought of in such terms, the question arises, what means are allowable in the attempt to discover general features of the *substantial* rules for expressions in our language, the rules which determine specific senses? The view of the matter on which this paper centres is that here we may legitimately approach our use of language from within, i.e. reflectively as self-conscious masters of it, rather than externally, equipped only with behavioural notions. Thus it is legitimate to appeal to our conception of what justifies the application of a particular expression; to our conception of what we should count as an adequate explanation of the sense of a particular expression; to the limitations imposed by our senses and memories on the kind of instruction which we can actually carry out in practice; and to the kind of consequence which we associate with the application of a particular predicate, to what we think of as the point or interest of the distinction which the predicate implements. The primary concern of this paper is with the idea, henceforward referred to as the *governing view*, that from such considerations can be derived a reflective awareness of how we understand expressions in our language, and so of the nature of the rules which determine their correct use. The governing view, then, is a conjunction of two claims: that our use of language is rightly seen, like a game, as a practice in which the admissibility of a move is determined by rule, and that general properties of the rules may be discovered by means of the sorts of consideration just described. What I am going to argue is that these theses are mutually incoherent.

The difficulty has to do with the fact that the second thesis of the governing view, concerning the means whereby general features may be discovered of the semantic rules which we actually follow, forces us to recognize *semantic incoherence* in our understanding of a whole class of predicates—elements whose full exploitation would force the application of these expressions to situations in which we should otherwise regard them as not applying. The second thesis requires us to recognize rules which, when considered in conjunction with certain general features of the situations among which their associated expressions are to be applied, issue in contradictory instructions. Nevertheless we succeed in using these expressions informatively; and it seems that to use language informatively depends on using it, in large measure, consistently. It follows that our use of these expressions cannot correctly be pictured purely as the implementation of rules of the character which the second thesis yields for them; these rules cannot be implemented by any consistent pattern of behaviour. The governing view is therefore incoherent; for if its second thesis is true, the semantic rules governing certain predicates are capable by consistent beings only of selective implementation and thus, contrary to the first thesis, are not *constitutive* of what we count as the correct use of these expressions.

The predicates in question are all vague; but their vagueness is not just a matter of the existence of situations to which it is indeterminate whether or not they apply. Rather it is something which Frege, under the guise of a favourite metaphor, constantly runs together with possession of borderline-cases, viz., the idea of lacking 'sharp boundaries', of dividing logical space as a blurred shadow divides the background on which it is reflected. The conflation is natural because the figure equally exemplifies the idea of the borderline-case, a region falling neither in light nor shadow. But there is no clear reason why possession of borderline-cases should entail possession of blurred boundaries. If, following Frege, we assimilate a predicate to a *function* taking objects as arguments and yielding a truth value as value, then a predicate with borderline-cases may be seen simply as a partial such function—which is consistent with the existence of a perfectly sharp distinction between cases for which it is defined and cases for which it is not. Borderline-case vagueness of this straightforward kind presents no difficulty for the governing view; it is merely that there are situations to which no response in terms of a certain range of predicates is determined by their associated semantic rules as

correct. In contrast, if the second thesis of the governing view is correct, then predicates with 'blurred boundaries' are, in typical cases, rightly regarded as semantically incoherent.

This incoherence is implicit in the very nature of their vagueness. Vagueness is hardly ever, as Frege and Russell thought, merely a reflection of our not having bothered to make a predicate precise. Rather, the utility and point of the classifications expressed by many vague predicates would be frustrated if they were supplied with sharp boundaries. The sorts of argument allowed by the second thesis of the governing view will transpire to yield support for the idea that such predicates are essentially vague. The thesis equips us to argue that lack of sharp boundaries is not in general merely a superficial phenomenon, a reflection of a mere hiatus in some underlying set of semantic rules. In almost all the examples one comes across lack of sharp boundaries is not the consequence of an omission, but e.g. a product of the kind of task to which an expression is put, the kind of consequences which we attach to its application or, more deeply, the continuity of a world which we wish to describe in purely observational terms. Lack of sharp boundaries is a phenomenon of semantic depth. It is not usually a matter simply of our lacking an instruction where to 'draw the line'; rather the instructions we already have determine that the line is *not* to be drawn.

This conclusion might seem a welcome contribution to our understanding of the nature of vagueness, even from the standpoint of the governing view, were it not that it comes out in the form that no sharp distinction may be drawn between cases where it is definitely correct to apply such a predicate and cases of *any* other sort. But that is obviously a paradoxical concept. Thus it is that someone who espouses the governing view simply has no coherent approach to the Frege-Russell view of vagueness. His second thesis furnishes him with conclusive reasons to reject the suggestion that vagueness is a superficial, eliminable aspect of natural language with no real impact upon its informative use. But it does so in such a way that he is constrained to regard many vague predicates as semantically incoherent—specifically, as prone to the reasoning of the Sorites paradox—so that, unless the Frege-Russell view is right, he cannot maintain his first thesis with respect to such expressions. Only if their vagueness were an incidental feature could he maintain that the *essential* semantics of such expressions conformed to his first thesis.

II

Let us then consider some examples of the Sorites paradox in order to be clear how the governing view cuts off traditional lines of solution, indeed, all lines of solution. To begin with the classical case: if a pile of salt is large enough to be fairly described as a heap, the subtraction of a single grain of salt cannot make a relevant difference; if $n+1$ grains of salt constitute a heap, so do n grains. Thus one grain, and, indeed, zero grains constitute a heap. To block the paradox, it seems we have to be able to insist that, for some particular value of n, $n+1$ grains of salt would amount to a heap while n grains would not. But that is simply not the sense of 'heap'. Exact boundaries for the concept of a heap, either in terms of the precise number of grains contained or, indeed, in terms of any other precise measure, simply have not been fixed. But without such boundaries, a transition from $n+1$ grains to n grains can never be recognized as transforming a case where 'heap' applies into a case where it does not. Here we gravitate towards the idea that lack of exact boundaries is, as such, an essentially incoherent semantic feature.

A second example is given by Essenin-Volpin.[2] Consider the typical span of time between one human heartbeat and its successor. Then the concept of childhood—the sense of 'child'—is such that one does not, within a single heartbeat, pass from childhood to adolescence. Not that we are children for ever; but at least childhood does not evaporate between one pulse and the next. Similarly for the transition from infancy to childhood, and from adolescence to adulthood. 'Infant', 'child', 'adolescent', 'adult' are thus all semantically incoherent expressions; for the sense of each of these predicates is such that, in a typical process of growing-up, their correct application will always survive the transition from one heartbeat to its successor or to its predecessor. So, by appropriately many steps of *modus ponens*, we may force the application of each of these predicates to cases we should otherwise regard as falling within the domain of one of the others.

As a third example, consider a series of homogeneously coloured patches, ranging from a first, red patch to a final, orange one, such that each patch is *just* discriminable in colour from those immediately next to it, and is more similar in respect of colour to its immediate

[2] A. S. Essenin-Volpin, 'Le programme ultra-intuitioniste des fondements des mathématiques', in *Infinitistic Methods (Proceedings of the Symposium on Foundations of Mathematics, Warsaw, 2–9 September* 1959) (Pergamon Press, Oxford, 1961), p. 203.

neighbours than to any other patches in the series. That is, marginal changes of shade are involved in every transition from a patch to its successor, and each such transition carries us further from red and closer to orange. Now, the sense of colour predicates is such that their application always survives a very small change in shade. If one is content to call something 'red', one will still be so content if its colour changes by some just discriminable amount. There is a notion of a degree of change in respect of colour too small to amount to a change *of* colour. Only if a substantial difference comes between two patches of colour shall we consider ourselves justified in ascribing to them incompatible colour predicates.

This, obviously, is to attribute semantic incoherence to colour predicates. We have an easy proof that all the patches in the example are red, or that they are all orange, or that they are all doubtfully either. Moreover any two colours can be linked by such a series of samples; so any colour predicate can be exported into the domain of application of one of its rivals.

What is involved in treating these examples as genuinely paradoxical is a certain *tolerance* in the concepts which they respectively involve, a notion of a degree of change too small to make any difference, as it were. The paradoxical interpretations postulate degrees of change in point of size, maturity and colour which are insufficient to alter the justice with which some specific predicate of size, maturity or colour is applied. This is quite palpably an incoherent feature since, granted that any case to which such a predicate applies may be linked by a series of 'sufficiently small' changes with a case where it does not, it is inconsistent with there being any cases to which the predicate does not apply. More exactly, suppose ϕ to be a concept related to a predicate, F, as follows: that any object which F characterizes may be changed into one which it does not simply by sufficient change in respect of ϕ. Colour, for example, is such a concept for 'red', size for 'heap', degree of maturity for 'child', number of hairs for 'bald', etc. Then F is *tolerant* with respect to ϕ if there is also some positive degree of change in respect of ϕ insufficient ever to affect the justice with which F applies to a particular case.

In essentials, then, the Sorites paradox interprets certain vague predicates as tolerant. But this might seem a tendentious interpretation. Not that there is any doubt that the predicates in question do lack sharp boundaries; and the antiquity of the paradox bears witness to how easy it is to interpret this as involving the possession by these

predicates of a principle of re-application through marginal change. But is this a correct interpretation? Because 'heap' lacks sharp boundaries, it is plain that we are not entitled to single out any particular transition from *n* to *n*–1 grains of salt as being the decisive step in changing a heap into a non-heap; no one such step is decisive. That, however, is not to say that such a step always *preserves* application of the predicate. Would it not be better to assimilate the situation to that in which bordering states fail to agree upon a common frontier? Their failure to reach agreement does not vindicate the notion that e.g. a single pace in the direction of the other country always keeps one in the original country. For they have at least agreed that there is to be a border, that *some* such step is to be a decisive one; what they have not agreed is where. If we regard the predicates in the example in the terms of this model, we shall conclude that their vagueness is purely a reflection of our intellectual laziness. We have, as it were, decided that a disjunction is to be true—at some stage, *n* grains will be a heap where *n*–1 grains will not—without following up with a decision about *which* disjunct is true. On this view, the notion that these predicates are tolerant confuses a lack of instruction to count it the case that a proposition is false with the presence of an instruction to count it true. This conflation would be permissible only if the semantic rules for our language were in a certain sense complete, that is, if we possessed instructions for every conceivable situation. But for there to be vague expressions in our language is, on this view, precisely for this not to be so.

Someone who holds the governing view is bound to reject this suggestion as a deep misapprehension of the nature of the vagueness of these predicates. The lack of sharp boundaries possessed by these examples is correctly interpreted as tolerance, provided that we may discover elements of their senses in accordance with the second thesis. It would be inconsistent with elements already present in the semantics of these predicates so to refine their senses that the Sorites reasoning was blocked. How is this?

'Heap' is essentially a coarse predicate, whose application is a matter of rough and ready judgement. We should have no use for a precisely demarcated analogue in contexts in which the word is typically used. It would, for example, be ridiculous to force the question of obedience to the command, 'pour out a heap of sand here', to turn on a count of the grains. Our conception of the conditions which justify calling something a heap is such that the appropriateness

of the description will be unaffected by any change which cannot be detected by *casual observation.*

A different argument is available for supposing colour predicates tolerant with respect to marginal changes in shade. We learn and teach our basic colour vocabulary ostensively. Evidently it is a precondition of the feasibility of so doing that we can reasonably accurately remember how things look. Imagine someone who can recognize whether simultaneously presented objects match in colour, so that he is able to use a colour-chart, but who cannot in general remember shades of colour sufficiently well to be able to handle without a chart colour predicates for which we are able to dispense with charts. Such a person might, for example, be quite unable to judge whether something yellow, which he was shown earlier, would match the orange object now before him. Thus, for such a man, an ostensive definition of 'yellow' would be useless; in order to apply 'yellow' as we apply it, he would have to employ a chart. We, in contrast, are able to dispense with charts for the purpose of making distinctions of colour of the degree of refinement of 'yellow'. Any object to which a colour predicate of this degree of refinement definitely correctly applies may be recognized as such just on the basis of our ostensive training. Plainly, then, it has to be a feature of the senses thereby bestowed upon these predicates that changes too slight for us to remember—that is, a change such that exposure to an object both before the change is undergone and afterwards leaves us uncertain whether the object *has* changed, because we cannot remember sufficiently accurately how it was before—never transform a case to which such a predicate applies into one where such is not definitely the right description. The character of our basic colour training presupposes the *total memorability* of the distinctions expressed by our basic colour predicates; only if single, unmemorable changes of shade never affect the justice of a particular basic description can the senses of these predicates be explained entirely by methods reliant upon our capacity to remember how things look.

For the tolerance of 'child', etc., the governing view affords a third type of argument. The distinctions expressed by these predicates are of substantial social importance in terms of what we may appropriately expect from, and of, persons who exemplify them. Infants, for example, have rights but not duties, whereas of a child outside infancy we demand at least a rudimentary moral sense; we explain the anti-social behaviour of some adolescents in terms of their being adolescents; and

we make moral and other demands of character on adults which we would not impose on the immature. Plausibly, these predicates could not endure such treatment, were they not tolerant with respect to marginal changes in degree of maturity—certainly with respect to the changes involved in the transition from one heartbeat to the next. It is *ceteris paribus* irrational and unfair to base substantial distinctions of right and duty on marginal differences; if we are forced to do so, e.g. with electoral qualifications, it is with a sense of injustice. Moreover it is only if a *substantial* change is involved in the transition from childhood to adolescence that we can appeal to this transition to explain substantial alterations in patterns of behaviour. That predicates of degree of maturity should possess tolerance is a direct consequence of their social role; very small differences cannot be permitted to generate doubt about their application without correspondingly coming to be associated with a burden of moral and explanatory distinctions which they are too slight to carry.

On the second thesis of the governing view, then, our embarrassment about where to 'draw the line' with these examples is to be viewed as a consequence not of any hiatus in our semantic programme but of the tolerance of the predicates in question. If casual observation alone is to determine whether a predicate applies, then items not distinguished by casual observation must receive the same verdict.[3] So single changes too slight to be detected by casual observation cannot be permitted to generate doubt about the application of such a predicate. Similarly, if the conditions under which a predicate applies are to be generally memorable, it cannot be unseated by single changes too slight to be remembered. Finally, very slight changes cannot be permitted to generate doubt about the application of predicates of maturity without contravening their moral and explanatory role. The utility of 'heap', the memorability of the conditions under which something is 'red', the point of 'child' impose upon the semantics of these predicates tolerance with respect to marginal change in the various relevant respects.

To allow these considerations is to concede that the vagueness of these examples is a phenomenon of semantic depth—that it is sacrificed at much more than the cost of the intellectual labour of the stipulation —and that it is a structurally incoherent feature. Two things follow. First, there is no special logic for predicates of this sort, crystallizing

[3] Not that it has to be the case that a definitely correct verdict can always be reached; but if it cannot, that in turn must be the situation with respect to each item in question.

what is distinctive in their semantics in contrast with those of exact predicates; for what is so distinctive is their inconsistency. Second, the fashion in which we typically use these expressions needs some other model than the simple implementation of rules, if these rules are to incorporate all the features of their senses which we should wish to recognize on the basis of the second thesis.

III

There is a fourth, and more profound way in which tolerance, according to the second thesis, would seem to arise. Colour predicates will again serve as an illustration. Plausibly, these predicates are in the following sense purely *observational*: if it is possible to tell at all what colour something is, it can be told just by looking. The look of an object decides its colour, as the feel of an object decides its texture, or the sound of a note its pitch. The information of one or more senses is decisive of the applicability of an observational predicate; so a distinction exemplified by a pair of sensorily-equivalent items cannot be expressed solely by means of such predicates. What is about to be illustrated is a feature of any predicate whose sense is purely observational in the fashion just adumbrated.

If colour predicates are observational, any pair of patches indistinguishable in colour must satisfy the condition that any colour predicate applicable to either is applicable to both. Suppose, then, that we build up the series of colour patches of the third example, interposing new patches to the point where every patch in the resultant series is indiscriminable in colour from those immediately adjacent to it. The possibility of doing so, of course, depends upon the non-transitivity of our colour discriminations. The observationality of 'red' requires it to be tolerant with respect to the kind of change involved in passing from any patch in this series to an immediate neighbour, so we have a Sorites paradox. If 'red' is observational, its sense must be such that from the premisses, that x is red and that x looks just like y, it follows that y is red, no matter what objects x and y may be. Thus we are equipped to conclude that each successive patch in the series is red, given only the true premiss that the first patch is red.

The memorability, then, of the conditions of application of 'red' requires that it be tolerant with respect to changes which, under favourable circumstances, we can actually directly discern. Now, however, it appears that even if our memories were to be as finely discriminating as our senses, colour predicates and others would still

possess tolerance; only the changes which their application tolerated would not be changes which we could directly discern in objects which underwent them. This tolerance has nothing to do with the limitations of our memories; it is a consequence of the observationality of these predicates.

These considerations are broadly analogous to what was said of 'heap': if we so fix the sense of a predicate that whether it applies has to do with nothing other than how an object seems when casually observed, then changes other than such as can be determined by casual observation cannot transform a case to which the predicate applies into one to which there is some question whether it applies. The point remains good if we omit the word 'casual'. But this fourth example is prima facie deeper-reaching, at any rate for someone who, like Frege, believes that language should be purified of vague expressions. The cost of eliminating predicates of casual observation would be no more than convenience; to require, however, that language should contain no expression tolerant in the manner of the fourth example would be to require that it contained no expressions of strictly observational sense. If we stipulated away the tolerance of colour predicates, we should have to forgo our whole present idea of what justifies the application of these predicates, viz. the *look* of a thing. In general, there would be no predicate whose application to an object could be decided just on the basis of how it looked, felt, sounded, etc. Might there not then be a higher price to pay, namely the jeopardizing of contact between language and empirical reality?

We shall return to the last thought. First we require to see how the governing view sustains the idea that there is a large class of predicates whose senses are purely observational. If we are to understand the scope of the fourth example, we also require to know under what circumstances we may expect our sensory discriminations to be non-transitive.

That we do intuitively regard the semantics of colour predicates as purely observational is beyond doubt; and simply illustrated by the fact that we should regard it as a criterion of lack of understanding of such a predicate if someone was doubtful whether both of a pair of objects which he could not tell apart should receive the same description in terms of it. We regard it as a criterion of understanding such a predicate that someone, presented under suitable conditions with an object to which it applies, can tell that it does so just on the basis of the object's appearance. Certainly, then, our ordinary conception of

how to tell that a particular colour predicate applies, of what justifies its application, would involve that these predicates are purely observational.

In addition, it is plausible to suppose that any *ostensively definable* predicate must be observational. If an expression can be ostensively defined, it must be possible to draw to someone's attention those features in his experience which warrant its application; and if this is possible, there can be no question of the expression applying to some but not others among situations which he cannot distinguish in experience. It would be a poor joke on the recipient of an ostensive definition if the defined expression applied selectively among situations indistinguishable from one which was originally displayed to him as a paradigm.

In general the connection between an expression's being observational—its applying to both, if to either, of any pair of observationally indistinguishable situations—and its being ostensively definable is as follows. The picture of acquiring concepts by experience of cases where they do apply and cases where they do not—a picture which surely has *some* part to play in a philosophically adequate conception of the learning of a first language—cannot be wholly adequate for concepts which differentiate among situations which look, feel, taste, sound and smell exactly alike. So if that picture is wholly adequate for any concepts, they must be concepts whose range of application does not include situations which experience cannot distinguish from situations which may not definitely correctly be regarded as falling within that range. To master the sense of a predicate is, at least, to learn to differentiate cases to which it is right to apply it from cases of any other sort. If such mastery can be bestowed ostensively, a comparison of two such cases must always reveal a difference which sense-experience can detect. The notion that the whole range of application of a predicate can be made intelligible by ostensive means presupposes that it is never the case that only one of a pair of objects, which the senses cannot tell apart, is characterized by it.

This is a clear, absolutely general connection. If there is in the conditions of the correct application of a predicate nothing which is incapable of ostensive communication, then the predicate must apply to both, if to either, of any pair of indistinguishable objects. But it seems manifest that adjectives of colour, and many others, do precisely not involve any such further condition of correct application; on the contrary, ostensive training would appear fully determinant of

their meaning—or, if it is not, it is the only training which we get. The governing view thus vindicates the observationality of colour predicates twice over: as a consequence both of our general conception of what justifies their application, and of the character of the training in their use which we receive.

The other question was to do with the scope of the phenomenon of non-transitive indiscriminability. Suppose that we are to construct a series of colour patches, ranging from red through to orange, among which indiscriminability is to behave transitively. We are given a supply of appropriate patches from which to make selections, an initial red patch, and the instruction that each successive patch must either match its predecessor or be more like it than is any other patch not matching it which we later use. Under these conditions it is plain that we cannot generate any change in colour by selecting successive matching patches; if indiscriminability is to be transitive, then if each patch in the first *n* selections matches its predecessor, the *n*th selection must match the first patch. The only way to generate a change in colour will be to select a non-matching patch.

When the series is complete, how will it look in comparison with the series of the fourth example? It is clear that we shall have lost what was distinctive of that series: the appearance of *continuous* change from red to orange. In the new series the shades are exemplified in discrete bands, containing perhaps no more than one patch, and all the changes take place abruptly in a transition from a patch to its successor. It thus appears that, were our judgements of indiscriminability to be universally transitive among samples of homogeneous colour, no field of colour patches could be ordered in the distinctive fashion now possible: i.e., so as to give the impression of a perfectly smooth change of colour. If matching generally behaved transitively among shades, no series of colour patches could give the impression of continuous transformation of colour; by contraposition, then, for matching to function non-transitively among a finite set of colour patches, it is sufficient that they may be arranged so as to strike us as forming a phenomenal continuum. This reasoning may obviously be generalized. Any finite series of objects, none of which involves any apparent change in respect of ϕ, may give an overall impression of continuous change in respect of ϕ only if indiscriminability functions non-transitively among its members.

The reasoning may in fact be generalized further. It can be shown (cf. 'On the Coherence of Vague Predicates') that the non-transitivity

of our discriminations may be seen as a consequence of the continuity of change, viewed as a pervasive structural feature of our sense-experience. The general lesson of the fourth example is thus as follows. If we attempt to mark off regions of a seemingly continuous process of change in terms of predicates which are purely observational—predicates of which it is understood that ostensive definition gives their whole meaning—these expressions are bound to display tolerance in a suitable series of stages selected from the process. An analogue of the fourth example may thus in principle be constructed for any ostensively defined predicate; for absolutely anything which it characterizes might undergo seemingly continuous change to a point where it could be so characterized no longer. The fourth example indicates a basic fault, as it were, lying deep in the relation between the nature of our experience and those parts of language by means of which we attempt to give the most direct, non-theoretical expression to it.

This conclusion rests upon two assumptions: that it is right to regard the senses of colour predicates, etc., as purely observational; and that this is a very fundamental fact about their senses, whose sacrifice would be possible only at great cost. The governing view, as we have seen, yields the first assumption. For the second, however, no argument has so far been presented; I merely voiced concern that 'contact' between language and the empirical world might be attenuated if the use of purely observational predicates was abandoned. Before this concern is evaluated, and the general implications assessed of stipulating away the tolerance, and so the observationality, of the relevant predicates, we must consider a general objection to the way in which all four examples have been treated.

IV

If it is conceded that the vagueness of these examples is correctly interpreted as tolerance, then plainly no consistent logic does justice to the semantics of such predicates. It is natural to suggest, however, that the argument for this interpretation may have overlooked an essential feature of this sort of predicate: that they typically express distinctions of *degree*. There are degrees of redness, of childishness, and, if a smaller heap is regarded as less of a heap, of heaphood.

What is it for the distinction between being *F* and not being *F* to be one of degree? Typically, it is required that the comparatives, 'is less/more *F* than', are in use and that iteration of one of these relations

may transform something *F* into something not *F*, or vice versa. In addition, the semantic relations between the comparatives and the simple descriptions, 'is *F*' and 'is not *F*', are such that if *a* is less/more *F* than *b*, then the degree of justice with which *a* can be described simply as *F* is correlatively smaller or larger than that with which *b* can be so described. That is, a twofold classification of possible states of affairs into those which would justify the judgment, '*a* is *F*', and those which would not, misses what is distinctive about the predicate whose application is a matter of degree. For that to be so is exactly for there to be *degrees* of such justice.

It is thus plausible to suppose that a logic for distinctions of this sort cannot be based upon simple bivalence. With such predicates there are, as it were, degrees of truth, whose collective structure is that of the set of degrees of being *F*. In this sense it is arguable that the examples do require a special, non-classical logic. But how did the earlier arguments for the tolerance of these predicates overlook that they expressed distinctions of degree?

The suggestion is that the paradoxical reasoning essentially depends upon the constraints of bivalence. Consider a pair of objects one of which, *a*, we are happy to describe as *F*, while *b* is slightly less *F* than *a*. How is *b* to be described? If our admissible descriptions are restricted to '*F*' and 'not *F*', if we *have* to say one or the other, then presumably we shall describe *b* as *F*. For if something is more like something *F* than something not *F*, to describe it as *F* is the less misleading of the two alternatives. But the justification with which '*F*' is applied in successive such cases successively decreases. We have no principle of the form: if *a* is *F*, and *b* differs sufficiently marginally from *a*, then *b* is *F*; with distinctions of degree there are no 'small changes insufficient to affect the justice with which a predicate applies'; they are, on the contrary, small changes *in* the degree of justice with which the predicate may be applied. Of course, we do have the principle: if the judgment that *a* is *F* is justified to some large degree, and *b* is marginally less *F* than *a*, then the description of *b* as *F* will be better justified than its description as not *F*. But that is not a paradoxical principle.

Anyone who thinks he here feels the cool wind of sanity fanning his brow would do well to be clear why we do not still have *this* principle: if *b* is marginally less *F* than *a*, then if the less misleading description of *a* is '*F*', the less misleading description of *b* is '*F*'. Yet if this principle is false, there must in any Sorites-type series be a last case of

which we are prepared to say that if we *had* to describe it either as *F* or as not *F*, the better description would be '*F*'. Why, then, is it usually embarrassing to be asked to identify such a case without any sense of arbitrariness?

Let us assign to '*a* is *F*' a *designated* value just in case '*F*' is a less misleading description of *a* than 'not *F*'. Then our embarrassment is exactly to identify a last object to which the application of '*F*' would receive a designated value. But now the suspicion arises that tolerance is with us still; only it is no longer the *truth* of the application of '*F*' that would survive small changes but its designatedness.

Is this suspicion justified? One thing is clearly correct about the assumption of bivalence: faced with a situation and a predicate, we have only two choices—to apply or to withhold. There is not a series of distinct linguistic acts in which we can reflect every degree of justification with which a predicate may be applied. The crucial practical notion to be mastered for a predicate associated with the distinction of degree is thus that of a situation to which the application of the predicate is *on balance* justified. Without mastery of this notion no amount of information about the structure of variations in the degree with which '*F*' applies entails how the predicate is to be used. Now of this notion may it not still be a feature that it always survives sufficiently small changes?—that if *a* and *b* are dissimilar only to some very small extent, then if describing *a* as *F* is on balance justified, so is thus describing *b*?

It is clear that all the previous considerations will apply, and that the introduction of a complex structure of degrees of justification will get us no farther. For among these degrees we have still to distinguish those with which for practical purposes the application of the predicate is to be associated; otherwise we have not in repudiating bivalence done anything to replace the old connection between justified assertion and truth. But plainly, once we attempt to make such a distinction, the arguments afforded by the governing view sweep aside this proposed solution to the Sorites paradox as an irrelevance. To rehearse the reasons: if we are to be able to *remember* how to apply '*F*', then differences too slight to be remembered cannot transform a situation to which its application is on balance justified into one which is not so; if we are to be able to apply '*F*' just on the basis of *casual observation*, the same applies to differences too subtle to be detected by casual observation; if the distinction between cases to which the application of '*F*' is on balance justified and others is to be made just on the basis of

how things look, or sound, etc., then any pair of indistinguishable situations must receive the same verdict; finally, if '*F*' is associated with moral or explanatory distinctions which we are unwilling to tie to very small changes, we shall likewise be unwilling to allow such changes to generate doubt about the status of a situation previously regarded as on balance justifying description as *F*. Of course the use here being made of the notion of a situation to which the application of '*F*' is 'on balance' justified is quite uncritical. But this is legitimate. For, as remarked, there must be *some* such notion if a many-valued logic for distinctions of degree is to have any practical linguistic application.

V

Let us turn then to the question whether we could not eliminate, at not too heavy a cost, the tolerance of observational predicates. The resulting predicates would no longer be strictly observational; hence the initial doubt whether such a purified language could engage with the observational world at all. On reflection, though, it is clear that the dislocation of language and the world of appearance generated by such a purification would not have to be as radical as that. When three situations collectively provide a counter-example to the transitivity of indiscriminability, there is nothing occult in the circumstance that they do so. It is an observationally detectable difference between indiscriminable situations that one is distinguishable from a third situation from which the other is not; the relation, '*a* matches *b* matches *c* does not match *a*', is an *observational relation*, i.e. one whose application to a trio of objects can be determined just by looking at them, listening to them, etc.

Observational concepts evidently require narrower criteria of re-application than indistinguishability, if they are to be purified of tolerance. But we should not jump to the conclusion that to provide such criteria will require surrender of observationality altogether, for the phenomenon which is causing the trouble is itself observational. Indeed, the *only* kind of observationally detectable difference which there can be between indiscriminable items is that one should be distinguishable from some third item from which the other is not. So if the class of expressions in question is to remain in contact with observation, we have to look for some form of stipulation which *exploits* the non-transitivity of indistinguishability to provide a basis for describing indiscriminable situations differently. No other

explanation can correspond to a distinction which sense-experience can determine to obtain, a distinction which we can simply be shown.

After such a stipulation, the question whether a pair of indiscriminable colour patches should receive the same colour description may turn on their respective relations of indiscriminability/discriminability with respect to some third patch. But now we have to take note of a striking aspect of the philosophical psychology of non-transitive matching: it does not seem to be possible to conduct experiments with non-transitively matching triads in *memory*. For suppose that a predicate, *F*, is defined ostensively by reference to some individual, *a*, which, it is noted at the time, perfectly matches another individual, *c*; it is understood that *F* is not to be applied to individuals which match *a* unless they also match *c*. Later the trainee comes across *b* which, so far as he can determine, matches *a* perfectly; the question is, does *b* match *c*? It is evident that the issue is only resoluble by direct comparison, and especially that it cannot be settled by memory, however accurate. For the most perfect memory of *c* can give no further information than that it looked just like *a*; which, when non-transitive matching is a possibility, is simply insufficient to determine whether it would match *b*. This, it must be emphasized, in contrast with our conclusions concerning the third example, is *not* a limitation imposed by the feebleness of our memories; it is a limitation of principle.

It thus appears that if we are to be able to exercise expressions whose application to matching individuals depends upon their behaviour in relation to a third, possibly differentiating individual, then we have to be able to ensure the *availability* of the third individual. Expressions of this species will be practicably applicable only in relation to a system of paradigms. So we can see, even in advance of attempting a specific stipulation to remove the tolerance of 'red' as displayed in the fourth example, that the kind of semantic construction it will have to be is going to tie the application of expressions of colour to the use of a colour-chart.

Let us then consider, as a test case, how we might go about the construction of such a chart. What we require of the chart is that it should enable us to identify a last red patch in any series of the type of the fourth example. There is one obvious way to achieve this, namely to devise a single ad hoc paradigm. It is plausible to suppose that we could complete a colour-chart for the red/orange region at least in the sense that anything which we should wish to regard as falling within

that region would match something on the chart. Consider, then, an arrangement of colour patches which form in this sense a complete colour-chart for the red/orange region and which are simply ordered by similarity, i.e. every patch on the chart more closely resembles its immediate neighbours than any other patches on the chart. Then a sharp red/orange distinction can be generated as follows. Select some patch towards the middle of the chart; then any colour patch matching something on the chart either matches the selected patch or it does not; if it does, it is red; if it does not, but matches a sample to the left of the selected patch, it is again red; otherwise, it is orange.

Naturally it could not be guaranteed that duplicates of this chart would always deliver the same verdict. Charts could look absolutely similar, and even satisfy the condition that the *n*th sample on either matched and was distinguishable from exactly the same samples on the other chart as its own *n*th sample, yet deliver discrepant results. But they would not often do so. Besides, the situation is not novel. Rulers, for example, sometimes give different results. A final criterion for one system is deposited in Paris; and we could do the same with a colour-chart.

Generalized, this proposal might seem quite ludicrous in practical terms. We are confronted with the spectacle of a people quite lost without their individual wheelbarrow loads of charts, tape-recordings, smell- and taste-samples and assorted sample surfaces. But this caricatures the proposal. There would be no need for all this portable semantic hardware. This is clear if we pursue the analogy with the use of rulers: it is true that, without a ruler, we can only guess at length; but after the introduction of an ad hoc paradigm for colours, the use of colour predicates will presumably be analogous not to that of expressions like 'two feet long', but rather to that of expressions like 'less than two feet long', i.e. expressions of a *range* of lengths. Of such expressions the criterion of application is still measurement; but unless the example is a peripheral one, we can tell *without* measuring what the outcome of measurement would be. Training in the use of paradigms might be essential if one is to grasp the sense of such expressions; but, once grasped, most cases of practical application could be decided without the use of paradigms—for most practical purposes, the wheelbarrow could be left behind.

It would appear, then, that if we adopted such stipulations as a general strategy, it would not have to affect our use of observational language very much at all. At present we can tell of anything red that

it is so just by looking at it. This would still usually be true after the proposed stipulation; and if the new distinction was suitably located, cases where it was not true would in general coincide with borderline-cases of the old red/orange distinction. The use of predicates so refined could thus greatly resemble their present use; the distinctions which they expressed would be empirically decidable; and there would be one crucial disanalogy—they would be tolerance-free.

It is apparent that exactly parallel considerations may be brought to bear upon the earlier treatment of the first and third examples. Even after a precise re-definition of 'heap', we would be able to learn to tell in most cases just by casual observation what verdict the new criterion would give if applied; it would seldom be necessary actually to count the grains. And the distinction between red and orange, supposing an exact distinction were drawn by means of a chart, would be unmemorable only within that small range of shades which could not by unaided memory be distinguished from the last red sample. It would thus appear that the cost of eliminating tolerance in cases of these two types need not after all be high, since we could expect to be able to tell in general just by looking at, etc., an item on which side of the dividing line it would fall.

If there need, after all, be no substantial sacrifice in endowing formerly observational predicates with exact boundaries, what has become of the alleged profound tension between phenomenal continuity and language designed to express how things seem to us? The answer, of course, is that it has simply been swept under the carpet. The possibility of our dispensing with paradigms for most practical purposes depends upon our capacity e.g. to distinguish between cases where we could tell whether or not 'red' applied just by looking and cases where we could not, where we should have recourse to a chart. But if we are able to make such a distinction, there can be no objection to introducing a predicate to express it. And then, it seems, the semantics of *this* predicate will have to be observational. On what other basis should we decide whether something looks as though comparison with a chart would determine it to be red than how it looks? Of any pair of colour patches which look exactly alike, if either looks as though the chart would deliver the verdict 'red', both must. So the new predicate, introduced to reflect our capacity to make this distinction, will be applicable to both members of any pair of matching colour-samples, if to either.

It is not that there is any compelling reason to have such a predicate;

only that there is no reason not to. If we were sometimes able to tell without using a chart whether something was red, it would surely be possible to make intelligible to us a predicate designed to apply in just such circumstances. So it transpires that a language all of whose observational concepts were based on paradigms would avoid containing tolerant predicates only by not containing means of expression of all the observational distinctions which we are in fact able to make. The dispensability of the wheelbarrow requires the exercise of observational concepts.

It would of course be absurd to propose that the tolerance of such new predicates—'looks as though it would lie to the left of the last red shade', 'looks as though it contains fewer than ten thousand grains', etc.—might in turn be stipulated away. Their meaning will not permit it; it cannot be allowed of things which look exactly alike that one may look as though it satisfies some condition which the other looks as though it does not, unless how a thing looks may not be determined by looking. The earlier discussion of the first and third examples involved an over-estimation of our interest in preserving the tolerance of the predicates involved only if we possess a coherent understanding of these new predicates; if the first and third examples do not, after all, pose a substantial problem for the governing view, it is because of our capacity to handle expressions falling within the scope of the fourth example.

VI

Let us, then, finally review the character of the difficulty for the governing view which originates in the fourth example.

It is a fundamental fact about us that we can learn to classify items according to their appearance, that we are able, consistently as it seems to us, to apply or to withhold descriptions just on the basis of how things strike the senses. In a discrete phenomenal world, there would be no special difficulty—no difficulty not inherent in the idea of a semantic rule as such—in viewing our use of such expressions as essentially nothing but the following of rules of which it was a consequence that indiscriminable phenomena should receive the same description. But if mutually exclusive use is made of a pair of such predicates, and if cases to which one applies permit of continuous transformation into cases where the other applies, it cannot be correct to represent the use made of either predicate just as the doing of what

is required by a set of rules with such a consequence. Yet we are forced—if the relevance is allowed of considerations to do with what we should regard as adequate explanation of such expressions, or with certain criteria which we should accept of misunderstanding such an expression—to attribute to the rules governing these predicates precisely such an implication; and *all* the phenomena which we confront in our world are in principle capable of seemingly continuous variation.

It will not quite do, though, to present the difficulty as that of the inadequacy of any inconsistent set of rules to explain a consistent pattern of behaviour. To begin with, it is unclear how far our use of e.g. the vocabulary of colours *is* consistent. The descriptions given of awkward cases may vary from occasion to occasion. Besides that, the notion of using a predicate consistently would appear to require some objective criteria for variation in relevant respects among items to be described in terms of it; but what is distinctive about observational predicates is exactly the lack of such criteria. So we may not lean too heavily, as though it were a matter of hard fact, upon the consistency of our employment of colour predicates. The point rather has to do with the fact that our use of these predicates is largely *successful*; the expectations which we form on the basis of others' ascriptions of colour are not usually disappointed. Agreement is generally possible about how colours are to be described; which is equivalent to saying that others *seem* to use colour predicates in a largely consistent way.

It is this fact of which the governing view can provide no account. A semantic rule is supposed to contribute towards determining what is an admissible use of its associated expression. The picture evoked by the first thesis of the governing view is that there is, for any particular expression in the language, a set of such rules *completely* determinant of when the expression is used correctly; such a set thus provides a model of the information of which a master of the use of the expression may be deemed to be in possession. Clearly, however, the feasibility of such a picture requires that the rules associated with an expression, about whose use we generally agree, be consistent. For if they issue conflicting verdicts upon the correctness of a particular application of the expression, it cannot be explained just by appeal to the rules why we agree that the application is e.g. correct.

The problem presented for the first thesis by the occurrence of tolerant predicates, or of any kind of semantically incoherent expression, is not that, in a clear-cut way, nothing can be done to implement

an inconsistent set of instructions. Strictly, of course, anything that is done will conflict with a part of them. But we can imagine a game whose rules conflict, but which is nevertheless regularly and enjoyably played to a conclusion by members of some community because, for perhaps quite fortuitous reasons, whenever an occasion arises to appeal to the rules, the players concur about which element in the rules is to be appealed to, so that an impasse never comes about. We need not enquire whether they have noticed the inconsistency in the rules. The point of the analogy is that in practice they always agree whether a move is admissible, as we generally agree whether something is red. The analogue of the first thesis in relation to this example is the notion that the rules completely determine when a particular move is admissible. But while it may be true that the authority of the rules can be cited for any of the moves the community actually make, it is plain that the rules alone do not provide a satisfactory account of the practice of the game. For someone could master the rules yet still not be able to join in the game, because he was unable to guess what sort of eclectic application of them an opponent was likely to make in relation to any given move.

An outsider attempting to grasp our use of a tolerant predicate would presumably not encounter exactly this difficulty; it would be clear that we were not prepared to allow remote consequences of its tolerance, inferred by means of reasoning of the Sorites type. The difficulty of principle for the first thesis, however, is the same. The rules of the game cannot provide an account of how the game is played, for it is possible that someone might grasp them yet be unable to participate. The semantic rules for an expression are supposed to provide an account of its correct use; they cannot do so if someone whose use of it differed radically from ours could still be thought of as in possession of exactly the same brief—as he can be, if it consists in an inconsistent set of instructions.

What, then, have we learned? The comparison of language with a game is an extremely natural one. What better explanation could there be of our ability to agree in our use of language than if, as in a game, we are playing by the same rules? We are thus attracted towards the assimilation of our situation to that of people to whom the practice of a highly ramified, complex game has been handed down via many generations, but of which the theory has been lost. Our central task, as philosophers of language, is to work towards the recovery of such a theory: a theory which will explain the mechanism

of our recognition of the senses of new complex expressions by displaying them as functions of the senses of their constituents and their mode of combination, which will explicate our apprehension of valid inferences—which, in short, will explicate the overall character of our mastery of the language game. What we have learned is that we probably cannot combine this conception of what a theory of meaning should accomplish with the notion that the investigation is something which, as masters of the language in question, we are better placed to carry out than an observer of our practice. We have to avoid appeal, at any rate, to a range of considerations which it is our antecedent prejudice to consider must be relevant: considerations to do with what we should deem a proper explanation of the sense of an expression, the criteria which we should employ for determining that someone misunderstands it, what we use the expression for, i.e., what issues turn on its application, the limitations imposed by our senses and memories on the information which we can absorb from our linguistic training, and our general conception of what justifies the application of the expression. And what privilege do we enjoy in the quest for a theory of meaning which an observer of our usage does not, if all these traditionally accepted guidelines for sense are dismissed? But we have seen that we must dismiss them if we want a coherent account of the senses of vague expressions. The methodological approach to *these* expressions, at any rate, must be more purely behaviouristic and anti-reflective, if a general theory of meaning is to be possible at all.

X

Existence and Tense

MICHAEL WOODS

THIS paper is concerned with the problems involved in the semantics of existence in giving a truth theory for English. My particular concern is with the difficulties that are presented by the phenomenon of tense for those aiming to give a Tarski-style semantics for English in accordance with the programme envisaged by Donald Davidson and in other recent work. I shall therefore be presupposing a Davidsonian framework, though what I say is presumably capable of adaptation to alternative semantic approaches.

It has long been recognized that tensed existence, or more precisely, statements that an individual has existed, does now exist, or will exist (relative to a certain time), present problems for the standard treatment of existence in quantificational logic. It has been suggested[1] that, whereas the classical thesis embodied in the dictum that 'existence is not a predicate' is correct so far as tenseless existence is concerned, if construed as the denial that 'exist' is a first-level predicate, tensed existence must be represented by a first-level predicate. Such a position is surely extremely counter-intuitive: the tensed and tenseless occurrences of 'exist' are surely connected. Moreover, what we say about 'exist' in its tensed uses ought to harmonize with a satisfactory account of tenses generally, and also ensure the right connection between the semantics of 'exist' and those of what appear to be the tensed analogues in English of the existential quantifier, i.e. 'There is', 'There was', 'There will be', etc.

I shall not attempt any general discussion of tenses in English, and hope that my account of tensed existence-statements will not be inimical to a general theory of tenses. A major interest will be to fulfil the second requirement—to preserve conformity with the idea that 'existence is what the existential quantifier expresses'. This latter doctrine has been associated with the thesis that 'exist' is not a (first-level) predicate. The arguments for that thesis have tended to appeal

[1] This has been suggested by Peter Geach.

to the idea that, if 'exist' is construed as a (first-level) predicate, certain sentences which in fact express contingent truths or falsehoods will no longer do so. Michael Dummett has recently shown[2] that such arguments are faulty in more than one way. In the first place, it is not clear how, if it is genuinely a mistake to treat 'x exists' as a genuine first-level predicate, we are in a position to say what the consequences would be of construing it as one. In this respect, 'exist' contrasts clearly with a predicate like 'rare'. The evident absurdity of inferring from 'Women who stammer are rare' that this woman stammerer is rare reveals that the logical form of sentences of the form '*F*'s are rare' is unlike that of a large class of other sentences which are superficially similar, and the difference will no doubt turn out to be that 'rare' is not a first-level predicate, true of individuals. But for precisely this reason, there is no sense in asking what the truth conditions of sentences containing it *would be*, *if* it were construed as a first-level predicate. Because 'numerous' is not a first-level predicate, we do not know what to make of a sentence like 'Sadie is numerous'. The parallel between 'exist' and 'numerous' has commonly been thought to be fairly close, but there are not the same surface indications that 'exist' is not a predicate true of individuals.

Further, as Dummett pointed out, the argument that, if 'exist' is construed as a (first-level) predicate, the truth conditions of sentences containing it must be wrongly represented overlooks the fact that, if 'exist' is construed as a predicate true of every individual, the truth conditions at least of general existential sentences will be the right ones. If 'Black swans exist' is construed as equivalent to 'Some black swans exist', and the latter sentence is treated in the way suggested by its surface grammar, it will express a truth if and only if there is something which is a black swan and exists; and since 'exist' is being taken as true of everything, there will be something which is a black swan and exists if and only if there is something which is a black swan. For similar reasons, 'No black swans exist' will be true if and only if nothing is a black swan. Moreover, there is no danger at all, if 'exist' is thus construed, of the unwelcome consequence that 'Black swans exist' will fail to express a contingent truth. The connection that, intuitively, there ought to be between existence and existential quantification is preserved.

If we turn our attention to singular existential sentences, the

[2] In *Frege: Philosophy of Language* (Duckworth, London, 1973), pp. 278–80.

acceptability of the consequences of treating 'exist' as true of everything is less clear. A good deal will depend on what semantic account is given of proper names and other singular terms. But it is certainly the case that, on the account under discussion, 'Aristotle exists' (taking the verb tenselessly) will express a truth, and equally, had the world been different in appropriate ways, might not have expressed a truth; even if it also has to be conceded that the proposition that it expresses, as things are, is not one that might have had a different truth value from the one it in fact has[3].

So far, then, there is no good reason for denying that 'exist', as it occurs in ordinary English, is a (first-level) predicate, any more than there is for denying that 'self-identical' is. It is also clear, however, that if the semantic account under discussion is correct, there is no need to take it as a *primitive* predicate; provided that the variables of quantification are construed as ranging over existing objects only (and the account under discussion plainly requires this) the required predicate can be defined using the apparatus of quantification and identity. So we may expect 'exist' not to figure in canonical representations of English sentences, being everywhere supplanted, in a familiar way, by '$(\exists x)(x = \text{—})$'.

Problems arise, as has long been recognized, when an attempt is made to give a semantic account of tensed assertions or denials of existence. Taking 'exist' as a predicate true of everything we seem quite uninstructed on how to understand its tensing. If it is true of everything that exists, how can anything exist at some times and not at others? This point can be underlined by appeal to the customary explanation of existence in terms of self-identity, or (equivalently) identity with something. An object can be identical with just one thing, itself; and its identity with *that* cannot vary over time.

One possible reaction to this is to introduce tense into the identity predicate. Such a manoeuvre may be thought to have something to commend it independently of the problem of the semantics of tensed existence. Prior[4] once suggested that certain things that we feel impelled to say in cases of branching or fusion, where *A* and *B* are apparently identical for a part of their respective careers and different for another part of them, supply an adequate motivation for tensing

[3] On this question, see the recent discussion in A. Plantinga, *The Nature of Necessity* (Clarendon Press, Oxford, 1974), pp. 144 ff.

[4] In 'Time, Existence and Identity', in *Proceedings of the Aristotelian Society*, lxvi (1965–6), reprinted in *Papers on Time and Tense* (Clarendon Press, Oxford, 1968).

the identity predicate. But it is doubtful how far such a two-term relation, variable over time, deserves to be called identity; and in so far as it is not rightly so regarded, its capacity for illuminating tensed assertions and denials of existence is limited.

The simplest approach is to treat 'exist', in its tensed uses, as a primitive predicate, amenable to tense in the way that other predicates are. If the classical analysis of tenseless uses of 'exist' in terms of identity is retained, a regrettable gap will appear between the semantics of the tensed and those of the untensed uses of the verb. Alternatively, the tenseless uses can be defined in terms of the tensed ones, and we shall have some such definition as the following:

$$(x \text{ exists (tenseless)}) =_{df.} (\exists t)(x \text{ exists at } t).$$

If we introduce a primitive, tensed existence predicate, questions will arise about the status of objects at times when they do not exist. It is natural, and common[5], at this point, to have the variables ranging over possible objects, which are actual at the time when the existence predicate is true of them. If, in addition, we allow that the variables range over *possibilia* of which the existence predicate is *never* true, we have the result that the existential quantifier will now have no essential connection with existence. Although a sentence of the form '$(\exists x)(x = a)$' *may* entail *a*'s existence, if it does so it will only be because individual constants have been assigned denotations in the class of existents, not because of the meaning of the existential quantifier. And it will not necessarily be a law that $(x)((x \text{ exists}) \leftrightarrow (\exists y)(y = x))$. Such a line has been taken by Cocchiarella[6]. If the notion of variables which range over merely possible objects is thought unacceptable, it may be laid down as an axiom that everything exists at some time or other, but then the connection between the meaning of the quantifiers and existence will be owed entirely to this axiom.

If the variables of quantification are allowed to range over *possibilia*, and an existence predicate is introduced true of some of them but not all (which may or may not be tensed), it is natural to introduce additional quantifiers which imply existence (or actuality). They may then be used to define the existence predicate, or they may themselves

[5] Among recent writers, Nino Cocchiarella and Richard Montague may be mentioned.

[6] In, for example, 'Some Remarks on Second Order Logic with Existence Attributes', in *Noûs*, ii (1968), 165–75.

be defined in terms of it. The first line is taken by Cocchiarella, the second by Nicholas Rescher[7].

If, on the other hand, the variables of quantification are allowed to range over individuals that exist (at some time or other), it will be natural to preserve the connection between existence and existential quantification by offering a semantic account of the quantifiers which will cater for the tensing of 'There is' locutions in English and which will enable these to be construed as asserting existence at particular times. This is what I now attempt to do, within a Tarskian framework. If, in the style of Tarski, truth is defined as satisfaction by all sequences, and we attempt to provide a recursive definition of truth for the sentences of natural language whose truth value varies over time, it will become necessary to relativize the truth predicate in several ways—certainly to a speaker and a time[8]. Whether relativization also to an utterance is required need not be raised here.

The truth predicate thus becomes a three-place one: what is defined is the truth of a sentence relative to a speaker and a time. Relativization to a speaker and time is obviously required to deal with pronouns like 'I' and 'you', and also demonstratives like 'this' and 'that', and no doubt many others, because the reference of these expressions is fixed relative to particular (actual or potential) utterances, and these are identified by reference to speakers and times. Since my concern is with tense, I shall ignore the complexities that arise here, and assume that the relativization of pronouns and demonstratives can be effected by appropriate speaker- and time-relative assignment clauses for indexical singular terms in the truth theory. The Tarskian definition of the truth predicate, in terms of satisfaction, which takes proper account of indexical expressions will be of the following form:

$$\text{True}(A, t, p) =_{df.} (s)(\text{Sat}(A, s, t, p))$$

where, of course, 't' ranges over times, 's' over sequences, and 'p' over persons (i.e. speakers). What we require is a theory which ensures that each sentence is, relative to a given person, at every time satisfied by all sequences or none. The relativization of the truth predicate to persons and times already imported by indexical singular terms already requires that the satisfaction predicate be a four-place one, true of quadruples of expressions, sequences, times, and persons.

[7] In 'On the Logic of Chronological Propositions', *Mind*, lxxv (1966), 75–96.
[8] Cf. Donald Davidson, 'Truth and Meaning', *Synthese*, xvii (1967), 319 ff.

However, in what follows I shall ignore the relativization to persons, as being irrelevant to tense, and treat satisfaction as if it were three-place and truth as if it were two-place.

The phenomenon of tense plainly introduces an additional relativization, over and above that imported by indexical singular terms. That is to say, given a fixed assignment to all singular terms, a given closed sentence will be satisfied by all sequences at some times and by none at others. Plainly this possibility will need to be provided for in the relevant satisfaction clauses for primitive predicates. Since satisfaction is relativized to a time, and the theory itself cannot contain sentences with indexical expressions, it is natural to envisage the clauses as having the following form for monadic predicates:

$$(t)((\text{Sat}\ (`F'\frown\alpha), s, t) \longleftrightarrow \text{At}\ (t)[F(s^*\ \alpha)])$$

(when 'α' is a variable ranging over terms) and similarly for predicates with more places. The idea behind this approach is to define in the clause for each primitive predicate in the object language the conditions in which it is true present-tensedly of an object.

This approach, which takes the present tense as basic, can then deal with the various other tenses by introducing suitable sentential operators, which may in their turn be defined using sentences with quantifications over times and an appropriate ordering of times. For example, where P is the (simple) past tense operator, so that $P(S)$ is the past-tense transform of the present-tense sentence S, we shall have a clause of the following form:

$$(t)((\text{Sat}(P(S), s, t)) \leftrightarrow (\exists t')(\text{Before}\ (t', t)\ \&\ \text{Sat}(S, s, t'))).$$

This ground has, of course, been well explored by tense logicians. What I am concerned with is what results from this treatment of tenses when we come to deal with the semantics of quantification.

I have been assuming that locutions of the 'There is—' or 'There are—' form in English are properly represented by the existential quantifier. As already mentioned, one striking feature of such sentences, which is clearly closely connected with tensed existence, is the occurrence of tense in the 'There is—' 'There are—' construction. Someone who says 'There are still giant pandas' is asserting their present existence, not the existence at some time or other of something of which it is tenselessly true that it is a giant panda. Similarly, there are past-tensed and future-tensed sentences like 'There were dodos at one time' or 'There will never again be a man who can perform this

task successfully'. In Tarskian semantics, the standard clause specifying the satisfaction conditions of the existential quantifier specifies that a sequence *s* satisfies the existential quantification of a formula A with respect to the variable '*x*' if and only if some sequence *s*′ which differs from *s* in at most the assignment to '*x*' satisfies A. Formally

$$(\mathrm{Sat}(\ulcorner(\exists a)(A)\urcorner, s)) \leftrightarrow (\exists s')(s' \overset{a}{\approx} s \;\&\; \mathrm{Sat}(A, s')).$$

It seems clear that this way of construing quantifiers will indeed make the truth value of existentially quantified sentences vary over time. If we consider a sentence like 'There were dodos', the present account will treat 'dodo' as a one-place predicate, true present-tensedly of an object if and only if that object belongs to its extension at the time in question. It will thus be true that there were dodos if and only if the predicate 'dodo' was true of something at some time in the past, relative to the time of utterance. Similarly, it is true now that there are driverless trains if and only if something now belongs to the extension of the predicate 'driverless train'.

However, although the truth of existentially quantified sentences will vary with time as a consequence of the time-relativization of the satisfaction clauses for predicates, will the required connection with the notion of *existence* be preserved? On the present account, 'There were dodos' will indeed entail the *past* existence of dodos (relative to the moment of utterance), while not entailing their *present* existence; but the reason for this is essentially connected not with the meaning of the existential quantifier, but with the special feature of the predicate 'dodo'. 'Dodo' is an example of a predicate which will apply, present-tensedly, to an object only while it exists, and, hence, to say that it applied to an object at a certain time in the past will imply that thing's existence at that time in the past. If we consider, instead, a predicate which may be true of an object at some times, and not true at others, irrespective of that object's existence, like 'famous', the absence of connection between the existential quantifier and existence will become apparent. For if it is true that something will be famous in the future, we shall have the truth of some existentially quantified sentence in the future, even though the object in question, to which the existentially quantified sentence owes its truth, will then have ceased to exist. More generally, the classical account of existential quantification, which has so far been modified only to the extent of making the satisfaction predicate a three-place one, will not leave room for a

sufficiently full-blooded concept of existence. Intuitively, some predicates are such that their ceasing to hold of an item is regarded as involving something's passing out of existence, others are not so regarded. If all predicates are treated semantically in the same way, so far as this feature is concerned, there seems no way of connecting existential quantification and existence.

A full discussion of this point, which I have expressed rather generally, would require a discussion of definite descriptions, which I have ignored in this paper. The difficulty that I have in mind is that if we take, for example, a sentence of the form 'The *F* no longer exists', and definite descriptions are treated in a Russellian way, the sentence, on the account under discussion, will have to be construed as saying that it was true of something at some time that it was (then) uniquely *F* and that it is no longer true of that thing that it is uniquely *F*. But where '*F*' is a predicate whose ceasing to hold of an object does not involve the object's ceasing to exist, the conditions required by this analysis may be fulfilled when it is false that the *F* has ceased to exist. The case of what are sometimes called 'phase sortals' will illustrate the point. If the small sapling that I had in my garden has not been destroyed but has grown into a large tree, it will not be true to say that the small sapling has ceased to exist merely because it has ceased to be a sapling; but it will be the case that it was true of something that it was the only small sapling in my garden, and that that is no longer true of anything. If a non-Russellian account of definite descriptions is adopted, they will presumably, in one way or another, be assimilated to proper names. 'The *F* exists' will then, on the account of existence under discussion, be represented as '$(\exists x)(x = \text{the } F)$', and this will vary in truth value provided that 'the *F*' is taken as denoting an object only if that object is *F* at the time of utterance. The same objections as before can then be raised against this as an analysis of existence. Of course, if the definite description in a sentence of the form 'The *F* no longer exists' is taken to involve a *past* tense, the problem will be how such a sentence can ever express a truth.

The distinction between those attributes that are existence-entailing and those that are not is stressed by Cocchiarella[9], who uses it to define an existence predicate and quantifiers distinct from the standard ones. His work is in the context of a system in which the variables of quantification are allowed to range over *possibilia*, which may or

[9] Op. cit.; see also 'Existence-Entailing Attributes, Modes of Copulation and Modes of Being in Second Order Logic', in *Noûs*, iii (1969), 33–48.

may not exist at any time at all, hence his concern is not solely with the problems of the tensing of existence. I want now to see how such distinctions may be represented within a Tarskian framework.

What we are primarily concerned with is sentences appropriate for the assertion or denial of existence at a particular time. We may thus approach the problem by considering things that have a *temporal. history*—that begin to exist at one time and cease to exist at another. For present purposes, we need not confront the issue of whether an object may possess a discontinuous career. Intuitively, a three-fold distinction can be made among the things that may be said of objects having such a history, and which are true of it at some times and not at others. In the first place, we may distinguish what can be true of an object only while it exists from those things which, though they may be true of an item at some times and not at others, may be true also at times when the item does not exist. Having singled out the class of predicates first mentioned, it is natural to go on to distinguish further, among those predicates which are true of an object only during periods of its existence, those which, if they are true of an object at all, are true of it throughout its existence.[10] We thus get a three-fold classification of predicates.

Among Type 1 predicates (predicates true, if at all, of an object throughout its existence, but only while it exists) will be sortal predicates like 'man' and natural-kind predicates in general, along with a large range of predicates represented by count-nouns in English. Among Type 2 predicates will belong 'asleep', 'is running', 'is observed', and in general those which imply some current causal interaction between what the predicate is true of and something else. Examples of Type 3 predicates, which may be true of something at different times both while it exists and while it does not exist, could be 'is famous', 'is forgotten', 'is referred to'. Falling outside this classification will be those predicates which are true of an object with a temporal history either at all times or at none, including the untensed or de-tensed predicates corresponding to those just mentioned. If it is construed in a tenseless way the truth of 'Aristotle is a philosopher' will not be relative to a time; but if 'philosopher' is construed as being true of Aristotle at some times and not at others, it will qualify as a Type 2 predicate, and therefore, since Aristotle no

[10] According to Prior (*Past, Present and Future*) such distinctions were made in the Middle Ages by Burleigh.

longer exists, 'Aristotle is a philosopher', taken present-tensedly, will no longer express a truth. What is in question is a three-fold classification of the predicates occurring in sentences whose relativity of truth value to time is, at least partly, attributable to tense.

So far, the phenomenon of tense has been dealt with by the relativization of the satisfaction predicate to times. An alternative approach is suggested by the occurrence of sentences with a definite temporal reference. In general it is permissible, with any tensed sentence, to insert an expression designating a particular time. Thus we may say that Bertrand Russell was alive on 1 January 1965. This leads on to the thought that 'alive' is really a two-place predicate, true of an object and a time. If we pursue this suggestion further, it becomes clear that the present tense has to be regarded as containing an implicit indexical 'now' filling the argument place for a time. 'Harold Wilson is alive' will require analysis as 'Harold Wilson is alive now', where 'now' fills the argument-place filled by a definite temporal specification in 'Harold Wilson was alive on 1 January 1974'. The various past and future tenses will then be explained in a parallel way to that of the previous account, with changes required to accommodate the fact that the relativization to time is now being treated as a feature of an individual predicate of the object language and not of the satisfaction predicate. Thus the simple past tense may be explained using an indexical predicate-forming operator. It will be true of something, x, that it was F if and only if, for some time t before now, 'F' is true of x and t, where 'F' is treated as a two-place predicate. In the case of all those predicates whose tensing is dealt with in this fashion, the effect will be that an ostensibly one-place predicate will become a two-place one, and, in general, every prima facie n-place predicate will be replaced by an $n+1$-place one.

The impact of this way of dealing with tense on the satisfaction clauses for such time-relativized predicates is in principle straightforward. If 'famous' is a predicate thought appropriate for this treatment, it will always be true, if it ever is, that a definite object is famous at a certain definite time, and an atomic open sentence containing the predicate 'famous' will, of course, be satisfied only by sequences which are such that a time gets assigned to the variable in the second argument place. The relativity to time of the truth value of different sentences will be simply a special case of that introduced by all indexical expressions. In fact it would be fair to say that, on this second approach, the semantics of tenses is assimilated to the

semantics of 'this' and 'that', since all tensed sentences will implicitly involve an occurrence of the indexical 'now'.

It might be thought that, if this method of explaining the semantics of tense is carried through consistently, there will no longer be any need to relativize satisfaction to a time, and satisfaction can once again, in the classical Tarskian way, be defined as a two-place predicate, true of pairs consisting of expressions and sequences. This, however, would be clearly mistaken; if truth is defined relative to a time (and also a speaker), it must be possible for the same sentence, even in the mouth of the same speaker, to be satisfied by all sequences at some time and by none at others. As was explained earlier, a relativization to a time is imported by indexical singular terms, like pronouns and demonstratives, and this second approach to tenses merely explains them by reference to an indexical term referring to the time of utterance. The full satisfaction clause for an apparently one-place predicate, which on the present approach is being given a second place for a time, will be as follows, when 'α' and 'β' are variables ranging over terms:

$$(t)[(\text{Sat}(\text{`}F\text{'}\frown\alpha\frown\beta, s, p, t)) \leftrightarrow (F(\langle s, p, t\rangle^*\alpha, \langle s, p, t\rangle^*\beta))].$$

(As will, I hope, be apparent, I am assuming that indexical singular terms can be dealt with by so defining the assignment function,*, that objects are assigned to terms by triples consisting of a sequence, a person and a time. But nothing of importance for present purposes depends on the detailed manner of dealing with indexical singular terms.)

If we now turn our attention to the treatment of existential quantification on this second approach to tensing, it would seem that, as with the first approach, it will be possible to give some explanation of tensed sentences involving the English analogues of the existential quantifier. To take the example considered previously, 'There were dodos', if the tense in this sentence is treated in accordance with the second approach, 'dodo' will need to be represented by a two-place predicate, true of an object and a time if and only if it is a dodo at that time. So 'There were dodos' will be represented in some such way as the following:

$$(\exists x)(\exists t)(\text{Before}\ (t, \text{now})\ \&\ \text{Dodo}(x, t)).$$

Once again, however, the implication of past existence will be carried by the meaning of 'dodo': 'dodo' is a Type 1 predicate, and is true of an object at a time only if it exists at that time.

Doubts may be raised about the capacity of the second approach to deal adequately with the phenomenon of tense when we consider sentences of the form 'There is (now) something which will be *F*', as contrasted with 'There will be something that is then *F*'. On the second approach there seems to be no basis for any differentiation between them. In both cases, the formal rendering will have to be as an assertion that, for some object *x*, and for some time in future *t*, *x* is *F*-at-*t*. Since only predicates are tensed, and not quantifiers, and the only predicate involved is '*F*', there is no room for differentiation.

Such examples, and the shortcomings, already mentioned, of the first approach, suggest that there is a good deal to be said for combining the features of both approaches: on the one hand, to introduce indexical sentence operators which exploit the relativization of the satisfaction predicate to a time so as to permit the tensing of the existential quantifier, and on the other to introduce tense into at least some predicates by adding a further argument place. If '*F*' is such a predicate, there will be room for a distinction between saying that it is now true of something that it is *F* at some time in the future, and saying that it will be true of something that it is *F* at that time. Formally, the difference will be that between

(1) $(\exists t)$ (Before (now, t) & At (t) $[(\exists x)(F(x, t))]$)

and

(2) $(\exists t)$ (Before (now, t) & At (now) $[(\exists x)(F(x, t))]$)

It is noteworthy that the different formal renderings are possible only because we give '*F*' an argument place for a time. If, instead, '*F*' had been a one-place predicate, the rendering of 'There will be something which is *F*', would have been:

$(\exists t)$ (Before (now, t) & At(t) $[(\exists x)(Fx)]$)

and there would have been no room for a distinct rendering corresponding to (2) above.

This, it seems to me, is a merit of the combined approach which exploits relativization of the satisfaction predicate to a time, and also relativizes some predicates to a time by adding a further argument place. For it will be natural to treat those predicates which are true of an object, if at all, only while it exists (Type 1 predicates) as not so relativized, and satisfied by objects only while they exist. This will enable us to explain the well-known general invalidity of the inference

from 'There will be something which is *F*' to 'There is something that will be *F*': where '*F*' is a Type 1 predicate, there will be no way of saying, when an object is *F* throughout its existence, that, *before* it comes into existence, there is already something which is going to be *F* in the future.

There are, in fact, several considerations which seem to me to tell in favour of the two-fold approach to the semantics of tense, apart from its capacity to deal with tensed existential quantification in English, and tensed existence. In the first place, if the three-fold distinction among predicates has some independent plausibility, it will be a merit in an account of the semantics of tense that such distinctions are represented by it. As I have already indicated, Type 1 predicates will not be relativized to a time by the addition of a further argument place, and the satisfaction clauses for such predicates will exploit the relativization of satisfaction to a time. Thus the clauses for such predicates will look like this:

$$\text{Sat}((\text{`}F\text{'}\frown\alpha), s, t) \longleftrightarrow (\text{At } (t)[F(s^* \alpha)])$$

(ignoring the relativization of the assignment function).

Both Type 2 and Type 3 predicates, on the other hand, will be relativized to a time, and the satisfaction clause for them will take the form already indicated.

The difference between them will appear in a difference in the way in which the two relativizations to a time interact with one another. Type 2 predicates were explained as those predicates which are true of an object only while it exists, if at all, but need not be true of it throughout the period of its existence. Hence, in the case of Type 2 predicates, the predicate will be satisfied by no sequence at a time where there is nothing existing at that time of which the predicate is true. Given that 'is flying to the moon' is a Type 2 predicate, it will be satisfied by no sequences at any time at which there is (then) nothing of which it is true that it is flying-to-the-moon-at-that-time.

Type 3 predicates, on the other hand, though they will receive the same sort of satisfaction clause, and satisfaction will, of course, as before, have an argument place for a time, will have the characteristic that if a sequence satisfies the predicate at one time it will do so at every time. For, given that an object is *F*-at-*t* at some time *t*, it will be true of that object that it is *F*-at-*t* at any other time. This will become clear if we take a Type 3 predicate like 'famous': it is clear that an object does not need to exist in order to be truly described as famous.

Given that Socrates no longer exists, it is still true of him that he is famous; so it is true of Socrates that he is famous-in-1975, and *that* is not something which is true of him at some times and not at others. In general, we have a Type 3 predicate where it is true of an object and time at one time only if it is true of that object and time at every time.

A further advantage of this approach is that it enables some sense to be made of the distinction already mentioned between those predicates whose ceasing to apply to something involves that thing's passing out of existence, and those which have no such implication. In order to mark that distinction, we need a semantic theory that will not give a blanket treatment of all assertions that there is nothing of which some complex predicate is presently true. If the existential quantifier in canonical renderings of English sentences, and the corresponding construction in the English sentences themselves, is to be regarded, as it most naturally is regarded, as expressing existence, some more elaborate account will be needed than one which simply locates all temporal reference in predicates, since it will be timelessly true or false that something answers to a complex description with all temporal references fully specified. If tenses are dealt with solely by the assigning of appropriate argument places for times in predicates, nothing will actually come into or go out of existence: it will simply be the case that predicates containing indexical expressions for times will determine different classes of objects at different possible times of utterance. On the other hand, with the first approach, with no internal tensing of predicates, each time a complex predicate ceases to be true of anything, those things of which it was true will have to be regarded as having passed out of existence, if the existential quantifier is to be regarded as expressing existence.

Another advantage that may be seen in a combination of the two approaches is that provision is made for sentences lacking subject-predicate structure to be tensed. Satisfaction clauses specifying the satisfaction of such sentences by sequences will be relativized to a time in an appropriate way if the satisfaction predicate is a three-place one. English sentences like 'It is raining' may be thought appropriate for such treatment. But whether or not such provision needs to be made for English, if the phenomenon of tense is intelligible independently of subject-predicate structure, an adequate semantic theory ought to take account of this.

If we return now to the problem with which we began, of the semantics of existence, the distinctions already made give some indication of

how it may be approached. Having distinguished Type 1 predicates as those which are true of objects with a temporal history, if at all, throughout the periods when they exist, and having represented them by one-place predicates, whose variation in extension is captured by the relativization of the satisfaction predicate to a time, there seems no good reason for not treating 'exist' as itself a Type 1 predicate. It will be distinct from all other Type 1 predicates in the respect that it will be true of everything, at some time. This is in line with the guiding principle that the variables of quantification range over existing things only. In the case of objects lacking a temporal history, this predicate will be true of them at all times. In terms of this one-place predicate, true of everything at some time, another predicate can be defined, expressing 'untensed' existence, true of everything *simpliciter*.

It is a consequence of this account that the existence predicate will be capable of definition by recourse to second-order quantification. For, although it will certainly not be the case that all Type 1 predicates are monadic, it will certainly be true that all predicates which are represented formally as being monadic will be Type 1, since they will necessarily lack internal relativization to a time. If we make the reasonable assumption that everything that exists has some genuinely monadic Type 1 predicate true of it while it exists—these, in the case of objects with a temporal history, will typically include 'sortal' or 'substance' predicates—it will be possible to define existence using second-order quantification. For it will be true that $(x)((x \text{ exists at } t) \leftrightarrow (\exists f)(fx \text{ at } t))$. If Type 1 predicates are distinguished from others in the way suggested, the existence predicate will be definable in the way suggested (the idea of which is, of course, not new), even though it is also true that many predicates hold present-tensedly of items even when they do not exist.

XI

States of Affairs

BARRY TAYLOR

I. STRUCTURE OF A THEORY OF STATES OF AFFAIRS

For a variety of semantical and metaphysical reasons, some better than others, philosophers have found it convenient to postulate extra-linguistic entities called *states of affairs* to serve as the descripta of sentences (closed formulae). In the somewhat vague terminology of these traditional theorists, each state of affairs is a logical complex having as 'constituents' the entities relevant for the truth of any sentence describing it. Some states of affairs *obtain*; such states of affairs are *facts*; and a sentence is true precisely in case it describes a fact.

Broadly, the aim of this paper is to give a precise explication of the traditional theory of states of affairs. Evidently, such a construction might follow one of two paths. One way would be to define a totality of entities to provide a stock of descripta for the sentences of any language whatever; in this case, for any language there will presumably be some states of affairs in the defined totality whose obtaining or otherwise is irrelevant to the truth values of sentences of the language. Alternatively, each language *L* might be regarded as bringing with it its own conception of the totality of states of affairs—the states of affairs, as we might say, *posited by L*, the obtaining or otherwise of any of which will have some ramifications for the truth values of sentences of *L*. A primary task for an explication of states of affairs following this second line would be to give a general method of constructing, for each language, the set of the states of affairs it posits.

The explication proposed in this paper will be along the second of the lines suggested; for obvious reasons, attention will be restricted to standard first-order languages, whose structure and semantics are well understood. The aim of the paper is thus, more precisely, to present a general method whereby, given a first-order language *L*, the theory of the states of affairs posited by *L* can be developed. The

proposed construction will utilize just set-theoretic apparatus along with standard semantical devices.

A little terminology enables us to state some restraints on the form of a theory which can plausibly be construed as a reconstruction of traditional views on states of affairs. Where S is a sentence, and t and t' terms, of a given language L, let $S(t/t')$ be the result of substituting t' for some occurrence of t in S; and call a sequence $S_1 \ldots S_n$ ($n \geqslant 1$) of sentences of L a *sentence-chain of* L *linking* S *and* S′ just in case

(*a*) S_1 is S and S_n is S'

and

(*b*) for each i ($1 \leqslant i < n$), either
(i) S_{i+1} is logically equivalent to S_i or
(ii) S_{i+1} is $S_i(t/t')$ for some coextensive closed terms t and t'.

To ensure a reasonable correspondence with traditional views, we now require that a theory of the states of affairs posited by L should define a set Σ of appropriate entities, a predicate of *obtaining*, and a relation of *description*, meeting the following conditions:

[Condition 1] To each sentence of L the description relation assigns a unique element of Σ.
[Condition 2] The description relation assigns the same element of Σ to sentences linked by a sentence-chain of L.
[Condition 3] If an element of Σ is described by a sentence of L, that element obtains iff the describing sentence is true.

These conditions are intended to ensure that an explication will preserve the main structural features common to traditional views, though there is one strand of traditional thinking which they deliberately fail to reflect. Proponents of states of affairs have commonly assumed the viability of the notions of intensionalist semantic theory in a way which may well seem unacceptable in a post-Quinean era; in this paper, I want to preserve as neutral an attitude as possible towards these suspect semantic concepts, and this desire is reflected in the stated conditions. Consequently, there is one thesis common to the traditional views which is actually contradicted by these conditions; for these theories usually hold in opposition to Condition 1 that only *synthetic* sentences of a given language describe states of affairs. I take it, however, that this common traditional thesis does not form an essential part of the semantic conception of a state of

affairs as an extra-linguistic sentential correlate, and is largely a consequence of the *epistemological* uses to which a theory of states of affairs has often been put; and in any case, our conditions do throw a sop to this traditional scepticism about the descriptive powers of purportedly analytic sentences, since a subset at least of these sentences, viz. the logical truths, will all be judged by a theory meeting Condition 2 to have trivially the same descriptum.

Intensional terminology is also implicit in two other theses commonly held by theorists of states of affairs: the negative thesis that e.g. such sentences as 'Quine is cordate' and 'Quine is renate' fail to describe the same state of affairs given the mere coextensiveness of the predicates 'is cordate' (= 'has a heart') and 'is renate' (= 'has kidneys'); and the positive thesis that e.g. 'Alfred is an aardvark' and 'Alfred is a groundhog' do describe the same state of affairs in view of the synonymy of the contained predicates 'is an aardvark' and 'is a groundhog'. These theses suggest that Condition 2 would more faithfully reflect the tradition if the notion of a sentence-chain it embodies were extended so as to allow links to be forged by substituting synonymous predicate-letters within earlier members of the chain. So Condition 2 as stated stops short of imposing the full requirement suggested by traditional views, for the sake of avoiding an outright commitment of the explication to intensional semantics; though of course this does not here involve any denial of traditional theses.

We seek, then, a general strategy for devising for any first-order language *L* a theory of the states of affairs posited by *L* whose internal structure will meet the Conditions 1–3. But if such a theory is going to be an adequate explication of traditional views, it will need to do more than simply meet these structural conditions; we must also require that it meets what might be called the Material Adequacy Condition, viz. that the entities it construes as states of affairs can reasonably be regarded as 'logical complexes' having as 'constituents' just the entities relevant for the truth of any sentence describing them. This last condition, though necessarily somewhat vague, will turn out to have a powerful if largely negative role; it rules out immediately, for example, any attempt to found a theory of states of affairs for *L* based on the conception of the states of affairs described by a given sentence *S* of *L* as the set of all sentences linked to *S* by a sentence-chain of *L*, though it seems clear enough that a theory based on this idea could easily meet all the other, structural, conditions.

II. DESCRIPTIONS AND STATES OF AFFAIRS

At this point, it becomes necessary to investigate the claim made in recent literature on states of affairs (particularly that influenced by the writings of Davidson) that granted sufficient richness in the primitive resources of *L*, metatheorems can be established which demonstrate that no theory of states of affairs for *L* can consistently satisfy all of Conditions 1–3 along with the Material Adequacy Condition. Evidently, if this claim can be made out, the programme outlined in the previous section is threatened: either some limitation must be imposed on the scope of the analysis, so that languages whose resources are powerful enough to sustain the troublesome metatheorems are exempted from the field of enquiry, or some modification must be made to the conditions we want a theory of states of affairs to meet. But first it behoves us to look closely at the relevant formal results; the more so since the manner of their statement in the recent literature has tended to be somewhat airy.

The metatheorems in question can be stated so as to concern languages which contain as primitives an identity predicate and a definite description operator, though for present purposes it suffices and turns out to be simpler if we consider operators somewhat less powerful than a standard definite description operator. A primitive definite description operator is a primitive syntactic device for forming a definite description from a variable (called the operator-variable) and any formula; let a primitive *basic* description operator be a primitive definite description operator functioning under the additional syntactic restraint that the operator-variable, and it alone, should occur free in the embedded formula, and call descriptions formed by means of such an operator *basic descriptions*. We can state the metatheorems we need to look at in terms of this terminology of 'basic descriptions', thus avoiding irrelevant semantic complexities attendant on the possible presence of free parameters in the formula embedded in the description; but the complications required to extend the results to languages containing a full-fledged description operator should seem obvious enough.

Call a basic description of a language *L rotten* (according to an interpretation *I* for *L*) just in case the formula embedded in the description fails (according to *I*) to be true of a unique element in the universe of *I*. Now any adequate semantic theory of a language with basic descriptions will of course have to treat a basic description

which is *not* rotten on a specified interpretation, as a designation of the unique element satisfying the formula embedded in the description; but a number of different treatments are possible for basic descriptions which turn out to be rotten. In order to obtain the metatheoretic results normally claimed to threaten the theory of states of affairs, we need, I think, to suppose ourselves dealing with languages whose semantic theory is *Strawsonian*, so that formulae containing basic descriptions rotten on the specified interpretation are reckoned truth-valueless on that interpretation. (The formal details of the elaboration of such a semantic theory are irrelevant here; we may however suppose them carried out by some such technique as van Fraassen's method of supervaluations.) Within such a framework, the natural way to define the logical truths so as to preserve the usual logical laws is to count as logically true those formulae which are true on all interpretations on which they are not truth-valueless; and accordingly formulae are logically equivalent just in case they have the same truth value on any interpretation on which both have any truth value at all.

The following metatheorem can now be established:

*M*1 *Let* L *be a language containing as primitives an identity predicate* = *and a Strawsonian basic description operator* ℩, *together with some closed singular term* t *which does not fail of reference.*[1] *Then there is a sentence-chain of* L *linking any two true sentences* S *and* S′ *of* L.

Proof. Consider the sentence-sequence $S_1^1 \ldots S_4^1$, where:

S_1^1 is S
S_2^1 is $(\iota x)(x = t \,\&\, S) = t$
S_3^1 is $(\iota x)(x = t \,\&\, S') = t$
S_4^1 is S'.

Here S_1^1 and S_2^1 are logically equivalent. (S_1^1 has a truth value only on interpretations for which the basic description $(\iota x)(x = t \,\&\, S)$ is non-rotten; since such interpretations must make both S_1^1 and S_2^1 true, they have the same truth value on any interpretations which assign truth values to both.) Similarly S_3^1 and S_4^1 are logically equivalent; and on the assumptions that t does not lack a reference and that both S and S' are true, the basic descriptions $(\iota x)(x = t \,\&\, S)$

[1] Sc. on the primary or 'designated' interpretation. (Similarly we use 'true' to mean 'true on the designated interpretation', etc.)

and $(\imath x)(x = t \,\&\, S')$ are coextensive. (Note that if t lacked a reference this would not hold since the identity

$$(\imath x)(x = t \,\&\, S) = (\imath x)(x = t \,\&\, S')$$

would not be *true*.) So $S_1^1 \ldots S_4^1$ is the desired sentence-chain.

A weaker result can be established independently by an argument of greater aesthetic appeal (since the sentence-chain constructed need not appeal to singular terms possibly extraneous to the sentences linked):

M2 Let L *be a language containing a primitive identity predicate* = *and a Strawsonian basic description operator* $\imath$. *Then there is a sentence-chain of* L *linking any two true sentences* S *and* S′ *of* L *respectively containing closed singular terms* t *and* t′.

Proof. Consider the sentence-sequence $S_1^2 \ldots S_6^2$, where:

S_1^2 is S
S_2^2 is $t = (\imath x)(x = t \,\&\, S(t/x))$
S_3^2 is $t = t$
S_4^2 is $t' = t'$
S_5^2 is $t' = (\imath x)(x = t' \,\&\, S'(t'/x))$
S_6^2 is S'.

Here S_1^2 and S_2^2 are logically equivalent, since S_1^2 has a truth value on precisely those interpretations on which both it and S_2^2 are true; and similarly for S_5^2 and S_6^2. Further, S_3^2 and S_4^2 are logically equivalent since both are logical truths; and by our assumptions about S and S' the terms t and $(\imath x)(x = t \,\&\, S(t/x))$ are coextensive as are t' and $(\imath x)(x = t' \,\&\, S'(t'/x))$. Hence $S_1^2 \ldots S_6^2$ is the desired sentence-chain.

What are the consequences of these metatheorems for the theory of states of affairs? The structural conditions 1–3 were framed with *standard* first-order languages in mind, and it seems reasonable that they should be modified if Strawsonian languages with truth-value gaps are to be considered; thus Condition 1 should be altered so as to require the assignment of descripta only to sentences which do not lack a truth value, and similarly Condition 2 should require sentences linked by sentence-chains to describe the same state of affairs only when the linked sentences both have truth values. But once these minor adjustments are made, it is evident that in view of the modified Conditions 1 and 2 and *M*1 an adequate theory of states of affairs for a language with identity, a Strawsonian basic description operator

and some referential singular term will need to assign the same descriptum to all true sentences of the language. Now the Material Adequacy Principle is admittedly vague; but if talk of the entities 'relevant' for the truth of a given sentence makes sense at all, then clearly arbitrary true sentences of a given language can have quite different entities relevant for their truth, and so by that principle ought to describe distinct states of affairs. So as a consequence of *M*1, there can be no theory of states of affairs adequate by the structural conditions 1–4 and the Material Adequacy Principle for a language containing a Strawsonian basic description operator, identity, and a referential singular term; and a similar conclusion can be reached independently by reflection on *M*2.

Yet these results have been obtained only within the somewhat bizarre context of a Strawsonian semantics for basic descriptions, with its rejection of the classical Bivalence Principle; and it remains to be seen whether they can be obtained in a more orthodox setting. The matter is clearly of some importance. For as things stand, it is apparently open for the friend of states of affairs to find fault with the vagaries of Strawsonian semantics rather than to modify or abandon his conception of states of affairs, perhaps taking the present difficulties as a hidden and unacceptable price to be paid for the Strawsonian rejection of bivalence. Accordingly, it behoves us to investigate the status of these results under a less radical semantic treatment of descriptions.

One way to incorporate a primitive basic description operator into a first-order language which does less offence to logical orthodoxy is to adopt a *Fregean* treatment of basic descriptions, whereby designations are provided for basic descriptions which turn out rotten on a given interpretation by some more or less arbitrary semantic convention, subject to the constraint that rotten descriptions embodying coextensive formulae turn out to designate the same element. (The simplest such convention might specify some element of the interpretation to serve as the element designated by all basic descriptions it makes rotten; or a more complex convention might be adopted whereby a rotten description is taken as designating the whole *set* of elements which satisfy the formula it embeds.) Formulae containing basic descriptions rotten on a given interpretation thus turn out either true or false on that interpretation, depending on the details of the formula and the semantic convention adopted; and the classical accounts of logical truth and equivalence can be maintained.

Now the metatheoretic results $M1$ and $M2$ have no direct analogues for languages whose basic description operators are Fregean, the reason being that certain logical equivalences which were crucial for the establishment of those results fail to hold within a Fregean semantic framework. Thus to establish $M1$ appeal was made to the logical equivalence of

(1) S

and

(2) $(\imath x)(x = t \,\&\, S) = t$

(where t is any closed term) but these are *not* logically equivalent on a Fregean semantics for basic descriptions, since (1) is false and (2) true on any interpretation which falsifies S and treats t as designating that element of the domain which is designated by basic descriptions embodying formulae true of nothing in the domain. Similarly, the proof of $M2$ relied on a logical equivalence between

(3) S

and

(4) $t = (\imath x)(x = t \,\&\, S(t/x))$

(where t is some closed singular term occurring in S); but again this logical equivalence fails within a Fregean framework, (3) being false and (4) true on an interpretation which makes S false, and t a designation of the element designated by rotten descriptions involving formulae with the empty extension.

Both of these crucial logical equivalences fail to hold because of the possibility of a given term's denoting the same element as basic descriptions involving formulae with the empty extension, and genuine equivalences can be obtained once steps are taken to forestall this possibility. So though (1) and (2) are not logical equivalents within a Fregean scheme, the sentences

(5) $S \,\&\, t \neq (\imath x)(x \neq x)$

and

(6) $(\imath x)(x = t \,\&\, S) = t \,\&\, t \neq (\imath x)(x \neq x)$

(where t is any closed term) *are* logically equivalent within that framework; and similarly the sentences

(7) $S \,\&\, t \neq (\imath x)(x \neq x)$

and

(8) $t = (\imath x)(x = t \,\&\, S(t/x)) \,\&\, t \neq (\imath x)(x \neq x)$

(where t is some closed singular term occurring in S) are Fregean equivalents, though (3) and (4) are not. And, although $M1$ and $M2$ have no precise parallels for Fregean languages, it turns out that these equivalences can be used to establish similar though weaker results. Corresponding to $M1$, we have

M3 Let L *be a language containing as primitives an identity predicate* $=$ *and a Fregean basic description operator* ι; *and let* t *be a closed term of* L. *Then, where* S *and* S′ *are true sentences of* L, *there is a sentence-chain of* L *linking the sentences*

$$S \,\&\, t \neq (\iota x)(x \neq x)$$

and

$$S' \,\&\, t \neq (\iota x)(x \neq x).$$

Proof. Take the sentence-sequence $S_1^3 \ldots S_4^3$, where for each i ($1 \leqslant i \leqslant 4$)

$$S_i^3 \text{ is } S_i^1 \,\&\, t \neq (\iota x)(x \neq x)$$

(cf. proof of $M1$).

Here S_1^3 and S_2^3 are logically equivalent, as are S_3^3 and S_4^3; and the truth of both S and S' guarantees that the basic descriptions in S_2^3 and S_3^3 are coextensive. Hence $S_1^3 \ldots S_4^3$ is a sentence-chain as desired.

(It is worth noting that $M3$, unlike the corresponding $M1$, needs no specific stipulation that t be a referring term since there is no place for terms lacking reference within a Fregean scheme. But the proviso which was added to (1) and (2) to obtain the logically equivalent (5) and (6) is in effect a Fregean analogue of the earlier requirement in $M1$.)

Similarly, corresponding to $M2$ we have:

M4 Let L *be a language containing as primitives an identity predicate* $=$ *and a Fregean basic description operator* ι. *Then where* S *and* S′ *are true sentences of* L *respectively containing the closed terms* t *and* t′, *there is a sentence-chain of* L *linking the sentences*

$$S \,\&\, t \neq (\iota x)(x \neq x) \,\&\, t' \neq (\iota x)(x \neq x)$$

and

$$S' \,\&\, t \neq (\iota x)(x \neq x) \,\&\, t' \neq (\iota x)(x \neq x).$$

Proof. Consider the sentence-sequence $S_1^4 \ldots S_6^4$, where for each i ($1 \leqslant i \leqslant 6$)

$$S_i^4 \text{ is } S_i^2 \,\&\, t \neq (\iota x)(x \neq x) \,\&\, t' \neq (\iota x)(x \neq x)$$

(cf. proof of $M2$).

This sequence is the desired sentence-chain, since the pairs (S_1^4, S_2^4), (S_3^4, S_4^4), (S_5^4, S_6^4) are logical equivalents, and under the hypothesis of the theorem the terms t and $(\imath x)(x = t \,\&\, S(t/x))$ are coextensive, as are t' and $(\imath x)(x = t' \,\&\, S'(t'/x))$.

These results demonstrate that description operators, in the presence of identity, generate problems for a theorist of states of affairs independently of a semantics which rejects bivalence. For—intuitively—different entities will be relevant for the truth of S_1^3 in the proof of *M*3 than are relevant for the truth of S_4^3, provided the truth-relevant entities for *S* differ from those for *S′*; so by the Material Adequacy Principle, S_1^3 and S_4^3 in *M*3 might need to have different descripta, as might the S_1^4 and S_6^4 of *M*4. But by those metatheorems, a theory of states of affairs meeting the earlier structural conditions will have to make each of these pairs of sentences co-descriptive. So the Material Adequacy Principle and the structural adequacy conditions are inconsistent when applied to languages with identity and a Fregean basic description operator.

We must conclude that a primitive description operator generates genuine problems for the notion of a theory of states of affairs meeting the conditions imposed in the last section, and that these problems cannot be dismissed as idiosyncracies of Strawsonian semantics. Indeed, although I have not established the point here, it seems to me that metatheoretic results disturbing for the theorist of states of affairs can be established for *any* reasonable semantic treatment of a primitive description operator. One thing to emerge clearly from this examination, however, is that the precise form that the disturbing metatheorems will take depends crucially on the details of the semantic account of descriptions adopted. This point has been insufficiently acknowledged in recent discussions in the literature, which appear to suggest that the arguments adduced in support of Metatheorems *M*1 and *M*2 will hold in any semantic framework—whereas they hold in fact, as far as I can see, only in the rarified atmosphere of Strawsonian semantics.[2]

But whatever the deficiencies of the literature, the conclusion that the primitive description operator is hostile to the adequacy conditions of the last section must stand; and so, short of abandoning the quest for a theory of states of affairs altogether, some plausible

[2] A further defect in many of these discussions is the use of a form of the argument employed here to establish Metatheorem *M*1 which relies on a spurious construal of mere set-theoretic equivalences as logical equivalences—a deplorable laxity.

modification in those conditions must be sought. Since furthermore the Material Adequacy Principle has been stated so vaguely, the modification must be to the structural conditions.

It is not difficult to find an appropriate alteration; the difficulty is plausibly located in the requirement embodied in Condition 2 that logically equivalent sentences should describe the same state of affairs. For 'logical equivalence' is itself not a concept altogether sharp, depending as it does for its elucidation on what Quine called a 'prior inventory' of the logical particles; and in the preceding pages the identity predicate and (primitive) description operator have tacitly been reckoned part of the logical vocabulary. This assumption itself might be reasonable enough; but it is no longer clear that the consequent notion of logical equivalence is such that the same objects are truth-relevant for all logically equivalent sentences, as consideration of pairs like (5) and (6) demonstrates, and *M*3 and *M*4 may be taken as confirming this suspicion. Accordingly, the problems generated by these metatheorems are avoided by recasting Condition 2 in terms of a notion of logical equivalence narrower than one which counts identity and the description operator as logical particles. The requisite notion is easily defined syntactically (the Completeness Theorem ensuring that this definition is equivalent to a semantic one): let a formula *A* be a *tight* logical truth just in case it is provable from some standard set of axioms for first-order logic exclusive of the identity axioms and any axioms on the description operator, and count S and S' *tightly equivalent* iff the biconditional $S \leftrightarrow S'$ is a tight logical truth. Now in the obvious way a sentence-chain linking sentences S and S' can be counted tight only if all the logical equivalences appealed to for its links are tight equivalences; and from now on we suppose Condition 2 reformulated with 'tight sentence-chain' replacing 'sentence-chain'.

Clearly, this modification draws the fangs of the metatheoretic results discussed in this section; in spite of them, there is now no contradiction in the idea of a theory of states of affairs consistently meeting the structural conditions and adequate by the Material Adequacy Principle even for languages with identity and a description operator as primitives. If the point appears to have been laboured, that is only because of the inordinate amount of importance attached to these results in the recent literature. We now turn to the main task in hand: that of presenting a construction meeting these conditions and applicable to any standard first-order language.

It turns out to be easier if we approach this task by means of a less ambitious construction which ignores the demand that tightly equivalent sentences should have the same descriptum and then look for modifications to meet this requirement. This initial construction is based on one presented in McKinsey, J., 'A New Definition of Truth', *Synthese*, vii (1948), 428 ff., though it differs somewhat in detail and the present difference of purpose enables a more straightforward presentation.

III. THE CONSTRUCTION

Let L be a first-order language having negation ($\sim$) and conjunction (&) as its primitive logical constants, and the universal quantifier ($\forall$) as its quantificational primitive; L will also contain a denumerable list of variables, predicate-letters P^n_j (using the superscript to indicate degree and the subscript for further differentiation) in finite supply, possibly along with individual constants and devices (functors, description operators) for constructing complex singular terms. Suppose that within a set-theoretic metalanguage M_L for L a 'designated' interpretation I for L has been defined (i.e. an interpretation under which the intuitive and intended meanings of formulae of L are preserved). In particular, suppose that a nonempty domain D for L has been specified as the range of variables of L (according to I); that a two-place functor * has been defined assigning, to each term t of L, an element $s^*(t)$ of D as its denotation (according to I) relative to a denumerable sequence s of elements of D; and that the notions of truth on the interpretation I and satisfaction on I by denumerable sequences of elements of D have been defined. Further, suppose that the metatheory assigns to each predicate-letter P^n_j of L an 'intension' $\text{Int}(P^n_j)$ and an extension $\text{Ext}(P^n_j)$ (relative to the interpretation I), and defines a functor Δ such that $\Delta(\text{Int}(P^n_j)) = \text{Ext}(P^n_j)$. (The metatheory for L may thus e.g. be thought of as developed along standard Tarskian lines, but incorporating enough of the Kripke apparatus to handle the theory of intensions for primitive predicates of L.)[3]

An initial construction of the theory of states of affairs for L can now be carried out in M_L as follows. First, we define an *atomic state*

[3] It will be observed that, although the various semantic concepts here introduced are relativized to I, this relativity is not reflected in the symbolism. The convenient policy of thus suppressing relativity to I will be adhered to in the symbolism to be introduced in the following pages; associated informal remarks will always make it clear where such relativity has been suppressed.

of affairs (*posited by* L *on* I) as any $n+1$-tuple $\langle \text{Int}(P_j^n)\ b_1 \ldots b_n \rangle$, where P_j^n is a primitive predicate of L and each b_i is an element of D; and then we take the set Σ of *states of affairs* (*posited by* L *on* I) as the intersection of the sets Σ' such that:

(i) if ξ is an atomic state of affairs, then $\xi \in \Sigma'$
(ii) if $\xi \in \Sigma'$, so is $\langle \sim, \xi \rangle$
(iii) if $\Gamma \subseteq \Sigma'$ and $|\Gamma| \leqslant |D|+1$, then $\Gamma \in \Sigma'$

(where, for any set y, $|y|$ is the cardinal number of y. This condition on cardinality ensures that Σ will contain elements appropriate as descripta, by the provisions below, for all the conjunctions and quantified formulae of L whilst not allowing too many unneeded elements into the set.)

Next we say that a state of affairs $\xi \in \Sigma$ *obtains* iff either

(i) ξ is $\langle \text{Int}(P_j^n)\ b_1 \ldots b_n \rangle$ and $\langle b_1 \ldots b_n \rangle \in \Delta\ (\text{Int}(P_j^n))$

or

(ii) ξ is $\langle \sim, \zeta \rangle$ and ζ does not obtain

or

(iii) ξ is a set of states of affairs, and every element of ξ obtains.

A description relation can now be defined between the sentences (closed formulae) of L and elements of Σ. First, a preliminary notion is needed. Let s, s' etc. be denumerable sequences of elements of D; using the functor * supposed available within M_L, we define the *state of affairs assigned* (*according to* I) *to a wff* A *of* L *relative to the sequence* s (Assig(A, s)) as follows:

(i) A is $P_j^n t_1 \ldots t_n$ for some terms $t_1 \ldots t_n$. Then Assig(A, s) is $\langle \text{Int}(P_j^n)\ s^*(t_1) \ldots s^*(t_n) \rangle$.
(ii) A is $\sim B$. Then Assig(A, s) is $\langle \sim, \text{Assig}(B, s) \rangle$.
(iii) A is $B \,\&\, C$. Then Assig(A, s) is $\{\text{Assig}(B, s), \text{Assig}(C, s)\}$.
(iv) A is $(\forall x_i)\ B$. Then Assig(A, s) is $\{\xi \mid (\exists s')(s' \text{ differs from } s \text{ in at most the } i\text{th place } \& \ \xi = \text{Assig}(B, s'))\}$.

It is now a simple matter to prove by induction on the length of S that

M5 For any sentence S *of* L *and sequences* s, s′, *Assig*(S, s) = *Assig*(S, s′).

In view of this metatheorem, we can define the *descriptum* according

to I of a sentence S (Desc(S)) as the unique state of affairs ξ s.t. for any sequence s, ξ = Assig(S, s).

This preliminary construction is obviously going to need some modification, since it fails to meet that part of Condition 2 which requires that tightly equivalent sentences should have the same descriptum. Thus e.g. Desc($\sim\sim S$) = $\langle\sim, \langle\sim$, Desc(S)$\rangle\rangle \neq$ Desc(S). On the other hand, it is a trivial matter to show that it does satisfy the other structural conditions, together with that part of Condition 2 which requires that S and $S(t/t')$ should describe the same state of affairs if t and t' are coextensive.

The status of this initial theory with respect to the Material Adequacy Principle bears looking at in more detail. A leading idea of the construction is an attempt to explicate traditional talk of states of affairs as 'logical complexes' with 'constituents' by set-theoretic means. Thus, the states of affairs described by atomic formulae are straightforwardly treated as sequences of the entities relevant for the truth of the formulae; the controversial feature here is the selection of 'intensions' as the truth-relevant predicative element, and the significance of this selection depends on the structure of the metatheory with which we have supposed L supplied and the philosophical assumptions behind it. If, *contra* Quine, it is assumed that it makes sense to talk of synonymies between natural-language predicates (or their first-order regimentations), then the 'intensions' of the semantic theory of L may be supposed to be assigned so as to function genuinely as the intensions of pre-Quinean semantics, so that first-order regimentations of natural-language predicates are assigned the same 'intension' precisely in case they are synonymous. The construction proposed will then follow traditional theorists both in the negative thesis that e.g. 'Quine is cordate' and 'Quine is renate' (or, more strictly, their first-order representations) fail to describe the same state of affairs despite the coextensive character of the predicates 'cordate' and 'renate', and also in the positive thesis that e.g. 'Alfred is an aardvark' and 'Alfred is a groundhog' *are* co-descriptive in view of the synonymy of their predicates. But the construction sketched is not in itself wedded to such a semantic view; a Quinean, sceptical of intensional notions, might prefer to treat all predicates of L as differing in 'intension' irrespective of whether or not they regiment purportedly synonymous natural-language predicates, and thus (say) to identify the 'intension' of each predicate-letter directly with the predicate-letter itself. The resulting theory of states of affairs would preserve at

least the negative thesis from traditional views, and should turn out to provide a useful if more austere Quinean analogue to traditional notions.

Granted this treatment of the states of affairs described by atomic sentences, the initial construction attempts to find set-theoretic operations which will locate a set containing the truth-relevant elements for complex sentences from sets of elements relevant for the truth of the sentences they contain. This is simple enough in the case of conjunctions and universal quantifications; but in considering negative formulae the construction runs into the traditional problem concerning 'negative facts'. This familiar headache is essentially generated by a tension between the Material Adequacy Principle and Condition 3: intuitively, the same elements are relevant for the truth of a sentence S and its negation $\sim S$, whence by the Material Adequacy Principle they ought to describe the same state of affairs; but S and $\sim S$ have opposed truth conditions, hence by Condition 3 must have different descripta. The present theory attempts to resolve this tension without doing too much violence to intuition by positing an additional, quasi-formal element (taken as the negation-sign itself) which is truth-relevant for a negated sentence $\sim S$ over and above those relevant for the truth of S itself; thus it may be said to acknowledge negative states of affairs as a distinct *sui generis* category.

A first step towards modifying this initial construction so as to ensure fulfilment of Condition 2 in its full strength is to define a relation $\approx$ of (I-relative) *equivalence* which will hold between the descripta of tightly equivalent sentences, i.e., to define $\approx$ so that we can establish as a metatheorem

M6 If S *and* S′ *are tightly equivalent, then* $Desc(\mathrm{S}) \approx Desc(\mathrm{S}')$.

It turns out that such a relation can be defined in the following way. (The procedure is based on a suggestion made in discussion by M. A. E. Dummett, and improves on an earlier method with which I experimented.) Let Σ^* be the set of atomic states of affairs in Σ, and let a *total state* (posited by L on I) be any subset of Σ^*; further, let the *actual* total state be that total state containing just the atomic states of affairs in Σ^* which in fact obtain. Then we can associate each state of affairs ξ in Σ with a set, T-states(ξ), of total states in such a way that ξ will obtain just in case the actual total state is an

element of T-states(ξ); this is recursively accomplished by the following definition:

(i) ξ is an atomic state of affairs. Then T-states(ξ) $= \{\Gamma | \Gamma \subseteq \Sigma^* \;\&\; \xi \in \Gamma\}$.
(ii) ξ is $\langle \sim, \zeta \rangle$ for some $\zeta \in \Sigma$. Then T-states(ξ) $= \mathscr{P}\Sigma^*$— T-states(ζ).
(iii) ξ is a set of members of Σ. Then T-states(ξ) $= \bigcap_{\zeta \in \xi}$ T-states(ζ).

The following metatheorem can now be proved:

M7 If T-states(Desc(S)) $\neq \mathscr{P}\Sigma^*$, *then there is an interpretation* I′ *for* L *such* that S *is false on* I′.

(The formal details of the proof are relegated to the appendix.) As an obvious corollary of this theorem, if *S* is a tight logical truth, then T-states(Desc(*S*)) $= \mathscr{P}\Sigma^*$. By the definition given above, and the standard definition of $\rightarrow$ in terms of $\sim$ and &, we have T-states (Desc($A \rightarrow B$)) $=$ ($\mathscr{P}\Sigma^*$—T-states(Desc(A)) $\cup$ T-states(Desc(B)); and putting these results together, if $A \rightarrow B$ is a tight logical truth, then T-states(Desc(A)) $\subseteq$ T-states(Desc(B)). Hence if *S* and *S′* are tightly equivalent then T-states(Desc(*S*)) $=$ T-states(Desc(*S′*)); and so we can define equivalence for states of affairs in such a way as to ensure provability of *M*6 by putting

Definition $\approx$: $\xi \approx \zeta \leftrightarrow$ *T-states*(ξ) $=$ *T-states*(ζ).

This definition can be used as the basis for a reformulation of the theory so as to guarantee that all the structural conditions imposed earlier are fulfilled. Thus states of affairs can be reconstrued as equivalence-classes on Σ under the relation $\approx$, with the descriptum of a sentence now reckoned as the equivalence-class to which its descriptum in the earlier sense belongs, and the new states of affairs construed as obtaining iff all their members obtain in the old sense; and the resulting theory can easily be shown to meet the imposed structural conditions. (The proofs that Conditions 1 and 3 are met are trivial; and given *M*6 it follows quickly that if *S* and *S′* are linked by a strict sentence-chain then Desc(*S*) $\approx$ Desc(*S′*), whence the modified theory must meet Condition 2.) Actually, however, there is little point in complicating the theory in this way beyond a desire to preserve the strict letter of the structural conditions; it seems more natural to adhere to the simpler conception of states of affairs as elements of Σ, and to rest content with talking of states of affairs as merely

equivalent in some cases where a more traditional theory would posit a strict identity. This, accordingly, is the course I shall take, simply noting in passing that a formal ruse would suffice to transform the theory into one more strictly conforming to the stated conditions and traditional views.

(Incidentally, it is also worth noting that an attempt might be made to convert the theory outlined into one strictly conforming to the structural conditions in a different way, namely by taking the set of states of affairs as $\mathscr{P}\Sigma^*$ and reconstruing the descriptum of each sentence S as T-states(Desc(S)). A moment's thought, however, should suffice to show that the resulting theory does violence to the Material Adequacy Principle; for e.g. the descriptum of a negated sentence $\sim S$ would turn out to have no constituents in common with the descriptum of S, whereas, as was pointed out above, intuitively the same elements are relevant for the truth of both these sentences.)

A couple of final points about this construction. As was noted above, it can be shown that sentences describe equivalent states of affairs if linked by a tight sentence-chain as (in effect) required by Condition 2; and it is fairly obvious that this result can be strengthened. Specifically: S and S' describe equivalent states of affairs if linked by an *extended* tight sentence-chain, i.e. by a sequence of sentences $S_1 \ldots S_n$ meeting our earlier requirements on a tight sentence-chain, with the additional proviso that S_{i+1} may be $S_i(P^n_j/P^n_k)$ if $\mathrm{Int}(P^n_j) = \mathrm{Int}(P^n_k)$. It will be recalled that, when Condition 2 was originally introduced, we discussed the possibility of stating it in terms of a wider notion of sentence-chain which permitted links to be forged by substitution of *synonymous* primitive predicates; and clearly, if the notion of 'intension' appealed to in the semantic metatheory of L is strong enough to explicate synonymy, this wider notion of sentence-chain will coincide with that of an extended tight sentence-chain. Hence the significance of this last result is that, if the metatheory embodies a rich enough notion of 'intension', the proposed construction will (effectively) satisfy the stronger form of Condition 2.

A more substantial metatheoretic result can also be stated using this extended concept of a sentence-chain. None of the structural conditions imposed in the first section laid down a *necessary* condition for two sentences having the same descriptum, and I think it is in the spirit of the tradition to allow some laxity in this respect. For the particular theory outlined here, however, it does turn out to be possible to give precisely the analogous necessary conditions for two sentences

describing equivalent states of affairs, at least for quantifier-free sentences; for it can be demonstrated that the converse of the last result also holds for quantifier-free sentences, i.e. we have

M8 If S *and* S′ *are quantifier-free and Desc*(S) ≈ *Desc*(S′), *then there is an extended tight sentence-chain of* L *linking* S *and* S′.

(For a proof, see Appendix.) The restriction to quantifier-free sentences *S* and *S′* here is necessary because, if the domain of *I* is finite, universal quantifications and conjunctions of *L* might turn out to have equivalent descripta even though unconnected by an extended tight sentence-chain. In allowing this possibility, the present account thus follows the anti-Russellian or Ramseyan strand of the tradition.

IV. APPLICATIONS OF THE THEORY

What is the use of a theory of the states of affairs posited by *L*? One primary reason for which states of affairs have been posited in the past has been to provide an analysis of the concept of truth for the sentences of the language under investigation; but it is obvious that a theory along the lines presented in the preceding section will be useless for such a purpose, since the semantic apparatus required before a construction of the states of affairs posited by *L* can be undertaken is sufficiently strong to permit a direct Tarskian elucidation of truth for *L* without detour through the theory of states of affairs. Similarly, states of affairs have sometimes been used in an epistemological context, in an attempt to elucidate a distinction between synthetic sentences (which describe states of affairs) and analytic ones (which do not); but the present theory was deliberately freed from a connection with doctrines of this sort with the adoption of Condition 1. So is there any philosophical purpose to which a construction like the present one can be put?

Recently, and particularly under the stimulation of the works of Davidson, a good deal of philosophical interest has been attached to the problem of using the techniques of formal semantics to elucidate the semantic properties of natural languages. Essentially, the aim of this programme is to find a method for paraphrasing the sentences of natural language into something like a first-order theory; the paraphrases are then treated as base structures within a hypothetical transformational syntax for the natural language, whose semantic properties are thus identified with those of the underlying 'first-order'

language as developed by formal techniques. It is evident enough, however, that the paraphrases appealed to may need to extend the standard first-order apparatus somewhat, and consequently that semantic methods beyond the straightforward Tarskian ones may need to be employed. It is in this area that I think the theory of states of affairs might be useful.

As an example of the sort of problem which the theory might be used to solve, consider the problem of the analysis of singular causal sentences such as

(9) Fischer's defeat of Spassky caused Brezhnev's wrath,

and suppose that within a first-order language L (supplied with a metatheory of the sort discussed at the beginning of the preceding section) we paraphrase

(10) Fischer defeated Spassky

as

(11) $D(f, s)$

and

(12) Brezhnev was wrathful

as

(13) $W(b)$.

(Complexities engendered by tense are of course avoidably ignored in these and succeeding paraphrases.)

An attractive syntactic proposal in order to handle (9) would then seem to be to extend the language L to L' by adding a new two-place sentential operator (say CAUSE); thus wffs of L would be counted wffs of L', and in addition

[FR L'] if A, B are wffs of L, then CAUSE (A, B) is a wff of L'.

(9) would then be paraphrased (into L') as

(14) CAUSE$(D(f, s), W(b))$.

The difficulties arise when we consider the semantic description of the operator CAUSE, i.e. the problems engendered by the attempt to extend the definitions of satisfaction (and truth) for L to embrace the additional formulae of L' introduced under FR L'. The precise

properties which an account ought to preserve will of course partly depend on the semantic concepts which are considered admissible; but at least we should want singular terms occurring within the scope of the operator to be portrayed as occupying extensional position, and to allow logically equivalent sentences to be substituted *salva veritate* for sentences occurring within its scope. Further, the truth conditions for (14) must be seen to require the truth of both contained sentences for the truth of the whole, even though the operator CAUSE must clearly not be truth-functional; and the semantic account must also not allow substitution of merely coextensive predicates within the operator's scope to guarantee preservation of truth value. (An intensionalist semanticist might further want to require on the other hand that substitution of synonymous predicates *will* preserve truth value.) It is because of scepticism about the possibility of a viable semantic account combining these features that the present analysis is rejected in the contemporary *locus classicus* on singular causal statements, viz. Davidson's 'Causal Relations' (*Journal of Philosophy*, lxiv (1967), 691 ff.).

It seems, however, that these semantic difficulties can be overcome if we suppose the theory of states of affairs posited by L developed along the lines suggested, and further suppose that the metalanguage M_L within which the semantic theory for L is defined contains a primitive metalinguistic two-place predicate Ca of causality holding between states of affairs. Such a predicate must be supposed to hold only between *facts*, and further to hold between all facts equivalent to facts between which it holds; in other words, we must suppose the formula

$$Ca(\xi, \zeta) \leftrightarrow \xi \text{ obtains } \& \ \zeta \text{ obtains } \& \ (\forall\xi')(\forall\zeta')(\xi \approx \xi' \ \& \ \zeta \approx \zeta' \rightarrow Ca(\xi', \zeta'))$$

is a proper axiom of M_L. (Of course, assuming causality as a primitive notion in no way vitiates the analysis for present purposes; cf. Davidson, op. cit.) Granted this apparatus, a clause can be added to the satisfaction definition for L to accommodate the additional sentences in L' bestowing on the operator CAUSE all the features considered desirable by stipulating that

> a sequence s of elements in the domain of I satisfies CAUSE(A, B) on the interpretation I iff Ca(Assig(A, s), Assig(B, s)).

This solution of the semantic difficulty does not in itself of course

vindicate the proposed analysis against its competitors; but it does illustrate the sort of use to which the theory of states of affairs can be put within the investigation of natural language. Indeed, if this approach to sentences like (9) is correct, then it may seem that singular terms of ordinary language like 'Fischer's defeat of Spassky' which refer to 'events' might plausibly be treated quite generally as designations of states of affairs, and this suggests a whole programme of analysis; N. L. Wilson, in 'Facts, Events and their Identity Conditions'[4] has taken some steps in this (anti-Davidsonian) direction. In any case, I hope I have said enough to indicate how the theory of states of affairs might turn out to have some fruitful applications in the semantic elucidation of ordinary language.

APPENDIX: PROOF OUTLINES FOR $M7$ AND $M8$

Proof of M7. For each element α of $\mathscr{P}\Sigma^*$ and wff A of L, let I' be an interpretation *induced by* α *and* A (relative to the designated interpretation I) iff

(i) the domain of I' = the domain of I

(ii) for each P^n_j, $\langle b_1 \ldots b_n \rangle \in \text{Ext}_{I'}(P^n_j)$ iff $\langle \text{Int}(P^n_j)\, b_1 \ldots b_n \rangle \in \alpha$

and

(iii) for each term t in A and sequence s, $s^*_{I'}(t) = s^*(t)$

(where subscripts indicate relativization of semantic apparatus to I'). Then, subject to the proviso in the Remark below, for each α and A there is an interpretation I' induced by α and A. Further, by induction on the length of A, we establish

Lemma 1. If I' is induced by α and A, then s satisfies A on I' iff $\alpha \in$ T-states(Assig(A, s)).

The theorem follows: if T-states(Desc(S)) $\neq \mathscr{P}\Sigma^*$, then for some $\alpha \in \mathscr{P}\Sigma^*$, $\alpha \notin$ T-states(Desc(S)), whence by Lemma 1 S is false on some I' induced by α and A.

Remark. Obviously there is for each α and A an interpretation I' meeting conditions (i) and (ii) above; further, if L contains no description operators, condition (iii) can also easily be met. If L contains a description operator, we may simply require by finitely many separate stipulations that for each description in A the appropriate instance of (iii) should hold. The resulting interpretation I' may then turn out to be nonstandard in its treatment of descriptions (since the referent

[4] Unpublished mimeograph; presumed forthcoming in a *Festschrift* for C. A. Baylis.

on I' of a description may not be a function of the extension on I' of the formula it embeds). But this does not affect the significance of $M7$ for the paper, since the tight logical truths must be true even on interpretations nonstandard in their treatment of descriptions.

Proof of M8. For each P_j^n, let $\overline{P_j^n}$ be some arbitrarily selected cointensive predicate-letter; similarly, for each closed term t, let $\bar{t}$ be some arbitrarily selected coreferential closed term; and let the *normalization* $N(S)$ of a sentence S be the result of replacing each P_j^n and closed term t in S by $\overline{P_j^n}$ and $\bar{t}$ respectively, Then clearly, for any S, S and $N(S)$ are linked by an extended tight sentence-chain of L; so to prove the theorem, it suffices to establish

Lemma 2. If S and S' are quantifier-free, and Desc(S) $\approx$ Desc(S'), then $N(S)$ is tightly equivalent to $N(S')$.

Call a sentence S *normal* iff $S = N(S)$; further, let a *normal valuation* for L be a Boolean valuation of all normal quantifier-free wffs of L. Then any normal quantifier-free sentence S is a tight logical truth iff for every normal valuation v, $v(S) = 1$. Let v be the normal valuation *induced by* an element α of $\mathscr{P}\Sigma^*$ iff for each normal atomic sentence S of L, $v(S) = 1$ iff Desc(S) $\in \alpha$. Then by induction on the length of S, we can establish

Lemma 3. If S is a normal quantifier-free sentence, then the normal valuations v such that $v(S) = 1$ are precisely those induced by elements of T-states(Desc(S)).

Lemma 4. For any sentence S, Desc(S) = Desc($N(S)$).

Lemma 2 follows. Suppose the hypotheses true; then by Lemma 4 Desc($N(S)$) $\approx$ Desc($N(S')$); so by Lemma 3, precisely the same normal valuations assign 1 to $N(S)$ as to $N(S')$; hence $N(S)$ and $N(S')$ are tightly equivalent.

XII

The *De Re* 'Must': a Note on the Logical Form of Essentialist Claims*

DAVID WIGGINS

I

'Necessity does not properly apply to the fulfilment of conditions by objects (such as the ball of rock which is Venus or the number which numbers the planets), apart from ways of specifying them . . .' So Quine writes in 'Reference and Modality'.[1] A little later in the same article he writes 'This means adopting an invidious attitude towards certain ways of specifying x . . . and favouring other ways as somehow better revealing the "essence" of the object . . . Evidently this reversion to Aristotelian essentialism is required if quantification into modal contexts is to be insisted upon . . .'

Quine mocks essentialism. But are his strictures levelled at unreflecting acceptance of the ancient Aristotelian ontology of three-dimensional changeable continuants in terms of which we are still doing our unthinking best to make sense of the everyday fabric of the world? Or does he maintain that, *even while we remain within that provincial ontology*, we have the choice to discriminate or not discriminate in favour of some of the concepts which the things we recognize fall

* This paper continues one of the themes of 'Identity, Designation, Essentialism, and Physicalism', forthcoming in *Philosophia* (1975) and in my contribution to the symposium 'Identity, Necessity and Physicalism' to appear in the *Proceedings of the* 1974 *Bristol Philosophy of Logic Conference* (ed. S. Körner and M. Welbourne, Blackwell, Oxford, 1975). It nowhere presupposes that paper. The stimulus to attempt the continuation came from trying to defend some of these contentions at the Corso Estivo di Filosofia 1974 in Montagnana, Italy. The appendix which Christopher Peacocke has very kindly agreed to write for the piece is some sign of the nature and extent of my great debt to him both as one of the discutants there and subsequently. I am also indebted to J. A. W. Kamp in the section on negation.

[1] *From a Logical Point of View* p. 151. Note also p. 148: 'To be necessarily greater than 7 is not a trait of a number but depends on the manner of referring to the number.' For the solution to Quine's paradox of the number of the planets see R. Cartwright, 'Identity and Substitutivity', in *Identity and Individuation* ed. M. K. Munitz (NYU, New York, 1971).

under: that we can somehow avoid giving preeminence to concepts constitutive of what it is to be this or that very kind of continuant (i.e. essences)?[2]

Quine's intention is not completely clear. But if it were to suggest the second of these two things, then I should object that nothing less than a universally agreed and deeply rooted system of deliberate discrimination in favour of substance-concepts, and against what are rated mere accidents, could explain the *definiteness* with which our culture has had to contrive to invest questions of persistence and identity through time.[3] Nor could anything less than this account for the measure of unanimity with which scientific discoveries are deployed to find objective answers for such questions.

In anti-essentialist writings one of the most striking admissions of the claims I have just made is to be found in Russell's chapter on 'Aristotle's Logic' in his *History of Western Philosophy*. As a statement of an archetypal idea from which so much of the anti-essentialism, indeed the anti-Aristotelianism, of modern philosophy derives, it deserves extended quotation.

Socrates may be sometimes happy, sometimes sad; sometimes well, sometimes ill. Since he can change these properties without ceasing to be Socrates, they are no part of his essence. But it is supposed to be of the essence of Socrates that he is a man . . . . In fact, the question of essence is one as to the use of words. We apply the same name, on different occasions, to somewhat different occurrences, which we regard as manifestations of a single 'thing' or 'person'. In fact however this is only a verbal convenience. The essence of Socrates thus consists of those properties in the absence of which we should not use the name 'Socrates'. The question is purely linguistic: a *word* may have an essence, but a *thing* cannot. The conception of 'substance' like that of 'essence' is a transference to metaphysics of what is only a linguistic convenience. We find it convenient, in describing the world, to describe a certain number

[2] Cp. *Word and Object* (M.I.T. Press, Cambridge, Mass., 1960), p. 92: 'We in our maturity have come to look upon the child's mother as an integral body who, in an irregular closed orbit, revisits the child from time to time.' Question: Do we have any alternative but to see *the child's mother* in such a way? Or is it just that we had the choice of conceptualizing or not conceptualizing the world in such a way as to articulate such entities as women and their children? It may have been the purpose of some essentialists to deny that we had the second choice, but it is not my purpose. To confuse the two questions and try to transform a negative answer to the first into a negative answer to the second is to perpetuate one of the principal confusions which nourish the dispute between realism and idealism.

[3] Cp. my *Identity and Spatio-Temporal Continuity* (Blackwell, Oxford, 1967), Part One, p. 7 and Part Two, pp. 30–4 (1st Edition), a passage justly criticized by Shoemaker and now wholly amended for the second edition. See also my 'Essentialism, Continuity and Identity', forthcoming in *Synthese* (1974–5).

of occurrences as events in the life of 'Socrates' and a certain number of others as events in the life of 'Mr Smith'. This leads us to think of 'Socrates' or 'Mr Smith' as denoting something that persists through a number of years, and as in some ways more 'solid' and 'real' than the events that happen to him . . . . He is not . . . really any more solid than the things that happen to him. 'Substance' when taken seriously is a concept impossible to free from difficulties . . . . 'Substance' in fact is merely a convenient way of collecting events into bundles . . . What is Mr Smith apart from . . . occurrences? A mere imaginary hook, from which the occurrences are supposed to hang. They have in fact no need of a hook, any more than the world needs an elephant to rest upon. . . . 'Mr Smith' is a collective name for a number of occurrences. If we take it as anything more, it denotes something completely unknowable, and therefore not needed for the expression of what we know. 'Substance', in a word, is a metaphysical mistake due to transference to the world structure of the structure of sentences composed of a subject and a predicate. I conclude that the Aristotelian doctrines with which we have been concerned in this chapter are wholly false, with the exception of the formal theory of the syllogism, which is unimportant.

Allowing Russell 'convenience' as a name of what is virtual practical necessity, and waiving several small points such as the age-old confusion of a substance with a we-know-not-what (the supposititious survivor of a hypothetical process of removal of 'mere attributes', presumably as 'not really' the substance's attributes), I find much as an essentialist to applaud in this passage. The ontology of substances, in terms of which we view ourselves and one another and the medium sized landmarks of human existence, is indeed in the peculiar but agreed sense a convenience. For all I know, Russell and other philosophers with a powerful talent for set-theoretical cum mereological construction really could dispense with this ontology and adopt in its place some purer and more homogeneous ontology of events.[4] But it is

[4] And physics is not the only place where we should lose something if we could never even *look outwards* from within the ontology of three-dimensional continuants. Philosophy has been well served by writers upon identity who have reminded us that there is another way of experiencing the world which, while it depends on our continuant ontology, finds a way to look somehow beyond it. Take for instance the closing words of *Du côté de chez Swann*, as rendered by Scott-Moncrieff:

The reality that I had known no longer existed. It sufficed that Mme Swann did not appear, in the same attire, and at the same moment, for the whole avenue to be altered. The places that we have known belong now only to the little world of space on which we map them for our own convenience. None of them was ever more than a thin slice, held between contiguous impressions that composed our life at that time; remembrance of a particular form is but regret for a particular moment; and houses, roads, avenues, are as fugitive, alas, as the years.

Here art and nostalgia in concert have wrought from absurdity (from the crass confusion which Cratylus, reduced to whistling and gesticulating by the impossibility of stepping into the same river even once, intentionally or unintentionally exposed

the virtue of Russell's account as I see it that he has no consistent desire to deny, and does seem to assert, that, *if* we insist on availing ourselves of the convenience of the ontology of continuants (which strictly he thinks we should not, but *if* we do) then we *shall* commit ourselves to conferring a special role upon the essences which give the principles of continuity of the continuants which are articulated in that conceptual scheme. That is meant to be one of the objections to the ontology of continuants. It is true that Russell's anxiety to cast doubt on the echt existence of so second-grade an existent as Mr. Smith or Socrates—note the imperfectly executed project of scare-quoting all the occurrences of their names—induces him to declare that the question is purely linguistic. ('A *word* may have an essence but a *thing* cannot'—which by no means follows from Socrates or Mr. Smith's being in the peculiar but agreed sense a convenience.) But Russell's primary purpose is to advertise the claims of a superior ontology. The matter is utterly different with the other and later philosophers, numbering perhaps thousands, who in middle-of-the-road fashion have resisted Russell's ontological prospectus. They have preferred to discuss ordinary continuants like Socrates or Mr. Smith or his briefcase rather than events but persisted in the idea that there is nothing more than convenience or confusion in the central role the essentialist assigns to *man* in the individuation of Smith or Socrates. What I am emphasizing is that this was not Russell's position. But it is characteristic of the philosophers I have in mind to view with suspicion, without rejecting or defying Socrates or Mr. Smith themselves as individual continuants, the essentialist contention that, whatever else they may be, these must be men. If any philosophers believe in a substrate of *we know not what*, it must I think be these latter day anti-essentialists. Certainly they are bad heirs to Russell. Without even noticing what they are doing, they have shifted the question of 'convenience' to a new place. They have transferred it from the point of embracing or not embracing the continuant ontology

long before Hume & Bergson reinvented it) something which transcends confusion, transcends even falsehood. In these words of Proust there is a truth scarcely by literal means communicable, but a truth nonetheless. But this is not to say that houses, roads and avenues are not after all persisting things—or even that Proust himself thinks that they are not. If we understand his claim perhaps we shall not find any inconsistency between the *Swann* passage and *Jean Santeuil*:

'Places are people, but people who do not change and whom we often see again after a long time in wonderment that we have not remained the same' (p. 534, trans. Hopkins, London 1955).

as a whole—which is where Russell more or less put it—to the entities themselves which that world-view articulates. But in seeming to allow that Socrates and Mr Smith—and hence they themselves?—need not be men (could then be anything?), they threaten the operation of the only ontology which (in their seasoned preference for what has been 'tested over the lifetime of the many generations of our ancestors'[5]) they are actually willing to try to understand.

There is of course one respect in which I sympathize with the philosophers I have just mentioned—this is the idea that the three-dimensional continuant ontology is neither worthless nor demonstrably confused. But if one takes it seriously, one must examine it seriously too. If it must make a distinction of essence and accident, as Russell and I seem agreed that it must, then so far as I am concerned that is sufficient excuse for some obstinate interest in essentialist claims. At least one thing we need then is to understand these claims better. Amongst the first questions we should try to answer is the question 'What is the logical form of *Socrates must be a man* or *Socrates is necessarily a man* or *Socrates cannot help but be a man*?'

II

It is not uncommon in philosophers of avowedly sceptical or anti-essentialist persuasion to make an exception in their stand against essentialism for such claims as that Socrates is necessarily Socrates.[6] This then, at least *ad homines*, is a good place to start upon the subject.

Consider Miss Barcan's infamous derivation[7]:

$$(1) \quad (x)(y)((x = y) \supset (Fx \equiv Fy)).$$

As one instance of (1), provided that the letter F may stand proxy for such modal properties of objects as *is necessarily identical with x*, we get

$$(2) \quad (x)(y)((x = y) \supset (\Box(x = x) \equiv \Box(y = x))).$$

But by the truth of $(x) \Box (x = x)$—reading $\ulcorner \Box \phi a \urcorner$ as saying that

[5] J. L. Austin, *Collected Papers* (Clarendon Press, Oxford 1961), p. 130.

[6] Cp. Terence Parsons 'Essentialism and Quantified Modal Logic', *Phil. Review*, lxxvii (1969).

[7] *J.S.L.*, xii (1947), 15.

$\ulcorner \phi a \urcorner$ is true of any world containing a[8]—and by the consequent superfluity of the third clause, viz.,

(3) $\Box(x = x)$,

(2) must entail

(4) $(x)(y)\,[(x = y) \supset \Box(y = x)]$.

What we make of this seems to depend on what view we take of possible worlds.

If we take the view that possible worlds are in thought *discovered*—a realist view, let us say—then there is probably a way to deny this conclusion (e.g. by qualifying (1)). For if we *discover* possible worlds, then we have to scrutinize them (as if with a telescope, Kripke would say) in order to determine which if any of the contents of a possible world correspond to the contents of our own world. The identities of the things in the discovered world are not then built into the very characterization of the world in the way in which the properties and relations involved in it are.[9] (For some reason the latter are always supposed to be unproblematically self-identifying.) Identity itself is then in some sense supervenient upon the other self-identifying features; and there is nothing anywhere in this conception of a possible world to rule out the idea of discovering in a possible world *twins* (e.g. Hesperus *and* Phosphorus) of what is in this world one individual (Venus). (4) need not then stand.

I cannot myself find in this realist view a compelling rebuttal of (4), even if it represents better than Kripke's postulational view of possible worlds what must have been the imaginings of the pre-Babylonian astronomers who had no idea that Hesperus was identical with Phosphorus. Why after all should identity be supervienient on other relations? And surely possible worlds are not really things we find or discover. Rather we make them. Surely again we could find contingent *sense* (whether or not we could often find truth) in the counterfactual 'You might have resembled me, the way I am, and

[8] Cp. Kripke 'Identity and Necessity' in Milton K. Munitz (ed.) *Identity and Individuation* (NYU, New York, 1971), p. 137. 'Let us interpret necessity here weakly. We can count statements as necessary if whenever the objects mentioned therein exist, the statement would be true.' I have discussed this reading in 'Identity, Designation, Essentialism, and Physicalism', op. cit., and tried to refute any attempt along these lines to reduce *de re* to *de dicto*.

[9] Cp. Jaakko Hintikka 'The Semantics of Modal Notions', *Synthese* xxi (1970); and as against this Kripke op. cit. and my 'Essentialism, Continuity, and Identity', op. cit.

been much less the way you actually are: even while I might have been more like you, as you actually are, than you were.'[10] But on a realist view, where resemblance arbitrates cross-world identity, this supposition cannot even be given the right meaning.

So *if* we see possible worlds as the right way to decide (4), I conclude that a postulational or constructional view of them may provide a sounder framework than the realist one. Within this framework there will be no more problem about identifying the individuals in a possible world—that is about identifying the entities in a supposition which one constructs oneself—than there ever is for one to know what named individuals one is thinking about.

On this view of possible worlds three things are immediately evident.

(a) No single individual can correspond to two distinct entities in another possible world. I may frame the supposition of Caesar's being a plebeian and crossing the Rubicon. I may frame the supposition of Caesar's being a plebeian and not crossing the Rubicon. But these are distinct possible worlds. If I try to combine them in one supposition for one possible world and twin Caesar in that world, then I am wide open to the charge of simply not having *made up my mind* what my counterfactual supposition about Caesar *was*.

(b) Some at least of the properties actually enjoyed by an individual in this world may vary in distinct possible worlds.

(c) Although a counterfactual conceiver never needs to establish his title to be constructing a supposition about a certain individual, he must guard in various ways against *destroying* the presumption that his counterfactual conceivings do relate to this or that individual. No individual can be just anything or have just any property you like in another possible world.

Point (b) is very obvious. As for (c), theorem (4) is quite insensitive to its further elaboration.[11] Point (a) is also, on one point of view, very obvious. But the trouble is that point (a) begs the question *immediately* against anyone who thinks (4) is false and that a typical informative identity-statement is contingent. Call him the contingency theorist. He will say, and not unjustly, that theorem (4) is simply packed into the very conception which yields principle (a). And he was not party to that conception.

[10] Cp. Fred Feldman 'Counterparts', *J.Phil.*, lxvii (1971).
[11] For which see my op. cit., 'Essentialism, Continuity, and Identity'.

A good way to have resolved the dispute between the postulational possible world theorist and the contingency theorist would have been to translate the derivation (1)(2)(3) ⊢ (4) back into the language of pure suppositions, and to have settled the matter independently of all commitment to the ontology of possible worlds. The trouble is that this is not as easy as Kripke may have led some people to suppose. 'Suppose that Hesperus were not Phosphorus. Well, Phosphorus is Phosphorus. And Hesperus is Phosphorus, moreover. So if Hesperus were not Phosphorus, Phosphorus would be not Phosphorus.' Yes, but surely not if Hesperus were *not* Phosphorus? Perhaps there is a better way to argue purely suppositionally for the necessity of identity, but it is difficult to see what argument there is for (4) which is purely suppositional and yet quite innocent of possible worlds. Something of persuasive and expressive power is lost in every attempt I have been able to make.

At this point the contingency theorist may go over to the attack and turn upon the derivation itself. He may question the definition of *necessarily identical with x*, and compare it with a definition like 'is thought to be Dr. Jekyll'. One would scarcely want a derivation analogous to that of (4) with the consequence that 'If Dr. Jekyll is Mr. Hyde, then Dr. Jekyll is thought to be Mr. Hyde', he will say. (Taking that sentence in its natural meaning.) The fact is, he will claim, that 'it is necessary that - - -' generates an opaque context at '- - -'; and that there was never any reason to suppose either that equivalents were intersubstitutable there, or that properties will be well defined by means of the replacement by variables or designations within the scope of this operator in '. . . necessarily (- - -)'. 'Necessarily' belongs with 'it is believed that - - -', 'it is hoped that - - -', 'it is probable that - - -', 'it is funny/amusing/unfortunate that - - -', and not with 'it is true that - - -', 'it is [not] the case that - - -', or 'not - - -'. It is true that the counterexamples to (4) can be reduced by the method of Russell and Smullyan[12] to proportions which are more manageable for the necessity theorist than they at first seemed; but this reduction in their number still leaves unsettled the question of the inter-substitution of variables and names for the same thing in 'necessarily' contexts. It is beside the point whether these are 'rigid designators'. Not even rigid designators are intersubstitutable in 'probably' contexts, so why should they be in for all one knows equally opaque 'necessarily'

[12] Smullyan, *J.S.L.*, xii (1947), using Russell's distinction of the primary and the secondary occurrence of a definite description.

contexts? Possible worlds are simply a way of concealing the whole difficulty from view, the contingency theorist will say.

So far, I think the contingency theorist has very much the edge over the necessity theorist. The only good way to defend (4) is to derive it in a context which is innocent even of the suspicion of opacity. But in fact—though nobody has bothered sufficiently with the contingency theorist to say this—there is a way to do this, taking off from a *must* in English which is both manifestly *de re*, and manifestly modifies predicates and relations. It is present in 'The number of the planets, which is nine, must be greater than seven'.[13] Applying this modifier to the relation of identity $(\lambda x)(\lambda y)(x = y)$ we get $\text{Nec}[(\lambda x)(\lambda y)(x = y)]$ or that relation which any r and any s have iff they are necessarily identical. Then we may reproduce the derivation of (4) in terms which are perfectly innocent even of the suspicion of quantifying into opaque contexts as follows:

(1) $(x)(y)((x = y) \supset (Fx \equiv Fy))$
(2λ) $(x)(y)((x = y) \supset ((x \text{ has } (\lambda z)[[\text{Nec}[(\lambda r)(\lambda s)[s = r]]], [x, z]]) \equiv (y \text{ has } (\lambda z)[[\text{Nec}[(\lambda r)(\lambda s)[s = r]]], [x, z]]))$
(3λ) $(x)(x \text{ has } (\lambda z)[[\text{Nec}[(\lambda r)(\lambda s)[s = r)]], [x, z]])$
(4λ) $(x)(y)((x = y) \supset (y \text{ has } (\lambda z)[[\text{Nec}[(\lambda r)(\lambda s)[s = r]]], [x, z]]))$.

This is cumbersome, but it is what the contingency theorist asked for. The definition of *necessarily identical with x* does not now depend at all on the apparatus of possible worlds. And the argument about (4) no longer moves round and round in a circle. The only conceivable point left to argue is whether there is a *de re* use of 'must' in English. But the onus is on the contingency theorist at last. He has to dispel as illusion what seems to be fact—that in English there exist many such *de re* uses.

III

Let us now revert to the sort of claim with which we embarked upon the subject. Cleaving to the *de re* use of 'must', nothing could now seem more natural than to read essentialist statements as having the forms

(5) $[\text{Nec}[(\lambda x)(\text{Man } x)]], [\text{Socrates}]$.
(6) $[\text{Nec}[(\lambda x)(\text{Heavenly body } x)]], [\text{Hesperus}]$.

Anything that is Socrates must be a man. Anything that is Hesperus cannot help but be a heavenly body.

[13] Cp. 'Essentialism, Continuity and Identity'.

But how does this notion of 'necessarily' work? Can we spell out in any systematic way its contribution to the truth grounds of the sentences in which it figures? Before we can get to such an account we need a better feel for the intuitive desiderata by which it should be constrained. I shall give three, [A], [B], [C] following.

[A] If 'necessarily' governs sometimes a predicate and sometimes a sentence, uses I will mark for the moment as *Nec* and $\Box$ without prejudice to ambiguity or the possibility of giving one overall account, then there is a natural way of explicating the old distinction of *de re* and *de dicto*.[14] It should be explicated in terms of the scope of 'necessarily' itself. And from this characterization we shall have it as a proper consequence, not as a stipulation, that *de re* necessity has a transparent subject-place.[15] The contrast with current logical terminology is worth stressing. Deliberately and explicitly most modal logicians at present characterize the difference of *de re* and *de dicto* not in terms of the scope of 'necessarily' but by a quite different mark, namely whether or not variables bound from outside lie within the scope of $\Box$. In the presence of a presumption of opacity in $\Box$ this is an unfortunate not to say prejudicial characterization (which may indeed help to explain the continuing suspicion of essentialism). It characterizes the *de re* in such a way as to make it sound impossible. The transparency of the '*a*' position in $\Box\phi a$, where the term is a rigid designator, looks like a dubious privilege simply legislated to it, so long as no distinction is provided between $\Box$ $((\lambda x)[\phi x], [a])$ or $\Box(\phi(a))$ and $[\text{Nec}(\lambda x)[\phi x]]], [a]$. Finally, if there is a distinction to be marked between $\Box(a = b)$ and $[\text{Nec}[(\lambda x)(\lambda y)(x = y)]], [a, b]$—and we shall suggest in due course that the former is never true except where *a* and *b* are such things as numbers—this will suggest that certain syntactical and semantical preliminaries should precede any inquiry into the essentialist commitments or non-commitments of quantified modal logic, it will explain the unclarity and formlessness of the results so far achieved, and it will account for the anomalies created there by such attributions as $(x)\Box(x = x)$.

[14] Cp. my *Identity and Spatio-Temporal Continuity*, op. cit., part III 3.2 (ii), old edition; P. T. Geach's 1967 paper on the identity of propositions, *Logic Matters* (Blackwell, Oxford, 1972), p. 174; R. Cartwright 'Some Remarks on Essentialism' *J.Phil.*, lxv (1968); R. Stalnaker and R. Thomason 'Abstraction in First Order Logic' *Theoria* xxiv (1968). For more recent statements of this point of view see my op. cit. 'Essentialism, Continuity, and Identity'; John Woods 'Essentialism and Quantifying In' in *Identity and Individuation*, ed. M. K. Munitz, op. cit.

[15] Cp. for this mark, Christopher Kirwan 'Essences: How good are the objections?', *Proc. Aristotelian Society* lxxi (1970–1).

[B] Like necessity, negation can be applied either to a predicate or to a sentence. Let us symbolize the first as *Neg* and the second with the tilde $\sim$. If we are to vindicate and correctly state the semantical difference of $\Box((\lambda x_i)(\phi x_i), [a])$ and $[\text{Nec}[(\lambda x_i)[\phi x_i]], [a]$, then the analogy is worth pursuing in detail between this pair and $\sim(\lambda x_i(\phi x_i), [a])$ and $[\text{Neg}(\lambda x_i(\phi x_i))], [a]$. (The symbols '$\sim$' and 'Neg' are like '$\Box$' and 'Nec' in being intended to leave open the question of a unifying account of 'not'.)

The philosophical literature is by no means devoid of attempts to distinguish predicate and sentence negation. Miss Anscombe, for instance, (who follows Bochvar is calling her distinction a distinction between 'external' and 'internal' negation) makes it the distinguishing mark of any proper name of an individual *a* that, where and only where *a* is designated by a proper name, there is no distinction of truth conditions to be found between $\sim[\phi[a]]$ and what might have been symbolized as $[\text{Neg-}\phi], [a]$.[16] Since she follows Russell's theory of descriptions, however, (and would presumably embrace Smullyan's extension of that to modal contexts) this need not represent any very substantial commitment to the predicate-negator/sentence-negator distinction. (Indeed it is all of a piece with Kripke's treatment of 'necessarily' contexts with rigid designators if, in consequence, no distinction of form is to be marked, where *a* is designated by a constant, between $\text{Neg-}\phi[a]$ and $\sim[\phi[a]]$.) A clearer or more committal use of the distinction is to be found however in Brian Medlin's interesting attempt to resolve by it the paradox of the origin of motion (instant of change).[17]

The train leaves at noon. Is noon the first moment of motion or the last moment of rest? Or both? Well, not both for in that case the train has contradictory properties at noon. But if noon is not both the first moment of motion and the last moment of rest—if indeed not both these things can even exist—which shall we say falls at noon? Unless both answers are equally good (which, since they are incompatible, means they are equally bad), either we must find a way out of the whole dilemma, and this is Medlin's approach, or we must find good reason for choosing between a Dedekindian section defined by a last

[16] *Introduction to Wittgenstein's Tractatus* (Hutchinson, London, 1959), Ch. 5. Cp. generally H. P. Grice 'Vacuous Names' in *Words and Objections* (ed. Hintikka and Davidson) Reidel, Dordrecht, 1969.
[17] *Mind*, 1964.

moment of rest and a Dedekindian section defined by a first moment of motion, in order to mark the instant of departure.[18]

Medlin's way out of the dilemma is to rule as follows:

(1) x was not-in-motion at $t \equiv t$ was either followed or preceded or both by a period during which x did not move.
(2) It is not the case that x was in motion at $t \equiv t$ was *both* followed *and* preceded by a period throughout which x did not move.

The definiendum in (1) is intended to be compatible, and the definiendum in (2) not compatible, with the definiendum in (3).

(3) x was in motion at $t \equiv t$ was either followed or preceded or both by a period throughout which x moved.

It is Medlin's intention that if t was followed by a period throughout which x did move then the definienda of (1) and (3) should be both true. Naturally, he holds that the definienda of (2) and (3) are not compatible.

I choose the example because it has the virtue of being completely independent of the problem of bearerless names, and because it is interesting. But all other reservations and comments are irrelevant to the question whether the distinction between (1) and (2) can be seriously made out. What must interest us is that the difference Medlin has tried to provide between (1) and (2) is described by him in terms of the distinction of sentence negation and predicate negation.

Suppose that we have a simple language L' with *in motion* as its sole primitive predicate, indexed variables of quantification $x_1, x_2, x_3 \ldots$ (but in framing certain recursions we shall restrict ourselves, for simplicity's sake, to x_1), the universal quantifier (x_i), the lambda-abstractor λ, conjunction &, the tilde representing sentence negation, and *Neg* representing a negator of the predicates abstracted by λ. Suppose truth is defined for this language in the standard way as satisfaction by all sequences of objects, where sequences are denumerably long and are functions from 1, 2, 3, 4 . . . to the entities which will occupy their first, second, third, fourth . . . places. Then satisfaction

[18] Cp. Aristotle, *Physics* VI. It does not seem to me irrational to prefer the former to the latter option, on the ground that there are no degrees of being at rest, *a fortiori* no infinitesimal degrees of it, while there are degrees of being in motion. (A line of approach which Professor G. E. L. Owen has informed me may be traced as far back as Proklos.) The speed of the train is a function from times to real numbers $\geqslant 0$; and the set of speeds which represent motions is open. So the set of times when x moves must be open too.

is defined as a relation between such sequences and well-formed formulas (designated here by the underlining of themselves, thus: $\underline{(\phi x_i)}$) as follows: For any sequence s,

1. $(s \text{ sat}\underline{(\text{in motion } (x_i))}) \equiv$ (the ith member of s, henceforth $s^*(\underline{x_i})$, is in motion).
2. $(s \text{ sat } \underline{A \;\&\; B}) \equiv (s \text{ sat } A) \;\&\; (s \text{ sat } B)$.
3. $(s \text{ sat } \underline{\sim A}) \equiv (\sim (s \text{ sat } A))$.
4. $(s \text{ sat}\underline{(x_i)(A)} \equiv$ (s sat A, and every sequence s' differing from s in at most the ith place, henceforth $s' \underset{i}{\approx} s$, sat A)
5. $(s \text{ sat}\underline{[(\lambda x_1)[A]][t]}) \equiv (s')\big(((s' \underset{1}{\approx} s) \;\&\; (s'^*(\underline{x_1}) = s^*(t)) \supset (s' \text{ sat } A)\big)$.
6. $(s \text{ sat}\underline{[\text{Neg}[(\lambda x_1)[A]]][t]}) \equiv [\text{Neg}(\lambda y)[(s')\big(((s' \underset{1}{\approx} s) \;\&\; (s'^*(\underline{x_1}) = y)) \supset (s' \text{ sat } A)\big)], [s^*(t)]$.

Finally we have the rule

$$R\colon\ \frac{v_1 \ldots v_n(A \equiv B),\ (\text{———}A\text{———})}{(\text{———}B\text{———})}$$

where 'v' ranges over the variables of L' and '(——— ———)' represents any context of L'.

The metalanguage is conceived here as built from the object language L' itself, and as enriched with 'satisfies' (defined ultimately by purely object-language sentences), quotational devices, and the other minimal resources of sequence theory which are absent from the object language but needed on the right hand side of such equivalences. $s^*(t)$ is the interpretation of the term t for the sequence s. As explained, this is the ith member of the sequence s if t is a variable. But it is some stipulated constant designation for all sequences if t is a constant. t, t' etc. are metalogical variables for terms (i.e. variables or constants). A, B are metalogical variables for wffs of L'.

By these definitions

(In motion (a))

and

$\sim$(In motion (a))

are equivalent to

$$[(\lambda x_1)\ (\text{In motion } x_1)],\ [a]$$

and

$$\sim([(\lambda x_1)(\text{In motion } (x_1))],\ [a])$$

respectively. Let us then ask how the last compares in respect of truth conditions with the internal negation of the first and third sentences above, sc.

$$[\text{Neg}[(\lambda x_1)(\text{In motion } (x_1))]],\ [a].$$

For any sequence s,

$$s \text{ sat} \underline{\sim[(\lambda x_1)[\text{In motion } (x_1)],\ [a]]}$$

if and only if

$$\sim\{(s')((s' \underset{1}{\approx} s)\ \&\ (s'^*(\underline{x_1}) = a) \supset (s' \text{ sat}\underline{(\text{In motion } (x_1))}\}.$$

This follows from (3) and (5) of the previous paragraphs. And note that by the general equivalence between any formula without lambda and some lambda formula this is equivalent to

$$\sim\{[(\lambda y)[(s')((s' \underset{1}{\approx} s)\ \&\ (s'^*(\underline{x_1}) = y) \supset (s' \text{ sat}\underline{(\text{In motion } (x_1))}]],\ [a]\}.$$

If we now look at the internal negation of the first and third sentences displayed in the present paragraph we shall find

$$s \text{ sat } \underline{[\text{Neg}(\lambda x_1)[\text{In motion } (x_1)]],\ [a]}$$

if and only if, by (6) and barely distinguishably from the condition for external negation,

$$[\text{Neg}[(\lambda y)[(s')((s' \underset{1}{\approx} s)\ \&\ (s'^*(\underline{x_1}) = y) \supset (s' \text{ sat}\underline{(\text{In motion}(x_1))}]]],\ [a]$$

But the whole difference we are interested in now depends on our understanding the difference between the internal and the external negation of *another* formula, one involving 'satisfies', within which the predicate for which Medlin explained the difference is not even used. Here we can get no assistance from Medlin's special definitions of 'in motion'.[19] We are struggling to answer a problem which has

[19] There would be a point in pursuing further the details of Medlin's own analysis of motion if the analysis were not plagued by the problem of regression. As Mr. Richard Sorabji has pointed out to me, a replica of the original problem reappears as soon as we ask 'At what point exactly did it cease to be true that not (x was moving) even

escaped from the point where Medlin began upon it and has reappeared in the metalanguage, namely the distinction *perfectly in general,* where ϕ is either simple or complex, between [Neg-ϕ], [a] and $\sim(\phi[a])$. The trouble is that, if we put on one side as irrelevant to Medlin's purposes the supposed case where t is a bearerless name, then it is impossible to conceive of the one being true without the other. Do $\sim$ and *Neg* then mean the same? Well, they are distinct in sense iff no common correct account can be provided for what they mean, i.e. of their truth conditions.[20] Can a common account be provided?

One standard way of unifying them would be roughly on these lines: s satisfies $(\underline{\text{Not } A[t_i, t_j \ldots}])$, where the square brackets hold places for any number of terms corresponding to the free variables in A, iff

(i) if A has no free variables, then s does not sat A;
(ii) if A has one free variable, then s does not sat $\underline{A[t]}$, which is equivalent to the condition that $s^*(t)$ is not A;
(iii) if A has two free variables . . .

Inasmuch as the outcome of (i) is to mate $\underline{\text{Not} A}$ with a truth condition indistinguishable from that given earlier for $\underline{\sim A}$; and inasmuch as the outcome of (ii) is to mate $\underline{\text{Not } A[t]}$ with something truth-conditionally indistinguishable from a truth condition given earlier for $\underline{[\text{Neg}(\lambda x_i)[A]], [t]}$; inasmuch as both of these things result, this unification succeeds. If it succeeds it justifies its own use in object and metalanguage of *Not* as a unitary concept of negation throughout. But what the proposal misses (and some might think it justifies them in ignoring the demand for such) is an account of the syntactical or structural difference which has made it so tempting for people to accept the idea that it can be true that it is not the case that El Dorado is in Venezuela and not true that El Dorado is not-in-Venezuela. And by this proposal, as in the present language of modal logic, specifically predicate modification (which frequently in natural languages takes on a special sense, as in e.g. '*in*⁀voluntary', '*s*⁀cortese'

---

though x was still not-moving?' A better way of fulfilling Medlin's purpose would have been to extend to the predicate *x is in motion at time t* an intuitionist treatment. Where t is specified as an instant it may be claimed that the predicate transcends all possible experience, and that the whole problem rests from the outset on an unjustified insistence on the applicability of the law of excluded middle to this predicate.

[20] See my 'Sentence Sense, Word Sense, and Difference of Word Sense' Steinberg & Jakobovits, *Semantics* (C.U.P., Cambridge, 1972). Compare also Sparshott, *Inquiry into Goodness* (Toronto University, Toronto, (1958)), and O. P. Wood *Mind* lxv (1956), 108 para 2.

etc.[21]) is not marked or distinguished as such. But it can be marked. Nor for reasons both given and yet to be given is marking it semantically otiose.

Suppose we think of a language with one negation sign *Not* and in which negations take the form:

$$\text{Not}\ [(\lambda x_i)[A]][t]$$

where A is any formula and t is a singular term. In the case where λx_i is vacuous, because x_i does not occur free in A, t is some arbitrary fixed term: let us say 'Λ'.[22] Then the external negation 'Not (Socrates is bald)' has the form

$$\text{Not}\ (\lambda x_i)[\text{Socrates is bald}][\Lambda]$$

and the internal negation 'Socrates is non-bald' has the form

$$\text{Not}\ (\lambda x_i)[x_i \text{ is bald}][\text{Socrates}].$$

The unifying interpretation is as follows:

$$s \text{ sat}\underline{[\text{Not}(\lambda x_i)[A]][t]} \text{ iff } (s')[((s' \underset{i}{\approx} s)$$
$$\& \ (s'^*(\underline{x_i}) = s^*(t)) \supset (s' \text{ does not sat } A)].$$

The satisfaction conditions for our two negations will turn out to be interderivable. But if we follow this second method, then the scope-difference on which we have insisted will correspond to two different *semantically interpreted* methods of building up two syntactically distinguishable structures. If we think the structural difference important we may perfectly rationally prefer the second rather less obvious method of unifying $\sim$ and *Neg*. It amounts to seeing each of them as a case of a single functor from predicates to predicates. (In the case of predicate negation the functor 'not' leads from the predicate to its complement. In the case of sentence negation the

[21] For a treatment of negation informed by some of the variety and richness of these phenomena see the first part of G. H. von Wright's 'On the logic of negation', in *Commentationes Physico-Mathematicae* (Helsingfors, 1959).

[22] Cp. John Wallace 'Belief and Satisfaction', *Noûs* vi (1972). If this device not only seems artificial or trivializing, but is also incompatible in a more than superficial way with what Frege established about the respective roles of predicate and sentence in predication, or if it detracts from some explanatory primacy supposedly attaching to the sentence; then all this may combine with the unacceptability of the first and simpler unifying account of *Not* to motivate us to resist the semantical unification of $\sim$ and *Neg* altogether. Analogous conclusions have sometimes been reached before (cp. Russell & Whitehead *Principia Mathematica* (2nd ed. Cambridge) *19, pp. 127–28). *Not* will not emerge as a mere pun. See first op. cit. note 20 above.

functor leads from predicates to predicates, from (e.g.) the universal predicate λx(Socrates is bald)—supposing Socrates *is* bald—to the null predicate Not[λx(Socrates is bald)].)

The parallel with □ and *Nec* is manifest. It is the tradition to use what is (in effect) the first of these two methods, and to blur the difference between *Necessarily Socrates is a man* and *Socrates is necessarily a man.* I am suggesting that, if any unification at all of □ and *Nec* is to be attempted, the second kind of method is to be preferred. I shall now mention three reasons why it is. This will bring us directly to the point of defining satisfaction for sentences with *Nec.*

[C] The first reason to want to distinguish Necessarily [$\phi[a]$] and ([Necessarily $(\lambda x_i)(\phi x_i)$], [a]) I have already given. Without the distinction, all arguments for and against (4) move round and round in a circle. A decision about (4) is a preliminary even to the construction of the possible-world semantics by which some philosophers and logicians seek to resolve such issues.

The second reason is this. An essential property of x is any property of x such that either x does not exist, or x has this property. (Or, in the language of possible worlds, a is necessarily F iff x is F in every possible world in which a exists). It follows, as night follows day, that existence itself (if it is a property at all, but modal logicians seem prepared to call it one, and 'x has something identical with it' looks like a complex first-level predicate) is an essential property. If we do not distinguish the sentence-scope and the predicate-scope of 'necessarily', however, and if we assign only one structure to 'Necessarily exists [a]', then we reach counterintuitive results. It is true that Kripke would encourage us to read this as saying only that a exists in all the worlds a exists in—much too innocuous an assertion.[23] But it is a bad effect of this ruling that it suits ill at least one standard reading of the English sentence (while not really providing for more than one reading), and that so many of the expressive resources of the modal language have then been used up before provision is made for the difference between *Necessarily seven exists* and *Necessarily Cicero exists.* But, as normally understood in English, the first sentence is true—seven is a necessary entity (does exist in every possible world)—and the second is false, because Cicero need not exist (and does not exist in every possible world).

Of course such difficulties have not gone unnoticed or unattended by modal logicians. My point here, as with the third point I shall

[23] Op. cit., p. 153.

make, is that the real root of the difficulty is to be found in logicians' studied disregard of the syntax of English modal language and of the *de re/de dicto* distinction which is so easily marked there.

The third reason to make the distinction I am urging concerns existential generalization, which has of course been subjected by modal logicians to complicated restrictions. Suppose we represent 'Cicero is necessarily a man' as '□ Cicero is a man' and suppose we do not distinguish in the way I urge between a *de re* and a *de dicto* version of the former claim. Now (Man(Cicero)) $\vdash_{\text{English}}(\exists x)(\text{Man } x)$. For 'Cicero' is a good name with a definite and determinate sense, transmitted to us by any sort of causal or apostolic succession you regard as relevant to naming.[24] The actual reference of this name fixes its sense. The merits or demerits in this regard of other names are irrelevant. But then it *must* hold that, *if* Cicero is a man, then men exist. Or so it would seem. IF we can conceive at all of a claim of the form '□ - - - *a* - - -' being true (where the '*a*' marks the place of a proper name of a contingent being), and to me it is far from clear that we *can* conceive of this if '□ - - -' makes the claim '- - -' with respect to every possible world; IF we can conceive of such a claim being true, then surely $\Box$ [(Man)(Cicero) $\supset$ $(\exists x)(\text{Man } x)$]. Wherever Cicero was a man there, surely, there would be men. Where could Cicero be a man without men, indeed without Cicero, existing? But then if $\Box$(Man(Cicero)), the indubitable modal principle $[(\Box p \ \& \ \Box(p \supset q)) \supset \Box q]$ gives $\Box\ (\exists x)(\text{Man } x)$. But this isn't true.

It would not alter the situation materially to render 'Cicero is necessarily a man' as

$$\Box((x)[(x = \text{Cicero}) \supset (x \text{ is a man})]).$$

For if existential generalization on the name 'Cicero' is as good as I have argued it is, then we have

$$(x)((x = \text{Cicero}) \supset (x \text{ is a man})) \vdash_{\text{English}} (\exists y)[(x)((x = y) \supset (x \text{ is a man}))]$$

and we have the necessitation of the corresponding conditional, which with the necessitation of the antecedent gives the necessitation of the consequent:

$$\Box(\exists y)[(x)((x = y) \supset (x \text{ is a man})].$$

[24] Cp. 'The Perils of Pauline', in P.T. Geach, *Logic Matters*, op cit., and Saul Kripke, 'Naming and Necessity', in *Semantics of Natural Languages*, ed. Harman & Davidson (Reidel. Dordrecht, 1971).

This is every bit as false as $\Box\,(\exists x)(\text{Man } x)$. It would not then have altered the situation, as I said, to have represented 'Cicero is necessarily a man' by $\Box((x)[(x = \text{Cicero}) \supset (x \text{ is a man})])$. And the complication would already have detracted from the clarity, such as it was, of the position that there is no need for my *de re*/*de dicto* distinction in sentences $\Box\phi a$ where the subject is named by a rigid designator.

The best way out, I claimed in 1967 and still claim, is to distinguish the *de re* and *de dicto* by the scope of 'necessarily' itself, and to distinguish two versions of 'Necessarily Cicero is a man'. Taken *de re* this is an unproblematic essentialist claim. Taken *de dicto* it is not even true.

What then is the right thing to say about the conditional claim already discussed, viz.

$$\text{Necessarily } ((x)((x = \text{Cicero}) \supset (x \text{ is a man})))\,?$$

Taken thus, *de dicto*, is it true or not? If it is true, and if my claim stands about existential generalization on 'Cicero', then as explained we get the false

$$\text{Necessarily } (\exists z)(x)(x = z \supset x \text{ is a man})).$$

The question such statements raise is whether we can even evaluate sentences containing proper names with respect to all worlds.

The point of view for which I should want to argue is this—there is nothing whatever wrong with existential generalization on well-defined names; but in my former claim about it the condition introduced by the capital IF is actually not satisfied. And whatever the merits or demerits of existential generalization, there are no truths of the form $\Box\,(\text{- - -}\, a \,\text{- - -})$ available (numbers apart) for the argument about E.G. which we have been discussing to work upon.

IV

With so much by way of motivation and constraints, it will be natural to propose to explicate the logical form of essentialist claims in the more austere framework of what Donald Davidson[25] has called a homophonic truth theory. Suppose we take that fragment of (very basic) English corresponding by translation rules to an applied predicate calculus of first level with denumerably many variables $x_1, x_2 \ldots$, the existential quantifier $(\exists x_i)$, and one single two-place predicate. The formal language will then be like that at the beginning

[25] See 'Truth and Meaning', *Synthese* xvii (1967), 304–23; 'Semantics for Natural Languages' in *Linguaggi Nella Società e Nella Tecnica* (Milan, 1970); and many subsequent articles.

of Wallace's 'On the Frame of Reference'—except that for the sake of subject-matter we may take 'identical with' in lieu of Wallace's two-place predicate 'before'[26]. But the example is purely illustrative in intent, designed only to exhibit a general semantical strategy before confronting (in the appendix) the full technical difficulty of adjoining the predicate modifier 'necessarily' to a richer language. To this formal language we now add the lambda abstractor for purposes of forming predicate abstracts like $(\lambda x_i)(\lambda x_j)$ $[x_i = x_j]$ and a predicate modifier *Nec* applicable to such predicate-abstracts thus:

$$[[\mathrm{Nec}(\lambda x_i)(\lambda x_j)\,[x_i = x_j]].$$

It is supposed that translation or transformation rules will be devised in due course to convert all the expressions of this extended applied predicate calculus of first level, and also of the metalanguage of which it forms one part, into correct expressions of some sort of basic English.

The goal of the truth theory will then be the familiar one: to define truth for all the sentences of the formal language just sketched in terms of the closure of a well-formed formula and its satisfaction by all sequences. To define satisfaction by sequences of open and closed formulae of the language, we avail ourselves of a metalanguage *ML* consisting of the language *L* itself supplemented by quotational devices and the now familiar quantum of set theory required to deal with sequences. That the object language is a part of the metalanguage duplicates on a miniature scale the large and important fact that our own position is that of English speakers attempting to characterize as far as is possible the semantical resources of English itself. The final almost transcendental objective is to state within English a systematic theory to mate with every English sentence a statement of the conditions under which it is true. The criterion of success in my own minute exercise is the Tarskian one suggested by Davidson: that the theory of satisfaction for *L* should suffice to prove within our metalanguage *ML*, for every closed expression *S* of *L*, an equivalence of the form

$$\mathrm{True}(S) \equiv p$$

where '*p*' holds a place on the right-hand side for the use of the very sentence mentioned on the left-hand side. Although officially our metalanguage is our object language *L* supplemented in the way

[26] *Synthese* xxi (1970).

indicated, we shall sometimes for purposes of exposition use something closer to the Basic English transforms which correspond to expressions of *ML*.

We think of the language *L* as determined by formation rules for the atomic predicate '=' and the usual recursion clauses for formulas containing the quantifier $(\exists x_i)$, and the propositional connectives. Then, in a highly delimited fashion, λ is introduced.[27] If A is an atomic wff with two free variables then $\underline{(\lambda x_i)(\lambda x_j)[A]}$ is an abstract, and $\underline{\text{Nec}[(\lambda x_i)(\lambda x_j)[A]]}$ is a modified abstract. Then, where t, t' are terms, both $\underline{[(\lambda x_i)(\lambda x_j)[A]], [t, t']}$ and $\underline{[[\text{Nec}(\lambda x_i)(\lambda x_j)[A]], [t, t']}$ are well-formed sentences. For purposes of the definition of satisfaction in L which now ensues, the variables s, s' range over sequences. $s^*(t)$ means *the interpretation for the sequence s of the term t.* $s^*(\overline{x_i})$ means, as before, *the ith member of the sequence s.* $s\left(\dfrac{i, j \ldots n}{x_{k_1}, x_{k_2} \ldots x_{k_m}}\right)$ means *the sequence obtained from s by substituting object* x_{k_1} *for the object at the ith place, object* x_{k_2} *for the object at the jth place* . . . (But to simplify matters we shall limit ourselves here to x_1 and x_2, and so to the first two places of any sequence).

In this style Wallace's atomic predicate recursion is as follows: (Sat 1): $(s)(s \text{ satisfies } \underline{[t = t']} \text{ iff } s^*(t) = s^*(t'))$.

The new recursions are as follows:

(Sat 2): $(s)(s \text{ satisfies } \underline{(\lambda x_1)(\lambda x_2)[x_1 = x_2], [t, t']} \text{ iff}$

$$\left[(\lambda x_1)(\lambda x_2)\left[s\left(\frac{1, 2}{x_1 x_2}\right) \text{ sat } \underline{[x_1 = x_2]}\right]\right], [s^*(t), s^*(t')]).$$

(Sat 3): $(s)(s \text{ satisfies } \underline{[\text{Nec}[(\lambda x_1)(\lambda x_2)[x_1 = x_2]]], [t, t']} \text{ iff}$

$$\left[\text{Nec}(\lambda x_1)(\lambda x_2)\left[s\left(\frac{1, 2}{x_1 x_2}\right) \text{ sat} \underline{[x_1 = x_2]}\right]\right], [s^*(t), s^*(t')]).$$

Note that *Nec* turns up here in exactly the same modifying role in the metalanguage as the metalanguage describes in the object language.

[27] In the exceedingly simple language *L*, λ is particularly easily dispensable. We introduce it only in order to pave the way for the consideration of more complex formal languages in which wffs of arbitrary complexity are admitted to the position between square brackets in $\lambda x_i\ \lambda x_j$ [. . .], the open sea outside the sheltered refuge of language *L*. For this problem see the Appendix by Christopher Peacocke.

Finally, following an idea of Richard Grandy[28] in the treatment of another problem, we state a rule of inference:

Rλ: If $\vdash((x_{i_1} \ldots x_{i_n})(A \equiv B))$
and if ——$(\lambda x_{i_1} \ldots \lambda x_{i_n})[A]$——,
then infer ——$(\lambda x_{i_1} \ldots \lambda x_{i_n})[B]$——.

Here the dash connotes any context of L and $\vdash$ connotes provability within the theory of satisfaction for L. With an eye to the second level extension of the theory we might now add a rule allowing the inter-substitution of abstracts standing for the very same property. But naturally the theory of satisfaction itself will provide no new rulings on property identity.

To make the system familiar and increase confidence in it, let us test it once or twice by the canon of Tarski's Convention T.

First we prove an equivalence. Suppose for any s, any z, and any y:

1. $s\left(\dfrac{1, 2}{z, y}\right)$ sat $\underline{(x_1 = x_2)}$.

Then by (Sat 1)

2. $s\left(\dfrac{1, 2}{z, y}\right)*(\underline{x_1}) = s\left(\dfrac{1, 2}{z, y}\right)*(\underline{x_2})$.

Hence, resting on 1,

3. $(z = y)$.

Therefore

4. $\left[s\left(\dfrac{1, 2}{z, y}\right) \text{ sat } \underline{(x_1 = x_2)}\right] \supset (z = y)$.

The same argument (using (Sat 1) right to left) will deliver 4 right to left and give the equivalence

5. $\left[s\left(\dfrac{1, 2}{z, y}\right) \text{ sat } \underline{(x_1 = x_2)}\right] \equiv (z = y)$.

Hence, since nothing depended on the particular choices of z and y,

6. $(s)(z)(y)\left[\left(s\left(\dfrac{1, 2}{z, y}\right) \text{ sat} \underline{(x_1 = x_2)}\right) \equiv (z = y)\right]$.

[28] See p. 143 of Richard Grandy, 'A Definition of Truth for Theories with Intensional Definite Description Operators' in *Journal of Philosophical Logic* i (1972). See Peacocke's Appendix for a necessary refinement of the rule.

Now let us try to prove, where 'h' is short for 'Hesperus' and 'p' is short for 'Phosphorus',

$$\text{True } \underline{[[(\lambda x_1)(\lambda x_2)[x_1 = x_2], [h, p]]} \text{ iff } [(\lambda x_1)(\lambda x_2)[x_1 = x_2]], [h, p].$$

Suppose then

$$s \text{ sat}\underline{[(\lambda x_1)(\lambda x_2)[x_1 = x_2]], [h, p]}.$$

Then by (Sat 2)

$$\left[(\lambda x_1)(\lambda x_2)\left[s\left(\frac{1, 2}{x_1, x_2}\right) \text{ sat}\underline{[x_1 = x_2]}\right], [s^*(\underline{h}), s^*(\underline{p})]\right].$$

Now substituting on the basis that $h = s^*(\underline{h})$ and $p = s^*(\underline{p})$, and using (6), taking 'x_1' for 'z' and 'x_2' for 'y', and employing our rule of inference, we obtain

$$[(\lambda x_1)(\lambda x_2)[x_1 = x_2]], [h, p].$$

The same argument will work in reverse to give the equivalence; as it will to prove the equivalence

$$\text{True } \underline{[\text{Nec}(\lambda x_1)(\lambda x_2)[x_1 = x_2], [h, p]]} \equiv$$
$$[\text{Nec}(\lambda x_1)(\lambda x_2)][x_1 = x_2]], [h, p].$$

For suppose

$$s \text{ sat}\underline{[\text{Nec}[(\lambda x_1)(\lambda x_2)[x_1 = x_2]]], [h, p]}.$$

Then by (Sat 3)

$$\left[\text{Nec}\left[(\lambda x_1)(\lambda x_2)\left[s\left(\frac{1, 2}{x_1, x_2}\right) \text{ sat}\underline{[x_1 = x_2]}\right]\right], [s^*(\underline{h}), s^*(\underline{p})]\right]$$

which, by the identity of h and p and the rule Rλ, yields

$$\left[\text{Nec}(\lambda x_1)(\lambda x_2)\left[s\left(\frac{1, 2}{x_1, x_2}\right) \text{ sat}\underline{[x_1 = x_2]}\right]\right], [h, p].$$

Again the argument is reversible.

A number of questions immediately arise. First extensionality. The proposal displays the terms in a *Nec*-sentence as manifestly open to intersubstitution of identicals and existential generalization. But what about predicates? Suppose that Gyges' magic ring of invisibility was and will be the only one ever extant, and suppose that Gyges never

had any other ring. Then (x) ((x is a ring of Gyges) $\equiv$ (x is a magic ring of invisibility)). Suppose that Gyges' ring was essentially a magic ring of invisibility. We do not want it to follow from this that Gyges' ring was essentially Gyges' ring. There might be two ways of blocking this inference.

The first way, which I have not explicitly adopted (though I am conscious of the possibility of some charge to the effect that the full dress semantics presented in the Appendix implicitly commits us to something like this), is to block predicate extensionality outright by proposing a relational view of predication. On this relational view we should see

$$[\lambda x_i(\phi x_i)],\ [a]$$

as saying that a and $(\lambda x_i)(\phi x_i)$ are in the relation of Participation. In more Fregean language, we might say that a falls under the concept $[\lambda x_i[\phi x_i]]$. It may then be proposed to allow substitutivity of properties (and relations) in a context just in case an abstract designates the very same property as the abstract which it would supplant designates. If $(\lambda x_i)[\phi x_i]$ and $(\lambda x_i)[\psi x_i]$ do not designate the same property, but do happen to be coextensive, then, in extensional contexts, $(\lambda x_i)[\phi x_i],[a]$ will of course *entail* $(\lambda x_i)[\psi x_i],\ [a]$ by an argument from a true premiss $(y)\{((\lambda x_i)[\phi x_i],\ [y]) \supset ((\lambda x_i)[\psi x_i],\ [y])\}$. But the conclusion so obtained is not on this view any application of substitutivity as such. On the other hand, if we have

$$[(\lambda x_i)[\phi x_i]] = [(\lambda x_i)[\psi x_i]]$$

and if

$$[\text{Nec}(\lambda x_i)[\phi x_i]],\ [a]$$

then

$$[\text{Nec}(\lambda x_i)[\psi x_i]],\ [a]$$

would be obtained. Although the theory for *Nec* will not rule whether $[(\lambda x_i)[\phi x_i]]$ and $[(\lambda x_i)[\psi x_i]]$ are or are not the same property, we are independently committed to this problem,[29] or so it may be said.

29 See e.g. Hilary Putnam 'On Properties' in *Essays in Honour of C. G. Hempel*, ed. Rescher (Reidel, Dordrecht 1969). It may be said that what results from the relational proposal is something viciously regressive; and it may be objected, in the spirit of Plato or Bradley, that if there was ever a good reason to view $\phi(a)$ as of the form $[\lambda x_i\,(\phi x_i)],\ [a]$ then there is an equally good reason to see in this last the more complicated form

a participates^1 in $\lambda x_i[\phi x_i]$

This is not the approach we have adopted. Confining the theory itself (if not always the informal exposition) to strictly first-level materials, we have simply replaced the full extensionality rule R by Rλ. (Grandy's rule as refined by Peacocke in the Appendix.) The undesirable substitution is then avoided because it is not provable in the truth theory for L that $(x)((x$ is a ring of Gyges$) \equiv (x$ is a ring of invisibility$))$.

John Wallace objects to the project of devising a homophonic truth theory for $\Box$ that the required recursions force upon us the necessitation of certain sentences which say that certain sequences satisfy certain expressions even though these expressions might have meant something quite different.[30] Is there a comparable objection to our theory for *Nec*? Suppose that h must be p, that h has to p [Nec[$\lambda x_1\, \lambda x_2$ $[x_1 = x_2]$]]. Ought it to follow, as it does by (Sat 3), that they necessarily have the property that (or that they must be such that) any sequence got by supplanting its first and second members by h and p respectively satisfies $\underline{[x_1 = x_2]}$, this last being one of the wffs of L which happen to express identity? Similarly (though outside the limited province demarcated by L) it might be objected: surely Caesar can be essentially a man without being essentially such that any sequence with Caesar in its second place satisfies $\underline{(\text{Man}(x_2))}$. For 'man' might not have meant man.

---

or

$(\lambda w)\ (\lambda y)\ [y$ participates^1 in $w]$, $[\lambda x_i\ [\phi x_i]$, $a]$

But why stop there? Surely this last has more structure to be uncovered. The trio a and $\lambda x_i[\phi x_i]$ and *participates*^{1} are related by the first's and the second's (in that order) falling under the third:

$[(\lambda r \lambda s \lambda t)\ [\langle s, t\rangle$ participates^2 in $r]]$, $[(\lambda w)\ (\lambda y)\ [y$ participates^1 in $w]$, $\lambda x_i[\phi x_i]$, $a]$

And why stop even there? What is sauce for the goose is sauce for the gander, and so on. But I reply that if the rationale of seeing (ϕa) as $(\lambda x_i)\ (\phi x_i)$, $[a]$ is to accommodate adverbial modification of ϕ, then at each stage in the regress we may ask 'Do we need adverbial modification of the predicate or relation which is to be hypostasized?' Of the predicates and relations we encounter at the first stage there is a vast potentiality for modification. Of the relations to be encountered at the second stage there may be some modification. Perhaps we should think of [Nec $(\lambda x_i)\ (\phi x_i)$], $[a]$ as saying that a necessarily-participates^1 in $(\lambda x_i)\ (\phi x_i)$. But by the time we reach the third stage there is not the same need to make arrangements to accommodate modification of *participate*^{2}. And here or hereabouts the regression may halt. As for ontological expensiveness, the enemies of predicate modification, e.g. Davidson (see 'The Logical Form of Action Sentences' in Rescher ed. *The Logic of Decision and Action* (Pittsburgh, 1967)), cannot easily complain. The counterpart of Davidson's theory of verb-adverbs for adjective-adverbs would be committed to quantification over states (as the analogue of events).

[30] 'On the Frame of Reference', op. cit., pp. 139–40.

There is a general problem here. If I couldn't help but stumble over the doorstep, and the doorstep is the one my grandfather stumbled on 50 years ago, then I couldn't help but stumble on the one he stumbled on, even if it was pure accident that that doorstep was lying in wait for me (had for instance been moved to a different house in a different town). Similarly if I owe (must pay) the grocer 5/6d and the grocer is my great uncle I must pay my great uncle 5/6d, even though it does not have to be that the grocer is my great uncle. There is here a tangled skein of large and potentially confusing issues; but it will be enough to detach one or two threads to answer the objection just mentioned. Let us confine the discussion to a difficulty already latent in recent discussions. Kripke maintains that it is a *de re* necessity for Elizabeth II to be the child of George VI, even if George VI did not need to beget Queen Elizabeth.[31] He is also inclined towards a claim which Chisholm had made and independently elaborated, that where a table, *T*, has a leg, *L*, *T* must *de re* have *L* as a part. Chisholm writes 'To say of the table that it is necessarily made up of the stump and the board is not to say of the stump and the board that they are necessarily parts of the table. And it is not to say that the stump is necessarily joined to the board'.[32] Never mind about the plausibility of this mereological essentialism. The point is that it is not meant to follow that while the leg exists the rest of the table must exist. It is supposed that the leg can exist even while the table exists no more.

One approach to this problem would be to do what certainly could be done for the table and leg problem and insist upon a fuller specification of the essential property. Chisholm's original claim might then be stated, with *t* ranging over times,

$$(t)((\text{table exists at } t) \supset (\text{leg composes table at } t))$$

and then rendered into

$$\text{Nec}[(\lambda y)(\lambda w)[(t)((y \text{ exists at } t) \supset (w \text{ composes } y \text{ at } t))]], \quad [\text{table, leg}].$$

[31] Cp. 'Naming and Necessity', op. cit., footnote 56. It would be a mistake to suppose that all such claims are as controversial as Kripke's here. Anyone who will use the concept of necessity at all will find it difficult to deny such claims as this: that Carr's catch was necessarily Carr's catch (Cp. Strawson's *Individuals* (Part II), (Methuen, London, 1959)), that Aspasia's smile necessarily belonged to Aspasia, that the event of Perikles speaking the funeral oration was necessarily Perikles' action. But Aspasia need never have smiled, nor did Perikles have to speak (do) the speaking of the funeral oration. Carr might have been a butter-fingers. Yet if anything is certain it is certain that $[(\lambda x)\ (\lambda y)\ [xRy]] = [(\lambda y)\ (\lambda x)\ [y \text{ converse-R } x]]$. And it would be perverse in the extreme to try to exclude the corresponding biconditional from provability within the theory of truth for *L*.

[32] 'Parts as Essential to their Wholes', *Review of Metaphysics* xxvi (1973).

This secures the intended asymmetry. But if I am right about existential generalization this strategy would not work for the necessity of origin doctrine (here again I am not inquiring into its plausibility[33]); and we can in any case solve the problem more generally within an obvious extension of our theory for *Nec*, by distinguishing

$$[\text{Nec}(\lambda x)(\lambda y)(x \text{ composes } y)], [\text{Leg, Table}],$$

—which is false and has all the undesired existential consequences since we can prove that $(x \text{ composes } y) \equiv (\exists z)(\exists w)((x = z) \,\&\, (w = y) \,\&\, (x \text{ composes } y))$—

$$[\text{Nec}(\lambda x)(x \text{ composes Table})], [\text{Leg}]$$

which is false too, and Chisholm's real claim,

$$[\text{Nec}(\lambda y)(\text{Leg composes } y)], [\text{Table}].$$

This last may or may not be false, according as Chisholm's and Kripke's doctrines are right or wrong. It is certainly different and, even in the obvious extensions of the theory of *Nec*, it will not entail the others.

Here ready made is the solution to the objection inspired by Wallace. What (Sat 3) suggests is not that the relational expression 'is' or '=', flanked by the variables 'x_1' and 'x_2', is such that it must be satisfied by any sequence with h and p in its first and second places, or that the English expression 'Man' prefixed to the variable 'x_2' is such that it must be satisfied by any sequence with Caesar as its second member. These claims might be defended in various ways (as Wallace's objection concerning a theory of truth for $\Box$ might perhaps be answered in various ways). But these things are not what (Sat 3) says or suggests. What (Sat 3) says is that certain individuals (via sequences) necessarily-satisfy certain expressions; not that those expressions are necessarily-satisfied-by those individuals.

There is left much unfinished business. We need a substantial theory of *Nec* (axioms for *Nec*, and good reasons to think the axioms are true), which will enable us to evaluate inferences which at the moment we can only check intuitively.[34] It would be premature however to attempt such a construction before clarifying the mutual relations of $\Box$ and *Nec*. *Nec* cannot it seems be defined by $\Box$, but the

[33] I do so in 'Essentialism, Continuity, and Identity', op. cit.

[34] E.g. of the kind informally essayed towards the end of the paper cited in the previous note.

reverse procedure needs to be attempted. Suppose, for instance, that arrangements were made, as they can be, for *Nec* to modify sentences (as O-place predicates). Then should we arrive at a notion which coincides with the intended meaning of □? Would the new construct mean 'necessarily' *de dicto*? (On this may hang the question whether □ and *Nec* may be unified in the way in which ~ and *Neg* can be. See III[B] above.) It remains to be seen, the question being additionally complicated, in spite of the impressive achievements of the possible-world semanticists, by the lack of cast-iron intuitions concerning the meaning or meanings of the English *de dicto* 'necessarily'. The point where our intuitions begin to falter about the notion of necessity which we express by that English word is, I think, just beyond the frontier marked by Lemmon's system SO.5[35]. Indeed, for that sort of reason, I still find myself needing to be dissuaded of the metalinguistic reading (after the manner of Quine) which takes *de dicto* 'necessarily' as some predicate (wider than *is provable*) of sentences.[36] If a metalinguistic reading were acceptable it would be possible to see a way forward.[37]

[35] See 'Is there only one correct system of modal logic', *Aristotelian Society Supp. Vol.* xxxiii (1959), 31.

[36] See Richard Montague 'Syntactical Treatments of Modality', in *Acta Philosophica Fennica* xvi (1963); W .V. Quine 'Three Grades of Modal Involvement' in *Ways of Paradox* (Random House, New York 1966), pp. 156–7, 164–6. Note that Montague's disproof of this reading of □ depends upon the *theoremhood*, in any system purporting to represent 'necessarily', of *Necessarily* ((*Necessarily* p) ⊃ p), a formula not present as a theorem in SO.5, which lacks the self-involuting properties of stronger systems: and note, what may be much more important, that Montague's argument ignores the real possibility that modal logic may in the end be forced to take account of a language-hierarchy solution to the semantical paradoxes.

[37] Cp. Donald Davidson 'On saying that' in *Words and Objections*, op. cit.

An Appendix to David Wiggins' 'Note'*

CHRISTOPHER PEACOCKE

MY aim in this appendix is to supply a truth theory for an object language containing the predicate modifier *nec* and to comment briefly on the philosophical and formal issues involved. Uses of syntactic distinctions without semantic theories to invest them with significance may be no more than attempts to draw distinctions where there are no differences.

The truth theory to be offered here is 'almost homophonic' in a sense to be made precise, and does not quantify over nonactual objects nor over worlds. In constructing such a theory, we have to take account of two features of *nec* that would not be found in the simplest conceivable predicate modifiers. The first is that *nec*, unlike *large*, can modify predicates of arbitrary finite degree. This has the consequence that while we might hope to build a finitely axiomatized theory around a satisfaction axiom of the form[1]

$$\text{sats}(s, \underline{[\text{large } \lambda x_i[A(x_i)]](t_1)}) \equiv B,$$

it would be a mistake to hope to do the same with

$$\text{sats}(s, \underline{[\text{nec } \lambda x_{i_1} \ldots \lambda x_{i_n}[A(x_{i_1}, \ldots, x_{i_n})]](t_1, \ldots, t_n)}) \equiv B;$$

for this last formula is at best a *schema*, with infinitely many instances. One way of seeing this quickly is to try to write out in primitive notation the structural-descriptive names occurring in these two formulae: if 'α_i' ranges over open sentences with free occurrences of the *i*'th variable ('var(*i*)'), the expanded version for the first case is

$$\text{`['}\frown\text{`large'}\frown\text{`}\lambda\text{'}\frown\text{var}(i)\frown\text{`['}\frown\alpha_i\frown\text{`]'}\frown\text{`]'}\frown\text{`('}\frown t_1\frown\text{`)'}.$$

In the second case we can produce nothing legitimate, '. . .' not being an object-language ('*OL*') expression.

* My thanks to David Wiggins for encouragement and advice at every stage in the writing of this appendix.

[1] Throughout I follow Wiggins' notation unless otherwise specified. s_i is the *i*'th element of sequence s; '$\frown$' is the concatenation functor.

The other fact to be accommodated is that we can iterate occurrences of *nec* in *OL* sentences. As with $\underline{\Box}$, the case is clearest when one occurrence of *nec* is separated from another embedded within it by a quantifier or other vocabulary. The claim that Socrates was necessarily born to someone who was necessarily human is wellformed, whether true or false; we would represent it by

$$[\text{nec}\ \lambda x_1[\exists x_2(x_2 \text{ bore } x_1\ \&\ [\text{nec}\ \lambda x_3[\text{human}\ (x_3)]](x_2)]]\ (\text{Socrates}).$$

The constraint this feature places on any truth theory for our *OL* is in effect that the satisfaction axiom treating *nec*, when applied to *OL* sentences containing embedded occurrences of *nec*, deliver at some point formulae of a form to which the axiom can be applied once again. The following is a very simple axiom we might try to add to Wiggins' (Sat 1) and (Sat 2) that would fail to meet this constraint: where ^{o} is a syntactic operation on abstracts such that $(\underline{\lambda x_1 \lambda x_2[x_1 = x_2]})^o = \underline{x_1 = x_2}$ and $(A)^o = A$ elsewhere, and where 'ϕ' ranges over abstracts,

$$\text{sats}(s, \underline{[\text{nec}\phi](t_1, t_2)}) \equiv \text{nec}\lambda x_1\lambda x_2[\text{sats}(\langle x_1, x_2\rangle, \phi^o)](s^*t_1, s^*t_2).$$

In the presence of rule $R\lambda$, this axiom can indeed deliver the biconditional

$$\text{sats}(s, \underline{[\text{nec}\lambda x_1\lambda x_2[x_1 = x_2]](t_1, t_2)}) \equiv \text{nec}\lambda x_1\lambda x_2[x_1 = x_2](s^*t_1, s^*t_2).$$

But it cannot handle *OL* sentences with one or more iterations of *nec*. For if we substitute '$[\text{nec}\lambda x_1\lambda x_2[x_1 = x_2]]$' for '$\phi$' in the axiom, we obtain on the right hand side within the abstract an expression which speaks of satisfaction of an abstract not followed by any terms, something for which satisfaction has not been defined. There is no immediately obvious way to alter the definition of '^{o}' that remedies the position.

We can avoid the pitfalls produced by the first of these two complications by using the syntactic variable '$\vec{t}$' over bracketed series of terms of the form $(t_1, \ldots, t_n)$; and we can avoid the second problem by having a separate recursion on the abstracts of *OL* in the theory, specifying inductively the conditions under which a sequence has the property correlated ('Corr') with a given abstract. Before launching into a general theory, we can illustrate the operation of the second idea in a simple context by using it to supplement (Sat 1)–(Sat 2) to

allow iterations of *nec*. The following three axioms and one inference rule suffice to accommodate iteration while keeping the theory purely homophonic:

$$\mathrm{Corr}(\underline{\lambda x_1 \lambda x_2[x_1 = x_2]})(x_1, x_2) \equiv \lambda x_1 \lambda x_2[x_1 = x_2](x_1, x_2) \qquad \text{(Sat 4)}$$

$$\mathrm{Corr}(\underline{\mathrm{nec}\ \phi})(x_1, x_2) \equiv \mathrm{nec\ Corr}(\phi)(x_1, x_2) \qquad \text{(Sat 5)}$$

$$\mathrm{sats}(s, \underline{\phi\ (t_1, t_2)}) \equiv \mathrm{Corr}(\phi)(s^*t_1, s^*t_2) \qquad \text{(Sat 6)}$$

Rule: if $\vdash \forall x_1 \forall x_2(\Sigma(x_1, x_2) \equiv \Omega(x_1, x_2))$, and Σ is an abstract or of the form Corr(——), and Ω is of one of these two forms, from

—— Σ——

infer

—— Ω——.

Thus by (Sat 4), Rule and (Sat 6)

$$\vdash(\mathrm{sats}(s, \underline{\lambda x_1 \lambda x_2[x_1 = x_2](t_1, t_2)}) \equiv \lambda x_1 \lambda x_2[x_1 = x_2](s^*t_1, s^*t_2); \qquad (1)$$

and by (Sat 4), Rule and (Sat 5)

$$\vdash \mathrm{Corr}(\underline{\mathrm{nec}\lambda x_1 \lambda x_2[x_1 = x_2]})(x_1, x_2) \equiv \mathrm{nec}\lambda x_1 \lambda x_2[x_1 = x_2](x_1, x_2). \qquad (2)$$

Hence by (2), Rule and (Sat 6)

$$\vdash \mathrm{sats}(s, \underline{\mathrm{nec}\lambda x_1 \lambda x_2[x_1 = x_2](t_1, t_2)}) \equiv \mathrm{nec}\lambda x_1 \lambda x_2[x_1 = x_2](s^*t_1, s^*t_2); \qquad (3)$$

by (2), Rule and (Sat 5)

$$\vdash \mathrm{Corr}(\underline{\mathrm{necnec}\lambda x_1 \lambda x_2[x_1 = x_2]})(x_1, x_2) \equiv \mathrm{necnec}\lambda x_1 \lambda x_2[x_1 = x_2](x_1, x_2); \qquad (4)$$

by (4), Rule and (Sat 6)

$$\vdash \mathrm{sats}(s, \underline{\mathrm{necnec}\lambda x_1 \lambda x_2[x_1 = x_2](t_1, t_2)}) \equiv \mathrm{necnec}\lambda x_1 \lambda x_2[x_1 = x_2](s^*t_1, s^*t_2);$$

and so on.

Combining the use of *Corr* and the use of '$\vec{t}$' we naturally reach this axiom for the general theory:

$$\text{sats}(s, \underline{\phi\vec{t}}) \equiv \text{Corr}(\phi)\#(s, \vec{t})$$

where

$$\#(s, \underline{(t_1, \ldots, t_n)}) = \langle s^*t_1, \ldots, s^*t_n \rangle.$$ [2]

This axiom is used in the theory stated below; it is seen there to involve assigning to *OL* sentences containing abstracts truth conditions that make predications of *sequences*. It is this that prevents the theory given from being fully homophonic (remarks on this aspect follow later).

I shall state a theory labelled '*T*1' and show its adequacy before going on to suggest a certain modification.

As with other adequacy proofs, we need a proper statement of the formation rules of the *OL* treated if we are at any point to proceed by induction on the length of *OL* sentences. We say, then, where '*h*', '*p*', 'x_1', 'x_2', . . . are terms of *OL*, where 't_1', 't_2', . . . range over all terms of *OL*, and '*r*' is a variable over *OL* proper names, that:

(i) $\underline{Ft_1}$ is a sentence

(ii) $\underline{t_1 = t_2}$ is a sentence

(iii) (α) $\underline{\lambda x_i[x_i = r]}$ is an abstract of degree 1

(β) $\underline{\lambda x_i[r = x_i]}$ is an abstract of degree 1

(γ) $\underline{\lambda x_i \lambda x_j[x_i = x_j]}$ is an abstract of degree 2 where $i \neq j$

(iv) $\underline{\lambda x_i[Fx_i]}$ is an abstract of degree 1

(v) if *A* is a sentence, so is $\underline{(\sim A)}$

[2] In this case the underlined dots really are innocuous. One way of clearly ousting them is this. First we dispense with the style of variable '$\vec{t}$' in favour of general variables and the syntactic predicate 'S' governed by these two axioms

$\forall t_1\ (\text{S}(\text{'('}\frown t_1 \frown \text{')'}))$
$\forall x \forall y\ (\text{S}(x \frown \text{')'}) \ \&\ \text{S}\ (\text{'('}\frown y).\supset \text{S}\ (x \frown \text{','} \frown y)).$

Then we can have the following two axioms containing '#', where we abbreviate with underlining:

$\forall t_1\ (\#\ (s, \underline{(t_1)}) = \langle s^*t_1 \rangle)$

$\forall x \forall y\ (\text{S}(\underline{x,y})) \supset \#\ (s, \underline{x,y})) = \langle \#\ (s, \underline{x})), s^*y \rangle).$

We have written no schemata here.

(vi) if A is a sentence, so is $\underline{(\exists x_i A)}$

(vii) if A and B are sentences, so is $\underline{(A \mathbin{\&} B)}$

(viii) if ϕ is an abstract of degree n, so is $\underline{[\mathrm{nec}\phi]}$

(ix) if A is a sentence containing all and only the variables $x_{i_1}, \ldots, x_{i_n}$ free, then $\underline{\lambda x_{i_1} \ldots \lambda x_{i_n}[A]}$ is an abstract of degree n, where $i_j < i_k$ for $j < k$.

(x) if ϕ is an abstract of degree n, then $\phi(t_1, \ldots, t_n)$ is a sentence.

For convenience we will assume that abstracts are always formed using the earliest available variables from the infinite list of variables. Thus $\lambda x_2 \lambda x_3[x_2 = x_3]$ is not counted as an abstract: rather we should write $\underline{\lambda x_1 \lambda x_2[x_1 = x_2]}$. Occasionally we write 'nec ϕ', not '[nec ϕ]'.

We assume classical first-order logic with identity for the metalanguage, treating the particular metalanguage abstracts used below as unanalyzed one place predicables for the purposes of logical axioms and inference rules. The following are the nonlogical axioms and rules of the theory, where 'ϕ' is a variable over abstracts, 'A' and 'B' over sentences, and '$\vec{\lambda}$' over expressions of the form $\lambda x_1 \ldots \lambda x_n$. (In the theory, *Corr* is taken to be defined only on abstracts, and *sats* only in relation to sentences; this permits the simple statements of, *i.a.*, *B*1 and *B*7.)

*B*0 $\quad \mathrm{Corr}(\underline{[\mathrm{nec}\phi]})s \equiv [\mathrm{nec}\ \mathrm{Corr}(\phi)]s$

*B*1 $\quad \mathrm{Corr}(\underline{\vec{\lambda}[A \mathbin{\&} B]})s \equiv \lambda s[\mathrm{sats}(s, \underline{(A \mathbin{\&} B)})]s$

*B*2 $\quad \mathrm{Corr}(\underline{\vec{\lambda}[\exists x_i A]})s \equiv \lambda s[\mathrm{sats}(s, \underline{(\exists x_i A)})]s$

*B*3 $\quad \mathrm{Corr}(\underline{\vec{\lambda}[\sim A]})s \equiv \lambda s[\mathrm{sats}(s, \underline{(\sim A)})]s$

*B*4 (α) $\mathrm{Corr}(\underline{\lambda x_i[x_i = r]})s \equiv \lambda s[\mathrm{sats}(s, \underline{x_i = r})]s$

(β) $\mathrm{Corr}(\underline{\lambda x_i[r = x_i]})s \equiv \lambda s[\mathrm{sats}(s, \underline{r = x_i})]s$

(γ) $\mathrm{Corr}(\underline{\lambda x_i \lambda x_j[x_i = x_j]})s \equiv \lambda s[\mathrm{sats}(s, \underline{x_i = x_j})]s$

*B*5 $\quad \mathrm{Corr}(\underline{\lambda x_i[Fx_i]})s \equiv \lambda s[\mathrm{sats}(s, \underline{Fx_i})]s$

*B*6 $\quad \mathrm{Corr}(\underline{\vec{\lambda}[\phi\vec{t}]})s \equiv \lambda s[\mathrm{sats}(s, \underline{\phi\vec{t}})]s$

*B*7 $\quad \mathrm{sats}(s, \underline{\phi\vec{t}}) \equiv \mathrm{Corr}(\phi)\#(s, \vec{t})$

*B*8 $\quad \mathrm{sats}(s, \underline{(A \mathbin{\&} B)}) \equiv .\ \mathrm{sats}(s, A) \mathbin{\&} \mathrm{sats}(s, B)$

*B*9 $\text{sats}(s, \underline{(\sim A)}) \equiv \sim\text{sats}(s, A)$

*B*10 $\text{sats}(s, \underline{(\exists x_i A)}) \equiv \exists s'(s' \approx s \ \& \ \text{sats}(s', A))$

*B*11 $\text{sats}(s, \underline{F}t_1) \equiv Fs^*t_1$

*B*12 $\text{sats}(s, \underline{t_1 = t_2}) \equiv s^*t_1 = s^*t_2$

*B*13 $s^*\underline{h} = h$; *B*14 $s^*\underline{p} = p$; *B*15 $s^*\underline{x_i} = s_i$

*B*16 $\exists s'(s' \underset{i}{\approx} s \ \& \ s'_i = x)$

There are two nonlogical inference rules; in the version prior to the modification to follow, they are, where 'v_1', 'v_2', . . . are variables over metalanguage variables of any style:

Rule *S*1: if *A* and *B* are open sentences all of whose free variables are among $v_1, \ldots, v_n$, and $\vdash \forall v_1 \ldots \forall v_n(A \equiv B)$, then from

——— $\lambda v_1 \ldots \lambda v_n[A]$ ——— one can infer

——— $\lambda v_1 \ldots \lambda v_n[B]$ ———.[3]

Here and below '$\vdash$' means provability in the theory, with the use of nonlogical axioms allowed.

Rule P: if $\vdash \forall s(\Sigma s \equiv \Omega s)$, where Σ is either an abstract or of the form Corr (——), and Ω is also of one of these forms, then from——— Σ ——— one can infer ——— Ω ———.

The rules are to be applied only if the results of application are wellformed. Finally, we set

$$\text{Tr}(A) =_{\text{df.}} \forall s(\text{sats}(s, A)).$$

We are now in a position to prove that for any closed *OL* sentence *A*, $\vdash \text{Tr}(A) \equiv A'$, where ( )$'$ is a certain syntactic operation on *OL* sentences defined as follows, where we omit underlining and some bracketing:

(a) $Ft_1{}'$ is Ft_1

(b) $t_1 = t_2{}'$ is $t_1 = t_2$

(c) $\lambda x_i[r = x_i]'$ is $\lambda s[r = s_i]$

(d) $\lambda x_i[x_i = r]'$ is $\lambda s[s_i = r]$

[3] The inspiration for this kind of rule comes from Richard Grandy's R3 at p. 143 of his 'A Definition of Truth for Theories with Intensional Definite Description Operators', *Journal of Philosophical Logic*, i (1972).

(e) $\lambda x_i \lambda x_j[x_i = x_j]'$ is $\lambda s[s_i = s_j]$

(f) $\lambda x_i[Fx_i]'$ is $\lambda s[Fs_i]$

(g) $(\sim A)'$ is $\sim(A')$

(h) $(\exists x_i A)'$ is $\exists x_i(A')$

(i) $(A \& B)'$ is $A' \& B'$

(j) $[\text{nec}\phi]'$ is $[\text{nec}\phi']$

(k) if A' is $R(x_{i_1}, \ldots, x_{i_n})$, where the x_{i_j} are all the free variables of A, then $(\lambda x_{i_1} \ldots, \lambda x_{i_n}[A])'$ is $\lambda s[R(s_{i_1}, \ldots, s_{i_n})]$

(l) $(\phi(t_1, \ldots, t_n))'$ is $\phi'\langle t_1, \ldots, t_n\rangle$.

It may be helpful if at this point we give a proof in $T1$ of an easy T-sentence, say

$$\text{Tr}(\underline{[\text{nec}\lambda x_1 \lambda x_2[x_1 = x_2]](h, p)}) \equiv [\text{nec}\lambda s[s_1 = s_2]]\langle h, p\rangle.$$

By $B4$ (γ),

$$\vdash \text{Corr}(\underline{\lambda x_1 \lambda x_2[x_1 = x_2]})s \equiv \lambda s[\text{sats}(s_1, \underline{x_1 = x_2})]s;$$

while by $B12$ and $B15$,

$$\vdash \text{sats}(s, \underline{x_1 = x_2}) \equiv s_1 = s_2.$$

Thus applying Rule $S1$, we get

$$\vdash \text{Corr}(\underline{\lambda x_1 \lambda x_2[x_1 = x_2]})s \equiv \lambda s[s_1 = s_2]s$$

and by this last formula, rule P and $B0$

$$\vdash \text{Corr}(\underline{[\text{nec}\lambda x_1 \lambda x_2[x_1 = x_2]]})s \equiv [\text{nec}\lambda s[s_1 = s_2]]s.$$

Applying Rule P to this and $B7$, we reach

$$\vdash \text{sats}(s, \underline{[\text{nec}\lambda x_1 \lambda x_2[x_1 = x_2]](h, p)}) \equiv [\text{nec}\lambda s[s_1 = s_2]]\langle s^*\underline{h}, s^*\underline{p}\rangle.$$

By $B13$ and $B14$ we can substitute in that formula 'h' and 'p' for '$s^*\underline{h}$' and '$s^*\underline{p}$' respectively, and then by first order logic, using the fact that 's' is not free in the right hand side of the resulting biconditional, we have

$$\forall s(\text{sats}(s, \underline{[\text{nec}\lambda x_1 \lambda x_2[x_1 = x_2]](h, p)})) \equiv [\text{nec}\lambda s[s_1 = s_2]]\langle h, p\rangle.$$

But this is the desired T-sentence, when '$\forall s(\text{sats}(s,\quad))$' is replaced by its abbreviation 'Tr( )'.

To prove adequacy generally, it suffices to show that for any sentence $A(x_{i_1}, \ldots, x_{i_n})$ and corresponding abstract $\lambda x_{i_1} \ldots \lambda x_{i_n} A(x_{i_1}, \ldots x_{i_n})$ (ψ, say) of OL,

$$\vdash \text{sats}(s, \underline{A(x_{i_1}, \ldots, x_{i_n})}) \equiv A(s_{i_1}, \ldots, s_{i_n})'$$

and

$$\vdash \text{Corr}(\psi)s \equiv \psi' s.$$

Proof: We proceed by induction on the length of A, the various cases arising from the formation rules (i)–(x). The induction hypothesis ('ind. hyp.') is available in cases (v)–(x).

(i) from $B11$, $B13$–$B15$, (a)
(ii) from $B12$, $B13$–$B15$, (b)
(iii) by applying consequences of $B12$–$B15$ to $B4$ by way of Rule $S1$: for instance, in case (iii)(γ) from $B12$ and $B15$,

$$\vdash \text{sats}(s, \underline{x_i = x_j}) \equiv s_i = s_j$$

hence by $B4$ and Rule $S1$,

$$\vdash \text{Corr}(\underline{\lambda x_i \lambda x_j [x_i = x_j]})s \equiv \lambda s[s_i = s_j]s$$

(iv) similar to (iii)
(v)–(vii) here the treatment is exactly that for these connectives and quantifiers found in Tarskian truth definitions: we use the ind. hyp., $B9$–$B11$ respectively, plus $B16$ in case (vi)
(viii) by ind. hyp.

$$\vdash \text{Corr}(\phi)s \equiv \phi' s$$

so by Rule P and $B0$

$$\vdash \text{Corr}(\underline{[\text{nec}\phi]})s \equiv [\text{nec}\phi']$$

which by (j) is what we wanted
(ix) by ind. hyp.

$$\vdash \text{sats}(s, \underline{A(x_{i_1}, \ldots, x_{i_n})}) \equiv A(s_{i_1}, \ldots, s_{i_n})'.$$

$A(x_{i_1}, \ldots, x_{i_n})$ can arise only from one of the formation rules (v)–(vii) or (x); for each of these cases, using the appropriate one of $B1$–$B3$ and $B6$ with Rule $S1$, we reach

$$\vdash \text{Corr}(\psi)s \equiv \lambda s[A(s_{i_1}, \ldots, s_{i_n})']s.$$

But by (k),

$$\lambda s[A(s_i, \ldots, s_{i_n})'] \text{ is } (\lambda x_{i_1} \ldots \lambda x_{i_n})[A(x_{i_1}, \ldots, x_{i_n})])'.$$

(x) if $A(x_{i_1}, \ldots, x_{i_n})$ is of the form $\phi(t_1, \ldots, t_n)$, then by ind. hyp.

$$\vdash \text{Corr}(\phi)s \equiv \phi' s;$$

and also by *B*7

$$\vdash \text{sats}(s, \underline{\phi(t_1, \ldots, t_n)}) \equiv \text{Corr}(\phi) \# (s, \underline{(t_1, \ldots, t_n)});$$

from the last two displayed formulae, Rule *P* and the definition of '#',

$$\vdash \text{sats}(s, \underline{\phi(t_1, \ldots, t_n)}) \equiv \phi' \langle s^* t_1, \ldots, s^* t_n \rangle.$$

which with *B*13–*B*15 yields what is by (*l*) required.

Thus some more sample T-sentences that are derivable in *T*1 are:

$$\text{Tr}(\underline{[\text{nec}[\text{nec}\lambda x_1 \lambda x_2[x_1 = x_2]]](h, p)}) \equiv [\text{nec}[\text{nec}\lambda s[s_1 = s_2]]]\langle h, p \rangle$$

$$\text{Tr}(\underline{\lambda x_1 \lambda x_2[\sim \exists x_3(x_3 = x_1 \;\&\; \sim [\text{nec}\lambda x_1 \lambda x_2[x_1 = x_2]]\,(x_3, x_2))](h, p)}) \equiv \lambda s[\sim \exists x_3(x_3 = s_1 \;\&\; \sim [\text{nec}[s_1 = s_2]]\,\langle x_3, s_2 \rangle)]\langle h, p \rangle.$$

Plainly this theory *T*1 has been constructed with an eye only to the derivability of the T-sentences, and not, for instance, with any concern to incorporate principles of inference appropriate only to *nec*; one could give an exactly parallel treatment for *possibly* as a predicate modifier. To argue for particular claims involving *nec* that are not guaranteed by the truth theory itself one will need to provide a substantive theory containing nonlogical and nonsemantical axioms that use, rather than mention, *nec*; this too is a task beyond anything attempted here.[4]

[4] What of the ontology of *T*1? In particular, is it committed to properties, and if so does it impute such an ontology to OL? This last query is not settled in the negative by the fact that *T*1 does not treat properties as entities that stand, or elements of entities that stand, in the satisfaction relation to OL expressions. This settles nothing since *T*1 also uses a concept of Correlation, and the critical question is what this use imports. Those who think this does expand the ontology required may be tempted to compare the case with this truth definition for a simple language where (they will say)

If, with David Wiggins, we wish to read

$$[\text{nec}\lambda x_1[\text{man}(x_1)]](\text{Socrates})$$

as a statement of the essentialist's claim that Socrates necessarily is a man, then given that nothing can really be a man (with a brain and central nervous system) without existing, the translation of this statement into the language of possible worlds must be 'In any world in which Socrates exists, he is a man'.

More generally,

$$[\text{nec}\lambda x_1 \ldots \lambda x_n[A(x_1, \ldots, x_n)]](t_1, \ldots, t_n)$$

would go over into

'In any world w in which all of $t_1, \ldots, t_n$ exist, $t_1, \ldots, t_n$ have the relation A in w.' (If we were to make similar existential provisions in the antecedent of this translation for terms occurring in $A(x_1, \ldots, x_n)$, all hope would disappear of finding a difference of truth conditions between any of $\text{nec}\lambda x_1\lambda x_2[Rx_1x_2](a, b)$, $\text{nec}\lambda x_1[Rax_1](b)$ and $\text{nec}\lambda x_1[Rx_1b](a)$.) But on the intuitive understanding of *nec* that these possible-world translations, despite their heavy ontology, crudely express, *T*1 certainly contains some false theorems. The problem lies with Rule *S*1.

One example suffices to show the general difficulty: it can be made vivid by supposing that '*h*' of the metalanguage names Hesperus and that '*F*' has the same satisfaction conditions as the English *man*. In classical first-order logic with identity, and so in *T*1, we can prove that

$$\exists x_2(x_2 = h)$$

and hence that

$$Fs_1 \equiv (Fs_1 \;\&\; \exists x_2(x_2 = h)).$$

---

although OL has no objectual quantification, a finite treatment of the infinitely many singular terms forces an assignment of entities:

$$\begin{cases} \text{den}(\underline{\text{Cleopatra}}) = \text{Cleopatra} \\ \text{den}(\underline{\text{father of } t_1}) = \text{father of den}(t_1) \\ \text{Tr}(\underline{t_1 \text{ is taller than } t_2}) \equiv \text{den}(t_1) \text{ is taller than den}(t_2). \end{cases}$$

But this analogy is question-begging since it is *identity* that occurs in the first two axioms here; in *T*1, the recursion for *Corr* uses only material biconditionals. The result of the argument seems to be a stand-off; which if anything puts the onus on those who regard *T*1 as imputing an ontology of properties to its OL.

Using this in tandem with Rule $S1$ we can easily prove that

$$\underline{\mathrm{Tr}(\exists x_3([\mathrm{nec}\lambda x_1[Fx_1]](x_3)))} \equiv \exists x_3([\mathrm{nec}\lambda s[Fs_1 \ \& \ \exists x_2(x_2 = h)]]\langle x_3\rangle)$$

is a theorem of $T1$. Certain essentialists will count this biconditional as false, its left being true and its right false; and everyone will count the resulting biconditional false if we work through the argument with '$\sim(Fx_1 \ \& \ \sim Fx_1)$' in place of '$Fx_1$'. Indeed, if we wish to count '$h = h$' as not true with respect to worlds in which Hesperus does not exist, then even the theorem

$$\underline{\mathrm{Tr}(\exists x_3([\mathrm{nec}\lambda x_1[Fx_1]](x_3)))} \equiv \exists x_3([\mathrm{nec}\lambda s[Fs_1 \ \& \ h = h]]\langle x_3\rangle)$$

is unwanted.

Plainly the difficulty is that in classical first-order logic with identity we can prove the biconditional linking a pair of sentences with different ontological commitments. On the model-theoretic conception of validity which this logic captures this is of course both unsurprising and desirable. But when we apply this logic to a language that is already interpreted, we cannot, *pace* Rule $S1$, expect the provable equivalence of open sentences A and B to sustain their substitutivity in *nec* contexts in all cases; for the truth value of sentences containing *nec* is sensitive to such differences in ontological commitment.

Here is a rule, Rule $S2$, which is motivated by such considerations and can supplant Rule $S1$:

If: A and B are open sentences all of whose free variables are among $v_1, \ldots, v_n$, and $\vdash \forall v_1 \ldots \forall v_n(A \equiv B)$, and

(i) B contains no individual constants not in A, excepting that

  (a) B may contain any individual constants that occur in the satisfaction and evaluation axioms for some expression a description of which occurs in A

  (b) B may contain names of OL expressions

(ii) as in (i), interchanging 'A' with 'B'.

then: from ——— $\lambda v_1 \ldots \lambda v_n[A]$ ——— one can infer ——— $\lambda v_1 \ldots \lambda v_n[B]$ ———.

The motivation for the main part of this rule also justifies the qualifying clauses (a) and (b). The satisfaction and evaluation axioms of the

theory do not express merely contingent truths about the language of which the theory treats, as we see clearly when we take into account the (so far) suppressed language parameter of *sats* and *, and are careful about scope: concerning the language L that is (regimented) English, necessarily any sequence satisfies x_1 *is larger than Hesperus* in L iff its first element is larger than Hesperus. Any language for which this does not hold is other than L. Qualification (b) need not worry us since *OL* expressions are expression *types* and do not fail to exist in any possible situation.

Let us say that theory *T*2 results from *T*1 when Rule *S*2 replaces *S*1. Then the reader can satisfy him or herself that *T*2 is also adequate by checking that all the applications of Rule *S*1 in our earlier adequacy proof are in fact also applications of Rule *S*2.

*T*2 remains of course only an almost homophonic theory. But it is worth noting that a very simple transformation ( )″, the inverse of the operation ( )′, applied to the right hand side p of any *T*2 T-sentence will yield the sentence p'' that is described on the left hand side; and moreover that p and p'' will be provably equivalent in theories that contain an analogue of Rule *S*2 and yield the infinitely many indubitable instances of the schema

$$\lambda s[A(s_1, \ldots, s_n)]\langle s_1, \ldots, s_n\rangle \equiv \lambda x_1 \ldots \lambda x_n[A(x_1, \ldots, x_n)](s_1, \ldots, s_n).$$

XIII

Is There a Problem about Substitutional Quantification?*

SAUL KRIPKE

THREE RECENT papers, two by John Wallace and one by Leslie Tharp,[1] have attempted to prove that the distinctions usually made between 'substitutional' and 'referential' quantification are untenable. Now I have not only been puzzled that able authors should advance such a thesis; I have also been surprised to find that many able readers of their papers have believed that they have succeeded, or may possibly have succeeded. Sample statements of the thesis are:

(1) Advantages which were supposed to attach to substitutional quantification by virtue of its 'lighter', less predication committed, recursion are all lost. The range for quantified variables and the bias toward extensionality are present in the derived recursion on satisfaction (Wallace (2), p. 208).

(2) Some of these writers see in the substitution interpretation an ontological neutrality . . . some a congenialness to intensionality and modality . . . that distinguish it from the satisfaction interpretation. If my claim is correct, these differences are illusory (Wallace (1), p. 251).

* A note on the history of this paper. I began it early in 1972, in a mood of dismay over the fairly common acceptance of the Wallace–Tharp thesis at my own university, and completed most of Sections 1–8 (except 2(*a*) and 5(*a*)) and some of Section 9. I then put the project aside for more constructive work. Subsequently I was further dismayed to see the Wallace–Tharp thesis disseminated in such papers as Davidson (1), and some friends urged that the work had value as an exposition of substitutional quantification and other fundamental logical matters. The editors of this volume invited me to complete the paper and publish it here. I did so in 1975, adding material and somewhat revising the earlier sections. Nevertheless at some points the history of the composition of the paper shows through. The recent exchange between Camp and Wallace (5) appeared too late for me to take account of it in the paper except for a brief postscript.

I should like to thank the editors of this volume for their crucial help in preparing the paper for publication against considerable pressure of time.

[1] Wallace (1) and (2) and Tharp. I should mention that my critical discussion of Tharp is largely confined to its second section; I find much less to criticize in the first and third sections. Wallace (1) deals with many topics in addition to substitutional quantification. I don't discuss his views on the others, even though I have many other points of strong disagreement (and some of agreement) with this ambitious paper.

(3) (In substitutional quantification) one appears to be defining truth in terms of linguistic entities alone, with no appeal to the objects over which the quantifiers range. However, there is an oversight here which Wallace has noted . . . If one could define truth in some way directly, appealing only to linguistic objects, or at least not appealing to all individuals, then this would be demonstrably different from the usual definition if one could show that no definition of satisfaction emerges. Unfortunately there appear to be difficult technical problems in constructing such definitions; and even if one finds examples, it may not be possible to get a satisfactory general picture (Tharp, p. 368).

The claim made thus seems to be that, contrary to the usual impression, a careful examination of truth definitions for the substitutional quantifier will show that these definitions, if they succeed at all, must make a covert appeal to some range for the variables. Further, Wallace apparently argues that the usual view that substitutional quantification into opaque contexts is unproblematic is incorrect; in fact, he seems to argue (Wallace (2), p. 209) that a truth definition for substitutional quantification will render all contexts quantified into transparent.

Wallace and Tharp do *not* quite seem to go so far as to claim that substitutional quantification is unintelligible, or that a truth definition for it is impossible. At best, they seem to claim rather that, intelligibly interpreted, it reduces to referential quantification. In the oral tradition, I have heard much stronger claims: that Wallace and Tharp have shown substitutional quantification impossible, or that truth theories for it violate Tarskian requirements. Such views have reached print. Davidson (1), pp. 79–80, citing Wallace and Tharp, says, 'Theories of truth based on the substitutional definition of quantifiers do not in general yield the T-sentences demanded by Convention T . . . substitutional theories have no evident virtue to set against their failure to satisfy Convention T.' Here Davidson endorses the claim; elsewhere, Davidson and Harman, in their introduction to their book (Davidson and Harman), attribute to Wallace the strong view that 'the "substitutional interpretation of quantification" cannot be squared with Convention T', without specifically endorsing it.

I see no merit in any of these claims, either stronger or weaker. My interest is as much in a methodological issue as in the substantive issue: I am interested in the papers by Wallace and Tharp as symptomatic, perhaps in an extreme way, of fairly common confusions

about formal mathematical and logical arguments and their relation to philosophical conclusions.

Two more preliminary remarks. First, as I shall emphasize later, Wallace and Tharp are ambiguous on whether various key quantifiers are substitutional or referential. This leads to differing interpretations of their claims, depending on whether they are talking about substitutional quantification or referential quantification. Since their thesis is supposed to be about substitutional quantification, I interpret them in this light. However, some of their theses read more plausibly when taken to be about referential quantification; such an interpretation is given in Section 10.

Second, I have largely framed the discussion of Wallace and Tharp within the philosophical framework they themselves (especially Wallace) presuppose[2]—Quine's views on ontological commitment and Davidson's ideas on the philosophical significance of a finitely axiomatized truth theory. I have done so in spite of considerable doubts and uncertainties as to whether these frameworks may not need fundamental modifications at key points, whether they are often misapplied, and whether different approaches might not be better. I have done so because a discussion of such fundamental issues might more than double the length of this paper, and since my views on these matters are often inconclusive. Let no one conclude that I completely endorse the framework, merely because I choose to meet Wallace largely on his own ground. Occasional indications of doubt of the framework, tips of the iceberg, surface from time to time.

Some of the discussions in the paper may be of interest in relation to either substitutional quantification or the Davidsonian programme as a whole, in addition to the specific issues raised by Wallace and Tharp. I would especially call attention to Section 5(*a*), where I sketch a proof that if substitutional quantification with sentential substitutes is allowed in the metalanguage, both the Tarskian problem of an explicit definition of truth and the Davidsonian problem of a finitely axiomatized truth theory become almost trivial, and have no relation to the problem of a recursive semantics for the object language.

[2] Tharp, here and elsewhere, indicates some doubts about the framework. In the discussion of substitutional quantification, however, he uses it. Both authors, of course, in denying the distinction between referential and substitutional quantification, are disagreeing with a view of Quine.

Wallace's working ontological doctrine appears to be that the ontology of a language is the Quinean ontology of a Davidsonian truth theory for it. I largely work within this postulate without committing myself to it.

1. STANDARD QUANTIFICATION AND SUBSTITUTIONAL QUANTIFICATION[3]

A (first-order) language based on the standard, or 'referential' quantifier, is usually defined as follows. We are given a (possibly empty, finite, or denumerable) list of primitive constants a_1, a_2, a_3, . . ., and a (possibly empty, finite, or denumerable) list of n-place function letters for each n, $\{f_i^n\}$. There is also a denumerable list of variables x_1, x_2, ... A *term* is defined by the clauses: the primitive constants and variables are terms; if $t_1, \ldots, t_n$ are terms, so is $f_i^n(t_1, \ldots, t_n)$. For each n, a similar list of primitive n-place predicates $\{P_i^n\}$ is given, and it is assumed there is at least one such predicate for at least one n. $P_i^n(t_1, \ldots, t_n)$ is an *atomic formula*. Formulae are defined as follows: atomic formulae are formulae; if ϕ and ψ are formulae, so is $\phi \wedge \psi$; if ϕ is a formula, so is $\sim\phi$; if ϕ is a formula so is $(\exists x_i)\phi$. ($(x_i)\phi$ can be defined as $\sim(\exists x_i)\sim\phi$).

Semantically, we interpret the standard quantifier as follows. A non-empty domain D is given; also we are given a function F mapping every primitive constant into an element of D, every n-place function letter into an n-place function from D^n to D, and every n-place predicate letter into an n-place relation on D. D is called the 'range' of the variables. Let $s = \{s_i\}$ be an infinite sequence of members of D. Then for each term t, the *denotation of t with respect to s* is defined by: the denotation of x_i is s_i; the denotation of a primitive constant is the corresponding element of D; the denotation of $f_i^n(t_1, \ldots, t_n)$ is $f(a_1, \ldots, a_n)$, where $f = F(f_i^n)$ is the function corresponding to f_i^n and $a_1, \ldots, a_n$ are the denotations of $t_1, \ldots, t_n$. For a term not containing variables the denotation is independent of s.

If $P_i^n(t, \ldots, t_n)$ is an atomic formula ϕ, we say that s *satisfies* ϕ iff the denotations of $t_1, \ldots, t_n$ with respect to s are related by the relation corresponding to P_i^n; s satisfies $\phi \wedge \psi$ iff s satisfies ϕ and satisfies ψ; s satisfies $\sim\phi$ iff s does not satisfy ϕ; s satisfies $(\exists x_i)\phi$ iff there is a sequence s' of members of D differing from s in at most the ith place which satisfies ϕ. A formula without free variables is *true* iff some sequence satisfies it.

The substitutional quantifier is formally similar to the standard, or 'referential' quantifier, but its semantics is very different; variables also play a quite different role. Throughout the present paper, I will emphasize this difference by using roman (unitalicized) letters for

[3] Although I will be fussier than usual about some notational matters, I won't be fussy about others where it seems to me there is no opportunity for confusion. In particular I will not be fussy about corners, quotes, etc.

substitutional variables, and $(\Pi \mathrm{x}_i)$ and $(\Sigma \mathrm{x}_i)$ for the universal and existential substitutional quantifiers. (x_i) and $(\exists x_i)$ will be the referential quantifiers and italicized variables will be referential. Only in this way can we avoid ambiguities. If some argument by Wallace and Tharp is to show that the two quantifiers are equivalent, let us not prejudge the issue by an ambiguous choice of notation. As we shall see, Wallace and Tharp do not take this precaution; and their failure to take it turns out not to be irrelevant to their arguments.

Let L_0 be a language. The sentences of L_0 are assumed somehow to be effectively specified syntactically: in the larger language L to be developed, an L_0-sentence will be called *atomic*. We assume that L_0 has a non-empty class C of expressions called the *substitution class*; the elements of C are called *terms*, but we do not assume that *terms* are to 'denote' any objects. Nor do we assume that they even be *syntactically* similar to the terms of a referential language. Terms could be any class of expressions of L_0, sentences, connectives, even parentheses (after Lesniewski).

Let $\mathrm{x}_1, \mathrm{x}_2, \ldots$ be an infinite list of variables not contained in L_0. Let A be a sentence of L_0. An expression A' obtained by replacing zero or more terms in A by variables is called an (atomic) *preformula* or *preform*. If the result of replacing variables by arbitrary terms in an atomic preformula is always itself a sentence of L_0, the preformula is an (atomic) *form*. (The sentences of L_0 are automatically forms, since they are the degenerate case with no variables.) In general there may not be an effective test for when a preform is a form. A simple sufficient condition for such a test to exist is the syntactic requirement that, in any sentence of L_0, replacement of any term by any other term still yields a sentence of L_0. In this case, every (atomic) preform is a form.

We wish to extend L_0 to a language L. If there is an effective test for the formhood of a preform, take all forms to be *atomic formulae* of L. Otherwise, specify some effectively given set of forms as *atomic formulae*. We assume that these include all the sentences of L_0, and that if $\phi(\mathrm{x}_{i_1}, \ldots, \mathrm{x}_{i_n})$ is an atomic formula, so is the result of replacing the listed variables with any others.

Given a notion of atomic formula of L, we now define the notion of an arbitrary formula inductively: an atomic formula is a formula; if ϕ and ψ are formulae, so are $\phi \wedge \psi$, $\sim\phi$, and $(\Sigma \mathrm{x}_i)\phi$. (It is assumed that the truth-functions and the existential substitutional quantifier are *new* notations, not to be found in L_0.) A formula without free

variables is called a *sentence* of *L*. *Formulae which are not sentences will be assigned no semantic interpretation; they merely play an auxiliary role.* (This contrasts with the referential case, where such formulae define relations and are 'satisfied' by sequences. Here we have no satisfaction, only truth.[4])

Formulae with free variables can also be called *forms*: usually, however, we reserve this expression for the atomic case. We also mention the notion of an *n*-ary *functor*: this is an expression with *n* variables, $x_{i_1}, \ldots, x_{i_n}$, such that, when arbitrary terms replace the variables, a term results. I allow the degenerate case where not all of the variables $x_{i_1}, \ldots, x_{i_n}$, or even none of them, appear in an *n*-ary form or functor.

We assume that truth has already been defined for sentences of L_0. We note that $\phi \wedge \psi$ is a sentence iff ϕ and ψ are; $\sim\phi$ is a sentence iff ϕ is; $(\Sigma x_i)\phi$ is a sentence iff ϕ is a formula containing at most x_i free. Then the extended truth conditions for sentences of *L* are:

(4) $\sim\phi$ is true iff ϕ is not;
(5) $\phi \wedge \psi$ is true iff ϕ is and ψ is;
(6) $(\Sigma x_i)\phi$ is true iff there is a term *t* such that ϕ' is true, where ϕ' comes from ϕ by replacing all free occurrences of x_i by *t*.

Plainly, granted that truth has been characterized for the sentences of L_0, (4)–(6) characterize truth for all of *L*. Let me formulate this theorem more exactly. Given *any* set *S* of sentences of L_0 which we take to be the set of 'true' sentences of L_0, there is a *unique* set S' (of truths for all of *L*) satisfying (4)–(6) and coinciding with *S* on L_0. There are two parts to this assertion, uniqueness and existence. To prove both halves we use induction on the complexity of the sentences of *L*, where the complexity of a sentence is defined as the number of truth-functions and quantifiers it contains. We now argue by induction on the complexity of a formula of *L* that any sets S' and S'' coinciding with *S* on L_0 and satisfying (4)–(6) coincide. That is, we prove by induction on *n* that if ϕ has complexity *n*, $\phi \in S'$ iff $\phi \in S''$. Let ϕ be a formula of *L*. If it has complexity 0, then $\phi \in S'$ iff $\phi \in S''$ iff $\phi \in S$ (since every formula of complexity 0 is in L_0, and S' and S'' both coincide with *S* on L_0). If the result is assumed for formulae of complexity

[4] Of course a formula with free variables can be interpreted semantically by observing that it becomes true if such and such terms replace the variables and false if other terms replace them. This, however, is merely a concept defined in terms of truth for sentences; unlike satisfaction in the case of referential quantifiers, it plays no role in the inductive definitions of semantical terms.

$\leqslant n$, let ϕ be a formula of complexity $n+1$. ϕ must contain a connective or quantifier, since its complexity exceeds 0. Suppose, say, ϕ is of the form $(\Sigma x_i)\psi$. Then if $\phi \in S'$, *i.e.* $(\Sigma x_i)\psi \in S'$, by (6) some formula ψ' is in S', where ψ' comes from ψ by replacing free occurrences of x_i by a term. Since ψ' has complexity n, by hypothesis $\psi' \in S''$. But then by (6) for S'', $\phi \in S''$. So $\phi \in S''$ if $\phi \in S'$. The converse is similar. The cases where ϕ is $\sim\psi$ or $\psi_1 \wedge \psi_2$ are proved in the same way.

This proves the *uniqueness* of any S' satisfying the given conditions. We now need to prove the *existence* of such an S' coinciding with S on L_0 and satisfying (4)–(6). We sketch the proof. As a lemma, we prove by induction on n that there is a set S_n which coincides with S on L_0 and satisfies conditions (4)–(6) for all formulae of complexity $\leqslant n$ (and contains only formulae of complexity $\leqslant n$). For $n = 0$, let S_n be the set of all formulae of complexity zero in S. Given an S_n satisfying the given conditions, I leave it to the reader as an exercise to show how to define a set S_{n+1} satisfying the given conditions for formulae of complexity $\leqslant n+1$ (the idea is obviously to adjoin new formulae of complexity $n+1$ in such a way that conditions (4)–(6) are still satisfied). We can now define S' as the union of all the S_n's and verify that it satisfies the required conditions (the proof is easiest if we prove as a lemma, parallel to the uniqueness proof in the preceding paragraph, that there is a *unique* S_n satisfying the conditions stated for S_n).

It should be noted that the proofs just given, both of the existence and of the uniqueness of an S' satisfying the given conditions for formulae of L, depended crucially on the assumption that substitutional quantification with the given substitution class is not already part of the notation of L_0.[5] Both the substitution class and the formulae of L_0 were given *in advance* before the language was extended to L. If we look at the argument given above, we see that it used crucially the assumption that the terms of the substitution class do not themselves contain the new style of quantifiers. Otherwise, for example, we would have committed a fallacy when we argued that if ϕ is $(\Sigma x_i)\psi$ and has complexity $n+1$, and ψ' comes from ψ by replacing x_i by a term t, then ψ' has complexity $\leqslant n$, for perhaps the introduction of the term t increases complexity if t itself contains

[5] L_0 can contain referential or substitutional quantifiers, and these can even occur in the terms, provided that the style of quantification being introduced to extend to L is a new one, notationally distinct from all of these.

many quantifiers. Theories in which the substitution class is allowed to include definite descriptions $\imath x\phi$ for arbitrary ϕ of L, aside from presenting problems of interpretation, violate this requirement. Failure to heed the requirement has been responsible for some of the worst misconceptions about substitutional quantification. *If the requirement is not fulfilled, we cannot prove, by the methods above, the existence and uniqueness of S'.* On the other hand, though we assumed that conjunction and negation were not part of L_0 either—largely so that we could think of all formulae of L_0 as atomic—this assumption was *not* needed in the proof of the existence and uniqueness of S' above. So we can apply our results to cases where this assumption is relaxed. Further, even for some substitution classes violating the condition that quantifiers not occur in terms,[6] there *may* be *another* proof, different from the one just given, of the existence and uniqueness of a set with the desired properties. Though in this case the set would probably not be said to be *inductively* defined, we could still say that substitutional truth was uniquely characterized and thus well defined. Such cases will be rather special.

Let me give an example.[7] Suppose the terms of the substitution class are taken to be the sentences not of L_0, but of L. Then the requirements needed to prove the theorem are plainly violated, since terms are being defined inductively along with L itself. The sentence $(\Sigma x)x$ will be true iff some sentence ϕ of L is true, where the complexity is arbitrary. $(\Pi x)x$ will be true if every sentence ϕ of L is true. Clearly the clauses no longer allow us to carry out the inductive argument given above and the substitution class in question is in general illegitimate. (The sentences of L_0, on the other hand, form a legitimate substitution class.) In rare special cases, however, the uniqueness of S' can be proved with the sentences of L as the substitution class. Suppose L_0 is extensional in the sense that sentences are always replaceable in any context by materially equivalent sentences *salva veritate*. Suppose further that L_0 contains at least one true sentence T and one false sentence F. Then it can be proved that there is a unique extension of the truth set for L_0 to a truth set for L satisfying (4)–(6). Further, it can be shown that L is extensional in the same sense as L_0, and that therefore $(\Sigma x)\phi$ is true if either ϕ' or ϕ'' is, where ϕ' and ϕ'' come from ϕ by replacing x with T or F, respectively.

Following Tarski, we can transform the inductive definition of S' as the unique set satisfying certain conditions into an explicit definition. Really this is an application of Russell's theory of descrip-

[6] Strictly speaking, the condition is that the substitutional quantifiers we are introducing into L not occur in terms; terms may contain referential or substitutional quantifiers with other styles of variables if these already occur in L_0.

[7] Small type indicates a digression from the main themes of the surrounding text.

tions: instead of saying that a sentence is true if it is a member of *the* set satisfying (4)–(6) (and coinciding with S on L_0), we say that a sentence is true if *there is* a set containing it and satisfying (4)–(6) and . . ..

I would have thought that any mathematical logician at this point would conclude that truth for L has been characterized uniquely. If someone asserts a formula ϕ of L, we know precisely under what conditions his assertion would be true. (Namely, that ϕ is a member of a set satisfying (4)–(6) and coinciding with S on L_0.)

Does Wallace really wish to deny that truth has been characterized for L? Some passages actually suggest that he does. In Wallace (1), for example, we find, 'I think that some philosophers will resist the idea that (1)–(3) (our (4)–(6)—S.K.) are not already an adequate account of truth conditions' (p. 233). Shouldn't they 'resist' this idea? *There is no hidden fallacy in the proof that conditions* (4)–(6) *uniquely extend a truth concept for* L_0 *to one for* L. (*If* Wallace means to deny this, he is wrong.)

Perhaps Wallace means that (4)–(6) are not enough by themselves; we must have the concept 'true in L_0' (the set S) already. This is true enough, but no lengthy disquisitions are needed to establish the point. It has nothing to do with substitutional quantification; it would remain true even if (6) and (Σx_i) were dropped from the language and only the truth-functions remained. *Of course* an inductive definition requires a basis; we can only use (4)–(6) to extend truth from L_0 to L. Who ever thought otherwise? The phenomenon is characteristic of *all* recursive definitions.

Now Wallace's main aims are to show a collapse of substitutional into referential quantification. There is one point which, indeed, deserves strong emphasis. This is that the use of substitutional quantifiers cannot *per se* be thought of as guaranteeing freedom from 'ontological commitment' (other than to expressions). It is true that the clauses (4)–(6) can be stated without mentioning entities other than expressions[8] *and the entities mentioned in characterizing truth for* L_0. *If* other entities are mentioned in characterizing truth for L_0, they still are used when the notion is extended to L. Note that, however, there is no reason to think that other entities are used in every truth characterization for every L_0; such an assumption would be obviously false.

[8] The *explicit* definition of truth in L involves quantification over sets of expressions also.

Wallace and Tharp, especially the former, seem to argue that the 'terms' must denote or a determination of truth conditions for L will be impossible. Since *any* class of expressions of L_0 can be the substitution class, and since L_0 can be any language, and since we can extend a truth concept for L_0 to L automatically, such a result would seem to mean that *any expressions of any language must denote*, a rather astounding result. True, for injudicious choices of the substitution class there will be very few *forms*. It is entirely feasible, however, to let the substitution class consist of the *sentences* of L_0 (see Section 5(*a*)). Does this provide an *a priori* proof of Frege's view that *sentences* denote? Suppose L_0 contains *connectives*, say primitive truth-functions $\wedge$, $\sim$, $\vee$, $\supset$, $\equiv$. The substitution class can consist of expressions where a sentence of L_0 is followed by a binary connective. Then $x\psi$, where ψ is a sentence, is a form, and $(\Sigma x)x\psi$ is implied by each of its instances $\phi_1 \supset \psi$, $\phi_1 \wedge \psi$, $\phi_2 \equiv \psi$, $\phi_2 \supset \psi$, etc. Is this supposed to mean that expressions such as '$\phi\supset$' denote? Usually they are not even regarded as significant units!

The same puzzlement arises with respect to *opacity*. Suppose the terms of L_0 *do* denote; the truth characterization for L_0 somehow uses the concept of denotation for all the terms. Then L_0 may contain *opacities*; codesignative terms may not be intersubstitutable in L_0 *salva veritate*. Yet this phenomenon, if it exists, will be entirely irrelevant to the extension of L_0 to L, and of truth for L_0 to truth for L. L will then contain 'substitutional quantification into opaque contexts'; this is why the conventional view asserts that such quantification is unproblematic. Wallace challenges this view. Does he challenge the theorem on which it is based (that a truth characterization for L_0 uniquely extends to L)? If not, there can be no trouble with truth for L which was not *already* trouble with truth for L_0. (See Section 3, the 'Giorgione' case, for a simple example of an opaque L_0.)

We find that we are faced with a dilemma. Either Wallace and Tharp actually deny the theorem that truth for L_0 can uniquely be extended to truth for L, in which case they have made a simple mathematical error; or they deny that this theorem shows that the (extensional) semantics of L has been fully explained, given one for L_0—some other restrictions are to be imposed. The imposition of additional restrictions is, indeed, a very fashionable activity among those working on Davidson's semantics. Is it very plausible? It is a simple *theorem* that the truth conditions for L_0, plus (4)–(6), determine those for L. If someone asserted a sentence ϕ of L, anyone who

could define truth for L_0 would know *precisely* under what conditions the assertion would be true. Can there really be additional requirements? Any working mathematical logician would regard the theorem under discussion as *settling* the question whether the (extensional) semantics of L has been intelligibly given.

Without looking any further at Wallace's and Tharp's arguments, I find myself saddled with a complex dilemma. Perhaps they do not really mean to deny that truth for L is intelligibly characterized, given truth for L_0, regardless of whether L_0 has opacities or any denoting terms. But is is hard for me to interpret them otherwise. Alternatively, they mean to impose additional requirements, which must be satisfied before they will admit that truth has been characterized for L. But then, since it is a theorem that truth has been characterized for L, it would seem that *either* (i) the additional criteria are unjustified, *or* (ii) they are directed toward some problem other than the intelligibility of 'true in L'[9] (if so, the other problem should have been clearly stated!), *or* (iii) the claims that truth in L (for arbitrary L, including L's with opacities and non-denoting terms) fails to satisfy the additional criteria are incorrect. The disjunction here is *not* exclusive. We will find below that *at least* (iii) is almost invariably the case. But before I had made *any* detailed examination of Wallace's and Tharp's arguments, I personally found myself faced with this dilemma. Something, I thought, must have gone wrong somewhere, since the substitutional truth definition is *plainly* a perfectly good inductive definition. The only question that remained, I thought (unless I was to be in for a rude and major shock) was to find, for particular arguments, *which* of (i)–(iii) was involved. Why didn't all other readers react the same way?

1(*a*). *Substitutional Validity*

The universal substitutional quantifier $(\Pi x_i)\phi$ can be defined as $\sim(\Sigma x_i)\sim\phi$. Just as $(\Sigma x_i)\phi$ can be regarded as the (possibly infinite) disjunction of the formulae resulting by replacing all free occurrences of x_i by a term t, so $(\Pi x_i)\phi$ can be regarded as their conjunction;[10] it is true if and only if all such instances are true.

[9] For example, some of Davidson's criteria—that a language not have infinitely many primitives—seem intended to show that a language violating them couldn't be a *first* language, rather than that it must be unintelligible.

[10] This should be taken with reservations. It means that $(\Pi x)\phi$ has the same truth conditions as a (possibly infinite) conjunction of all its instances; it does not mean that $(\Pi x)\phi$ could be formally derived from the set of its instances as an infinite conjunction could be in infinitary logic. See Dunn and Belnap.

We have so far been talking about particular first-order referential or substitutional languages. The language of the *pure predicate calculus* can be formulated for both. It contains a denumerably infinite list of variables (italicized for referential, unitalicized for substitutional), and denumerably infinite lists of n-place *predicate* and *function* letters P_i^n and f_i^n, for each $n \geqslant 0$.[11] If $n = 0$, f_i^n is a *constant* and P_i^n is a *sentence* letter. Further, the notations include), (, $\wedge$, $\sim$, and the existential quantifier (either $(\exists x_i)$ for each i or $(\Sigma \mathrm{x}_i)$ for each i). The formation rules are well known. A closed formula ϕ of the pure referential predicate calculus is *valid* iff it comes out true under any interpretation, no matter what non-empty domain D is taken to be the range of the variables, no matter what elements of D are assigned to the constants in ϕ, no matter what n-ary relations on D are assigned to the n-place predicate letters in ϕ, and no matter what n-ary functions, mapping D^n into D, are assigned to the n-ary function letters in ϕ. Similarly, a closed formula ϕ of the pure substitutional predicate calculus is valid iff it comes out true when we take any language L_0 and non-empty substitution class C, extend L_0 to L as above, and replace any constant in ϕ by a term in C, any n-ary function letter f_i^n by an n-ary functor of L_0, and any n-ary predicate letter $(n \geqslant 0)$ P_i^n by an n-ary form of L_0. (Instead of '(atomic) form of L_0' we could have said '(arbitrary) form of L' without changing the extension of the notion of validity.) In like manner, we can define the notion of a finite or denumerable list of formulae $\phi_1, \phi_2, \phi_3, \ldots$ having a formula ψ as a logical consequence in both cases.[12]

A formula of a particular substitutional language L is *valid* iff it comes by substitution of forms of L for predicate letters, functors for function letters, terms for constants, sentences of L for sentence letters, from a valid formula of the pure substitutional predicate calculus. Similarly for the referential case. Similarly for both the substitutional and the referential consequence relations.

The important fact is this: *one and the same formal system* can be used to prove all the valid formulae of both the pure referential and the pure substitutional predicate calculi. If a formula is valid in the

[11] We use the terms 'predicate letter', 'function letter', etc., even for substitutional languages, where predicates and functions are *not* involved. We hope this won't mislead.

[12] For the given notion of logical consequence, the difficulties raised by Dunn and Belnap don't arise. The usual predicate calculus is an adequate formalization of the consequence relation even with infinitely many premises. (See also footnote 10.)

one sense, it is valid in the other (ignoring our convention on italics, ∃, and Σ; or replacing the one notation by the other). A similar remark applies to the consequence relation. The phenomenon is a familiar one in mathematical logic: an uninterpreted formal system admits several different interpretations which validate all its theorems. The familiar first-order predicate calculus has not only the given interpretations but others; a certain 'Boolean-valued' interpretation is useful in independence proofs in set theory. In the present paper, unlike those of Wallace and Tharp, we have adopted notational conventions to make it clear at each point which quantifier—the referential or the substitutional—is in question. (When we deal with an *uninterpreted* formal system, or when the interpretation is unimportant, we use *referential* quantifier notation.)

2. A FORMAL TRUTH THEORY

2(*a*). *Requirements for a Theory*

If we wished to formalize the theorem of Section 1 directly, then to define the set S' and prove its existence and uniqueness we need set theory, at least a theory of sets of expressions of L. This is the approach favoured by Tarski (he deals, of course, with a *referential* language), who defines truth explicitly in a language of higher order, or alternatively, a set-theoretic language.

Donald Davidson, for various philosophical reasons, has tended to advocate a variant version of Tarski's approach which requires less ontology and less richness in the metalanguage.[13] The approach has become so popular that it has almost become confused in some writings with Tarski's original approach. Davidson proposes taking the truth predicate T(x) as primitive (*satisfaction* would be primitive if a referential language were the object language). Instead of defining truth explicitly, we characterize it by a *finite* set of axioms; they will state such recursive clauses as (4)–(6). The result could be a truth theory for the object language in one of two senses. (i) The axioms 'implicitly define' truth in the following sense. We assume that the referential variables of the metalanguage have 'intended' domains and the substitutional variables intended substitution classes. Further, we assume all the predicates, function symbols, and other vocabulary of the 'old' metalanguage (before the new primitive predicate T(x),

[13] The possibility of a formulation of Davidson's type was, however, well known to logicians. The philosophical emphasis on such a formulation is due to Davidson.

and such auxiliaries as satisfaction if present, are introduced) have fixed intended interpretations. Then the requirement is that all interpretations of the 'new' vocabulary (the 'old' being 'fixed') which make the axioms true make the extension of T(x) be the set of true formulae of L, and that there be at least one such interpretation. (ii) The following alternative criterion is preferred by Davidson, and is largely followed by Wallace and Tharp. (In Wallace (2), Wallace relaxes the finite axiomatizability requirement somewhat.) Here the criteria of success are twofold: (a) that the new axioms have a true interpretation, where the old vocabulary gets the intended interpretation and T(x) gets interpreted as satisfied by just the true closed sentences of the object language; (b) that for each closed sentence of the object language ϕ, $T(\bar{\phi}) \equiv \phi'$ be a logical consequence of the axioms, where ϕ' contains only 'old' vocabulary ('Convention T'). In the case where the metalanguage contains the object language, we may go so far as to require that ϕ' *be* ϕ (the 'homophonic' case); if, *antecedently* to the truth theory, we have a canonical translation of the metalanguage into the object language, we can demand that ϕ' be the canonical translation of ϕ into the metalanguage; but in the general case, we can say little more than the above and let the truth theory itself determine the translation of the object language into the metalanguage.[14]

The advantages of the approaches under (i) or (ii) are that usually an ontology in the metalanguage of *sets* of expressions is not required; usually a much weaker ontology suffices, since we don't demand an *explicit* definition of truth.

Now (ii) implies (i), since half of (iia) is explicitly the existence half of (i), and (iib) implies the uniqueness half (if we assume that one of the axioms asserts or implies that T(x) is true *only* of sentences of L). On the other hand, 'trick' axiom sets can be found where (i) holds but (ii) does not. Tharp essentially gives *one* such case (see Section 9), which, however, requires infinitely many axioms; finite examples can also be produced easily. (If (ii) were weakened so that (iia) did not

[14] Caveats: (a) The truth theory doesn't really determine a translation of the object language into the metalanguage, since in general for a given ϕ, there is more than one formula ϕ', satisfying all the given criteria, such that $T(\bar{\phi}) \equiv \phi'$ is provable. (b) Although Davidson imposes a finite axiomatizability requirement, all we need to ensure that the implicit definition can be turned into an explicit definition in a finite set-theoretic language is the weaker condition that only finitely many axioms contain the 'new' vocabulary being inductively defined. The requirement that there be only finitely many axioms containing no 'new' vocabulary is not needed. I return to both these points in Section 5 below.

incorporate half of (i) but were replaced, say, by the requirement that the axioms be consistent, (ii) wouldn't imply (i) either.) Now in the cases where (i) and (ii) diverge, is it obvious that we should prefer (ii) to (i)? Wallace and Tharp seem to assume so.

As we stated (i) and (ii) above, we presupposed that the notion of truth for L was somehow given in advance and could be used to state the adequacy conditions (i) and (ii). This of course is impossible if we are trying to *define* truth for L rather than presupposing the notion in advance. In the latter case, we revise condition (i) simply to state that the axioms are true with *some* interpretation of T(x) and the other 'new' predicates, the old vocabulary remaining fixed, and that all such interpretations give the same extension to T(x). In this case the axioms *implicitly* define *a set*, which we *take* to be the set of truths of L; and in a language with quantifiers over *sets* of expressions we can easily define the set of truths as the unique set satisfying the axioms. In condition (iia), we would simply require that there be *an interpretation* of the 'new' predicates, with the 'old' vocabulary retaining its intended interpretation, which makes all the axioms true. As far as T(x) is concerned, requirement (iib), plus the axiom $(x)(\mathrm{T}(x) \supset \mathrm{Sent}(x))$ guarantees that T(x) shall have a unique extension. It is, however, condition (i), not the stronger condition (ii), which is needed to convert the axiom set into a higher-order definition of a truth concept for L. In those rare trick cases where (i) and (ii) diverge, it seems to be dubious that the definition should be pronounced unsuccessful on those grounds. After all, it could then be converted to an explicit set-theoretic definition of truth in L, and this is the requirement assumed in standard mathematical logic. Since, however, Davidson may have given, from his own point of view, special arguments for (ii) rather than (i), and since we rarely need to make much capital out of the distinction, we shall not argue the issue at length.

Confusion over the issue of (i) versus (ii) in *Tarski*'s theory has arisen because of the tendency to identify Davidson's project and Tarski's. Tarski wished to give an explicit definition in a higher-order language. If condition (i) is satisfied we can easily get such an explicit definition of truth as the unique interpretation of T(x) satisfying the axioms. The existence and uniqueness of such a set can be either taken as an axiom or proved from more fundamental principles.

What about Tarski's Convention T? There is no problem in proving $\mathrm{T}(\bar{\phi}) \equiv \phi'$ where ϕ' contains only old vocabulary, since T(x) has been explicitly defined in terms of the old vocabulary. The only problem that

can arise is the case where the object language has a *prior* interpretation in the metalanguage. Say, for example, it is contained in the metalanguage. Then I cannot see why *Tarski* need prohibit, if the worst comes to the worst, taking $\phi \equiv \phi'$ as an axiom, and thus deducing $T(\bar{\phi}) \equiv \phi$ from $T(\bar{\phi}) \equiv \phi'$.[15] This would involve a separate new axiom for each ϕ, but, as far as I am aware, *Tarski* never requires that his results be provable in finitely axiomatised theories. In most of his work, Tarski is endeavouring to give an explicit definition of truth for a given object language in a metalanguage in which all formulae are of finite length. It is this project, not a finite axiomatizability requirement, that leads him to give recursive definitions of semantical notions. As far as I can see, there is no requirement that results about the explicitly defined semantical concepts (including the T-sentences) be proved in a finitely axiomatized theory.

Tarski states his main results in higher-order languages, which are conventionally axiomatized using schemata. In the one section of his paper (§5) where he seriously discusses taking truth as *primitive* in an axiomatic theory, he actually postulates each sentence $T(\bar{\phi}) \equiv \phi$, precisely the *bête noire* of the Davidsonian approach!

None of this is to argue that the additional special requirements of the Davidsonian programme may not have philosophical justification—this is an issue I can't completely discuss. However, given the almost mystical reverence with which Tarski and Convention T are invoked in Wallace's papers,[16] and the sense of awe they are intended to create in the reader, it is important to emphasize that there are important differences between the programme of Davidson, Wallace, *et al.*, and Tarski's original ideas. Working logicians, when they do semantical or model-theoretic work, are closer to Tarski's original paper than to Davidson; but there are some differences of emphasis with Tarski's original paper also, which, for example, is more heavily involved with the theory of types than logicians are today.

2(*b*). *The Theory*

We saw above essentially that condition (i) (in the weak form where we had no prior concept of truth) was fulfilled by (4)–(6) (suitably formalized, and with 'true in L_0' in the 'old' vocabulary). Is condition (ii) also fulfilled? It is the purpose of this section to sketch the verification that, of course, it is. That is, we wish to show that the Davidsonian condition (ii) for a truth theory is satisfied.

[15] Of course in many typical cases we will actually deduce $\phi \equiv \phi'$ from more fundamental principles.

[16] See for example the panegyrics in Wallace (2): 'It may strike the reader that Convention T is an astonishingly powerful intellectual device . . .' (etc.) (p. 202). Wallace's expressed admiration for the achievements of modern logic is of course sincere, and I share it (not always for his reasons). But these achievements should not be used to terrorize the reader, in the manner of the legendary Eulerian use of algebra (see Section 11(*b*)). I fear that this may be an unintended effect of Wallace's style of exposition.

We need a metalanguage M for L. M is to contain *referential* quantifiers ranging over arbitrary (well- or ill-formed) strings of indecomposable (atomic) symbols of L; such an ontology of expressions is part and parcel of the project of defining the class of 'true' expressions of L, and (6) straightforwardly gives the truth conditions of $(\Sigma x_i)\phi$ in terms of the existence of a certain term. The ontology used to give the semantics of a substitutional object language is not the null ontology, but, at least, an ontology of expressions. A larger ontology may be required if it is needed to give a truth definition (or here, truth theory) for L_0; see below.

In their clear and very helpful exposition of substitutional quantification Dunn and Belnap argue that not even an ontology of expressions is required since, they say, the quantifiers in the metalanguage may be construed as substitutional also. (See Dunn and Belnap, p. 184 point 4.) Such an argument seems to me to be a typical example of the unfortunately mechanical way in which Quine's criteria of ontological commitment are often applied: referential quantifiers carry an ontological commitment while nothing else ever does. There are two possibilities for the interpretation of the supposed substitutional metalanguage. Presumably the substitutional quantifiers of the metalanguage are supposed to have (structural descriptive) names of the expressions of the object language as substitutes. Then either the interpretation of the metalanguage is such that these terms are thought of as denoting expressions of the object language or it is not. In the former case, as Wallace correctly argues, and the present paper explains in Section 3, the difference between substitutional quantifiers with names of expressions as substitutes and referential quantifiers ranging over expressions is negligible, and the first type of quantifier carries as much 'ontological commitment' to expressions as does the second. In the latter case (if another interpretation is indeed possible), then the metalanguage may in fact carry no ontological commitment to expressions of the object language. In this case, however, what justifies us in calling the language M a *metalanguage* for the object language, L, at all? If nothing in M purports in any way to refer to, or quantify over, expressions of L, how can a formal theory phrased in M possibly say anything whatever about the semantics of L? If the ontology of M is really supposed to be the null ontology, the formula $T(x)$ can no longer be interpreted as a *predicate* satisfied by exactly the true sentences of L, but it is rather a *form* of M with no interpretation whatsoever. How then can the theory phrased in M be said to be the theory of *truth* for the language L?

The view that the metalanguage for a substitutional object language could be devoid of ontological commitment, which probably is by no means peculiar to Dunn and Belnap, is typical of the way philosophical conclusions are often drawn by a mechanical application of technical criteria, while basic conceptual distinctions and the purposes of these criteria are lost sight of. Those who argue in this way should be compared

to the proverbial fanatics who redouble their (technical) efforts when they have forgotten their (philosophical) aims.

In the preceding discussion I have been following one aspect of the terminology of Dunn and Belnap which in fact I find objectionable. Dunn and Belnap write as if a metalanguage, *M*, giving the semantics of an object language, *L*, were simply an uninterpreted formal language, whose formation, and perhaps transformation, rules are given to us but whose interpretation is left open. In this terminology, a truth theory seems to be an uninterpreted formal system which is supposed to have some relation or other (what relation?) to the object language. On the contrary, if we are giving either a truth definition or an axiomatic recursive truth characterization for an object language, *L*, to say that we have thus given the semantics of *L* we must give it in an interpreted language we already understand. (This is a special case of the 'great fundamental principle' that definitions must be stated in language which is already understood.) On this use of the term 'metalanguage', then, there is little room for saying that the metalanguage *could* be interpreted this way and *could* be interpreted that way. The metalanguage is already interpreted, though theorists may give different theories of its syntactic and semantic structure. Note that in this sense, since a homophonic truth theory for an object language is couched in a metalanguage which contains it, such a theory can be said to give us the semantics only of languages which we antecedently understand.

The discussions by Wallace and Tharp, and perhaps some of the rest of the Davidsonian literature, seem to me to exhibit an unfortunate tendency to treat the issue of a truth theory for a disputed form of language as a purely formal project in which the metalanguage can be as uninterpreted as the object language. Such a standpoint is almost inevitable when one is concerned with homophonic truth theories for languages whose intelligibility is under dispute. It should be emphasized that such uninterpreted homophonic truth theories are completely irrelevant to questions of intelligibility since the metalanguage is not antecedently understood (and thus is not even a metalanguage in the sense of the preceding paragraph). To demonstrate that an object language is intelligible we can give its semantics in a language which we antecedently understand (English is a good candidate) and homophony is irrelevant. The lack of a sharp formulation of the notion of a metalanguage in many discussions blurs our comprehension of whether these discussions are directed to questions of intelligibility or to some other question. For further discussion of the possible role of homophonic truth theories see the beginning of Section 5.

We use Greek letters α, β, . . ., as variables ranging over arbitrary strings of individual symbols of *L*. (We assume that the expressions of *L* are all concatenates of a finite number of individual symbols; the variable x_i can be identified with letter 'x' followed by *i* strokes.) We assume that *M* contains, for each individual (atomic, indecomposable) symbol *e* of L_0, a constant $\bar{e}$ denoting *e*; also *L* contains one binary function letter '$\frown$' for concatenation and one dyadic

predicate letter '=' for identity. It is well known that these resources suffice for a theory of the elementary syntax of *L*, and that each expression of *L* is denoted by a structural descriptive name for it, built up from the names of the individual symbols using concatenation. We assume that axioms for elementary syntax are given. To develop a truth theory for *L* in *M*, we then formalize (4)–(6), in obvious notation, as

$$(7)\ (\alpha)\,(T\overline{(\sim\alpha)} \equiv \sim T(\alpha))$$
$$(8)\ (\alpha)(\beta)(T\overline{(\alpha\wedge\beta)} \equiv (T(\alpha) \wedge T(\beta)))$$
$$(9)\ (\alpha)(\beta)(\text{Formula}\ (\alpha) \wedge \text{Variable}\ (\beta) \supset$$
$$(T(\overline{(\Sigma\beta)\alpha}) \equiv (\exists\gamma)(\exists\alpha')(T(\alpha') \wedge \text{Term}\ (\gamma) \wedge \text{Subst}\ (\alpha', \alpha, \gamma, \beta))))$$

Here we use the horizontal bar similarly to Quine's corners; '$\overline{(\sim\alpha)}$' denotes the negation of α and is defined as '$\bar{(} \frown \bar{\sim} \frown \alpha \frown \bar{)}$', where '$\bar{(}$', '$\bar{\sim}$', and '$\bar{)}$' are the primitive constants of *M* denoting left parentheses, negation, and right parentheses, respectively. The interpretation of (7)–(9) should be obvious from the fact that they formalize (4)–(6).

Now in addition to (7)–(9) we obviously need a basis clause for atomic sentences, i.e., for sentences of L_0:

$$(10)\ (\alpha)(\text{AtSent}\ (\alpha) \supset (T(\alpha) \equiv R(\alpha))).$$

Here $R(\alpha)$ formalizes the truth conditions for L_0, which we assumed were already given.

Does the metatheory involve an ontology of expressions alone? As stated, it does, since $R(\alpha)$ was taken as primitive. If arbitrary predicates of strings (or, if Gödel numbering had been used, arbitrary number-theoretic predicates) are allowed there can be nothing wrong with this; ontology can be saved with a sufficient ideology. Suppose, however, we wish not to take $R(\alpha)$ as primitive but to define it in terms of more basic primitives. After all, $R(\alpha)$ is itself a truth predicate for a primitive language L_0, and for each particular language L_0 we may wish this predicate to be explained. The definition of $R(\alpha)$ in more basic terms depends heavily on the choice of L_0; we can in general say nothing specific about $R(\alpha)$ other than what has been said above. Whether the definition of $R(\alpha)$ requires us to extend the ontology of the metalanguage beyond an ontology of expressions alone depends both on the choice of L_0 and on the question of what predicates of expressions (or, alternatively, via Gödel numbering, of

numbers) we are willing to take as primitive. In *the most favoured case* we can drop R(α) and define the class of true atomic strings without introducing any new vocabulary or ontology not already in the metalanguage; in this case, no one could conceivably quarrel with the claim that our axiomatic theory involves an ontology of expressions alone. Otherwise, we can add either new predicates true of strings, or new ontology, or both, to the metalanguage *M*. *If* we extend the ontology of the metalanguage, and add a new binary predicate of denotation to the metalanguage, relating the terms to some of the new entities, and postulate that every term denotes one of the new entities, *and* certain additional conditions to be detailed in the first half of Section 3 are satisfied, then we can say, as we will in Section 3, that the substitutional quantifiers of *L* are in a sense equivalent to referential quantifiers. Otherwise, the new ontology may have nothing to do with the terms or alleged denotata for them. For example, if we introduce quantifiers over *sets* of strings of symbols of *L* into *M* we can define many sets of strings which were not definable before; and perhaps the set of true sentences of L_0 will be among them. This does not mean that the new ontology of sets of expressions of L_0 has anything to do with alleged or real 'denotations' of the terms. All in all, no general thesis that *M* does or does not use an ontology of expressions alone, or that a denotation relation is or is not introduced, seems justified. The answer depends on both L_0 and the stock of primitive predicates of strings.[17] Only if

[17] In Davidson (1), p. 79, when Davidson states that substitutional languages 'do not in general yield the T-sentences demanded by Convention T', he acknowledges that 'there are exceptions in the case of object languages whose true atomic sentences can be effectively given'. Wallace, in footnote 25 to Wallace (1), acknowledges that there are exceptions to his general thesis 'when truth in the object language is decidable'. (He lists other exceptions, but they are almost always subsumable under this one.) Davidson's condition is weaker than Wallace's, since he requires only that atomic truth, not truth in general, be effectively characterizable. Number theory is a case where truth is decidable for atomic sentences but not for sentences in general; Wallace specifically rejects it as a candidate for substitutional quantification (see Sections 8 and 9).

I am not sure what Davidson has in mind that motivates him to make his specific exception. The non-homophonic truth theory of this section and the homophonic truth theories of Section 5 are all completely general and involve no effectiveness restrictions. Suppose, however, we place the tightest possible restriction upon the resources of the metalanguage: it is to contain quantification only over strings of symbols of the object language—with no other substitutional or referential quantifiers—and an ideology of concatenation and identity alone, plus the predicate T(α). This, then, is what we called 'the most favoured case' in the text. Such restrictions are unmotivated and unnecessarily severe, but *perhaps* Davidson has something like this in mind. If such a restriction is imposed, then we can characterize substitutional truth only for those substitutional languages whose true atomic sentences can be specified using concatenation, identity and quantification over expressions alone; to say this

R(α) itself is taken as primitive can we get a quick and automatic answer.

Let me give an example of what I just called the 'most favoured case'. The terms of L_o are arbitrary strings of the letters '*a*' and '*b*'. A formula of L_o is anything of the form $M(t_1, t_2)$, where t_1 and t_2 are two terms. Such a formula counts as true whenever the first string is the mirror image of the second; for example, *M*(*abb*, *bba*) is true while *M*(*abb*, *bab*) is false. This truth characterization for L_o is indeed syntactic, and the truth characterization can then be extended to the larger language *L* by means of (7)–(9) (or (4)–(6)). Note that no question arises of any 'denotations' for the 'terms'—the terms are merely uninterpreted strings of the letters '*a*' and '*b*'. Nor do the substitutional variables have any 'range'.

Do truth theories of the kind given in this section satisfy 'Convention T' ((iib) above)? Since the metalanguage here does not contain the object language, what is required is that for each ϕ of *L* (the object language), there should be a statement ϕ' of *M* (the metalanguage) which does not contain the predicate 'T', and such that $T(\overline{\phi}) \equiv \phi'$ should be provable. ϕ', then, can be regarded as the 'translation' of ϕ into M, giving its truth conditions. It is easy to see that, for each ϕ of L_o, such a ϕ' is forthcoming. To take a simple example, if ϕ_o is atomic, the theory proves:

$$\text{(11)}\quad T(\overline{(\Pi x_1)(\Sigma x_2)\phi_o}) \equiv (\alpha)(\text{Term}\,(\alpha) \supset (\exists\beta)(\text{Term}\,(\beta) \wedge (\exists\gamma)(\text{Subst}\,(\gamma, \overline{\phi_o}, \alpha, \beta, \overline{x_1}, \overline{x_2}) \wedge R(\gamma)))).$$

Here Subst $(\gamma, \overline{\phi_o}, \alpha, \beta, \overline{x_1}, \overline{x_2})$ says that γ comes from $\overline{\phi_o}$ by substituting terms α and β, respectively, for the variables x_1 and x_2. The reader is invited to work out these and other examples for himself. He is also invited to verify, in the case of the mirror-image language and any other case where R(α) is defined purely in terms of elementary syntax, that the ϕ' of *M* giving the truth conditions for a ϕ of *L* is always a statement about the elementary syntax of *L*.

---

is essentially just to repeat the restriction. This restriction is *not* equivalent to effectiveness of the set of true atomic sentences, as follows from the well-known results of Gödel, Post, Church, Turing, *et al.* I can't imagine any more severe restriction upon the metalanguage since here I have given it the minimal ontology and vocabulary necessary to treat the syntax of the object language. The fact that the mirror-image language given as an example in the text below does have a recursively specifiable set of true atomic sentences should not mislead here. Effectiveness of a class of sentences implies their definability in a restricted metalanguage of the type mentioned here, but not conversely.

Now Wallace (1) states substantially the conditions (7)–(9) and claims that he has demonstrated their inadequacy. Where does his error lie? It is hard to say from an examination of his text. He never even mentions the idea, which should have been obvious, of a general basis clause (10), even though in Wallace (2) he clearly and explicitly recognizes that a substitutional truth theory must start from such a truth characterization for the atomic sentences. Instead, in Wallace (1), he assumes that (10) is to be replaced by infinitely many instances, giving the truth conditions for each atomic formula separately. We shall discuss such theories below in connection with Tharp's paper; in the present context it suffices to observe, as Wallace recognizes in Wallace (2), that a truth theory for L should start out from some general characterization of the truth conditions for atomic sentences, as in (10). This recognition would have been easier if, following *Tarski* rather than Davidson, we were searching for an *explicit definition* of truth; truth can hardly be said to be definable for L if it is not defined already for L_0.

Another possible source of error may lie in a search for a *homophonic* truth theory, that is, one which yields consequences of the form $T(\bar{\phi}) \equiv \phi$. (7)–(10) can hardly do this, since ϕ is not in the metalanguage M! All we can possibly demand *here* is that to each ϕ of L a ϕ' of M is associated, where ϕ' does not contain the predicate $T(x)$ and $T(\bar{\phi}) \equiv \phi'$ is provable. ϕ' then gives the truth conditions of ϕ and can be regarded as the 'translation' of ϕ into M. Such a truth theory is often much more useful than any homophonic truth theory. A homophonic truth theory is useful only to someone who already understands L. The non-homophonic theory given in this section corresponds to the intuitive way the substitutional quantifier, and its truth conditions, would be explained to someone who did not have this notion already, but did understand truth in L_0, plus the notions of elementary syntax, including concatenation and (referential) quantification over expressions. He can then give the truth conditions for each sentence of the ill-understood object language in language he *does* understand. In just the same way, a homophonic truth theory for German would be intelligible only to someone who already understood German; a Frenchman ignorant of German would be more interested in a truth theory for German in French as a metalanguage, in which the truth conditions for each German sentence are given in French. We shall discuss the question of a homophonic truth theory for the substitutional quantifier below.

Finally Wallace proposes to illuminate the error in regarding (4)–(6) as adequate recursive conditions by criticizing Peter Geach, who claims that (6) does indeed specify truth conditions for an interpretation of the existential quantifier: 'The difference between what Geach requires of truth conditions and what is required by Tarski's Convention is easy to state: by Geach's lights, an ordinary sentence involving no semantical terms may have its truth conditions given by a sentence that contains semantical terms, indeed, the concept of truth itself; by Tarski's lights, not. The Tarski demand is that a theory of truth explain partial definitions on the right sides of which no semantical terms appear' (Wallace (1), pp. 233–4).

Wallace seems here to be mistaken. If, by asserting that the concept of truth itself appears in the truth conditions, he means that the ϕ' such that $T(\bar{\phi}) \equiv \phi'$ is provable contains the T-predicate itself, he is wrong. We saw that ϕ' contains no such thing. Perhaps he means to refer to $R(\alpha)$ (truth for atomic sentences, or for L_0). There is no need to assume, however, that $R(\alpha)$ *must* be taken as primitive, or that, if it is defined, its (explicit) definition *must* involve 'semantical terms'. Why should it, in general? We discussed above the possibilities of defining $R(\alpha)$; in some cases *no* new vocabulary was needed. But, *in general, if Wallace's demands can be satisfied for* L_0, there is a finitely axiomatized theory of truth for L_0 which satisfies condition (ii) above, and, in particular, yields for every ϕ of L_0 a ϕ' containing no semantical terms such that $R(\bar{\phi}) \equiv \phi'$ is provable. But this means (*via* the fact above that (ii) implies (i)) that $R(\alpha)$ is implicitly definable in terms of non-semantical vocabulary. We can then, using quantifiers over *sets* of expressions,[18] convert the implicit definition into an explicit one, still without using semantical terms, in the manner of Tarski (see Section 1 and the beginning of the present section). So it seems that *either* Wallace's conditions are *already unsatisfiable for* L_0, *or* they can be satisfied for L, provided quantifiers over sets of expressions are allowed. In the former case, the blame should not attach to the innocent (6), any more than to (4) and (5), but to (10). (Actually, since L_0 can have minimal structure, in practice a truth definition for L_0 almost always comes much more easily and with less apparatus than *via* the Tarski procedure above, even in the case where L_0 contains opaque constructions, the case which motivates

[18] If the axioms involve an auxiliary notion of satisfaction, then we need, strictly speaking, quantifiers over sets of ordered pairs of infinite sequences and expressions. We ignore this in the text. The point is that quantifiers over sets of an appropriate kind are involved.

Geach. In particular, if we use the general Tarskian procedure sketched above, the theory will yield sentences $T(\bar{\phi}) \equiv \phi'$, where ϕ' may contain quantifiers over sets of expressions; in practice, by additional devices, such higher-order quantification can almost invariably be eliminated for the truth conditions of particular sentences of L if it could be eliminated for particular sentences of L_0. We give an example early in the next section.)

Although Wallace's claim against Geach appears to be mistaken, it is instructive to examine the force of the claim had he been correct. Does he propose a reasonable requirement?

Although Wallace refers to his condition as 'the Tarski demand', I know of no place where it is stated in any of Tarski's writings; and for reasons to be given immediately, I doubt that he could have stated any such thing. Davidson, in Davidson (4), p. 19, regards the condition as a partial replacement for the genuinely Tarskian demand that the sentence in the metalanguage which gives the truth conditions of a sentence in the object language be a 'translation' of the object-language sentence; or, in his phrase, that it 'draw upon the same concepts' as the sentence whose truth conditions it states. As a special case, then, if $T(\bar{\phi}) \equiv \phi'$ is to be provable in the metalanguage, ϕ' should not contain semantical terms unless ϕ does; otherwise it wouldn't match ϕ in content. He attributes the condition to Wallace, not Tarski.

So stated, the demand is alien to Tarski's project, where truth and all other semantical terms were supposed to be explicitly defined in terms of non-semantical vocabulary. (This is what all the shouting originally was about!) Tarski's metalanguages contain no semantical terms. Of course this fact means that Wallace's condition is trivially fulfilled, but it is fulfilled vacuously and is useless as a restriction which is intended to formalize the demand that ϕ' 'draw upon the same concepts' as ϕ. All in all, it would have been less misleading if Wallace had called the demand 'the Wallace demand'.

Presumably Wallace and Davidson intend the restriction to be applied to theories formulated in the Davidsonian style, where some semantical terms are to be taken as primitive. In the homophonic case, where the theory proves $T(\bar{\phi}) \equiv \phi$, the demand once again is fulfilled but is of course unnecessary as an additional stipulation. So presumably the demand was put forth for non-homophonic theories, which prove $T(\bar{\phi}) \equiv \phi'$. Here the demand should not be confused with the requirement placed under (ii) above in Section 2(*a*) that ϕ' contain only 'old' vocabulary. This means that the semantical concepts which are being recursively characterized by the axioms must not occur in ϕ'—a condition which is necessary in order to prove that the axioms do indeed implicitly define these concepts, given the old vocabulary—but there is no requirement that the 'old' vocabulary should not include 'semantical' terms which are not being recursively characterized, whether or not they occur in ϕ.

How reasonable, then, is Wallace's demand for non-homophonic Davidsonian truth theories? At first blush it seems eminently plausible. If ϕ' is a 'translation' of ϕ, how can ϕ' contain 'semantical' vocabulary if ϕ does not? (Indeed, how can ϕ' contain 'geographical' vocabulary if ϕ does not?) But consider a Davidson-style theory of truth for a language with *demonstratives*. Can it yield anything better than ' "This is bigger than that" is true in the mouth of a speaker *s* at a time *t* iff *the thing he refers to by* "this" *at t* is bigger than the thing *he refers to by* "that" *at t*'? (See Weinstein.) Can a Davidsonian theory of *ambiguity* produce anything better than ' "John went to a bank" is true in the mouth of *s* at time *t* iff either the word "bank" *meant* (or, *had as its extension*) (in *s*'s mouth, at *t*) the monetary depositories and John went to a monetary depository (before *t*), or it *meant* the sides of rivers and John went to a side of a river'?[19] Even if these results *can* somehow be improved, do we really know in *advance* that Wallace's condition *must* be met? (I don't see why we should even *expect* this, unless indeed we expect fulfilment of the stronger condition that *all* semantical vocabulary must be explicitly definable in other terms, in which case the condition once again is trivialized.) It is one thing for Wallace or anyone else to choose to work within a given set of technical requirements and see if they can be fulfilled. It is another thing to use them as a stick to beat opponents without giving them a rigorous justification.

A technical requirement should be imposed only with caution. It is *not* sufficient that a requirement (a) be impressively technical in formulation, (b) have a vague initial ring of plausibility to it, and (c) rule out approaches you happen to dislike.

Finally, suppose we had accepted Wallace's condition, and that either his technical claim against Geach was correct, or better, we for some reason preferred to take $R(\alpha)$ as primitive. How much force would the condition have in this context? If we already knew that quantification was not 'semantical', the result would be damning. But perhaps all the result would show is that substitutional quantification, unlike referential, is a 'semantical' notion. Dunn and Belnap report (p. 184, point 5) that, independently of Wallace, many have regarded substitutional quantification as metalinguistic. Perhaps the results would show that these people were right. Wallace's condition can have any force only for a previously understood vocabulary which we are certain has no semantical terms.

3. SOME RELATIONS BETWEEN THE SUBSTITUTIONAL AND THE REFERENTIAL QUANTIFIERS

Let us consider one case where $R(\alpha)$ (in (10)) is indeed defined in a way which requires an extra ontology, and a denotation relation

[19] In Davidson (4), Davidson treats the ambiguity case by such a phrase as 'condition *C* is fulfilled' in place of my explicitly semantical condition about the meaning of the particular token of the word 'bank'. I can't really see what condition *C* is supposed to be but such a semantical condition (or a projected but of course far from available analysis thereof). Like remarks apply to his use of the term 'demonstration' in many papers.

between terms and objects. Suppose that a denotation function is given, assigning, to each term t, a 'denotation' $\delta(t)$. Let D be the set of all denotations of terms. Then if referential quantification over D, and a denotation function or relation, are used to define $R(\alpha)$ and thus to state (10), we can no longer claim that the metalanguage involves an ontology of expressions alone. In this case, let us explore the relation between the substitutional quantifiers and standard quantifiers ranging over D.

Let $\phi(x_1, \ldots, x_n)$ be a formula with the free variables listed. Normally, a formula with free substitutional variables is assigned no interpretation. If denotations are present, however, we might take $\phi(x_1, \ldots, x_n)$ to be *satisfied* by an n-tuple $\langle a_1, \ldots, a_n \rangle$ if and only if $\phi(t_1, \ldots, t_n)$ is true, where $\delta(t_i) = a_i$. Unfortunately, such a definition can be carried out only in the special case where each formula is (referentially) *transparent*: where replacement of one term by a codesignative term leaves truth values unchanged. If opacity (non-transparency) intervenes, then the truth conditions depend not only on $a_1, \ldots, a_n$, but also on the choice of the terms $t_1, \ldots, t_n$ to designate them. Now it can be shown by induction that, provided each sentence of L_0 is transparent, so is each sentence of L. The induction, however, depends on the fact that the only constructions available in L are the truth-functions and the substitutional quantifier; it would fail if intensional operators such as necessity or the propositional attitudes were added.

In L as it stands, however, opacity can arise only as the product of opacity in L_0. Let me give an example of the latter. Suppose the denotations of the terms in L_0 are people, and L_0 consists of formulae of the form $P(t)$, where '$P(t)$' can be read 't was so-called because of t's size', where 't' in both cases should be replaced by a specific term. Then a statement of the form '$P(t)$', where t is a term, can be defined to be true iff $\delta(t)$ was called by the term t because of the size of $\delta(t)$. Here quantification over people and the denotation relation enter essentially into the specification of the truth conditions for L_0, yet the atomic formulae of L_0 are opaque. As Quine has emphasized, 'P(Giorgione)' will be true and 'P(Barbarelli)' false, even though Giorgione = Barbarelli.[20]

[20] Philosophically, of course, greater interest has attached to opacity as a result of intensional operators such as 'necessarily', 'Jones believes that', etc. I don't primarily deal with such examples, because a rigorous treatment would demand a treatment of the semantics of such operators. It is much simpler, and sufficient for many expository purposes regarding substitutional quantification and opacity, to consider the case

Suppose that (a) a totally defined denotation function is given for all the terms of L and (b) all formulae in L are transparent. Let D once again be the set of denotations of the terms. Then, for each atomic formula $\phi(\mathrm{x}_1, \ldots, \mathrm{x}_n)$, we can define the *induced relation* corresponding to the formula to be the relation which holds between $a_1, \ldots, a_n \in D$ if $\phi(t_1, \ldots, t_n)$ is true, where $\delta(t_i) = a_i$. We can say further that a sequence $s = \{s_i\}$ of elements of D satisfies a formula if the formula becomes true when each free occurrence of a variable x_i is replaced by a term t_i denoting s_i. Then the following result holds: *satisfaction, under the definition just given, of a formula of L satisfies all the inductive conditions stated in Section 1 for satisfaction by a referential quantifier ranging over D.* So, in the special case where (a) and (b) are postulated in the metatheory, there is indeed little difference between a substitutional quantifier and a referential quantifier ranging over the set of denotata.[21]

If (a) holds but (b) does not, such a conclusion fails. Indeed, if L contains opaque constructions and also contains identity,[22] a formula of the form

$$(12)\quad (\Sigma \mathrm{x}_1)(\Sigma \mathrm{x}_2)\,(\mathrm{x}_1 = \mathrm{x}_2 \wedge \phi(\mathrm{x}_1) \wedge \sim \phi(\mathrm{x}_2))$$

will be true, since there will be terms t_1, t_2 and a formula $\phi(\mathrm{x})$ such that $t_1 = t_2$, $\phi(t_1)$, and $\sim\phi(t_2)$ will all be true. No formula of the form (13) can be true:

$$(13)\quad (\exists x_1)(\exists x_2)(x_1 = x_2 \wedge \phi(x_1) \wedge \sim \phi(x_2)).$$

where opacity comes in in the atomic formulae and all operators are extensional. I do touch on such intensional operators in Section 6, but a systematic treatment of their mesh with substitutional quantification is beyond the scope of this paper.

[21] There are cases where the theorem just stated is formally correct but may lead to a somewhat 'unhappy' interpretation of L. We can't elaborate, but such a case may arise where L contains intensional operators but no opacities for the trivial reason that no two terms are codesignative. We ignore such issues in the text.

[22] We must be careful about 'identity' in a substitutional language. In languages where assumption (a) above holds, it is strictly speaking a *form*, $\mathrm{x}_1 = \mathrm{x}_2$, which, for any two terms, t_1, t_2, yields a truth $t_1 = t_2$ iff $\delta(t_1) = \delta(t_2)$; the term 'identity' somewhat misleadingly suggests a *predicate*. In the absence of (a), there is no obvious general way to interpret '='; how, for example, should it be introduced into a language with a substitution class consisting of sentences of L_0? Above, we interpreted the formal system of the pure predicate calculus, not the predicate calculus with identity, for arbitrary substitutional languages.

Wallace (1), following other authors, gives a purported *definition* of identity. It is well known that for referential languages the success of the definition depends upon an identification of indiscernibles. For substitutional languages, though the definition yields the usual *formal* properties of identity, it gives intuitively incorrect results except if (a) and (b) are both satisfied. For example, if (a) holds but (b) does not, formula (12) shows that the definition fails.

For (13) to be true $x_1 = x_2 \wedge \phi(x_1) \wedge \sim \phi(x_2)$ would have to be satisfiable. But any sequence satisfying $x_1 = x_2$ must assign the same value to x_1 and x_2; hence it must assign the same truth value to $\phi(x_1)$ and to $\phi(x_2)$. The differences between the substitutional and the standard quantifier here are dramatic. And notice that the truth characterization for L goes through smoothly even if L_0 contains opaque formulae.

Even if L does contain opaque formulae, a particular formula $\phi(x_1, \ldots, x_n)$ of L may be transparent; and we can define the n-place relation it induces on D in the obvious way.

It would be useful for the reader to carry out a truth theory in the style of Section 2(*b*) for a particular object language containing opaque contexts. Suppose the object language, L, contains just two forms: $P(x)$ is the pseudo-predicate 'is so called because of its size' and $Q(x)$ is some ordinary predicate, say 'is fat'. Suppose the terms are built out of two atomic terms a and b using a single binary functor, f, so that the terms are $a, b, f(a, a)$, $f(b, b), f(a, b), f(f(a,a),a)$, etc. Since the terms are to be thought of as denoting, the metalanguage must contain referential quantifiers ranging over the denotata of the terms, and a function symbol for the function denoted by f (say use f itself). Also, let a and b be used in the metalanguage as names for the denotata of a and b in the object language. We also need—as a first approximation—a denotation function, δ. Axioms will state $\delta(\bar{a}) = a$, $\delta(\bar{b}) = b$ and

$$(\alpha)(\beta)(x)(y)((\delta(\alpha) = x \wedge \delta(\beta) = y) \supset \delta(\overline{f(\alpha, \beta)}) = f(x, y)).$$

Now $R(\alpha)$ can be explicitly defined if appropriate predicates are available in the metalanguage. Namely, we define $R(\alpha)$ to hold if and only if either α is a formula of the form $P(t)$ where t is a term and $\delta(t)$ is called by the term t because of the size of $\delta(t)$, or α is of the form $Q(t)$ and $\delta(t)$ is fat. Note that now $R(\alpha)$ has been eliminated as primitive notation and that the metalanguage contains only referential quantifiers and no opacities, but the metalanguage had to be expanded to include referential variables ranging over the denotata of the terms rather than just variables ranging over expressions alone. All this illustrates some of the themes of the preceding paragraph. It is a simple example of how substitutional quantification can be used to 'quantify into' opaque contexts in a straightforward way.

So far, the theory with $R(\alpha)$ eliminated has required the use of a primitive denotation function, in possible violation of the restrictions imposed by Wallace on the use of primitive semantical terms. (Actually, Wallace would probably regard such a pseudo-predicate as 'is so called because of his size' as semantical, so that the left-hand sides of T-sentences mentioning sentences containing it already mention sentences containing semantical vocabulary and thus there is no objection to the right-hand sides containing semantical vocabulary also, even if we accept Wallace's requirement.)

It is instructive to see how such a semantical term can be eliminated. The full machinery of Tarski's explicit definitions of truth, with their quantification over arbitrary sets of expressions, is not required in this case. Let the metalanguage contain variables ranging over arbitrary finite sequences of objects previously admitted into its ontology. Then we can say that a term t denotes an object x if and only if there is a finite sequence, σ, of pairs $\langle\langle t_1, x_1\rangle \ldots \langle t_n, x_n\rangle\rangle$ where each pair of the sequence is either one of the pairs $\langle \bar{a}, a\rangle$ or $\langle \bar{b}, b\rangle$, or is of the form $\langle \overline{f(t_i, t_j)}, f(x_i, x_j)\rangle$ where the pairs $\langle t_i, x_i\rangle, \langle t_j, x_j\rangle$ occur previously in the sequence, and where the pair $\langle t, x\rangle$ is one of the pairs in σ. So given quantification over finite sequences we can define the denotation relation explicitly and can eliminate all semantical vocabulary from the definition of R(α). Very simple definitions of R(α) of this kind are usually possible when L is a language of very simple structure, as is often the case in applications. It would be a very instructive cxercise for the reader to verify his understanding of the key concepts by earrying out the construction just sketched in detail.

One special case where every term denotes is the *autonymous interpretation*: let every term of L be interpreted as denoting itself. Opacity is then ruled out vacuously, since no two terms are codesignative. The substitutional quantifiers can then be interpreted as quantifiers ranging over (autonymous) expressions. This interpretation can be used to illuminate the close *formal* correspondence between the Π and Σ quantifiers, and the ( ) and $\exists$ quantifiers. I assume, however, that this trivial interpretation is *not* all that Wallace is claiming when he argues that satisfaction invariably lurks in the background of the substitutional quantifier. Indeed, even without the autonymous interpretation, it is clear that every substitutional formula is equivalent to one involving referential quantifiers over expressions; this fact was emphasized in Section 2. The utility of the substitutional quantifier lies in the fact that while the referential quantifiers over terms take *names* of terms as substitutes, the substitutional quantifiers take the terms themselves, which can be denotationless or can denote other things.

Now let us consider the converse problem regarding the referential quantifier. When can a substitutional language be found which is equivalent? If there are terms t in a language built up with referential quantifiers, then sometimes the truth conditions for the referential quantifier will satisfy the analogue of (6): whenever $(\exists x_i)\phi$ is true, where ϕ contains only x_i free, some substitution instance ϕ' of ϕ is true. This condition is necessary and sufficient for it to be the case that every statement of the referential language will retain its truth

value when the referential quantifiers are replaced by substitutional quantifiers with the terms t as the substitution class. (Even if (6) is satisfied, however, we *cannot* draw this conclusion if the terms include arbitrary definite descriptions and thus are not a legitimate substitution class in the sense of Section 1.) An obvious set of jointly *sufficient* (but not necessary) conditions for such a situation to obtain is that every element of the range D of the variables be *nameable*—be denoted by some term. (This statement applies to referential languages in the sense of Section 1; it would not apply if the language were extended to allow various intensional constructions such as a belief operator.) The conditions are *not* necessary. This situation hardly represents the general case; Quine has rightly emphasized that referential quantification theory can be done without using terms at all. And even in this special case, a replacement of referential quantifiers by substitutional quantifiers with the old terms of the referential language as the substitution class cannot be said to eliminate the range D from the semantics of the language, if the atomic formulae are interpreted using a denotation relation for the terms.

One case where every element of D is nameable is the referential metalanguage M used in Section 2: each expression is denoted by its structural descriptive name. Because of this, the referential quantifiers used in M could have been replaced by substitutional quantifiers, provided the structural descriptive names are still interpreted as denoting expressions. The set of all expressions satisfying the formula $\mathrm{T}(\alpha)$ can then be defined—opacity does not arise in M even if it is present in L—and will coincide with the set of true sentences of L.

4. MIXTURES OF THE SUBSTITUTIONAL AND REFERENTIAL QUANTIFIERS

In this section we sketch how a language L' can contain both a substitutional quantifier and a referential one. Two-sorted languages with two standard quantifiers, ranging over different domains, are familiar. The semantics of a language with two substitutional quantifiers with two different substitution classes should be obvious.

Suppose one quantifier, ranging over a non-empty domain D and represented by *italicized* variables $x_1, x_2, \ldots$, is referential, while the other quantifier, represented by *roman* variables $\mathrm{x}_1, \mathrm{x}_2, \ldots$, is substitutional, with substitutes in some substitution class C. Then we must give a recursive definition of satisfaction, not truth, where the sequence $s = \{s_i\}$ assigns a value to the ith *italic* variable but does

not assign values to the roman variables. Satisfaction is to be defined for formulae containing no free *roman* variables.

We assume that, for each atomic formula without free roman variables $A(x_{i_1}, \ldots, x_{i_n}, t_1, \ldots, t_n)$ (where the t_i are elements of C), satisfaction is somehow defined outright. Note, for example, that a formula $A(x_1, t)$, with just one free variable x_1 and one term, defines a *set* (*not* a relation!) on D; but the set may depend on t and be different if t is replaced by another term. Semantically, for each term t, a subset $\chi(t)$ of D is assigned to $A(x_1, t)$.

If ϕ and ψ are formulae without free roman variables, we stipulate:

(14) s satisfies $\sim\phi$ iff s does not satisfy ϕ.

(15) s satisfies $\phi \wedge \psi$ iff s satisfies ϕ and s satisfies ψ.

(16) s satisfies $(\exists x_i)\phi$ iff there is an s', differing from s at most at the ith place, such that s' satisfies ϕ.

Finally, let ϕ be a formula with at most one roman variable x_i free. Then we stipulate:

(17) s satisfies $(\Sigma \mathrm{x}_i)\phi$ iff s satisfies ϕ', where ϕ' is like ϕ except that some term t replaces all free occurrences of x_i.

Note that the free *italic* variables play a genuine semantical role, but the free *roman* variables do not: formulae with free roman variables are assigned no interpretation.

For formulae with no free variables, italic or roman, truth can be defined in terms of satisfaction in the usual way. It would not be possible, in the present context, to proceed by a recursion on truth alone, because of the italicized variables. (Consider the semantics of formulae with both types of bound variables such as $(x_1)(\Sigma \mathrm{x}_1)\phi$.)

The considerations in this section can be formalized in a metalanguage with quantifiers ranging at least over expressions of the object language, and elements of D and sequences of them. In favoured cases this will be all the ontology needed; but more will be needed if more is used to define satisfaction for the atomic formulae. I leave the actual formalization to the reader.

5. A HOMOPHONIC TRUTH THEORY

As I emphasized in Section 2, the truth characterization given in the first two sections is not meant to be homophonic and cannot be, since the metalanguage M does not contain the object language; rather it gives the truth conditions for the substitutional quantifier in terms of (standard) quantification over expressions. Homophonic

truth theories are intelligible only if the object language is antecedently understood. Explanations of the type in Sections 1 and 2 illuminate the object language for someone who does not antecedently understand it.

Why, then, should we be that interested in homophonic theories? If definitions of the type of Section 1 are available (more so, if they are easily formalized as in Section 2), hasn't truth been characterized for the object language? I think the answer is affirmative. Why worry whether a homophonic theory is available? There is the following possible consideration. Someone may argue that if only a theory of the type of Section 2 is available and homophonic theories are lacking, this shows that the structure of the object language is merely 'surface structure'. Really, it will be said, the ϕ of the object language is a disguised rendering of the ϕ' which gives its truth conditions in the metalanguage. Perhaps substitutional quantification is merely a misleading formulation of metalinguistic assertions with referential quantifiers over expressions. I don't see how damaging this would be to substitutional quantification, since its meaningfulness would be conceded. Nevertheless, since the proposed criterion for a language being merely disguised notation has some plausibility, and since the question of a homophonic truth theory always has its own technical interest, I will explore this question in the present section.

In Wallace (1), Wallace argues just this way with respect to the 'possible-worlds semantics' for modal logic. Since the modal operators disappear in the metalanguage, he argues, they are mere misleading surface structure in the object language.[23] *Perhaps* the concluding paragraph in Wallace (1), Section III, hints at an analogous suggestion for substitutional languages, though usually Wallace seems to be making the much stronger claim that substitutional quantification cannot be interpreted at all unless it collapses into referential quantification with a domain consisting of denotations of the terms.

How plausible, however, *is* the criterion? A Davidsonian truth theory for natural languages typically yields such T-sentences as: 'I love you' is true in the mouth of a speaker s at a time t iff s (tenselessly) addresses a person s' at time t and s loves s' at t. On the right-hand side no tenses, or personal pronouns, appear. Is a Davidsonian then committed to the view that tense, personal pronouns, indexicals, demonstratives, and the like are all misleading surface structure in English and that English is 'really' a language which contains only eternal sentences without indexicals or

[23] I don't actually concede Wallace's premiss that a truth theory with the modal operators themselves in the metalanguage is impossible, but I don't need to argue the point here, so in the text I write as if this premiss were assumed.

tenses? Certainly Davidson in Davidson (3) didn't think so. The parallel is especially interesting because of the formal similarity between modality and tense.

It is worth observing that even for homophonic truth theories, the basis clauses plus the recursion clauses are usually insufficient by themselves to yield $T(\bar{\phi}) \equiv \phi$, but are ordinarily geared to some non-homophonic translation of ϕ into the metalanguage. For example, in standard referential quantification, what we would derive directly is not something like $T(\overline{(x_1)(x_1 \text{ is fat})}) \equiv (x_1)(x_1 \text{ is fat})$, but rather something like $T(\overline{(x_1)(x_1 \text{ is fat})}) \equiv$ there is a sequence s such that every sequence s' differing from s in at most the first place has a fat first member. Extra axioms then are needed to restore homophony. Though with these extra axioms the claim that the formula on the right of a T-sentence gives the 'true structure' of the formula whose truth conditions it gives can be maintained, I am somewhat puzzled at the intuition behind the claim. For one would think that the naive intuition that supports this criterion would hold that the semantical structure of a sentence is given by the basis and recursive clauses alone, or at least that if a T-sentence can be derived from them, the right hand side of *that* T-sentence would give the 'true semantical structure' of the formula mentioned on the left. Why should that formula give a bogus structure and auxiliary axioms be required to get back to the 'true' structure? (And since the T-sentence derivable most directly from the recursive clauses gives the 'wrong' structure, and some other T-sentence derived with the aid of auxiliary axioms gives the 'right' structure, how are we in general to choose which T-sentence gives the 'right' structure? An indefinite number will be derivable.[24]) Surely no one really thinks that the 'true' structure of quantification over individuals is quantification over sequences, or that a formula superficially beginning with one universal quantifier has as its 'true' structure a complex formula with one existential quantifier followed by one universal quantifier.[25] For more on the necessity of auxiliary axioms to ensure homophony, see the end of Section 10.

[24] The basis and recursive clauses by themselves yield some formulae $T(\bar{\phi}) \equiv \phi'$, where ϕ' differs considerably in structure, ontology, etc., from ϕ. (Actually the choice of ϕ' is in no obvious way uniquely determined here, though there is often a 'natural' candidate in practice; but let that pass.) Then with the help of some additional axioms whose conjunction is ψ we may obtain $T(\bar{\phi}) \equiv \phi$, but we could even more easily use them to obtain $T(\bar{\phi}) \equiv (\phi' \wedge \psi)$, etc. The required target formula is far from 'revealed' by the truth theory; it appears that we have to specify it in advance. Exactly how, then, is the truth theory supposed to *reveal* the 'true underlying structure'? I suspect that a great deal more work has to be done to make such a view coherent and plausible.

[25] Note also that the structure directly revealed by the recursive clauses will be different for '$(x_2)(x_2$ is fat)' and '$(x_1)(x_1$ is fat)'. I don't mean by this simply that different variables will appear on the right than appeared on the left, but rather that different predicates will; for example we will have 's differs from s' in at most the *second* place' etc. Note also that the quantificational structure of the right-hand side formulae may well be more complex than suggested in the text when various predicates are unpacked, e.g. 'differing from s in at most the second place' may involve quantification over numbers; 's' has a fat first member' would seem to have the form '$(\exists x)(\text{Member}(s', x, 1) \wedge \text{Fat}(x))$' where 'Member' is a three-place predicate relating sequences, things and numbers; etc. The 'structure' of '$(x_1)(x_1$ is fat)' directly revealed by the recursive clauses is a wondrous object.

Once again I must protest against the easy imposition of formal criteria, usually polemically motivated, without giving them a careful and detailed justification.

Before I consider the question of a homophonic truth theory for *L*, let me mention a more or less mechanical way in which a non-homophonic truth theory can be made homophonic. First, extend the metalanguage so that it contains the object language. Next, add to the old truth theory as axioms all statements of the form $\phi \equiv \phi'$, where ϕ is in the object language and ϕ' is its translation into the metalanguage. Then, since $T(\bar{\phi}) \equiv \phi'$ followed from the old axioms, $T(\bar{\phi}) \equiv \phi$ follows from the new ones.

Such a device violates the *finite axiomatizability* requirement stressed by Davidson and by Wallace, since there are infinitely many axioms $\phi \equiv \phi'$. But it satisfies the following weaker requirement (if the old theory did so)—only finitely many axioms contain 'T' (or any other auxiliary 'new' vocabulary such as satisfaction). Such a weaker requirement is sufficient to exclude the trivial truth theory which takes all the statements $T(\bar{\phi}) \equiv \phi$ as axioms. It also is sufficient to allow the implicit definition given by a truth theory to be turned into an explicit definition in a higher-order language. Since the exclusion of the trivial truth theory is the main justification currently advanced for the finite axiomatizability requirement,[26] perhaps it should be replaced by the weaker. Probably a better procedure yet—at this juncture—would be to abandon the practice of setting down arbitrary 'requirements' with weak or vague justifications, and to evaluate each proposal on its merits. The trivial truth theory would be ruled uninteresting because it is just that—trivial: it does not reveal illuminating structure.[27] Once again the moral: an author should not seek to impose his own formal requirements on others,

[26] Davidson (3) gives a fairly elaborate philosophical argument for the finite axiomatizability requirement, which he nonetheless calls a 'bold hypothesis'. Wallace (1) and Wallace (2), which are later, simply cite the requirement as a means of excluding the trivial truth theory. My impression is that this version is more common in recent work.

[27] Actually, as I mentioned above, Tarski proposes just this theory as an axiomatic theory of truth for the one case where he at first thought that truth was not explicitly definable. The T-sentences $T(\bar{\phi}) \equiv \phi$ were by no means considered trivial at the time of Tarski's paper. They showed that for each ϕ the question whether ϕ is true was not a fuzzy metaphysical one but is equivalent to asking the question 'ϕ?' itself. Tarski thought it quite illuminating that a formal theory of truth with each axiom $T(\bar{\phi}) \equiv \phi$ can be set up, especially in the presence of infinitary rules.

It is true that the theory with each sentence $T(\bar{\phi}) \equiv \phi$ as an axiom reveals no recursive semantic structure. If *that* is our project it must be excluded. But we will see in Section 5(*a*) that some finitely axiomatized theories are in the same boat.

unless they have a very careful justification. Perhaps finiteness criteria can meet this test, and they undoubtedly have led to fruitful and appealing work; but I am uncertain.

Having said this, I shall explore what can be done within the strict constraints of finiteness. We must make some restrictions on L not needed for the project of Section 2. Let us call the substitution class of L—the set of its terms—'C_1'. Then restrictions on C_1 must be adopted which will be stated below. At the moment, we will assume that *there is a finite list of atomic forms (with free roman variables) such that every formula of* L_0 *comes from a formula on the list by substituting terms for free variables*. Below, I will make the simplifying assumption that one form $\phi_0(\mathrm{x}_1, \mathrm{x}_2)$, with two free roman variables, suffices. The treatment can easily be generalized to a finite list.

To set up the metalanguage M', we assume that M' has two types of variables—the roman substitutional variables of L, and Greek variables ranging over strings of symbols of L. So M' is a language of the type discussed in the previous section. We assume, as in the case of M, that M' possesses, for each single symbol e of L, a primitive constant $\bar{e}$ denoting e. M' also possesses a binary function symbol, interpreted as concatenation. We can call any expression built up out of Greek variables or constants $\bar{e}$ using concatenation zero or more times an expression of class C_2. Then, given an assignment of expressions of L as values to the Greek variables, a term of class C_2 denotes an expression of L. Each expression e of L is denoted by its structural descriptive name $\bar{e}$ in M'. The atomic formulae of M' are of three types: every atomic formula of L (with or without free roman variables) is an atomic formula of M'; if s_1 and s_2 are expressions of class C_2, $s_1 = s_2$ is an atomic formula of M'; if x_i is a roman variable, and s is in C_2, $Q(\mathrm{x}_i, s)$ is an atomic formula of M' and $Q(t, s)$ is an atomic formula for each t in C_1. The formulae of M' are defined as comprising the smallest class containing the atomic formulae and closed under the specifications: if ϕ and ψ are formulae, so are $\sim\phi$, $\phi \wedge \psi$, $(\Sigma \mathrm{x}_i)\phi$, and $(\exists\alpha_i)\phi$. Clearly every formula of L is a formula of M'.

'$=$' is semantically interpreted as the identity relation on the range of the Greek variables. $Q(t, \alpha_i)$, where t is in C_1, and α_i is a Greek variable, defines for fixed t a set of expressions of L: in fact, we take it to define the set whose sole element is t itself. In other words, $Q(t, \alpha_i)$ is to be satisfied when and only when α_i is assigned t itself as

value. More generally, then, $Q(t, s)$ will be true, where s is in C_2, relative to a sequence assigning a value to each Greek variable, precisely if s, relative to this assignment, denotes the term t. In particular, $Q(t, \bar{t})$ will always be true. If t_n is any term in C_1 other than t, $Q(t_n, \bar{t})$ will be false. Notice that the *form* $Q(\mathrm{x}_i, \alpha)$ gets no interpretation whatsoever.

As axioms, we adopt various axioms adequate to set up a theory of the elementary syntax of L, and (7)–(9) for the semantics of the truth-functions and the substitutional quantifier. (10), however, is supplanted by the following basis clause, which eliminates the need for the old $\mathrm{R}(\alpha)$:

$$(18)\quad (\Pi \mathrm{x}_1)(\Pi \mathrm{x}_2)(\alpha_1)(\alpha_2)(Q(\mathrm{x}_1, \alpha_1) \wedge Q(\mathrm{x}_2, \alpha_2). \supset . \mathrm{T}(\overline{\phi_o(\alpha_1, \alpha_2)}) \equiv \phi_o(\mathrm{x}_1, \mathrm{x}_2)).$$

We need various special axioms governing the Q-predicate:

$$(19)\quad (\Pi \mathrm{x}_1)(\exists \alpha_1)(Q(\mathrm{x}_1, \alpha_1) \wedge \mathrm{Term}\ (\alpha_1)).$$

$$(20)\quad (\Pi \mathrm{x}_1)(\alpha_1)(\alpha_2)(Q(\mathrm{x}_1, \alpha_1) \wedge Q(\mathrm{x}_1, \alpha_2). \supset . \alpha_1 = \alpha_2).$$

$$(21)\quad (\alpha_1)(\mathrm{Term}\ (\alpha_1) \supset (\Sigma \mathrm{x}_1)\ Q(\mathrm{x}_1, \alpha_1)).$$

We also need axioms sufficient to derive all the formulae $Q(t, \bar{t})$; in conjunction with (20), these will be sufficient to determine the extension of $Q(t, \alpha)$ for each t. Such axioms are infinite in number, but under the restrictions on L we have adopted, they can be derived from a finite number of instances. For example, in the case of the mirror-image language, where the terms are finite strings of the two letters a and b, the axioms will read:

$$(22a)\quad Q(a, \bar{a}).$$

$$(22b)\quad Q(b, \bar{b}).$$

$$(22c)\quad (\Pi \mathrm{x}_1)(\Pi \mathrm{x}_2)(\alpha_1)(\alpha_2)(Q(\mathrm{x}_1, \alpha_1) \wedge Q(\mathrm{x}_2, \alpha_2). \supset . Q(\mathrm{x}_1\mathrm{x}_2, \alpha_1 {}^\frown \alpha_2)).$$

If, on the other hand, the terms are precisely the expressions: $a, fa, ffa, fffa$, etc., where f is a one-place functor symbol, then the appropriate axioms are:

$$(23a)\quad Q(a, \bar{a});$$

$$(23b)\quad (\Pi \mathrm{x}_1)(\alpha_1)(Q(\mathrm{x}_1, \alpha_1) \supset Q(f\mathrm{x}_1, \bar{f} {}^\frown \alpha_1)).$$

A like treatment applies wherever the terms are built up out of finitely many simple terms using a finite number of operation symbols.[28]

We remark that (21) will be redundant in the presence of (19) and (20), and of the axioms entailing $Q(t, \bar{t})$ for each t, provided that the axioms for elementary syntax (concatenation theory) are sufficiently powerful.

The point of the Q-formulas is to provide a device like quotation in M': $Q(t, \alpha)$, for each term t, systematically represents a formula satisfied by t alone. Originally (4)–(6) (or (7)–(9)) were geared to a non-homophonic theory of truth for L; $Q(t, \alpha)$, and the axioms governing it, restore needed connections.

The important result regarding the theory given above is this. If $Q(\mathrm{x}_1, \ldots, \mathrm{x}_n)$ is a formula of L with just the Roman variables indicated free,

$$(24)\quad (\Pi \mathrm{x}_1) \ldots (\Pi \mathrm{x}_n)(\alpha_1) \ldots (\alpha_n)(Q(\mathrm{x}_1, \alpha_1) \wedge \ldots Q(\mathrm{x}_n, \alpha_n) \,.\supset.\, \mathrm{T}(\overline{\phi(\alpha_1, \ldots, \alpha_n)}) \equiv \phi(\mathrm{x}_1, \ldots, \mathrm{x}_n)).$$

In particular, if $n = 0$:

$$(25)\quad \mathrm{T}(\bar{\phi}) \equiv \phi.$$

The reader is invited to carry out an inductive proof of (24)—by induction on the complexity of ϕ—for himself. (The induction starts with (18) as basis.) (25) is the homophonic truth paradigm of Tarski.

Now an error may arise in the interpretation of $Q(t, \alpha)$. Since each statement of the form $Q(t, \bar{t})$ is true, someone might conceivably be tempted to misread $Q(\mathrm{x}_1, \alpha_1)$ as 'is denoted by', basing the reading on the truth of such statements as

(25) Cicero is denoted by $\overline{\text{Cicero}}$,

which expresses a relation between a man and an expression.

[28] It should be emphasized that this condition has nothing to do with any recursive semantic structure for the interpretation of the terms. When it is violated it can often be reinstated by a simple change of notation. For example, if the substitution class consists of infinitely many primitive constants 'a_1', 'a_2', . . ., the condition is violated. But it will hold if the primitive constant 'a_n' is rewritten as 'a' followed by n vertical strokes, where the single symbol 'a' and the vertical stroke '|' is new notation. This introduces no semantic relations between the terms that did not exist before. It is a purely syntactic device.

If the condition is not easily achieved and we wish a finitely axiomatized theory entailing all the formulae $Q(t, \bar{t})$, it is best to introduce a new style of substitutional variable whose substitutes are not just the terms but arbitrary well- or ill-formed strings of symbols of the object language. For an example, see Section 5(a) below.

Any such temptation is erroneous. $Q(\mathrm{x}_1, \alpha_1)$ does *not* define a relation; for each t, which may be substituted for x_1, the result is a *monadic* predicate with one free referential variable whose extension is $\{t\}$. The $Q(t, \alpha)$ formulae are well-defined, for example, for the mirror-image language, in which obviously no denotations are assigned to the terms, and the substitutional variables have no 'range'. The semantics of $Q(t, \alpha)$ is clear *without assuming that terms have denotations.*

What if denotations *are* assigned to the terms in the interpretation of L? We saw in Section 3 that a substitutional formula can be said to induce a relation, provided that the terms have denotations and the formula is transparent. Now even if the first condition holds, the second does not. Although

(26a) $Q(\text{Cicero}, \overline{\text{Cicero}})$

and

(26b) $Q(\text{Tully}, \overline{\text{Tully}})$

are true,

(27) $Q(\text{Cicero}, \overline{\text{Tully}})$

is false, as is apparent from the truth conditions for the formulae. The truth of (26b), together with the falsity of (27), means that the Q-formulae are opaque. So *even if L is interpreted so that the terms denote,* $Q(\mathrm{x}_1, \alpha_1)$ does not define the relation 'is denoted by', *nor any other relation.* Note further that if *some terms denote and others do not,* they are *not* distinguished by $Q(t, \alpha)$. For example,

(26c) $Q(\text{Zeus}, \overline{\text{Zeus}})$

is as true as (26a) and (26b).

We must therefore be careful not to misinterpret such an axiom as (19), either by a misreading of the substitutional quantifiers as referential or by misreading $Q(\mathrm{x}_1, \alpha_1)$. A reading of (19) such as 'Everything is denoted by a term' would be guilty of *both* errors. Rather (19) should be read as the infinite conjunction of all formulae $(\exists\alpha_1)(Q(t, \alpha_1) \wedge \text{Term}\,(\alpha_1))$; and each such formula is true because $Q(t, \alpha_1) \wedge \text{Term}\,(\alpha_1)$ is satisfied by the assignment of t itself to α_1 as value. Similar remarks apply to (20) and (21).

Wallace (1) gives a formal homophonic truth theory for the substitutional quantifier very similar to our theory in M'. His treatment

of the subject is vitiated, however, if I understand him correctly, by a (mis)reading of $Q(t, \alpha)$ as 'is denoted by'. He follows this misreading with a correlative misinterpretation of (19) as 'Everything has a name', which is then triumphantly cited to show that the substitutional truth theory collapses into a referential one.

One caveat regarding (19), or for that matter all the formulae (19)–(23). Wallace gives the impression that the necessity in a theory of the present kind for such an axiom as (19) reveals a hidden lacuna in the recursive clauses (4)–(6). Although they appeared adequate by themselves for an account of truth conditions, it emerges that they are insufficient; special additional axioms such as (19) are required. Any such impression is erroneous. The recursive clauses (4)–(6) were geared either to an explicit definition of substitutional truth in the style of Section 1 or to a non-homophonic truth theory in the style of Section 2(*b*): they characterize truth in a metalanguage containing referential quantifiers over expressions but not containing the object language. When we aim for a homophonic theory in the present section special axioms such as (19) are required, not to make a truth theory possible at all, but to postulate the needed connection between the referential variables of the metalanguage and the substitutional variables of the object language so as to restore homophony. The clauses (4)–(6) naturally are geared to yield T-sentences of the form $T(\bar{\phi}) \equiv \phi'$ where ϕ' is a sentence of the metalanguage distinct from ϕ. We need (19)–(23) to obtain $T(\bar{\phi}) \equiv \phi$. See the passage in small type at the beginning of the present section, and the concluding paragraphs of Section 10, for a demonstration that this kind of situation is a typical one. Almost all truth theories, including those for referential quantification, are 'naturally' geared to a non-homophonic translation, and special additional axioms are generally required to restore homophony. Wallace has *not* discovered a special feature of substitutional quantification, unnoticed by those who thought the recursive clauses (4)–(6) were sufficient.

If the reader has any lingering tendency to misread $Q(t, \alpha)$, let him consider a modified metalanguage M'', which we sketch in a rough way. The formation rules of M'' are like those of M' with the following modifications. (i) First, the formulae $Q(t, \alpha)$ are dropped. (ii) Second, the class C_2 of terms is enlarged by the stipulation that if t is any term of class C_1, the result of placing t within single quotes—which we write as 't'—will be a term of class C_2, interpreted as denoting t. (Only the terms of L, and not other expressions of L, are enclosed in quotes). Then the expressions of class C_2 are to be built up out of Greek variables, primitive constants for

atomic expressions of L, and quoted terms, using concatenation. The simple atomic formulae of M'' are then: the sentences of L_o, and the formulae $s_1 = s_2$, where s_1 and s_2 are expressions of class C_1. Atomic formulae in general are defined as the result of replacing terms of class C_1 in simple atomic formulae by roman variables. *The replacement is allowed even for terms enclosed within quotes.* Thus the quotation-name of a term functions in a manner radically different from its structural descriptive name: a structural descriptive name of a term does not contain that term as a part; this is clear for the structural descriptive name of a complex term such as $\bar{a} \frown \bar{b}$, and we have adopted the viewpoint that for an atomic term such as 'a', '$\bar{a}$' is also an unstructured atomic term. The quotation of a term, in contrast, *is regarded as containing that term as a part.* So if L is the mirror-image language, where the terms are finite strings of 'a' and 'b', " '$\mathrm{x}_1 a$' = 'x_2' " is well-formed because " 'ba' = 'b' " is.

Arbitrary formulae of M'' are built up out of atomic formulae in the usual way: If ϕ and ψ are formulae, so are $\phi \wedge \psi$, $\sim\phi$, $(\exists\alpha_i)\phi$, and $(\Sigma \mathrm{x}_i)\phi$.

Now $Q(t, \alpha_i)$ can be *defined*, for M'', as 't' = α_i. The fact that $Q(t, \alpha_i)$ can be interpreted without assuming that the terms of L have denotation, and that it is opaque even if they do, is amply brought out by the definitions. $Q(t, \alpha_i)$ bears a relation to the quotation of t analogous to the relation between Quine's 'Mosesizes' and the name 'Moses': in the one case we have a *predicate* true only of t, in the other case we have a term denoting t.

Actually, the presence of quotation in M'' allows us to simplify the axioms. We assumed above that all sentences of L_o come by substitution from a single dyadic atomic formula $\phi_o(\mathrm{x}_1, \mathrm{x}_2)$. Assume further that the formula in question can be written as '$F(\mathrm{x}_1, \mathrm{x}_2)$'—that is, we assume that all atomic formulae of L_o can be written as the concatenation of the letter F, a left parenthesis, a term, a comma, a term, and a right parenthesis. This involves no loss of generality; if L_o is not written that way already, it can be rewritten in this form. (The simplification makes it easier to state (28) below, but it is not essential.) Then we can replace (18) by:

$$(28)\quad (\Pi \mathrm{x}_1)(\Pi \mathrm{x}_2)(\mathrm{T}(\bar{F} \frown \bar{(} \frown \text{'}\mathrm{x}_1\text{'} \frown \bar{,} \frown \text{'}\mathrm{x}_2\text{'} \frown \bar{)}) \equiv F(\mathrm{x}_1, \mathrm{x}_2)).$$

Note that here and elsewhere a quoted variable is *not* interpreted as denoting the variable. (28) is true iff each of its instances is, where the variables are to be replaced by terms inside and outside the quotes.

(19) can be replaced by:

$$(29)\quad (\Pi \mathrm{x}_1)\ \mathrm{Term}\ (\text{'}\mathrm{x}_1\text{'}).$$

(20) can be dropped; it is the analogue of the assumption that there is at most one Mosesizer, which is superfluous if a term 'Moses' is used. (21) remains as it is, using the definition of $Q(\mathrm{x}_1, \alpha_1)$. As before, it is superfluous in the presence of powerful enough syntactic axioms, and the other axioms. (22a)–(22c) should now read:

(30a) 'a' = $\bar{a}$.
(30b) 'b' = $\bar{b}$.
(30c) $(\Pi \mathrm{x}_1)(\Pi \mathrm{x}_2)$('$\mathrm{x}_1\ \mathrm{x}_2$' = '$\mathrm{x}_1$' $\frown$ 'x_2').

Similarly, (23a) and (23b) become:

(31a) 'a' = $\bar{a}$.
(31b). (Πx_1)('fx_1' = $f \frown$ 'x_1').

(30a)–(30c), which are designed for the mirror-image language, allow us to prove all statements of the form 't' = $\bar{t}$, such as 'ab' = $\bar{a} \frown \bar{b}$. I leave to the reader the derivation of the Tarski sentences (25).

The $Q(t, \alpha)$ language has one advantage over the language with a quotation functor. Confusions always arise over quoted *variables*: are we naming the variable, or quantifying into the functor? The $Q(t, \alpha)$ language seems less likely to engender confusion.

5(*a*). *Another homophonic substitutional truth theory*

So far, I have been following Wallace's exposition as closely as possible. The only substitutional quantifiers in the metalanguage are those of the object language. Actually, if arbitrary substitutional quantifiers are allowed in the metalanguage, the task of finding a finite truth theory is almost trivial.

Let L be any object language subject to two conditions: it has only finitely many atomic (indecomposable) symbols, and certain strings of atomic symbols are singled out as closed symbols of L. Extend L to a metalanguage M''' as follows. The symbols of M''' include $\exists$, (,), Σ, $\sim$, $\wedge$, Greek variables α, β, γ, α_1, α_2, . . ., roman variables x, y, z, x_1, x_2, . . ., sentence variables p, q, p_1, p_2, ... The Greek, roman, and sentence variables are assumed to be new symbols, not to be found in L. If any of the other symbols are already in L, we need not duplicate them in extending L to M'''. Below we will use σ as a special metavariable over strings of symbols of L; it is part of our informal metalanguage for describing M''', but it is not part of the formal notation of M''' itself. In particular, it should not be misconstrued as a Greek variable of M'''. Other symbols added to L include constants $\overline{e_1}$, . . ., $\overline{e_n}$ (one for each of the atomic symbols e_1, . . ., e_n of L) and one binary letter f. *Terms*[29] (referential) are defined inductively to include *Greek* variables, constants, and $f(t_1, t_2)$ for any terms t_1, and t_2. Usually we write $t_1 \frown t_2$ for $f(t_1, t_2)$. A closed term is one containing no Greek variables. There is one primitive two-place predicate of identity and a one-place predicate of truth

[29] The use of the term 'term' here is different from the typical use in previous sections. And so is the use of the letter 't' and its subscripted or primed variants as a variable ranging over arbitrary terms of M'''. The terms 't' here are *not* in the substitution class of either style of substitutional quantifier, but they are substitutes for the referential (Greek) variables. Thus where before we wrote '$Q(t, \alpha)$', here we write '$Q(\sigma, t)$' and the like. I hope no confusion will be engendered.

applied to Greek variables, and forms $Q(\mathrm{x}, \alpha)$ and $Q(\mathrm{p}, \alpha)$. Formulae are defined as follows: A formula of L is a formula (of M'''); if t_1 and t_2 are terms, $t_1 = t_2$ and $\mathrm{T}(t_1)$ are formulae; any sentence variable is a formula; if ϕ and ψ are formulae, and x, p, and α are roman, sentence and Greek variables, respectively, $\sim\phi$, $\phi \wedge \psi$, $(\Sigma \mathrm{x})\phi$, $(\Sigma \mathrm{p})\phi$, and $(\exists\alpha)\phi$ are all formulae; if σ is any string of symbols, each of which is either one of the atomic symbols of L, a sentence variable, or a roman variable, and t is a term, then $Q(\sigma, t)$ is a formula. (Notice that even if L contains quantifiers, they are *not* applied to arbitrary formulae of M'''.)

In the interpretation, $\overline{e_1}, \ldots, \overline{e_n}$ denote, respectively, $e_1, \ldots e_n$. Roman variables are substitutional variables whose substitution class consists of arbitrary (including ill-formed) strings of symbols of L. Sentence variables are substitutional variables whose substitution class consists of the (closed) sentences of L. Greek variables as usual range over arbitrary well- or ill-formed strings of symbols of the object language L. 'f' is interpreted as the concatenation function. The denotation rules for terms are obvious: *closed* terms are structural descriptive names of (well- or ill-formed) strings of symbols of the object language. If σ is a string of symbols of L, and α is a Greek variable, $Q(\sigma, \alpha)$ is a one-place predicate satisfied by σ alone. The interpretation of everything else is obvious. The task is to prove $\mathrm{T}(\bar{\phi}) \equiv \phi$ for each (closed) sentence of L. Axioms:

(32) $Q(e_1, \overline{e_1}), \ldots, Q(e_n, \overline{e_n})$.

(33) $(\Pi \mathrm{x}_1)(\Pi \mathrm{x}_2)(\alpha_1)(\alpha_2)(Q(\mathrm{x}_1, \alpha_1) \wedge Q(\mathrm{x}_2, \alpha_2) \,.\supset .\, Q(\mathrm{x}_1\, \mathrm{x}_2, \alpha_1 \frown \alpha_2))$.

(34) $(\Pi \mathrm{p})(\alpha)(Q(\mathrm{p}, \alpha) \supset (\mathrm{T}(\alpha) \equiv \mathrm{p}))$.

(Exercises: (i) Why couldn't we have just postulated $(\Pi \mathrm{p})(\mathrm{T}(\bar{\mathrm{p}}) \equiv \mathrm{p})$? Because $\bar{\phi}$, the structural descriptive name of ϕ, does not contain ϕ as a proper part. The situation would be simpler if M''' contained a quotation function and the task was simply to prove $\mathrm{T}(`\phi') \equiv \phi$ for each ϕ. Here we follow Tarski and prove $\mathrm{T}(\bar{\phi}) \equiv \phi$ for structural descriptive names $\bar{\phi}$. I also preferred, following previous practice, to let M''' contain referential (Greek) variables ranging over strings of symbols of L rather than substitutional variables with structural descriptive names as substitutes.

(ii) Why have two styles of substitutional variable, when one substitution class contains the other? After all, for referential variables, if the range of a variable is given, separate variables over any subdomain are superfluous: they can be replaced by variables over the entire domain, in the style $(x)(SD(x) \supset \phi(x))$, where $SD(x)$ is a predicate true exactly of the subdomain. In the present case, we might replace (34) by either $(\Pi \mathrm{x})(\alpha)(Q(\mathrm{x}, \alpha)$

$\wedge$ Sentence(α) . $\supset$. T(α) $\equiv$ x), where 'Sentence(α)' is a unary predicate true exactly of the closed sentences of L; or, alternatively, (Πx)(α)(Sent(x) $\wedge$ Q(x, α) . $\supset$. T(α) $\equiv$ x), where 'Sent(x)' is a form yielding a true closed sentence when a sentence is substituted for the variable and a false sentence when any other string of symbols of the object language is substituted. The trouble in both cases is that T(α) $\equiv$ x becomes ill-formed when x is replaced by strings which are not sentences, and thus is not a form.)

Here, following the Davidsonian tradition, we took T(α) as primitive. But we could, following Tarski more closely, *explicitly* define 'T(α)' in the metalanguage as '(Σp)(Q(p, α) $\wedge$ p)' (and, of course, drop it as a primitive). It would then be even more in the spirit of Tarski to replace (34) in this case by more fundamental principles from which it can be proved. The following will do:

(35) $(\Pi p_1)(\Pi p_2)(\alpha)(Q(p_1, \alpha) \wedge Q(p_2, \alpha) \;.\supset.\; p_1 \equiv p_2)$.

Actually, (35) should really probably be replaced by stronger, more fundamental principles still; but to do so we would be forced to change the formation rules of M'''.

Ever since Davidson's seminal paper, Davidson (3), the problem of giving a recursive procedure, showing how the meaning of whole expressions of a language L depends on the meanings of their parts, has come to be identified with the problem of giving a finitely axiomatized truth theory for that language. The present section seems to present a counterexample to any sweeping identification of this kind. The truth theories of this section are undoubtedly finitely axiomatized. They reveal nothing about the structure of L: no structure was assumed. Perhaps with some stated restriction, proponents of the claim can make it clearer.

Both the truth theory and the explicit truth definition presented in this section have strong formal resemblances to Ramsey's famous theory and to the theory rejected in Tarski (bottom of p. 158 to p. 162). It is the failure of this theory which leads Tarski to conclude (bottom of p. 162) that '*the attempt to construct a correct semantical definition of the expression "true sentence" meets very real difficulties*' (Tarski's italics). Whatever difficulties there may have been with these constructions, I believe I have shown in this section that these difficulties can be met using substitutional quantification and the formula Q(p, α).

On pp. 161–2 Tarski suggests that paradoxes may result if we try to set up truth theories in the way he rejects. An extensive parallel literature has recently arisen on the similar supposed problem that 'substitutional quantification plus quotation leads to the Liar Paradox', and possibly other paradoxes as well. Such authors as Binkley and Harman propose

desperate restrictions on the use of quotation to avoid the alleged paradox. Much of the literature attributes the 'paradox' to Quine, although I am unaware of any published source.

All derivations of the 'paradox' rely upon the device of taking the substitution class for a substitutional quantifier in a substitutional language, L, to consist of all sentences of L itself, including sentences containing the very substitutional quantifier in question. Such a substitution class violates the restriction placed upon substitution classes in Section 1 in the most elementary way, and obviously an inductive proof in the style of Section 1 that truth for the substitutional language is uniquely defined is impossible. The case in question is, therefore, not a legitimate substitutional language in the sense of Section 1, and gives no case for supposing that substitutional quantification leads to any paradoxes.

When Marcus[30] (who states that she derives her observations from an unpublished letter from van Fraassen) correctly observed that this kind of so called 'substitutional quantifier' violates the restrictions needed for an inductive definition (Marcus, pp. 246–7), her work came to be regarded by some as just another proposed restriction, perhaps the least drastic, to block the 'paradox'. Why wasn't it simply called the exposure of a fallacy?

In my opinion, the way to do substitutional quantification with sentences as substitutes is to let the substitution class consist of the sentences of the ground language L_0, not the language L. This was the procedure adopted in the present section, with the object language, L, playing the role of L_0, and the metalanguage M''' playing the role of L. If we wish substitutional quantifiers whose substitutes are sentences of the language L, we can extend L to a larger language, L', with a new style of substitutional quantifier whose substitutes are sentences of L. This process can be iterated indefinitely, adding a new style of substitutional quantifier at each stage. The resulting language strongly resembles Russell's ramified theory of types for propositions, but is based upon substitutional quantification. The ramified theory of types for 'propositional functions' can be interpreted in a similar way, using a suitable generalization of substitutional quantification which is beyond the scope of this paper.[31] The possibility of such substitutional or quasi-substitutional interpretations of the ramified theory of types is just *one* way of casting doubt on Quine's repeated assertion that Russell's ramified theory of types provides no significant ontological gain over ordinary set theory. It also casts doubt on his assertion that the ramified theory of types is irrelevant to the semantic paradoxes it was designed to solve, since it was precisely the failure to ramify which gave trouble to the pseudo-substitutional language.

6. SATISFACTION, PSEUDO-SATISFACTION AND OPACITY

Wallace (1) has claimed to find satisfaction in the metatheory of substitutional quantification. Clearly the claim cannot refer to meta-

[30] The recent interest in substitutional quantification stems largely from Prof. Marcus's persistent advocacy.

[31] One treatment of the relation between predicative set theory and substitutional quantification can be found in the last section of Tharp.

languages such as *M*, nor to the mechanical way of extending *M* to give a homophonic truth theory, as in the beginning of Section 5. So apparently it is intended to apply to a metalanguage like *M′*.

Now, first, Wallace observes that just as truth is paradigmatically characterized by schema (25), so satisfaction (of formulae with one free variable) is paradigmatically characterized by

$$(36)\quad (x_1)(\mathrm{R}(x_1, \overline{\phi(x_1)}) \equiv \phi(x_1)).$$

Any two-place predicate $\mathrm{R}(x_1, \alpha)$ satisfying (36) for each formula $\phi(x_1)$ whose sole free variable is x_1 will have the satisfaction relation as its extension (or more strictly, its extension will coincide with satisfaction on the set of all pairs of individuals and formulae with one free variable: nothing in (36) precludes its extension containing pairs $\langle a, b\rangle$ where b is not such a formula).[32]

Now in *M′* we can define P-Sat (x_1, α_1) as short for $(\exists\alpha_2)(\exists\alpha_3)$ $(Q(\mathrm{x}_1, \alpha_2) \wedge \mathrm{T}(\alpha_3) \wedge \text{Subst}\,(\alpha_3, \alpha_1, \alpha_2, \overline{\mathrm{x}_1}))$. Then it can be shown that

$$(37)\quad (\Pi\mathrm{x}_1)(\text{P-Sat}(\mathrm{x}_1, \overline{\phi(\mathrm{x}_1)}) \equiv \phi(\mathrm{x}_1))$$

is a theorem of *M′* for each formula $\phi(\mathrm{x}_1)$ with one free substitutional variable.

Wallace concludes immediately that P-Sat(x_1, α_1) has satisfaction as its extension. Unfortunately, such a conclusion can be based only on a confusion of (37) with (36). P-Sat(x_1, α_1), which, because of the formal similarity of (36) and (37), we can call the 'pseudo-satisfaction formula', is a form with one free substitutional variable. We can conclude that it induces any relation at all only if (i) *all* the terms are assigned denotations and (ii) it is transparent. As in the case of the *Q*-formulae, it is easy to see that even in the exceptional case where (i) holds, (ii) will not; the reason is that the definition of P-Sat involves the opaque form $Q(\mathrm{x}_1, \alpha_2)$.

Nevertheless, perhaps Wallace still has some hope. He writes (Wallace (2), p. 208): 'The point is that informal arguments involving satisfaction can be carried out in the formal semantics.' Perhaps some such arguments can be carried out using (37) instead of (36)—after all, the two schemata are formally analogous.

[32] Actually, no binary predicate satisfying (36) can be satisfaction in the strict technical sense, since the latter is a relation between *sequences* and open sentences. The kind of relation which satisfies (36) is a relation between an object and a formula with just one free variable. In the present section, I follow Wallace's terminology and call such a relation satisfaction. For more on the distinction in question here, see Section 10.

The only sample Wallace gives is:

> '(Ay)(y satisfies "Jones believes that x is an airedale" if and only if Jones believes that y is an airedale).

In particular

> a^* satisfies "Jones believes that x is an airedale" if and only if Jones believes that a^* is an airedale.

But "satisfies" is an extensional predicate, so if

$$a^* = b^*$$

we have

> a^* satisfies "Jones believes that x is an airedale" if and only if b^* satisfies "Jones believes that x is an airedale".

whence by one more application of the general principle,

> Jones believes that a^* is an airedale if and only if Jones believes that b^* is an airedale'

(Wallace (2), p. 209).[33]

This astounding result would render belief contexts referentially transparent.

If (Ay) is interpreted as (Πy) and satisfaction is replaced by pseudo-satisfaction, the fallacy is evident: pseudo-satisfaction, unlike satisfaction, is *not* transparent. Wallace's argument, therefore, cannot be formalized in M'.

One might inquire whether the opaque $Q(t, \alpha_1)$, which causes all the trouble, might be replaceable by a transparent construction. The possibility which immediately comes to mind is $Q'(t, \alpha_1)$, defined as satisfied whenever α_1 is assigned any term coreferential with t. (Q' is well-defined *only* if all terms denote.) Unfortunately, if Q were replaced by Q', (24) would become false whenever $\phi(x_1, \ldots, x_n)$ is itself opaque. Q'-formulae are thus unusable unless the object language has no opacities to begin with. (Indeed, one of the defects of the discussion in Wallace (2) is that after 'proving' (in my opinion, fallaciously) a conclusion about elementary number theory—an extensional language—Wallace feels entitled to draw immediate

[33] Wallace states that his argument 'is closely related to ones given by Quine', and is inspired by unpublished formulations by Sandra Lynne Peterson (now Sandra Peterson Wallace).

conclusions about the general case, including intensional languages. Surely it should have struck him that the cases may well be different.)

6(*a*). *Scope and Opacity; Referential* vs. *Substitutional Quantification into Opaque Contexts*

Would Wallace's argument for transparency work if (Ay) were a referential quantifier rather than a substitutional quantifier? In this case, the fallacy in the argument was essentially pointed out by Russell in his famous paper 'On Denoting', published in 1905. Russell, as is well known, analysed a formula of the form $\psi(\iota x\phi(x))$, where $\phi(x)$ is atomic, as

$$(38)\quad (\exists y)((x)(y = x \equiv \phi(x)) \wedge \psi(y)).$$

Here the analysis is unambiguous if $\iota x\phi(x)$ is the only definite description present. If more than one is present—say the formula is $\psi(\iota x\phi(x), \iota x\phi'(x))$—the formula is ambiguous depending on the order in which the descriptions are eliminated, but the results are logically equivalent. If $\psi(x)$ is not atomic, however, there are more serious possibilities of ambiguity. Say, for example, $\psi(x)$ is $C\chi(x)$ where 'C' is a unary sentence connective, such as negation, necessity, or, in Wallace's example, belief. Then $C\chi(\iota x\phi(x))$ may be analysed as either of the following:

$$(39)\quad (\exists y)((x)(y = x \equiv \phi(x)) \wedge C\chi(y));$$
$$(40)\quad C((\exists y)((x)(y = x \equiv \phi(x)) \wedge \chi(y))).$$

Russell disambiguated, in *Principia Mathematica*, by a scope notation. (39) was written as

$$(39')\quad [\iota x\phi(x)]C\chi(\iota x\phi(x))$$

and (40) as

$$(40')\quad C[\iota x\phi(x)]\chi(\iota x\phi(x)).$$

The scope operator indicates to what context the elimination of descriptions should be applied.

Russell pointed out that (39) and (40) are *not* logically equivalent. However, if C is an extensional connective, such as negation, we can prove $(\exists !x)\phi(x)\ .\supset .\ (39) \equiv (40)$ (where $(\exists !x)\phi(x)$ abbreviates $(\exists y)(x)(y = x \equiv \phi(y))$. If C is intensional, say necessity or belief, not even this simple sentence is provable. Further, the law $(y)\psi(y) \wedge$

$(\exists!x)\phi(x)$. ⊃ . $[\imath x\phi(x)]\ \psi(\imath x\phi(x))$ is valid: the scope of the description is the entire context $\psi(y)$. The notion of scope, and similar remarks, of course apply if connectives with more than one place and quantifiers are present, giving more ambiguities in a scopeless notation.

Now in Wallace's argument, from the premiss

(41) $(y)(y$ satisfies 'Jones believes that x is an airedale' if and only if Jones believes that y is an airedale),

if we take 'a^*' to abbreviate a Russellian description, with the existence and uniqueness conditions fulfilled, we can deliver (assuming that 'a^*' is non-vacuous)

(42) $[a^*](a^*$ satisfies 'Jones believes that x is an airedale' if and only if Jones believes that a^* is an airedale).

Using the extensionality of 'if and only if' we can drive the scopes inward a bit (provided 'a^*' is non-vacuous):

(43) $([a^*]\ a^*$ satisfies 'Jones believes that x is an airedale') if and only if $[a^*]$ (Jones believes that a^* is an airedale).

The argument can then be completed to show that in

(44) $[a^*]$ Jones believes that a^* is an airedale

the position of a^* is transparent.

However, the conclusion is harmless and could have been proved directly. Suppose 'a^*' abbreviates '$\imath x\phi(x)$'. Then (44) expands, in Russell's theory, into:

(45) $(\exists y)((x)(x = y \equiv \phi(x)) \wedge$ Jones believes that y is an airedale).

Here the predicate $\phi(x)$ is not within the scope of any intensional construction and can be replaced by any coextensive predicate. What would have been disastrous is the conclusion that the position of 'a^*' is transparent in

(46) Jones believes that $[a^*]$ $(a^*$ is an airedale)

or equivalently, analysed by Russell's theory,

(47) Jones believes that $(\exists y)((x)(x = y \equiv \phi(x)) \wedge y$ is an airedale).

But no such conclusion is forthcoming, and no such conclusion *could* be forthcoming from the nature of the case.[34]

Now Wallace, in Wallace (1), advocates the adoption of Russell's theory of descriptions. But it would make no difference if descriptions, or some other category of singular terms, were taken as primitive. The main point is that the distinction between (46), which gives the content of Jones' belief—'that a^* is an airedale'—and (44), which asserts *of* the actual referent of 'a^*' that Jones believes that *it* is an airedale, exists in the nature of things and must be expressed somehow in an adequate notation. The distinction is manifest if 'a^*' abbreviates, say, 'Smith's favourite pet'. The medieval logicians called this the distinction of *de dicto* and *de re*, though the terminology is misleading in that it suggests a twofold distinction when in fact more than two scope possibilities can arise if intensional constructions are iterated. Notice that the *de re* interpretation can be expressed in the metalanguage by the assertion that a^* satisfies 'Jones believes that x is an airedale'. In the object language, if singular terms such as descriptions are taken as primitive, it is best to provide the notation with explicit scope indicators. These scope indicators can be used to distinguish (46) and (44); if vacuous descriptions, or non-denoting singular terms, are allowed, scope will make a difference even in extensional contents. Note also that (46), unlike (44), is not 'about' the referent of 'a^*'—say, Smith's actual favourite dog—at all; on Frege's theory of sense and reference, it can be said to be about the 'sense' of 'a^*'. And the rule for substituting singular terms for the universal quantifier will be: $(x)\phi(x) \supset [a^*]\phi(a^*)$ (or $(x)\phi(x) \wedge \exists x(x = a^*) \,.\supset.\, [a^*]\phi(a^*)$ if empty terms are allowed).

What if the object-language notation doesn't contain explicit scope indicators? Then the most natural convention assigns all terms the minimum scope. (For if $\phi(a^*)$ is atomic, there is no ambiguity of scope: $\phi(a^*)$ must be $[a^*]\phi(a^*)$. If $\sim\phi(a^*)$ is to be the negation of $\phi(a^*)$, then it must be $\sim[a^*]\phi(a^*)$; $[a^*]\sim\phi(a^*)$ is not the negation of $[a^*]\phi(a^*)$. This argument generalizes to all cases.) The *de re*

[34] Of course, if there is a class C of terms which are all indifferent to scope distinctions—i.e., when a large-scope sentence is equivalent to a small-scope sentence—then, using the transparency of the large-scope version, we can show that all contexts are transparent with respect to the terms of the class. Some writers seem to have denied this, but the conclusion follows from the analysis above.

interpretation—(44)—must be expressed in a roundabout way. One appropriate formulation is: $(\exists x)(x = a^*$ and Jones believes that x is an airedale).[35]

Note that if $\phi(x)$ is a complex formula containing many intensional operators $(x)\phi(x)$ will not in general imply $\phi(a^*)$; for if $\phi(x)$ is complex, the scope of a^* in the scopeless notation will not be interpreted as all of $\phi(a^*)$. Rather we will have $(x)\phi(x) \supset (\exists x)(x = a^* \wedge \phi(x))$ (or $(x)\phi(x) \wedge (\exists x)(x = a^*) \,.\supset.\, (\exists x)(x = a^* \wedge \phi(x))$ if empty terms are allowed). The reason for this complication is the absence of explicit scope indicators in the object language.

This leads to an important difference between the substitutional quantifier and the referential. If $(\Pi x)\phi(x)$ is interpreted as the infinite conjunction of all formulae $\phi(a^*)$, then of course $(\Pi x)\phi(x)$ *will* entail $\phi(a^*)$ no matter how complicated $\phi(a^*)$ is. Here $\phi(a^*)$ is *de dicto*; in each of its occurrences, a^* has minimum scope. The contrast with the referential quantifier is dramatic. Another contrast, mentioned already, is the possible truth of formulae such as (12).

Perhaps it would be worthwhile to mention in what the problem of referential quantification into intensional contexts consists. The problem does *not* consist in some kind of threatened collapse into extensionality, as in Wallace's argument; arguments attempting to show this have all turned on scope fallacies. (Indeed, given the modern model theory of intensional logic, it can be shown, wherever this theory applies, that such arguments *must* turn on scope fallacies.) The problem about such quantification lies elsewhere. Given an intensional unary sentence connective such as 'it is necessary that' or 'Jones believes that', it is consistent for a philosopher to hold that he understands this operator as applied to closed sentences, but not as applied to open sentences with free referential variables. To understand them, he would have to understand their satisfaction conditions. Even if a singular term 'a^*' denoting an object y is available, one cannot assume that y satisfies 'Jones believes Fx' or 'Necessarily Fx' if and only if '$F(a^*)$' expresses a belief of Jones or a necessary truth; for whether '$F(a^*)$' expresses either may be highly sensitive to the choice of the singular term 'a^*' to denote y, especially if

[35] Subtle differences may or may not appear between this roundabout formulation and a formulation with explicit scope notation, in connection with the issue of vacuous singular terms, depending on the conventions adopted. See Stalnaker and Thomason (1) and (2) for a theory in which the explicit scope indicators differ from the roundabout treatment. It seems to me that Stalnaker and Thomason somewhat exaggerate the importance of such distinctions, which in any case can be obliterated by a change of convention. I ignore them in the text.

definite descriptions are included. This much restates the opacity of such contexts and the distinction of *de dicto* and *de re*. Now some philosophers have felt that *de re* belief and *de re* necessity are unintelligible unless they are reduced to their *de dicto* counterparts, or at least, the entailment relations between a *de dicto* and a corresponding *de re* statement of modality or belief are clarified. Quine, for one, has emphasized his opinion that *de re* necessity ('essentialism') is unintelligible even if its *de dicto* counterpart were assumed intelligible.

None of these questions arise for the substitutional quantifier. In this case, the intelligibility of substitutional quantification into a belief or modal context is guaranteed provided the belief or modality is intelligible when applied to a closed sentence. The reason is that, in the theory of substitutional quantification as given by (4)–(6), the truth conditions of closed sentences always reduce to conditions on other closed sentences. As Quine has pointed out, even for a context as opaque as quotation, where no one thinks that satisfaction for referential variables makes any immediate sense, substitutional quantification is immediately intelligible. It was just such possibilities which were exploited in Section 5; and it is the ability to avoid all *de re* considerations and interpret quantifying into such contexts solely in terms of *de dicto* belief and modality which has been a principal motivation for interest in the use of substitutional quantification in such contexts.

The present writer, being primarily interested in the question of *de re* modality, is less attracted to substitutional quantification here, though of course I grant its intelligibility. Substitutional quantification is here, as always, not a *rival* theory to referential quantification but could be combined with it in a single system. Indeed we could imagine a system in which each and every term of the substitution class C denotes, and the domain D of the referential quantifiers coincides with the set of all denotata of terms in C. Even so, all the following schemata would have true instances if the language contains intensional operators:

(48a) $(\Sigma \mathrm{x}_1)(\exists x_1)(\mathrm{x}_1 = x_1 \wedge Fx_1 \wedge \sim F\mathrm{x}_1)$
(48b) $(\Sigma \mathrm{x}_1)(F\mathrm{x}_1) \wedge (x_1) \sim Fx_1$
(48c) $(\exists x_1)(Fx_1) \wedge (\Pi \mathrm{x}_1) \sim F\mathrm{x}_1$.

For example, for (48c), $(\Pi \mathrm{x}_1) \sim F\mathrm{x}_1$ is the infinite conjunction of all formulae $\sim Ft$, where each term has *innermost* scope, while $(\exists x_1)Fx_1$ will be true iff some instance $[t]Ft$ is true,where t has outermost

scope. If the context *Ft* contains intensional connectives, both may be true.

The reader should work this out, given an appropriate class of terms as substitutes and range for variables, depending on the considerations of the present section.

One might have supposed, given the way Wallace argues here, that he is unfamiliar with the received distinction between *de dicto* and *de re* as applied to belief. Others of his papers[36] show that he does not lack familiarity with the distinction. In these papers, he not only recognizes the distinction, but inclines to think that *de re* belief is not only intelligible but should be taken as the basic notion, without any demand that it should be reduced to *de dicto*. *Perhaps* he somehow is under the impression that the *de dicto–de re* distinction can be made out for the notation of intensional abstraction he borrows from Quine but cannot be made out in a notation which takes belief as a sentence connective. *If* this is his impression, he is mistaken.[37]

7. 'SUBSTITUTIONALISM'; WHICH QUANTIFIER IS 'RIGHT'?

Some have characterized my treatment of the metalanguage M' in Section 5 as follows: 'So you are saying that a substitutionalist could

[36] E.g. Wallace (4).

[37] Many of the matters concerning scope treated in this section are familiar, but Wallace's argument has led me to believe that even at this late date a brief exposition might not be superfluous. For a treatment of scope distinctions in modal contexts—which, however, antedates the modern model theory for modal logic and therefore does not deal with semantical matters—see Smullyan. For an elegant treatment in which singular terms are taken as primitive but a scope indicating device is present in the object language, see Stalnaker and Thomason (1) and (2). For a clear treatment where singular terms are taken as primitive but explicit scope indicating devices are absent—so that we need the kind of circumlocution mentioned in the text to get the effect of large scope—see Thomason. The paper by Thomason and the papers by Stalnaker and Thomason do not treat the connection between their languages with singular terms as primitive and the original scope devices of Russell. This is very unfortunate in both cases, since the motivation for various of the conditions they place on singular terms becomes clearer when it is observed that they are equivalent to conditions which provably obtain when singular terms are regarded as abbreviated notation in the manner of Russell. In Thomason's paper this leads to an exaggerated conception of the differences in expressive power between his treatment and a treatment such as that in Kripke, where singular terms and definite descriptions do not appear in primitive notation. In the Stalnaker and Thomason papers the absence of a comparison is especially surprising, since the explicit problem which motivates their elegant treatment is that of scope. It is true that both Thomason and Stalnaker and Thomason differ from Russell when vacuous singular terms are involved; but this is a relatively peripheral issue which should not obscure the fact that in many crucial respects the three styles of treatment say essentially the same thing.

As far as I know there are no published formal or model-theoretic treatments of substitutional quantification into modal contexts, and hence of the contrast with referential quantification indicated in the text. (See (48a)–(48c).) Such a rigorous treatment would be beyond the scope of this paper; perhaps I will undertake it elsewhere.

argue that the quantifiers in Wallace's metalanguage should be read substitutionally also.'

I would not construe Section 5 in this fashion. I do not know what philosophical position 'substitutionalism' is, but the treatment in Section 5 did not depend on any special philosophical position. I regard substitutional quantification and referential as both intelligible; as was emphasized in Section 4, a single language can contain both. In the present paper, we have distinguished the notions by two different notations.

Now the point of Section 5 was that, if a truth theory is to be homophonic, the metalanguage *must* contain the object language; and any formula in the object language must be interpreted in the metalanguage the same way as it was before. In particular, if certain variables in the object language are substitutional, they *must* remain so in the metalanguage. Therefore, the interpretation we gave for $Q(x, \alpha)$ is *forced* on us, since its first variable is substitutional. It is not just that we *need* not read it as Wallace does; we are *prohibited* from his referential reading. All this is a matter of correct logical procedure, not of a philosophical position.

I have often heard the issue of 'substitutionalism' put in the following way: 'Which quantifier is right, the substitutional or the referential?' Or alternatively, the query goes: 'What is the proper interpretation of the quantifier, referential or substitutional?' What can these queries mean? And what does the phrase 'the quantifier' mean in the second formulation?

One construal would refer the queries to some uninterpreted formal system or systems. If they refer to uninterpreted first-order quantification theory (the pure predicate calculus) the answer has already been given: both the substitutional and the standard interpretations make all theorems valid. If the formal system is some particular uninterpreted axiomatic first-order theory, such as elementary number theory or set theory, it is well known that often a variety of non-isomorphic standard (referential) interpretations make all the theorems true; and if appropriate terms are available, one or several substitutional interpretations may be possible. And of course, *other* interpretations, differing from both the 'referential' and the 'substitutional', are possible; for example, the 'Boolean-valued' interpretations mentioned in Section 1(*a*). The point is that an uninterpreted formal system is just that—uninterpreted; and it is impossible to ask for the 'right' interpretation.

Of course some particular formal systems may be incapable of a substitutional interpretation even though they have a referential one. As Quine has observed, if $(\exists x)\phi(x)$ is provable in the system but $\sim\phi(t)$ is provable for every expression t which can be substituted for x so as to yield a meaningful sentence $\phi(t)$, it is manifestly impossible to give the system a substitutional interpretation, but if its formation rules are standard and it is formally consistent a referential interpretation is possible. If $\sim\phi(t)$ is provable for every expression in a class of expressions C, while $(\exists x)\phi(x)$ is provable, it is impossible to make all the theorems true and interpret the quantifier as substitutional with substitution class C. These conditions are sufficient, but demonstrably not necessary, for a consistent first-order theory to lack a substitutional interpretation (or a substitutional interpretation with substitution class C) which makes all its theorems true.

What about the opposite problem? Are there theories which have a substitutional interpretation but no referential one? The possibility of regarding the terms as denoting autonymously, as mentioned at the end of Section 3, may suggest a negative answer, and indeed I think the possibility of such an interpretation is one reason why logicians whose interests are primarily mathematical have not felt called upon to explore substitutional quantification as a separate model–theoretic subject. In spite of this possibility, I think that there are cases where a substitutional intepretation is smooth and a referential interpretation is at least messier. Consider the case where the substitution class consists of sentences of L_0, as mentioned above. A referential interpretation of quantifiers with sentential substitutes guarantees philosophical controversy. Do the variables range over propositions, or perhaps sentences or truth values? Are the entities in the range *denoted* by sentences? Don't connectives now play a triple role, as sentence connectives, function symbols, and predicates? (In Frege's system, they *did* play such a triple role.) I by no means wish to prohibit or downgrade systems with, say, propositional quantifiers, nor to suggest that the philosophical objections to them are legitimate; and sometimes (if the restrictions on admissible substitution classes are violated) a substitutional interpretation won't be feasible anyway. But it is certainly true that it is easier, within otherwise conventional bounds, to give a substitutional interpretation of some such systems than to give a referential one. Even worse classes of substitutes can be devised. (See Section 1.) On the whole, whatever its applications to natural language, I think

substitutional quantification will yield a rich and interesting class of sophisticated systems not as easily interpretable in the orthodox referential manner.

If the system is, on the other hand, an interpreted formal system, then the interpretation will specify whether the variables and quantifiers are referential, substitutional, or something else. In some special cases, as we emphasized in Section 3, a substitutional interpretation may be 'equivalent' to a referential one. This fact is no more puzzling than the logical equivalence of $P \wedge P$ and $P \vee P$ and of $(\exists x)(\exists y)(Fx \wedge Fy)$ and $(\exists x)(\exists y)(Fx \vee Fy)$ in spite of the fact that conjunction and disjunction are different.

Finally, the issue may concern the correct interpretation of certain English expressions, such as perhaps 'there is a . . .', 'there are', 'there exists', etc. Now I cannot go into all the ramifications of this issue here, but several things may be meant. For example, the issue may be whether these expressions 'carry any ontological commitment'. But what can this issue be? Can there be a serious question whether someone who says 'there are men' or 'there exist such things as men' thereby commits himself to the view that *there are men* or that *there exist such things as men*? After all 'there exist men' is true if and only if *there exist men*; what further question can there be? Someone might *perhaps* maintain that 'there are' in various *special* usages may be interpreted as resembling the use of 'there are' in 'there are rabbits' only in 'surface grammar' and lacks any 'ontological commitment'; and he might even try a substitutional interpretation to make his point. It would be something else to argue that 'there are rabbits' is not true if and only if *there are rabbits*: to deny this is comparable to denying that 'John is tall' is true if and only if *John is tall.*

What indeed can the question whether 'there are rabbits' makes any 'ontological commitment' to rabbits mean? Wasn't the term 'ontological commitment' *defined* by such examples as 'there are rabbits'? No, it will be replied, ontological commitment was defined with respect to first-order referential languages, and the question is whether English should be interpreted by translation into such a language, or into a substitutional language which makes no ontological commitments. Not so. We did *not* learn quantification theory as our mother tongue. Somehow or other the weird notation '$(\exists x)$' was explained to us, by teachers or books, either by such examples as ' "$(\exists x)$ Rabbit (x)" means "*there is an* x which is a rabbit" ', or

by a formal definition of satisfaction, couched in English, such as the one above in this paper: 's satisfies "$(\exists x_i)$ Rabbit (x_i)" iff *there is an* s' differing from s in at most the ith place which satisfies "Rabbit (x_i)" '. And the quantifiers will be said to range over a *non-empty* domain D, where the technical term 'non-empty' is explained by saying that D is non-empty iff *there is an element* in D, or the equivalent. *If* the interpretation of the English 'there are' is completely in doubt, the interpretation of the formal referential quantifier, which depends on such explanations, must be in doubt also; perhaps the explanation the teacher used when he taught it to us was couched in a substitutional language, and we spoke such a language when we learned his interpretation! Perhaps referential quantifiers themselves are therefore really substitutional! Nonsense: we speak English, and the whole interpretation of the referential quantifiers was *defined* by reference to 'there are' in its standard employments. A Martian hearing us can doubt whether our assertion 'there are rabbits' makes any commitment to the existence of rabbits. *We* cannot doubt this.

None of this is to deny that *some* English usages which are superficially existential *may* really have another interpretation ('there is a good chance'? 'there are three feet in a yard'? etc.), or that the substitutional quantifier may play a role here. (In fact, I am sceptical about the role of the substitutional quantifier for interpreting natural language.) It *is* to say that anyone who doubts or denies that English has any resources for making genuinely existential assertions has cut the ground out from under his feet; he has no way even of *formulating* the question at issue. The alleged 'issue', then, is bogus.

Even aside from this consideration, isn't it clear that when we say 'there is a rabbit outside', there may be no name in our language, say 'Jones', which makes 'Jones is a rabbit outside' true? If we ask 'Is there life on Mars?', do we ask whether we can *name* any life on Mars? Is the question answered negatively if we can show that every sentence '——is alive on Mars', where the '——' is replaced by a name, is false? Even our hypothetical Martian, who understands no English, might soon be able to conclude by such observations that the English 'there are' is not in general a substitutional quantifier. (Wallace asks, at the end of Wallace (2), whether in ordinary language, 'everything has a name'. He regards this question as difficult; unlike the technical points made in his paper, it supposedly has as yet no definitive answer. On the contrary, isn't the answer obvious? Don't almost all things lack names in our language? (Consider grains

of sand, rabbits, stones, . . .) I am puzzled. Perhaps Wallace uses 'name' in some generalized sense, including, say, definite descriptions. But then the whole notion of substitutional quantification, as we defined it in Section 1, doesn't apply, because of the restriction that the terms must be given in advance of *L*. And it seems obvious to me that our existential assertions make no commitment to nameability even in this extended sense.)

Wallace concludes his discussion of substitutional quantification in Wallace (1), p. 237, as follows:

'The limits of substitutional quantification brought out in this section, if they are limits, are subtle. They do not bar someone from saying "there are men" and meaning that some substitution instance of "*x* is a man" is true-in-English. Of course not: *someone* might say "bububu" and mean that. But if someone's sentence does mean that, then it has the structure, ontology, and truth conditions that the sentence

(49) some substitution instance of "*x* is a man" is true-in-English

has in my language and not the structure and truth conditions the sentence

(50) there are men

has there.'

Now I do not understand this passage, nor do I see how it could possibly follow from the considerations which preceded it, even if—and we have seen that such is hardly the case—they are otherwise unexceptionable. Presumably 'my language' is English, and the argument is supposed to yield a non-trivial, substantive conclusion about English. Now, the conclusion might have been that in no *possible* language could 'there are men' have the truth conditions of (49); but such a conclusion Wallace quite rightly denies, and for the right reason. If so, presumably the conclusion is that *in English* (49) and (50) have different ontologies, structures, truth conditions, etc., even though in some possible language their truth conditions would have been the same. One would think that the conclusion, then, will depend on some empirical facts about English, as opposed to a logically possible other language. Yet in the preceding argument, not one empirical fact about English is mentioned, nor is

any special reference made to English; all the considerations are abstract considerations about truth definitions. Suppose Wallace had instead decided to draw some conclusion about German: if his argument worked, it should be possible to draw a substantive empirical conclusion about the German 'es gibt Menschen' without mentioning any specific empirical facts about German, an argument which could establish its conclusions to someone who understood no German and knew nothing about the linguistic habits of Germans! Surely such a procedure is absurd.

Perhaps Wallace's argument is supposed to be fleshed out with some empirical but unstated premisses about English, though it is hard for me to see what these might be, and they surely should have been stated explicitly. Perhaps, on the contrary, the 'my language' of (49) and (50) is not English, but some artificial language invented by Wallace (obviously similar, in some of its vocabulary and syntax, to English since, e.g., (50) is a sentence of both languages; and mysteriously referring to English in (49)). If so, surely Wallace should specify the syntax and semantics of this language, and explain how the preceding considerations of his paper are relevant to it, and why any conclusion about this artificial language is interesting.

8. WALLACE AND THARP ON SUBSTITUTIONAL NUMBER THEORY

In Wallace's second paper, Wallace (2), and in Tharp's paper, the burden of the argument is devoted to elementary number theory. Wallace and Tharp both argue that although to all appearances the (uninterpreted) system of elementary number theory can be interpreted substitutionally with an ontology of expressions alone, a closer analysis shows that this is not so; a covert appeal to an extra-linguistic ontology is said to be hidden in the substitutional definition. The discussion involves a large number of mathematical intricacies, which are said to yield the stated result. In this section, we discuss the conceptual basis of the Wallace–Tharp treatment of number theory; in the next section, we examine their mathematical arguments.

Now the Wallace–Tharp treatment of a substitutional truth definition for number theory follows a much simpler line than the formal lines of either Section 2 or Section 5. Wallace and Tharp, taking number theory as the object language, choose as the meta-language the extension of the object language formed by adding just one new predicate $T(x)$, interpreted as the truth predicate for the object language. They then discuss the problem of giving, on this

basis, a truth characterization, presumed to be the homophonic one. Since the object language is to be a part of the metalanguage, formulae not containing T(x) must be interpreted the same way in both.

Now an initial problem should be evident: how is the metalanguage supposed to be adequate for a truth theory of the object language, when unlike the languages of Sections 2 and 5 it contains no variables ranging over *expressions* of the object language, but only the variables of the object language?

The reader may well smile at the ignorance betrayed by the question. It is well known, it may be replied, that for object languages containing number theory new variables in the metalanguage are superfluous. Modern logic has shown this by the technique of *arithmetization.* Gödel showed that each expression of the object language can be correlated with a number, and that syntactic relations between expressions, under this correlation, correspond to arithmetical relations between numbers. This is the well-known technique of *arithmetization.* So, *provided the object language contains variables ranging over numbers (and associated arithmetical predicates) and the metalanguage contains the object language*, the technique of arithmetization shows that special variables in the metalanguage ranging over expressions of the object language are unnecessary.

The joker in this argument lies in the italicized phrase of its final sentence. It is *precisely under dispute* whether the object language (the formal system of number theory, substitutionally interpreted) contains variables ranging over the natural numbers, and whether the metalanguage needs variables ranging over numbers, or can get along with variables ranging over expressions alone. The view Wallace and Tharp oppose maintains that the object-language variables have no 'range' at all! Clearly, something has gone awry here. How can we treat the matter without begging all the crucial questions? First, the variables in the object language should be written substitutionally; the substitution class will consist of the numerals: 0, 0′, 0″, . . . The metalanguage does need referential variables, over expressions of the object language (for the need of these, see Section 2(a) above). Could we replace these, *via* a Gödel numbering, with referential variables ranging over numbers? No, because the whole *question* was whether an ontology of *numbers*, in the metalanguage, was needed in *addition* to an ontology of expressions: we cannot ask *this* question while we are identifying expressions with numbers.

Wallace and Tharp have thus begged the question twice: first by treating the object-language variables as referential variables ranging over numbers rather than as substitutional variables with numerals as substitutes; second, by taking the referential variables of the metalanguage to range over Gödel numbers instead of over strings of symbols of the object language. In ordinary contexts, identification of expressions with their Gödel numbers is harmless; the two structures are isomorphic and any differences other than structure are irrelevant for mathematical purposes. In the present context, however, where the question appears to be whether numbers need appear in the metalanguage in addition to expressions or whether the latter alone suffice (Tharp, for one, clearly formulates the problem in this way), we must be presupposing a point of view according to which numbers and expressions are distinct entities despite the identity of structure. (In any event, if the identification of numbers and expressions were the innocent technical device Wallace and Tharp assume it to be, nothing but convenience would be lost if we dropped the identification.)

There are two ways of doing the job properly. We can, as in Section 2, take the object language to be substitutional number theory with numerals as substitutes, and take the metalanguage to have only *referential* quantifiers over strings of symbols of the object language; in this case, we must forego homophony. Alternatively, in the style of Section 5, we can take the object language as before, but let the metalanguage contain both substitutional variables with numerals as substitutes *and* referential variables ranging over strings of symbols of the object language (neither could be replaced by referential variables over numbers, which do not appear in the metalanguage at all!); then we aim for a homophonic theory. If we take either alternative the result is clear. The homophonic treatment goes through smoothly, as a special case of Section 5. The non-homophonic treatment, as in Section 2, goes through smoothly also. We saw in Section 2 that the only danger of introducing an ontology other than one of expressions came if R(α) (truth for atomic sentences) was to be defined rather than taken as primitive. In the present case, the most decisive possible answer is forthcoming: R(α) (truth for atomic sentences of number theory) is definable in a purely syntactic manner with the apparatus of quantification over expressions, names for indecomposable symbols of the object language, concatenation, and identity alone. (This was the 'most favoured case'

of Section 2(*b*).) So no ontological problems can conceivably arise here: an ontology of expressions alone *is* sufficient for the truth theory.

Thus even if Wallace's and Tharp's mathematical claims were perfectly correct—and we will see in the next section that this is far from the case—their treatment would be rendered irrelevant by fundamental conceptual errors.[38] (In Wittgenstein's phrase, the 'decisive move in the conjuring trick' was made at an early and unnoticed point in the discussion.) The uninterpreted formal system of elementary number theory *can* receive a perfectly good substitutional interpretation. Moreover, if we are willing to assume an ontology of numbers and can thus set up the definition of satisfaction for referential number theory, with a modest logical apparatus we can prove that substitutional number theory and referential number theory have the same truths. To put the matter more exactly, sentences of substitutional number theory retain their truth values when the Σ and Π quantifiers are replaced by referential quantifiers interpreted as ranging over numbers (and the associated forms and functors are reinterpreted as predicate and function symbols, etc.).

How significant is this result? In my opinion, not very. As we said before, numbers and expressions *do* form essentially isomorphic structures. As Quine and others have often remarked, from the structural and mathematical point of view any progression can serve as the numbers. Such progressions are readily available in an ontology of expressions; if '*a*' is any symbol, the number *n* can easily be identified with a string of *n* consecutive *a*'s. Further, as Quine has shown (Quine (1)), the arithmetical operations such as addition and multiplication can be defined in terms of quantification over expressions, names of atomic expressions, concatenation, and identity alone. Any result using substitutional quantification to the effect that an ontology of numbers can be dispensed with in favour of an ontology of expressions is thus pretty idle from the mathematical point of view. The numbers could have been identified with expressions in the first place, or (using Gödel numbering) we could have done it the other way round. Substitutional quantification is irrelevant here.

[38] Of course there is nothing wrong with truth theories of the kind they treat if no ontological issue about numbers *vs.* expressions and referential *vs.* substitutional quantification is under dispute. Wallace attributes to Hilbert and Bernays a theory of the kind Wallace and Tharp use. I assume that Hilbert and Bernays gave such a theory independently of the issues Wallace and Tharp discuss.

One parting remark to illustrate the doubly question-begging aspect of Wallace's and Tharp's treatment of number theory. Both Wallace and Tharp lay great stress on a formula which they both read as 'every number is named by a numeral'. They attach great significance to the question whether this formula is used in the proofs of Tarski T-sentences. Now if the object language is read properly, that is substitutionally, the formula in question has the form $(\Pi x)(\Sigma y)A(x, y)$, where $A(x, y)$ is a binary form: any ontological reading of it is question-begging and incorrect. (The case of (19) above is similar except that here *all* the quantifiers are substitutional.) But even if the formula had been referential, $(x)(\exists y)A(x, y)$, the reading would be tendentious and misleading. As Wallace remarks (Wallace (1), p. 234) $A(x, y)$ is a simple numerical formula, say $y = 2{\cdot}3^x$, and $(x)(\exists y)A(x, y)$ is a trivial theorem of arithmetic. What significance can the use of this formula have in a proof that the use of any other arithmetical formula (say, the Chinese remainder theorem) would not have? The significance and interpretation Wallace and Tharp attach to the formula is imposed from the outside, *via* the identification of Gödel numbers with expressions. It has nothing to do with a straightforward reading of referential number theory itself.

9. MATHEMATICAL CLAIMS ABOUT FORMAL NUMBER THEORY

In this section, I wish to discuss, as independently as possible of the philosophical considerations of the previous section, some of the mathematical claims made in Wallace (2) and Tharp[39]. (Wallace will be discussed cursorily, for reasons stated below; Tharp at somewhat greater length.) I should emphasize that the preceding section was already enough to refute the Wallace–Tharp treatment of number theory. Here I wish to examine their technical claims.

The central technical claim of Wallace (2), on which he rests all his philosophical discussion, states that a certain 'naive' theory of truth fails to prove the Tarski T-sentences, while a certain sophisticated theory does so. The theories are stated in the manner indicated in the previous section: expressions are identified with their Gödel

[39] In this section I follow the convention of writing the variables in the italicized (referential) style. For the reasons in the preceding section, I regard the papers under discussion as systematically ambiguous between referential and substitutional interpretations of the quantifiers. Since such questions of interpretation are largely irrelevant to the purely mathematical issues, I will follow the convention stated above at the end of Section 1(*a*).

numbers, the metalanguage is supposed to contain the object language, yet somehow the quantifiers in the metalanguage are referential (over numbers) while those in the object language are substitutional (or are they?). At any rate, the formation rules of the metalanguage add a single predicate $T(x)$ to the object language, whose formation rules are those of number theory. The 'naive' theory of truth, which apparently fails to yield the T-sentences, is essentially the natural formalization, in these terms, of (4)–(6) (Section 2 above) for the inductive definition of substitutional quantification, plus a basis clause (x) (AtSent $(x) \supset (T(x) \equiv R(x))$), where $R(x)$ is a recursive number–theoretic predicate whose extension is the set of Gödel numbers of true atomic sentences. It is asserted—a fact which Wallace conjectured since 1968 but was proved only recently by Tharp—that the naive theory fails to yield the Tarski T-sentences. A 'sophisticated' theory, like the 'naive' theory except that the basis clause for the atomic sentences uses the so-called 'denotation' relation (actually a purely arithmetical relation), is said to yield the T-sentences. Doubts that *both* claims can be correct are immediate: the 'sophisticated' theory is just a reformulated form of the 'naive' theory, since the basis clause using the 'denotation' relation is obviously *equivalent* to a certain recursive characterization of the atomic sentences.

We need not dwell at length on the resolution of this contradiction. Wallace in Wallace (3), crediting the information to David Kaplan,[40] has acknowledged the falsity of most of his claims about the 'naive' theory. If a 'natural' recursive truth characterization is given for the atomic sentences, *all the Tarski T-sentences* $T(\bar{\phi}) \equiv \phi$ are derivable, contrary to Wallace's claim. Owing, however, to the Gödelian incompleteness of number theory, it is possible to find artificial recursive characterizations of atomic truth, which are coextensive with the 'natural' ones, but whose coextensiveness with these cannot be proved in number theory. The artificial characterizations sometimes have the following weakness: the homophonic sentences $T(\bar{\phi}) \equiv \phi$ may be unprovable, and all we are able to prove is $T(\bar{\phi}) \equiv \phi'$, where (i) ϕ' is a formula of the *object* language (not containing the 'T' predicate), and (ii) ϕ' is equivalent to ϕ, but the fact cannot be proved in formal number theory. It is arguable that even such an artificial theory represents a non-homophonic but legitimate

[40] I thank Kaplan for calling my attention to Wallace (2) and to the fact that its central theorem is erroneous.

truth theory for arithmetic, relative to a non-homophonic 'translation' of arithmetic into itself. At any rate, homophony is easily restored by the addition of a single true number–theoretic axiom asserting the coextensiveness of the artificial atomic truth characterization with a natural one. So the central technical claim of Wallace (2), which he constantly calls a 'hard logical fact' fatal to the substitutionalists, is in fact false. Since Wallace has now acknowledged the true situation, we omit the proofs.

Other technical claims apparently made in this paper are dubious as well. On p. 210, Wallace discusses whether the substitutional truth theory for analysis (second-order arithmetic) is true: apparently he means, whether every true existential statement of analysis is satisfied by a *nameable* (definable) real (set of integers). According to Wallace, 'the decision whether a naive substitutional theory is true . . . for analysis . . . seems to require determination, independent of an account of truth, of the ontology of the object language. And this seems difficult, really it is impossible.' This is 'what makes the controversy resist resolution'. (Wallace (2), p. 210.) If I have understood the question correctly, however, it is by no means lost in such a philosophical fog. The question whether every true existential formula of analysis is instantiated by a real definable in analysis is in fact demonstrably *independent* of the usual axioms for Zermelo-Fraenkel set theory. Various proposed additional axioms, however, such as the axiom of constructibility, imply an affirmative answer. However, for the reasons set forth in Section 1 above, even such an affirmative answer would not imply that a recursive substitutional truth definition coinciding with the (referential) notion of true sentence of analysis is possible; for a definition in terms of definable reals would not reduce more 'complex' cases to 'simple' ones (since the definitions of the reals may be arbitrarily complex). However, the question whether such a recursive substitutional definition is possible admits a sharp mathematical answer; see the next section. Usually I feel that Wallace and similar writers have an excessive tendency to try to reduce philosophical questions to technical ones. In this case Wallace seems to mix in vague philosophical considerations where the problem is precise and mathematical, and can be treated by precise techniques.

Now although Tharp and Wallace agree that Tharp has proved the main technical claim of Wallace (2), they don't appear to have read each other's papers carefully. In fact, Tharp correctly states that Wallace's 'naive' theory yields all the Tarski sentences (he calls the proof 'a routine logical exercise'), and his own result, which he mistakenly takes to be Wallace's conjecture in Wallace (2),[41] is different

[41] Tharp's theorem *is* relevant to Wallace's discussion in Wallace (1), which mentions truth theories which start by postulating $T(\bar{\phi}) \equiv \phi$ for each atomic ϕ. See Section 2(*b*) above.

and correct. The correct result is the following. If, in the 'naive' theory, we replace the recursive truth characterization for the atomic sentences by the infinite sequence of axioms $T(\bar{\phi}) \equiv \phi$ for each atomic formula ϕ, and leave all else unchanged (including the analogues of (4)–(6) above), the Tarski sentences $T(\bar{\phi}) \equiv \phi$ are no longer derivable for arbitrary ϕ, and remain underivable even if all true sentences of arithmetic are added. Tharp's proofs of these results use Gödel's theorem, modular arithmetic, and non-standard models. The philosophical reader may well tend to conclude that results requiring such sophisticated tools must have a deep and unsuspected significance. And it may be surprising that the infinite collection of sentences $\{T(\bar{\phi}) \equiv \phi\}$ for atomic ϕ, which together have the force of a truth characterization for the atomic sentences, should have less logical force than $(x)\,(\mathrm{AtSent}\,(x) \supset (T(x) \equiv R(x)))$.

Actually, the situation is not at all mysterious, and the use of sophisticated tools in Tharp's proofs is completely unnecessary. The following example illustrates the problem. Suppose we add to number theory a single primitive predicate $P(x)$, and take $P(0)$, $P(1)$, $P(2)$, . . . as new number-theoretic axioms. The new axioms have the force that $P(x)$ holds for each number; yet does $(x)P(x)$ follow by the usual deductive rules? Plainly it does not. A formal proof has only finitely many steps, and cites only finitely many axioms. So if $(x)P(x)$ were deducible, it would have to be deducible from a *finite* number of axioms $P(\boldsymbol{m}_1), \ldots, P(\boldsymbol{m}_n)$.[42] Clearly it is not deducible from a finite number of such instances; in fact, if we interpret $P(x)$ as true only of $m_1, \ldots, m_n$, each of the finitely many axioms will be true, but $(x)P(x)$ will be false. Similarly, one can prove, for example, that from $P(0)$, $P(2)$, $P(4)$, $P(6)$, . . . we cannot use the usual formal rules to deduce $(x)(\mathrm{Even}(x) \supset P(x))$.

Exactly the same phenomenon has arisen in Tharp's case. Tharp proposes to replace the general truth characterization $(x)(\mathrm{AtSent}(x) \supset (T(x) \equiv R(x)))$ by the infinite set of all statements $T(\bar{\phi}) \equiv \phi$ for each atomic ϕ; in effect, he proposes to replace the general statement by each of its instances.[43] Now it is easy to see that from this infinity

[42] If m is a number, $\boldsymbol{m}$ is the numeral in the formal language of number theory which denotes m.

[43] Literally, the instances of the general statement would be $\mathrm{AtSent}(\boldsymbol{m}) \supset .\ T(\boldsymbol{m}) \equiv R(\boldsymbol{m})$, for each m. We can show that this is equivalent to $T(\bar{\phi}) \equiv \phi$ for each atomic ϕ as follows. If m is not the Gödel number of an atomic formula, then $\sim(\mathrm{AtSent}(\boldsymbol{m}))$ is provable in number theory and the axiom $\mathrm{AtSent}(\boldsymbol{m}) \supset .\ T(\boldsymbol{m}) \equiv R(\boldsymbol{m})$ was already provable and therefore redundant. If m is the Gödel number of an atomic sentence ϕ, then the antecedent $\mathrm{AtSent}(\boldsymbol{m})$ is provable, so the axiom is

of axioms, not even (*) $T(\overline{(\exists x)(x \neq x)}) \equiv (\exists x)(x \neq x)$ can be deduced, even in the presence of recursive clauses like (4)–(6). If (*) were provable, since $\sim(\exists x)(x \neq x)$ is provable, we could also prove (**) $\sim T(\overline{\exists x)(x \neq x})$. Such a proof would have to use only finitely many axioms, $T(\overline{\phi_1}) \equiv \phi_1, \ldots, T(\overline{\phi_n}) \equiv \phi_n$, for particular atomic formulae $\phi_1, \ldots, \phi_n$. But this is manifestly impossible; to ascertain the falsity of $(\exists x)(x \neq x)$, we must know the truth value of *all* the atomic statements $0 = 0, 1 = 1, \ldots$ More rigorously, we give the following interpretation to the predicates: all predicates except 'T' are interpreted as usual. '$T(x)$' is interpreted as coinciding with truth in the ordinary sense for $\phi_1, \ldots, \phi_n$; it is false of (the Gödel numbers of) all other atomic formulae. For complex formulae, we then determine the extension of '$T(x)$' recursively by conditions (4)–(6). Clearly all the axioms (including $T(\bar{\phi}_1) \equiv \phi_1 \ldots, T(\bar{\phi}_n) \equiv \phi_n$, (4)–(6), all number–theoretic truths, and the induction schema) are satisfied, but $T(\overline{(\exists x)(x \neq x)})$ comes out *true* under the proposed interpretation, so (**) is not deducible. This is *all* that is required for a completely rigorous proof of Tharp's result.

Of course, if we allow an infinitary rule (the ω-rule) which infers a universal statement $(x)A(x)$ from its instances, $A(0), A(1), \ldots,$ then the problem no longer arises, either with our primitive predicate $P(x)$ or in Tharp's case. Nor can it be denied that Tharp's axioms *implicitly define* truth in the sense outlined above in Section 2 (see (i) in the beginning of the section); it is the *unique* predicate making the axioms true, the intended interpretation of the domain and the other predicates being fixed. The same holds for the axioms $P(0)$, $P(1), \ldots$; these *implicitly* define $P(x)$ as the predicate true of all numbers. From this point of view, both the non-derivability of $(x)P(x)$ from its instances and the non-derivability of the truth schema from Tharp's axioms reflect familiar deductive deficiencies of finitary systems.

Intuitively, the point can be put in terms of an analogy. A finite mind may well be able to verify each statement $P(0), P(1), \ldots$ without knowing $(x)P(x)$ (e.g., an oracle tells him each instance when asked, but not the generalization; or $P(x)$ means 'x is not an even number which fails to be the sum of two primes', and each instance

---

equivalent to its consequent $T(m) \equiv R(m)$. Since m is the Gödel number of ϕ, this can be rewritten equivalently as $T(\bar{\phi}) \equiv R(\bar{\phi})$. Since $R(\bar{\phi}) \equiv \phi$ is provable for any atomic ϕ, this last formula is equivalent to $T(\bar{\phi}) \equiv \phi$.

is verifiable by computation but the general statement has not been proved). The reason is that a finite mind will know only finitely many statements at a time. Such a situation is well formalized by the usual finitary rules. A mind who can somehow 'survey' all the instances together, rather than just knowing a finite number at a time, will know $(x)P(x)$; in effect, he has the ω-rule. The same comments differentiate between a hearer who in any finite time can be told $\mathrm{T}(\bar{\phi}) \equiv \phi$ for each particular (atomic) ϕ, and one who has a general truth characterization for all atomic sentences.

Wallace and Tharp are plainly quite aware that even in Tharp's theory, the ω-rule would suffice to deduce all the required T-sentences; also that truth has been implicitly defined. Why don't they discuss whether their criteria are not too strict, and one or both of these conditions sufficient? With respect to the ω-rule Wallace is confident that Tarski prohibits any such rule, that the ω-rule could not be used in a truth theory, and that only the usual first-order rules may be allowed. (See Wallace (2), p. 201, (3).) Perhaps some of Tarski may have led to such an interpretation,[44] but actually there is considerable contrary evidence in Tarski. In p. 258, last sentence, to p. 261, top, Tarski advocates introducing the ω-rule into the theory of truth at some length. In another paper, 'On the concept of logical consequence', pp. 409–11, Tarski argues that any concept of logical consequence that does not include the ω-rule is inadequate. Of course Tarski's views are by no means sacrosanct, and Wallace may well have good arguments for requiring finitary rules (say, 'since our minds are finite'). However, Wallace would have done better to give these arguments and not simply cite Tarski as authority for his own restrictions. We would discuss this matter further were it not that the question of the ω-rule seems largely irrelevant, since we could have started out with the axiom $(x)(\mathrm{AtSent}(x) \supset (\mathrm{T}(x) \equiv \mathrm{R}(x)))$ to begin with.

The main question is: what significance does all this have for substitutional quantification? After all, exactly the same problems would arise for *referential* quantification if someone insisted on replacing the characterization of satisfaction for primitive predicates by its instances: for instance, we replace $(x)(y)(\mathrm{Sat}(\langle x, y\rangle, \overline{w = z}) \equiv x = y)$ by $\mathrm{Sat}(\langle 0, 0\rangle, \overline{w = z})$, $\mathrm{Sat}(\langle 1, 1\rangle, \overline{w = z})$, . . ., $\sim\mathrm{Sat}(\langle 0, 1\rangle, \overline{w = z})$, $\sim\mathrm{Sat}(\langle m, n\rangle, \overline{w = z})$(for $m \neq n$), etc. Why is

[44] For example, in his paper 'Some observations on the concepts of ω-consistency and ω-completeness', pp. 294–5, Tarski speaks much more negatively about the ω-rule than he does in the passages I cite in the text. And of course there are passages where he defines 'consequence' by the usual deductive rules.

the phenomenon of special interest in the substitutional case?[45] Perhaps to show that an inductive substitutional definition of truth in number theory is impossible without a definition of atomic truth? We hardly needed Tharp's theorem for that; *no* inductive definition is possible unless it starts out with a general characterization of the atomic (basis) case.

Tharp proves a correct theorem; he suggests that philosophically significant conclusions follow. What is unstated is exactly *what* the philosophical conclusions are, and *how* they follow from the theorem. Surely even in the present technically oriented period of philosophy, such a task is not dispensable. As we have quoted in the beginning of this paper, Tharp regards his result as showing that there 'appear to be difficult technical problems' in constructing substitutional definitions without appealing to a range for the quantifiers. His result, however, is irrelevant to the quite general treatment in Sections 2 and 5 above. Tharp is far from the first mathematician to be led into an excessively complicated proof of a simple theorem (it has happened to the best), but in the present instance the complications obscure the fact that Tharp's result is merely a special case of a simple general situation, unlikely to be of much philosophical interest and having no special relation to substitutional quantification, or even to truth theories, as such. The phenomenon in question can be expected to arise *whenever* a universal axiom is replaced by its particular instances. (See the next section for further discussion.)

So, aside from the problems of Section 7, Wallace's main result on number theory is startling but false, while Tharp's is true but obvious and of no special relevance to substitutional quantification.

10. TRUTH AND SATISFACTION

Another interpretation of Wallace's and Tharp's papers is possible, which is compatible with a great deal, though not all, of what they say, and is at any rate of some technical interest. This interpretation takes them to be dealing with referential object languages, *not* (as they seem to say) substitutional object languages. Consider the following problem about *referential* quantification. Tarski defines truth for languages based on referential quantification not directly, but *via* a recursive definition of satisfaction. Would it have been

[45] It escapes me why, in papers where finite axiomatizability and non-triviality are usually at a premium, it is suddenly demanded that the single axiom $(x)(\mathrm{AtSent}(x) \supset . (\mathrm{T}(x) \equiv \mathrm{R}(x)))$ be replaced by the infinity of axioms $\mathrm{T}(\bar{\phi}) \equiv \phi$ for atomic ϕ.

possible for him to avoid it, and define truth directly? If so, would satisfaction be definable in terms of truth?

These questions, which seem to be a leading theme of Wallace (1), concern languages formulated using *referential* quantifiers, *not* substitutional quantifiers. But substitutional quantification comes in as follows: The truth definition for substitutional quantification proceeds by a direct recursion on truth. But we have seen above (Section 3; for number theory, Section 8) that under certain conditions the true sentences under a referential interpretation of the quantifiers satisfy the recursive clauses of a substitutional truth definition. To put the matter differently, if the universal and existential quantifiers over the domain are *reinterpreted* as substitutional quantifiers (of the Π and Σ type) with a given substitution class, exactly the same formulae become true. In this case we can use the *substitutional* recursive clauses to give an *extensionally correct* recursive characterization of truth for the *referential* object language.

Now in some cases it is certainly possible to give a metalanguage where truth is definable (for a given referential object language) but satisfaction is not. For example, since (as Tarski has shown) the elementary theory of the reals is complete and decidable, if we Gödel number expressions (harmless here!), truth for the elementary language of the reals is definable in elementary number theory: in fact, it is a recursive predicate. But satisfaction of course is not *definable* since the required ontology (the reals) is not available in the metalanguage. Even if the set of true sentences of a language were not recursive but arithmetical, the set of truths would be definable in number theory, but satisfaction would not be, if the associated ontology outstrips that of number theory.[46] In general, the set of true sentences will be definable in various metalanguages whose ontology is just the integers (for example, metalanguages taking truth for the object language as a primitive predicate!). Satisfaction will not be definable unless the ontology of the object language is just the integers. So if the problem is whether 'every truth definition necessarily . . . yields . . . a definition of satisfaction' (Tharp, pp. 363–4), the answer is surely negative. (Tharp himself mentions one counterexample.)

Wallace's and Tharp's discussions, however, indicate that they

[46] Such examples are easily constructed. I mention them because Wallace does concede (Wallace (1), footnote 25) that his theses do not apply to languages with an effectively decidable truth predicate. If he concedes this, he should clearly have made the same concession at least for languages with an arithmetical truth predicate.

have a somewhat different question in mind. Their problem can be appreciated this way. Suppose, in a favoured case, a substitutional recursion defines a truth concept coextensive with a referential one. Then the definition can be carried out by a recursion on truth alone; and a formal truth theory can be given along the lines of Section 2. Let us suppose that the $R(x)$ of the basis clause is taken as primitive. Such a truth theory contains only referential quantifiers over expressions of the object language and therefore (except in the exceptional case where this ontology is adequate) contains no concept of satisfaction.

Suppose we wish, however, not merely to give an extensionally correct substitutional truth definition for a referential object language but to *show* that it coincides in extension with the referential truth definition. If we wish to do so, we must plainly extend the metalanguage. There are two possibilities. (i) We could explicitly introduce the referential truth predicate also and try to add formal axioms which imply the coextensiveness. That is, we already have $T_1(\alpha)$, satisfying the substitutional clauses above: suppose we introduce another predicate $T_2(\alpha)$, satisfying the recursive clauses of a *referential* truth theory. (To do this, we must introduce a primitive predicate of satisfaction, since this is the subject of the recursion, and define $T_2(\alpha)$ in terms of it. Quantifiers over the domain of the object language must be introduced into the metalanguage to do this.) We can then ask for new axioms which will imply $(\alpha)(T_1(\alpha) \equiv T_2(\alpha))$. (ii) Suppose we extend the original metalanguage (with $T_1(\alpha)$) *only* to contain the object language in addition; so that the extended metalanguage contains two styles of referential quantifier, one over expressions of the object language and one over the domain of the object language. Then we cannot express $(\alpha)(T_1(\alpha) \equiv T_2(\alpha))$, since $T_2(\alpha)$ is no longer in the metalanguage. But we still can get a similar effect by considering the infinite set of statements $T_1(\bar{\phi}) \equiv \phi$ for each closed formula ϕ of the object language. We can see this in two ways. First, if satisfaction, with the appropriate recursive clauses, and $T_2(\alpha)$ were defined, then $T_2(\bar{\phi}) \equiv \phi$ will be provable for each ϕ; so $T_1(\bar{\phi}) \equiv \phi$ will be provable for each particular ϕ if and only if $T_1(\bar{\phi}) \equiv T_2(\bar{\phi})$ is provable for each ϕ. So the relation of $T_1(\bar{\phi}) \equiv \phi$ for each ϕ to $(\alpha)(T_1(\alpha) \equiv T_2(\alpha))$ is, in effect, similar to the relation, discussed in Section 9, of a universal statement to its instances. To put the matter differently: for any particular statement ϕ in any language, and any predicate $A(x)$, to say $A(\bar{\phi}) \equiv \phi$ is to say that $A(x)$

coincides with truth as far as ϕ is concerned; if $A(\bar{\phi}) \equiv \phi$ is a schema correct for all ϕ, then $A(x)$ is coextensive with truth. In the case at hand, since the ϕ's are interpreted referentially, *all* statements of the form $T_1(\bar{\phi}) \equiv \phi$ will be true if and only if the substitutional truth characterization is coextensive with the referential one. Except for the caveats of Section 8, we have in effect found a way of asking the question of the coextensiveness of the substitutional and the referential truth characterizations without explicitly introducing the latter concept.

Suppose we try to prove the coextensiveness, as formulated in either (i) or (ii). We have already extended the formation rules of the metalanguage beyond those of Section 2; do we need additional axioms beyond the axioms of Section 2? Of course we do. Those axioms merely guaranteed that substitutional truth be recursively characterized; they said nothing about its coextensiveness with referential quantifiers over any specified domain. And there is, of course, no general theorem to the effect that a substitutional quantifier with an *arbitrary* substitution class yields the same truths as a referential quantifier over an *arbitrary* (unrelated!) domain; some stipulation must connect the two. A necessary and sufficient condition for the coextensiveness was given in Section 3; referential and substitutional quantification, for a given domain D and substitution class C, will be coextensive if and only if the *referential* quantifier satisfies the analogue of clause (6) above for C (an existential formula is true if a substitution instance is). Such an axiom, however, obviously cannot be expressed directly in the metalanguage contemplated under (ii) above. However, as stated also in Section 3, usually we think in terms of two simple *sufficient* conditions connecting the domain and the substitution class: that every element of the domain be denoted by an element of the substitution class, and that every element of the substitution class denote an element of the domain. Symbolically, if 'Den(x, α)' means 'x is denoted by α' and is added to the notation of the metalanguage:

(51) $(x)(\exists\alpha)(\text{Term}(\alpha) \wedge \text{Den}(x, \alpha))$.

(52) $(\alpha)(\text{Term}(\alpha) \supset (\exists x)\text{Den}(x, \alpha))$.

Wallace postulates precisely these two conditions. (Actually, he seems to suppose that the second is derived from more basic axioms.) Other axioms tell us what the denotations of particular terms are.

Wallace stresses the necessity of adding a primitive relation of denotation and a postulate such as (51).

About this argument, some initial comments. First, this interpretation of Wallace's discussion in Wallace (1) must be carefully distinguished from the interpretation given above in Sections 2 and 5. (Both interpretations are supportable from his text.) In those sections, we took Wallace to be dealing with a *substitutional* object language, and to be arguing that a proper truth theory somehow collapses it into a referential one: there we judged Wallace's arguments to be inadequate, and, in particular to *misidentify* a certain form $Q(\mathrm{x}, \alpha)$ as a denotation predicate (indeed, as a binary predicate at all). In the present section, Wallace is interpreted as dealing with an admittedly *referential* object language, and the 'denotation' relation is *not* misidentified. There is no question of *proving* the 'surprising' conclusion that the object language is referential, for this 'conclusion' is *assumed*. Second, the ontological questions are settled by stipulation. It is *assumed* that the variables of the object language range at least over the domain D, and that the metalanguage contains the object language. So our metalanguage, even before 'denotation' is introduced, takes the ontology of the object language for granted. Third, the conclusion is not particularly that a denotation relation and the assumption (51) are needed for the substitutional recursion. It is rather that, *to prove that substitutional truth coincides with referential truth*, we need some additional assumptions, the most natural method being to introduce a denotation relation and (51). Once Wallace's conclusion is formulated in this way, it is a result that I at least assumed everyone knew from the outset. Wallace's argument may trade on its oscillation, in his own mind and the reader's, between an argument for dramatic but false conclusions about a substitutional object language and an argument for (more or less) correct but weak conclusions about a referential object language.

Even here, Wallace's conclusions are a bit too strong. Wallace argues that, since denotation is available, we can define, say, '$\mathrm{Sat}_1(x, \overline{A(y)})$' by '$(\exists\alpha)(\mathrm{Den}(x, \alpha) \wedge \mathrm{T}_1(\overline{A(\alpha)})$', and can even prove the schema (*) $\mathrm{Sat}_1(x, \overline{A(y)}) \equiv A(x))$ using (51). The same method allows us to define $\mathrm{Sat}_n(x_1, \ldots, x_n, \overline{A(y_1, \ldots y_n)})$ for each *fixed n*. Here, however, we don't have a single satisfaction relation, but a different n-place relation for each n. Satisfaction in Tarski's sense (and Wallace's) is by infinite *sequences* of objects of the domain D

of the object language, and these are not available in the ontology of the metalanguage, which needs only quantifiers over the domain and over expressions. Indeed if D is denumerable, the infinite sequences of objects in D are non-denumerable in number and therefore cannot all be mapped in $1 - 1$ fashion into D. So not even a coding device (or 'ontological reduction') could possibly construe all the infinite sequences of elements of D as elements of D. Note that it is the single satisfaction predicate, not the infinitely many distinct predicates, which is needed for a recursive theory of referential truth. (So even here it is untrue that the theory enables us to define all the predicates and ontology used in the standard satisfaction recursion; in fact it gets along with a somewhat weaker ontology.)

We could improve the situation by changing the notion of satisfaction. A slightly more cumbersome notion, still workable for a recursive characterization of referential truth, takes sequences of elements of D of arbitrary *finite* length as satisfiers. Even these are not in the ontology of the object language, but at least cardinality considerations will not be a problem for coding if D is infinite. Even so, there may be nothing in the vocabulary of the metalanguage which suffices to code the finite sequences of elements of D into elements of D. What we can do is represent any finite sequence of expressions by an expression. We can then define a finite sequence $\langle t_1, \ldots, t_n \rangle$ of terms as 'satisfying' a formula $A(x_1, \ldots, x_n)$ if $A(t_1, \ldots, t_n)$ is true. Really this relation is a purely linguistic relation between expressions and could have been defined without reference to the ontology of the object language at all. But when the denotation relation is available, we can define, for a finite sequence of terms σ, a function $\psi(m, \sigma)$ giving the denotation of the mth term of the sequence. In this way, finite sequences of terms can in a sense be thought of as representing finite sequences of objects (in a many-one fashion). Nevertheless, the situation regarding satisfaction is more delicate than Wallace suggests. Indeed a satisfaction predicate of the usual Tarskian kind is unavailable still.

The Wallace–Tharp treatment of number theory, even interpreted from the point of view of the present section, has special problems. Their convention of assuming that the object-language variables range over numbers and identifying expressions with their Gödel numbers is not nearly so bad as it was when number theory was interpreted as substitutional. Under the present referential interpretation of the object language, the variables do indeed range over

numbers. Perhaps it may seem innocuous to identify expressions with their Gödel numbers, so that the metalanguage can contain the object language in a simple way (only one new predicate). However, the interesting part of Wallace's argument was that to prove $T_1(\bar{\phi}) \equiv \phi$ for each ϕ we must *adjoin* a denotation relation to the metalanguage and an axiom $(x)(\exists\alpha)(\mathrm{Den}(x, \alpha))$. In the treatment of number theory all these questions are simply begged. Denotation is identified with a simple recursive relation between numbers, which was already in the object language anyway, such as $y = 2{\cdot}3^x$. The new axiom becomes a truth of arithmetic such as $(x)(\exists y)(y = 2{\cdot}3^x)$, easily proved in number theory. Wallace and Tharp are aware of these facts, but they do not conclude, as they should have, that key questions are being begged by the convention of Gödel numbering, innocuous as it may be in most contexts. It would have been better to set up a metalanguage with two styles of variables, one for numbers and another for expressions, so as to avoid begging questions as nearly as possible.

Second, Tharp in particular states the problem in a non-standard terminology which was highly confusing at least to the present reader. As I recalled above, he states that the general problem is whether 'every truth definition . . . yields . . . a definition of satisfaction'. For the special case of number theory, Tharp first proves that his own theory with infinitely many axioms $T(\bar{\phi}) \equiv \phi$ for atomic ϕ fails to yield the T-sentences. He then comments: 'the workable substitutional truth definition (theory?—S.K.), which states the base case in a general way . . ., differs only in appearance from a definition explicitly in terms of satisfaction. One may define the predicate "y satisfies x" by saying that the formula which results from substituting the numeral for y in x is true. It seems likely that any reasonably natural definition of truth along substitutional lines which yields the Tarski biconditionals will use the fact that every element is named by a numeral, and so yield a definition of satisfaction' (p. 368). All this is puzzling. First, no matter what the deductive strength of the truth theory (in particular, even if it is Tharp's unsuccessful theory), we can *always* define satisfaction (really, not satisfaction but the binary relation called 'Sat_1' above) by 'saying that the formula which results from substituting the numeral for y in x is true'. This definition is always *there*, and satisfaction is always *definable* in terms of truth (all the auxiliary apparatus is purely number–theoretic, thanks to the 'innocuous' identification of expressions with Gödel

numbers), regardless of any axioms. Tharp seems to write as if (explicit) definability were a matter of what axioms are assumed, when it is of course a matter of the *expressive power* of the *language* rather than the *deductive power* of a *theory*. Nor do Tharp's comments make sense when interpreted as about *implicit* definability, which *is* dependent on the axioms of a theory. As Tharp is well aware, even the axioms of his *unsuccessful* theory implicitly define truth, in the sense that truth is the only interpretation of the predicate $T(x)$ which makes all the axioms true (the range of the quantifiers, and the interpretations of the number-theoretic predicates, being fixed as standard). Satisfaction (really, here, Sat_1), being explicitly definable from truth, is implicitly defined also.

Although Tharp constantly speaks of *definability*[47], he really is obviously thinking of provability. He is not really asking whether the *predicate* Sat_1 is *definable* in terms of truth, but whether all instances of the *schema* (*) $\mathrm{Sat}_1(x, \overline{\phi(y)}) \equiv \phi(x)$ are *provable* in the theory. Yet his account is still puzzling. 'It seems likely that any reasonably natural definition (should read: theory—S.K.) of truth along substitutional lines which yields the Tarski biconditionals will use the fact that every element is named by a numeral, and so yield a definition (theory!—S.K.) of satisfaction.' What does it matter what facts the proof of the Tarski biconditionals uses? Thanks to the identification of expressions and Gödel numbers, the fact in question is *there*, *provable* in number theory; it will be present to help prove the schema (*) whether it was used to prove the Tarski biconditionals or not.

Tharp writes: 'One would expect the problem of giving an interesting definition of substitutional quantification . . . to be related to the problem of defining truth without defining satisfaction. If one could define truth directly, appealing only to linguistic objects . . . this would be demonstrably different from the usual definition if one could show that no definition of satisfaction emerges. Unfortunately there appear to be difficult technical problems in constructing such definitions . . .' Once again 'definition' seems to be used in a non-standard way. Tharp really seems to be asking, not whether truth can be defined without defining satisfaction, but whether all instances of the Tarski T-schema can be provable without all instances of (*)

[47] In the *third* section of his paper, page 370, discussing another topic, Tharp indicates that he is well aware of the received terminology on definability *vs.* provability, and uses it. ('Our negative result is a matter of definability and not merely provability.') This fact makes his loose terminology in the second section all the more puzzling.

being provable (for a suitable definition of Sat_1), in a finitely axiomatizable theory. (He had already shown this possible without the finite axiomatizability requirement.) In particular, he seems to write as if some 'substitutionalists' had hoped, asserted, or presupposed that his unsuccessful theory would be an example of this, a conjecture he refutes by showing it doesn't yield Tarski's schema in general. Now I know of no one in particular whose hopes were dashed in this way. But it should be clear that any such hopes would in any event have been misguided. Suppose some finitely axiomatizable extension of number theory *did* yield the Tarski T-sentences $T(\bar{\phi}) \equiv \phi$ for each closed ϕ, but not the schema (*) for Sat_1. Would this phenomenon be a virtue, or make it an interesting theory? $\text{Sat}_1(x, y)$ is explicitly definable in terms of $T(x)$. Since all sentences $T(\bar{\phi}) \equiv \phi$ are derivable, the predicate $T(x)$ can only be interpreted as truth, and $\text{Sat}_1(x)$ can only be interpreted as satisfaction (for one variable). So the formulae (*), whether or not *derivable*, are all *true* (and would be derivable if we had an ω-rule). If they are not derivable, this only indicates the deductive weakness of the theory, not that in some interesting sense truth is definable but satisfaction is not.

The question Wallace and Tharp are trying to answer here about substitutional number theories can be answered rather sharply, and favourably to their desires.[48] Suppose we adjoin the single primitive predicate $T(x)$ to number theory, and extend the axioms of number theory by adding the induction schema for formulae in the extended language,[49] the Tarski schema $T(\bar{\phi}) \equiv \phi$ for each ϕ, and the arithmetized analogues of (4)–(6). *Then each instance of the schema* (*) *is formally derivable.* (I omit the proof, which is elementary but rather long). No wonder it proves difficult to find a theory which implies each of these axioms without implying (*)! The proof, however, depends heavily on particular properties of number theory, even on the identification of expressions with Gödel numbers, and I have no idea of any extension to more general contexts. Further, the result fails if only the formulae $T(\bar{\phi}) \equiv \phi$ are taken as axioms, without assuming (4)–(6).[50] (The proof of this is similar to that of Tharp's result in Section 9.) For all I know, some finitely axiomatizable

[48] The proofs they give at most would show that certain attempts (not particularly plausible ones!) to prove the T-sentences without (*) fail. There is little evidence given that another attempt wouldn't succeed.

[49] This is Wallace's standard relaxation of the finite axiomatizability requirement for number theory. We allow the induction schema plus finitely many additional axioms.

[50] The proof also depends upon the presence of the induction schema.

theory, in the vocabulary of number theory plus T(x), implies T($\bar{\phi}$) $\equiv \phi$ for each ϕ without implying all instances of (*). If so, however, such a theory does not yield an interesting 'definition of truth without defining satisfaction'. It will fail to prove some formula which must be *true* in any standard models of its axioms; perhaps it may even lack standard models altogether. It will be a piece of pathology of purely technical interest.

These questions about number theory aside, Wallace has raised an interesting technical question: Under what conditions, if any, can a finitely axiomatizable theory, couched in a metalanguage containing a referential object language, yield all sentences T($\bar{\phi}$) $\equiv \phi$, without yielding, for some predicate '$\mathrm{Sat}_1(x, y)$' of the metalanguage, a corresponding (one-variable) satisfaction schema like (*) (and its generalization to n variables, for each n)? Wallace essentially discusses one particular way of doing this (substitutional quantification, plus a denotation relation, with (51)). Surely, however, he does not expect this to be the most general situation. Tharp writes: 'I must confess that although it seems extremely plausible to me that there should be reasonable examples (where we have the T-schema but not (*)), I have been unable to find one'. My own confession is even more embarrassing. If my memory is correct, a few years ago, when I first worked on the problems of this paper, I found some interesting examples. Now I find myself unable to recall either the examples or their proofs.

What philosophical morals can be drawn? In the concluding section of Wallace (1), he draws (p. 248) ontological conclusions: any finitely axiomatized truth theory 'reads concepts, objects, and identity into the language interpreted'. We have seen in previous sections that any such conclusion is unjustified for substitutional object languages: on the interpretation in the present section, the object languages are *assumed* to be referential, and the metalanguages are *postulated* to contain the ontology of the object languages, so all ontological questions are settled *in advance*. Another philosophical interpretation of the results seems to be suggested by Davidson (2). This paper suggests (p. 758) that 'the semantic theory of truth as developed by Tarski deserves to be called a correspondence theory because of the part played by the concept of satisfaction; for clearly what has been done is that the property of being true has been explained . . . in terms of a relation between language and something else'. In the spirit of this view, perhaps attempts to get a direct

recursive definition of truth, without any auxiliary concept such as satisfaction, could be said to correspond to a 'coherence' theory of truth, since the truth of any one sentence will depend only on the truth of others.[51] The issue will then not be whether certain entities *exist*, nor whether the variables of the object language range over them, but whether they must be invoked to define truth. Wallace's discussion could then be taken thus: For certain referential languages a substitutional (therefore 'coherentist') characterization of truth is coextensive with the satisfaction definition. To prove the co-extensiveness of this coherentist definition with a referential truth definition for each ϕ (i.e. of $T(\bar{\phi}) \equiv \phi$ for each ϕ), we may often need to invoke a relation of denotation, and thus a certain relation between language and the world, after all.

If we confine ourselves to special referential theories, however, stronger results can be stated. A simple one was first pointed out to me by Harvey Friedman, and is very closely related to a result stated by Tharp in his paper. Suppose the ontology of the language includes all sets of integers (or sets of expressions, if we do not identify expressions with integers), and that membership of a number in a set of numbers is expressible in the object language. Then no finite set of axioms, with $T(x)$ as sole additional predicate, implicitly defines the set of (Gödel numbers of) true sentences of the object language. Suppose some finite set of axioms implicitly defined truth, in the sense that the set of truths was the unique interpretation of $T(x)$ making all the axioms true (or even in the sense that any two interpretations of $T(x)$ coincide with the truths on the integers). Let A be the conjunction of all these axioms, and let A' come from A by replacing '$T(x)$' throughout by '$x \in y$', where 'y' is a new variable. Then we could explicitly define truth by the formula $(\exists y)(A' \wedge x \in y)$, contrary to the theorem on the indefinability of truth. A similar argument can prove that truth is not implicitly definable even with the aid of auxiliary predicates, provided that these auxiliary predicates are true of numbers only.

Tharp proves (p. 365 of his paper) a very similar result by very similar methods, but the conclusion he states is (roughly) that no finite set of axioms involving $T(x)$ alone, or $T(x)$ with auxiliary predicates of numbers alone, can yield the T-sentences by the usual deductive rules. Since some axioms implicitly define truth without

[51] I do *not* wish to *commit* either Davidson or myself to this correspondence. It does seem to be in the spirit of Davidson (2).

actually yielding the T-sentences in this sense (see, e.g., Tharp's unsuccessful theory, or the case Wallace treats, where denotation and the additional axioms are needed for the proof of the T-sentences, but not for the implicit definition), the result is stated in a somewhat weaker form than necessary. It would have been equivalent had he allowed the ω-rule. The present result shows that no direct recursive definition of truth is possible, not just that the T-sentences will not be formally derivable. It seems stronger, for languages of the kind specified, than Wallace's results, for this reason and also for the reason that Wallace nowhere argues that the T-sentences may not be derivable by other methods than the one he gives.

For a large and significant class of referential languages, the result of Friedman and Tharp shows that no direct recursion on the concept of truth, or on other properties of expressions, would implicitly define truth over the object language. This certainly illuminates (in my opinion, better than Wallace's remarks) the question why Tarski was forced to do his recursion on some concept, like that of satisfaction, which defines a relation between expressions and other objects. Does it support the correspondence theory against the coherence theory? The result is indeed suggestive, but we should be cautious in giving a philosophical interpretation to a technical result. Even slight changes in technical definitions can change the technical situation greatly; and perhaps another technical notion might be as suggestive a model for the coherence theory as the present one. The surest way of examining coherence theories must still be by a direct examination of the actual arguments and doctrines of their historical advocates. Although I have not done so, I suspect that such an examination would reveal that no sophisticated technical result is needed to refute them.

A concluding technical note: I suspect that many readers of Wallace's paper have thought that the necessity of such additional axioms as (19), (51), and (52) for homophonic truth theories is a special feature of substitutional truth theories: homophonic referential theories proceed by direct application of the recursive clauses, while Wallace has exposed the common illusion that substitutional truth theories can do this. Such a contrast is incorrect. We saw in Section 2(*b*) that the recursive clauses plus a basis clause yield a perfectly good non-homophonic substitutional truth theory. On the other hand, if we are interested in homophony, the standard treatment of referential truth theories if anything requires even more special additional axioms (beyond the basis and recursive clauses) than do the substitutional theories of Section 5 and the present section. First, as I

mentioned above (p. 357), referential theories naturally yield roughly such T-sentences as

$$T(\overline{(x)Fx_1}) \equiv (\exists s)(\text{Sequence}(s) \wedge (s')((\text{Sequence}(s') \wedge s \approx s') \supset F(\text{first-term-of-}s'))).$$

But there is yet a further problem. As I have said, ordinary sequences of the elements of the domain, D, of a referential object language are not themselves in D. (In Wallace (1), Section II, it seems to be tacitly assumed that sequences of elements of D are themselves in D, which is true at best in very special cases.) So the referential quantifiers in the metalanguage must range over a larger domain, D', which includes (at least) the elements of D *and* sequences of them. D itself can be singled out as a subset by a primitive predicate $D(y)$. Then, the right-hand side of the formula previously derived should really read:

$$(\exists s)(\text{Sequence}(s) \wedge (y)(\text{Term of}(s, y) \supset D(y)) \wedge (s')((\text{Sequence}(s') \wedge (y)(\text{Term of}(s', y) \supset D(y)) \wedge s \underset{1}{\approx} s') \supset F(\text{first-term-of-}s'))).$$

(Here both 's' and 'y' are metalinguistic variables ranging over the larger domain D'.) Using additional axioms beyond the basis and recursive clauses, we can then derive $T(\overline{(x_1)Fx_1}) \equiv (y)(D(y) \supset F(y))$. We have still not achieved homophony, and could not achieve it unless the notational resources of the metalanguage are extended to include the object-language variables which range over D. The metalanguage then becomes a language with two styles of quantifier, as is the language M' of Section 5. We then need two additional axioms. Let x be an object-language variable ranging over D and let y be a metalanguage variable ranging over D'. Then the two additional axioms are $(x)(\exists y)(D(y) \wedge x = y)$ and $(y)(D(y) \supset (\exists x)(x = y))$. Using these axioms we can finally deduce $T(\overline{(x_1)Fx_1}) \equiv (x_1)Fx_1$. The formal similarity of these axioms to (19) and the like should be evident. They are needed, like the axioms in the substitutional case, to connect two different styles of variable. What is interesting is that in the referential case we need a considerable amount of work even to derive the intermediate stage $T(\overline{(x_1)Fx_1}) \equiv (y)(D(y) \supset F(y))$. I suspect that if everything were done in detail there would be more auxiliary work in the standard treatment of the homophonic referential case than there is in the homophonic substitutional case. Although other treatments of referential quantification, differing in various ways from this standard one, are possible, I know of none which gets by with the basis and recursive clauses alone, and requires no additional axioms.[52]

[52] *Some*, but not all, of the extra axioms can be dispensed with if we are willing not to separate the recursion in the original one-sorted language from the extension to a two-sorted language. We could then *define* $D(y)$ as $(\exists x)(x = y)$ and then dispense with the axioms $(x)(\exists y)(y = x \wedge D(y))$ and $(y)(D(y) \supset (\exists x)(x = y))$. In like manner, in M', Section 5, we could have *defined* Term (α) as $(\Sigma x)(Q(x, \alpha))$, and (19) and the like would become theorems; in the present section we could define Term(α) as $(\exists x)$Den(x, α) and dispense with (51) and (52). In all cases the procedure is somewhat artificial. In

11. SUMMARY AND CONCLUSIONS

11(*a*). *Substitutional Quantification*

There never was any problem about substitutional quantification. For any class of expressions C of a language L_0, we can extend the language by adding substitutional quantification with this class of expressions as the substitution class, whether or not some, all, or none of the expressions in the class denote, and whether or not (if some terms denote) L_0 contains referential opacities. The truth conditions for every sentence in the extended language are completely determinate if those of L_0 were. *All this was already proved in Section* 1. The claims against substitutional quantification, therefore, must have involved additional criteria, and it was hard to see how such criteria would override the straightforward results of Section 1.

It turns out, however, that all the additional criteria Wallace and Tharp propose can be met, so their adequacy need not be discussed. A non-homophonic truth theory was presented in Section 2; a homophonic one in Section 5. Indeed, if the substitution classes of the metalanguage include sentences of the object language, and strings of symbols of the object language, the problem of a finite homophonic truth theory for an *arbitrary* language is trivial (Section 5(*a*)). (The observation is not without interest for the Davidson programme.) All this, once again, is independent of whether terms do or don't denote, or even have the syntactic appearance of denoting.

The arguments to the contrary typically turned out to depend on confusion between substitutional and referential quantification. The main substitutional truth theory of Section 5 was essentially presented also by Wallace, but simply misread, etc. These were not the only errors.

I should emphasize that the point is *not* simply that some particular arguments against the intelligibility of substitutional quantification have been refuted, but maybe better ones will come along later. The

---

the case of Section 5 and the present section, it means that we no longer define the notion of a term in a purely syntactic manner (in terms of concatenation and identity alone). Nevertheless the trick shows that Wallace's main additional axioms are theoretically dispensible, though a careful analysis would show that the fact is of little significance. The other axioms for referential quantification mentioned above are not so easily dropped.

One attractive alternative not explored, and feasible in most cases, keeps the ontology the same in object language and metalanguage (unless *expressions* need to be added to the ontology), and codes finite sequences of the domain into the domain by adding further *vocabulary* (ideology). We don't discuss how generally this can be carried out; the axiomatic treatment is of a different kind.

issue of whether truth conditions have been given for substitutional languages is one of mathematical fact, not philosophical opinion. The central theorem of Section 1 *already shows that we have determinate truth conditions for substitutional quantification, independently of any considerations about denotation or opacity.* Any argument to the contrary, therefore, *must* be fallacious: it puts its proponents in the camp of the circle squarers and the angle trisectors. Indeed, the proofs that circle squarers and angle trisectors cannot succeed are mathematically much more difficult than the proof of the theorem of Section 1.

Another interpretation of Wallace and Tharp, taking them to be dealing with referential quantification and satisfaction, was given in Section 10. Interesting questions arise in connection with this interpretation, but I won't summarize the conclusions.

Perhaps I have misinterpreted Wallace and Tharp, and they meant to advance some thesis other than the ones I attributed to them. If so, I give my apologies to these authors for the misinterpretation; but since I know many others have shared these interpretations, the present paper will have at least served the useful purpose of dispelling the misimpressions that resulted. At present I can think of no negative general thesis regarding substitutional quantification resembling those of Wallace and Tharp which is both true and interesting. Perhaps I have missed one.

In my opinion, the most interesting applications of substitutional quantification are likely to come in connection with systems like the metalanguage of 5(*a*) where the expressions of the two substitution classes do not even have the *syntactic appearance* of being names of an ordinary kind. Note how, where the proof of the existence of finitely axiomatized truth theories using a *referential* metalanguage requires the recursions of a Tarski, the substitutional truth theory in 5(*a*) is almost trivial. Any confused belief that referential and substitutional quantification are the same should be dispelled by considering this case.[53] (I recommend as an exercise to any reader with lingering Wallace–Tharp tendencies that he construct metametalanguages, with appropriate truth theories, for the metalanguage of 5(*a*) along the lines of Sections 1, 2, 5, and 5(*a*) itself.) Since the truth theories of Section 2 'translate' substitutional quantification into

[53] Attention to the various purely formal differences between substitutional and referential quantification mentioned in the paper should also help to dispel confusion. See especially the formulae (48a)–(48c) in Section 6(*a*).

referential quantification over expressions, in theory the former is dispensable. But in terms of formal economy, the situation can be different.

Some of our apparently existential locutions *may* even sometimes be correctly interpreted substitutionally, as many have advocated. In fact I doubt that such an interpretation is often possible, but I cannot explore the matter here.

11(*b*). *An Elementary Methodological Sermon*

Plainly I have given the Wallace–Tharp papers a far more meticulous examination than I need to establish my main substantive conclusion. (See, for example, on just one relatively peripheral issue, the remarks on Wallace's treatment of Geach: the main point—the technical inadequacy of Wallace's criticism—is supplemented by several others which follow it in small type. The main point, of course, if correct, is sufficient to refute Wallace; so are some of the others.) I had two reasons for my procedure. First, I didn't want any major errors to go uncorrected, for fear that readers will retain some misleading impressions. (I fear I may have missed some nonetheless; in any event, I specifically limited myself to those portions of the papers which attack substitutional quantification.) Second, I thought that a thorough discussion would call attention to a few elementary methodological morals. I am uncertain how much the vices in the Wallace–Tharp papers extend to the rest of the technical philosophical literature; they *are* extreme examples, and a discussion of the extent to which their methodological defects are or are not present elsewhere is obviously beyond the scope of this paper. Nevertheless, the ability of the authors, and the reputation of the results, already give me some disquiet about the role of technical argument in current philosophy. For the papers under review are papers written by two sincere working practitioners who doubtless thought that they were defending common sense, and papers which, if they were not generally accepted, attracted some notice and approbation. If I am right, these papers make several fundamental errors. Something has gone badly wrong. What morals can be drawn?

It should go without saying that care should be taken not to rest a philosophical discussion on a mathematical falsehood. Wallace offends badly in this respect, as witness the technical errors detailed above—see especially the trivially false 'hard logical fact' on which the entire philosophical discussion in Wallace (2) is based. Tharp, a trained

mathematical logician, offends far less on this score and does not state false theorems; but even he manages to convey several misleading technical impressions, enumerated in Sections 9 and 10. Certainly his statement that difficult technical problems stand in the way of a substitutional truth definition is incorrect. It is ridiculous when philosophers base their work on false or ill-digested mathematical 'facts'. An example, removed from the present discussion, is the impression, still widespread among philosophers though diminishing, that the paradoxes have reduced set theorists to comparing a large number of differing systems embodying different, completely unintuitive, approaches to the paradoxes. In fact, essentially one system, Zermelo-Fraenkel set theory, is seriously studied by working set theorists; and most set theorists today regard it as based upon an intuitive idea. Yet many philosophical morals have been drawn from the alleged plethora of competing and unintuitive approaches.[54]

Just as important, perhaps even more so, is the necessity to keep basic conceptual distinctions in mind. In my opinion, Wallace and Tharp offend very badly on this score. Substitutional quantification is constantly confused with referential, as in Wallace's tendentious misreading of (19). Expressions are mechanically identified with their Gödel numbers, even in discussions where the issue is supposed to be whether an ontology of numbers is dispensable in favour of one of expressions. (Of course, the identification is unexceptionable in standard contexts, where this is not at issue.) The almost tautological condition that a truth theory, if it is to be homophonic, must be phrased in a metalanguage which contains the object language (with the object language interpreted as it was before), is ignored. Tharp interchanges the notions of definability and provability in a confusing way. It is important, in discussions of logico-philosophical issues, not to lose sight of basic, elementary distinctions by covering them up with either genuine or apparent technical sophistication. We must not ignore the conceptual woods through excessive attention to the technical trees.

Philosophers should not confuse their own particular philosophical doctrines with the basic results and procedures of mathematical logic.

[54] The misimpression is somewhat less open to censure than the errors of Wallace and Tharp. First, it is an error about the present practice of the set-theoretic community and may be more nearly accurate as a report of set-theoretic opinion a few decades ago (though even so regarded it has its defects). Second, it can be argued that the set theorists *should* regard Zermelo-Fraenkel as completely unintuitive, or *should* study a plethora of competing approaches. I would disagree, but the issue would become (quasi-) philosophical.

Davidsonians have had an excessive tendency to ignore the distinction between their own goals and methods and those of Tarski. As Wallace rightly states (Wallace (2), p. 200), Tarski's work has been widely accepted by logicians (with modifications). It is therefore important—not just for historical accuracy—that writers should not confuse their own particular philosophical doctrines with Tarski's work, or with the results of modern logic. For to challenge a particular set of philosophical doctrines is one thing; to challenge the basic results of modern logic is another. By reading one's own doctrines into classical results one may give an authority to these doctrines they do not really possess. We have seen that Wallace constantly attributes views and requirements to Tarski which cannot be found in Tarski and many of which—as in the cases of finite axiomatizability requirements and the prohibition of the ω-rule—sometimes seem to be explicitly repudiated by Tarski. (There is a correlative evil: some philosophical writings of an anti-formalist tendency attribute the particular philosophical views of Russell, Quine or the Vienna Circle—to mention three examples—to 'the formal logicians'.)

It should be worth emphasizing what the role of truth in contemporary logic is. Once a formal language has been defined syntactically, the main *semantic* demand is that an *explicit definition* (*characterization*) *be given* (*in understood language*) *of which sentences are true*. (If relevant, other concepts, such as satisfaction, truth-in-a-model, etc., may be defined also.) For an example, see Section 1 on substitutional languages. Then, given any sentence ϕ of the language, we have been told under precisely what conditions it is true, and in that sense, understood its sense. (Philosophers of strongly 'intensionalist' views may think more is required.) Tarski's Convention T applies only when the object language in question is one we *already* understand, perhaps by some informal translation procedure into natural language (this was the case for quantificational languages when Tarski wrote) or by *another* truth definition (see the example in Section 2). In this case we must verify that the defined concept—T(x)—really is truth in terms of our *prior* understanding of the language. A necessary and sufficient condition for a truth definition to be extensionally correct is that each T-sentence $T(\bar{\phi}) \equiv \phi$ be true. To know this we must prove each such sentence. There is no special restriction on *how* the T-sentences are to be proved.

In the case where a language is being introduced, an explicit definition of truth (and other semantical notions if relevant) is the necessary

and sufficient condition for the language to have a mathematically defined (extensional) semantics. There is no other requirement. Otherwise, the language can be interpreted by informal English explications: semantics will then be left at the level of informal intuition. Prior to Tarski's work, semantics was generally regarded as only susceptible to such informal treatment.

None of this is to attack Davidson for deviating from Tarski *per se*. Additional restrictions, etc. may be relevant *if we have different purposes in mind from those of the previous paragraphs*. The purposes of any additional restrictions should be stated carefully and explicitly. Davidson is well aware, and sometimes makes clear, that his purposes differ from Tarski's. (Indeed Tarski's original purpose seems to be to show that truth can be defined mathematically, and that Convention T gives a precise criterion of the success of the definition. Thus he combated the impression that truth was a 'fuzzy' unscientific concept. This purpose differs somewhat from that of contemporary logic given above, and more so from Davidson's.) Davidson seems especially concerned in his early papers with criteria for a language's being learnable as a first language. Later, he emphasizes other concerns. Nevertheless, his own writings, and Wallace's much more so, sometimes tend to encourage confusion of Tarski's original ideas, or their understanding by today's logicians, with later philosophical doctrines and technical restrictions. It is important not to confuse violation of the technical criteria of some recent philosophers with violation of the principles of modern logic itself. It would perhaps be desirable to adopt explicit terminology to distinguish 'Davidson's Convention T'—with its finite axiomatizability requirements etc.—from Tarski's original Convention T. The former, though it has undoubtedly led to some fruitful work, involves much more controversial philosophical doctrines than does Tarski's.

The tendency to propose technical criteria with the aim of excluding approaches one dislikes should be curtailed. Here I may be more controversial than I was in stating the almost platitudinous morals given above. Some writings, especially those of Wallace, have proposed technical requirements with the explicit or implicit aim of finding 'objective' criteria to exclude approaches they wished in advance to reject.[55] We have seen the pitfalls of this technique in several places

[55] Wallace's writings are perhaps close to unique in their bold exhibition of this tendency. It is present, though less blatantly, in other writings on the Davidsonian programme. Much more common in the philosophical community, however, is the

above. Often, both the claim that the condemned theories must fail to satisfy the criteria and the claim that the preferred approach will satisfy the criteria are *simultaneously* defective.

Several issues are involved here. Once it has been conceded that truth for a formal language has been explicitly defined, each sentence of the language has determinate truth conditions and is in this sense intelligible. Any other criteria (for a formal language) must, therefore, be directed toward some problem other than intelligibility and should be explicitly and carefully stated. Usually formal criteria are motivated, or at least defended, by some intuitive underpinning. Philosophers often become so overjoyed, however, when they have found formal criteria for the success of some project that its intuitive basis is often disregarded, like a ladder which can easily be kicked away after it has been climbed. Occasionally technical criteria are advocated just because they are technical criteria: it is as if it were thought that any technical criterion, however loosely defended, is superior to a mere (!) philosophical argument. Quine, for example, in his well known discussion of ontological reduction in Quine (2), states various possible criteria of reduction, adopting one which supposedly includes well-known cases and excludes undesired cases, with very little discussion of the question why one criterion or another is philosophically well motivated.

Any such tendency should surely be resisted. If a criterion such as finite axiomatizability of a truth theory is identified with the intuitive notion of revealing recursive structure in the semantics of the object language, we must *not* enthusiastically conclude that the loose philosophical notion can be forgotten in favour of its technical 'explication'. On the contrary, the intuitive notion must always play a dominant role, lest theories which intuitively do reveal recursive structure but are infinitely axiomatized are dismissed, while finitely axiomatized theories which reveal no recursive structure are embraced. (Examples of both kinds exist.)

In writings such as Wallace's, one senses the frequent presence of attempts to find technical criteria to exclude formalisms which have really been rejected in advance. Such attempts have a strong propensity to go awry. *Unless a technical criterion has been given a rigorous philosophical justification which really justifies us in maintain-*

---

tendency to respect technical criteria just because they are technical, though the criteria are not particularly chosen with a polemical purpose.

ing it a priori, I suggest that *if* an author wishes to work under its constraints, he should regard it as a *hypothesis* within which he chooses to work. It should constantly be checked against its intuitive motivation, and can justify itself by the fruitfulness of the work to which it leads (which must be compared with rival approaches) and the consonance in practice of the formal criterion with its original intuitive motivation. It should rather rarely be used to prohibit others from exploring other approaches. Theories should generally be praised or condemned by their concrete fruits, not by sweeping criteria casually imposed in advance. It seems to me extremely unlikely that any rich, well explored formal languages will at this late date be properly condemned for failure to satisfy some simple criterion.[56]

It should be emphasized that Davidson, for example, often presents his programme in just the spirit I am advocating; in Davidson (3) he calls it a 'bold hypothesis'. Although I cannot treat the matter in detail here, I am convinced that the justifications do indeed make a hypothetical treatment appropriate; they do not justify his or allied requirements as requirements we can impose *a priori*. Unfortunately, there is often a transition, sometimes even in Davidson's own writings, to a view that the programme contains *a priori* requirements which can be used to condemn alternatives, though elsewhere he gives the impression of disclaiming any such intention.

Philosophers should maintain a proper scepticism of attempts easily to settle linguistic or other empirical questions by quick a priori formal considerations. A good example of such an attempt is Wallace's proposal, discussed at the end of Section 7, to decide what he acknowledges to be the purely empirical question of the structure and ontology of 'There are men' in English by reference to formal considerations alone. A popular philosophical legend asserts that Hegel gave an *a priori* philosophical proof that there were exactly seven planets. I do not know whether this story is true (I have a stronger impression that some of Galileo's contemporaries did argue in this

[56] I have spoken of formal theories of natural language without really discussing my own attitudes. I find myself torn between two conflicting feelings—a 'Chomskyan' feeling that deep regularities in natural language must be discoverable by an appropriate combination of formal, empirical, and intuitive techniques, and a contrary (late) 'Wittgensteinian' feeling that many of the 'deep structures', 'logical forms', 'underlying semantics' and 'ontological commitments', etc., which philosophers have claimed to discover by such techniques are *Luftgebaüde*. I don't know how to resolve the tension, but I have let the first tendency be taken for granted in this paper. Nevertheless, though to a considerable extent I can work with them and I certainly do not regard them as completely meaningless, I don't really think that such phrases as 'logical form' have been sufficiently well explained to be used uncritically in philosophical discussion.

way), but it is certainly true that some recent philosophical authors are so enamoured of formal logic that they write as if it can be used to settle admittedly empirical questions about English with a minimum of empirical work. (Of course no one really believes such a thesis, baldly stated.) It is extraordinary that some who place the greatest emphasis on scientific rigour invoke it to justify such a technique. Take any such piece of writing in hand. Does it contain any empirical evidence regarding the actual behaviour of English speakers? Does it contain any intuitive evidence, based on our linguistic intuition or our understanding of the language as English speakers? If the answers to all such questions are negative (or are only minimally affirmative), then the work need not necessarily be committed to the flames, but it should be regarded with a critical and sceptical eye whatever its formal ingenuity. A purely *a priori* proof that English must have such and such a structure can succeed only if it proves that every possible language must have this structure; cases of success are likely to be rare. If we do not maintain a cautious attitude to such *a priori* linguistics, future generations may well regard us with the same bemusement that the Hegel of legend presently receives for his *a priori* astronomy.

Finally, *philosophers should have a better sense of both the power and the limitations of formal and mathematical techniques.* Let us review the situation which produced the papers of Wallace and Tharp. Underlying these papers there is an ever-present fear that it will be shown, using substitutional quantification, that *nothing exists*, or at least that *English assertions never commit us ontologically to anything but expressions.* The argument comes from an application of criteria for ontological commitment. Wallace and Tharp surely take themselves to be defending plain common sense against such assertions, and surely they are right to wish to do so. Unfortunately, they think the rescue must come in a drastic way—substitutional quantification must be proved unintelligible at all costs, lest it serve to show that our ontology collapses. A delicate application of Tarski's restrictions—an application which admittedly would have failed if infinitary rules were allowed—comes to the rescue and shows that the substitutional quantifier must be interpreted using a hidden concept of denotation. We can thank Tarski, and the intricacies of Convention T, for being able to claim that our discourse is committed to the existence of ships and molecules, of buildings and lemons, after all. Any scientist who naively thought his investigations

led to genuinely existential conclusions must similarly be grateful for Tarski's work.

Isn't there something *comical* about this dispute, in the sense that Kierkegaard thought that the Hegelian system was comical? Is it really credible that an astronomer who claims to have discovered a new planet, or a common man who believes in the existence of many other things, will find that substitutional quantification shows that he has no 'ontological commitment' to any such entities? And is it really credible that it is Tarski's Convention T which is needed to come to the rescue? Surely a little common sense is needed to check the philosophical tendency to build formal castles in the air. And surely it should have been implausible in advance that such elementary formal considerations can bear such a tremendous philosophical weight.

Remarkably, genuinely relevant formal work sometimes gets ignored in highly technical and 'formalistic' philosophical discussions. First (see the present paper), greater attention to the detailed consequences of technical criteria would act as a check against the tendency to propose them rashly. In particular, surely those who are drawn to finite axiomatizability demands should pay greater attention to the extensive technical literature on finite axiomatizability and non-finite axiomatizability than they do.

Another example: Montague and Kaplan, and Montague, following Gödel, have proved sharp results showing that if propositional atittudes or modalities are treated as properties of sentences paradox will result unless special precautions are taken. Yet the extensive quasi-technical literature advocating such treatments (or treatments using inscriptions, utterances, etc.), generally simply *ignores* the results rather than specifying how they are to be overcome.

Of course, an argument, once it is stated, can be refuted only after a detailed examination of it. It is not sufficient to dismiss the methodology as insane or counter-intuitive, even though my plea is that common-sense considerations ought to guide technical work more than they do. So in examining Wallace and Tharp I had to engage in the very kind of mathematical prestidigitation which I assert has carried too much weight for its own sake in recent philosophy. One can only examine arguments on their own ground. And I have said relatively little about the other side of the dispute, the side Wallace and Tharp rightly wish to refute. Why did anyone think that the existence of substitutional quantification created the danger of ontological collapse? Phobic and insane though this fear may be,

one cannot remove it without examining the arguments which engendered it. Some beginnings have been made in Sections 2 and 3, where I emphasize that neither a general doctrine that a referential metalanguage for a substitutional object language requires an ontology of expressions alone nor a general doctrine that other entities are always needed seems appropriate, and especially in Section 7 where I stress the unintelligibility of the supposed 'question' whether English quantification is ever referential at all. But a great deal more would need to be done: we would need a careful examination of the merits and demerits of Quine's and other criteria for 'ontological commitment' and 'ontological reduction', and of the applications various writers have made of these criteria. Only such an examination would finally alleviate the fears of those who sense that delicate logical constructions may engender an ontological collapse. I should stress that I am in full agreement with Wallace and Tharp that no such ontological collapse could be forthcoming from substitutional quantification alone. It is only the methology of their attempt to prove this thesis that I find objectionable.

A rather well known mathematical legend describes an encounter between the eminent *philosophe* Denis Diderot and the great mathematician Leonhard Euler, who were simultaneously in residence at the St. Petersburg court of Catherine the Great. Some of the courtiers were shocked by Diderot's atheism and, in an attempt to embarrass him, arranged a confrontation with Euler, who, they said, had a mathematical proof of the existence of God. When the confrontation took place in front of the entire court Euler argued:

$$\text{`\textit{Monsieur,}}\ \frac{a+b^n}{n} = x;\ \textit{donc Dieu existe. Répondez!'}$$ [57]

Diderot, who was utterly innocent of algebra, was at a loss for a reply and left the court in disgrace.

In fairness to Diderot, it should be mentioned that the incident surely never took place as described.[58] In fact Diderot was the author of several learned mathematical essays. If we do not take care, however, some of our philosophical discussions are in danger of coming to resemble the legendary confrontation. I have seen cases where a very simple, almost mathematically trivial technical trick has captured a philosopher's imagination and been used as if it were the key

[57] 'Sir, $\frac{a+b^n}{n} = x$; therefore God exists. Reply!'

[58] I rely on Gillings's scholarly account of the history of the tale.

that easily and mechanically unlocked doors that were forever closed to ordinary philosophical investigation. I have more than once heard philosophical arguments in which a technical result—sometimes mathematically garbled, sometimes technically sound—has been cited as if it directly led to a philosophical conclusion without the necessity of other premisses. It is not even always clear whether or not the proponent regards his argument as enthymematic. Yet when the argument is interesting, it is as often the suppressed philosophical premisses as it is the mathematical result which ought to be the focus of the dispute. And, of course, readers should take care not to be cowed by complicated-sounding symbolic argument in the manner of the legendary Diderot.

I wish to emphasize again that none of my general methodological remarks can be used as a substitute for arguments in particular cases. One cannot, for example, dismiss a proposed technical criterion on the grounds that 'technical criteria should be regarded with suspicion'; one must examine the particular arguments offered for it. I only wish to plead that arguments should indeed be offered and examined; one should not have an exaggerated respect for a technical criterion merely because it is a technical criterion.

In recent but past times some circles of English-speaking philosophy, especially in Great Britain, were said to have greatly underestimated the applicability of formal and logical techniques to philosophical questions. I assume that such an attitude is shared by few of the readers of the present volume, so that I hardly need defend the genuine philosophical contribution made by modern logic here. To some extent the pendulum seems to have swung again in the other direction, and cautions of a different kind are required. Logical investigations can obviously be a useful tool for philosophy. They must, however, be informed by a sensitivity to the philosophical significance of the formalism and by a generous admixture of common sense, as well as a thorough understanding both of the basic concepts and of the technical details of the formal material used. It should not be supposed that the formalism can grind out philosophical results in a manner beyond the capacity of ordinary philosophical reasoning. There is no mathematical substitute for philosophy.

POSTSCRIPT

After this paper was virtually completed, I saw the recent exchange between Camp and Wallace in *Noûs*, May 1975. The substitutional truth

theory in the third section of Camp's paper seems to be closely related to the homophonic theory, couched in M'', given in Section 5. Camp, however, seems to regard his theory as an *alternative* to Wallace's. Wallace, he says, provides a workable theory if only referential quantifiers are allowed in the metalanguage, while his theory uses substitutional quantifiers in the metalanguage. He thus seems to miss one of the main points—that in a homophonic truth theory for a substitutional language the metalanguage, since it contains the object language, *must* contain substitutional quantifiers, and that Wallace is misreading a substitutional form, $Q(t, \alpha)$, as if it were the denotation relation. Camp also uses a primitive quoting device rather than $Q(t, \alpha)$, and fears that the presence of such devices must be severely restricted so as to avoid paradox (p. 175). As against the impression that substitutional quantification plus quotation leads to paradox, see the concluding paragraphs of Section 5(*a*).

Wallace replies, in effect, that some such formula as $(\exists z)(z = x \wedge Q(z, \alpha))$ already defines denotation, even if $Q(z, \alpha)$ is opaque and does not. The fallacies from the standpoint of the present paper are obvious. First, the formula in question should be written $(\mathrm{z})(\Sigma \mathrm{z} = \mathrm{x} \wedge Q(\mathrm{z}, \alpha))$ and, if intelligible at all, would be a form which does not define a predicate unless it is already assumed that each and every term denotes. Second, the use of the symbol '=' is also problematic unless a denotation is *already* provided for all the terms: see footnote 22.

Unfortunately the interchange between Camp and Wallace reached me too late to study it thoroughly and give it a more detailed evaluation than is contained in the preceding brief remarks. The paper by Belnap and Grover, of which I was completely unaware, was called to my attention even later. It contains a detailed theory of the mesh of substitutional quantification with a quotation functor—not the '$Q(t, \alpha)$' device characteristic of Sections 5 and 5(*a*). Although they appear not to give an axiomatic treatment, in contrast to those sections, they do explicitly state that substitutional quantification into quotation with sentential substitutes enables us to give an explicit definition of truth in a metalanguage without using any techniques of recursive semantics. Since they have a quotation functor, they state as the preferred form of Convention T that $(\Pi \mathrm{p})(\mathrm{T}(\text{`p'}) \equiv \mathrm{p})$ be provable, in apparent contrast to 5(*a*) exercise (i) in small type. I have been unable to compare their treatment with the axiomatic treatment of 5(*a*) in detail, but their discussion (which antedates 5(*a*) by several years) may wholly or partially anticipate the main point of 5(*a*) and may even suggest ways in which it could be improved. The paper by Grover in the same volume appears also to be highly relevant to the discussion of the so-called 'paradoxes' of substitutional quantification into quotation.

BIBLIOGRAPHY

N. D. Belnap and D. L. Grover, 'Quantifying in and out of Quotes' in H. Leblanc (ed.), *Truth, Syntax and Modality* (North-Holland, Amsterdam, 1973).

R. Binkley, 'Quantifying, Quotation and a Paradox', *Noûs*, iv (1970), 271.

J. L. Camp, 'Truth and Substitution Quantifiers', *Noûs*, ix (1975), 165.

D. Davidson, (1) 'In Defense of Convention T' in H. Leblanc (ed.), *Truth, Syntax and Modality* (North-Holland, Amsterdam, 1973), p. 76.

D. Davidson, (2) 'True to the Facts', *Journal of Philosophy*, lxvi (1969), 748.

D. Davidson, (3) 'Truth and Meaning', *Synthese*, xvii (1967), 304.

D. Davidson, (4) 'Semantics for Natural Languages' in Davidson and Harman.

D. Davidson and G. Harman (eds.), *The Logic of Grammar* (Dickenson, Encino and Belmont, 1975).

J. M. Dunn and N. D. Belnap, 'The Substitution Interpretation of the Quantifiers' *Noûs*, ii (1968), 177.

R. J. Gillings, 'The So-Called Euler–Diderot Incident', *The American Mathematical Monthly* (1954).

D. L. Grover, 'Propositional Quantification and Quotation Contexts' in H. Leblanc (ed.), *Truth, Syntax and Modality* (North-Holland, Amsterdam, 1973).

G. H. Harman, 'Substitutional Quantification and Quotation', *Noûs*, v (1971), 213.

S. A. Kripke, 'Semantical Considerations on Modal Logic', *Acta Philosophica Fennica*, xvi (1963), 83.

R. B. Marcus, 'Quantification and Ontology', *Noûs*, vi (1972), 240.

R. Montague, 'Syntactical Treatments of Modality with Corollaries on Reflexion Principles and Finite Axiomatizability', *Acta Philosophica Fennica*, xvi (1963), 153.

R. Montague and D. Kaplan, 'A Paradox Regained', *Notre Dame Journal of Formal Logic*, i (1960), 79.

W. V. Quine, (1) 'Concatenation as a Basis for Arithmetic' in *Selected Logic Papers* (Random House, New York, 1966).

W. V. Quine, (2) 'Ontological Reduction and the World of Numbers' in *Ways of Paradox and Other Essays* (Random House, New York, 1966), p. 199.

B. A. W. Russell, 'On Denoting', *Mind*, xiv (1905), 479.

A. F. Smullyan, 'Modality and Description', *Journal of Symbolic Logic*, xiii (1948), 83.

A. Tarski, *Logic Semantics and Metamathematics* (Clarendon Press, Oxford, 1956).

L. H. Tharp, 'Truth, Quantification and Abstract Objects', *Noûs*, v (1971), 363.

R. H. Thomason, 'Some Completeness Results for Modal Predicate Calculi' in K. Lambert (ed.), *Philosophical Problems in Logic* (Reidel, Dordrecht, 1970), p. 56.

R. H. Thomason and R. C. Stalnaker, (1) 'Modality and Reference', *Noûs*, iv (1968), 359.

R. H. Thomason and R. C. Stalnaker, (2) 'Abstraction in First Order Modal Logic', *Theoria*, xxxiv (1968), 203.

J. Wallace, (1) 'On the Frame of Reference' in D. Davidson and G. Harman (eds.), *Semantics of Natural Language* (Reidel, Dordrecht, 1972), p. 219.

J. Wallace, (2) 'Convention T and Substitutional Quantification', *Noûs*, v (1971), 199.
J. Wallace, (3) 'Nonstandard Theories of Truth' in Davidson and Harman.
J. Wallace, (4) 'Belief and Satisfaction', *Noûs*, vi (1972), 85.
J. Wallace, (5) 'Response to Camp', *Noûs*, ix (1975), 187.
S. Weinstein, 'Truth and Demonstratives', *Noûs*, viii (1974), 179.

Notes on the Contributors

J. A. Foster is a Fellow of Brasenose College, Oxford.

Donald Davidson is a Professor of Philosophy at The Rockefeller University and Princeton University.

John McDowell is a Fellow of University College, Oxford.

Michael Dummett is a Fellow of All Souls College, Oxford.

Brian Loar is an Assistant Professor of Philosophy at the University of Michigan.

Christopher Peacocke is a Junior Research Fellow of The Queen's College, Oxford.

P. F. Strawson is Waynflete Professor of Metaphysical Philosophy in the University of Oxford, and a Fellow of Magdalen College.

Gareth Evans is a Fellow of University College, Oxford.

Crispin Wright is a Fellow of All Souls College, Oxford.

Michael Woods is a Fellow of Brasenose College, Oxford.

Barry Taylor is a Lecturer in Philosophy at the University of Melbourne.

David Wiggins is Professor of Philosophy at Bedford College, London.

Saul Kripke is a Professor of Philosophy at The Rockefeller University, and an adjunct lecturer at Princeton University.